Profit Without Honor
White-Collar Crime and the Looting of America

Second Edition

Stephen M. Rosoff
University of Houston, Clear Lake

Henry N. Pontell
University of California, Irvine

Robert H. Tillman
St. John's University

Prentice
Hall

Upper Saddle River, New Jersey 07458

Library of Congress Cataloging-in-Publication Data

Rosoff, Stephen M.
    Profit without honor : white-collar crime and the looting of America/Stephen M.
Rosoff, Henry N. Pontell, Robert Tillman.—2nd ed.
        p.   cm.
    Includes bibliographical references and index.
    ISBN 0-13-028685-0
    1. White collar crimes—United States. 2. Fraud—United States. I. Pontell, Henry N.,
1950   II. Tillman, Robert.   III. Title.

HV6769 .R667 2002
364.16'8'0973—dc21   2001034603

Publisher: Jeff Johnson
Executive Assistant: Brenda Rock
Executive Acquisitions Editor: Kim Davies
Assistant Editor: Sarah Holle
Managing Editor: Mary Carnis
Production Management: Clarinda Publication Services
Production Editor: Rosie Jones
Interior Design: Cindy Miller
Production Liaison: Adele Kupchik
Director of Manufacturing and Production: Bruce Johnson
Manufacturing Buyer: Cathleen Petersen
Creative Director: Cheryl Asherman
Senior Design Coordinator: Miguel Ortiz
Formatting: The Clarinda Company
Director of Marketing Communication and New Media: Frank Mortimer, Jr.
Marketing Manager: Ramona Sherman
Printer/Binder: R. R. Donnelley and Sons, Inc. (Harrisonburg, Va.)
Copy Editor: Robyn Durand
Proofreader: Nancy Hayes
Cover Designer: Anthony Inciong
Cover Illustration: Lisa Zador SIS/Images.Com
Cover Printer: Phoenix Color Corporation

Pearson Education LTD.
Pearson Education Australia PTY, Limited
Pearson Education Singapore, Pte. Ltd.
Pearson Education North Asia Ltd.
Pearson Education Canada, Ltd.
Pearson Educación de Mexico, S.A. de C.V.
Pearson Education—Japan
Pearson Education Malaysia, Pte. Ltd.

10 9 8 7 6 5 4 3 2
ISBN 0-13-028685-0

*In memory of **Lillian Rosoff***
A woman of resonant kindness and quiet courage

Contents

Preface

In the short time that has passed since the first edition of this book was published in 1998, there have been—as one surely would expect—significant new developments in the study of white-collar crime. Promissory note sales scams, hardly a blip on the radar a few years ago, are now being called the number one fraud in the United States. Congressional hearings have exposed the flagrant deceit of the sweepstakes industry. The biggest embezzlement in American history and the biggest swindle ever uncovered have both occurred, as well as the largest price-fixing fine ever meted out. New environmental horror stories have surfaced involving an obscure deadly substance, beryllium. The disastrous Firestone tire debacle has outraged the nation, and a major bribery scandal has clouded the 2002 Winter Olympics in Salt Lake City.

Computer crime has continued to emerge as the nation's fastest growing category of crime. Two recent cyber-attacks have brought the Internet to its knees. One damaged an estimated 45 million PCs; the other crippled most of the major e-commerce sites, and each attack was launched by a *15-year-old boy*. "Pump and dump" schemes have exploded on the Internet, and "identity theft" has become part of the popular lexicon. Perhaps most ominous, organized crime has smelled the "new economy" and has forced its way to the feeding trough. The first edition described Wall Street brokers acting like organized criminals. This edition depicts organized criminals acting like Wall Street brokers.

The late 1990s also witnessed a resurgence of insider trading along with the merger-mania that characterized the so-called greed decade of the 1980s. Of course, one of the biggest and most important antitrust cases in American history—*U.S.* v. *Microsoft*—has been tried and has yielded a stunning verdict. All of these cases and many others are considered in this updated edition.

So, once again, *Profit Without Honor* seeks to elucidate a very broad subject that only seems to get broader: white-collar crime. How broad? Its domain stretches from the small price-gouging merchant to the huge price-fixing cartel. It can breed in an antiseptic hospital or a toxic dump. It is at home on Main Street, Wall Street, Madison Avenue—sometimes even 1600 Pennsylvania Avenue.

Yet, as Americans demonize the Crips and the Bloods, recoil at the Unabomber, and obsess over O. J. Simpson, white-collar crime still remains the "other" crime problem. The reason for this relative indifference is that the true costs of upperworld misconduct are largely unrecognized. Compared with murderers, terrorists, and urban gangsters, white-collar criminals do not seem to scare the public very much.

Even the economic expense—by far the most identifiable cost—is typically underestimated by the average citizen. Annual losses from white-collar crime are probably 50 times greater than losses from ordinary property crime. For example, the price of bailing out a single corrupt savings and loan (S & L) institution surpassed the total losses of all the bank robberies in American history. The bill for the entire S & L bailout ultimately may exceed a *trillion* dollars. (To put that figure in perspective, consider that a million seconds is about 11 days; a trillion seconds is about 30,000 years.) Indeed, the price-tags attached to some white-collar crimes are so staggering that they are difficult to comprehend. They evoke memories of the late Senator Everett McKinley Dirkson's wry quip: "A billion here, a billion there; and pretty soon you're talking about real money!"

Monetary expenditures are only the tip of the topic. The "looting" in the subtitle of this book refers to more than larceny; it implies destruction, too. This book argues for an expanded definition of white-collar crime because such crime is not just property crime on a grand scale. It entails higher and more enduring levels of costs—particularly physical and social costs. These less conspicuous effects carry a heavy payment that cannot be measured with a calculator.

White-collar crimes do not leave a chalk outline on the sidewalk or a blood spatter on the wall, so the American public, in its understandable preoccupation with street crime, often has overlooked the violent aspects of elite deviance. In his polemic book, *Thinking About Crime*, James Q. Wilson marginalizes white-collar crime, lumping it together with "victimless" crimes such as gambling and prostitution. He states that most citizens (including himself) do not consider white-collar offenses to be very serious compared with street crime. Wilson's intuition about the predominance of such a belief is quite correct. The belief itself, however, is utterly wrong. *White-collar criminals cause more pain and death than all "common criminals" combined.*

A likely explanation for the inadequate attention can be derived from a cognitive rule-of-thumb known as the *availability heuristic*. It stipulates that there is a common human tendency to judge the likelihood of occurrences in terms of how readily instances come to mind. Vivid events stick in our memories, and their greater ease of recall misleads us to overrate their frequency relative to less dramatic, but actually more pervasive events. The physical harm wrought by some forms of white-collar crime can be slow and cumulative—like the mythic "death of a thousand cuts." In other words, the human suffering caused by corporate cupidity frequently can take years to materialize, in contrast to the graphic suddenness which usually characterizes street violence. Consequently, it is easy for people to misperceive the extent of the injuries caused. As this book will delineate, environmental crime, hazardous workplaces, medical malfeasance, and unsafe products are lethal manifestations of what Ralph Nader calls "postponed violence."

As for social costs, they are the most insidious and difficult to measure. The victims here are not limited to endangered employees, mistreated patients, or injured consumers, but include all of society—from its component institutions to its transcendent culture. Indeed, a case could easily be made that *every* category of white-collar crime depicted in this book manifests a deleterious effect on some social institution and thereby inflicts damage on society as a whole. To cite just two instances, the insider trading scandals detailed in Chapter 6 have eroded public faith in the American economy; and the crimes by the government described in Chapter 8 have devalued the democratic process.

It should also be noted that much of the existing white-collar crime literature focuses on offenders—those who commit these crimes, their motives and methods. This is certainly an illuminating perspective, but not the only perspective. This book seeks to shed light on the *victims* of white-collar crime as well. Victimology is a critical element because it helps give the problem the personal relevance it has sometimes lacked. The more predatory white-collar crime is perceived to be, the less likely it will continue to be dismissed as a mere appendix to the crime problem.

One additional preliminary comment seems appropriate, and it concerns the style of the chapters that follow. We have chosen to present our material in an occasionally flippant and hopefully engaging manner. But despite its intermittent irreverence, this is a serious book on an important subject. It is not difficult to write mordantly about con artists charging people $30 for a "solar clothes dryer," then mailing them a piece of rope and some clothespins (Chapter 2), or greedy doctors billing Medicare for pregnancy tests performed on elderly males (Chapter 10), or religious charlatans peddling trashy "holy shower caps" to thousands of devout proselytes (Chapter 5). It is likewise easy for readers to ridicule those who are duped by such flagrant deceit. Thus, it is worthwhile to bear in mind an old maxim: when you slip on a banana peel it is tragedy; only when *someone else* slips does it become comedy. A reiterate lesson of this book is that white-collar crime spares no one. Everybody reading this sentence (or writing it, for that matter) has been somebody's victim. Each of us would do well to remember just how much alike a window and a mirror can be.

ACKNOWLEDGEMENTS

The authors gratefully acknowledge the efforts of an energetic platoon of students who ably served as research assistants as this book was being prepared and prepared again.

At the University of Houston-Clear Lake, they are (in alphabetical order): **(FIRST EDITION)** Pam Biggs, Chrissie Blevin, Robbie Cartwright, Susan Dinbali, Mykal Le, Monica Madrid-Hall, Tom Mayfield, Bill McCollum, J. J. McKinzie, Becky Richter, Sarah Smith, and Dave Weimer. **(SECOND EDITION)** Brenda Birdow, Shannon Boudreaux, Monica Contreras, Monique Dasant-Crawford, Debra Kalmbach, Tammy Merrimon, Kevin Morgan, Stephen Morrison, Marian Olivarez, Julie Patterson, Emilia Satsky, Antonia Vasquez, Elizabeth Wade, Pearline Williams, and Jamison Wise.

At the University of California, Irvine, they are **(FIRST EDITION)** Steven Rennie, Cindy Guttierez, and Shauhin Talesh. **(SECOND EDITION)** Helena Rene, Pei-San Tsai, Paul Rodriguez, Jennifer Cabatbat, Erin Morgan, Frances Lee, Denise Chang, Linda Shen, and Tai-Ling Tsai.

Thank you all for work well done.

Numerous colleagues have generously contributed their special insights. Notable among them are John Dombrink, Kitty Calavita, Paul Jesilow, and Marc Turk of UC Irvine, Otto Reyer of Western University of Health Sciences, Bill Black of the University of Texas, Austin, Susan Will of John Jay College of Criminal Justice, Kevin Walsh of Sam Houston State University, and Tom Kellow of the University of Houston.

The authors also appreciate the efforts of several scholars who reviewed the first edition of this book and offered their judicious evaluations. This second edition has benefited from their professionalism. They are (in alphabetical order): Curtis Clarke, Athabasca University; Lynn Cooper, California State University, Sacramento; David Shichor, California State University, San Bernadino, and Ernie Thompson, University of Houston, Clear Lake.

We would like to thank our editor at Prentice Hall, Kim Davies. Our production editor, Rosie Jones, at Clarinda Publication Services provided her considerable talents, along with a remarkable measure of personal interest and attention. She is a consummate professional.

In addition, Angela Peters of UH-Clear Lake and Marilyn Wahlert and Judy Omiya of UC Irvine provided superb administrative and secretarial support.

To Frank Belsky, a friend like no other, sincere appreciation for many valuable suggestions. To Barbara Levine, whose sharp eye is a treasure, thanks for giving so graciously of your time.

And to the inimitable Gilbert Geis, profound gratitude for your encouragement and inspiration.

Stephen M. Rosoff
Henry N. Pontell
Robert H. Tillman

About the Authors

Stephen M. Rosoff is associate professor of sociology and Director of the Graduate Criminology Program at the University of Houston—Clear Lake. He received his Ph.D. in social ecology from the University of California, Irvine. He has written extensively on white-collar crime and professional deviance, particularly in the areas of medical fraud and computer crime. He is co-author of two forthcoming books: *Contemporary Legal Issues: Whose Rights? Who's Right?* (Roxbury Press) and *Deviance and Deviants* (Prentice Hall).

Henry N. Pontell is professor of criminology, law and society in the School of Social Ecology at the University of California, Irvine. He received his Ph.D. in sociology from the State University of New York at Stony Brook. A widely recognized authority on white-collar crime, including financial institution fraud and crime in the health care industry, and writer in a number of areas of criminology and sociology, in 2001 he received the Association of Certified Fraud Examiners Cressey Award for major lifetime contributions to the study, detection and deterrence of fraud. His recent books include: *Big Money Crime: Fraud and Politics in the Savings and Loan Crisis*, and *Contemporary Issues in Crime and Criminal Justice: Essays in Honor of Gilbert Geis*.

Robert H. Tillman is associate professor of sociology at St. John's University in New York City. He received his Ph.D. in sociology from the University of California, Davis. He is the author and co-author of several books on white-collar crime, including: *Global Pirates: Fraud in the Offshore Insurance Industry* (Northeastern University Press, forthcoming); *Broken Promises: Fraud by Small Business Health Insurers* (Northeastern University Press); and *Big Money Crime: Fraud and Politics in the Savings and Loan Crisis* (University of California Press).

Introduction

As a freckle-faced 13-year-old, Darlene Gillespie was one of the nine original Mouseketeers on television's *Mickey Mouse Club.* So popular was young Darlene that, while dozens of mouse-eared moppets came and went, she was kept on for the show's entire 1955–1959 run. She was even featured in her own serial: *Corky and White Shadow.*[1] The Disney publicity department proclaimed she had "more bounce to the ounce than a bottle of soda pop."[2] In 1998, she bounced right into federal court.

As an unfreckled 56-year-old, Darlene Gillespie was convicted on 12 counts of conspiracy, securities fraud, mail fraud, obstruction of justice, and perjury.[3] Gillespie and her boyfriend, who was also convicted, operated a scheme to make money in the stock market without paying for any stock.[4] The couple had bought more than 194,000 shares valued at $827,000 by writing checks on closed and overdrawn accounts.[5] They also had created a fictional person to make their transactions, then lied about this nonexistent agent to the Securities and Exchange Commission.[6] In 1999, Gillespie was sentenced to 2 years in prison.[7]

Darlene Gillespie's stunning fall from *Mouseketeer* to *racketeer* is just a striking example of the pervasiveness of white-collar crime in our society. On any given day, one might pick up a newspaper and read stories reporting bribery scandals among politicians at every tier of government, crooked deals involving Wall Street financiers, or the raffish schemes of predatory con artists. And these are only the stories that make it into the press. Beyond them are innumerable cases of corruption, fraud, and abuse that are never uncovered or reported. Yet, when most Americans talk about the "crime problem," they envision images of the violent murders, rapes, assaults, and robberies relentlessly portrayed in television "docu-dramas" and in gory detail by the tabloid press. The public's fears are not unwarranted; street crime remains at intolerably high levels in the United States. The problem is that these concerns can eclipse our understanding of other kinds of crime—particularly white-collar offenses that are in many less obvious ways much more harmful to society as a whole.

This book surveys the forms, causes, and consequences of white-collar crime. In it, the authors strive to give the reader a sense not only of the relevant social scientific theories but of the mechanics of white-collar crime: how these schemes work, who perpetrates them, and how they are tied to the environments in which they occur. The authors also hope to convey the scope of "upperworld" criminality, to demonstrate the degree to which it has become ingrained in our major social institutions and our culture.

THE HISTORY OF A CONCEPT

The term "white-collar crime" is a social science construct that has transcended its academic roots and entered the public lexicon. Its origin can be precisely located. In 1939, Professor Edwin Sutherland of Indiana University delivered the presidential address to the American Sociological Society, in which he argued for the need to expand criminological thinking to include behaviors and persons not generally thought of—either by the public or by most scholars of the time—as crime and criminals. As he later explained in a classic book, most theories of crime focus on those offenses committed in overwhelming disproportion by members of the social underclass. Sutherland contended that such an exclusive perspective ignores the fact that "persons of the upper socioeconomic class engage in much criminal behavior; that this behavior differs from the criminal behavior of the lower socioeconomic classes principally in the administrative procedures used in dealing with the offenders."[8] He called these offenses white-collar crimes, a metaphor meant to distinguish the occupational status of those who worked in office buildings from those who worked in factories or practiced other "blue-collar" trades or were unemployed.

Sutherland defined white-collar crime as "crimes committed by a person of respectability and high social status in the course of his occupation."[9] With this definition, he connected two distinct elements: the social status of the offender and the occupational mechanism by which the offense is committed.

In Sutherland's view, prevailing theories about the causes of crime were based on naïve assumptions regarding the validity of official statistics gathered from public institutions like courts and prisons, which have always overrepresented the poor and the powerless. Sutherland asserted that those statistics were prone to extreme bias because they failed to reflect two important facts. First, "persons of the upper socioeconomic class are more powerful politically and financially and escape arrest and conviction to a greater extent than persons who lack such power."[10] Second, and more important to Sutherland, the justice system is inclined to employ a very different procedural apparatus for dealing with white-collar offenders.

> Persons who violate laws regarding restraint of trade, advertising, pure food and drugs, and similar practices are not arrested by uniformed policemen, are not tried in criminal courts, and are not committed to prisons; this illegal behavior receives the attention of administrative commissions and of courts operating under civil or equity jurisdiction. *For this reason such violations of law are not included in the criminal statistics nor are individual cases brought to the attention of scholars who write the theories of criminal behavior* [emphasis added].[11]

Sutherland supported his position with data that revealed substantial numbers of criminal and administrative violations among the biggest corporations in America. He further concluded that "the financial cost of white-collar crime is probably several times as great as the cost of all the crimes customarily regarded as the 'crime problem.'"[12] As an illustration, he noted that "an officer of a chain grocery store in one year embezzled $800,000, which was six times as much as the annual losses from 500 burglaries and robberies of the stores in that chain."[13]

Sutherland's work was groundbreaking, forging a new theoretical path and setting a research agenda for many future scholars. Indeed, his development of the concept of white-collar crime exemplifies what Peter Berger has labeled the "debunking motif" in sociology. The process of debunking involves "looking for levels of reality other than those given in the official interpretations of society."[14] In fundamentally altering the study of crime by focusing attention on an elite form of lawbreaking previously ignored by criminologists, Sutherland thus debunked theories "which blamed such factors as poverty, broken homes, and Freudian fixations for illegal behavior."[15]

It must be noted, however, that Sutherland's ideas were not incubated in a vacuum, but rather reflected the historical context in which they developed. Sutherland was 56 years old when he delivered his influential speech in 1939, so much of his intellectual germination took place in the early part of the twentieth century, an era that witnessed an acceleration of the shift of the United States from a rural, agrarian society to an urban, industrial one. A major part of that transformation, of course, was the emergence of modern corporations as the dominant force in the American economy.

The increasing power of a handful of big companies and their seeming immunity to laws designed only to restrict the behavior of deviant individuals had led to the "public's dawning sense of vulnerability, unease, and anger."[16] That outrage eventually inspired a popular social movement to expose the abuses of big business. At the turn of the twentieth century, journalists known as muckrakers began to write shocking accounts of outrageous corporate conduct. Upton Sinclair, for example, published *The Jungle,* a scathing critique of the meatpacking industry in 1904, in which he detailed the horrendous conditions faced by immigrant workers desperate for a weekly wage.[17] Sinclair's exposé of unsanitary practices spurred the establishment of the Food and

Drug Administration, the first federal agency empowered to create and enforce standards in the food processing industry (Chapter 2).

Around the same time, other journalists took aim at the monopolies that were establishing strangleholds on major sectors of the economy. The expanding corporations of the late nineteenth century had discovered a simple truth: It was more profitable to collude than to compete. The culmination of this assault on the free market was the formation of national trusts, through which various companies would fix prices or pool their operations under a single administration in order to eliminate competition. In an effort to curb such conspiracies, Congress passed the Sherman Antitrust Act of 1890 (Chapter 2). Although very few cases were prosecuted during the early years of the Act, corporations were at least forced to rethink their strategies and turn toward a more "legitimate" form of expansion, the merger. Between 1895 and 1908, thousands of companies disappeared as they were gobbled up by larger firms.[18]

The corporation which came to symbolize the strategic use of mergers and trusts was the Standard Oil Company, headed by John D. Rockefeller. By ruthlessly destroying his competitors, Rockefeller created an empire that controlled virtually the entire American petroleum industry. Ida Tarbell, a muckraker whose own father had been ruined by Rockefeller, chronicled the gluttony of Standard Oil. Her articles helped ignite public sentiment against Rockefeller and encouraged President Theodore Roosevelt to "bust" the Standard Oil trust. In 1909, the courts finally ordered Standard Oil to dissolve itself into a number of smaller companies.[19]

Still other writers decried the increasing concentration of economic power among rapacious oligopolies. Frank Norris' thinly fictionalized book, *The Octopus,* described how four powerful companies had conspired to control the vast railroad empire of the American West.[20] In *Other People's Money, and How the Bankers Use It*, Louis Brandeis, who would later become a distinguished Supreme Court Justice, warned of a "financial oligarchy" run by a network of interlocking directorates, through which officers of investment banks, life insurance companies, and railroad corporations sat on each other's boards, conducting transactions that benefited the members of what Brandeis called the "Money Trust."[21] The result was an economy run by and for the members of this elite group, who had become, in Brandeis' words, "masters [of] America's business world, so that practically no large enterprise can be undertaken successfully without their participation or approval."[22] Brandeis singled out banker J. P. Morgan for the harshest criticism. Morgan epitomized the nineteenth Century robber baron, and his House of Morgan symbolized "monopolistic and predatory control over the financial resources of the country."[23]

An even more direct influence on Sutherland's work was a 1907 book by sociologist E. A. Ross. In his book titled *Sin and Society*, Ross vividly expressed his dismay about corrupt business practices: "Nationwide is the zone of devastation of the adulterator, the rebater, the commercial freebooter, the fraud promoter, the humbug healer, the law-defying monopolist."[24]

Behind all this corruption was a social type that Ross called the *criminaloid*, who enjoys a public image as a pillar of the community and a paragon of virtue; but beneath this veneer of respectability could be found a very different persona, one that is committed to personal gain through any means. Ross' criminaloid is clearly the antecedent of Sutherland's white-collar criminal.

The 1920s were a bonanza for white-collar crime. The feeding frenzy unleashed by an exploding economy attracted bold and ingenious predators. An especially remarkable figure was con artist extraordinaire Charles Ponzi, a turn-of-the-century immigrant and former fruit peddler. Although his spectacular career was relatively brief, he remains one of the most influential white-collar criminals in American history. The mendacious strategy he developed has inspired past, present, and no doubt future generations of swindlers.

In 1919, Ponzi announced that his Financial Exchange Company of Boston would guarantee an incredible 50% return to investors within 45 days. The plan ostensibly was to purchase international postage coupons in countries where the exchange rate was low and then resell them in countries with higher rates. It was a primitive form of the technique now known as arbitrage—which was refined so deviously by Ivan Boesky in the 1980s. Within 6 months, Ponzi had persuaded 20,000 investors to give him nearly $10 million. The secret of Ponzi's smoke screen was that he paid off early investors with new investors' money, thereby attracting more and more investors. At its height, his company had a *daily* cash flow of $250,000—a phenomenal amount for that time.[25] The mathematics of pyramid scams, however, gives them a relatively short lifespan. Soon after the *Boston Globe* published a sensational exposé in 1920,[26] Ponzi was arrested, convicted of fraud, sentenced to 4 years in federal prison, and later deported. He died a pauper in 1949 in Brazil, where he had run a hot-dog stand.[27] Eighty years later, pyramid investment scams that promise income from the recruitment of others, rather than from the sale of a product, are still commonly known as Ponzis.[28]

C A S E   S T U D Y

Ponzi Schemes—What's Old Is New

If anything, Ponzi schemes are now bigger than ever. According to one prosecutor: "There's a pyramiding frenzy going on in the United States, and hundreds of millions of dollars are exchanging hands."[29] In 1997, businessman Steven Hoffenberg was handed a whopping 20-year sentence by a federal judge in New York for what some were calling *the biggest swindle in American history.* The defendant was also ordered to pay restitution and fines totaling nearly *half a billion dollars.* Hoffenberg, who operated a bill collection company named Towers Financial, admitted that he had defrauded investors of $462 million in a gigantic Ponzi. He had lured thousands of small, vulnerable investors into buying high-interest notes that were paid off with money from subsequent investors. The pyramid collapsed in 1993. Many of Hoffenberg's victims were elderly retirees. One victim, for example, was forced to return to work at the age of 84 after losing his life's savings.[30]

(Continued)

Other recent Ponzi cases include:

❖ A California company, Credit Development International, claimed that for an initial investment of $130 and monthly payments of $30, consumers could obtain unsecured credit cards with high limits and make as much as $18,000 per month by recruiting other participants. The Federal Trade Commission (FTC) found these claims to be false, calling them a mask for a Ponzi scheme.[31]

❖ Three salesmen for another California company, Metro Display Advertising, were convicted of fraud after they swindled 1200 people out of $46 million. The company owned bus shelters in Los Angeles and Las Vegas. Investors paid $10,000 and were assured of hefty returns of up to 20% each year. It was nothing more than a classic Ponzi, in which money from new investors was used to pay earlier investors.[32]

❖ Yet a third California firm, FutureNet Online, settled charges with the FTC for their illegal marketing practices of Internet access devices. Consumers paid fees ranging from $195 to $794 to become FutureNet distributors. But most of the income they were promised did not come from sales of the devices (which are available at major retailers for less money). "Instead the promised income could only come from fees paid by newly recruited distributors who would in turn recruit more distributors, and continue to seek and recruit and collect fees from an endless 'downline' of new distributors."[33] As with any pyramid program, 90% of investors lost money.[34]

❖ Houston police raided a meeting of the Jubilee Celebration Paradigm and seized more than $730,000 from participants. The operation was part of a multimillion-dollar, nationwide pyramid scheme. To join, one needed to pay $2000 in cash and recruit two more members.[35] A few months later, police raided another pyramid meeting in Houston. This time it was the Ya-Ya Girls, an operation which persuaded women to invest $5000 in hopes of getting a return of $40,000.[36]

❖ One of Charles Ponzi's most nefarious reincarnations was David Burry, who defrauded relatives and neighbors out of more than $25 million, much of it the retirement savings and children's college funds of lifelong friends. He used their money to buy luxury cars and homes, a 48-foot yacht, a private helicopter, and other conspicuous trappings of wealth.[37] Burry was the owner of CF Foods, a wholesale candy distributor. The company, like Burry, appeared to be very successful; but it was a classic Ponzi. Burry promised investors returns of 18% to 30% but instead of generating sales and profits, he simply paid off some old investors with money from newer investors and pocketed the rest.[38] The sense of personal betrayal was devastating. David Burry was known in his community as a man who gave generously to charities and attended church regularly every Sunday. He even attended Bible classes, although he evidently missed the one covering the Fifth Commandment: Thou shall not steal.

❖ Perhaps the fastest growing fraud in the United States involves the sale of fraudulent promissory notes, mostly to the elderly. Promissory notes are a form of

(Continued)

short-term debt that companies use to borrow cash, akin to an "IOU." A loophole in securities laws exempts some 9-month promissory notes from regulatory scrutiny. Investors are promised a "risk free" return of between 9% and 12%, which is enticing but not so high as to cause alarm. The notes often are purported to be "bonded" by foreign insurance companies, which are fake.[39] The Securities and Exchange Commission alleges that this is just another complicated Ponzi, in which only early investors see any return on their money[40]; later investors lose everything. Thousands of victims have incurred known losses of nearly $500 million.[41] According to one state official: "Two years ago, promissory note fraud 'wasn't even on the list of Top 10 scams. This year it's No 1.'"[42] A recent example would be Brian Russell Stearns, a Ponzi artist who swindled 300 Texans out of more than $50 million by peddling promissory notes and other fake financial instruments.[43] Most of the victims were residents of his wife's hometown of Brady, Texas—a town best known until then for its annual goat cook-off.[44]

❖ People who recently received e-mails with a subject line that read, "Hotter than anything you've ever seen,"[45] probably thought it was one of those tacky sex ads. But it was worse. It was a pyramid investment offer:

> Follow the simple instructions and in two weeks you will have US $10,000 in your bank account. Because of the LOW INVESTMENT, SPEED and HIGH POTENTIAL, this program has a VERY HIGH RESPONSE RATE![46]

According to the U.S. Postal Inspection Service, 80% of the scams involving junk e-mail (known as "spam") are for pyramid schemes.[47] E-mail has provided a perfect new environment for one of the most rudimentary cons—the chain letter. Chain letters can sound so seductive, until one does the math. For example, if you are number six in the chain, the letter must go five more rounds before you move to the top of the list. If everyone is expected to send the chain to five other persons, who each in turn must send it to five others, and so on, that means that almost *10 million people* have to respond before you collect a dime.[48] Good luck.

International financier Ivar Kreuger, a contemporary of Ponzi, was even more audacious. By switching around assets and liabilities or creating entirely fictitious assets, Kreuger swindled his shareholders and moneylenders out of $500 million.[49]

Public skepticism about the morality of big business, which had been fostered by writers like Brandeis and Ross, intensified during the Great Depression of the 1930s. The stock market crash of 1929 had laid bare the reckless speculation and rampant frauds that had fueled the economic boom of the 1920s. One sardonic journalist of the time quipped: "If you steal $25, you're a thief. If you steal $250,000, you're an embezzler. If you steal $2,500,000, you're a financier.[50]

In 1933, the nation was rocked by a monetary crisis that eventually led to the closure of over 500 banks. This was before the establishment of federal deposit insurance, so depositors simply lost their money in one stroke, wiping out the life savings of thousands of working men and women. Quite understandably, there was great public resentment toward banks and bankers, an attitude that was captured in the bitter lines of a popular folk song about the colorful bank robber, Pretty Boy Floyd:

> Now as through this world I ramble,
> I see lots of funny men,
> Some will rob you with a six gun,
> And some with a fountain pen.
>
> But as through this life you travel,
> And as through your life you roam,
> You won't ever see an outlaw
> Drive a family from their home.

From "Pretty Boy Floyd." Words and music by Woody Guthrie.[51]

As Guthrie's lyrics suggest, the notorious gangsters who captured the public's attention during the 1930s often became unlikely folk heroes because, in a perverse way, they exemplified the populist spirit of defiance of big business and big government. Part of the admiration of "public enemies" was probably based on a few well-publicized acts of community benevolence. Pretty Boy Floyd, for example, was noted for distributing turkey dinners to the poor on Thanksgiving Day. But another aspect of that popularity undoubtedly stemmed from the deep antipathy that many victims of the Depression felt toward big business and their sense, however misguided, that outlaws represented the struggles of the common man. This, then, was the environment in which Sutherland developed his ideas about white-collar crime—an environment where the battered masses were openly hostile to the economic elite.

Despite its resonance, however, Sutherland's message did not spark an immediate stampede of academic attention. Indeed, it was not until the 1970s that his ideas would be more fully applied to empirical research. This delay was caused mainly by historical circumstance. Sutherland's seminal work, *White Collar Crime,* was not published until 1949. It coincided with the dawn of an era of conformity which spanned nearly 20 years, during which the populist anti-authority spirit was replaced by an atmosphere of public confidence in the ability of corporate America to guide the country to new heights of prosperity. Even within the discipline of sociology, the dominant theoretical position was functionalism, a perspective that focused on societal equilibrium and the maintenance of the status quo, rather than on inequality and flaws in the social system.

Often enough this faith in the good intentions of corporate America proved to be misplaced. The "Great Salad Oil Swindle" of 1963 stands out as such an instance. The Allied Crude Vegetable Oil Refining Corporation devised an elaborate and ingenious way of vastly inflating its inventory of salad oil.

[The company] filled many of its vats with water, adding only a top layer of oil. Pipes connected the vats underground, so that the layer of oil could be shifted across the vats as needed during the inventory observation procedure.[52]

By the time this massive hoax was uncovered, Allied had sold its financiers $175 million worth of phantom salad oil.[53]

During this same era, a similar deception was perpetrated by the flamboyant Texas wheeler-dealer Billie Sol Estes. Estes had cornered the liquid fertilizer (anhydrous ammonia) market in 1959 by dropping his retail price from $100 per ton to $20, running his competitors out of business. Because his wholesale cost was $80, the price war inevitably drained Estes' capital and he could not pay his bills. His wily solution was to keep borrowing large amounts of money from his creditors. Estes later explained: "You borrow enough from a banker and you no longer have a creditor. . . . You get into somebody deep enough, and you've got a partner."[54]

As collateral Estes used government contracts he had received to store surplus grain in his warehouses, along with his assurances that he would be receiving many additional contracts, with the help of his friend and political benefactor, then-Senator Lyndon Johnson of Texas. Estes later "borrowed" millions more from other lenders, this time using as collateral suspicious mortgages he held on huge metal tanks in which his liquid fertilizer was stored. Unlike the "Great Salad Oil Swindle," it was not the *contents* of the tanks that did not exist—it was the tanks themselves. They had not even been built.

Estes was arrested and later convicted on a bevy of charges related to his invisible assets. In 1963, he was sentenced to 15 years in federal prison.[55] Lyndon Johnson, who had adroitly distanced himself from his former crony, was never formally implicated and remained largely untouched by the scandal. Twenty months later, he was the president of the United States.

Despite such revelations as the oil and fertilizer tank frauds, and the huge electrical equipment price-fixing conspiracy detailed in Chapter 2, most Americans of that time were less inclined to view business as a problem than as a solution. This mood changed abruptly, however, during the late 1960s and early 1970s, when social unrest once again brought into question the legitimacy of those holding power. A number of important events reinforced this renascent skepticism: the Watergate scandal, the unpopular Vietnam War, stories of unlawful conduct on the part of the Central Intelligence Agency (CIA) and the Federal Bureau of Investigation (FBI). The complicity of large corporations in these abuses of power served to discredit the integrity of the economic, as well as the political, elite. Surveys conducted during this period found that the public's trust in business and political leaders had diminished significantly. One poll reported, for example, that the proportion of Americans who indicated "a great deal of confidence" in the people running major companies declined from 55% in 1966 to just 16% in 1976.[56]

A by-product of this revival of mass cynicism was a heightening of interest in white-collar crime. In the 1970s, the Justice Department undertook some unusually vigorous prosecutions of white-collar offenders, including such corrupt politicians as Vice-President Spiro Agnew, several state governors, and White House budget director Bert Lance.[57] Even the FBI, which had never before demonstrated much passion in this area, substantially increased its budget for white-collar crime investigations.[58]

The disillusionment with political and business leaders in the 1970s also generated a resurgence of academic work on white-collar crime, as sociologists and criminologists rediscovered many of the notions raised by Sutherland decades earlier. An important study by Clinard and Yeager[59] utilized some of Sutherland's empirical methods to reveal high levels of lawbreaking among major American corporations. A number of other studies documented the dynamics of white-collar criminality in such industries as securities,[60] automobiles,[61] liquor,[62] and prescription drugs.[63]

In addition, criminologists undertook examinations of the justice system's response to white-collar crime, testing the hypothesis that higher status offenders received preferential treatment.[64] Theorists also began to look for the sources of white-collar criminality in organizational characteristics[65] and to acknowledge the uniqueness of corporate crime.[66]

And then came the 1980s, a period that spawned white-collar crimes of such unprecedented magnitude that it was already dubbed the "greed decade" before it was half over. In 1983, the FBI investigated 1825 cases of white-collar crimes involving losses of $100,000 or more. In 1988, the number had jumped to 3448, an increase of 89% in 5 years.[67] The excesses of this era were often attributed to a cultural shift in which Americans became dominated by unbridled material ambition. Business schools and BMW dealerships prospered, while public schools decayed and urban streets became war zones. Many observers believed that this change in values was a reflection of a presidential administration whose philosophy stressed nineteenth century rugged individualism, in which the right of the individual to prosper outweighed the collective welfare of society. The primary role of government became the elimination of any obstacles to profit. The "greed is good" credo, quoted at the beginning of this chapter, extolled winning by any means. It is now evident that a favorite means was white-collar crime.

Some offenders became household names. On Wall Street, investment broker Ivan Boesky illegally manipulated the stock market and in the process redefined the crime of insider trading. On an even grander scale, junk bond guru Michael Milken started a chain reaction that buried the American economy under massive debt when he oversold billions of dollars worth of high-risk securities to banks, insurance companies, and other financial institutions. In California, perfidious entrepreneur Charles Keating plundered the Lincoln Savings and Loan Association, causing the biggest bank failure in American history and contributing heavily to a numbing bailout of the S & L industry at the expense of innocent taxpayers. The unholy trio of Boesky, Milken, and Keating all went to prison, and their respective stories are chronicled in detail in subsequent chapters. But they were only high-profile representatives of a time when a stunned public witnessed a seemingly endless procession of revelations about misconduct at all levels of business and government.

Consider, for example, the rise and fall of Barry Minkow. This book will relate many case studies of white-collar crime—some notorious, some obscure. But none is more astonishing nor more reflective of the anything-for-a-buck mentality that permeated the 1980s than the tale of a young man, barely out of his teens, who created a make-believe company and came within weeks of swindling some of the savviest grownups on Wall Street out of $80 million.

C A S E   S T U D Y

The $80 Million Kid

In 1981, a 16-year-old Los Angeles high school student and aspiring body-builder named Barry Minkow borrowed $1500 and formed a carpet cleaning company he named ZZZZ Best (pronounced Zee-Best). The largely unregulated carpet cleaning business has long been riddled with questionable practices, from deceptive advertising to "bait-and-switch" telephone solicitations, through which glib hustlers can double or triple a low-priced contract by talking customers into costly extra services after entering their homes. Minkow, boyishly charming, intensely ambitious, and completely unscrupulous, had been learning the business part-time since he was 14 and was now eager to go out and swindle people on his own.

ZZZZ Best initially was a failure. Minkow ignored the day-to-day cost controls required of any new enterprise in favor of reveling in the flashy role of teenage tycoon. By the time he turned 17, he was heavily in debt. His curious solution was to open a second location, which he financed by stealing his grandmother's jewelry. As his bills mounted and Minkow could no longer even meet his payroll, he turned to insurance fraud to raise cash. In 1983, he kicked a hole in his office door and reported that he had been robbed. He contacted his adjuster and claimed the loss by theft of several $1000 "Corwell Triple-Vac Dual-Pump Water-Heated Steam Cleaners," a nonexistent machine for which he produced fake invoices. His staged break-in netted Minkow about $16,000. He would later repeat this scam a number of times at other ZZZZ Best locations.

In order to secure new loans, bank officers demanded financial statements and tax returns. Because Minkow had never prepared or filed either, he resorted to counterfeiting. He used bogus paperwork, along with his talent for inventing impressive-sounding but fictitious equipment, to entice a $30,000 loan from a private investor, a reputed mobster. In addition, Minkow stole over $10,000 worth of blank money orders, which he used to pay off some of his more pressing debts. He also began resorting to credit card fraud by adding zeroes to customers' bills.

In retrospect, it seems incredible that ZZZZ Best managed to stay afloat; yet somehow it continued to operate. Still too young to buy a drink, Minkow drove a new sports car and purchased an expensive condominium. His parents were now working for him; he insisted that they call him Mr. Minkow.

Had Barry Minkow been arrested at this point—as he clearly should have been—the story of ZZZZ Best would hardly be worth telling. Minkow could have

(Continued)

been dismissed as a precocious sociopath whose childish greed was hopelessly overmatched in the adult world. But it seemed that it was the adult world that was overmatched. In 1985, Minkow found a way to elevate a sleazy little scam to major white-collar crime status. If lenders were willing to believe in a company that barely existed except on forged documents, why not make ZZZZ Best even bigger and more attractive to investors?

Using stolen insurance company stationary, Minkow awarded himself hundreds of thousands of dollars in fictitious fire and water damage restoration contracts. One of his most outrageous claims was that he had successfully bid on a $3 million contract to restore an eight-story building in the small town of Arroyo Garden, California. The tallest building in Arroyo Garden was only three stories high. Asked by lenders for pictures of the job site, Minkow provided photographs shot from shoe level and cropped at the roof of the building, creating the illusion of additional stories. This crude ploy somehow satisfied bank loan officers. Nobody seemed to wonder how these million-dollar contracts were falling into the lap of a 19-year-old kid. A federal prosecutor would later observe that, if carpet cleaning were really so profitable, he would have tossed his desk out the window and changed careers.[68]

In 1986, Minkow decided to make ZZZZ Best a public corporation. "If the public could be persuaded to buy large amounts of ZZZZ Best stock—as investors surely would after that stock had been hyped by a salesman as good as Barry had become—it would provide new sources of cash that *would not have to be paid back*."[69] It was the very essence of the "creative financing" that propelled the 1980s. However, because his doctored financial statements could never survive scrutiny from the Securities and Exchange Commission (SEC), he utilized a backdoor method, known as a shell route. ZZZZ Best merged with Morningstar Industries, an inactive Utah mineral exploration firm, and acquired Morningstar's publicly owned shares in exchange for stock in the newly-formed corporation. Minkow personally received 76% of the shares. He was now worth *$12 million* on paper. The mayor of Los Angeles declared November 8, 1986, Barry Minkow Day.

ZZZZ Best had never been anything more than a preposterous Ponzi scheme, a pyramid swindle in which money was raised continually from new investors to pay off old investors. Minkow made it look as easy as Ponzi had six decades earlier. By April 1987, ZZZZ Best stock was selling for $18 a share. The company's book value (total shares multiplied by price per share) was $210 million. Barry Minkow was now worth *$109 million* on paper.

In 1987, less than a month after Minkow's twenty-first birthday, he met with the preeminent Wall Street firm of Drexel, Burnham, Lambert, whose junk bond department, led by superstar Michael Milken, had revolutionized the high-yield, high-risk securities industry by fueling a voracious takeover binge driven by massive debt. Drexel agreed to raise $80 million, via junk bonds, for ZZZZ Best to buy out KeyServ, a Philadelphia-based cleaning service which operated in 43 major markets under contract to Sears, Roebuck, & Company. "By buying KeyServ, ZZZZ Best could get off the Ponzi treadmill, take advantage of the revered Sears name,

(Continued)

pay off its other debts, do away with the nonexistent damage-restoration business, and (theoretically) live happily ever after."[70]

Drexel also proposed a future deal in which it would raise an astounding $650 million for ZZZZ Best to launch a hostile takeover of Service Master, a multi-billion dollar commercial cleaning contractor. Barry Minkow did not even have to ask.

Thanks to a number of television appearances in which he showcased his manic charisma, Minkow became something of a media celebrity. Influential magazines like *Newsweek, Inc.,* and *American Banker* ran features on the emerging legend of an entrepreneurial prodigy. Far less flattering, however, was an investigative report published in the *Los Angeles Times* on May 22, 1987, that would forever puncture the ZZZZ Best myth and collapse Barry Minkow's phony little empire. It was all laid out in the 1200-word article.[71] Within a month, ZZZZ Best stock plummeted from $18 to $6. The world had finally seen the real Barry Minkow and his perversion of the American dream.

In July, 1987, Minkow resigned from ZZZZ Best at the age of 22, citing ill health. Shares were now selling for mere pennies. In 1988, he was indicted by a federal grand jury and the case of *United States v. Barry J. Minkow* went to trial. In the words of one attorney: "It's astounding that a fellow who's hardly shaving could cause a financial debacle of this kind."[72] Minkow was charged with bank, stock, and mail fraud, money laundering, racketeering, conspiracy, and tax evasion. ZZZZ Best, a company once purported to be worth hundreds of millions of dollars, auctioned off its entire assets for only $62,000—not even enough to cover Minkow's bail. He was convicted on all 57 counts and received a stiff 25-year prison sentence. Some time later, when Assistant U.S. Attorney Maury Leiter was touring the new federal detention center in downtown Los Angeles, he heard one of the prisoners call his name. It was Barry Minkow:

> "Hey, Mr. Leiter—how do you like the place?"
> "It seems very nice," the prosecutor said.
> "It's real nice," Barry agreed. "The carpets are real clean, too. And they're gonna stay that way, for a long, long time."[73]

If the 1980s was the greed decade, the 1990s might well be dubbed the "betrayal decade." The huge institutionalized corruption that marked the S & L collapse and the insider trading scandals may not have been as manifest, but stories surfaced again and again of persons abusing their positions of trust to deceive and betray. Indeed, the signature phrase of the 1990s may have been uttered by the victim of a multimillion-dollar embezzlement: "I'm hurt and angry that our trust was betrayed."[74]

Barry Minkow served as a kind of poster-boy for white-collar crime in the greed decade. Regrettably, there is no shortage of candidates to represent the betrayal decade. One worthy successor might be Russell Erxleben, a football hero who exploited his fame and traded his honor for 30 pieces of foreign currency.

C A S E   S T U D Y

Russell Erxleben—All-American Crook

Russell Erxleben was a legend in the annals of Texas football, first in high school and later as a three-time All-American placekicker and punter (1976–1978) at the University of Texas, Austin. He still holds the record for the longest field goal in collegiate history—67 yards! He was a first-round draft pick of the NFL's New Orleans Saints, one of the few kickers ever drafted so high. When his 10-year professional football career ended in 1988, he spent most of his time overseeing some real estate investments and playing golf. He was looking for a new career and became involved in a number of short-time ventures in telecommunications, oil and gas, and seafood processing,[75] all of which reportedly failed.[76]

Then, in the early 1990s, Erxleben agreed to invest a little money in the foreign currency exchange market through a broker friend in Houston. This exotic market seemed to ignite the competitive juices in the ex-jock. He worked hard to learn as much as he could about the process. He learned that currency trading is a huge operation. "Approximately $1.5 trillion is traded in the foreign exchange market every day, with about 18% of that occurring in the United States."[77] He also discovered that "[f]oreign currency trading is not a well-known investment vehicle in the United States, except at the institutional level. A piddley amount of trading is done for U.S. consumers at the retail level."[78]

Brokers make money for clients by predicting currency fluctuations. In other words, if a broker makes a Swiss franc buy, for example, he or she is betting that the Swiss franc price will drop. Experienced brokers will carefully look for certain events known to trigger interest rate changes, such as statements by the Federal Reserve Bank or by key foreign governments. Successful currency traders also attend to more subtle signs or even their own well-honed instincts.[79]

"Erxleben learned the process the hard way, forking over his own money and losing quite a bit early on."[80] But he chose not to punt and slowly began to have some trading success. By 1996, Erxleben was the president of his own currency trading firm, Austin Forex. In a 1997 interview with the *Austin Business Journal,* the company's chief administrative officer said: "Russell has a God-given talent. This is not the kind of thing you can pick up from books."[81]

Erxleben's football fame obviously lent him a built-in advantage as a start-up entrepreneur. His name had immediate recognizability in a state where football is almost a religion. Before long, Erxleben was making a lot of money for himself and his clients. In its first year, Austin Forex had an annual average return of 100%.[82] In that one year, the company's trading value had soared from 11 clients and $500,000 to 80 clients and over $5 million. The firm moved to plush new offices and had 15 full-time traders in its employ.[83] The *Austin Business Journal* extolled Erxleben's work ethic and "conservative principles."[84]

As word of his success spread, new clients arrived. Austin Forex now required a minimum investment of $20,000. People cashed in life insurance policies

(Continued)

and college savings accounts to increase their contributions.[85] In Erxleben's words: "I can't build a company if people lose money."[86]

If the Erxleben tale ended here it would be a nice little "All American" success story—the local boy making good a second time. But this is not a book about success stories; it is a book about criminals and their victims. The *Austin Business Journal* feature that lionized Erxleben came out on October 17, 1997. Within a few months, he was being investigated by the Texas State Securities Board and a federal grand jury.[87] On September 11, 1998, Austin Forex, already under the control of a temporary receiver, closed its doors forever.[88]

The court-appointed receiver reaffirmed that Austin Forex was nothing more than a Ponzi: "It appeared to me that Austin Forex had no sources of income other than investors' money, so any funds paid to investors came from other investors."[89]

Erxleben attempted to put the company into Chapter 11 protection, but at a bankruptcy hearing in November 1997 a warning letter written to Erxleben by one of his lawyers was presented as evidence:

> Recruiting new investors to satisfy old investors while the problem grows bigger and bigger is the essence of a classic Ponzi or pyramid scheme. It is fraudulent beyond any doubt and may very well subject you to both civil and criminal liability.[90]

Largely as a result of this damning evidence, a federal bankruptcy judge ruled against Erxleben and denied his company court protection.[91] Erxleben was later sued by a group of his investors, who accused him of defrauding them of $1 million.[92] In May 1999, he agreed to a $4.7 million dollar settlement, which included stiff punitive damages.[93] How the plaintiffs could ever hope to collect seemed highly problematic. Austin Forex, which had taken in $50 million from about 800 investors, now had only $400,000 in cash.[94]

His lawyer argued: "Mr. Erxleben lost the money in trading. He did not put money in his pocket. He does not have a hidden fund of cash. He just made a lot of bad trades and lost the money."[95] Investigators had once suspected that Erxleben had squirreled away a tidy sum in some offshore bank account but eventually concluded that "he had simply been very ill-equipped for the complicated and highly volatile world of currency trading and lost all the money."[96]

According to Erxleben, he had done nothing illegal. He was as wrong about that as he was about the vagaries of the currency market. Losing money in bad investments may not be illegal, but what *is* illegal is not telling clients about their losses and sending them false financial statements, accusations Erxleben did not dispute.[97] It was also illegal to mislead investors by lying about how successful his company's investments were, about the risks involved, and about how their investments would be used.[98]

In late 1999, Erxleben agreed to plead guilty to federal charges of conspiracy and fraud and agreed to cooperate with efforts to recover clients' money. "It

(Continued)

was the right thing to do," he said. "I never intended to defraud anybody, but in the process I broke the law. The bottom line is, I have to stand up to it, take my medicine and try to get through this the best I can."[99] His clients were not moved a bit by his apology. In the words of one: "The guy's just a real problem case. I don't think he truly understands the extent of his wrongdoing; nor does he care."[100]

So which was the "real" Russell Erxleben: the contrite incompetent revealed in the first quote or the conscienceless crook portrayed in the second? The question was perhaps answered in August 2000 when Erxleben, still awaiting sentencing on his fraud and conspiracy convictions, was cited for contempt. A judge found him guilty of impeding efforts to recover assets from Austin Forex. Erxleben had refused to respond to nine separate court orders since his plea bargain a year earlier.[101] All Austin Forex assets were supposed to have been liquidated and returned to investors. But Erxleben—Mr. "I have to take my medicine"—failed to report items such as Rolex watches, diamond rings, and promissory notes purchased with company funds.[102] He had also cashed savings bonds bought by his failed company and concealed information about a bank account held in his wife's name.[103] He was handed a 6-month jail sentence, pending appeal.[104]

On September 18, 2000, Russell Erxleben was sentenced to 7 years in federal prison. He was also fined $1 million and ordered to pay $28 million in restitution.[105] He remained free on bond during a series of technical delays. However, his bond was revoked and he was locked up in October after he allegedly threatened the life of an ex-friend and former investor.[106]

When Austin Forex was riding high, Erxlaben once preached: "You cannot come into this business with a little money." What he neglected to add was that if you trusted him, you could not expect to come *out* of that business with *any* money.

According to a study conducted by the Association of Certified Fraud Examiners, white-collar crime actually appeared to be on the upswing in the 1990s.[107] The group's 1998 survey of 600 fraud auditors reported that eight out of ten believed that white-collar crime had worsened over the previous 5 years.[108] Perhaps emblematic of the decade was the tax fraud imprisonment of Catalina Vasquez Villalpando. Tax evasion is a fairly routine offense; except in this case Ms. Villalpando was the *treasurer of the United States;* thus, all the paper money printed in the United States between 1990 and 1994 bears the signature of a convicted felon.[109]

From the California cell biologist who faked his research findings, which supposedly linking electric power to cancer, in order to win a $3.3 million grant from the federal government[110] to the world-famous Thoroughbred farm accused of killing a champion stallion to collect on a $35 million insurance policy,[111] the decade of 1990s was a cornucopia of perfidy.

Even Salt Lake City, long considered a bastion of traditional American morality, the capital of a state where Bill Clinton finished *third* in the 1992 presidential election,[112] was not immune. Its bid for the 2002 Winter Olympics "[turned] the city of the Latter-Day Saints into a by-word for present-day scandal."[113]

An Olympic-Sized Scandal

Salt Lake City, Utah, had been pursuing the Winter Olympics for 30 years. Its first bid was in 1966 when it took a run at the 1972 games. This initial quest was so inept it bordered on comical. For example, the bid committee commissioned a translation of its promotional literature into French, including a geographical description of Utah describing its location in the "Great Basin of the West." For some reason, the translator used the phrase "Grand Basin," which in French meant that Utah was in the "Toilet of the West."[114] Needless to say, the bid was unsuccessful.

Over the years, a feeling grew within the Salt Lake City Olympic Committee that they were out of the loop, that something about their style did not dovetail with the practices and expectations of the International Olympic Committee (IOC). For example, when bid committee officials from the city arrived at an IOC meeting in Puerto Rico in 1989, they brought nothing with them but their serious ambitions and some Salt Lake City souvenir letter openers to distribute to the IOC. Thomas K. Welch, the head of the bid committee, recalls:

> When we arrived there, the Greeks were entertaining on their yacht, with gorgeous hostesses. Atlanta had rented a mansion, shipped in furniture from Atlanta and called it the Atlanta House. Toronto had set up a whole wing out by the pool and were serving breakfasts, lunches and dinners to the I.O.C. . . . Everyone was giving wonderful gifts—I think there were crystal vases and jewelry. Bid cities each had limousines. We showed up with nothing—on a bus.[115]

Welch says that on the eve of the vote for the 1998 games he was approached by the son of an IOC member, who offered to swing several votes to Utah for $35,000.[116] The bid committee refused, probably because they did not have the money. Nagano, Japan, with its second-rate facilities and mediocre snow, won by four votes.[117] At that point, Salt Lake City boosters decided to play by the unwritten rules of the Olympic movement and "do whatever it took to woo the Olympics."[118]

"Whatever it took" turned out to be at least $1.2 million bestowed upon IOC members and their families.[119] For example, the head of Canadian Olympic Association allegedly was given a free face-lift valued at $50,000 by the Utah bid committee in exchange for her support.[120] The bribes and payoffs to the IOC also included "scholarships, free medical care, expensive firearms, help with a lucrative property deal and, it is rumored, nights with prostitutes."[121]

The bid committee determined that the swing votes on the IOC belonged to its African members. They knew that no Olympic bid had ever been successful without African support, so they lavished particular attention on those delegates. An agreement was made to provide training and support for Sudanese athletes.[122] The IOC delegate from the Republic of the Congo received more than $70,000 in cash and an estimated $200,000 in "benefits."[123] The IOC delegate from Kenya received direct payments totaling $34,650.[124] "The children of I.O.C. members from Mali and Cameroon received more than $100,000 each in bogus scholarships and

(Continued)

payments."[125] A grandson of the Algerian delegate received a payment of $14,500.[126] The wives of delegates from Mauritius and Togo were given trips to Europe.[127] The son of an IOC member from Swaziland showed up regularly at the bid committee's Salt Lake City offices, opened the door and asked: "Where's my check?" And checks were cut.[128]

> From February 1993 to February 1996, the bid committee paid installments of $500 that totaled $14,500 to a Raouf Scally, who was thought to be a relative of an I.O.C. member. Local Olympic officials still have no certain idea who Scally is or what North African country he came from.[129]

But the handouts were by no means limited to African delegates. Three couples with IOC ties, including delegates from Australia and Guatemala, were given a trip to the Super Bowl valued at $20,000.[130] Other delegates were treated to trips to New York City, Las Vegas, and Disneyland.[131] The husband of the Finnish delegate received a $33,750 consulting fee from a Utah engineering firm.[132] Thomas Welch himself set up the Korean delegate's son with sham consulting work at a local communications company, with the bid committee paying most of his salary. The bid committee even arranged for the Korean delegate's daughter to perform with the Utah symphony.[133] The daughter of the Ecuadorean delegate was enrolled in the phony Salt Lake Organizing Committee (SLOC) "scholarship program" and received $23,000 in "living expenses." She was not even a student; she was a 44-year-old divorcee.[134]

Salt Lake City was officially awarded the 2002 Winter Olympics in 1995. But what should have been the end of the story turned out to be only the beginning. The tale went public when a Salt Lake City television journalist was given a draft copy of a letter written in 1996 on Salt Lake Olympic Committee (SLOC) stationary by its vice-president, David Johnson, addressed to the daughter of an IOC official. The young woman had been receiving money for tuition, rent, and expenses for 3 years. But now that the bid had been secured, her gravy train was about to pull out of the station.

> "Under the current budget structure, it will be difficult to continue the scholarship program with you. . . . The enclosed check for $10,114.99 will have to be our last payment for tuition."[135]

The letter set off the biggest corruption scandal in the history of the Olympics and became "the story that launched a thousand stories."[136]

Among those stories launched were reports that began surfacing immediately about corruption in past successful Olympic bids, including Nagano,[137] Atlanta,[138] and Sydney.[139] The governor of Utah declared: "Olympic corruption didn't start here, but it must end here."[140]

Fallout continued from the evolving scandal. At least two major sponsors of the 2002 games—Johnson & Johnson and John Hancock Insurance—withdrew their sponsorship,[141] and the Senate Commerce Committee held hearings to con-

(Continued)

sider stripping the IOC of its tax-exempt status. The committee denounced the IOC but chose to hold off on any action until the Committee had time to enact promised reforms. Those reforms began in 1999 when the IOC expelled six of its members—leaving only 106 members remaining.[142]

Welch and Johnson were investigated under the Utah commercial bribery statute but were never charged. The state claimed it could find no evidence that the men committed a crime because there seemed to be no victim.[143] But the Justice Department saw it differently. After a 19-month probe,[144] Welch and Johnson were indicted by a federal grand jury for felony conspiracy, fraud, and racketeering.[145] They were also accused of diverting $130,000 for their personal use.[146] Both men defiantly maintained their innocence. They insisted that everything they did had been done with the tacit approval of the Utah business and political figures with whom they dealt. They claimed that other Olympic officials knew what they were doing and that unnamed politicians were "involved."[147] Johnson's attorney argued: "It was open and notorious that people in the IOC were treated like royalty."[148] Welch's lawyer added that his client had done nothing more than any other representative from any other city wooing the IOC had done.[149]

The trial was scheduled to begin in June 2001.[150] The charges against each defendant carry a combined sentence of up to 75 years in prison.[151] Because no one denies the payments that were made, it will be up to a jury to decide if crimes were committed or if the Salt Lake City Olympic bid was simply a winning strategy in a fiercely competitive game. The defense characterizes the payoffs as "goodwill gifts."[152] Prosecutors assert that it was "unmistakably bribery."[153]

Another sign of the betrayal decade was the proliferation of embezzlement, a crime of flagrant betrayal. For example, Donald Bunsis, a once-trusted lawyer and financial adviser, was sentenced to 15 months in federal prison in 1997 after he embezzled more than $2 million from elderly clients, many of them long-time friends.[154]

The decade also witnessed three separate trade groups that were victimized by trusted insiders. In the early 1990s, the Washington-based Edison Electric Institute discovered that one of its employees had siphoned off more than $600,000 by inventing fake vendors and opening checking accounts in their names.[155] In 1997, the chief financial officer of the California-based American Electronics Association diverted more than $800,000.[156] And two years later, the president of the Washington-based Natural Gas Supply Association pleaded guilty to charges that he had embezzled $2.8 million. He had created a number of fictitious "consultants" and had pocketed their hefty fees.[157] According to the prosecutor, most of the stolen money went to "food, drink, [and] travel."[158]

Also in 1997, the chief financial officer of a California meat exporting company confessed to the "wrongful taking" of between $85 million and $95 million.[159] Although his annual salary was "only" $150,000, his lifestyle was strikingly ostentatious by any standards—he even owned his own nightclub, Club Cha Cha. His estranged wife, who allegedly had received 70% of what he pilfered, was even more conspicuous in her consumption. She reportedly owned 20 Thoroughbred horses, an exotic car dealership, and several huge estates in exclusive locales. Each of her homes was decorated with sumptuous furniture and rare antiques. One had a giant aquarium containing sharks; another had precisely landscaped pens filled with llamas, emus, and ostriches.[160] By some accounts, this alleged embezzlement is believed to be the *biggest* ever in the United States.[161]

Perhaps the most memorable embezzlement of the 1990s, however, was not the biggest—only the oddest.

C A S E   S T U D Y

Prell for Ponies?

In 1994, *Forbes* magazine ran a glowing feature on a little-known entrepreneur named Roger Dunavant, who had taken over Straight Arrow Products, a small Bethlehem, Pennsylvania manufacturer of horse-care products. In an act of unaccountable inspiration, Dunavent had begun marketing the company's horse shampoo, *Mane 'n Tail*, for human use.[162] If the concept seems a little silly, it is far sillier to note that people actually started buying this stuff and washing their hair with it—in droves. Straight Arrow's sales went from $500,000 in 1990 to $44 million in 1994.[163]

Dunavant became a celebrity. *People* magazine shot him taking a bubble bath with his kids. Ernst & Young named him a 1995 Manufacturing Entrepreneur of the Year. *Advertising Age* even featured Straight Arrow as one of its 1996 Marketing 100.[164]

Straight Arrow had begun in Phil and Bonnie Katsev's kitchen in 1971. When the equestrian couple divorced, Bonnie Katsev became the sole owner. In the early 1990s, tired of running the business, she sold half the firm to her head salesman, Roger Dunavant, and half to her 23-year-old son Devon.[165] Devon Katsev had little interest in the business. "Although he had idly taken a few courses at a local community college and had attended welding school to learn how to fit pipes, the long-haired dreamer thought mainly of becoming a rock star."[166]

Dunavant's imaginative marketing strategy "transformed Straight Arrow from a steady seller of equine products to a fast-growing cosmetics firm for humans."[167] He took his horse shampoo to drugstores, supermarkets, and department store chains. He also began to hype *Mane 'n Tail* with outrageous lies. He told reporters that *Mane 'n Tail* made his hair grow so fast that he had to cut it every week. He said that doctors were recommending the shampoo to chemotherapy patients.[168]

By this time, Dunavant was routinely representing himself as the sole owner of Straight Arrow, even though he owned only half the company. He started

(Continued)

covering his personal expenses with company funds. As his alleged misappropriations went unnoticed, he began transferring assets from Straight Arrow into firms owned by his family. Straight Arrow also began leasing office space "at four times market value from a company partly owned by his wife."[169] *Forbes*, which once hailed Roger Dunavant, now called him "a classic con man."[170]

"While Dunavant pillaged Straight Arrow, his 'partner' Katzev didn't notice a thing."[171] Between 1990 and 1994, Dunavant granted himself $7.3 million in compensation. During this same period, Devon Katzev, who owned half the firm, happily received $600 per week, plus $300 per month in car allowance.[172] Katzev, sounding a bit like the Jeff Spicoli character in *Fast Times at Ridgemont High*, would later testify in court: "I was kind of, like, my hair's long, I'm in this rock status. I was, like, all right."[173]

But in 1993, young Katzev got serious. He had heard rumors about how his partner was looting the company. He finally took a good look at the books and hit Dunavant with a lawsuit.[174] "In February 1996 Dunavant was ordered to repay Straight Arrow $4.5 million. As court-ordered audits of Straight Arrow's books continue, he may be coughing up a lot more."[175]

Dunavant was fired from his job and Katzev was named Straight Arrow's president. Katzev vowed to make Straight Arrow what it once was; but it may have been too late. The circus was leaving town. Wal-Mart had already moved *Mane 'n Tail* off its beauty shelves and into its pet department.[176] A Wal-Mart spokesman explained: "The trend didn't last."[177] The national sales manager for a rival firm agrees: "The horse-shampoo fad is over."[178]

MEASURING WHITE-COLLAR CRIME

Since the 1930s when the FBI first began collecting crime statistics in its Uniform Crime Reports, the federal government has poured billions of dollars into the creation of databases that measure traditional or "street" crimes. As a result, American criminologists now have access to an array of sophisticated data sets that allow them to study crime from a number of perspectives: reported versus unreported crimes; consequences to victims; trends over time; and geographic distributions across the national level or down to individual city blocks. By contrast, government agencies—federal, state, and local—have devoted relatively few resources to gathering data specific to white-collar crime. There are virtually no systematic counts, for instance, of the numbers of white-collar offenses that occur in a given year or the number of individuals arrested for these offenses. Indeed, it is disappointing that we have progressed so little since Sutherland first criticized the class biases in official crime statistics.

At least part of the problem results from the difficulties in arriving at a precise definition of white-collar crime. Deciding which crimes are and which are not white-collar crimes sometimes is not an easy matter to resolve. Even more encumbering is the fact that most white-collar crimes are never reported, constituting a substantial, but unmeasurable, "dark figure." While many street crimes, such as theft, assault, and rape, also go unreported, the numbers are undoubtedly much greater for white-collar crimes because in so many cases, victims are not even aware that they have been victimized. When large manufacturers conspire to fix prices, for example, consumers know only that the cost of their purchases has increased, not that it has done so artificially because of illegal, anticompetitive practices.

Another reason why the government has failed to produce better data on white-collar crime is ideological. Until recently, most officials simply did not consider these offenses to be as serious as street crime, believing that data collection should be directed toward the kinds of traditional crimes typically committed by the lower class. From this perspective, systematic efforts to count crimes committed mainly by middle- and upper-class businessmen are stifled in order to avoid stigmatizing respectable members of the business community.[179]

For all the reasons just noted, researchers have been forced to generate their own statistical data on white-collar crime in order to determine its prevalence—that is, the extent to which it occurs in the population as a whole. These efforts usually have taken one of three forms: cross-sectional studies of large corporations, industry-specific studies, and victimization surveys. The first two types of analysis have relied on the official records of regulatory and law enforcement agencies. Victimization surveys, on the other hand, have sought to measure the public's exposure to white-collar crime.

Cross-Sectional Studies

In his pioneering 1949 study, Sutherland examined the records of criminal and civil courts, as well as administrative agencies, seeking adverse decisions against the 70 biggest manufacturing, mining, and mercantile corporations over the 70-year period up to 1945. "Adverse decisions" consisted of criminal convictions, civil judgments, and actions taken against a company by a regulatory agency or commission.[180] Such a methodology provides an overly conservative measure of corporate criminality, because as we have noted, most white-collar crimes are never reported or sanctioned, and because many of the infractions that are detected are settled out of court. Nonetheless, these data can provide at least a sense of the extent of crime among the corporate elite.

Sutherland found that every one of the 70 corporations in his sample had incurred one or more adverse decisions, with the two most prolific transgressors incurring a total of 50 violations each. Combined, the firms under considerations recorded 980 violations and of these, 158 (16%) were criminal offenses. Looked at in another way, 41 of the 70 corporations (60%) had been convicted on criminal charges, averaging four convictions each. Sutherland remarked that "in many states persons with four convictions are defined by statute to be 'habitual criminals,'" implying that many major corporations would also qualify for that label which would customarily be applied to "common" criminals.[181]

In the 1970s, Marshall Clinard and Peter Yeager updated and expanded Sutherland's analysis by conducting a similar study of the 477 largest publicly owned manufacturing corporations in the United States. They examined criminal, civil, and administrative actions either initiated or completed by 25 federal agencies against these companies in 1975 and 1976. Offenses included: administrative violations (e.g., failure to report information to authorities), financial violations (e.g., illegal payments), labor violations (e.g., occupational safety and health violations), manufacturing violations (e.g., the marketing of unsafe products), and illegal trade practices (e.g., price fixing). Clinard and Yeager found that three-fifths of the 477 manufacturers had at least one action initiated against them in the 2-year period under consideration. Moreover, they found that crime was highly concentrated among certain firms. Just 38 companies were responsible for 52% of all recorded violations, with the heaviest concentration in the oil, pharmaceutical, and automobile industries. The data further indicated that larger corporations were more likely than smaller ones to have committed offenses.[182]

The Clinard and Yeager study was followed by several analyses conducted by journalists, each producing congruent findings. One investigation considered federal criminal cases, limited only to bribery, fraud, illegal political contributions, tax evasion, or antitrust violations, against the 1043 companies that were on the *Fortune* magazine list of the 800 largest industrial corporations at some point between 1970 and 1990. Even using this restrictive range of offenses, 117 (11%) of the companies or their executives—had been charged with at least one of those crimes during the period in question. Interestingly, only 50 executives from just 15 companies actually were sentenced to jail in connection with these cases.[183] Another investigation reported that among the nation's 500 largest corporations, 23% had been the subject of criminal or civil actions for serious misconduct over a 10-year period. Among the 25 biggest companies, 14 had incurred criminal convictions or civil penalties in excess of $50,000.[184]

Viewed together, all these cross-sectional studies indicate that white-collar crime is relatively commonplace among large corporations, especially if one also considers the dark figure of unreported offenses. This does not necessarily mean, of course, that unlawful acts are being committed on a daily basis by these companies. But the findings do suggest that at some point, most major firms, or their executives, will be accused of committing business crimes.

Industry-Specific Studies

Industry-specific studies have confirmed the findings of Sutherland and Clinard and Yeager that criminal and civil penalties tend to be concentrated in certain industries. We will examine some evidence from several major industries with relatively high rates of criminality.

First, consider defense contractors—firms that are repeatedly awarded lucrative contracts by the federal government for defense-related work. Included in this category are such companies as General Dynamics, Lockheed, and McDonnell Douglas that build the fighter planes, aircraft carriers, and sophisticated weapons for the U.S. Army, Navy, and Air Force. A study of the top 100 defense contractors (based on the values of their contracts in 1985) conducted by the General Accounting Office (GAO) found that half of these firms had been the subject of criminal investigations by the Justice Department between 1982 and 1985. These investigations centered on cases of suspected defense procurement fraud involving allegations of overcharging, defective products, and conflicts of interest. Furthermore, 28 of the 100 contractors had been the targets of multiple investigations.[185]

Next, consider the securities industry. Generally, we think of securities fraud in terms of the high-profile insider trading cases on Wall Street, or the heavily publicized stock swindles of crooks like Barry Minkow,[186] or sensational scandals like that of futures trader Nicholas Leeson, who single-handedly caused the failure of Britain's ancient Baring Bank in 1995, when he lost $1.24 billion in unauthorized transactions.[187] It would be short-sighted, however, to exclude other segments of this industry. In the 1980s, rigged trading was also uncovered on the Chicago Mercantile Exchange and the Chicago Board of Trade.[188] Not to be overlooked are the thousands of brokers around the country who handle accounts for small, individual investors. How honest are they? Little empirical evidence on this subject existed until a 1992 study, conducted by the Securities and Exchange Commission (SEC), probed trading practices at 161 branch offices of 9 large brokerage firms. Together, these firms accounted for 49% of all customer accounts in the United States. The SEC reported instances of "excessive trading, unsuitable recommendations, unauthorized trading, [and] improper mutual fund switching" at one-quarter of the offices it examined.[189] Investigators selected 14 branch offices of one of the 9 firms for closer scrutiny. At eight of those offices, they found evidence of routine broker misconduct in handling the accounts of elderly clients.[190]

In late 1995, criminal charges were filed against 11 securities salesmen in a nationwide Justice Department crackdown on "rogue brokers."[191] Among the charges were allegations that the brokers traded securities in customers' accounts without permission and stole from customers by altering trading statements. Some victims reportedly lost their life savings or their children's college funds. Attorney General Janet Reno called the alleged crimes an "inhumane and serious threat to the investment industry."[192] Even more recently, Merrill Lynch agreed to pay a $750,000 fine to settle state charges in Massachusetts that "it failed to properly oversee one executive who committed fraud and another who mismanaged clients' portfolios."[193]

But the problem is not limited to a handful of major securities dealers. Half of the 101 small- and mid-sized brokerages examined by the SEC in 1995 had hired persons with disciplinary histories. The report noted lax supervision by many firms, which pay little attention to the illegal conduct of some unsavory traders in their employ. Many "rogue brokers" dodge from one Wall Street address to another, honing their sleazy sales pitches.[194] In one case, regulators identified a broker with a history of unsavory practices and customer complaints who worked at six firms in 1 year.[195] The chairman of the SEC put it bluntly: "The industry is not policing its own ranks."[196]

Examples from other industries abound. A study by a global business investigations and intelligence firm reports that nearly 40% of senior managers at Internet companies have questionable backgrounds, such as criminal convictions or organized crime connections.[197]

Finally, consider the S&L industry of the 1980s, which became institutionally corrupt on a scale seldom witnessed. Between 1980 and 1992, hundreds of S&Ls were forced to shut down because of insolvency. One major study found suspected fraud at two-thirds of the 686 insolvent S&Ls that were under the supervision of the Resolution Trust Corporation in 1992—losses due to fraud at each of those institutions averaged over $12 million.[198]

Thus, although white-collar crime is no stranger to the entire corporate world, it is clearly concentrated in specific industries whose structures are conducive to criminality. As we shall see in later chapters, these "criminogenic" industries create both opportunities for crime and conditions that conceal illegal acts from the authorities.

Victimization Surveys

Another way to measure the extent of white-collar crime is to ask members of the public about their exposure to it. Victimization surveys have been used for many years to gain more accurate information about the prevalence of street crime. Only recently, however, has this method been used to collect data on white-collar crime. A survey conducted in 1991, for example, asked respondents about personal fraud, defined as "the misrepresentation of facts and the deliberate intent to deceive with the promise of goods, services, or other financial benefits that in fact do not exist or that were never intended to be provided."[199] Of the more than 1,200 subjects randomly selected for the sample, nearly *one-third* reported that they had been the targets of an attempted or successful fraud in the previous year, with a mean loss of $216. The most common forms described were scams involving "free prizes," followed by automobile repair rip-offs (Chapter 2).[200]

THE COSTS OF WHITE-COLLAR CRIME

Given the paucity of official data on white-collar crime, it is not surprising that precise estimates of the economic costs of such offenses are also difficult to determine. Nevertheless, a number of government agencies and private organizations have offered estimates that can help ascertain the magnitude of the problem. The victimization survey cited in the previous section, for example, estimated that personal frauds alone, such as repair scams and free prize swindles, cost American taxpayers about $40 billion annually. In 1974, the U.S. Chamber of Commerce produced a similar $40-billion estimate for the following aggregated offenses: bribery, fraud, kickbacks, payoffs, computer crime, consumer fraud, illegal competition, deceptive practices, embezzlement, pilferage, receiving stolen property, and securities theft.[201]

In 1976, Congress's Joint Economic Committee "estimated that the short-term direct dollar costs of certain white-collar crimes—not including product safety, environmental, chemical, and antitrust violations—is roughly $44 billion a year."[202] If we add to that figure the $30 billion to $60 billion lost annually to antitrust violations[203] and the approximate $25 billion cost to taxpayers for fraud committed against federal agencies,[204] we derive a conservative estimate that increases the cost of white-collar crime in the 1970s to at least $100 billion. Taking inflation into account, that cost today would probably be closer to $250 billion, a figure consistent with more recent projections by the Senate judiciary committee.[205]

To appreciate just how much $250 billion is, consider that the U.S. Bureau of Justice Statistics estimated in 1992 that the monetary costs to all victims of personal crimes (e.g., robbery, assault, larceny) and household crimes (e.g., burglary, motor vehicle theft) totaled $17.6 billion in that year. This figure includes "losses from property theft or damage, cash losses, medical expenses, and amount of pay lost because of injury or activities related to the crime."[206] *Yet even that inclusive total represents only 6% of the projected annual losses from white-collar crime.*

The overall cost differential between white-collar crime and street crime can be underscored as well by the notorious case of Lincoln Savings and Loan, the fraudulent thrift institution run by Charles Keating. After the bank was seized by federal regulators, the price of paying off Lincoln's debts eventually climbed to $3.4 billion.[207] According to the FBI, the losses from all bank robberies in the United States in 1992 was $35 million,[208] about 1% of Keating's misappropriation. Thus, it is likely that the total costs of all American bank robberies in the last 100 years is less than the cost of bailing out a single corrupt S & L.

In addition, some costs of white-collar criminality cannot be measured in dollars and cents, including the physical consequences of crimes such as industrial pollution, the illegal dumping of toxic wastes, injuries and deaths of workers exposed to illegal hazards on the job, and unsafe products marketed to consumers. There are also social and political costs. When influential business executives, powerful politicians, and respected professionals are seen flaunting the system, often suffering little or no punishment for their misdeeds, the average citizen's respect for the law is weakened. One legal scholar has referred to this effect as the "demoralization costs" of the unequal sanctioning of wealthy criminals: "When persons are treated unequally in an area in which they believe equal treatment is a right, both they and their sympathizers (a potentially much larger group) suffer psychic injury that may lead them to reduce their contributions to society, or to take anti-social actions in revenge."[209] Such "anti-social actions" could take the form of property crime committed by members of the underclass, who hear stories about preferential treatment of elite offenders and get a message that "crime pays."

PUBLIC PERCEPTION OF WHITE-COLLAR CRIME

One of the reasons why the government pays so little attention to white-collar crime is that members of the public do not express nearly the same degree of outrage over such crime as they do over street crime, which has become the overriding social issue of our time. Surveys have found that Americans tend to view white-collar crime as a problem, but not a particularly severe one.[210] A 1979 survey, for instance, reported that residents of a small Midwestern community ranked white-collar offenses as far less serious than street crimes involving the theft of property worth $25 or more.[211] Evidently, despite the billions of dollars lost to white-collar crime each year, most Americans still do not accord it a very high priority on their lists of pressing concerns—even today, beneath the rubble of the "greed decade."

Such relative apathy may in turn be explained by the fact that many business crimes are complex and confusing; they often manifest no clear-cut villains and victims the way that street crimes and even political scandals do. To illustrate this important point, compare the public responses to two events. In 1992, the media revealed that one of the many "perks" provided to members of the U.S. House of Representatives was check-writing privileges at a quasi-bank run by the federal government. In sharp variance with the rules enforced at "real" banks, congressional depositors were not required to have sufficient funds in their accounts in order for their bank to cover their checks, which permitted many members of Congress to "bounce" large checks routinely and without penalty.[212] Indeed, records reveal that representatives have been bouncing checks at the House bank as far back as 1830.[213] In a 12-month period between July 1989 and June 1990, 8331 bad checks were written,[214]—an average of 19 per member. When the so-called "Rubbergate" story broke in the press, the popular reaction was one of anger, disgust, and demand for reform. A cry of "throw the bums out" swept the country, causing considerable alarm among incumbent legislators, many of whom lost their seats in 1994.

Contrast this reaction with the public's response to another scandal that had occurred the preceding year, when the media reported that a major Wall Street investment firm, Salomon Brothers, had "rigged" the U.S. treasury bond market.[215] Salomon was one of a select group of buyers allowed to bid on government securities in what is called the "primary market." Those bonds are then resold on a "secondary market" to the public at large. In order to ensure that the primary market remains competitive, federal regulations prohibit individuals or firms from purchasing more than 35% of any bond issue. But on at least three occasions, Salomon traders far exceeded that limit by submitting camouflaged bids in the names of clients. Salomon thus effectively cornered the treasury bond market and in the process, illegally inflated its profits.[216]

Despite the serious economic ramifications of its violations, there were no widespread cries to ban Salomon Brothers from the government securities market. Radio talk shows did not fill the airwaves with the voices of angry callers demanding more accountability on Wall Street. Officers at big investment firms did not fear that their jobs were in jeopardy by an incensed citizenry. In fact, just a few months after the bond scandal, brokerage executives enjoyed the largest increase in their compensation packages in years.[217]

Clearly, there were substantial differences in the public repercussions generated by the sensational "Rubbergate" and the less sensational Treasury bid-rigging cases. The former involved behaviors that most people could understand and relate to. Ordinary persons are well aware that if they write checks on accounts holding insufficient funds, they face at the very least a financial penalty from their bank and perhaps even criminal sanctions. The consequences of bond market manipulation, however, are much more difficult to visualize and comprehend.[218]

Yet, the injury caused by Salomon Brothers was substantially greater than a bunch of checks kited by irresponsible politicians. Salomon's unlawful practices increased the interest that the government—that is to say, the taxpayers—had to pay out to investors. Over time, the ensuing losses will run into billions of dollars. Just as it was with the Boesky, Milken, and Keating cases, the treasury bond scandal came with a delayed detonator. It is an insidious feature of many white-collar crimes that, like Carl Sandburg's fog, they creep in "on little cat feet,"[219] often going unnoticed by a distracted public until the bill comes due.

ABOUT THIS BOOK

The chapters that follow provide detailed descriptions of numerous forms of white-collar crime. This book covers a broad spectrum in order to illustrate the pervasiveness of upper-world criminality across a wide range of institutions, including business, government, the medical profession, even religious organizations, and involving a remarkably diverse set of actors—including captains of industry, politicians, doctors, cops, and computer hackers. The authors have attempted to infuse each chapter with a historical perspective by describing some selected cases from the past in order to illustrate that white-collar crime is not solely a contemporary social problem but has a long and vivid history.

Chapter 2 focuses on some of the deceptive practices that affect many of us directly as consumers. It is a lengthy chapter because consumer fraud is the most prolific of all white-collar crimes. A variety of examples are presented of scams perpetrated by crooked auto repairmen, slick telemarketers, and sleazy merchants. Also emphasized is how some unlawful schemes are carried out at high corporate levels in the form of price fixing, price gouging, and false advertising.

Chapter 3 details the sale of dangerous or defective products to consumers by greedy manufacturers who are fully aware of the potential for harm. Also described are unscrupulous quacks who peddle worthless, and sometimes deadly, medicines and cures. Many of these practices punctuate the fact that some forms of white-collar crime are just as violent as the more dramatic crimes of murder, rape, and robbery.

Chapter 4 explores two other categories of "violent" white-collar crime. The deliberate pollution of the natural environment has become one of the most prevalent of all corporate offenses. We will examine some of the pernicious effects of the tons of lethal chemicals and toxic waste that are dumped illegally in the United States every year. In addition, an amoral trend in this area, as we shall see, is the export of these hazardous substances to Third World countries, whose citizens often have no freedom to protest. This chapter also reviews some of the punitive weapons developed by lawmakers, courts, and regulators in recent years in an attempt to combat such virulent attacks on the environment. A related kind of white-collar crime occurs in the workplace environment, when an employer knowingly permits unsafe conditions to exist. The chapter looks at the tragic consequences to workers of on-the-job exposure to asbestos, radiation, poisons, and deadly pesticides. It examines, as well, the reasons why federal and state officials generally have failed to curb habitual violations by permitting employers to exploit legal loopholes that enable them to evade responsibility for the suffering they cause. Here, too, we will see how American companies have begun to export hazardous work conditions overseas, where safety regulations are much more lax.

The social cost of white-collar crime refers to an erosion of the vital trust that people place in their elite institutions. If the public comes to believe that those institutions are corrupt, that the "game is rigged," then it becomes more difficult for society to carry out its basic functions. Chapters 4 through 8 examine social institutions whose legitimacy has been weakened by extensive fraud. **Chapter 4** contains a comprehensive overview of the insider trading scandals that shook Wall Street during the 1980's. Attention will be given to the manner in which those crimes weakened the confidence of investors in the securities markets and posed a serious threat to the entire American economy.

Chapter 5 considers the corruption of two other vital cultural institutions: the mass media and religion.

Chapter 6 contains an examination of securities fraud, including a comprehensive overview of the insider trading scandals that shook Wall Street during the 1980s. Attention will be given to how those crimes weakened the confidence of investors in the securities markets and posed a serious threat to the entire American economy.

Chapter 7 investigates the S & L scandals of the 1980s, along with related frauds within fiduciary enterprises such as pension funds and insurance companies. It argues how changes in government policies, particularly deregulatory legislation, opened the doors wide to misappropriation, in what may well have been the most costly set of white-collar crimes ever committed.

Chapters 8 and 9 focus on the abuses of power that occur within political institutions. Criminologists recently have become more interested in lawless activities undertaken on behalf of the government and its leaders. **Chapter 8** chronicles cases of crimes through which organizations and agencies have sought to achieve covert governmental goals through unethical or illegal means. Subtopics include the use of unknowing or unwilling human "guinea pigs" for officially sponsored medical experimentation, violations of the domestic sovereignty of other nations, and the surveillance and persecution of American citizens by agents of the government. Watergate, the Iran-Contra Affair, and the infamous Tuskegee study of men with untreated syphilis all serve as jarring examples of offenses in these areas.

Chapter 9 analyzes the proliferation of political corruption in the United States, concentrating on the structural features of certain institutions and organizations that facilitate malfeasance on the part of individual politicians and officials. Corruption is surveyed across all branches of government—executive, legislative, and judicial—and across all levels of authority—federal, state, and local. Separate consideration is given to police corruption, which represents a unique fusion of white-collar crime and street crime.

In the S & L debacle, as we have noted previously, the ultimate victims were taxpayers, because they had to pick up the tab in the form of massive financial bailouts of failed S&Ls. **Chapter 10** explores another form of white-collar crime in which taxpayers ultimately foot the bill: Medicaid fraud. Medicaid is the government-funded health benefit program that provides medical care to the needy. Special attention is given to the structure of Medicaid (and similar programs), which seems to encourage abusive practices by physicians and other healthcare professionals.

One of the fascinating aspects of white-collar crime is the way in which new technologies create opportunities for new types of thievery. Nowhere has this been more evident than in the area of computer crime, thought to be the fastest-growing form of crime. **Chapter 11** describes a variety of computer-based offenses, including high-tech embezzlement, military and industrial espionage, long-distance telephone toll frauds, and software piracy operations that attack the security of the burgeoning "information superhighway" and threaten the so-called new economy.

Finally, **Chapter 12** seeks to tie together the sundry topics of the preceding chapters by addressing fundamental issues and questions regarding societal, institutional, and organizational causes of white-collar crime. Major sociologic and criminologic explanations are considered, along with the distinctive manner in which law enforcement agencies, the mass media, and the general public respond to white-collar crime. The chapter also examines broader economic, environmental, and human consequences, stressing the need for popular recognition that white-collar crime can be enormously destructive in both direct *and indirect* ways.

This book concludes, however, on a more optimistic note by focusing on some effective strategies for controlling corporate lawlessness. The authors will argue that things may not be as hopeless as they appear. Ordinary citizens have more resources at their disposal than they may realize to combat what too often seems to be the insatiable greed of the white-collar criminal.

NOTES

1. Quoted in Anderson, Dennis. "Mouseketeer Darlene Goes on Trial Today." *Houston Chronicle*. November 30, 1998: A3.
2. *Ibid.*
3. "Former Mouseketeer Guilty in Stock Swindle." *New York Times*. December 12, 1998: A10.
4. Anderson, *op. cit.*
5. *New York Times,* December 12, 1998, *op. cit.*
6. Anderson, *op. cit.*
7. "Former Mouseketeer Will Be Jailed for Fraud." *New York Times*. March 12, 1999: A20.
8. Sutherland, Edwin H. *White-Collar Crime: The Uncut Version*. New Haven, Conn.: Yale University Press, 1983; 7.
9. *Ibid.,* p. 7.
10. *Ibid.,* p. 6.
11. *Ibid.,* p. 7.
12. *Ibid.,* p. 9.
13. *Ibid.,* p. 9.
14. Berger, Peter. *Invitation to Sociology: A Humanistic Perspective*. New York: Anchor, 1963; 38.
15. Geis, Gilbert and Goff, Colin. "Introduction." In Sutherland, *op. cit.*, p. ix–x.

16. McCormick, Richard. "The Discovery that Business Corrupts Politics." *American Historical Review* 86, 1981: 256.

17. Sinclair, Upton. *The Jungle*. New York: Harper and Brothers, 1951.

18. Fligstein, Neil. *The Transformation of Corporate Control*. Cambridge, Mass.: Harvard University Press, 1990.

19. Yergin, Daniel. *The Prize*. New York: Simon and Schuster, 1991.

20. Norris, Frank. *The Octopus: A Story of California*. New York: Penguin, 1986.

21. Brandeis, Louis. *Other People's Money, and How the Bankers Use It*. New York: Kelly, 1971; 4.

22. *Ibid.*, p. 4.

23. *Ibid.*, p. 4.

24. Ross, E. A. *Sin and Society: An Analysis of Latter-Day Inequity*. New York: Houghton, Mifflin, 1965; 54.

25. *Crimes of the 20th Century: A Chronology*. New York: Crescent Books, 1991.

26. "Ponzi Secret Dark to French Bankers." *Boston Globe*. August 2, 1920: 1, 3.

27. Russell, James. "Ponzi-Like Schemes Snare Unwary Around the World." *Miami Herald*. August 8, 1994: 1K.

28. As recently as 1995, the Foundation for New Era Philanthropy was accused of operating a massive Ponzi scheme in which charitable organizations were promised they would double their endowments in just 6 months with large matching gifts from anonymous donors. "These donors apparently didn't exist and new contributions are alleged to have been used as the source to 'double' the old contribution" (Johnston, Jeffrey L. "Following the Trail of Financial Statement Fraud." *Business Credit* 97, October 1995: 47).

29. Zuniga, Jo Ann. "3 Arrested in Pyramid Scheme." September 9, 2000: 35A.

30. "Convicted Fraud Gets Genuine Punishment." *Houston Chronicle*. March 8, 1997: 3C.

31. Federal Trade Commission. "CDI Pyramid Promoters Settle FTC Charges." www.ftc.gov. February 16, 1999.

32. Mulkern, Anne C. "Three Convicted in Pyramid Scheme." *Orange County Register*. August 21, 1998: 2.

33. Federal Trade Commission. "Pyramid Defendants Settle FTC Charges." www.ftc.gov. December 22, 1998.

34. *Ibid.*

35. Asher, Ed. "Arrests Crack Fraud Scheme, Authorities Say." *Houston Chronicle*. December 13, 1999: 1A, 6A.

36. Zuniga, *op. cit.*

37. Raghavan, Sudarsan. "Man's Exemplary Ways Deceive Many." *Houston Chronicle*. January 8, 2000: 23A.

38. *Ibid.*

39. Knox, Noelle. "Note Fraud Explosion Targeted." *USA Today*. May 31, 2000: 1A.

40. Williams, Krissah. "More Scams Take Money From Elderly." *Houston Chronicle*. June 2, 2000: 1C, 10C.

41. Knox, Noelle. "Task Force Scours for Note Fraud." *USA Today*. June 2, 2000: 1B.

42. Quoted in Knox, May 31, 2000, *op. cit.*, p. 1A.

43. Hughes, Polly R. "Jury Decides Texas Grifter a Pro at Cons." *Houston Chronicle*. February 9, 2001: 1A, 14A.

44. *Ibid.*

45. Weise, Elizabeth. "Spam Scam Slams a Chain of Fools." *USA Today*. February 8, 2000: 3D.

46. *Ibid.*

47. Miller, Leslie. "Senders of Junk E-Mail Warned." *USA Today*. February 6, 1998: 1D.

48. Weise, *op. cit.*

49. Schilit, Howard M. "Can We Eliminate Fraud and Other Financial Shenanigans?" *USA Today* 123, September 1994: 83–84.

50. "The National City Bank Scandal." *The Nation*. March, 1933: 248.

51. Leventhal, Harold and Guthrie, Marjorie. *The Woody Guthrie Songbook*. New York: Gosset and Dunlap, 1976; 186–187.

52. Marvin, Mary Jo. "Swindles in the 1990s: Con Artist are Thriving." *USA Today*, September 1994: 83.

53. Schilit, *op. cit.*

54. Quoted in Moore, Evan. "Billie Sol Estes: Last One Standing." *Texas (Houston Chronicle Magazine)*. June 23, 1996: 10.

55. Estes was paroled in 1971 after serving 8 years. He returned to prison in 1979 for tax evasion. He was released again in 1984.

56. Orr, Kelly. "Corporate Crime, the Untold Story." *U.S. News & World Report*, September 6, 1982: 29.

57. Katz, Jack. "The Social Movement Against White-Collar Crime." In Bittner,

Egon and Messinger, Sheldon (Eds.), *Criminology Review Yearbook*. Volume 2. Beverly Hills, Calif.: Sage, 1980: 161–181.

58. Webster, William. "An Examination of FBI Theory and Methodology Regarding White-Collar Crime Investigations and Prevention." *American Criminal Law Review* 17, 1980: 276.

59. Clinard, Marshall and Yeager, Peter. *Corporate Crime*. New York: The Free Press, 1980.

60. Shapiro, Susan. *Wayward Capitalists*. New Haven, Conn.: Yale University Press, 1984.

61. Leonard, William and Weber, Marvin. "Automakers and Dealers: A Study of Criminogenic Market Forces." *Law and Society Review* 4, 1970: 407-424.

62. Denzin, Norman. "Notes on the Criminogenic Hypothesis: A Case Study of the American Liquor Industry." *American Sociological Review* 42, 1977: 905–920.

63. Braithwaite, John. *Corporate Crime in the Pharmaceutical Industry*. London: Routledge and Kegan Paul, 1984.

64. For examples see: Wheeler, Stanton, Weisburd, David, and Bode, Nancy. "Sentencing the White-Collar Offender: Rhetoric and Reality." *American Sociological Review* 47, 1982: 641–649; Hagen, John, Nagel, Ilene, and Albonetti, Celesta. "Differential Sentencing of White-Collar Offenders." *American Sociological Review* 45, 1980: 802–820.

65. Gross, Edward. "Organizational Crime: A Theoretical Perspective." In Denzin, Norman (Ed.). *Studies in Symbolic Interaction*, Volume I. Greenwich, Conn.: JAI Press, 1978; 55–85; Schraeger, Laura and Short, James. "Towards a Sociology of Organizational Crime." *Social Problems* 25, 1978: 407–419; Wheeler, Stanton and Rothman, Mitchell. "The Organization as Weapon in White-Collar Crime." *Michigan Law Review* 80, 1982: 1403–1426.

66. Coffee, John. "No Soul to Damn, No Body to Kick: An Unscandalized Inquiry into the Problem of Corporate Punishment." *Michigan Law Review* 79, 1981: 386–457.

67. Sheehy, Sandy. "Super Sleuth—White-Collar Criminals Beware: Ed Pankau Is Looking for You." *Profiles*. July 1992: 38–40.

68. Domanick, Joe. *Faking It in America: Barry Minkow and the Great ZZZZ Best Scam*. Chicago, Ill.: Contemporary Books, 1989.

69. *Ibid.*, p. 126.

70. Akst, Daniel. *Wonder Boy: Barry Minkow—The Kid Who Swindled Wall Street*. New York: Charles Scribner's Sons, 1990; 5.

71. Akst, Daniel. "Behind 'Whiz Kid' Is a Trail of False Credit Card Billings." *Los Angeles Times*, May 22, 1987: Sec. IV, pp. 1, 3.

72. Akst, 1990, *op. cit.*, p. 270.

73. *Ibid.*, p. 272. Barry Minkow, still not yet 30, was paroled in 1994 after serving 5 years. While incarcerated, he underwent a self-proclaimed religious conversion and conducted evangelical Bible classes for small groups of inmates. Whether this represented a sincere spiritual transformation or just another scam, only God and Minkow know for sure. But many who remember the "old" Barry (including investors who lost their life's savings in the ZZZZ Best collapse) remain skeptical.

74. Quoted in: Ivanovich, David. "How Big Embezzlement Surfaced." *Houston Chronicle*. July 2, 1999: 1C, 8C.

75. Orman, Neil. "Kicking up Profits." *Austin Business Journal*. October 20, 1997: 1–5.

76. "Erxleben Offers to Settle Huge Lawsuit." www.amarillonet.com. May 5, 1999.

77. Orman, *op. cit.*, p. 2.

78. *Ibid*; p. 3.

79. *Ibid.*

80. *Ibid*; p. 3.

81. Quoted in *Ibid*; p. 3.

82. *Ibid.*

83. *Ibid.*

84. *Ibid.*

85. *Ibid.*

86. Quoted in *Ibid*; p. 2.

87. "Erxleben Loses Bid to Retain Papers." www.austin360.com. December 3, 1998.

88. "Ex-Kicker Erxleben Reaches Settlement." sportinggreen.com. May 4, 1999.

89. Quoted in *Ibid.*

90. Quoted in www.austin360.com.

91. *Ibid.*

92. www.amarillonet.com, *op. cit.*

93. www.sportinggreen.com, *op. cit.*

94. amarillonet.com, *op. cit.*

95. Quoted in Ibid.

96. www.austin360.com, November 2, 1999.

97. *Ibid.*

98. "Judge Approves Former Longhorn, Saints Kicker Plea Deal." www.reporternews.com. November 23, 1999.

99. "Former Longhorn, Saints Kicker Pleads Guilty." www.totalcollegesports.com. November 2, 1999.

100. Quoted in www.austin360.com, November 2, 1999, *op. cit.*

101. "Erxleben Ordered to Jail for Contempt of Court." sports.excite.com. August 17, 2000.

102. "Ex-Saints Kicker Erxleben Facing Jail Sentence." www.totalsports.net. August 17, 2000.

103. "Former Saints' Kicker Guilty of Contempt." www.sunherald.com. August 17, 2000.

104. sports.excite.com, *op. cit.*

105. "Erxleben Sentenced for Securities Fraud." infoweb7.newsbank.com. September 19, 2000.

106. "Ex-UT Kicker in Fraud Jailed for Alleged Threats." *Houston Chronicle*. October 1, 2000: 22A.

107. "Collared." *Houston Chronicle*. August 15, 1998: 38A.

108. *Ibid.*

109. "Former U.S. Treasurer Sentenced to Prison, Fined for Tax Evasion." *Houston Chronicle*. September 14, 1994: A11.

110. Safire, William. "Bureaucratic Bunglers Going Unpunished." *Houston Chronicle*. July 27, 1999: 18A.

111. Truex, Alyn. "Paradise Lost." *Houston Chronicle*. February 6, 2000: 1B, 13B. Tedford, Deborah. "Calumet Farms Officials Found Guilty of Bribery." *Houston Chronicle*. February 8, 2000: 1A, 8A.

112. "City of Latter-Day Scandal." *The Economist*. 350. January 30, 1999: 42.

113. *Ibid.*

114. Johnson, Kirk. "Tarnished Gold." archives.nytimes.com. March 11, 1999.

115. Quoted in *Ibid.*

116. *Ibid.*

117. *The Economist, op. cit.*

118. *Ibid.*

119. Johnson, *op. cit.*

120. O'Hara, Jane. "A Woman Under Fire." *Maclean's*. March 29, 1999: 34.

121. *The Economist, op. cit.*, p. 42.

122. Sullivan, Bill. "Salt Lake Bribe Probe Implicates 10." *Houston Chronicle*. February 10, 1999: 1B. 5B.

123. *Ibid.*

124. *Ibid.*

125. Johnson, *op. cit.*

126. Sullivan, *op. cit.*

127. *Ibid.*

128. Johnson, *op. cit.*

129. *Ibid.*

130. *Ibid.*

131. *Ibid.*

132. *Ibid.*

133. *Ibid.*

134. *Ibid.*

135. Quoted in Shepard, Alicia C. "An Olympian Scandal." *American Journalism Review* 21; April, 1999: 20.

136. *Ibid.*

137. Shepard, *op. cit.*

138. Monroe, Sylvester. "Olympics: IOC Bribery Scandal Widens." *Time* 134. August 30, 1999: 20. Hosenball, Mark. "A New Olympics Mess." *Newsweek*. September 20, 1999: 28.

139. Drozdiak, William and Shipley, Amy. "Sidney Official Offered Money on Eve of IOC Vote." *Washington Post*. January 23, 1999: D1. Dusevic, Tom. "Rough Track to 2000." *Time International* 153, February 8, 1999: 34.

140. Quoted in Sullivan, *op. cit.*, p. 5B.

141. "Johnson & Johnson Withdraws 2002 Olympic Sponsorship." *Washington Post*. April 19, 1999: D2. Shipley, Amy. "Sponsor Pushing for IOC Reforms." *Washington Post*. April 21, 1999: D1.

142. Wilson, Stephen. "Olympic Panel Ousts 6 in Corruption Scandal." *Houston Chronicle*. January 25, 1999: 1A, 8A.

143. Foy, Paul. "Utah Probe Didn't Back Olympic Case." dailynews.yahoo.com. February 8, 2001.

144. Foy, Paul. "No Plea Bargain." abcnews.com. July 13, 2000.

145. "Two Former Bid Leaders Indicted in Salt Lake City Investigations." www.cnn.com. July 20, 2000. "Ex-Olympic Officials Indicted." abcnews.com. August 7, 2000. "Arraignments Set Stage for Olympic Bribery Trial." cnn.com. August 7, 2000.

146. Foy, Paul. "Ex-Officials Charged in Olympic Bribery." *Houston Chronicle*. July 21, 2000: 2A.

147. "Ex-Olympic Officials Indicted." abcnews. com. August 7, 2000.

148. Quoted in Foy, Paul. "Lawyers Argue Over Olympic Charges." dailynews. yahoo.com. February 8, 2001.

149. Foy, Paul. "Olympic Bribery Trial Continues." dailynews.yahoo.com. February 8, 2000.

150. "Olympic Magistrate Has Full Plate." msnbc.com. January 2, 2001.

151. "Arraignments Set Stage for Olympic Bribery Trial." cnn.com. August 7, 2000.

152. "Government Targets Olympic Bidders." msnbc.com. December 14, 2000.

153. *Ibid.*

154. Fried, Joseph P. "Financial Advisor Sentenced to 15 Months and Restitution." *New York Times.* March 10, 1997: B3.

155. Ivanovich, *op. cit.*

156. *Ibid.*

157. *Ibid.*

158. Quoted in *Ibid.*, p. 8C.

159. Gilmore, Janet. "Embezzler Comes Clean." *New York Daily News.* March 30, 1997: 1, 12.

160. *Ibid.*

161. *Ibid.*

162. Conlin, Michelle. "King Lear?" *Forbes* 158. September 23, 1996: 126–127.

163. *Ibid.*

164. *Ibid;* p. 126.

165. *Ibid.*

166. *Ibid;* p. 126.

167. *Ibid;* p. 126.

168. *Ibid.*

169. *Ibid;* p. 127.

170. *Ibid;* p. 127.

171. *Ibid;* p. 127.

172. *Ibid.*

173. Quoted in *Ibid;* p. 127.

174. *Ibid.*

175. *Ibid;* p. 127.

176. *Ibid.*

177. Quoted in *Ibid;* p. 127.

178. Quoted in *Ibid;* p. 127.

179. For an example of this rationale, see the testimony of Richard Sparks before the House Committee on the Judiciary Subcommittee on Crime, in "White-Collar Crime," 95th Congress, 2nd Session, July 19, 1978: 162–165.

180. Sutherland, *op. cit.*

181. *Ibid.*

182. Clinard and Yaeger, *op. cit.*

183. Ross, Irwin. "How Lawless are Big Companies?" *Fortune.* December 1, 1980: 57-64.

184. Orr, Kelly. "Corporate Crime: The Untold Story." *U.S. News and World Report.* September 6, 1982: 25–29.

185. U.S. General Accounting Office. *Defense Procurement Fraud: Cases Sent to the Department of Justice's Defense Procurement Fraud Unit* (GAO/GGD-86-142FS). Washington, DC: SEC, 1994.

186. What young Barry Minkow was to the 1980s, sixty-ish Robert Reed Rogers may be to the 1990s. Rogers, with at least a 20-year history of involvement in suspected scams, from precious metals to healthcare, was the CEO of Comparator Systems, a tiny Los Angeles company that was accused by the SEC in 1996 of one of the biggest stock swindles of the decade. Rogers' firm supposedly had developed a fingerprint identification device that would let businesses and governments quickly and affordably verify that people are who they claim to be. Not only was this machine slow and inefficient, Comparator did not even own it. Rogers allegedly stole a prototype from a Scottish inventor.

Blessed with superb salesmanship, Rogers attracted a throng of investors, including a high-ranking FBI agent, a Harvard astronomer, the former U.S. Ambassador to Italy, the crown prince of Yugoslavia's displaced royal family—who later committed suicide in the Comparator workshop—as well as many retirees and other small investors. The company had been publicly traded since 1979. Its initial offering was underwritten by the Denver-based penny stock specialist Blinder & Robinson, known derisively as "Blind'em and Rob'em." The founder of this sleazy (and now defunct) operation, Meyer Blinder, would later be convicted of racketeering and securities fraud. Eventually, Comparator had an incredible 600 million outstanding shares. By comparison, IBM (one of the largest corporations in the world) has 540 million outstanding shares.

Beginning in February 1996, false rumors generated by unknown sources began flooding the Internet claiming that Comparator was negotiating a major deal with MasterCard International. When Comparator stock began to rise, Rogers fueled the fire with press releases that the company was negotiating with other important potential customers, including several foreign governments and large hospital chains wishing to provide technological assurance that mothers went home with the right babies. The result was a trading frenzy never before witnessed on Wall Street.

Over just 3 days in May, Comparator stock soared from 6 cents a share to nearly $2, about a 3000% gain. It was the most active stock ever traded on the Nasdaq exchange, accounting for a quarter of Nasdaq's total volume over the 3-day period. Market regulators halted trading of the stock after it was discovered that Comparator had no customers and no commercially viable products.

On June 11, Comparator was delisted from the Nasdaq market. Some brokers, however, continued to quote the stock over the phone, and the following day a remarkable 2.2 million shares were traded. One dealer was bidding a mill (one-tenth of a penny) for the shares. One best not doubt that hope springs eternal.

And if one ever doubts that America is still the land of opportunity, one need only take note that a company with worthless assets, a product it did not own, and a 29-person payroll it had not met in 11 years, became "valued" at $1 billion in 72 hours. (From Henry, David and Schmit, Julie. "The Big Lie." *USA Today*, June 7, 1996: 1B–3B; Miller, Greg and Lee, Don. "Comparator Conundrum: Honest Mistake or Con Job?" *Los Angeles Times*, June 8, 1996: A1, A26–A28; Henry, David. "Nasdaq Takes Comparator off Market." *USA Today*. June 12, 1996: 1B; Henry, David. "Comparator Still Finds Some Takers." *USA Today*, June 13, 1996: 1B.)

187. Day, Jacqueline. "Courting Disaster or Simply Business as Usual." *Bank Systems & Technology* 32, April 1995: 38–41; Millman, Gregory J. *The Vandal's Crown: How Rebel Currency Traders Overthrew the World's Central Banks*. New York: Free Press, 1995.

188. Langberg, Mike. "White Collar Crime Erodes Faith in Business." *San Jose Mercury News*. February 12, 1989: 1E.

189. U.S. Securities Exchange Commission. *The Large Firm Project*. Washington, DC: SEC, 1994; p. ii. A dramatic example of alleged criminal abuses at major firms was a Paine-Webber broker who killed himself after he was accused of swindling three Beverly Hills clients out of a total of $115,000 (Kadetsky, Elizabeth. "A Tale of Two Scandals." *Working Woman* 19, September 1994: 9–10).

190. *Ibid.*

191. Woodyard, Chris. "Local Stockbrokers Charged with Fraud." *Houston Chronicle*. December 1, 1995: 1C, 3C.

192. *Ibid.*, p. 1C

193. "Brokerage to Pay Fine Over Two Execs' Actions." *Houston Chronicle*. May 16, 2000: 5C.

194. Baldo, Anthony. "Sweeping the Street." *Financial World* (Special Edition). August 16, 1994: 61–63.

195. Lowry, Tom. "SEC: Half of Brokerages Use 'Rogue' Traders." *USA Today*. March 19, 1996: 1A.

196. Quoted in *Ibid.*, p. 1A

197. Barnes, Cecily. "Questionable Pasts Follow Internet Executives, Study Finds." CNET.com. October 26, 2000.

198. Pontell, Henry, Calavita, Kitty, and Tillman, Robert. *Fraud in the S&L Industry: White-Collar Crime and Government Response*. Final Report to the National Institute of Justice, Washington, D.C., 1994.

199. Titus, Richard, Heinzelmann, Fred, and Boyle, John. "Victimization of Persons by Fraud." *Crime and Delinquency* 41, 1995: 54.

200. *Ibid.*

201. U.S. Chamber of Commerce. *A Handbook on White-Collar Crime: Everyone's Loss*. Washington, DC: U.S. Government Printing Office, 1974.

202. Conyers, John. "Corporate and White-Collar Crime: A View by the Chairman of the House Subcommittee on Crime." *American Criminal Law Review* 17, 1980:288.

203. *Ibid.*

204. U.S. General Accounting Office. "Federal Agencies Can, and Should, Do More to Combat Fraud in Government Agencies" (GGD-78-62). Washington, DC: U.S. Government Printing Office, 1978.

205. U.S. Congress, Senate Committee on the Judiciary. "White-Collar Crime." 99th Congress, 2nd Session, Part 1. February 27, 1986.

206. Titus, et al., *op. cit.*, p. 59

207. Granelli, James. "Forecast Is for $3.4 billion to Liquidate Lincoln Savings." *Los Angeles Times*. October 31, 1993: D1.

208. Federal Bureau of Investigation. *Uniform Crime Reports for the United States, 1992*. Washington, DC: U.S. Government Printing Office, 1993.

209. Coffee, John. "Corporate Crime and Punishment: A Non-Chicago View of the Economics of Criminal Sanctions." *American Criminal Law Review* 17, 1980: 448.

210. Rossi, Peter, Waite, Emily, Bose, Christen, and Berk, Richard. "The Seriousness of Crimes: Normative Structure and Indi-

vidual Differences." *American Sociological Review* 39, 1974: 224–237.

211.   Cullen, Francis, Link, Bruce, and Polanzi, Craig. "The Seriousness of Crime Revisited." *Criminology* 20, 1982: 83–102.

212.   Schwarzkopf, LeRoy C. "Rubbergate/Kitegate: The House Bank Scandal." *Government Public Review* 19, 1992: 307–309.

213.   Kuntz, Phil. "Check-Kiting at the House Bank: How It Worked, How It Didn't." *Congressional Quarterly Weekly Report.* February 29, 1992: 446–451.

214.   Gugliotta, Guy. "Congress: Membership Has Its Privileges." *Washington Post National Weekly Edition.* October 7–13, 1991: 15.

215.   Egan, Jack. "A Bond Scandal that Won't Stop." *US News and World Report* 111, September 16, 1991: 48–49.

216.   U.S. Congress, Senate Committee on Banking, Housing, and Urban Affairs, Subcommittee on Securities. "The Activities of Salomon Brothers, Inc., in Treasury Bond Auctions." 102nd Congress, Session 1, September 11, 12, 1991.

217.   "Surging Paychecks on Wall St." *New York Times.* April 14, 1992: D1.

218.   Another complex treasury bond scandal also erupted in 1994, when the investment banking firm of Kidder Peabody announced that it had suspended the head of its bond trading desk. The 36-year-old "superstar" was accused of creating $350 million in phantom profits, while concealing $100 million in losses. The latter figure was later revised upward to $210 million, making it one of the largest Wall Street brokerage house losses ever. The alleged swindler specialized in what is called "strips" trading. A "strip" is a bond that is broken up into its component parts—principal and interest—which are then traded separately. It is a perfectly legitimate practice when done properly. However, Kidder Peabody charged that the rogue trader had discovered a glitch in its computer system which allowed him to "strip" treasury bonds into zero coupon bonds and then illegally convert the "zeros" back to treasury bonds, recording them as bogus profits.

This case appears to be yet another of those warped Horatio Alger stories so indigenous to Wall Street. When the accused had started at Kidder in 1991, after being fired by two other investment firms, he was reportedly sleeping on the floor of his one-room Manhattan apartment. Two years later, he had "earned" $9 million in bonuses.

In 1996, the SEC began holding lengthy hearings on the scandal. The targeted suspect denied any wrongdoing, characterizing himself as the victim of an attempt by Kidder Peabody to pin huge losses suffered by its highly visible mortgage department on an African American scapegoat. In light of the evidence, most financial analysts found this defense spurious, although Kidder Peabody was roundly condemned for lax supervision and flawed accounting procedures. When the dust settles, it may very well turn out that the accused was both a crook *and* a scapegoat (Bary, Andrew. "Trading Points: Kidder Management's Excuse: Don't Blame Us, We're in Charge." *Barrons* 74, April 25, 1994: MW10–MW11; Queenan, Joe. "A Sure Tip-Off." *Barrons* 74, May 2, 1994: 54; Spiro, Leah N. "Why Didn't Kidder Catch On?" *Business Week* 3369, May 2, 1994: 121; "Kidder Peabody: Curioser." *Economist.* 331, June 11, 1994: 102–105; Celarier, Michelle. "Computer Fraud on Wall Street." *Global Finance* 8, July, 1994: 44–49; Mack, Gracian. "Another Scandal on Wall Street." *Black Enterprise* 24, July, 1994: 41–42; Spiro, Leah N. "They Said, He Said at Kidder Peabody." *Business Week* 3384, August 8, 1994: 60–62; Zecher, Joshua. "Kidder Fiasco Alarms Wall Street." *Wall Street & Technology* 12, September, 1994: 36–42; Weathers, Dianne. "Street Life." *Essence* 25, November, 1994: 81–82; Kerr, Ian. "The Fall of the House of Kidder." *Euromoney* 309, January, 1995: 30–34; "Wall Street Wiz Says Ex-Bosses Knew About $350 Million in Phony Deals." *Jet.* 87, March 13, 1995: 38; "Ex-Kidder Trader: Bond Profit Strategy Not Wrong." *Houston Chronicle.* May 26, 1996: 2C).

219.   Sandburg's poetic metaphor was first applied to white-collar crime by David Wise, describing the crimes of Watergate (*The Politics of Lying.* New York: Vintage Books, 1973; *x.*).

Crimes Against Consumers

> *First Con Artist:*   When it came time to measure a job, he'd cut the yardstick and glue it back. He took out seven inches so his square footage would always be higher.
> *Second Con Artist:*   Are you serious?
> *First Con Artist:*   Nobody ever looks at a yardstick to see how long it is. The man was a genius.

From *Tin Men* (1987). Screenplay by Barry Levinson.

On March 8, 1999, the U.S. Senate Permanent Subcommittee on Investigations convened hearings on the predatory marketing practices of sweepstakes companies. The chairperson, Senator Susan M. Collins, characterized that industry's tactics as "increasingly deceptive and increasingly aggressive."[1] She cited scores of vulnerable consumers who had squandered their life's savings on magazine subscriptions after being given the false impression that they were "guaranteed winners" of or "finalists" for a multimillion dollar prize. Senator Collins noted: "The disclaimer is in very small print and in a shaded background that doesn't show up."[2]

The first day of the hearings featured witnesses describing the experiences of their aging parents or in-laws who depleted their savings, pursuing prizes but never winning. One woman testified that her elderly mother had spent about $40,000 on subscriptions in just 2 years. Another woman told the committee that her 86-year-old father had pleaded with her not to attend the hearings. "He is concerned that I am ruining his chances of winning."[3]

Patti McElligott of Tyler, Texas, said her late father-in-law had more than 158 magazine subscriptions, including 32 subscriptions to U.S. News and World Report. Even after the retired Army officer died, McElligott said she received a sweepstakes promotion declaring that his "estate is a winner."[4]

The most dramatic moment occurred when Eustace Hall, a 65-year-old retired medical technologist, broke down and sobbed while detailing his sweepstakes addiction. He had spent over $15,000 on contests since 1992 trying to help put his daughter through law school. He had been forced to return to work, refinance his house, and tap his pension. He had never won a dime.[5]

He pointed to a letter he had received from Publishers' Clearing House, a major sweepstakes firm, in 1997. The letter stated that he was on the firm's "Best Customer List" and informed him of an upcoming contest.

In the personalized letter, contest manager Dorothy Addeo wrote that she was "in a bit of hot water" because her boss wanted to know why "someone as nice as Eustace Hall doesn't win." Her mission, she said was to "personally guarantee" that Hall be a winner.[6]

Hall took this "personal guarantee" at face value. He believed his loyalty in ordering a multitude of subscriptions from Publishers' Clearing House had finally been rewarded. He had no idea that this same "personal guarantee" had been mailed to *9 million* other customers.[7]

Computer-generated personalized letters are a standard marketing ploy in the sweepstakes industry. The letters are skillfully constructed to draw the elderly, the retired, and the disabled into a seemingly personal relationship with the contest manager, typically a fictitious individual whose "signature" appears on each letter. Publishers' Clearing House admits that it is all made up. But Christopher Irving, the company's director of consumer affairs, argues: "In terms of using a fictitious name, that's standard business practice followed by many, many, many companies."[8] A news release from Publishers' Clearing House ridicules its critics: "Shhhhhh! Don't tell, but Betty Crocker, Uncle Sam, and Josephine the Plumber aren't real people either."[9] True. But Betty Crocker has never promised consumers anything more grandiose than flakier piecrust, not $5 million, as Eustace Hall was "guaranteed."

When Deborah J. Holland, senior vice-president of Publishers' Clearing House, testified on the second day of the hearings, she dismissed Hall's letter: "This was advertising, a promotion, just like 'ring around the collar.'"[10] Committee member Senator Carl Levin saw it very differently: "You lied to a customer."[11]

C A S E   S T U D Y

"Family" Values

In December 1997, an elderly California man got off a plane in Tampa, Florida, for the *second* time in 4 months.[12] On each occasion he had expected to be greeted by television personality Ed McMahon, who was going to make him a millionaire a dozen times over. The 88-year-old retired steamfitter had received spec-

(Continued)

tacular news: RICHARD LUSK, FINAL RESULTS ARE IN AND THEY'RE OFFICIAL: YOU'RE OUR NEWEST $12 MILLION WINNER.[13]

The man was overjoyed. He would soon be able to care properly for his bedridden wife of 65 years. It seemed too good to be true but it *had* to be true. "After all, the familiar face of Ed McMahon was on the envelope. Lusk trusts Ed McMahon."[14] But where was Ed? Not in Tampa.

Ed was evidently not in Tampa either when a 53-year-old woman desparately borrowed money in order to fly to Florida with her two daughters from her neighborhood in the slums of Baltimore in order to collect the $11 million Ed told her she had "won." Her letter had been even more urgent: COME FORWARD IN THE NEXT 5 DAYS—OR LOSE IT ALL. WE ARE WAITING FOR THE $11 MILLION WINNING NUMBER TO ARRIVE AT OUR TAMPA FLORIDA HEADQUARTERS.[15] So highly personalized was the message that it included documents that looked like official government papers, even threatening prosecution if anyone but her tampered with the letter.

A 76-year-old Florida woman living on Social Security with her disabled husband thought that the hundreds of precious dollars she had invested in magazine subscriptions had reaped a spectacular dividend when she received a mailing that read: YOU STAND ALONE AT THE TOP—YOU'VE SWEPT PAST 200,000+ OTHER WINNERS WITH OUR FIRST $11,075,000 PRIZE IN HISTORY.[16] She called the nearby American Family prize center to find out when she should come to collect her check. "[She] was told that the office was guarded and closed to the public."[17] Her grand prize turned out to be less than grand. In fact, it turned out to be nothing.

These sad stories are hardly unique. Since 1994, more than 20 people, mostly elderly, have arrived in Tampa with stars in their eyes. "The stars soon turned to tears."[18] One sympathetic airport police officer has seen it too many times.

> We take them aside and show them the fine print—and sometimes it takes us quite awhile to find the disclaimer. We say, "See this little fine print? See where it says: Only if you have the winning number? Then they start crying.[19]

This heartless ruse is the work of American Family Publishers, a New Jersey-based company that half-owned by the giant Time Warner conglomerate. Its business is selling magazine subscriptions—millions of magazine subscriptions. For its efforts it receives 90% of the price of a subscription.[20] Huge ongoing sweepstakes are its signature marketing tool; it mails out an incredible 200 million promotional letters each year.

American Family employs two high-profile shills to help bait its traps: McMahon and the ubiquitous media mogul Dick Clark, whose earlier brushes with questionable ethics are described in Chapter 5. McMahon resorts to defensive semantics when his role is criticized. He insists: "[T]here is a 'may' and an 'if' qualifying every sentence in American Family's promotions."[21] Clark appears to be less

(Continued)

defensive. When he was asked if he had any misgivings about endorsing the sweepstakes, Clark replied: "None whatsoever."[22]

Nineteen percent of American Family's customers are over age 65. In fact, the company has offered to sell the names and addresses of about 470,000 senior citizens, classified as "repeat customers," to other contests.[23] The elderly seem to be especially susceptible to American Family's seductive deceit. A Georgia Tech professor, specializing in aging and memory, explains: "Cognitive processes change in the normal course of aging . . . and those changes may leave some elderly people less able than they once were to evaluate sweepstakes pitches."[24] He also speculates that the elderly constitute a generation that may be misled more easily than younger generations. "They're less cynical about what they read and more trusting about what they see."[25] One retiree with a fixed monthly income of about $900 took a 26-hour bus trip to Tampa to collect his promised jackpot. He acknowledged that he spends as much as $200 a month on magazines hoping to win the sweepstakes. "I run out of food now and then the fourth week of every month."[26]

The deceptive enticements that the company has perfected are blared at the elderly, and the not-so-elderly, by Clark and McMahon in big bold letters:

❖ **[Addressee's name], it's down to a 2 person race for the $11,000,000—You and one other person were issued the winning number—whoever returns it first gets it all.**

❖ **We have reserved an $11,000,000 sum in your name.**

❖ **Are you willing to risk letting your alternate take it all?[27]**

❖ **A mammoth fortune is at stake here—more money than you can possibly imagine. Don't risk letting $11,075,000 slip through your hands.[28]**

The "*if* you hold the winning number" disclaimers, however, are "typically in tiny print that is difficult for the elderly to read."[29] As a Senator Collins observed: "People should not need a law degree or a magnifying glass to read the rules."[30]

Early in 1998, Florida filed suit against American Family, Ed McMahon, and Dick Clark, claiming that their marketing scheme duped millions of Americans into buying unneeded magazines and tricked countless consumers into believing that they were sweepstakes winners. A major allegation was the company's use of deceptive language to mislead customers into thinking that they had no chance of winning without buying magazines. By law, making a purchase cannot elevate a contestant's odds in a legitimate sweepstakes.

American Family denied any wrongdoing, claiming that more than 400 winners have received more than $77 million since the company entered the sweepstakes market in 1978.[31] But it was time for damage control. Barely 6 weeks later, an agreement was announced under which American Family would stop promoting its sweepstakes with the slogan: "You're our next winner." The company further agreed to display prominently a "No Purchase Necessary" statement and offer customers a money-back guarantee. The agreement was the culmination of a coordinated multistate effort.[32] Thirty-two states would each receive $50,000.

(Continued)

Florida and three other states, which rejected the agreement, reached a much heftier $4 million settlement with American Family in 1999.[32]

These state settlements, however, did not include lawsuits filed by disgruntled individual consumers, which continued to pile up. American Family repeatedly declared that it would not settle private lawsuits.[34] When a federal court in New Jersey consolidated these cases into dozens of class action suits,[35] American Family filed for Chapter 11 bankruptcy protection.[36]

Finally, in late 1999, American Family Publishers raised the white flag. The company offered to pay out $33 million to settle all outstanding claims.[37] Under the agreement, approved by the federal court, anyone who had spent more than $40 in a single year since 1992 purchasing magazine subscriptions from American Family, and who had believed that their purchases had improved their odds of winning, could file for a refund.[38] In addition, every American Family customer since 1992 would be entered automatically in a $1 million sweepstakes with 10 people, chosen at random, receiving $100,000 each.[39] The company also agreed that future mailings would disclose the odds of winning, clearly state that no purchase is necessary, and print the rules in large type. It further agreed to discontinue its use of official-looking "government" documents.[40]

As of this writing, Florida is still investigating whether American Family violated criminal racketeering statutes, alleging that American Family "defrauded customers by repeatedly billing them for the same subscription and not paying them refunds when subscribers died."[41]

Susan Caughman, CEO of American Family, insists "It was not our intention to be deceptive."[42] Many law enforcers strongly disagree. The attorney general of Connecticut rebuts Ms. Caughman's astonishing contention: "This is consumer deception at its worst."[43] This sentiment was echoed succinctly by another one of American Family's "best customers," a 73-year-old New Jersey widow who subscribed to 20 magazines per year: "We were snookered."[44]

Dial F for Fraud

In 1990, more than 1.5 million American families found post cards in their mailboxes announcing: **ONE OF THE FOLLOWING PRIZES IS BEING HELD IN YOUR NAME!** The message seemed to guarantee that the addressee would receive a Mercedes automobile, a $10,000 cashier's check, a full-length mink coat, or a Hawaiian vacation for two simply by calling a 900 telephone number, at a cost of only $9.90.[45] A subsequent federal investigation revealed that the chance of someone winning any prize other than the Hawaiian vacation was effectively nonexistent. Moreover, winners of the "free" trip had to pay for their own airfare at greatly inflated prices through participating hotels. "The conditions were so unfair that less than one percent of those winning the vacation claimed their prize."[46] This transparent rip-off generated over $800,000 in telephone charges. According to the U.S. Postal Inspection Service, another 900 number sweepstakes scheme "bilked 170,854 callers out of $1.7 million in six weeks at $9.95 a pop."[47] As one personal finance writer has asserted: "It's not a prize if you pay for it."[48]

The burgeoning 900 number telephone industry illustrates how easily old crimes like consumer fraud can dovetail with new technology. From its benign inception in 1980,[49] when the first 900 number flashed on television screens during the Carter-Reagan presidential debate and invited viewers to vote for the winner by placing a 50-cent call, pay-per-call telephone services have become a billion-dollar key to American pocketbooks. In 1991, there were more than 10,000 "900 programs" in the United States, an increase of over 3000% in just 3 years.[50] About 17% of American households make at least one 900 call each year.[51] One waggish columnist has declared: "I have seen the future, and it costs $2 for the first minute and $1 for each minute thereafter."[52]

This is not to say that all 900 number services are fraudulent. Many legitimate businesses provide useful information or technical support to customers on a pay-per-call basis. There is now even a service called Tele-Lawyer, which dispenses legal advice for $3 per minute.[53] However, the opportunities for consumer abuse are rampant, as the following vignettes amply attest:

❖ A Seattle television advertiser told children to "call Santa Claus" by holding their phone up to the television speaker, which then emitted electronic tones that automatically dialed a 900 number and billed the household.[54]

❖ The developmentally disabled son of a North Carolina couple ran up over $9000 in charges in less than a month by dialing a pay-per-minute "chat line." Apparently, the women at that 900 service had persuaded the young man to give them his home number because, according to his mother, "[W]e're getting collect calls from them in jail asking for bail money!"[55]

❖ For a $2.99 call to a 900 telephone number, a Houston company offered American citizens the opportunity to win a free ride on the Russian space station. So many calls came in from around the country that the telephone system handling them collapsed.[55]

❖ An 11-year-old Tennessee boy answered the telephone and was told that he could win a free vacation trip for his parents if he would call a 900 number and answer the question: "What is the name of Batman's car?" He immediately called the number, correctly identified the Batmobile, and was then instructed to call another 900 number. "Eight months later, all his parents had received was a $120.72 phone bill."[57]

❖ For a $10 phone call, a Cleveland entrepreneur promised to fax a personalized message to Saddam Hussein during Operation Desert Storm. He claimed the proceeds would be used to help clean up the Persian Gulf oil spill and sponsor a welcome-home parade for American troops.[58]

❖ A Houston firm hired people responding to a help wanted ad to pose as psychics on a 900 "hotline." Many of those who called these "psychics" reportedly were desperately distraught—in some cases even suicidal—over personal or medical problems. They were offered a free 2-minute reading. When their free time elapsed, however, an additional 10 minutes would cost $32; employees were trained to keep callers on the line as long as possible. A spokesman for the company defended the service, arguing that it was "like counseling for poor people, the ones who can't afford $150 an hour for a shrink."[59] The only flaw in that philanthropic defense is that customers placing a 40-minute call to his phony network could be charged the same $150 psychiatrists' fee to hear advice from an unemployed pool cleaner.

❖ The 909 long distance prefix for the Caribbean is also a favorite of electronic "junk mail" scams. Victims frequently find 909 messages on their pagers and, not recognizing the international prefix, return the call, only to find a recording of someone providing worthless information while "talking very slowly."[60] In one case, unwitting callers were connected to a male impotency hotline recording, which produced hefty charges on their next phone bill.[61] An even more reprehensible version of this scam is worked by crooks who leave messages on telephone answering machines, either angry warnings about a nonexistent overdue bill or shocking news that a family member has been killed. In either case, stunned victims are instructed to call a "909" number immediately. In 1 month, one promoter raked in $50,000 by billing "customers" $100 per call.[62]

Live "sex lines" now account for an estimated 5% to 10% of all "900" minutes logged.[63] One firm offered recorded sexually explicit 900 messages at "regular long-distance rates." It neglected to mention that the call was to the Netherlands Antilles.[64]

A particularly devious form of predation involves the unauthorized use of these "phone sex" services by minors, which reportedly is now epidemic. Promoters target teenage boys, drowning in their own testosterone. "And though all sex numbers say, 'You must be 18 to call,' who's checking?"[65] A 15-year-old Ohio boy once rang up a *$40,000* bill in 1 month by incessantly calling the Ultimate Pleasure Connection.[66]

The Myth of the Free Market

Deceptive Sweepstakes and dishonest 900 number[67] practices represent, of course, only two specks in the expansive universe of consumer abuse, for of all the myriad forms of white-collar-crime, crimes against consumers are the most prolific.[68] Only a relatively small number of adult patrons may be inclined to dial "900" sex lines at $10 per minute; but from the humble roll of mints each of us has purchased to the costly new car most of us have or will one day buy, we are all consumers.

Indeed, the modern capitalist state is fueled by the profits generated by the consumption of goods and services. Proponents of a pure free-market economy contend that, left to itself, the economy affords consumers sufficient protection, because unrestrained competition reduces prices and impels producers to improve the quality and safety of their goods and services.[69] These assertions, however, are based on an idealized *laissez-faire* model, which as even the most libertarian economists would concede, has never existed. As we shall see later in this chapter, true competition has been more illusory than real in many markets.

Opponents of government regulation and legal intervention also argue that because most businesses are law-abiding, there is no need for state controls. This position seems no more logical than proposing to raze our prisons, because most citizens are law-abiding.

A few hidebound theorists still adhere to the venerable rule of *caveat emptor* (let the buyer beware). "[They] point out that the best interests of consumers are served by giving them goods and services at the lowest possible price, and letting them decide whether or not to take the risk of getting unsatisfactory goods at low prices."[70] The flaw in such reasoning is that modern markets are often too complex for buyers to adequately understand the costs and risks of purchases. The *caveat emptor* doctrine, established by Roman law in the early years of the Empire, was predicated on the notion that purchasers could inspect the quality of goods before agreeing to buy. The problem then, as it still is today, was the risk for latent defects.[71] Furthermore, the assumption that cheapness is all the consumer wants is misguided.[72]

Crimes against consumers carry a heavy social cost. "Breakdowns in dealings between buyers and sellers affect the quality of life, the quantity of life, the reality of justice, and the credibility of government."[73] It is worth recalling that, to the tiny Lilliputians of Johnathan Swift's *Gulliver's Travels*, fraud was considered a far more serious crime than theft and was usually punished by death. Common sense and simple precautions, Swift wrote, can deter the thief; "but Honesty hath no Fence against superior Cunning."[74]

Thus, it is imperative that somewhere between the stifling governmental interference that has failed miserably in noncapitalist economies and the hands-off policy implied by the *caveat emptor* rule, a balance must be struck. American consumers, seeking nothing more than fair value in the marketplace, deserve to be protected. At the very least, a superordinate doctrine of *caveat venditor* (let the *seller* beware) must be institutionalized.

In this chapter, we will consider three broad categories of crimes against consumers: (1) consumer fraud, (2) false advertising, and (3) price fixing. As will be the case in subsequent chapters, such gross classification serves as a way to organize a substantial volume of material in a convenient, but necessarily arbitrary, format. Obviously, there is considerable overlap among the categories. *All* crimes against consumers could be treated as fraud, for example, in that they all involve deceptive practices. For our purposes, however, consumer fraud is operationalized as those relevant crimes which do not fall distinctly within the other five categories.

CONSUMER FRAUD

Consumer fraud has been condemned since Biblical times.[75] In the thirteenth century, Thomas Aquinas, in his *Summa Theologica*, condemned "a man who sells a lame horse as a fast one."[76] Seven hundred years later, a United States senator concluded that nearly one-quarter of all the money spent by American consumers was for "nothing of value."[77] Consumer fraud entails the use of deceit, lies, or misrepresentations to entice customers to buy goods or services.[78]

Sometimes, we read about instances so preposterous that even the solemn Thomas Aquinas might have struggled to suppress a grin.

❖ For years, one urban furniture store held a "Going Out of Business" sale every Friday. The owner invariably changed his mind over the weekend and opened for business as usual on Monday.[79]

❖ A "disabled" young man selling magazine subscriptions house-to-house, purportedly to pay for an operation, was observed by one homemaker literally jumping from his car, running around to the other side, pulling out a pair of crutches, and then hobbling up to her door.[80]

❖ 28,000 people shelled out $80 million to a company called Culture Farms in order to get rich quick by "growing smelly milk cultures on their windowsills."[81]

❖ A New Jersey jewelry company marketed "Faux Black Culture Pearls," with ads that featured terms like "brilliant," "fiery," and "dazzling." It also promised to include a "certificate of authenticity." Because "faux" is the French word for "false," the firm was actually guaranteeing that this cheap plastic piece of costume jewelry was *authentically false*.[82]

❖ A Texas mail-order firm ran newspaper ads throughout the country asking bald people to send samples of their remaining hair for an expert "scalp analysis" in order to determine if their locks could be restored. "Apparently they felt they could help everyone who applied . . . including the National Better Business Bureau employee who mailed hair from his cocker spaniel."[83]

❖ Other mail order companies have advertised a "solar clothes dryer" and sent customers a small piece of old-fashioned clothesline and some clothespins. For $3.95, customers have purchased a "universal coat hanger" and received a 10-cent nail.[84]

❖ Yet another disreputable mail-order company stated in its ad: "Money returned if not satisfactory." When disgruntled customers sought a refund, they received a notice stating: "Your money is entirely satisfactory and we therefore decline to return it."[85]

❖ A woman entered one of those ubiquitous "You May Be a Winner" sweepstakes and "won" a mink coat. Unfortunately, it was made from the fur around the animal's genital area. According to a consumer advocate: "It had a unique odor when it rained."[86]

❖ A Chicago dance studio, which targeted lonely widows, reportedly sewed small Coke bottles into the pants of male instructors in a way designed to make the women think that their teachers had become sexually aroused by dancing with them.[87]

Stories like these conform to the Hollywood image of the roguish con artist. However, there is a visceral meanness to many consumer frauds that belies any endearing stereotype. There is surely nothing roguish, for example, about some private adoption agencies that collect advance payments of $20,000 or more with no intention of ever finding babies for desperate infertile couples[88]; or phony finance companies that collect up-front fees from the creditless poor and then disappear without providing the promised loans[89]; or "affinity" swindlers who perpetrate investment frauds against victims who are linked to them by religion or ethnic background[90]; or crooked land promoters who beguile elderly couples into squandering their life's savings on retirement property located in barren deserts or uninhabitable swamps.[91]

Likewise, there is nothing amusing about post-disaster scam artists. When Hurricane Hugo hit the South Carolina coast in 1989, phony contractors canvassed neighborhoods collecting up-front material fees for needed repairs. After the "contractors" disappeared, their complaining victims did not even know their names or the names of their companies. A local consumer advocate recalls: "Some would have no better ID to report than 'He was driving a dark pickup.'"[92]

A veteran police investigator has observed, "Society has come to view those who fall prey to confidence criminals as either greedy, gullible, or brain dead."[83] But although it is reassuring to believe that only the foolish can be swindled, "it often is the people who think they are too smart to fall for a scam who end up cheated."[94] Even persons whose judgment and business acumen are otherwise beyond reproach have been swindled in misleading franchise deals, worthless "rare" coin investments, fictitious vacation packages from bogus travel agencies, and innumerable other shady schemes. Individuals as sophisticated as filmmaker Woody Allen, author Erica Jong, the late sportscaster Don Drysdale, and even the noted economist Arthur Laffer reportedly have been victimized.[95] The truth is that anyone is vulnerable. Virtually all of us have been ripped off at one time or another, often again and again, sometimes without ever knowing it. A state securities commissioner has warned: "No one is safe—your doctor, the retired couple next door or the man who picks up your garbage."[96]

In a Harris poll, business managers were asked to choose the industry they believed required the most attention from the consumer movement. The landslide "winner" was auto repairs.[97] A Roper poll reported that 70% of respondents believed that they were "quite often" or "almost always" deceived or overcharged by auto mechanics.[98] A former chairman of the Senate Consumer Subcommittee has reported that letters about auto repairs comprise the largest category of complaints that the congressional panel receives.[99] The Federal Trade Commission has charged that 30% of the billions of dollars Americans spend annually to fix their cars goes for unnecessary work.[100] "By simple arithmetic this means—however incredible it may seem—that every day of the year auto repair shops cheat Americans out of $57 million."[101]

Many of those frauds are committed by greedy mechanics in independent repair shops. An unfortunate Mexican tourist brought his expensive French-made Citroën to a Dallas shop, which replaced a number of parts at a cost of $850. When that car later was dismantled by a city consumer affairs investigator responding to the owner's complaint, it was discovered that several of the "replaced" parts had in fact never been replaced at all. They simply "had been buffed down to their shiny metallic surface in an apparent attempt to make them look new."[102]

In 1987, an investigative reporter drove a 3-year-old Oldsmobile Cutlass across the country, stopping at 225 garages in 18 states. The car had been meticulously prepared before departure and was in perfect running order, "engine tuned, transmission serviced, new spark plugs, brakes shock absorbers, struts, fan belts and hoses."[103] Every vital component had been checked and, if there were any doubt about its reliability, replaced. Before each stop, the reporter pulled a single spark plug wire loose. At 56% of the garages, mechanics performed unnecessary work or charged for repairs not done. Estimates ran as high as $495. Some mechanics even deliberately sabotaged the vehicle in order to fatten repair bills.[104]

Far more troubling, however, is that much of the auto repair fraud that has been uncovered implicates major corporate chains, whose stature and public trust are far removed from fly-by-night garages. Criminologist Paul Jesilow had research assistants bring a perfectly functioning car battery to 338 California sites for testing, including such corporate giants as K-Mart, Goodyear, and Firestone. All the confederates employed in the study were female, because women are believed to be particular targets of auto repair fraud. The battery was pre-tested and post-tested by the researchers and was found able to sustain a 200-volt load for 15 seconds, the equivalent to starting a car on a very cold day with the heater and radio running. Nevertheless, nearly 10% of the sites recommended the purchase of a new battery.[105]

Probably the most well-documented case of auto repair fraud involved Sears, Roebuck & Company, one of the country's biggest retailers. In 1990, prompted by a growing number of complaints, the California Department of Consumer Affairs launched an 18-month undercover investigation of billing practices at 33 Sears automotive repair centers. In its final report, the department described how its agents had been overcharged nearly 90% of the time by an average of $223.[106] Agents had taken 38 cars with worn brakes but no other mechanical defects to Sears centers throughout the state. In 35 cases, they were told that additional and more expensive repairs were required.

> The worst example was in the San Francisco suburb of Concord, where an agent was overcharged $585 to have the front brake pads, front and rear springs, and control-arm bushings replaced. In other instances, cars were returned damaged or even unsafe, with loose brake parts or improperly installed coil springs.[107]

The report blamed Sears' commission-based pay schedule, which rewarded unnecessary work. Earlier the company had cut mechanics' hourly wages and put them on piece-work incentives, while simultaneously pressuring service advisers to meet sales quotas.[108] Sears initially denied all allegations, but soon hoisted the white flag and began placing full-page newspaper ads conceding (albeit in the passive voice) that "mistakes" had occurred. It rescinded commission payments for automotive service advisors.[109] In 1992, in what was believed to be the largest consumer fraud settlement ever reached,

Sears agreed to provide refunds for overcharged customers throughout California, reimburse the state $3.5 million to cover the cost of the investigation, and contribute $1.5 million to mechanic training programs. In addition, the company pledged to distribute $46.6 million in coupons to disgruntled consumers nationwide.[110]

C A S E   S T U D Y

A Very "Shifty" Business

Another company with a deplorable record is AAMCO, the largest chain of transmission specialists in America. AAMCO's television commercials typically feature a benevolent service manager telling a relieved customer[111] that his or her car needs only an inexpensive adjustment, rather than a new transmission. As Woody Allen observed in the movie *Annie Hall*: "Boy, if life were only like this!" Unfortunately, real life is nothing like this—at least in the transmission business.

In 1967, the attorney general of Minnesota filed suit against AAMCO's parent firm, accusing the chain of "selling high-priced rebuilt transmissions or expensive overhauls when a minor adjustment would have solved the customer's problems, charging for transmissions that were never installed, and stealing parts from cars they inspected."[112]

Among the many brazen abuses uncovered by investigators was the case of an 18-year-old woman who, like so many consumers, knew little about automotive mechanics. "She would no more doubt the word of a 'transmission specialist' than she would question the diagnosis of her family physician."[113] When a St. Paul AAMCO manager told her that her 4-year-old car needed a rebuilt transmission at a cost of $300, she agreed to pay. Because AAMCO does not extend credit, it turned her contract over to a loan company which charged her $380 in 24 monthly installments. Four weeks later, her car would not shift into reverse, and she returned to AAMCO. The shop demanded another $300, claiming that its 6-month warranty was voided because her transmission had been damaged by a service station mechanic who adjusted her carburetor.[114]

A far less trusting young man, who had taken his car to another St. Paul AAMCO shop, was told that he needed a $250 repair.

> He paid the shop $23 for disassembly and "inspection" and another $10 for storage, and had the car towed—with its transmission in a box in the trunk—to another repair shop. Mechanics there told him that half his transmission had been stolen and replaced with junk parts.[115]

The former foreman of a Minneapolis AAMCO shop testified about repairing a car that would not shift because the pressure regulator valve was stuck. The customer was told that he needed a rebuilt transmission, which he agreed to pur-

(Continued)

chase. The shop, however, simply cleaned the valve, spray-painted the original transmission blue, and reinstalled it. The customer ended up buying his own transmission for $200.[116]

The year after the Minnesota suit, the attorney general of New York also filed charges against AAMCO. By 1970, charges had also been filed by the Federal Trade Commission (FTC).

One witness in the New York investigation was a man who had resigned after only 1 day as manager of a newly opened AAMCO shop in Syracuse. He told investigators how he had fixed one car by installing a 30-cent part. The training supervisor instructed the new manager to phone the customer and tell him that his transmission was burned out and that he needed a new one, at a cost of $225. When the man refused, the supervisor made the call himself.[117]

Other witnesses described a three-step sales program used to defraud customers, which allegedly was taught in classes at AAMCO corporate headquarters.

> The first step was to persuade the customer to leave his car and have the transmission disassembled for inspection. The second step was to convince him that his transmission was burned out, often by showing him junk parts the salesman claimed were from his car or by "salting" the transmission pan with metal shavings. The third step was to sell him a rebuilt transmission or overhaul, starting at $250 or higher.[118]

The FTC complaint against AAMCO, as well as the suits filed by Minnesota and New York, were settled out of court. AAMCO denied any guilt but agreed to all the terms set down by the prosecutors. The firm reportedly has since changed its management programs.[119] Whether this settlement had any long-term deterrent effect upon the transmission business seems questionable. Nearly 20 years later, in 1989, the New Jersey Consumer Affairs Division brought charges against eight transmission shops for performing unnecessary repairs. The intervening years may have witnessed countless fads and fashions, but consumer fraud, it seems, never goes out of style.

Telemarketing Fraud

Another form of consumer fraud becoming increasingly more invasive is the telemarketing swindle. In 1988, aggressive con artists were using telephones to reach out and cheat consumers of an estimated $10 billion.[120] In 1992, the total was revised upward to $15 billion.[121] By 1995, the figure had swollen to more than $40 billion,[122] and a survey commissioned by the Consumer Protection Network reported that 90% of Americans had been targeted at least once.[123] One could argue that heavy selling has supplanted heavy breathing as the defining feature of the modern obscene phone call.

Of course, not all phone sales are made by crooks. Many reputable companies utilize telemarketing to promote their products and services. But the assortment of telephone scams is bewildering. At the lower end of the scale, supplies of "miracle" vitamins are peddled for $100 or more; "Unfortunately, the product is generally worth around $30—if it arrives at all."[124] Similarly disingenuous was a company that called families with an "exciting" announcement that they had won a powerboat. "Predictably, the $200 shipping costs tangibly exceeded the less than $50 value of a rubber inflatable boat with a battery-driven eggbeater-like engine."[125]

At the higher end, thousands of dollars are sucked into bogus investments in precious and strategic metals, oil and gas drilling, coins, gems, foreign currencies, penny stocks, and just about anything else with an allure of big profits.[126] A Georgia woman, for example, invested $10,000 in a $2.00-per-share gold-mining corporation pitched over the phone by a penny stock brokerage firm. A year later, the stock had fallen to 20 cents. When the victim belatedly checked out her investment, she discovered that the company owned some land near a gold mine—but did not own the mine.[127]

Two Texas men, operating a bogus company called National Listing Service, were convicted of fraud and conspiracy in 1999 after they cheated 27,000 property owners out of $9 million. Using county records to obtain the names of persons who had purchased time shares or property in resort areas, the defendants contacted their victims and promised that they could quickly sell the properties at a huge profit for a marketing fee of only $695. No sales were ever made and the telemarketers simply pocketed the fees.[128] Although $9 million is a lot of money, it hardly moves the needle on the swindlers' Richter Scale. A single rare coin operation has bilked customers out of more than $200 million.[129]

The most ruthless telemarketers are nothing if not opportunistic; they will exploit any misfortune, from natural disaster, to illness, to war, to death. Following natural disasters, con artists often call local residents under the pretext of charity solicitations and pocket the donations.[130] Customers have also been given the ghoulish chance to reap big profits by supposedly investing in life insurance policies taken out on persons with AIDS.[131] Unauthorized telemarketers have solicited contributions for a San Diego summer camp for young burn victims; the camp never received a penny of the proceeds.[132]

Global tensions likewise generate a receptive environment for fraud. The conflict in the Persian Gulf in 1991 enabled swindlers pushing domestic energy investments to "play on Americans' fear of dependence on foreign oil."[133] When two Virginia firefighters were killed in a terrible 1996 warehouse fire, telemarketers began calling local residents claiming to be raising funds for the families of the victims. Predictably, neither of the families ever received any money.[134] And when the work of renowned Spanish painter Salvador Dali jumped in value following the artist's death, reams of fake Dali prints were sold to unsuspecting investors. A Virginia chiropractor bought seven counterfeit prints for $8700.[135] "Salvador Dali fakes are so common now that the Better Business Bureau . . . refers to complaints as 'Hello, Dali' calls."[136]

Perhaps the most cynical opportunism of all involves the targeting of the elderly. According to a congressional subcommittee, senior citizens, who comprise about 12% of our population, make up at least 30% of fraud victims.[137] The reason for such disproportionate selection is that high-pressure telemarketers know that the elderly often have substantial savings, lump-sum pensions, or home equity. America's over-65 population has a combined personal income of more than $800 billion and accounts for almost 75% of the net worth of the nation's households.[138] Also, the elderly tend to be home more often than younger people. Moreover, studies indicate that the longer one remains on the phone the better the chance a telemarketer has of making a sale. Older people are products of a generation that stressed politeness, so they are less inclined to hang up abruptly.[139]

Many senior citizens not only have cash but are desperately lonely—an enticing combination for telemarketers determined to test the boundaries of sleaze. Elderly Florida residents were willing to pay $20,000 for a lifetime's worth of dance lessons: "Some were too frail to walk."[140] In St. Louis, similarly incongruous long-term dance lesson contracts were sold for between $80,000 and $250,000.[141]

In 1994, an 85-year-old woman was referred to the National Fraud Information Center (NFIC) by a private mail carrier after she had called to have a $20,000 check delivered to some "nice man" in Florida. "When interviewed by the NFIC counselor, the woman was unable to tell what the $20,000 was for. 'They just told me to send it, and that's what I mean to do,' she replied."[142]

An 80-year-old New York woman sent thousands of dollars to a Chattanooga, Tennessee, telemarketing operation because she had become "addicted" to the attention they paid her.

> "I've been a widow for 19 years. It's very lonely. They were nice on the phone. They became my friends.[143]

One older couple lost their entire life's savings of $350,000 to a relentless rare coin operation.[144] A 72-year-old former school superintendent was fleeced of $225,000 in a commodities contract scam run by a precious metals firm in Newport Beach, California. Another Newport Beach commodities dealer swindled $10,000 from a Baptist minister in rural upstate New York.[145] Con artists generally favor warmer climates, and Newport Beach, located on the coast of upscale Orange County, has become the "Emerald City" of telemarketing fraud. "An office-space glut in swindler-riddled Orange County enables crooks to negotiate several months of free rent, then skip out to a new site when the payments come due."[146] The FBI estimates that there are 5000 "boiler rooms" (see below) in Southern California alone.[147]

Likewise, Houston has become a hub for fraudulent telemarketing schemes because of a surplus of offices and the availability of 30-day leases. For example, a con man named Samuel DeBlasio ran a telemarketing operation in Houston between 1992 and 1993 that cheated more than 3300 people, most of them elderly, out of $3 million. DeBlasio and the 128 telemarketers he employed contacted people around the country informing them that they had "won" Ford Explorers. When targets called DeBlasio's office to confirm their prizes, they "were told they would have to send money—the amounts ranged from $3.98 to $6000—to cover the taxes on the prize and the shipping costs."[148] No prizes were ever delivered. DeBlasio was convicted in federal court in 1996 and received the harshest prison sentence ever meted out for telemarketing fraud—14-years. In his statement to the court, DeBlasio insisted that he was just an aspiring entrepreneur and had done nothing wrong.[149]

At the heart of telemarketing fraud are the infamous "boiler rooms"—spartan offices containing little else but banks of telephones[150] manned by glib hustlers working their way through computerized "sucker lists" with carefully scripted pitches.

> Once they get you on the phone, salesmen quickly activate your greed glands. That is accomplished by asking a simple question, such as "If you could make 30 percent on your savings in the next three months without taking any risks, would you be interested?" Only Mother Teresa would say no.[151]

The classic telephone swindle consists of three calls known as the *front*, the *drive*, and the *close*.[152] The front will introduce the customer to the scheme. The salesman tries to learn how much money the "mark" has or, more precisely, how much of it he can grab. He promises to send descriptive literature, which usually arrives a few days later and consists of an impressive-looking folder containing a great deal of unspecific material but little concrete information. The drive comes shortly after the folder is received. Now the salesman makes his hard sell, bombarding the target with empty slogans and statistics. The close follows within a short time. The salesman tries to create a sense of urgency, and it is then that many worn-down consumers finally cave in.

Victims are called "marks" because, once fleeced, they are marked as lifelong targets. A recurring form of telemarketing fraud is the "reload" scam, in which swindlers take a second shot at consumers who already have been victimized.[153] Their pitch is brazen but can be psychologically compelling to someone desperate to recoup painful financial losses.

> Hello, Mrs. Luckless? This is John DeRoach with the Guys-Next-Door Brokerage, and I'm calling you today because I understand you lost a lot of money with the Trust-Is-Us Coin Co. . . . Yeah, they were real crooks. . . $10,000, huh? Tsk, tsk, tsk. What a shame. Well, I've got a program here with a legitimate company that will allow you to double your money and make up your losses. All we need to get started is $5,000. . . ."[154]

An especially despicable variation on reload is the so-called rip and tear scam. Here, telemarketers call previous victims, posing as law enforcement agents. They offer to help recover some of the victim's losses if the victim will pay an official fee for the recovery effort.[155]

The Attack of the Toner-Phoner

One of the biggest and most incredible telemarketing assaults on an individual target ever reported was a variation of the reload technique, combining elements of traditional business fraud with outright blackmail.[156] The office manager for a small school district in a Philadelphia suburb received a long-distance call from a California office-supplies distributor. She ordered some green felt-tipped pens that teachers had been requesting and, when the shipment subsequently arrived with an invoice, she wrote out a check for a few hundred dollars and sent it to the company.

After she placed several more legitimate orders, a company representative, calling himself "Mr. Chester," an alias of indicted fugitive Marc Suckman, contacted her and told her that because she was such a good customer they would like to send her a pocket tape recorder as a token of their appreciation. This gift-giving ploy is a "hook" frequently used by office supplies hustlers, who are sometimes called "toner-phoners" for the copy machine accessories many of them push. She agreed to accept this inexpensive present, a seemingly innocuous decision that ultimately would ruin her life.

A few weeks later, Mr. Chester phoned to say he was shipping the balance of her order. In fact, there was no balance, because she had not placed an order; but Mr. Chester convinced her that she had done so and was thus obligated. Once she acquiesced, Mr. Chester began calling monthly, pressing one order after another on her. When cartons of colored markers began filling the storage closet, leaving little room for other supplies, she informed Mr. Chester that the school district did not need any more pens. She was told that there was an outstanding balance of nearly $4000, for which he demanded a final check to close out the account. When she balked at this absurd claim, Mr. Chester threatened that if she did not pay that amount he would inform the school board that she had solicited a personal gift for placing the orders. He had no idea how effective this threat would be.

> [S]he was terrified of losing her job . . . Her two kids were approaching college age and she and her husband, a mailman and part-time coach at the school, were saving every penny to pay for tuition.[157]

She agreed to settle the fraudulent account, believing that she had heard the last of Mr. Chester. However, as any less naïve person could have predicted, he called back a month later, claiming a new outstanding balance of $4200. When she resisted, Mr. Chester threatened to reveal that she had already sent his company an unauthorized check for goods she never received. She paid that bill and others that followed—sometimes three per month. She covered up her coerced embezzlement by juggling computer records and whiting out names on canceled checks.

Eventually, the deficit grew so gargantuan that she could no longer balance the books, even dishonestly. When a new superintendent discovered the financial discrepancies, she was arrested by the FBI and quickly confessed. Over just a 3-year

(Continued)

period, she had sent Mr. Chester (Suckman) over 130 checks totaling more than *$2 million*—about a third of the school district's entire budget—in payment for absolutely nothing. And all she had ever personally gained from her illegal efforts was a cheap Taiwanese tape recorder, batteries not included.

As the staggering costs of telemarketing fraud spiral upward, law enforcers have begun to allocate more attention and resources to this problem. Between 1995 and 1998, an FBI operation dubbed Double Barrel produced criminal charges against nearly 1000 telemarketers. Double Barrel utilized retired FBI agents and postal inspectors, as well as senior citizens recruited by the American Association of Retired Persons (AARP), to pose as previous marks targeted by reload scams. They recorded the phone calls for evidence. These volunteers produced over 11,000 recordings of conversations with scammers.[158] In the words of one FBI agent assigned to Double Barrel:

> "The tapes are the best evidence we've ever had. You've got them saying, 'I can guarantee you're going to win that car. What color would you like, Mabel?' You can get all the lies on tape."[159]

One AARP volunteer, who has produced about 3000 recordings, adds: "When you know you're taping them, it's really kind of comical. They're hanging themselves."[160]

Two of the most notable figures caught in the Double Barrel were John A. Field, III and Marcus K. Dalton. Field is a former federal prosecutor and former director of enforcement for the U.S. Commodity Futures Trading Commission, who switched from fighting crime to committing crime. His operation sold units of the imaginary United Currency Exchange Ltd. of London. Field also served as something of a guru to con artists, advising telemarketers on how to structure their offerings to avoid scrutiny from federal regulators.[161] Dalton, who is considered one of the country's most prolific securities fraud artists, admitted to selling at least $80 million in bogus securities, "including phony wireless cable operations, bridge loans to finance a wireless venture in American Samoa, and fraudulent shares in Treasure Chest Television, a children's programming investment."[162]

. . . And the Poor Get Poorer

People in financial difficulty are often easy prey because of their desperation. Fraudulent loan companies purchase lists of persons experiencing hard times, such as those involved in foreclosure proceedings, and either telephone them or mail them loan applications guaranteeing approval in exchange for upfront fees. One such company operated in Arizona in the summer of 1991. It received 1702 loan applications, each accompanied by a $249 "fee." When one does the math, one finds that "this modestly-sized scheme grossed almost

$425,000 in just 90 days."[163] The Better Business Bureau estimates that advance-fee loan scams cost consumers more than $1 million each month.[164]

Unscrupulous players in the burgeoning home equity loan business constitute another example of how financially desperate people can be exploited by so-called bird dog salesmen. The market for high-rate second mortgages to disadvantaged consumers is estimated at $35 billion.[165]

> Hundreds of thousands of homeowners have been victimized in the past decade. Tens of thousands have lost their homes; still more have seen their equity sucked out by exorbitant fees and usurious interest rates charged by predatory mortgage companies . . . Many are targets because they are old or illiterate. Others are vulnerable simply because they are poor.[166]

An elderly Alabama man with a poor credit history was given a home equity loan for $1353. The interest was so high and bloated with so many fees, charges, and points (a point equals 1% of the mortgage principal) that his effective annual rate was 61.4%.[167] A Georgia woman took out a $5000 home improvement loan at such high interest that she had to refinance the loan twice. "By the third loan, she would have been required to repay a total of $63,000 if she had not declared personal bankruptcy."[168] After receiving her loan, a California woman faced monthly payments of $2000—on an income of $1000.[169]

As in the preceding case, some second mortgages are structured so that repayment is impossible. The real goal is foreclosure. The firm can then resell the house to another buyer who cannot afford the payments, and the cycle begins again. It is not unusual for a finance company to resell the same home four or five times.[170]

Many of these companies are owned or backed by "respectable" banks, who are lured by the big money in home equity loans but repelled by the dirtiness of the business. Participation by proxy allows mainstream financial institutions to enjoy the best of both worlds—usurious profits and clean hands. This symbiosis was illustrated by Fleet Financial, New England's largest bank, when it extended a $7.5 million line of credit to one of that region's most notorious lenders, Resource Financial. According to a study, three-quarters of the families who borrow money from Resource lose their homes.[171] When a reporter asked Fleet vice-president Robert Lougee, Jr. about his bank's complicity in the mass foreclosure game, he declared: "These people may be poor and illiterate, but no one puts a gun to their head and tells them to sign."[172]

In a Pennsylvania case, Transamerica Financial Services and the prestigious Mellon Bank paid a $6.2 million settlement after the two companies were accused of a kickback scheme involving loans to low-income applicants.[173] Transamerica Financial Services has a history of exploiting the poor. In 1990, the company foreclosed on the home of an impoverished, mentally disabled Arizona widow who was unable to repay a loan at a rate of $499 per month. Her total income was $438 per month. A judge halted the foreclosure, ruling that Transamerica "knew or should have known" that the woman was not competent when she signed the loan paper.[174]

Another popular way to fleece the poor is through disreputable vocational schools. Telemarketers plunder the federal student loan programs, which have been described as "a multi-billion-dollar swamp of fraud."[175] At a school for medical assistants in Atlanta, "many poor black single mothers had gone into hock for $4,800 for the promise of a well-paying job in a doctor's office."[176] The entire school consisted of a reference center holding a handful of books and supplies, and a large "boiler" room containing 75 telephones where recruiters solicited students.[177]

These schools are pitched as steppingstones to a better life. A typical script goes: "Listen, young lady, you have two children and no husband. What are you ever going to do with your life?"[178] The sad truth is that these fraudulent training programs dump sincerely motivated students on a treadmill that leads nowhere, burdened with tuition debts they cannot ever pay. For example, a Texas woman was recruited by a truck-driving school. She later learned that she could not even qualify for a state commercial license because she only has one foot.[179]

A Georgia trade school charges over $4000 to train students to work as aides in nursing homes, a position that pays barely more than minimum wage. "The public vocational school down the street also trains aides—for $20."[180] Another school charges $3,000 to train armed security guards. The state requires only 12 hours of training to obtain a license, but the school's program fills up 300 hours, largely padded with old war movies.[181]

FALSE ADVERTISING

Closely related to consumer fraud is the practice of false advertising.[182] A renowned British writer has observed: "Advertisements are now so numerous that . . . it [has] therefore become necessary to gain attention by magnificence of promise."[183] The remarkable thing about this comment is that it was penned by Dr. Samuel Johnson in *1759.*

In theory at least, the multi-billion dollar American advertising industry serves as a conduit between businesses' need to inform and the public's need to know. Many critics contend, however, that in practice advertising provides very little useful information to consumers, whose desire to evaluate products and services in a knowledgeable way remains largely unfulfilled.[184] The reason for this is that advertising has become—or perhaps has always been—more a tool for manipulation than education. Indeed, of the three advertisement categories classified by the Federal Trade Commission (FTC), *informative* ads are probably the least visible. Far more ubiquitous is a second category, *puffing* ads, featuring self-serving ballyhoo or irrelevant celebrity endorsements.[185]

The third and most insidious category, *deceptive* ads, is characterized by misleading or untrue claims,[186] sometimes supported by rigged tests and photographic trickery.[187] While the industry as a whole may be fair game for criticism, deceptive practices warrant the most serious attention. Puffery can be used as a shield to avoid accountability for a claim about a product or service[188] and may confuse or even offend the sensibilities of consumers; but false advertising crosses the line between exaggerative license and unmitigated fraud.

The FTC's authority over the advertising industry predates the advent of network television.[189] Thus, every television commercial ever run has been subject to FTC regulation. Many consumer advocates have given the FTC and other regulatory agencies low overall grades in this area through the years, but the government has displayed occasional flashes of toughness.

In the 1960s, for example, Shell Oil mounted an advertising campaign built around a unique ingredient it called "Platformate," that supposedly gave its gasoline significantly greater mileage. In its commercials, Shell showed a car running on fuel with Platformate crashing through a paper wall, while identical cars lacking Platformate in their equally full tanks ran out of gas well before the barrier. The government stepped in after it was pointed out that Platformate was just a concocted name given by Shell to a type of additive contained in all comparable gasolines. In other words, the test cars without Platformate had run on a substandard fuel that did not exist commercially.[190] The major gasoline producers have, in fact, repeatedly violated the limits of permissible puffery over the years. In 1996, for example, the FTC accused Exxon of falsely advertising that its 93 Supreme Premium gasoline could reduce automobile maintenance costs.[191]

In the 1970s, the FTC ruled that the makers of the popular over-the-counter pain reliever, Anacin, had deceptively advertised their product by making a slew of false claims. Consumers were told, for instance, that Anacin (a blend of aspirin and caffeine) could relieve depression, stress, nervousness, and fatigue, which it could not; could bring relief within 22 seconds, which it could not; was recommended more often by physicians than aspirin, which it was not; and was the strongest nonprescription analgesic available, which it was not.[192] In a similar 1999 case, the FTC ordered Norvartis, the world's second-largest pharmaceutical manufacturer, to run advertisements correcting earlier claims that its Doan's back-pain pills are better than other analgesic medicines.[193]

In the 1980s, the Beech-Nut Nutrition Corporation, a leading manufacturer of baby foods, advertised its apple juice as "100% fruit juice." This apple juice was also said to contain no sugar. In fact, it was loaded with sugar. What it did not contain was apple juice. When stories of Beech-Nut's appalling deception began to surface, the company shipped its entire remaining 26,000-case inventory to the Caribbean, where the juiceless juice was sold to unwitting parents. Over a 10-year period, Beech-Nut had been able to "extract as much as $60 million from consumers"[194] for what one of its own scientists later called "a fraudulent chemical cocktail"[195] masquerading as baby food. In 1988, Beech-Nut's president and vice-president of operations were convicted of violating federal food and drug laws.[195]

In a similar 1995 case, the owner of Carrington Foods was ordered to pay a $78,000 fine after a felony conviction for misbranding. Packages of Miss Sally's Stuffed Crabs bore bright stickers proclaiming "More Crabmeat Than Ever." Miss Sally's product not only did not contain more crabmeat than ever, it contained no crabmeat whatsoever.[197]

The intensity of state and federal regulation seemed to increase a bit in the 1990s, but whether this reflects tougher enforcement policies or just more willingness by advertisers to test the limits of tolerable hyperbole is not altogether clear.

A survey of recent cases includes the following:

❖ Kayser-Roth, manufacturers of No Nonsense Pantyhose, agreed to pay a monetary penalty for making unsupported claims regarding the amazing durability of its hosiery.[198] Investigators, who were unable to replicate the product's virtual indestructibility demonstrated on television, concluded that No Nonsense commercials were nonsense.

❖ The Home Shopping Network reached a settlement with the New York attorney general's office, under which it agreed to curb deceptive advertising of jewelry. The network generally flashes a "retail value" on the screen and then cuts its "sale price" far below that figure. The state had alleged that the suggested retail prices were "drastically inflated."[199] Jewelry is the "bread-and-butter" of electronic shopping, leading in sales volume and profit margin. In an even more recent case, Home Shopping was slapped with a $1.1 million fine by the FTC for airing advertisements making unsubstantiated claims for skin care, weight loss, and premenstrual syndrome and menopause products.[200]

❖ Commercials for premium-priced Alaska Ice Cream promised "the extraordinary taste of the Great Frozen North." Containers featured polar bears and ice-blue fjords, along with an Anchorage address and a folksy history of the product's Arctic origin. The only problem was that Alaska Ice Cream is made in Michigan and distributed from a warehouse in the Bronx. In response to complaints from Alaska's attorney general, the company dropped its phony provenance.[201]

❖ NordicTrack, a major marketer of indoor exercise equipment, agreed to settle an FTC complaint regarding fatuous claims the company's ads made about how much weight NordicTrack users could expect to lose.[202] The FTC has also obtained a settlement agreement from Jenny Craig, Inc. in response to charges of deceptive advertising in connection with the Jenny Craig diet program's claims about weight loss, price, and safety.[203]

❖ The FTC settled charges with Schering-Plough Healthcare Products, the marketer of Coppertone Kids sunscreens for children. Ads for 6-Hour Waterproof Sunblock were deemed deceptive in their claims that one application provides 6 hours of protection from the sun for children engaged in sustained vigorous activity. The FTC charged that such a claim was unsubstantiated and untested by the company. The director of the FTC's Bureau of Consumer Protection said: "You can't use a smokescreen to sell a sunscreen."[204]

❖ The FTC also settled charges against computer makers Dell and Micron for disseminating misleading ads about computer leases. Both companies had placed important cost information in "inconspicuous or unreadable fine print or omitted such information altogether."[205] Apple was similarly found to have engaged in false advertising in its "Apple Assurance" campaign. Apple Assurance offered consumers free access to live, free technical support for as long as they own their Apple product. According to the FTC: "Apple, however, subsequently began charging these consumers $35 for such access."[206]

❖ R. J. Reynolds agreed to modify its advertising for Winston "no additives" cigarettes. The FTC alleged that Reynolds implied, without any reasonable basis, that Winston cigarettes are safer to smoke because they contain no additives. Reynolds agreed to make a prominent disclosure in future Winston ads: **No additives in our tobacco does NOT mean a safer cigarette.** According to the FTC: "[T]here's no such thing as a 'Safe Smoke.'"[207]

❖ Providian Financial, one of the largest credit card issuers in the United States, agreed to pay at least $300 million to consumers to settle claims that it used deceptive advertising practices. Providian's Guaranteed Savings Rate Program promised customers a lower rate than they had been receiving on balances transferred from other cards. But according to the federal Office of the Comptroller of the Currency (OCC), some customers actually ended up with *higher* rates than before.[208]

❖ The FTC sued SlimAmerica, Inc. for false claims about the company's "Super-Formula" diet pills, as advertised in newspapers, magazines, and on the Internet.[209] A 90-day supply of Super Formula sold for $129.95. Ads promised that Super-Formula is "absolutely guaranteed to blast up to 49 pounds off you in only 29 days."[210] Also included was an endorsement by Howard Retzer, MD. According to the FTC, the company made between $5.3 million and $17.7 million from the sale of Super-Formula. A federal judge ruled that the product was worthless and that the company's claims (and "Dr." Retzer's credentials) were misrepresented.[211] SlimAmerica was ordered to reimburse thousands of defrauded customers $8.3 million.[212]

❖ Kevin Trudeau, a deft huckster whose infomercials once flooded late-night television, was fined $1 million by the FTC for false and misleading pitches he made on behalf of six products. The products included the Mega Memory system, which claimed it could teach anyone to have a photographic memory; the Sable Hair Farming System, which claimed it could prevent or reverse baldness; Eden's Secret Nature's Purifying Product, which claimed to cure illnesses and cause weight loss; and the Addiction Breaking System, which claimed that a series of gestures such as tapping the face and rolling the eyes could end addictions to alcohol, tobacco, and drugs.[213] Trudeau is an old hand at lawbreaking, with a record of prior felony convictions for larceny and credit card fraud.[214] An FTC assistant director commented: "Just because it's on television, doesn't mean that it's true."[215]

Celebrity Endorsements: Would I Lie to You?

In 1990, Actor Lloyd Bridges was sued by customers who had been cheated by an investment company for whom the veteran star had done print ads and television commercials. After the company went bankrupt and its officers were thrown in jail, victims went after Bridges.[216] When a Chicago court ruled that endorsers could be held liable under Illinois consumer fraud law, even for innocent misrepresentations, the case was quickly settled. The established precedent has sobering implications for celebrity endorsers, like Dick Clark and Ed McMahon, who do not personally bother to substantiate the truthfulness of information they communicate to consumers.

FTC guidelines now require celebrity endorsers to base their endorsements on honest beliefs formed from personal findings or experience.[217] In 2000, Robin Leach, the ebullient bon vivant who hosted television's *Lifestyles of the Rich and Famous,* reached a settlement with the Justice Department over his endorsement of fraudulent vacation packages on behalf of two crooked Florida-based companies. Consumers in 12 states had received certificates bearing Leach's picture and the message: "Robin Leach says Pack Your Bags!" The certificate told recipients they had won a luxury Florida vacation and a bonus cruise to the Bahamas, featuring a Las Vegas-style casino. Leach claimed the trips were the "vacation experience of a lifetime."[218] This "free" 7-day trip actually cost "winners" $1000,[219] and the luxurious "beachfront" hotel was a dump 5 miles from the beach.[220] The "cruise" consisted of a daylong ride on a car ferry whose "on-deck pool" contained no water,[221] and the Vegas-style "casino" was a bingo parlor.[222] An assistant attorney general in one of the targeted states, said: "Robin Leach promised champagne wishes and caviar dreams. We think consumers got Kool-Aid and tuna fish."[223]

One of the fastest growing market segments in the United States is in the area of nutrition. Anyone who doubts how health-conscious many Americans have become need only observe grocery shelves now stocked with such improbably-named products as Spam Lite and Lo-Fat Twinkies. But as the demand for healthier foods has increased, so has the use of misrepresentation in advertising and labeling. Even when such claims as "cholesterol free," "high fiber," and "low sodium" are strictly accurate, they may still be confusing. For one thing, such claims do not necessarily mean that a product is healthy.[224] For example, certain brands of peanut butter advertised as "cholesterol free" are nonetheless high in saturated fats, which can raise blood cholesterol levels.[225]

Two cases, both decided in 1994, illustrate typical objections to questionable nutritional claims. In one instance, the FTC ruled that Stouffer Lean Cuisine frozen foods had made deceptive "low sodium" assertions in a $3 million advertising campaign.[226] In the second case, the Hillshire Farms division of the Sara Lee Corporation agreed to pay a $130,000 fine and change the advertising of its "lite" meat products. According to the government's allegations, the company had misleadingly suggested that several products were low in fat when they were not.[227]

Another deceptive labeling practice involves the term "natural." Some cosmetics companies, for instance, make their products "natural" merely by adding tiny amounts (perhaps 0.1%) of herbal extract mixtures that provide no benefit to the consumer.[228]

No type of deceptive advertising has generated more public outrage than that aimed at children. The United States is one of the few countries in the world which permits advertisers to sell products to children via television.

Most nations consider this practice to be immoral. In fact, a recent survey by *Advertising Age* magazine reported that 62% of Americans want children's ads taken off the air entirely.[229] The average American child, who spends a staggering amount of time watching television, views about 25,000 commercials year.[230] The majority are for food products of negligible nutritional value, mainly heavily sugared cereals, soft drinks, and candy. The American Academy of Pediatrics has called for a ban on children's food ads, maintaining that such messages are contributing to a national obesity problem.[231]

Many of the remaining ads are for toys. Any parent who has ever cleaned out a closet full of long-abandoned playthings that a young son or daughter had once pleaded for readily understands that most toys are junk. Shoddily constructed and easily broken, they are rarely able to perform as advertised. In an "attitude inoculation" study led by Norma Feshbach, elementary school children were shown commercials for a toy, then immediately were given the same item. Feshbach challenged them to make the toy do what they had just witnessed on television; they seldom could.[232]

Children, who are so easy to persuade, are "an advertiser's dream."[233] They are hopelessly overmatched against skilled teams of animators, professional writers and juvenile actors, child psychologists, and cinematographers employing a menu of special effects,[234] all designed to manipulate them. Peggy Charren, founder of Action for Children's Television (ACT) has written: "The ads feature more children and better animation than the programs they interrupt. Children like commercials, and corporations know how to take advantage of this sad fact of life."[235] In response to criticism, the best the toy companies and television broadcasters can do is argue weakly that commercials help parents teach their children "consumer skills."[236]

Even older children can be highly vulnerable to dishonest media promotions. Consider the sensational scandal surrounding the pop-singing duo, Milli Vanilli. "Milli Vanilli was the stage name for two young performers, Robert 'Rob' Pilatus and Fabrice 'Fab' Morvan, who had come out of nowhere, released their hit album and won the 1990 Grammy Award for best new artist." [237] In their year of stardom, according to one mind-boggling estimate, Milli Vanilli generated revenues of $200 million.[238] Then it was revealed that Pilatus and Morvan were only nice-looking, lip-synching front-men for an unscrupulous music producer. They had not sung a single note on their recordings or videos. Milli Vanilli would have been more aptly named Phoni Baloni.

The primary victims of this fraud were adolescent girls, who had lavished their adoration and consumer dollars on Rob and Fab. Ironically, Milli Vanilli's hit album was titled "Girl You Know it's True."

Bait and Switch

Some years back, the *New York Times* reported a story about a woman who had responded to a bedding store's published advertisement offering a full-size Sealy superfirm mattress for $48. When a salesman showed her the item, it was leaning against a storeroom wall, soiled and looking, in the customer's words, "like one of those mattresses on the sidewalk waiting for a sanitation pickup."[239] What the woman had encountered was one of the oldest and most durable forms of false advertising: the bait and switch.

The FTC defines bait and switch as "an alluring but insincere offer to sell a product or service which the advertiser does not intend or want to sell."[240] The merchant's objective, of course, is to switch the buyer to another higher-priced, more profitable item. For example, a Virginia dealer reportedly spent many hundreds of dollars each month advertising Singer sewing machines at remarkably low prices, yet never sold one. Customers would be shown a beat-up, obsolete model (the bait), which the salesman would immediately disparage. Disappointed shoppers were then pressured to buy a less well-known and more expensive brand (the switch).[241]

Bait and switch is the mainstay of some sleazy retail stores. In sales parlance, their advertised merchandise is "nailed to the floor."[242] The manager of one such business is said to have pointed to a portable television and warned his sales staff: "Any guy who lets that set go out the door goes with it."[243]

Some researchers have concluded that bait and switch is ultimately a self-destructive strategy with built-in disincentives.[244] In other words, they argue that once a store gets a bad reputation resulting from the practice, it will suffer financial losses.[245] However, this prediction is flawed, because the assumption that consumers are "effortlessly rational" is naïve.[246] With almost any variety of consumer fraud, pride or cognitive dissonance sometimes thwarts rationality. Cognitive dissonance, a psychological construct, refers to the internal conflict which often results when an individual receives information that contradicts fundamental personal beliefs.[247] Thus, if a person holding a competent and prudent self-image is "ripped off," a state of cognitive dissonance is created. That state may be relieved—that is, returned to cognitive balance—either by modifying one's self-image ("I guess I'm not so smart after all!") or by reinterpreting the event ("I wasn't really ripped off!"). The latter may be the more attractive, though less rational, option, because it is more ego-supporting than the former. Simply put, many people just cannot admit to being duped, not even to themselves.

PRICE FIXING

Price fixing is criminalized under the Sherman Antitrust Act of 1890, one of the most important pieces of legislation in American history. The Act came of age in 1911 with the dissolution of the immense Standard Oil and American Tobacco empires. Over time, additional federal regulations were enacted (most notably the Clayton Act and the Federal Trade Commission Act), and states now have their own antitrust statutes as well. The most visible case in recent years was the 1982 break-up of the vast AT&T telephone monopoly. In 1994, the antitrust division of the Justice Department prosecuted 60 criminal cases.[248]

Antitrust laws prohibit practices that unreasonably deprive consumers of the advantages of competition, the *sine qua non* of capitalism.

When competitors agree to fix prices, rig bids or allocate customers, consumers lose the benefits of competition. The prices that result when competitors agree in these ways are artificially high; such prices do not accurately reflect cost and therefore distort the allocation of society's resources. The result is a loss not only to U.S. consumers and taxpayers, but also the U.S. economy. [249]

In a truly competitive market, businesses attract consumers by holding prices down and keeping quality up. When competitors conspire to fix prices, however, consumers pay higher prices for inferior goods and services. In other words, collusive arrangements among nominal competitors unlawfully maximize corporate profits at the consumer's expense.

The illegality of price fixing has not often deterred its practice. A study of 582 large American corporations concluded that "violations of the nation's antitrust laws are common in a wide variety of industries."[250] Recent cases in which price-fixing sanctions were applied by courts or administrative agencies include such diverse industries as steel,[251] lead smelting,[252] glass,[253] oil drilling,[254] natural gas,[255] trash hauling,[256] road building,[257] electrical contracting,[258] commercial explosives,[259] disability insurance,[260] urology services,[261] athletic shoes,[262] residential doors,[263] scouring pads,[264] plastic dinnerware,[265] toys,[266] video games,[267] motion pictures,[268] infant formula,[269] soft drinks,[270] white bread,[271] and Passover matzo. [272]

One reason for the failure of deterrent measures is that the government's commitment to regulation of price fixing has been erratic. The intensity of enforcement has depended on the political regime and the prevailing ideology in Washington at a particular time.[273] Studies report that price fixing is most apt to occur during Republican administrations because of that party's traditional pro-business, antiregulatory philosophy.[274] During the 8 years of the Reagan administration in the 1980s, for instance, the number of antitrust suits filed by the federal government shrank from 142 to 19.[275] On the other hand, studies also indicate that Republican judges tend to impose harsher sentences for individual antitrust offenders than Democratic judges, perhaps because Republican judges are generally less inclined to side with criminal defendants.[276]

Regarding antitrust enforcement, the 8 Clinton years during the 1990s can perhaps be characterized as schizophrenic. On the one hand, the second half of that decade spawned the re-emergence of the merger-mania that defined the 1980s. By 1995, proposed mergers that might have been unthinkable just a few years before were flying past the Justice Department, sometimes without even slowing down: Exxon and Mobil;[277] Chevron and Texaco;[278] BP and Amoco;[279] BP Amoco and Atlantic Richfield;[280] Reading & Bates and Falcon Drilling;[281] Dow and Union Carbide;[282] Time Warner and Turner Broadcasting;[283] AOL and Netscape;[284] Time Warner and AOL;[285] IBM and Lotus;[286] Disney and Capitol Cities/ABC; Westinghouse and CBS; Unilever and Bestfoods;[287] Kimberly-Clark and Scott Paper; Chemical Banking and Chase Manhattan;[288] American International Group and

SunAmerica;[289] WorldCom and MCI;[290] AT&T and Teleport;[291] United Airlines and US Airways;[292] Continental Airlines and Delta Airlines;[293] American Airlines and TWA;[294] and the Union Pacific and Southern Pacific railroads. [295] Critics contend that such deals would give too few companies too much control of important markets or products. If the Age of the Monopoly is over, the Age of the Oligopoly appears to be alive and well.

Even the regional telephone companies formed by the breakup of the AT&T monopoly appear to be heading toward reconglomeration. On April 1, 1996, Southwestern Bell and Pacific Telesis announced a proposed merger.[296] Just 3 weeks later, Nynex and Bell Atlantic announced merger plans.[297] In 1998, a merger was proposed between SBC Communications (formerly Southwestern Bell) and Ameritech (another former "Baby Bell").[298] And in 2000, the Federal Communications Commission approved the merger of Bell Atlantic and GTE, a union that would create the largest local telephone company in the United States.[299]

On the other hand, the 1990s also witnessed an abundance of stiff sanctions and record-breaking fines for price fixing and other antitrust violations. For example, in the largest civil antitrust settlement ever up to that time, 37 brokerages involved in a massive price-rigging conspiracy agreed in 1998 to pay $1.03 billion to investors who were overcharged for Nasdaq-listed stocks. The companies making payouts included the biggest names in the securities world: Merrill Lynch, Goldman Sachs, Salomon Smith Barney. The case revolved around the practice of quoting stocks for customers to the nearest quarter of a dollar, rather than the nearest eighth, thus generating extra profits.[300]

The current record, as of this writing, for the largest class action settlement of an antitrust case is the $1.05 million dollars imposed in 1999 on seven pharmaceutical companies that virtually control the vitamin market in the United States. These firms had conspired for years to raise and fix vitamin prices worldwide. The settlement followed 14 prosecutions by the Justice Department's antitrust division that had led to $875 million in criminal fines.[301]

In 1999, oil-field services companies Smith International and Schlumberger became the first companies in 16 years to be found guilty of criminal contempt in violation of an antitrust decree.[302] The companies had formed a joint fluid drilling venture in violation of a court order. Each firm was fined $750,000 but was allowed to continue operating the joint venture in exchange for payment of a $13.1 million civil penalty.[303]

In 1996, Archer Daniels Midland (ADM), the grain- and soybean-processing conglomerate whose products are found in everything from shampoo to soft drinks, agreed to pay a then-record $100 million price-fixing fine involving lysene (used in animal feed) and citric acid (used in food and beverages). In exchange, the government agreed to drop potentially far more costly antitrust charges relating to high-fructose corn syrup, ADM's most important product.[304] Despite the size of the fine, financial analysts concluded that ADM—long known as one of the most powerful and politically connected corporations, doling out enormous political contributions to both Democrats and Republicans[305]—had made a "good deal." The company held over $2 billion in cash at the time, so the fine was less than might have been antici-pated had the corn syrup investigation continued. In fact, ADM's stock ac-tually *rose* following the settlement.[306]

ADM's corporate culture was perfectly captured in a meeting between an ADM executive and a foreign competitor which was secretly taped by the FBI: "We have a saying here in this company that penetrates the whole com-pany. Our competitors are our friends. Our customers are the enemy."[307]

In 1998, the ADM record for the largest antitrust fine fell was sur-passed when UCAR International, the *country's* largest producer of graphite electrodes, which provide the heat source for steel mills, was fined $110 mil-lion after it admitted scheming to fix prices.[308] That record fell a year later when SGL Carbon Aktiengesellschaft, the *world's* largest producer of graphite electrodes, became the fourth member of the carbon-graphite cartel fined by the Justice Department for price-fixing. The fine in this case was $135 million. Robert J. Koehler, CEO of the German-based corporation, also agreed to pay a $10 million fine, the largest antitrust fine ever levied against an individual.[309]

Another $135 million fine was imposed on Mylan Laboratories, the country's second-largest manufacturer of generic drugs, after it was found to have fixed prices of two widely prescribed antianxiety medications. The com-pany had conspired to control ingredients for the two drugs; then raised prices by as much as *3000%*. The price of one drug was raised from $7.30 for a bottle of 500 tablets to $190. The second drug's price rose from $11.36 for a bot-tle of 500 to $377.[310] Mylan chairman Milan Puskar agreed to the settlement but continued to dispute the accusations: "We continue to believe we acted properly."[311] One can only wonder how Mr. Puskar defines "improper."

Perhaps appropriately enough, it was the pharmaceutical industry that shattered the record for antitrust fines in 1999, when the Swiss pharma-ceutical giant Hoffman-LaRoche paid a $500 million fine for its part in a global price-fixing conspiracy.[312] That year, the Justice Department's antitrust divi-sion raked in an unprecedented $1 billion in fines and penalties.[313] How long this current record stands will depend on the final outcome of one of the most important antitrust cases in American history: *U.S. v. Microsoft*.

C A S E   S T U D Y

Microsoft = Macro-Monopoly?

No company symbolizes the "new economy" of the late twentieth and early twenty-first centuries like Microsoft, whose meteoric rise to market supremacy is legendary. Founded in 1975 by Bill Gates and Paul Allen, it started with three em-ployees and $16,005 in revenues. By 1991, its Windows operating system was on more than 90% of the personal computers (PCs) in the world. By 1998, the company had a market cap of $263 billion,[314] and Gates, whose assets totalled an estimated

(Continued)

$58 billion, was hailed as the richest person on the planet—perhaps the wealthiest man who has ever lived.

The success of Microsoft, however, quickly became a source of enormous controversy. Admirers of the company pointed to it as the perfect exemplar of successful modern capitalism. One noted economist, writing in defense of Microsoft, maintains: "[R]unning other companies out of business and gaining market share is what capitalistic competition is all about."[315] Other scholars echo this sentiment, characterizing Microsoft's aggressive marketing practices simply as "brutally competitive."[316]

Critics, however, accused the company of ruthlessly squashing competitors like bugs on a windshield. This bug metaphor would probably not be lost on Rob Glaser, a former Microsoft executive and CEO of RealNetworks (a company which makes software for sending video over the Internet). Glaser told the Senate Judiciary Committee that Microsoft had placed a "bug" in its rival Windows program that "broke" RealNetwork's software.[317] According to a Silicon Valley antitrust lawyer, "The only thing the robber barons did that Bill Gates hasn't done is use dynamite against their competitors."[318]

Consumer advocates also accused of Microsoft of price-gouging. They point out that at a time when computer prices were falling sharply, Microsoft's prices for its operating systems more than doubled. "In 1990 the operating system represented about 4 percent of the price of a computer; today the system makes up over 12 percent."[319] Former Senator Howard Metzenbaum, chairman of the Consumer Federation of America, is one of Microsoft's harshest critics:

> Because of its monopoly, Microsoft can skimp on quality. It ships products with avoidable defects, sells upgrades that are often of marginal value and is not pushed to develop truly innovative products. Microsoft has repeatedly imitated the innovative leaders in the industry and then driven them out of the market.[320]

In 1991, the Federal Trade Commission undertook an investigation of whether Microsoft had monopolized the market for PC operating systems. When it concluded that investigation 2 years later, the FTC turned the case over to the antitrust division of the Justice Department. The following year, the case was seemingly settled with a consent decree, under which Microsoft agreed to give computer makers more leeway in using software from competitors.[321]

When Microsoft launched Windows 95 in 1995, it did not include an Internet browser. Its fledgling Explorer browser had to be purchased separately. But by the end of the year, Gates had shifted Microsoft's corporate strategy toward the Internet, and the company began distributing Internet Explorer for free. When Explorer 4.0 was launched in 1997, it took dead aim at Netscape Communication, the dominant player in the browser market. The strategy was simple and effective: Microsoft demanded that computer manufacturers install Internet Explorer as a condition of installing Windows 95.[322] Such a practice is known as "bundling."

(Continued)

In its 1994 agreement with the Justice Department, Microsoft had consented not to require computer manufacturers to install "separate" products. Microsoft was permitted only to bundle "integrated" products with Windows. For example, Windows Explorer, which organizes files, was viewed as an "integrated" component of Windows.[323]

In 1997, the Justice Department sued Microsoft. It contended that Internet Explorer was a "separate" product and thus its bundling violated the consent decree. The government argued that Explorer was clearly separate from Windows because: (1) it could be "uninstalled" without compromising the operation of Windows, and (2) Microsoft had given away Internet Explorer for years as a distinct, stand-alone product.[324]

Two months after the suit was filed, a U.S. district court judge issued a preliminary injunction ordering Microsoft to stop forcing PC makers to install its browser. Six months later (June 1998), however, a federal appeals court overturned the injunction.[325] It was a shorted-lived victory for Microsoft, because the cork was now out of the bottle, and the case against Microsoft had moved well beyond bundling.

A month before the injunction was lifted, the Justice Department and 20 state attorneys general sued Microsoft, this time charging that the company had illegally used its monopolistic power to hurt competitors and stifle innovation in the software industry.[326] A steady stream of accusations began appearing in court papers and leaked press accounts depicting Microsoft "not as a tough negotiator but as a back-alley enforcer.[327]

Gates was accused of masterminding a conspiracy to kill off a rival company, Netscape, levering his monopolistic control over one market to take over another.[328] The government alleged that Microsoft had employed predatory practices against a virtual "Who's Who" of high tech: Netscape, Apple, Intel, AOL, and Compaq, as well as others.[329] The government's chief counsel, David Boies, announced that he intended to ask every witness to stake his or her credibility on whether Windows constitutes a monopoly. He declared: "I doubt even [Microsoft's] witnesses will be able to keep a straight face."[330]

Microsoft, however, strongly rejected being labeled as the dreaded *M* word (monopoly). Although by 1998 its Windows and DOS systems controlled 97% of the world market, it asserted that monopoly and market share are not the same.[331] It questioned how the government could possibly be acting in the best interests of consumers by forcing it to stop giving away its product for free.[332] The company further argued that it had integrated its browser into its new Windows 98 operating system so it cannot be separated as a stand-alone product.[333] Microsoft's chief counsel, William Neukom, denounced the government's case as "desperate" and "cynical."[334]

And so, on October 19, 1998, one of the most important antitrust trials in American history began. How important? The *New Republic* put it in perspective: "[T]his is not merely an argument about one company or one very, very rich man. At its heart, the Microsoft monopoly trial will determine who writes the business rules of cyberspace—the government or Microsoft."[335]

(Continued)

Before the trial was an hour old, the packed courtroom got to see and hear that "very, very rich man." Not in person; Gates never attended the trial. The lawyer representing the states who had joined in the suit charged Gates with a "lack of intestinal fortitude" to testify.[336] But he had been deposed on videotape several months earlier. At the time, government lawyers had complained that Gates had been "evasive and non-responsive."[337] Boies now offered a persuasive illustration of the Gates stonewalling style by showing a brief clip from the deposition. Gates, looking "at once deeply uncomfortable and deeply bored"[338] was asked by an unseen interrogator, "Have you ever read the complaint in this case?"[339] Gates replied, "No."[340]

Two hours of excerpts, culled from his 20-hour deposition, made Gates (according to *Time*) "look like he was the worst CEO in America."[341] He was asked about a damning piece of evidence: an e-mail he had written about Microsoft's plans to use Apple Computer to "undermine" archrival Sun Microsystems. He responded that he could not remember sending the message and had no idea what he could have meant by it. And although Microsoft had held two well-documented negotiations with Netscape in 1995, Gates claimed he had only learned of these negotiations from an article in the *Wall Street Journal*.[342]

> [I]t was a difficult line to swallow. Gates as a fuzzy- headed amnesiac? This is a man revered . . . for his awesome "bandwidth" (geek speak for intelligence). Gates' memory is so capacious that at age 11, he astounded friends and family by memorizing all 107 verses of the Sermon on the Mount. He's so driven and detail oriented that he favors baths over showers so he can study while he soaks.[343]

Gates was so disingenuous that the presiding judge laughed out loud—along with the rest of the courtroom—at a particularly blatant obfuscation, when Gates asked the meaning of the word "we."[344]

> The Gates in the video . . . paused for 20 seconds or more while formulating some answers. When the going got tough, he rocked back and forth in his chair like a toy dog in a car window. He testily parsed fine distinctions (Microsoft's "deal" with Apple vs. their "relationship") and professed to be nonplussed by common Anglo-Saxon words ("I have no idea what you're talking about when you say 'ask.'").

Boies' strategy seemed clear: Expose the boss as a liar and thus erode the company's credibility. Time and again, Gates claimed to have been out of the loop during discussions and key meetings. And time and again, his taped testimony was contradicted by memos and e-mails written by him, each one enlarged on a 10-foot video screen. Regarding the negotiations with Netscape that Gates claimed to have learned of from the *Wall Street Journal*, Boies presented an internal Microsoft e-mail that Gates had written on the same day as the meeting. "I think there is a very powerful deal of some kind we can do with Netscape."[345]

Netscape turned down Gates' proposal that Microsoft would agree not to develop a rival browser for non-Windows operating systems if Netscape agreed to

(Continued)

stay out of the Windows market. Netscape co-founder Marc Andreesen would later compare the unsuccessful meeting to "a visit from Don Corleone. I expected to find a bloody computer monitor in my bed the next day."[346]

Using Microsoft's own paper trail, "the government portrayed a company obsessed with crushing its competitors . . . and willing to use every tool at its disposal, including threats and financial inducements to force or persuade other companies to drop any planned or existing alliances with Netscape."[347] Microsoft's legal team derided such evidence as "snippets." Their repeated use of this term became a running joke. In fact, an anti-Microsoft group had "Free the Snippets" buttons made up and handed them out to reporters at the courthouse.[348]

But the snippets Boies chose were "killers." For example, Gates was quoted in an e-mail that recaps a meeting he held with AOL executives: "How much do we need to pay you to screw Netscape?"[349]

One of the government's most compelling witnesses against Microsoft was Apple vice-president Avadis Tevanian. In 1997, the two archrivals had entered into a stunning partnership when Microsoft helped bail Apple out of a financial slump with an infusion of $150 million.[350] Tevanian recounted a series of 1997 meetings in which Microsoft intimidated Apple. Microsoft allegedly had threatened to withhold its business software, Microsoft Office, from the Apple's signature Macintosh computer. The price tag for Microsoft's continued cooperation was making Internet Explorer Apple's default browser.[351]

Tevanian also alleged that Microsoft had demanded that Apple stop making its QuickTime multimedia software for Windows-based computers. According to Tevanian, Microsoft again used the same threat: It would pull support for Microsoft Office, which was critical to Apple.[352]

> Tevanian recounted a sinister moment in which an Apple executive, surprised by a Microsoft demand that the company drop [QuickTime], asked, "Do you want us to knife the baby?" "Yes," the Microsoft executive reportedly replied, "we're talking about knifing the baby."[353]

He added that when Apple refused to abandon QuickTime, Microsoft sabotaged it so it would have problems running on computers using Internet Explorer.[354] To punctuate Tavanian's testimony, the government introduced a handwritten note from Apple's chief financial officer, which read in part:

> "Apple needed to ensure that Microsoft would continue to provide MS Office for Mac, or we were dead. . . . They were threatening to abandon Mac. [The] trading card was making Internet Explorer [the] default browser."[350]

Conspicuously absent among the roll call of witnesses were the PC manufacturers, "the most obvious victims of alleged Microsoft coercion."[356] Some industry insiders contend that the PC makers were silenced by the very power the government was seeking to curb.[357] According to one former CEO, "Nobody in the PC business wants to be near this."[358] A noted antitrust attorney adds, "They couldn't

(Continued)

find anyone brave enough to come forward and risk the wrath of Microsoft."[359] Boies quoted a Hewlett-Packard memo to Microsoft:

> "If we had a choice of another supplier based on your actions in this area," writes an HP exec, "you would not be our supplier of choice." But of course HP has no choice. That's the point.[360]

Compaq, the number one PC maker, even agreed to testify *for* Microsoft, despite itself being a past victim of Gates' bullying tactics. In 1996, Compaq had entered into a deal with America Online that would have displayed AOL's screen before the familiar Windows screen. According to a Compaq insider, when Microsoft threatened, Compaq backed down.[361] Furthermore, the company attested in Justice Department depositions that Microsoft had applied serious pressure when Compaq attempted to put Netscape's browser on its computers alongside Windows.[362]

Closing arguments from both sides ended in September 1999. On November 5, Judge Thomas Penfield Jackson, a Republican and Reagan appointee, delivered his first finding of fact. In a blistering ruling, Judge Jackson declared that Microsoft *is* a monopoly that stifles competition and hurts consumers. He agreed with nearly all the government's allegations.[363] By this time it had become clear what sanctions the government was seeking. It wanted to impose the antitrust version of the "death penalty"[364]—the breakup of the company into what were already being dubbed "Baby Bills."[365]

The court's second finding of fact was issued on April 3, 2000. In another stinging rebuke, Judge Jackson ruled that Microsoft "maintained its monopoly power by anticompetitive means and attempted to monopolize the Web browser market."[366] Jackson said that Microsoft had put an "oppressive thumb on the scale of competitive fortune."[367]

The final and most dramatic finding of fact was announced on June 7, 2000. Calling Microsoft "untrustworthy"[368] and an "unrepentant lawbreaker,"[369] Judge Jackson ordered the software giant to be split into two companies. Bill Gates called the ruling "an unwarranted and unjustified intrusion."[370] The imposed breakup was, of course, stayed pending appeal—a process believed likely to take years. Microsoft expressed firm confidence that it would ultimately prevail. Bill Gates seemed especially lifted by the case's shift to the appellate courts: "I'm reminded of the old saying, 'Today is the first day of the rest of your life.'"[371]

In September 2000, the U.S. Supreme Court declined to "fast track" the Microsoft appeal by hearing it immediately. It handed the case to the federal appellate court in Washington, DC. Although there seems to be little doubt that the Supreme Court will ultimately decide the fate of Microsoft, this decision was seen as a victory for the company. The DC court had already sided with Microsoft in an earlier case, and the current Supreme Court has an unpredictable record on antitrust cases.[372]

Allowing the appeal to proceed sluggishly may also benefit Microsoft in another way. In 2001, a pro-business Republican administration took control of the Justice Department. It seems possible that in this new political environment, the

(Continued)

government may be more willing to accept a less drastic settlement, or perhaps even drop the case entirely.

However, if the judgment of the court should prevail and Microsoft is split up, its arrogant "admit-nothing" strategy will almost certainly rate as "one of the greatest blunders in American corporate history."[373] Most antitrust experts agree that the case could have been settled early and easily had Microsoft conceded the obvious, made a few concessions, taken a slap on the wrist, and vowed to sin no more.

Instead, it bet on Bill Gates, whose testimony quickly degenerated from haughty invincibility to Clintonesque nitpicking over the meaning of simple words to outright prevarication. "Petulant, self-pitying, convinced of his own righteousness, Gates had no intention of admitting his company had done anything wrong. Instead, he decided to stonewall, and in the process he became the prosecution's star witness."[374]

Two frequent targets of major antitrust litigation are the oil industry and the airline industry. In response to the oil shortage of 1972–1973, which drove up retail prices to scarcely believable levels, four states (California, Oregon, Washington, and Arizona) filed class-action suits against seven major oil corporations. The suits alleged that the shortage had resulted from an unlawful conspiracy among Exxon, Shell, Mobil, Texaco, Chevron, Unocal, and ARCO to fix the price of gasoline.

After 17 years of legal maneuvers, the so-called Seven Sisters began settling the cases. In January 1992, Exxon agreed to pay the plaintiffs $9.9 million.[375] In April, ARCO, Texaco, and Unocal agreed to pay a total of $63 million.[376] The following year, Chevron, Mobil, and Shell finally settled, just days before a scheduled trial, for a total of $77 million.[377] Although none of the defendants admitted any wrongdoing and the $150-million combined settlement was far less than the billions sought, the attorneys general of the four states considered the agreements a hard-earned victory for long-suffering consumers.

While the Seven Sisters were dragging their fourteen feet through the judicial system, another class-action suit was being filed in federal court, this one aimed at the country's leading airlines. The defendants were charged with using an electronic fare database to fix prices. Among the specific allegations against American, Continental, Delta, Northwest, PanAm, TWA, United, and US Air was that fares were kept artificially high because airlines sent coded signals to competitors announcing future fare hikes that each would match.[378]

By 1992, all the companies except PanAm (which had gone out of business) agreed to out-of-court settlements, releasing them from the case.[379] The terms of the settlements were controversial and very unpopular with consumers. The $458 million that the airlines had put up in return for passengers dropping price-fixing claims was in the form of discount coupons rather than cash. Instead of getting refunds, the 10 million ticket buyers who had flown with the affected carriers from 1988 through mid-1992 would have to pay the airlines more money in order to recoup past losses. The coupons, moreover, expired just 3 years after the settlement and were useful for only a small portion of the price of full-fare tickets: at best 10%. Some frequent fliers calculated that they would have to buy as many as 60 round-trip, undiscounted tickets in order to get full credit for the coupons they were owed.[380] In addition, applications for coupons required filling out a complicated claim form containing four pages of fine print.

> [P]eople who filled out the simplest Form A, which involved no itemization, got a $25 voucher, four $10 vouchers and one for $5, for a total of $73. Those who filled out Form B got two $25 vouchers, two for $10 and one $9, for a total of $79. Those who itemized on Form C got $79, plus 0.232 percent (0.00232) of their claims.[381]

Most ordinary travelers expressed a strong sense of frustration with this gibberish. One typical customer received $159 worth of coupons, but after wrestling with all the complex requirements, she concluded: "They are valueless."[382] Analysts estimated that fewer than 10% of the coupons would ever be redeemed by individual consumers.

The only major beneficiaries were large corporations. IBM, for example, received $3.3 million in discounts. "Their coupons were delivered in filing cabinets rather than envelopes."[383] The other big winners were the plaintiffs' lawyers, for whom the settlement had provided $14 million in fees. One business magazine suggested puckishly that those attorneys be paid in *coupons*.[384]

Although price fixing is a crime, it is usually punished (as in the preceding examples) by means of corporate fines and administrative sanctions that are negotiated out-of-court. This policy rests on the notion that public exposure serves as a deterrent even when formal sanctions are weak.[385] Given the seemingly neverending proliferation of price-fixing cases, however, such an assertion seems questionable. Yet, judges have been reluctant to impose criminal sanctions, especially jail sentences, on individual antitrust violators.[386] Consequently, jail sentences may have little deterrent effect because of their infrequent use and relative lightness.[387]

One form of price fixing that *has* yielded criminal sanctions in a number of cases is the practice of bid-rigging. Perhaps offenses in this area are taken more seriously by the criminal justice system because the government itself is most often the victim, rather than individual consumers. Such was the case in the 1950s when manufacturers of heavy electrical equipment made a mockery of free enterprise.

C A S E   S T U D Y

The Great Electrical Conspiracy

Except for Watergate (Chapter 8), no white-collar crime in American history probably has been analyzed more thoroughly than the so-called Great Electri-

(Continued)

cal Conspiracy. Although it is often treated as a single crime, like Watergate, it actually consisted of a cluster of interrelated conspiracies. At least 20 distinct product lines were involved, and a network of more than 40 manufacturers were implicated.[388]

The collusion that would become a cultural norm within the electrical equipment industry emerged, not from a tradition of cooperation, but out of a climate of ferocious competition. In 1954, the Westinghouse corporation developed an improved transformer, which enabled it to jump into a market that had long been dominated by General Electric. To recapture its position, GE launched an all-out price war, slashing prices on transformers and many other electrical products to below cost. The ensuing battle cost the bigger companies millions of dollars and devastated smaller manufacturers.[389] When the price wars became incompatible with top management's demands for higher profits,[390] the industry's response was a decision to conspire rather than compete.

Instead of submitting competitive sealed bids for lucrative government contracts, executives began holding secret meetings at which they would agree in advance on prices and divide up the contracts among their respective firms. The customary sealed bids were thus reduced to a charade, because the "low" bid and winning bidder had been predetermined. The companies had effectively formed an illegal cartel, a flagrant violation of the Sherman Antitrust Act.

The scheme came unglued in 1959, when a communication miscue within the cartel resulted in the submission of identical, supposedly competitive bids to the federally controlled Tennessee Valley Authority (TVA). The TVA is the largest generator of electricity in the United States and a purchaser of enormous amounts of electrical power equipment. When this story broke, the press demanded an investigation. The Justice Department examined TVA records and discovered 24 other instances of matching bids over a 3-year period. Some of these bids were figured down to one 1/100th of a cent.[391]

The investigation soon revealed that bid-rigging was by no means peculiar to the TVA. It had become an endemic way of life industry-wide.[392] Over the years, electrical manufacturers had cheated taxpayers out of perhaps as much as a billion dollars by keeping prices at an unnecessarily high level.

> It represents real money, just as would money obtained through a bank robbery (in fact, hundreds or thousands of robberies). Whenever a municipal government was overcharged $250,000 for a turbine, its taxpayers had to make up the difference. Whenever a power and light company bought a generator for 10 percent more than it was really worth, its customers paid correspondingly more for the energy they consumed.[393]

Ultimately, fines totaling about $2 million were handed out, primarily to GE and Westinghouse. Given the pecuniary magnitude of the crimes, the amount seems insignificant. Criminologist Gilbert Geis, whose work first ignited academic interest in the case, has noted that a $400,000 fine levied at General Electric would be equivalent to a man who earns a $175,000 per year receiving a $3 parking ticket.[394]

(Continued)

In 1961, 45 executives from 29 corporations were indicted for criminal conspiracy. All either admitted their guilt or pleaded *nolo contendere* (no contest). Thirty-one were convicted, of whom seven received jail sentences of 30 days.[395] Four were vice-presidents, two were division managers, and one was a sales manager.[396] The other 24 convicted defendants were given suspended sentences. Good behavior earned the incongruous convicts a 5-day reduction in their terms. During their brief stay, they were described as "model prisoners." In fact, a warden called them "the most intelligent prisoners" he had housed all year.[397]

One aspect of this case which has long intrigued researchers was the unanimous rejection of any criminal self-identity among those convicted. For example, an officer of the Allis-Chalmers corporation explained that he had participated only because he had believed it had been part of his duty. In a memorable quote, one General Electric executive described the agreements as "illegal but not criminal."[398] Yet if one examines the dynamics of the conspiracy—the clandestine meetings, the frequent use of public telephones, the fake names and secret codes—one recognizes techniques and behaviors that are strikingly characteristic of organized crime.

Many of the defendants further argued that they had been performing a positive service to the economy by stabilizing prices. In other words, "they shifted blame to the market structure rather than to themselves." [399] Self-serving neutralizations are, of course, typical of most criminals—of any-colored collar.

Westinghouse stood by its offending executives, calling each a "reputable citizen," a "respected and valued member of the community," who had not acted for personal gain.[400] This denial of individual benefit offers no hint of the likely professional rewards attached to profitable bid-rigging. In sharp contrast, General Electric fired all its convicted officers, condemning them for violating the company's purportedly strict ethical policy. Many observers, however, felt that GE was scapegoating its former executives for the sake of public relations. When one of the defendants was asked if he thought he had been "thrown to the wolves" by top management, his answer was yes.[401]

Since the heavy electrical equipment scandal, bid-rigging has remained one of the most irrepressible of all antitrust violations. "Despite repeated waves of federal and state enforcement, it reappears with remarkable consistency."[402] In the 1980s, more than half the criminal cases filed by the antitrust division of the Justice Department concerned the rigging of sealed-bid procurement auctions.[403]

In 2000, almost all of the companies that supply food to New York City's schoolchildren were charged by the Justice Department in a bid-rigging scheme that overcharged the city at least $21 million. Thirteen companies and 22 individuals were accused of conspiring to fix prices on more than $200 million worth of food. As of this writing, 6 companies and 12 individuals have agreed to plead guilty.[404]

The dairy industry has been the most conspicuous violator in recent cases. Since the early 1980s, companies have conspired to rig the bids to supply milk to schools and other public institutions (including, ironically, prisons) in a number of states. More than 100 people and companies have been convicted of bid-rigging charges related to school milk prices,[405] at least 18 persons have gone to prison.[406] The initial investigation took place in Florida in 1988, where seven dairies "allegedly negotiated with their competitors to determine which would win each school contract and at what price, after which the other firms submitted bids higher than that of the designated winner."[407]

A year later, the scandal crossed into neighboring Georgia, where that state's attorney general declared "there was a 'significant likelihood' that local school districts . . . had been the victims of violations of antitrust laws and that suspected bid-rigging could have cost the districts 'tens of millions of dollars' over the 10-year period being investigated by his office."[408]

By 1993, unmistakable evidence had been uncovered in at least 20 states that executives at some of the biggest national and regional dairy companies had conspired to rig bids on federal and state milk contracts, sometimes for decades.[409] For example, the giant Borden corporation agreed to pay a $5.2 million fine after it admitted to antitrust charges relating to bid-rigging in its contracts with American military installations.[410]

Price Gouging

Another reprehensible practice falling under the general price fixing rubric is price gouging. This term refers to "the practice of taking extraordinary advantage of consumers because of the bias of the law, monopoly of the market, or because of contrived or real shortages."[411] A vivid example could be seen immediately following Hurricane Andrew, which devastated Florida in 1992, when prices on urgently needed supplies were raised to outrageously high levels.[412] The same greedy scenario was replayed after the serious earthquake that struck Los Angeles in 1994. Many local merchants immediately doubled and even quintupled prices on essential items such as bottled water and batteries.[413]

In 2001, a federal jury ordered Exxon Mobil Corp. to pay $500 million to 10,000 gas station owners in 35 states whom they had overcharged for 40 billion gallons of gasoline over a 12-year period. The company had created a discount program that charged cash customers less than credit card users but added 4 cents per gallon to the station owner's price. The company had pledged to cut wholesale prices to offset the surcharge, but circumvented its agreement by manipulating wholesale prices in a way that effectively erased any benefit to owners. As of this writing, Exxon Mobil is appealing the huge verdict.[414]

Price gouging includes spiraling price increases divorced from economic reality. This appears to have been the case when the price of infant formula shot up 155% during the 1980s, while the price of milk rose only 36%.[415]

Price gouging reflects corporate opportunism at its most ruthless. When a worldwide shortage of sugar caused sharp price increases for American manufacturers several years ago, products using sugar understandably rose in price concomitantly. The cost of soda, for example, increased by 15 to 25 cents per can. Less understandably, however, when the sugar shortage ended and prices returned to normal, the cost of soda remained at its higher, shortage-created level. Furthermore, in an illustration of how willing corporations are to exploit consumers by gouging prices whenever possible, diet soda (which contains *no* sugar) had also jumped in price. Moreover, *all* the major soft drink companies employed the same strategy, suggesting price fixing as well.[416]

Cereal manufacturing is an $8-billion-per-year industry, with over 200 brands on grocery shelves. It is an enormously profitable business, where the cardboard box sometimes costs producers more than the cereal inside.[417] Since the early 1980s (when the government dropped a lengthy investigation),[418] prices have risen 90% (twice the increase for other foods),[419] with "little apparent relation to true costs."[420] In 1995, a New York congressman called on the FTC to re-investigate possible antitrust violations. Speaking from the cereal section of a local supermarket, surrounded by $4 boxes of Rice Krispies, Frosted Flakes, Honey Nut Cheerios, and the like, he declared, "When I come down this aisle, my blood pressure goes up 10 points."[421] One investigative report was titled "Snap, Crackle, and Price-Fixing?"[422] In 1999, both Kellogg's and General Mills announced new price increases for their cereals—at a time when farm prices were falling.[423]

The pricing practices of the American pharmaceutical industry have come under particular scrutiny. The United States is the only Western nation that does not control the cost of prescription drugs. Perhaps as a consequence, accusations of price gouging have been leveled at that industry for decades. In 1978, ABC News reported, for example, that the Mylan Pharmaceutical Company was producing three versions of the antibiotic drug erythromycin, each a different color but otherwise *identical*. "The pink version is the generic and sells for $6.20; the yellow pills are marketed by Smith-Kline and sell for $9.20; and the orange ones are called Bristamycin and are marketed for $14.00."[424] A 1993 ABC News program reported that the price of an inexpensive drug used to worm sheep was raised 10,000% when it was discovered that the drug could be used to treat colon cancer in humans.[425]

Since 1980, prices for prescription drugs have risen three times faster than prices for all other products.[426] "The increases have forced millions of Americans of limited means to stop taking the medicines they need."[427] Senior citizens use the most prescription drugs of any age group—about 30% of the total annual sales in the United States. According to one U.S. Senator: "Over 5 million people over 55 now say they are having to make choices between food and their prescription drugs."[428] A 1986 survey by the American Association of Retired Persons (AARP) reported that 18,400,000 respondents over age 65 said that they had trouble paying for their presciption medications.[429]

A scathing congressional report released in 1991 attacked the "excessive and unreasonable profits"[430] generated by pharmaceutical corporations. This report noted that the drug industry's average 15.5% profit margin more than triples the 4.6% margin of the average Fortune 500 company. It was projected that if prices continued to spiral at the current rate, a prescription that had cost $20 in 1980 would rise to over $120 in the year 2000, a 500% increase.[431]

In 1999, 19 pharmaceutical companies agreed to pay more than $176 million to settle a class action lawsuit alleging that they gouged the public by overcharging pharmacies for medicines while cutting prices for health maintenance organizations (HMOs) and big volume buyers such as mail order drug firms. This was the second time in 3 months that a court had found that major drug manufacturers had conspired to destroy competition between retailers and HMOs.[432]

Drug manufacturers contend that soaring prices reflect huge research and development (R & D) expenses, which compel them to plow most of their profits into R & D. According to the Pharmaceutical Manufacturing Association, the average cost to bring a new drug to market in 1990 was $231 million. Critics counter that drug companies lump marketing research costs into their R & D budgets and that promotional and advertising expenditures actually exceed those associated with true R & D.[433]

The alleged excesses within the pharmaceutical industry raise disturbing questions about where the line between profit and profiteering is drawn. In the words of a California congressman, "Never have so few made such gross amounts of money from so many sick people."[434]

As the pharmaceutical industry's record toward the elderly demonstrates, price gouging is often directed at the easiest targets. Likewise, the poor, especially those who are members of minority groups, have long been singled out for victimization.[435]

When the President's Commission on Civil Disorders[436] issued its report on urban rioting in 1968, one of its most significant (although largely unnoticed) findings was that ghetto residents suffered constant abuses by local merchants. "[M]ost big purchases—furniture, appliances, cars, home improvements—are grossly overpriced." [437]

In the 1990s, racial tensions were attributed to the "systematic exploitation of minorities by banks, insurance companies, department stores, and other businesses." [438] For instance, drivers who happen to live in certain inner-city ZIP code areas usually pay higher auto insurance rates, regardless of their driving records. Bankers systematically "redline" entire neighborhoods, refusing to lend money to residents, who are then forced into the waiting arms of rapacious finance companies that charge sky-high interest rates.

Pawnshops, long a traditional symbol of inner-city usury, have staged a remarkable and very profitable comeback, doubling in number since the mid-1980s. At least five national pawnshop chains are now publicly traded on the New York Stock Exchange. One of the largest, Cash America (with over 250 units), charges up to 200% annual interest on its loans.[439]

The crude slum gougers described by the President's Commission may be less conspicuous today, but they are still prowling the fringes of the economic mainstream, culling the weak from the herd like practiced predators. Some have found new places to lie in ambush—behind store signs blaring

RENT-TO-OWN. The rent-to-own industry developed about 30 years ago as a way to skirt new usury laws designed to limit interest rates that inner-city merchants were charging consumers who bought on credit. "By redefining such transactions as rentals with 'the option to buy,' rent-to-own dealers are free to charge interest rates of 100, 200, even 300 percent."[440] No wonder business reportedly has been booming. How else could one buy a $400 set of children's bunk beds for $16.99 per week for 78 weeks, for total of $1325?[441]

Rent-to-own dealers defend their business as the only one willing to help low-income people who are shunned by banks and department stores. The leader of the industry's trade association has pledged, "Our customers have as much right to the American Dream as anyone else."[442] Unfortunately, they have to rent it.

Knockoff Rip-offs

A special type of price-gouging involves the covert substitution of low-quality counterfeit versions of brand-name consumer products, known as knockoffs. The MGM-Grand Hotel in Reno, for example, once refilled 16,000 bottles with cheaper liquor over a 14-month period.[443]

The knockoff business is booming. In 1982, world-wide losses to American manufacturers owning to counterfeiting or trademark infringement totalled $5.5 billion. In 1995, the annual cost had ballooned to $200 billion.[444] For example, in that year Procter & Gamble discovered counterfeit diluted bottles of its popular Head & Shoulders Dandruff Shampoo on shelves at a large supermarket chain.[445]

The most flagrant counterfeiting practice is probably the bootlegging of videotapes, video games, and computer software (Chapter 11), but knock-offs pervade a variety of other markets as well. Shoddy facsimiles of upscale furniture can be purchased at a fraction of the price. Often these pieces are superficially indistinguishable from the real thing until they begin to fall apart in a few years.[446] The garment industry (where the term knockoff was coined) has a long tradition of perfectly legal imitation, because clothing designs generally are not protected by copyright laws.[447]

Usually knockoffs are marketed as such, and consumers knowingly sacrifice quality for style. However, when the designer is counterfeited along with the design, a knockoff becomes a rip-off. For example, consumers have been victimized by bogus labels misrepresenting Levi, Jordache, and Guess jeans; couturiers Gucci, Cartier, and Ralph Lauren;[448] and even garments misappropriating the official National Football League insignia.[449] A recent study reports that 10% to 20% of e-commerce sites that sell luxury items are offering knockoffs, from fake Calvin Klein jeans to ersatz Rolex watches.[450]

Consumers commonly fall prey to illicit knockoff jewelry. A single operation by U.S. customs officials seized 500,000 fake designer watches.[451] As a callow teenager years ago, one of the authors purchased a "Bulova" wristwatch at a bargain price from a street vendor. It was not until the watch stopped running a few months later that he realized the tiny trademark read "Bolivia."

NOTES

1. Quoted in Mayer, Caroline E. "Senate Panel to Open Sweepstakes Hearings." *Washington Post*, March 8, 1999: A5.
2. Quoted in *Ibid.*, p. A5.
3. Quoted in CNN "Senate Probes Magazine Sweepstakes." www.cnn.com. March 9, 1999: 2.
4. *Ibid.*, p. 2.
5. Zagorin, Adam. "Sweepstakes Under Scrutiny." *Time*, March 22, 1999: 71.
6. Mayer, Caroline E. "Sweepstakes Industry Defends Its Practices." *Washington Post*, March 10, 1999: E4.
7. Mannix, Margaret. "Congratulations, You're a Loser." *U.S. News & World Report*, March 22, 1999: 74.
8. Quoted in *Houston Chronicle*, "OK, but Ed McMahon Is Real—Isn't He?" April 15, 1999: C1.
9. Quoted in *Ibid.*, p. C1.
10. Quoted in Mayer, March 10, 1999, *op. cit.*, p. E4.
11. Quoted in *Ibid,.* p. E4.
12. "Dick Clark, Ed McMahon Listed in Fla. Suit Against Sweepstakes." *Atlanta Journal and Constitution.* February 3, 1998: 4E.
13. McCormick, Darlene and Stidham, Jeff. "Man Believes He Won Prize Again." *Tampa Tribune.* January 31, 1998: 1; Kennedy, Helen. "Sweepstakes Sparks Suits." *New York Daily News.* February 15, 1998: 8.
14. Kennedy, Helen. "You're a Winner!" *Houston Chronicle*, February 22, 1998: 5A.
15. *Ibid.*
16. "For Sweepstakes 'Winners,' Millions Are a Mirage." *New York Times.* March 8, 1998: 30.
17. Wilborn, Paul. "Sweepstakes Player Sues for 'Winnings'." *St. Petersburg Times.* January 21, 1998: 1A.
18. *Ibid.*
19. Quoted in *Ibid.*, p. 4A.
20. Lowry, Tom. "Sweepstakes Giant Agrees to Tone Down Mailings." *USA Today.* March 17, 1998: 1B.
21. Quoted in Kennedy, *op. cit.*, p. 4A.
22. Quoted in *Ibid.*, p. 4A.
23. "Sweepstakes Firm Accused of Preying on the Elderly." *Wall Street Journal.* November 9, 1998: 13C.
24. Quoted in Biederman, Patricia W. "Elderly Subscribe to Contest Obsession." *Los Angeles Times.* February 7, 1998: A1.
25. Quoted in *Ibid.*, p. A1.
26. Quoted in Wilborn, Paul. "Contest Hopeful Buses from N.Y." *St. Petersburg Times.* August 12, 1998: 1B.
27. Lowry, Tim. "Settlement Won't End American Family Woes." *USA Today*, March 20, 1998: 2B.
28. Mayer, Caroline. "Sweepstakes." *Washington Post.* March 1, 1999: 6D.
29. Lowry, March 20, 1998, *op. cit.*, p. 2B.
30. Quoted in Mannix, *op. cit.*, p. 74.
31. Sharp, Deborah and O'Donnell, Jayne. "Lawsuit Calls 'You're a Winner' Mailings a 'Ruse.'" *USA Today.* February 3, 1998: 1A.
32. Lowry, March 20, 1998, *op. cit.*
33. "American Family Set to Pay Out $4 Million in Settlement Accord." *Wall Street Journal.* June 2, 1999: B16.
34. Lowry, March 20, 1998, *op. cit.*
35. White, Erin. "Sweepstakes Concern Seeks Creditor Shield." *Wall Street Journal.* November 1, 1999: B1.
36. Johnson, Greg. "Sweepstakes Operator Seeks Court Protection." *Los Angeles Times.* October 30, 1999: C1; Wilborn, Paul. "Sweepstakes Settlement Expected." *St. Petersburg Times.* October 30, 1999: 1A; "Sweepstakes Operator Makes Bankruptcy Filing." *New York Times.* October 30, 1999: C1.
37. "American Family Will Pay $33 Million in Settlement." *Wall Street Journal.* December 10, 1999: C14.
38. *Ibid.*, Nathan, Sara. December 10, 1999: 1B.
39. *Ibid.*
40. *Ibid.*
41. *Ibid.*, p. 1B. Florida's attorney general has also alleged that American Family has offered to sell nearly 470,000 names of senior citizens to other contests.
42. Quoted in *Ibid.*, p. 2B.
43. Quoted in *Ibid.*, p. 2B.
44. Quoted in *Ibid.*, p. 1B.
45. Sutton, Remar. "Dial '900' for Trouble." *Reader's Digest.* 139, August, 1991: 39–43.
46. *Ibid.*, p. 41.
47. Davis, Kristin. "You Have Definitely Not Won." *Kiplinger's Personal Finance Magazine.* July, 1992: 56.
48. *Ibid.*, p. 56.
49. Pay-per-call telephone services actually pre-date the 900 area code by several years. As early as 1974, New Yorkers

could phone a service called Dial-a-Joke and for a small fee hear comedian Henny Youngman deliver a sampling of his dusty one-liners.

50. Cobb, Nathan. "Dialing for Dollars." *St. Paul Pioneer Press.* July 4, 1991: 1F.

51. Gibson, William E. "Agencies Try to Put Dial-It Abuse on Hold." *Ft. Lauderdale Sun-Sentinel.* April 18, 1990: 1A.

52. Quoted in Cobb, *op. cit.*, p. 1F.

53. *Ibid.*

54. Mills, Mike. "FCC Proposes Clampdown on 900-Number Services." *Congressional Quarterly.* March 16, 1991: 664–666.

55. Sutton, *op. cit.*, p. 39.

56. Belkin, Lisa. "Offer of Free Voyage in Space Sends 2 on Trip to Texas Jail." *New York Times.* February 7, 1991: B13.

57. Sutton, *op. cit.*, p. 39.

58. Mills, *op. cit.*

59. Sallee, Rad. "Workers See No Future as Psychics on Hot Line." *Houston Chronicle.* April 7, 1996: 30A.

60. Stoeltje, Melissa F. "'Electronic Junk Mail'." *Houston Chronicle.* October 23, 1996: 10D.

61. *Ibid.*

62. *Ibid.*

63. Cobb, *op. cit.*

64. Crowe, Rosalie R. "Telemarketing Scams Boom: Few Report Losses." *Phoenix Gazette.* July 7, 1992: B4.

65. Sutton, *op. cit.*, p. 42.

66. Mills, *op. cit.*

67. In 1994, federal regulators proposed a crackdown on companies—mainly adult entertainment providers—that misleadingly charge customers large sums for services on toll-free *800* numbers. ("'800' Numbers Revoked." *New York Times.* August 11, 1994: D6.)

68. Glick, Rush G. and Newsom, Robert S. *Fraud Investigation: Fundamentals for Police.* Springfield, Ill.: Charles C Thomas, 1974.

69. Goldring, John. *Consumers or Victims?* Sidney, Australia: George Allen & Unwin, 1982.

70. *Ibid.*, p. 20.

71. Reitz, John C. "A History of Cutoff Rules as a Form of *Caveat Emptor*: Part II—From Roman Law to the Modern Civil and Common Law." *The American Journal of Comparative Law* 37, 1989: 247–299.

72. *Ibid.*

73. Best, Arthur. *When Consumers Complain.* New York: Columbia University Press, 1981; 3.

74. Swift, Jonathan. *Gulliver's Travels* (2nd Ed.). New York: Norton, 1961; 39. This book was originally published in 1726.

75. "Ye shall not steal, neither deal falsely, neither lie to one another." (*Leviticus* 19:11).

76. Aquinas, Thomas. "On Fraud Committed in Buying and Selling." In Monroe, Arthur E. (Ed.), *Early Economic Thought.* Cambridge, Mass.: Harvard University Press, 1930; 60.

77. Quoted in Thio, Alex. *Deviant Behavior* (3rd Ed.). New York: Harper & Row, 1988; 432.

78. *Ibid.*

79. Cartwright, Joe and Patterson, Jerry. *Been Taken Lately?* New York: Grove Press, 1974.

80. *Ibid.*

81. Linden, Dana W. "Closing In." *Forbes* 15, June 7, 1993: 52.

82. York, Pamela. "'Faux' Fools Victims." *Postal Inspection Service Bulletin.* Spring 1990: 11–14.

83. Cartwright and Patterson, *op. cit.*, p. 57.

84. Marvin, Mary Jo. "Swindles in the 1990s: Con Artists Are Thriving." *USA Today Magazine.* September 1994: 80–84.

85. Quoted in Cartwright and Patterson, *op. cit.*, p. 66.

86. Quoted in Kubiske, Daniel E. "Congratulations! You May Be a Fraud Victim!" *Everyday Law.* May 1989: 24.

87. *Ibid.*

88. Lewin, Tamar. "Undelivered Adoptions Investigated in 3 States." *New York Times.* March 22, 1992: 16.

89. Nieves, Evelyn. "Region's Quick-Cash Frauds Snare Desperate Consumers." *New York Times.* February 7, 1992: A1; "Protect Yourself Against Advance-Fee Loan Scams." *Consumers' Research.* December 1991: 16–19.

90. Marvin, *op. cit.*, p. 83. Deepak Gulati, an Indian immigrant in New York City, for example, sold bogus 12% promissory notes to his countrymen. Gulati's operation was a run-of-the-mill Ponzi scam, using funds from new investors to pay dividends to earlier ones. There was nothing run-of-the-mill, however, about the $3.2 million Gulati stole from his fellow immigrants.

91. Cartwright and Patterson, *op. cit.*

92. Razzi, Elizabeth. "Scams That Add Insult to Injury: When Big Disasters Strike, Petty Chiselers Are Close Behind." *Kiplinger's Personal Finance Magazine.* May 1994: 88.

93. Marvin, *op, cit.*, p. 80.

94. *Ibid.*, p. 80.

95. Bekey, Michelle. "Dial S-W-I-N-D-L-E." *Modern Maturity.* April 1991: 31–89.

96. Harris, Marlys. "You May Already Be a Victim of Fraud." *Money* 118, August 1989: 74–91.

97. Seib, Gerald F. "Dallas Ordinance Against Car Repair Frauds." In Johnson, John M. and Douglas, Jack D. (Eds.), *Crime at the Top: Deviance in Business and the Professions.* Philadelphia: J. B. Lippincott, 1978; 319–322.

98. Glickman, Arthur P. *Mr. Badwrench: How You Can Survive the $20 Billion-a-Year Auto Repair Ripoff.* New York: Wideview Books, 1981.

99. *Ibid.*

100. *Ibid.*

101. Blumberg, Paul. *The Predatory Society: Deception in the American Marketplace.* New York: Oxford University; Press, 1989. A government survey was even more damning. It found that "53 percent of the money spent on car repairs was wasted because of overcharges, work not performed, wrong repairs, and incompetent work" (Thio, *op. cit.*, p. 432).

102. Seib, *op. cit*, p. 320.

103. Sikorsky, Robert. "Highway Robbery: The Scandal of Auto Repair in America." *Reader's Digest.* May 1987: 91.

104. *Ibid.*, p. 91–99.

105. Jesilow, Paul, Geis, Gilbert, and O'Brien, Mary Jane. "Experimental Evidence that Publicity Has No Effect in Suppressing Auto Repair Fraud." *Sociology and Social Research* 70, 1986: 222–223.

106. "California Accuses Sears of Bilking Auto Service Customers." *National Petroleum News.* V 84, August 1992: 21–22.

107. Yin, Tung. "Retailing: Sears Is Accused of Billing Fraud at Auto Centers." *Wall Street Journal.* June 12, 1992: B1.

108. Quinn, Judy. "Employee Motivation: Repair Job." *Incentive* 166, October 1992: 40–46.

109. Fisher, Lawrence M. "Company News: Sears Ousts Chairman of Auto Division." *New York Times.* December 19, 1992: 39.

110. Ringer, Richard. "Company News: A President for Sears Automotive." *New York Times.* April 13, 1993: D15.

111. In early AAMCO commercials, the relieved customer was none other than Zsa Zsa Gabor.

112. Cartwright and Patterson, *op. cit.*, p. 30.

113. *Ibid.*, p. 29.

114. *Ibid.*

115. *Ibid.*, p. 30.

116. *Ibid.*

117. *Ibid.*

118. *Ibid.*, p. 31.

119. *Ibid.*

120. Miller, Thomas J. "Telemarketing: Reach Out and Cheat Someone." *State Government* 61, 1988: 98–99.

121. Crowe, *op. cit.*

122. Hassell, Greg. "A Hang-Up About Phone Solicitors." *Houston Chronicle.* March 13, 1996: 1C; Block, Sandra. "Scam Victims Get Help from FBI, AARP." *USA Today.* December 5, 1996: B1.

123. Ramirez, Anthony. "A Crackdown on Phone Marketing." *New York Times.* February 10, 1995: D1.

124. Bekey, *op. cit.*, p. 32.

125. Miller, *op. cit.*, p. 98.

126. *Ibid.*

127. Harris, *op. cit.*

128. Tedford, Deborah. "2 Guilty in Telemarketing Fraud Case." *Houston Chronicle.* October 14, 1999: 14A.

129. Miller, *op. cit.*

130. Smith, Marguerite T. "Guard Against Charity Scams." *Money* 23, February, 1994: 19. Also see Goldstein, Linda. "FTC Targeting Charitable Solicitation Fraud." *Telemarketing* 12, June, 1994: 18–19.

131. Marvin, *op. cit.*

132. Hager, Robert. "Charity Frauds Use Real Sob Stories." *MSNBC.com.* December 14, 1998.

133. Bekey, *op. cit.*, p. 36.

134. Hager, *op. cit.*

135. Harris, *op. cit.*

136. Bekey, *op. cit.*, p. 40. In 1995, the U.S. Postal Inspection Service outraged the art world when it announced plans to auction off more than 12,000 *fake* Dali prints it had seized from a major art fraud operation. Asked if the forgeries could re-enter the art market after purchase, a spokesman for the Postal Inspection Service replied: "I'm sure anything

is possible." (Blumenthal, Ralph. "Government Sale of Fake Dalis Raises Ire." *Houston Chronicle*. November 7, 1995: 4D.)

137. In addition to telemarketing fraud, the elderly have always been the favorite target of classic confidence swindles, such as the "pigeon drop" and the "phony bank examiner." For a description of these and other "con games" run on older victims, see Friedman, Monroe. "Confidence Swindles of Older Consumers." *Journal of Consumer Affairs* 26, 1992: 20–46.

138. Wangrin, Mark. "Addressing the Elderly: Senior Citizens a Popular Target for Mail Marketers." *Austin American Statesman*. June 19, 1994: A1.

139. Kahn, K. Pica. "AARP Warns Older Adults About Scams." *Houston Chronicle 50 Plus Supplement*. September 24, 1999: 1, 9.

140. Seeman, Bruce T. "Swindlers Target Lonely, Unwary Seniors." *Miami Herald*. July 8, 1993: 1BR.

141. Tighe, Theresa. "Swindlers Zero in on Elderly: Older People Have Assets and the Vultures Know It." *St. Louis Post-Dispatch*. January 30, 1994: 1D.

142. Barker, John. "Consumer Fraud." *Credit World* 82, 1994: 32.

143. "Phone Swindlers Dangle Prizes to Cheat Elderly Out of Millions." *New York Times*. June 29, 1997: 17.

144. Tighe, *op, cit.*

145. Harris, *op. cit.*

146. Bekey, *op. cit.*, p. 32.

147. Leeds, Jeff. "Officials Put Pressure on Telemarketers." *Los Angeles Times*. August 20, 1998: A23.

148. Tedford, Deborah. "Swindler Gets 14-Year Prison Term." *Houston Chronicle*. March 9, 1996: 1A.

149. *Ibid.*

150. It seems appalling that telephone companies, which often subject individual customers to exhaustive credit checks, require next to nothing in the way of disclosure from businesses requesting "800" numbers.

151. Harris, *op. cit.*, p. 79.

152. *Ibid.*

153. Crowe, *op. cit.*

154. Harris, *op. cit.*, p. 77.

155. Huffstutter, P. J. "Dozens in O.C. Held in Telemarketing Fraud Inquiries." *Los Angeles Times*. December 18, 1998: C1, C8.

156. The description of this case is gleaned from: Moore, Thomas. "A New Scam: Tele-Blackmail." *U.S. News & World Report*. June 11, 1990: 51–52.

157. Moore, *op. cit.*, p. 52.

158. "Nearly 1,000 Telemarketers Arrested in $2\frac{1}{2}$ Year Probe." *Los Angeles Times*. December 18, 1998: A41.

159. Quoted in "FBI Uses New Wrinkle to 'Scam' Con Artists." *Houston Chronicle*. June 29, 1998: 3A.

160. Quoted in *Ibid.*, p. 3A.

161. "Ex-O.C. Man Pleads Guilty to Telemarketing Fraud." *Los Angeles Times*. December 18, 1998: C10.

162. *Ibid.*, p. C10.

163. "Protect Yourself Against Advance-Fee Loan Scams." *Consumers' Research*. December 1991: 17.

164. *Ibid.*

165. Hudson, Mike. "Robbin' the Hood." *Mother Jones* 19, July 1994: 25–29.

166. Hudson, Mike. "Stealing Home." *Washington Monthly*. June 1992: 23.

167. Crosier, Louis. "Home Equity Scams Foreclose on the American Dream." *Public Citizen*. Summer 1994: 10–12.

168. *Ibid.*, p. 12.

169. *Ibid.*

170. *Ibid.*

171. *Ibid.*

172. Quoted in *Ibid.*, p. 25.

173. Hudson, *op. cit.*

174. Quoted in *Ibid.*, p. 27.

175. Hardie, Ann. "Bad Trade Schools Rip Off the Poor—and Taxpayers." *Atlanta Journal & Constitution*. January 28, 1990: 1A.

176. *Ibid.*

177. *Ibid.*

178. Quoted in *Ibid.*

179. *Ibid.*

180. *Ibid.*, p. A1.

181. *Ibid.*

182. For a more precise legal definition of deceptive advertising, see: Preston, Ivan L. "The Definition of Deceptiveness in Advertising and Other Commercial Speech." *Catholic University Law Review* 39, 1990: 1035–1039.

183. Quoted in Clark, Charles S. "Advertising Under Attack, Part Two." *CQ Researcher* 18, 1991: 673.

184. Swagler, Roger M. *Caveat Emptor: An Introductory Analysis of Consumer Problems*. Lexington, Mass.: D.C. Heath, 1975.

185. Thio, *op. cit.*

186. A recent example would be the Home Shopping Network's commercials for

baseballs autographed by Hall-of-Fame catcher Johnny Bench. Viewers were told that the baseballs were worth $129 but were available at the "sensational" price of $49.95. A sports collectible price guide puts the value of a Bench-autographed ball at $35. Both the Home Shopping Network and Bench himself were cited for misrepresentation by the New York City Consumer Affairs Agency. ("And Here's the Pitch." *New York Times.* October 8, 1993: B12.)

187. An example of deceptive cinematography would be a 1979 case, in which the nation's largest toy maker was found guilty of running a misleading ad which showed a toy horse standing on its own—by means of special camera techniques and film editing—when the horse, in fact, could not stand. (Eitzen, D. Stanley and Timmer, Doug A. *Criminology: Crime and Criminal Justice.* New York: John Wiley & Sons, 1985.)

188. Simonson, Alexander and Holbrook, Morris B. "Permissable Puffery Versus Actionable Warranty in Advertising and Salestalk: An Empirical Investigation." *Public Policy & Marketing* 12, 1993: 216–233.

189. Swagler, *op. cit.*

190. "The Platformate Illusion." *Consumer Bulletin.* January 1968: 26.

191. Woodyard, Chris. "Exxon Accused of High-Octane Lies." *Houston Chronicle.* September 18, 1996: 1C, 8C.

192. Clinard, Marshall B. and Yeager, Peter C. *Corporate Crime.* New York: Free Press, 1980.

193. "FTC Orders Novartis to Run Ads Retracting Claims About Doan's." *Los Angeles Times.* May 28, 1999: C5; "Maker of Pills May Appeal Order on Ads." *Houston Chronicle.* May 30, 1999: 17A.

194. "Bad Apples: In the Executive Suite." *Consumer Reports.* May 1989: 294.

195. Quoted in *Ibid.*, p. 294.

196. Traub, James. "Into the Mouths of Babes." *New York Times Magazine,* July 24, 1988: 18–20, 37–38, 52–53.

197. Henkel, John. "Seafood Maker Fined for Misbranding." *FDA Consumer* 29, November 1995: 33–34.

198. Schwartz, Nelson. "Snags Are Showing for Kayser-Roth's Claims for Stockings; No Nonsense Pantyhose Drew Unseemly Stares in Illinois when Foote, Con Ads Ran." *Wall Street Journal.* June 30, 1992: B8.

199. Robichaux, Mark. "Home Shopping Agrees to Revise Policy on Jewelry." *Wall Street Journal.* May 6, 1994: B8.

200. "Home Shopping Network to Pay Fine." *Los Angeles Times.* April 16, 1999: C2.

201. Richards, Bill. "Picture the Polar Bears, Clean Air, Ice-Blue Fjords of . . . Long Island?" *Wall Street Journal.* February 27, 1995: B1.

202. Walsh, Sharon. "FTC Cites NordicTrack for Making False Claims." *Houston Chronicle.* February 16, 1996: 10A.

203. "FTC Reaches Settlement with Jenny Craig to End Diet Program Advertising Litigation." www.ftc.gov. May 29, 1997.

204. Quoted in "Company Settles FTC Charges: Ads for Coppertone Kids Sunblock Were Deceptive." www.ftc.gov. February 18, 1997.

205. "Dell Computer and Micron Electronics Settle FTC Charges that Ads Misled Consumers About the Costs of Leasing Computers." www.ftc.gov. May 13, 1999.

206. "Apple Computer Settles FTC Charges that Its 'Apple Assurance' Program Was Deceptive." www.ftc.gov. January 26, 1999.

207. FTC Accepts Settlement of Charges That Ads for Winston "No Additive" Cigarettes Are Deceptive." www.ftc.gov. March 3, 1999; "RJR Agrees to 'No Additive' Explanation on Ads." *Los Angeles Times.* March 4, 1999: C6.

208. Dugas, Christine. "Providian to Pay $300M to Settle Deception Charges." *USA Today.* June 29, 2000: 1B.

209. "$8.3 Million Refund Ordered in False Advertising Case." *Mealey's Litigation Report* 2, August 12, 1999; p.1.

210. Hladky, Mary. "Federal Judge Weighs in on Fraudulent Diet Drug Program." *The Legal Intelligencer.* July 21, 1999: 4.

211. *Mealey's Litigation Report* 2, *op. cit.*

212. "Diet Pill Company ordered to Refund $8 Million." *Baltimore Sun.* July 20, 1999: 5A; "Dissatisfied Dieters Can Get Money Back for Pills." *Atlanta Journal and Constitution.* July 21, 1999: 6F.

213. Gillis, Michael. "False-Claims Complaints Settled by TV Pitchman." *Chicago Sun-Times.* January 14, 1998: 9. "Infomercial Pitchman, Associates Fined $1 Million." *Houston Chronicle.* January 14, 1998: 3C.

214. Gattuso, Gregg. "DRTV Host Charged in Pyramid Scheme." *Direct Marketing* 59, May 1996: 10–11.

215. Quoted in Gillis, *op. cit.*, p. 9.

216. "Endorser Liability." *ABA Journal*. May 1990: 24, 29.

217. Florida Attorney General News Release. "Robin Leach to Restrict Promotional Activities Under Agreement." June 19, 2000.

218. "Robin Leach Reaches Settlement With State." *Milwaukee Journal Sentinal*. June 20, 2000: 2B.

219. "Michigan Joins Suit Against Leach." *Montreal Gazette*. July 16, 1999: C10.

220. Robin, Joshua. "Robin Leach's Pitch Panned." *Seattle Times*. June 20, 2000: B3.

221. "Robin Leach Settles Endorsement Suit." *Chicago Sun-Times*. June 21, 2000: 52.

222. *Ibid.*

223. Quoted in Robins, *op. cit.*, p. B3.

224. Jouzaitis, Carol. "Read Those Labels Carefully and You Still May Be Misled." *Chicago Tribune*. June 18, 1990: 4.

225. *Ibid.*

226. "F.T.C. Warning for Stouffer." *New York Times*. October 5, 1994: D18.

227. "Ad Settlement by Sara Lee." *New York Times*. August 8, 1994: D8.

228. Goldemberg, Robert L. "Nature's Miracles." *Drug & Cosmetic Industry* 157, November 1995: 46–49.

229. Clark, Charles S. "Advertising Under Attack, Part One." *CQ Researcher*, 18, 1991: 659–670.

230. Choate, Robert B. "How Television Grabs Kids for Fun and Profit." In Heilbronner, Robert L. and London, Paul (Eds.). *Corporate Social Policy*. Reading, Mass.: Addison-Wesley, 1975; 181–186.

231. Clark, Pt. 1, *op. cit.*

232. Myers, David G. *Social Psychology* (3rd Ed.). New York: McGraw-Hill, 1990.

233. *Ibid.*, p. 264.

234. Favorite tricks include speeding up the film or tape to make the toy appear faster and more powerful than it is, and utilizing wide-angle lenses and extreme close-ups to make it look much bigger.

235. Quoted in Clark, Pt. 1, *op. cit.*, p. 666.

236. Myers, *op. cit.*

237. Stevens, Amy. "The Mouthpiece: Class-Action Lawyers Brawl over Big Fees in Milli Vanilli Fraud; They Line up Teen 'Victims' of the Lip-Synching Duo; Judge Notes Strong Odor, Rob and Fab or Fab and Tide?" *Wall Street Journal*. October 24, 1991: A1.

238. *Ibid.*

239. Blumenthal, Ralph. "When Buying a Bed, Beware." *New York Times*. February 22, 1979: C1, C8.

240. Quoted in Howard, p. 218.

241. Johnson and Douglas, *op. cit.*

242. *Ibid.*, p. 29.

243. *Ibid.*, p. 29.

244. Nelson, Phillip. "Advertising as Information." *Journal of Political Economy* 82, 1974: 729–754.

245. Gerstner, Eitan and Hess, James D. "Can Bait and Switch Benefit Consumers?" *Marketing Science* 9, 1990: 114–124.

246. Nagler, Matthew G. "Rather Bait than Switch: Deceptive Advertising with Bounded Consumer Rationality." *Journal of Public Economics* 51, 1993: 360.

247. Akerlof, George A. and Dickens, William T. "The Economic Consequences of Cognitive Dissonance." *American Economic Review* 72, 1982: 307–319; see also: Festinger, Leon. *A Theory of Cognitive Dissonance*. New York: Harper and Row, 1957.

248. Fix, Janet L. "Justice Dept. Fixated on Price Fixing." *USA Today*. September 8, 1995: 1B.

249. U.S. Department of Justice. "Antitrust Enforcement and the Consumer." Washington, DC: U.S. Government Printing Office 1992: 1.

250. Clinard, Marshall B. et al. *Illegal Corporate Behavior*. Washington, DC: Government Printing Office, 1979; 184. It should also be noted that price fixing is not confined to products; prices for services may be fixed as well. In 1990, three Arizona dentists were convicted of conspiring to fix the price of managed-care contracts. This was the first time in more than 50 years that price fixing charges had been filed against healthcare providers. ("Both Sides 'Win' Appeal of Price-Fixing Convictions." *Modern Healthcare*. September 2, 1992: 96.)

251. Bryant, Adam. "USX Must Pay $630 Million in Price-Fixing." *New York Times*. May 29, 1993: 33.

252. "Quexco to Settle FTC Charges." www.ftc.gov. May 14, 1999.

253. "Major Glass Makers Convicted by Jury in Price-Fixing Case." *Wall Street Journal*. December 24, 1991: B4.

254. U.S. Department of Justice. "Antitrust Enforcement and the Consumer." Washington, DC. U.S. Government Printing Office, 2001.

255. "Gas Concerns to Settle Suit." *New York Times*. September 26, 1990: D4.

256. U.S. Department of Justice, *op. cit.*

257. *Ibid.*

258. *Ibid.*

259. *Ibid.*

260. "Two Leading Providers of Disability Insurance Agree to Resolve FTC Antitrust Concerns." *www.ftc.gov*. May 18, 1999.

261. "Chicago-Area Doctors, Firms Settle FCT Charges Over Fixing Prices for Kidney Stone Treatment." www.ftc.gov. January 8, 1998.

262. "Keds to Pay to Settle Suits." *New York Times*. September 28, 1993: D7; "New Balance Shoe Agrees to Settle Price-Fixing Complaint." sddt.com. June 13, 1996.

263. "Premdor to Pay Fines Totaling $6 Million in Price-Fixing Case." *Wall Street Journal*. June 15, 1994: A8.

264. "Company News: U.S. Says Miles Will Pay Fine in Price Fixing." *New York Times*. October 29, 1993: D3.

265. "Plastic Ware Price Fixing." *New York Times*. June 10, 1994: D4.

266. "FTC Upholds Charges that Toys "R" Us Induced Toy Makers to Stop Selling Desirable Toys to Warehouse Clubs." www.ftc.gov. October 14, 1998; "Attorney General Montgomery Sues Toys 'R' Us and Major Toy Manufacturers for Price-Fixing." www.ag.ohio.gov. November 17, 1997.

267. Tomasson, Robert E. "Nintendo to Pay $25 Million in Rebates in Price Fixing." *New York Times*. April 11, 1991: D1.

268. U.S. Department of Justice, *op. cit.*

269. Pear, Robert. "Company News: Mead Johnson to Pay $38.76 Million Settlement." *New York Times*. July 3, 1992: D3. Also: Ramsey, Ross. "Makers of Baby Formula Settle with State for $1.5 Million." *Houston Chronicle*. November 18, 1995: 1A, 18A; "Abbott to Settle Formula Price-Fixing Claims." *Houston Chronicle*. May 25, 1996: 3C.

270. U.S. Department of Justice, *op. cit.*

271. "Mrs. Baird's Bakeries Guilty of Price-Fixing." *Houston Chronicle*. February 15, 1996: 1C.

272. Kosher Food Firm is Fined $1 Million in Price-Fixing Case." *Wall Street Journal*. May 20, 1991: B5.

273. Wood, H. Dan and Anderson, James E. "The Politics of U.S. Antitrust Regulation." *American Journal of Political Science* 17, 1993: 1–39.

274. Simpson, Sally S. "Cycles of Illegality: Antitrust Violations in Corporate America." *Social Forces* 65, 1991: 943–963.

275. Hage, David. "Hidden Monopolies." *U.S. News & World Report*. February 3, 1992: 42–48.

276. Cohen, Mark A. "The Role of Criminal Sanctions in Antitrust Enforcement." *Contemporary Policy Issues*. October, 1989: 36–46.

277. Owen, Jane D. "Founder Surely Would Be Troubled by ExxonMobil." *Houston Chronicle*. May 31, 2000: 23A.

278. Ivanovich, David. "Chevron, Texaco Agree to Merge." *Houston Chronicle*. October 16, 2000: 1A.

279. "BP and Amoco in Oil Mega-Merger." *news.BBC.co.uk*. August 11, 1998.

280. Oppel, Richard A., Jr. "BP Amoco, Arco Push for Deal OK." *Houston Chronicle*. January 14, 2000: 1C, 3C. "Oil Merger Gets OK." *ABCnews.com*. April 13, 2000.

281. Davis, Michael. "Reading & Bates, Falcon to Combine." *Houston Chronicle*. July 11, 1997: C1. While neither of these corporations may be a household word, their merger creates the largest offshore drilling company in the world.

282. Moore, Angela. "Chemistry Now Right for Dow, Union Carbide Merger." biz.yahoo.com. February 2, 2001.

283. Lieberman, David. "FTC Questions Time Warner CEO." *USA Today*, March 1, 1996: 1B.

284. "Judge Questions role of AOL Deal." www.msnbc.com. October 14, 1998.

285. Geewax, Marilyn. "AOL-Time Warner Deal Approved." *Houston Chronicle*. January 12, 2001: 1C; Silverman, Dwight. "Mega-Merger to Unite AOL, Time Warner. *Houston Chronicle*. January 11, 2000: 1A.

286. Lundquist, Eric. "Lotus CEO Sees Lots of Growth Ahead." dailynews.yahoo.com. January 17, 2001.

287. "Unilever Agrees to Buy Bestfoods for $20.3 Billion." *Houston Chronicle*. June 7, 2000: 1C.

288. Fix, Janet L. "Even Big Mergers Don't Ring Antitrust Alarms." *USA Today*. August 31, 1995: 1B.

289. "Insurance Titans Set to Merge in $16.4 Billion Transaction." *Houston Chronicle*. August 21, 1998: 3C.

290. Reggie, James. "SBC, Ameritech Merger a Step Toward New Ma Bell." *Houston Chronicle*. June 22, 1998: 19A.

291. *Ibid.*

292. Valdmanis, Thor. "United to Buy US Airways." www.usatoday.com. May 24, 2000.

293. "Continental-Delta Merger Talks." cbs. marketwatch.com. February 3, 2001.

294. "Competition vs. Jobs." www.abcnews. com. February 1, 2001.

295. Henderson, Pam. "Will Rail Mergers Leave You Sidetracked?" *Farm Journal* (Central Ed.) 119, December 1995: Z8–13. See also: Phillips, Don. "Rail Merger: Is Too Much Power Being Placed in Too Few Hands?" *Houston Chronicle*. October 22, 1995: 15A; "Merge with Care: Success of Two Railroads' Union Depends on Safeguards." *Houston Chronicle*. April 6, 1996: 30A.

296. Shiver, Jube, Jr. "Two More Baby Bells Plan to Join." *Houston Chronicle*. April 22, 1996: 1A, 6A.

297. Lynch, David. "2 Phone Giants to Merge." *USA Today*. April 22, 1996: 1A. See also: Henry, David. "Bell-Nynex Deal Receives Static." *USA Today*. April 23, 1996: 1B.

298. Reggie, *op. cit.*

299. *Ibid.*

300. Neumeister, Larry. "$1 Billion Nasdaq Settlement OK'd." *Houston Chronicle*. November 10, 1998: 1C, 12C. "Judge Approves $1 Billion Nasdaq Price-Fixing Settlement." www.nandotimes.com. November 10, 1998.

301. O'Donnell, Jayne. "Vitamin Makers to Settle." *USA Today*. November 3, 1999: 1B.

302. Davis, Michael. "Smith, Schlumberger Hit With Fines." *Houston Chronicle*. December 10, 1999: 1C, 3C. The last company to be cited for contempt of an antitrust decree was the Boston dairy firm H. P. Hood, which was fined $102,000 in 1983, after it acquired control of three other New England dairies in violation of a 1981 consent decree.

303. *Ibid.*

304. Kelley, Matt. "Price-Fixing by Company Brings $100 Million Fine." *Houston Chronicle*. October 15, 1996: 1A, 8A.

305. Eichenwald, Kurt. *The Informant: A True Story*. New York: Broadway Books, 2000.

306. Willette, Anne. "Archer Daniels Midland OKs Record Price-Fix Fine." *USA Today*. October 15, 1996: 1A.

307. Quoted in Galvin, John. "The New Business Ethics." *Smart Business* 13, June 2000: 88.

308. Sniffen, Michael J. "Steel Supplier Fined $110 Million for Price-Fixing." www. detnews.com. April 8, 1998.

309. Cox, Meki. "$135 Million Fine in Price-Fixing Case." *Orange County Register*. May 5, 1999: C3.

310. Bernstein, Sharon. "Drug Maker to Settle Case for $135 Million." *Orange County Register*. July 13, 2000: C1.

311. Quoted in *Ibid.*, p. C1.

312. Galvin, *op. cit.*

313. *Ibid.*

314. "The Tale of the Gates Tapes." *Time*. November 16, 1998: 74.

315. Thurow, Lester C. "Microsoft Case Is About a Good Capitalist Practice: Running Your Competition Out of Business." *USA Today*. November 3, 1999: 31A.

316. McKenzie, Richard B. and Shughart, William F., II. "Is Microsoft a Monopolist?" *Independent Review* 3, Fall 1998: 165.

317. Cortese, Amy, Garland, Susan B., and Hamm, Steve. "The Case of the Missing PC Makers." *Business Week*. September 21, 1998: 38, 40.

318. Quoted in McKenzie and Shughart, 166. The statement was probably a reference to a complaint lodged by the American Banana Company early in the twentieth century. Archrival United Fruit was accused of using dynamite to blow up American Banana's Central American facilities in order to preserve its domination of the banana export market.

319. Metzenbaum, Howard and Cooper, Mark. "Consumers Ought to Fret About Microsoft Monopoly." *Houston Chronicle*. October 20, 1998: 19A.

320. *Ibid.*, p. 19A.

321. "Important Dates in Antitrust Battle." *USA Today*. April 3, 2000: 6A.

322. McKenzie and Shughart, *op. cit.*

323. *Ibid.*

324. *Ibid.*

325. Elhauge, Einer. "Microsoft Won Appeal, but Decision Was Incorrect." *Houston Chronicle*. July 2, 1998: 35A.

326. Brinkley, Joel. "States Plant to Sue to Stop Windows 98." *Orange County Register*. April 30, 1998: 1. One of the original 20 plaintiff states, Texas, would later withdraw from the suit.

327. Mitchell, Russ. "Finally, the Trial Is About to Begin." *U.S. News & World Report* 125, October 19, 1998: 48.

328. Wolfe, Richard. "What's at Stake in the Microsoft Trial?" *New Republic* 22, November 16, 1998: 22; Wilson, Dave. "Feds' 1st Blow: Video of Gates." *Orange County Register.* October 20, 1998: C1, C12.

329. Taylor, Chris. "Gates in the Dock." *Time* 152, October 19, 1998: 68, 69.

330. Quoted in *Ibid.*, p. 69.

331. *Ibid.*

332. Miller, Greg and Helm, Leslie. "Microsoft Case Tried in Court of Public Opinion." *Los Angeles Times.* May 20, 1998: D1, D10.

333. "U.S. May Seek Wider Actions Against Microsoft." *Los Angeles Times.* October 8, 1998: C3.

334. *Ibid.*

335. Wolfe, *op. cit.*, p. 22.

336. Sandberg, Jared. "Storming Gates." *Newsweek.* November 2, 1998: 42.

337. Quoted in *Los Angeles Times.* "Government Lawyers Grill Bill Gates for a Second Day." August 29, 1998: D2.

338. "High Noon." *Fortune.* November 23, 1998: 162.

339. Quoted in *Ibid.*, p. 162.

340. Quoted in *Ibid.*, p. 162.

341. "The Tale of the Gates Tapes." *Time.* November 16, 1998: 74.

342. *Ibid.*

343. *Ibid.*, p. 74.

344. "Gates' Taped Pretrial Testimony Provokes Laughter From Judge." *Los Angeles Times.* November 17, 1998: C3.

345. *Fortune, op. cit.*, p. 163.

346. Quoted in "Microsoft: Case Turns on Allegation of an Attempt to Split Browser Market." *Orange County Register.* October 20, 1998: C1, C12.

347. Brinkley, Joel and Lohr, Steve. "Strong Evidence Contradicts Gates." *Houston Chronicle.* October 20, 1998: 1C, 10C.

348. *Fortune, op. cit.*

349. Quoted in *Fortune, op. cit.*, p. 163. Ironically, in the middle of the trial, AOL announced plans to buy Netscape for $10 billion.

350. Eun-Kyng, Kim. "Apple: Microsoft's $150 Million Partnership Had a Sinister Side." *Orange County Register.* November 2, 1998: 12.

351. Shiver, Jube, Jr. "Microsoft Threatened Apple, U.S. Contends." *Los Angles Times.* October 28, 1998: C3.

352. Eun-Kyng, *op. cit.*

353. *Time,* November 16, 1988, *op. cit.*, p. 74.

354. Eun-Kyng, *op. cit.*

355. Quoted in *Ibid.*, p. 12.

356. Cortese et al., p. 38.

357. *Ibid.*

358. Quoted in *Ibid.*, p. 38.

359. Quoted in *Ibid.*, p. 38.

360. *Fortune, op. cit.*, p.164.

361. *Ibid.*

362. *Ibid.*

363. Bridis, Ted. "Federal Lawyers Want Microsoft Split Three Ways." *Houston Chronicle.* January 13, 2000: 1C, 8C.

364. *Ibid.*

365. "Baby Bills" is obviously a tongue-in-cheek reference to Gates' name and the regional telephone companies that emerged from the break-up of AT&T in the 1980s. These new companies quickly became known as "Baby Bells."

366. Quoted in Silverman, Dwight. "Federal Judge Says Microsoft Broke the Law." *Houston Chronicle.* April 4, 2000: 1A.

367. Ignatius, David. "There Was a Hero in Microsoft Case—the Judge." *Houston Chronicle.* April 6, 2000: 27A.

368. Davidson, Paul. "Microsoft Split Ordered." *USA Today.* June 8, 2000: 1A.

369. *Ibid.*

370. Quoted in *Ibid.*, p. 1A.

371. Quoted in Davidson, Paul. "Microsoft Awaits a New Hand." *USA Today.* June 8, 2000: 1B.

372. Davidson, Paul and Biskupic, Joan. "Microsoft Case Sent to Appeals Court." *USA Today.* September 27, 2000: 1B.

373. Bray, Hiawatha. "Microsoft Madness." *Houston Chronicle, Zest Magazine.* February 11, 2001: 23.

374. *Ibid.*, p. 23.

375. "Exxon Corp.: Gasoline Price-Fixing Case Is Settled for $9.9 Million." *Wall Street Journal.* January 15, 1992: B4; "Exxon Moves to Settle Suits for $9.9 Million." *New York Times.* January 15, 1992: D4.

376. "Three Oil Companies to Pay $63 to 4 Western States." *Wall Street Journal.* April 23, 1992: A4.

377. "3 Oil Concerns in Settlement." *New York Times.* January 12, 1993: B20.

378. "Class-Action Status Granted in Airline Price-Fixing Suit." *Wall Street Journal.* August 8, 1991: A5.

379. "NWA, TWA Agree to Alter Pricing Action." *Wall Street Journal*. June 21, 1991: B1; "2 Airlines Settle Claims." *New York Times*. June 24, 1991: D2; "Company News: Continental Air in Settlement." *New York Times*. June 16, 1992: D5; Pulley, Brett and O'Brian, Bridget. "More Airlines to Settle Suit on Price-Fixing; Delta, Unites of UAL, AMR and US Air Agree to Pay Cash, Discount Coupons." *Wall Street Journal*. June 23, 1992: A3.

380. McMenamin, Bridgid. "Paper for Us, Money for Them." *Forbes*. October 26, 1992: 272–274.

381. Wade, Betsy. "Practical Traveler; An Unhappy Lot of Plaintiffs." *New York Times*. January 22, 1995: Sec. 5, p. 4.

382. Quoted in *Ibid.*, Sec 5, p. 4.

383. *Ibid.*

384. McMenamin, *op. cit.*

385. Scott, Donald W. "Policing Corporate Collusion." *Criminology* 27, 1989: 559–584.

386. Cohen, *op. cit.*

387. Among individual antitrust offenders sentenced to jail between 1975 and 1980, the average time served was about 1 month in misdemeanor cases and 3 months in felony cases.

388. Baker, Wayne E. and Faulkner, Robert R. "The Social Organization of Conspiracy: Illegal Networks in the Heavy Electrical Equipment Industry." *American Sociological Review* 58, 1993: 837–860.

389. Herling, John. *The Great Price Conspiracy: The Story of the Antitrust Violations in the Electrical Industry*. Washington, DC: Robert B. Luce, 1962.

390. Scherer, Frederick M. *Industrial Market and Economic Performance* (2nd Ed.). Boston, Mass.: Houghton Mifflin, 1980.

391. Herling, *op. cit.*

392. Geis, Gilbert. "The Heavy Electrical Equipment Antitrust Case of 1961." In Geis, Gilbert (Ed.), *White-Collar Criminal: The Offender in Business and the Professions*. New York: Atherton, 1968; 103–118.

393. Pontell, Henry N., Rosoff, Stephen M., and Goode, Erich. "White-Collar Crime." In Goode, Erich, *Deviant Behavior* (4th Ed.). Englewood Cliffs, NJ: Prentice-Hall, 1994; 345–371.

394. Geis, *op. cit.*

395. Lewis, Anthony. "7 Electrical Officials Get Jail Terms in Trust Case." *New York Times*. February 7, 1961: 1, 26.

396. *Ibid.*

397. Quoted in *Ibid.*, p. 105

398. Conkun, John E. *"Illegal but not Criminal:" Business Crime In America*. Englewood Cliffs, NJ: Prentice-Hall, 1977.

399. Pontell, et. al., p. 357.

400. Geis, *op. cit.*, p. 110.

401. *Ibid.*

402. Howard, Jeffrey H. and Kaserman, David. "Proof of Damages in Construction Industry Bid-Rigging Cases." *The Antitrust Bulletin* 34, 1989: 359.

403. Porter, Robert H. and Zona, J. Douglas. "Detection of Bid-Rigging in Procurement Auctions." *Journal of Political Economy* 101, 1993: 518–538.

404. Bacon, John. "Companies Admit NYC School Lunch Ripoffs." *USA Today*. June 2, 2000: 3A.

405. Schmidt, Peter. "Bid Rigging Among School Suppliers Becoming 'Pervasive,' Experts Fear." *Education Week* 13, September 22, 1993: 1, 18.

406. Hage, David, Boroughs, Don L., and Black, Robert F. "Hidden Monopolies." *US News & World Report* 112, February 3, 1992: 42–48.

407. "Milk Distributor in Florida Pleads Guilty to Conspiracy Charge in Bid-Rigging Case." *Education Week*. May 11, 1988: 5.

408. Schmidt, Peter. "Justice Department Probing Milk Bid-Rigging in Georgia." *Education Week* 8, May 24, 1989: 4.

409. Henriques, Diana B. "Evidence Mounts of Rigged Bidding in Milk Industry." *New York Times*. May 23, 1993: 1.

410. "Borden Fined $5.2 Million." *New York Times*. September 15, 1993: D11.

411. Eitzen and Timmer, *op. cit.*, p. 302.

412. Seligman, Daniel. "Hurray for Avarice." *European Economic Review* 36, May, 1992: 146.

413. Razzi, *op. cit.*

414. "Jury Orders Exxon to Pay $500 Million." *Houston Chronical*. February 21, 2001: 1c, 2C.

415. "The Sour Tale of Baby-Formula Pricing." *Consumer Reports* 58, October 1993: 626.

416. *Ibid.*

417. Hightower, Jim. *Eat Your Heart Out*. New York: Crown, 1975. Hightower points out that two cereals produced by General Mills—*Wheaties* and *Total*—are nearly identical. *Total* is *Wheaties* with three-

fourths of a cent worth of sprayed-on vitamins. The only other difference is that *Total* retails for about 40% more than *Wheaties*.

418. Baldwin, Deborah. "The Cornflake Cartel." *Common Cause Magazine*. Summer 1993: 32–36. In 1972, the FTC filed a complaint for price fixing against the country's four largest breakfast cereal companies. Those companies—Kellogg's, General Mills, General Foods (Post), and Quaker Oats—controlled 91% of the market at that time. (Sobel, Lester [Ed.], *Corruption in Business*. New York: Facts on File, 1977.

419. Schulte, Brigid. "Snap, Crackle and Price-Fixing?" *Miami Herald*. March 8, 1995: 1A.

420. "Congressmen Seek Inquiry into Cereal Pricing Method." *Wall Street Journal*. March 8, 1995: A12.

421. ABC News 20/20. *Transcript #1512*. Denver, Colo.: Journal Graphics, 1995; 6.

422. Schulte, *op. cit.*

423. "Cereal Prices Rising." www.WCVB.com. April 23, 1999.

424. Eitzen and Timmer, *op. cit.*, p. 303.

425. ABC News. "Bitter Pill to Swallow." Television Program: *Primetime Live* 290, March 25, 1993.

426. Warden, Chris. "The Prescription for High Drug Prices." *Consumers' Research Magazine* 75, December 1992: 10–14.

427. Rovner, Julie. "Prescription Drug Prices." *CQ Researcher*, July 17, 1992: 599.

428. Quoted in *Ibid.*, p. 600.

429. Pryor, David. "Prescription Drug Industry Must Be Reformed." *USA Today Magazine* 122, March 1994: 74–75.

430. Quoted in *Ibid.*, p. 600.

431. *Ibid.*, p. 599–624.

432. Lite, Jordan. "Drug Companies Settle Price-Gouging Suit." *Orange County Register*. February 20, 1999: G2.

433. *Ibid.*

434. Quoted in *Ibid.*, p. 614.

435. Caplovitz, David. *The Poor Pay More: Consumer Practices of Low-Income Families*. New York: Free Press, 1967.

436. The Commission was chaired by Governor Otto Kerner of Illinois, who would later go to prison for bribery (Chapter 9).

437. Miller, James N. "Slum Swindlers Must Go!" *Reader's Digest*, November 1969: 169.

438. Green, Mark. "How Minorities Are Sold Short." *New York Times*. June 18, 1990: A21.

439. Hudson, *op. cit.*

440. *Ibid.*, p. 22.

441. *Ibid.*

442. *Ibid.*, p. 22.

443. *Ibid.*

444. Young, Catherine and Light, Larry. "Out! Out! Damned Knockoffs." *Business Week* 3441, September 11, 1995: 6.

445. Gilgoff, Henry. "Rip-offs of Popular Products Victimizes Both Consumers and Manufacturers." *Newsday*. August 27, 1995: 1; Eldridge, Earle. "Bogus Shampoo Scalps Consumers." *USA Today*. August 17, 1995: 1B.

446. Owens, Mitchell. "The Knowable Knack of the Knockoff." *New York Times*. June 17, 1993: 61.

447. Daria, Irene. "Fashion's One-Two Punch: The Knockoff." *Glamour* 41, April 1993: 199.

448. *Ibid.*; Engardio, Pete, Vogel, Todd, and Lee, Dinah. "Companies Are Knocking Off the Knockoff Outfits." *Business Week* 3071, September 26, 1988: 86–88.

449. Weber, Joseph. "Here Comes the Blitz on Knockoff Artists." *Business Week* 3350, December 13, 1993: 8.

450. "Cyberscams." *Business 2.0*. March, 1999: 8.

451. Engardio et al., *op. cit.*

CHAPTER 3

Unsafe Products

> *Lawyer:*   You mean there might be a report that's no longer in existance?
>
> *Auto Executive:*   There might be eight-legged mice on Venus. That's another question I can't answer.
>
> *Lawyer:*   It's very easy for you to make jokes, Mr. Grazier. You have both your arms and legs.

From Class Action: (1990). Screenplay by Carolyn Shelby, Christopher Ames, and Samantha Shad.

During television's Golden Age, the distinguished broadcaster Edward R. Murrow hosted a celebrity interview program called *Person to Person.* One week in 1954, Murrow's guest was movie star Humphrey Bogart. The two men were chain-smokers, so the image beamed to millions of primitive black-and-white screens became so progressively cloudy that many viewers probably began turning knobs in a frantic effort to fix their sets. Within 10 years, Bogart and Murrow were both dead of smoking-related cancer.[1]

For decades, smoking has been recognized as the primary preventable cause of death in the United States. For much of that time, it was popularly perceived more as a psychologically gratifying habit than a physical addiction. Then, in 1994—exactly 40 years after Bogart and Murrow's exhibition of synchronized puffing—the Food and Drug Administration (FDA) leveled an extraordinary accusation against the tobacco industry. "Simply put, the agency asserted that the reason many cigarette smokers find it close to impossible to break the habit is because the industry *makes* it close to impossible."[2]

It had always been assumed by the majority of the American public that the nicotine in cigarettes was only the residue of the nicotine that occurs naturally in tobacco. Few consumers would have suspected that additional nicotine might actually be sprayed on tobacco as it is processed. The commissioner of the FDA cited "mounting evidence" that nicotine is an addictive drug—5 to 10 times more potent than cocaine—and that cigarette manufacturers boost its levels to satisfy this addiction. A government pharmacologist has said of nicotine: "It works like a drug, it looks like a drug, it is a drug pure and simple."[3]

Although tobacco companies publicly assert that nicotine is merely a flavor molecule, even they privately admit that it is a drug.[4] An internal memorandum from the Philip Morris corporation acknowledges that cigarettes, in effect, are nothing more than "nicotine-delivery systems."[5]

An R. J. Reynolds memorandum states: "Nicotine is known to be a habit-forming alkaloid, hence the confirmed user of tobacco products is primarily seeking the physiological 'satisfaction' derived from nicotine.[6] Another confidential internal memo written in 1963 by the general counsel for the Brown & Williamson tobacco company declares: "We are in the business of selling nicotine."[7] When this latter document was obtained by the press in 1994, Brown & Williamson's response was: "We continue to maintain the position that cigarettes aren't addictive."[8] However, a former top scientist for Brown & Williamson testified under oath that "the company's lawyers repeatedly hid damaging scientific research."[9] One memo explicitly discussed "burying" unfavorable test results.[10] Another uncovered memo (this one from 1958) reveals that Philip Morris executives rejected an internal report urging the company to remove benzopyrene, a known carcinogen, from its cigarettes.[11] And in the 1970s, "an industry scientist discovered how to remove harmful carbon monoxide from cigarette smoke but industry lawyers suppressed the research."[12]

Nevertheless, the Tobacco Institute still insists that "smoking . . . has yet to be proven to have a causal role in the development of diseases."[13] However, memos from the 1960s indicate that the industry's own research had concluded by then that smoking causes lung cancer and heart disease; these studies were never made public until they were "leaked" more than 30 years later.[14] Among other things, corporate documents revealed that "the industry destroyed results of its own product testing when the results showed 'biological activity,' a euphamism for ill-health effects."[15]

When the heads of the seven major American tobacco companies[16] were subpoenaed before a congressional committee in 1994, they were pelted with case histories of people who had died from the effects of smoking. All expressed sorrow over those deaths but denied that any of the deceased had been addicted to cigarettes. William Campbell, then president of Philip Morris, swore under oath, "I really don't accept that smoking is addictive."[17] Later, however, he was forced to concede at the hearing that his company had suppressed publication of a 1983 study involving rats, conducted by its own scientists, which demonstrate that nicotine *is* addictive.[18] In 1996, three former Philip Morris employees charged that the company routinely manipulated nicotine levels in its cigarettes. One of them, a former plant manager, said that tobacco was monitored for nicotine every hour of the day, and if it fell below desired levels, the tobacco was reblended and the nicotine was boosted.[19] These whistleblowers' sworn affidavits once again contradicted testimony by the CEO of

Philip Morris, who had told Congress under oath that his company "does not manipulate nor independently control the level of nicotine in our cigarettes."[20]

In 1998, the big lie was again exposed when a California company, DNA Plant Technology (DNAP), pleaded guilty to conspiring with Brown & Williamson to boost nicotine levels in tobacco. "DNAP illegally shipped and smuggled genetically altered seeds to Brazil, where Brown & Williamson grew a tobacco plant called Y-1 that contained twice the amount of nicotine in naturally cured tobacco."[21]

Following the congressional hearings, the American Medical Association (AMA), in its sharpest attack ever on the tobacco industry, declared that cigarette makers had "duped" the public by concealing decades of research on the harmful effects of smoking.[22] The AMA concluded: "No right-thinking individual can ignore the evidence of tobacco industry duplicity. We should all be outraged."[23]

The tobacco industry "has used its money to distort the truth, influence politicians and intimidate any who would expose its secrets."[24] And while the industry has complained vociferously of the use of scare tactics by its enemies, it has long resorted to scare tactics of its own. Tobacco companies warn that "health Nazis" are out to bankrupt stockholders and put tens of thousands of employees on welfare.[25]

Once-secret Philip Morris documents reveal that the company has even used the threat of economic reprisals to intimidate drug firms marketing smoking cessation products. For example, when Merrill Dow Pharmaceuticals began marketing Nicorette gum in 1984, Philip Morris retaliated by canceling chemical purchases from Merrill Dow's parent company, Dow Chemical. In order to appease Philip Morris, Dow agreed to tone down its marketing of Nicorette and target only a narrow band of smokers who have been trying to quit, rather than attacking cigarettes directly or imploring all smokers to quit.[26] In a memo, Dow assured Philip Morris that it was "committed to avoid contribution to the anti-cigarette effort."[27] Dow's reward for its capitulation was a resumption of chemical orders from Philip Morris.

Although there have been a number of product liability and wrongful death suits filed against tobacco companies, no plaintiff had ever collected a dime in damages stemming from the use of tobacco until 1996.[28] The industry had won every previous case on the grounds that smokers knowingly accept the risks of smoking.[29] Even a 1995 case, in which a plaintiff suing Lorillard Tobacco was awarded $2 million by a California jury after claiming that he had contracted cancer from cigarettes, was an anomaly. California law protects tobacco companies against lawsuits for smoking-related illness or death, but in this case the disease was *not* attributed to tobacco but to the *asbestos* used in filter tips.[30] In 1996, however, a Florida man with lung cancer was awarded $750,000 by a circuit court jury in a suit against Brown & Williamson.[31]

Perhaps spurred by the Florida verdict, the first retreat was sounded in the tobacco wars a few weeks later when Liggett Group (one of the smallest of the major tobacco firms) announced it was settling claims in a massive class action suit filed by a woman on behalf of her 47-year-old husband, who had died of lung cancer, and 50 million other smokers.[32] The widow had declared that she wanted the industry to pay for its "deception" over the addictiveness of nicotine.[33] Liggett agreed to pay 5% of its pretax income, up to $50 million a year, to fund programs to help smokers quit the habit. The other companies named in the suit emphatically declined to participate in the proposed settlement.[34] Industry leader Phillip Morris USA thundered, "We intend to fight and win."[35] Two months later, the tobacco industry did indeed win a major victory when a federal appeals court threw out the class-action suit.[36] The plaintiffs vowed to carry their fight to the Supreme Court, and announced plans to file 50 separate state class actions suits.

By 1997, 22 states had also filed suit against the tobacco oligopoly seeking to recoup millions of dollars in public funds spent to treat smoking-related health problems. Once again, Liggett broke ranks when it was announced that, as part of a settlement with these states, the company would publicly acknowledge on its packages that cigarettes *are* addictive and do cause cancer. This time, Liggett reportedly agreed to pay the states $25 million up front, plus 25% of its pretax profits for the next 25 years. Liggett further pledged to turn over what was called a "treasure trove of incriminating documents," including marketing memoranda and lawyers' notes from 30 years of meetings with other tobacco companies. Within weeks, the first of such documents was released to the public. A 1960s memorandum revealed how the tobacco industry weighed what it termed "ethnic factors":

> "Spanish and Negro groups like to purchase only the best of everything—they are not looking for bargains . . . [T]here must be a racial slant in the marketing efforts" toward Hispanics and blacks, while "promotion must be smart and sophisticated" for the Jewish market.[37]

A 1981 R. J. Reynolds marketing plan stated, "The majority of blacks . . . do not respond well to sophisticated or subtle humor in advertising."[38] A 1973 Reynolds marketing profile included a study of black smokers ages 14 to 20.[39]

The most serious charge raised against the tobacco industry involves its covert campaigns to addict teenagers to nicotine in order to create lifetime smokers. A lawyer who has represented many sick smokers argues that the formula is as simple as it is treacherous: "As smokers get older, as smokers die, as smokers quit because they're sick, or for other reasons, there is only one source of replacement smokers—and that is kids."[40] One Philip Morris memo flatly declared, "Today's teenager is tomorrow's potential regular customer."[41]

The tobacco companies are well aware that 90% of adult smokers began smoking as teenagers.[42] Moreover, a 1996 study reports that underage smokers (12 to 17 years old) are three times more likely than adults to be influenced by cigarette advertisements.[43] One of the Liggett documents recommended new packaging concepts for cigarettes to make them more appealing to youngsters.[44] A corporate memo reveals that the R. J. Reynolds Tobacco Company "proposed marketing cigarettes to 14- to 18-year-old smokers as early as the 1970s."[45] A series of 1972 documents from Brown & Williamson discuss that company's efforts to attract young smokers with honey-flavored and cola-flavored cigarettes.[46] Another Reynolds memo, from 1988, discussed the company's plans "to saturate areas where young people gathered, such as fast-food restaurants, video-game arcades, and outdoor basketball courts, with billboards and posters promoting its products."[47]

Yet another Reynolds memo even suggested that teen rebellion might make the risks of smoking more attractive to that underage market":[48]

> We are . . . unfairly constrained from directly promoting cigarettes to the youth market [identified as] the approximately twenty-one-year-old and under group.

> We should simply recognize that most of the "21 and under" group will inevitably become smokers and offer them an opportunity to use our brands.

> The beginning smoker and inhaler [called the "learning smoker"] has a low tolerance for smoke irritation, hence the smoke should be as bland as possible.

> [Cigarettes] should be marketed as a way to fight "stress" and other pressures of the teen years.[49]

R. J. Reynolds has denied that this memo reflects company policy, but it frequently has been singled out for marketing practices that target under-age smokers, particularly its Joe Camel cartoon campaign.[50] Because ciga-rette advertising is banned on television, tobacco companies also pay Holly-wood producers to place their lethal products in films, especially action movies that are popular with teenagers. Philip Morris reportedly paid $350,000 to plug its cigarettes in a James Bond thriller, appropriately titled "License to Kill."[51]

A study by the Centers for Disease Control and Prevention (CDC), re-leased in 1996, reports that the percentage of high school students who smoke now exceeds the percentage of smokers in the adult population.[52] A 17-year-old Connecticut girl, whose neighbor happens to be the CEO of Phillip Morris, artic-ulated the plight of the teenaged nicotine addict: "I try and try, but I can't quit."[53]

Victor Crawford, a former lobbyist for the Tobacco Institute, whose job it was for many years to protect cigarette makers from restrictions, changed sides in 1991 after developing throat cancer. His new message to young con-sumers was blunt and personal:

> "[H]e said that for about five years in the 1980s, he was part of a well-organized campaign that used 'some of the smartest people in America' to figure out 'how to get you to smoke.' . . . 'As tobacco kills off people like me, they need kids like you to replace me.'"[54]

Crawford, once a 2½-pack-a-day smoker, died of cancer in 1996 at the age of 63. His widow said that he had felt "tremendous remorse" about his role in promot-ing smoking: "He realized that it was wrong, that you don't market death."[55]

After lengthy negotiations, in 1987 the tobacco industry agreed to a proposed settlement with the attorneys general of 40 states, which had been seeking compensation for decades of smoking-related health costs.[56] Under the agreement, the tobacco companies would pay damages of $368 billion.[57]

The next time tobacco executives appeared before Congress to discuss the proposed settlement, they conceded for the first time in a public forum that nicotine *is* addictive.[58] A few months later, however, Congress rejected the settlement and the deal was declared "dead" by the chairman of RJR Nabisco (parent company of R. J. Reynolds), as his company and four other major tobacco firms withdrew from the deal. The Clinton administration and Congress had tried to raise the settlement to $516 billion and place even tougher restrictions on the industry than those agreed to by the states.[59]

Four states—Minnesota,[60] Texas,[61] Florida,[62] and Mississippi[63]—settled separately with the tobacco industry in 1997 and 1998 for a combined $40 billion.[64] By 1999, the remaining states had signed on to a $206 billion settlement,[65] the largest civil settlement in American history. The companies also agreed to spend $1.7 billion to finance antismoking advertising and to study youth smoking, and to eliminate any advertising that appeals to children.[66]

Nothing in the agreement with the states precluded individual lawsuits, however, although such cases had seldom proved successful. Up to then, tobacco companies had won all but 6 of the more than 1000 lawsuits filed by individuals since the 1950s.[67] Even in Florida, where the $750,000 jury award discussed earlier transpired, two subsequent cases involving similar plaintiffs with smoking-related cancer had failed.[68] But two of the tobacco industry's six losses came back to back in 1999. Cases in San Francisco and Portland had resulted in judgments totaling $131 million.[69] It seemed to some observers that momentum was starting to build against the companies.

Big Tobacco faced an even more serious threat from class action litigation, a largely untested arena. Prior to 1998, only one class action suit against industry had been tried, brought by flight attendants who claimed that second-hand smoke had made them ill. In that case, the companies agreed to a $300 million settlement to establish a research foundation.[70] A 1997 class action suit filed in Pennsylvania had not been tried; it had been thrown out by a federal judge on technical grounds.[71] And was considered a big win for Big Tobacco. But it may have been the last hurrah. Florida had launched its own class action suit, and this one *would* go to trial.

C A S E   S T U D Y

Lots of Zeros

When jury selection began in Florida in 1998 for a $200 billion smoker's class-action suit against the nation's cigarette makers, it was the proverbial "high noon" for Big Tobacco. The industry had come prepared to fight. There would be no pre-trial settlement, as in the flight attendants case the previous year. "That was a different time," a spokesman for R. J. Reynolds declared.[72]

(Continued)

The smokers charged that the tobacco industry had made a defective product and had conspired to deceive the public about smoking-related illnesses.[73] The lawsuit alleged: "Cigarettes are a product that when used as directed will inevitably cause death and disease to a large percentage of its users."[74] Hundreds of the plaintiffs were in the courtroom on the first day, some of them with portable oxygen tanks. "Questioning began amid a steady backdrop of coughing, wheezing, and the sound of electronic voice boxes."[75]

At the center of the suit was the issue of addiction, the same ground on which the earlier Pennsylvania class action had been dismissed. Plaintiffs claimed that it was impossible for them to kick the habit. In the words of one of their attorneys, "The essence of the conspiracy and fraud of these defendants has been to get smokers hooked on nicotine as young as possible and make lifelong customers of them."[76]

The attorney for Philip Morris argued: "You can't defraud somebody by hiding something they already knew."[77] He pointed out that health concerns about smoking had been raised as early as 1604 and that cigarettes were already being called "coffin nails" in the nineteenth century.[78] The industry further maintained that those who want to quit can do so. Industry lawyers challenged the plaintiffs' addiction claim by contending that 46 million people had quit smoking for good during the previous 30 years.[79]

On July 7, 1999, after 8 months of testimony, the Florida jury dealt a crushing blow to Big Tobacco, finding that cigarette manufacturers had conspired to "mislead smokers about the addictive and deadly nature of their product."[80] The verdict ruled that cigarette makers had "acted with reckless disregard"[81] and "engaged in extreme and outrageous conduct."[82]

Although there were only nine named plaintiffs, the suit had been brought on behalf of as many as 500,000 sick Florida smokers.[83] Legal experts believed that the case had opened the door for similar class action suits in other states. The executive director of Citizens for a Tobacco-Free Society proclaimed, "The Marlboro Man just fell off his horse into quicksand."[84]

The second phase of the trial concluded in April 2000, when three plaintiffs, who had been chosen to represent the hundreds of thousands of smokers in the potential class action, were awarded $12.7 million in compensatory damages by the same jury.[85] Legal experts predicted that this verdict would be a harbinger of a huge punitive damage award against the tobacco industry when that jury began the third phase of the trial: the determination of damages on behalf of the entire Florida class.

The predictions could not have been more prescient. On July 14, 2000, the tobacco industry was ordered to pay $145 billion to Florida smokers who had become ill or had died as a result of their addiction to cigarettes. It was the largest jury award in U.S. history.[86] The damages were apportioned against the defendants according to their market share, ranging from $74 billion against Philip Morris down to $790 million against Liggett Group.[87] After reading the breakdown, the judge muttered, "Lots of zeros."[88]

(Continued)

Many judicial authorities, as well as the tobacco attorneys, expected the spectacular award to be overturned or at least trimmed drastically. But 4 months later, a circuit judge upheld the verdict, rejecting claims that the amount would bankrupt the tobacco industry.[89] The bankruptcy threat was also dismissed by the founder of Smokefree Educational Services, a former Wall Street executive:

> Cigarette makers "can raise the price of cigarettes tomorrow and take in as much money as they need to pay," he said. "They have the luxury that smokers are addicted."[90]

Since the verdict, the tobacco industry has tried mightily to reshape its image. As part of its $100 million corporate image campaign, Philip Morris has unveiled a new website, on which it unequivocally states for the first time that there is an "'overwhelming medical and scientific consensus that cigarette smoking causes' diseases including lung cancer, emphysema and heart disease."[91] The company also has finally conceded at tobacco hearings held by the World Health Organization in 2000 that cigarettes are addictive.[92] Most remarkable of all, Philip Morris now refers to nicotine as a "drug" and has even said that the company could accept some regulation of tobacco by the DA.[93]

But for all the belated admissions, it is still not clear when—or even if—the Florida damages will be paid. Meanwhile, thousands of other suits, both individual and class action, remain pending. The tobacco industry firmly expects to win the Florida case on appeal and hopes to get bailed out of future class actions by Congress. In any event, prolonged appellate litigation is likely to outlive the plaintiffs. Big Tobacco's timetable for paying off all the Florida claims is about 75 years.[94]

Among the individual lawsuits against big tobacco, the costliest thus far occurred in 2001 when a Los Angeles jury ordered Philip Morris to pay more than $3 billion in damages to a cancer-stricken Marlboro smoker. After a two-month trial and a full week of deliberations, the jury found the country's biggest cigarette maker guilty on all eight of the plaintiff's claims—including negligence, misrepresentation, fraud, and selling a defective product.[95] The verdict far exceeded any previous award to an individual smoker. Philip Morris called the verdict "outrageous," and some legal experts have predicted that the huge punitive damages would be reduced by the courts. But the jury was quick to defend its judgement. One juror explained: "We got to that figure because we thought that figure would hurt them."[96] Another juror declared: "We want them to be responsible for their product. We want them to put on their product: 'It kills.'"[97]

The tobacco industry symbolizes the "postponed violence" of white-collar crime. Although it is less obvious, less immediate, and less directly traceable to its perpetrators than the violence associated with street crime, it is no less devastating to its victims.[98] Even if one excludes tobacco from the equation, the statistics are grim. "According to the National Commission on

Product Safety, 20 million Americans have suffered injuries from using unsafe consumer products."[99] Of those victims, 110,000 are permanently disabled, and 30,000 are dead.

Using automobile manufacturing as a model, we can identify two basic elements of corporate disregard for consumer safety: (1) resistance against safety devices, and (2) defects in design. The first element may be illustrated by the early refusal of General Motors (GM) to install safety glass in its cars. In 1929, the president of GM dismissed safety glass as too costly. His response to efforts promoting that product's use in windshields: "We are not a charitable institution."[100]

The second element, faulty design, is illustrated only too well by the Ford Pinto debacle of the 1970s. Pre-production crash tests had established that the Pinto's fuel system ruptured easily in rear-end collisions, causing an explosion. However, Ford had already begun tooling assembly-line machinery for the Pinto, so management, desperate to compete with Volkswagen for the emerging subcompact market, chose to manufacture the car as it was.[101]

Ford could have replaced the gas tanks with safer ones at a cost of $11 per car but decided that this expense would not be cost-effective.

> This decision was based on the following calculations. The $11 repairs for all Pintos would cost $137 million but 180 burn deaths and 180 serious burn injuries and 21,000 burned vehicles would cost only $49.5 million (each death was figured at $200,000 and each injury at $67,000). Therefore, the company could anticipate a saving or profit of $87.5 million by continuing to make and sell the cars that were expected to kill or injure several hundred people.[102]

Fiery crashes involving Pintos began to occur with alarming regularity. Ford's liability estimates, however, were way off the mark. Liability suits against the Pinto increased and judgments were routinely found against Ford. "In 1978, a jury in California awarded $127.8 million—including $125 million in punitive damages—to a teenager badly burned when his 1972 Pinto burst into flames after being hit in the rear by a car traveling 35 miles an hour."[103] That same year, the Department of Transportation announced that its tests had proved that the Pinto was unsafe and ordered a recall.

Ford's indifference to human life remains a testimony to the great paradox of white-collar violence: "A human being who would not harm you on an individual face-to-face basis, who is charitable, civic-minded, loving, and devout, will wound or kill you from behind the corporate veil."[104]

The same criminal justice system that unhesitatingly locks up murderers and muggers seems ill-equipped to deal with cases like that of the Pinto. Ford was charged, under the doctrine of corporate criminal liability, with reckless homicide in an Indiana trial. But the company was acquitted after mounting a successful million-dollar defense based on the scary premise that the Pinto was no more dangerous than other comparably sized cars of its time.[105] In 1979, an angry writer observed, "One wonders how long Ford Motor Company would continue to market lethal cars were [chairman] Henry Ford II and [president] Lee Iacocca serving 20-year terms in Leavenworth for consumer homicide."[106]

If anything positive emerged from the Pinto tragedies, it is that automakers are probably far more reluctant today to ignore design defects *post facto,* as Ford did. For example, in the face of a problem remarkably reminiscent of the Pinto, Navistar International, the nation's largest manufacturer of school buses, was quick to recall tens of thousands of vehicles in 1992 after government tests showed that the fuel tanks could rupture, producing a fire hazard in a collision.[107]

On the other hand, the continuous occurrence of such recalls still raises serious questions of how willing auto manufacturers are to put consumer safety ahead of bottom-line considerations *pre facto.* In 2000, Ford was in trouble again. A federal judge took the unprecedented step of ordering the recall of 1.7 million Ford cars and trucks sold in California, accusing the automaker of concealing a dangerous design flaw that can cause the vehicles to stall in traffic. Never before had a federal judge ordered an automotive recall.[108] Ford had already settled (without admitting any wrongdoing) dozens of personal injury and wrongful death lawsuits in which one of its vehicles was suspected of stalling.[109]

Ford's woes continued that same year when Bridgestone Corporation, the maker of Firestone tires, announced a recall of up to 20 million ATX, ATX II, and Wilderness tires. Although the tires in question were used by various automakers and were popular replacement tires, most were found as original equipment on Ford's best-selling Explorer sport utility vehicle as well as its Ranger and F-series pickup truck.[110] At the time of the recall, the National Highway Traffic Safety Administration (NHTSA) was investigating the role of these tires—specifically tread separation—in crashes that had caused 46 deaths, making it the deadliest flaw ever to result in a product recall.[111] This was Firestone's second time around the recall block. Several years earlier, its 500 series radial tires had a serious defect which caused the steel belt to separate from the tire, leading to "thousands of accidents, hundreds of injuries, and 34 known fatalities."[112] In the end, Firestone was fined a token $50,000.

Because of the magnitude of the ATX/Wilderness recall, it proceeded very slowly. Indeed, in the 2 weeks following the announcement, three more people were killed, in separate accidents, while riding on the recalled tires.[113] Within a month the suspected death toll had risen to 88.[114]

Ford was also rebuked for its failure to notify the government when it had begun replacing Firestone tires on its sport utility vehicles in 10 Middle Eastern countries, Malaysia, Thailand, and Venezuela *a year earlier.* Federal law requires companies to notify NHTSA regulators if they believe they have discovered a product defect.[115] Ford employees in other countries had raised serious questions about the quality of Firestone tires, as well as the tiremaker's integrity, 19 months before the American recall.[116]

But most of the blame was ascribed to Firestone. Company documents revealed that it had received more than 1500 legal claims, dating back to 1997, for property damage, injuries, and deaths resulting from failures of its ATX and Wilderness tires. Yet in response to numerous inquiries from Ford, Firestone repeatedly blamed abuse by customers, who underinflate their tires or overload their vehicles.[117] "What Firestone appears to have missed is that sport utility vehicles require more reliable tires than cars because they are more likely to roll over when they lose a tire."[118]

Since their problems have been so visible, the automobile and tire industries serve as familiar exemplars of corporate violence, but they are by no means the only businesses which have threatened the health and lives of innocent consumers. Ralph Nader and other consumer advocates have long decried the willingness of manufacturers to risk personal injury in order to trim production costs. For example, in 1985, a 13-year-old Minnesota boy had both his arms amputated while operating a forage blower, a farm machine that throws grain up into a silo. This horrifying accident could have been prevented by a safety guard which would have cost the manufacturer $2. These simple devices that automatically stop a spinning shaft when it is jammed are required in many European countries, but not in the United States.[119]

The list of consumer products known to be dangerous and defective runs on and on. A leather protection spray recently left over 1000 people in 18 states complaining of respiratory ailments.[120] About the same time, a Chicago manufacturer recalled 10,000 gas furnaces with faulty vent systems, which had been linked to 10 carbon monoxide deaths.[121] J. C. Penney had to recall 1.4 million electric food processors after some of them had started unexpectedly and amputated the fingers of a number of owners.[122]

A product as innocuous as a fisherman's worm-shocker may actually have taken more lives than the Pinto. In 1993, the federal government announced the recall of an electronic device used by fishermen to shock worms to bring them to the surface of the ground for use as bait. Over a 20-year period, such devices reportedly had caused the deaths by electrocution of more than 30 people, mostly children.[123]

Children, in fact, are of special concern to those who work in the area of consumer safety.[124] Greenpeace, the environmental watchdog group, has issued a list 28 vinyl children's products that it says contains dangerous levels of lead and cadmium.[125] The National Highway Safety Administration has recalled nearly a million children's car seats because of tests showing that push-button latch releases could jam in a crash, making it difficult to remove a child.[126] The Consumer Product Safety Commission (CPSC) convinced the Gerber corporation to recall about 10 million of its NUK pacifiers because they could fall apart and choke young children.[127] Fisher-Price recalled 420,000 of its Snuggle Light dolls after 5 children choked on the dolls' cloth caps.[128]

A 2000 investigation offered disturbing news. In the previous 3 years, 75% of the most dangerous problems that led to recalls of products used by children were never voluntarily reported to the government.[129] Cosco, for example, did not even recall a defective stroller until a year after the company had received 3000 complaints of lock failure that resulted in more than 200 reports of injuries to infants.[130] The mother of one of those 200 children stated, "It's scary that parents can have children that have been injured after the company knew it was a problem. . . . It's scary that companies can get away with it."[131]

According to the CPSC, Baby's Dream Furniture, a Georgia company, waited until it had received eight reports of children having their fingers amputated or crushed in its cribs before it reported the problem. The cribs were, of course, recalled, and the company agreed to pay $200,000 in civil penalties.[132]

What happens to products after they are found to be safety hazards? Unlike socks in the dryer, they do not simply disappear into some mysterious land of the lost. Sometimes, they are simply sold again. In 2000, a California company was fined $75,000 for selling previously recalled sweaters that were so flammable "they burned faster than newspaper."[133]

In 1977, the Environmental Defense Fund asked the CPSC to halt the sale of garments treated with TRIS, a flame retardant commonly used in children's sleepwear. TRIS was found to be a potent carcinogenic (cancer-causing) chemical. The group cited tests done by the Cancer Institute, declaring that "the evidence is conclusive that this is as clear a case of a carcinogen as we are going to find."[134] The government agreed and 2 months later halted the further sale of any TRIS-treated clothing.[135] But this was not the end of the TRIS story. According to a congressional committee report issued the following year, approximately 2.4 million TRIS-treated garments were shipped overseas to be sold in underdeveloped countries following the domestic ban.[136] This practice—known as "dumping"—is a common response by American manufacturers of hazardous products that are banned from the domestic market.[137]

Adulterated Food

In 1905, Upton Sinclair published *The Jungle,* an electrifying exposé of unsanitary practices inside the American meat-packing industry. Consider just one brief excerpt from the book:

> [T]here was a trap in the pipe, where all the scraps of meat and odds and ends of refuse were caught, and every few days it was the old man's task to clean these out, and shovel their contents into one of the trucks with the rest of the meat![138]

Sinclair further described how spoiled meat was sold, how slaughtered livestock were piled into decaying storerooms overrun with rats, and how sausages were stuffed with dung. He reported that workers sometimes would fall into rendering vats and be overlooked for days, until only their bones could be fished out. The rest of their remains would end up in consumers' pantries, mixed into containers of lard.

Although food has been regulated in the United States since the nineteenth century,[139] early legislation had proved to be ineffectual. *The Jungle* served as a catalyst for the enactment of tougher federal laws, such as the Food and Drug Act and the Meat Inspection Act of 1906.[140] The latter piece of legislation, however, only applied to meat sold in interstate commerce. Meat processed and sold within a single state (roughly 25% of all the meat consumed in the United States) was not subject to the law. The consequences of this loophole have been described graphically:

> Surveys of packing houses in Delaware, Virginia, and North Carolina found the following tidbits in the meat: animal hair, sawdust, flies, abscessed pork livers, and snuff spit out by the meat workers. . . . Such plants were not all minor operations; some were run by the giants—Armour, Swift, and Wilson.[141]

In response to such disgusting conditions, the Wholesome Meat Act was passed in 1967, requiring that states must at least match federal inspection standards.[142] But the siren song of the cash register continued to entice abuses. Hormel, for example, used to repackage and resell stale meat returned by retailers.

> When the original customers returned the meat to Hormel, they used the following terms to describe it: "moldy liver loaf, sour party hams, leaking bologna, discolored bacon, off-conditioned hams, and slick and slimy spareribs." Hormel renewed these products with cosmetic measures. . . . Spareribs returned for sliminess, discoloration, and stickiness were rejuvenated through curing and smoking, renamed Windsor Loins, and sold in ghetto stores for more than fresh pork chops.[143]

In 1970, the General Accounting Office (GAO) investigated 40 meat plants previously cited for sanitation violations by the U.S. Department of Agriculture (USDA) and found that 30 of them had not been cleaned up. "In these plants, the GAO found cow or pig carcasses contaminated with cockroaches, flies, rodents, livestock stomach contents, mouse droppings, rust or moisture."[144] "The GAO's understated conclusion: 'A serious problem of unsanitary conditions exists in the food-manufacturing industry.'"[145]

Although there are 7000 full-time federal meat inspectors, nonmeat food processing plants are inspected on average only once every 10 years.[146] A panel of experts, in a 1998 report to Congress, called for a major overhaul of the nation's food protection systems.[147]

Currently, about 5000 American deaths a year[148] and 76 million cases of food poisoning[149] are associated with tainted food. The poultry industry is considered especially pathogenic because of its susceptibility to *Salmonella* bacteria, the leading cause of foodborne sickness.[150] *Salmonella* usually produces nonlethal, flu-like symptoms, but in certain cases it can be more deadly, particularly to children, the elderly, and people with weakened immune systems.[151] According to one estimate, at least half the chickens sold in retail stores harbor *Salmonella*.[152] At processing plants, birds often become contaminated by fecal and urine wastes. Typically, a single individual checks 60 to 70 slaughtered chickens per minute.

For decades, there has been no question that more inspectors, more thorough examinations of carcasses, and improved standards of sanitation are desperately needed.[153] In 1996, a crucial first step was taken when the USDA drafted new meat inspection rules calling for increased microbial testing for *Salmonella* in place of the traditional "sniff and poke" method.

But *Salmonella* is not the only health problem linked to the poultry industry. Poultry is also highly susceptible to *Campylobacter* bacterium, which is considered the leading bacterial cause of food-borne illness, with an estimated 2 million to 8 million cases of *Campylobacter*-linked cases reported each year.[154] In 1997, the CDC estimated that *Campylobacter* infects between 70% and 90% of all chickens. Although not considered as deadly as *Salmonella*, it can cause illnesses equally as debilitating and has been linked to a serious paralytic disease. *Campylobacter* is responsible for as many as 800 deaths a year.[155]

Having considered the state of meat production then and now, we must not overlook the issue of future health risks. An increasingly popular technique, known as forced molting, prolongs the fertility of older birds. Hens are starved for a week or more in order to make them lose their feathers, after which they lay more eggs. The danger here is that molted birds are *5000 times* more susceptible to *Salmonella* than normally fed birds.[156] The introduction of recombinant DNA-derived growth hormones for use in meat production raises even newer questions about meat safety. Most of these compounds are steroid or sex hormones. Steroids are fat-soluble, implying that residues could be carried through meat into human tissues.[157] Because scientists do not completely agree on how growth hormones work, their ultimate safety will be determined by a generation of consumers thrown into an expendable role once occupied by medieval food-tasters.

In addition to meat and poultry, the Food and Drug Act granted the federal government broad regulatory powers over the entire food industry. For instance, concerns have been raised about the seafood industry, which has generated a number of health and safety problems related to natural viral and bacterial pathogens,[158] as well as toxic and chemical contamination from marine environments polluted with sewage, pesticides, and industrial chemicals.[159] In 1993, seafood accounted for 20% of all reported incidents of food illnesses the United States.[160] The FDA estimates that 114,000 Americans suffer seafood poisoning each year.[161]

In the biggest documented case of food poisoning ever, 224,000 persons became ill in 1994 from eating bacteria-tainted Schwann's ice cream made at a Minnesota plant. It took 2 years for officials to trace the source, milk tanker trucks which had previously carried salmonella-infected egg products.[162]

Daily newspapers frequently carry stories about recalls of hazardous food products. Even granola bars, the emblematic snack food of health-conscious "yuppies," have been adulterated. Sixteen hundred cases of bars were recalled in 1993 because they contained particles of metal.[163]

If there is one grocery product above all in which consumers have a right to expect purity, it is baby food, yet even this industry has failed to measure up to the public's trust. An analysis conducted by two environmental groups in 1995 found traces of pesticides in 53% of the baby food they tested. The study included samples from all the major baby food manufacturers were included in the study. Among the pesticides detected were neurotoxins and "probable human carcinogens."[164] According to the National Academy of Sciences:

> Children are more susceptible than adults to most pesticides. . . . [If they] are exposed to compounds that act in the nervous systems during periods of vulnerability, they can be left with lifelong deficits. If they're exposed to carcinogens, it can set the stage for cancer later."[165]

The public-be-damned attitude of food packers is epitomized by the H. J. Heinz Company, which recalled 12,000 cases of baby food from retailers after complaints that the jars contained pieces of rubber. According to a company spokesman, Heinz did not notify consumers about the recall *because tests showed the rubber was not a health hazard.*[166] That may be so, but what are the chances that the chairman of the board would let *his* child eat rubber?

Dangerous Drugs and Devices

Drugs, of course, were covered by the 1906 Food and Drug Act. Unfortunately, effective regulation was even slower to develop in the pharmaceutical arena than was the case with food (Chapter 2). Many drugs of dubious safety were sold without prescriptions until well into the 1930s.[167] The event most responsible for galvanizing public sentiment toward more rigorous protection was the deaths in 1937 of 107 children who were poisoned by a "cure-all" tonic known as Elixer Sulfanilamide.[168] After that incident, the law was changed to require the testing of all new drugs to establish their safety. The FDA is empowered to oversee the determination of potential therapeutic benefits and the associated risks of medication.

Pharmaceutical manufacturers are also regulated by common law tort doctrine, making them subject to strict liability,[169] that is, product liability is imposed even in the absence of any purposeful intent to harm. An example of tort liability is the widely used anti-obesity drug treatment fen-phen (a combination of the drugs fenfluramine and phentermine). American Home Products, which marketed the dangerous fenfluramine part of the fen-phen combination under the brand name Pondimin (phentermine has not been associated with health problems and remains on the market), became the target of a class action lawsuit in 1999 involving thousands of fen-phen users. American Home had pulled Pondimin off the market in 1997 at the request of the FDA, after a Mayo Clinic study linked it to potentially fatal heart valve damage. Dozens of fen-phen cases had been settled quietly out of court, but the same week the large class action suit was filed in New Jersey, a jury awarded a 35-year-old Texas woman $23 million after she successfully argued that American Home Products had concealed evidence that its diet drug caused valvular heart disease. The plaintiff blamed American Home Products for the lifetime of heart problems she now faces, including the inevitable surgery she will require to replace two heart valves as her ailments progress.[170]

Another well-publicized liability case involved the drug Bendectin, which was once commonly prescribed (until 1983) to treat the nausea and vomiting associated with morning sickness in pregnant women. Bendectin became the target of many tort lawsuits alleging that it caused horrible birth defects in the children of some mothers who took the drug.[171] Eventually, the manufacturer withdrew Bendectin from the market and submitted to a $110 million class action settlement.

The Bendectin controversy revived painful memories of the most tragic case of an inadequately tested drug ever, the nightmarish story of thalidomide. Developed in Europe, thalidomide was a sleeping potion for which the pharmaceutical firm of Richardson-Merrell purchased the American sales rights in 1959. In 1961, Merrell learned that the drug had been withdrawn from the German market because it was suspected of causing terrible birth defects. "Even so, Merrell continued to distribute free pills to doctors who gave them to patients, including pregnant women."[172]

Despite heavy pressure by Merrell,[173] the FDA successfully kept thalidomide off the American market based on the unfavorable foreign reports. Merrell, of course, did not realize it at the time, but the FDA had saved the company. Had thalidomide been approved, Merrell unquestionably would later have been sued out of existence,[174] because by 1962, it was conclusively recognized that thalidomide was a teratogen (from the Latin word for "monster")—a drug which causes congenital malformation in fetuses.

About 8000 thalidomide babies were born in 46 countries. Their distinctive range of deformities was described by the *Sunday Times* of London in a 1979 story about surviving victims who were by then in their teens: "Some have no arms, just flippers from the shoulder; some no legs, just toes from their hips; some have limbless trunks, with just a head and body."[175]

Most of these births occurred outside the United States. The relatively small number of American thalidomide babies was limited to those whose mothers had been given free samples, such as a 16-year-old unwed high school student in Los Angeles,[176] and those whose mothers had taken the drug overseas during pregnancy, such a New York woman who had given birth at a U.S. Army hospital in Spain.[177]

Obviously, the United States was extraordinarily fortunate that the FDA had refused to approve thalidomide. Nevertheless, Merrell-Richardson's conduct was irresponsible by any conscionable standard. The company had no information about thalidomide's effects in early pregnancy when it had begun testing the drug on humans by distributing it to private physicians to give to their patients. "[B]ut it repeatedly assured doctors that the drug was safe for everyone—*including* pregnant women."[178] The company had never bothered to conduct tests on pregnant animals; however, some of the toxicity tests it did perform on nonpregnant animals had yielded alarming results. When thalidomide was administered in syrup form to six female rats, they all died. When administered to 30 male rats, 23 died within a day. When given to a healthy dog, the animal twitched and vomited for nearly 3 hours and died the next morning. Merrell never revealed these findings to the FDA and continued its clinical trials on humans, eventually distributing 2.5 million thalidomide tablets to 1267 doctors. At the time, both figures were the highest ever recorded for clinical trials in the United States.[179]

In an incredible postscript, thalidomide was finally approved by the FDA in 1998 as a treatment for leprosy. Although there are believed to be fewer than 100 lepers in the United States, doctors would also be free to prescribe it for other purposes. And because thalidomide has shown some promise as a possible treatment for cancer and AIDS, it is likely that its use will extend well beyond a handful of leprosy patients. However, the FDA imposed unprecedented restrictions.

> The FDA is requiring doctors who prescribe thalidomide and pharmacies that sell it to register with the agency and undergo specific training on how to warn patients about the drug's dangers. Female patients will not get a prescription without a pregnancy test, and they must undergo regular pregnancy tests throughout the use of the drug. Women will also have to agree to use two reliable forms of contraception. . . . All patients will view a disturbing video warning delivered by a thalidomide victim.[180]

Although the FDA stressed its confidence that the safeguards would be effective, the head of its Center for Drug Evaluation and Research added, "No drug is 100% safe."[181] In the case of thalidomide, that would seem to be a stunning understatement.

Pharmaceutical manufacturing is the only American industry with a safety record arguably worse than that of its automakers. Richardson-Merrell, the company that sought to bring thalidomide to the United States, had the ignominious distinction of simultaneously marketing a second disastrous "wonder" drug, MER/29, a cholesterol inhibitor intended for use by heart disease patients. First marketed in 1960, MER/29 had become Merrell's biggest-selling prescription drug within a year and it was used by nearly 400,000 Americans.[182] When a rival firm, conducting comparative tests using MER/29, reported that laboratory animals had developed cataracts in their eyes, Merrell dismissed those results, claiming its own tests had produced no cataracts whatsoever. Yet at that time, Merrell already knew that 25 out of 29 rats in its own laboratories had incurred eye damage after receiving the drug.[183] In 1962, a technician employed by Merrell admitted that she had been ordered by a company executive to falsify her report of a study in which MER/29 had apparently caused blindness in laboratory monkeys.[184]

By the time MER/29 was taken off the market in 1962, at least 5000 people had suffered serious side effects from the drug. When a Richardson-Merrell vice-president and two laboratory supervisors were charged with fraud, they entered the familiar "no contest" plea. Each defendant could have received up to 5 years in prison, but a sympathetic judge gave them only 6 months probation. The company was fined $80,000; it had made an $18 million profit that year.[185]

Twenty years later, another pharmaceutical giant, Eli Lilly, marketed a painkiller called Oraflex for the treatment of arthritis. Evidence later showed that Lilly had known that 26 deaths had been linked to the drug overseas. The company never shared this information with the FDA when it had applied for permission to sell Oraflex in the United States. Within 6 months of its introduction, Oraflex was withdrawn from the American market after reports of new deaths began circulating. In 1985, Lilly pleaded guilty of attempting to conceal illegally the lethal hazards of Oraflex. "The total punishment handed out for a crime that is believed to have killed 49 people and injured 916 more was a $25,000 fine for Lilly and a $15,000 fine for one executive."[186]

In a recent southern California case, a physician and two employees of a pharmaceutical laboratory pled guilty to charges that they conspired to falsify test results used by the FDA to determine the safety and effectiveness of a variety of drugs.[187] The falsified results involved almost a dozen human clinical trials for birth control drugs and drugs used to treat asthma, diabetes, and sinusitis. The laboratory was hired by major drug firms to perform the tests. In one study, the lab created dozens of fake patients. In others, the researchers used their own blood and medical data from their own family members to submit bogus test results to the drug companies and the government. The apparent motive was to save money and time when legitimate test subjects were difficult to locate.[188]

C A S E   S T U D Y

Halcion Daze

In January, 1992, the world watched as President George Bush vomited and fainted at a state dinner in Japan. Although his aides quickly attributed the president's collapse to the flu, questions persisted about the possible side effects of the controversial sleeping pill Halcion, which Bush acknowledged that he took occasionally. Some Halcion critics openly speculated that the drug could even be connected to Bush's familiar fractured speech patterns that comedians loved to lampoon. Observers were particularly intrigued by a garbled campaign address the president delivered in New Hampshire about a month later, in which he referred to the Nitty Gritty Dirt Band as the "Nitty Ditty Nitty Gritty Great Bird."[189]

The strange tale of Halcion is yet another instance of an alleged cover-up on the part of a major pharmaceutical manufacturer, in this case, Upjohn. "Over the years, at least 100 law suits have been filed by users of the drug or their family members, as psychotic episodes and even homicides were blamed on its use."[190] Once the world's most popular sleeping pill, Halcion has since been banned in a number of countries, including Britain,[191] Norway,[192] and The Netherlands.[193] Halcion is the trade name for triazolam, a type of benzodiazepine which includes other popular sleep hypnotics, as well as tranquilizers such as Valium.[194] Upjohn first synthesized Halcion in 1969 and submitted a new drug application to the FDA the following year.[195] The company believed that Halcion was potentially more profitable than any sleeping pill ever produced. It knocked people out fast but cleared

(Continued)

the body so quickly that users did not experience the next-day hangover character-istic of barbiturates or other benzodiazepine hypnotics.[196] Early tests, however, raised plenty of red flags. A researcher at the University of California–Irvine College of Medicine found cases of amnesia among his subjects who were given Halcion.[197] A renowned medical scientist at the University of Edinburgh in Scotland reported that Halcion could cause harsh episodes of "rebound anxiety" in patients as the drug wears off.[198] He later described Halcion as "brain poison."[199]

A 1979 corporate memo written by an Upjohn executive tacitly acknowl-edged that the drug's approval was in trouble: "[T]he FDA will never approve Halcion without tremendous pressure. We have the people willing to exert the pressure but we must orchestrate it."[200] The company was particularly well-equipped to exert such pressure. "[A] former deputy commissioner of the FDA who had become a senior vice-president at Upjohn had meetings and telephone conversations with FDA personnel who were involved in a review of the drug's approval."[201] In November 1982, Halcion was approved by the FDA and became available by prescription in the United States the following spring.

Seldom, however, has such a potent drug been approved under more ques-tionable circumstances. It is now known that the findings of the original domestic research trial in 1972–1973 omitted about a third of the adverse reactions suffered by a group of Michigan prison inmates who were used as subjects.[202] Upjohn has characterized the omissions as "transcription errors."[203] In another early test, a Houston psychiatrist fudged his results by enrolling himself, his nurse, and at least 14 patients multiple times in the same study under different initials. When he was asked why so many subjects shared the same birth date, he lied, claiming he had utilized sets of twins.[204] An FDA audit has also revealed that a Vicksburg, Missis-sippi, psychiatrist fabricated a 6-month clinical trial. The agency has found no evi-dence that patients involved in this study ever actually took Halcion, although the doctor submitted a highly favorable report on the drug.[205]

The debate reached the public agenda when a San Francisco writer ques-tioned the FDA's approval of Halcion in a widely discussed magazine article. She described the intense reaction she had experienced with Halcion: "[After two weeks], my heart pounded and I was on the verge of tears much of the time. The slightest danger, such as having to make a left turn in traffic, put me in a sweat."[206] Her therapist, having heard only good reports about Halcion, never considered taking her patient off the drug. After 6 months, she "became convinced that the world was on the brink of nuclear war or invasion from space."[207]

In the face of such negative publicity, a memorandum written by Upjohn's marketing department recommended a "containment" strategy to protect sales. The first suggested tactic was to attribute the mounting criticism to the controver-sial Church of Scientology, an easy target as a scapegoat because of its campaigns against certain prescription drugs.[208]

In December 1991, an FDA official undertook an investigation of Halcion's safety. He spent 3 months in Upjohn's Michigan headquarters examining records

(Continued)

and interviewing employees. He concluded that Upjohn had "engaged in an ongoing pattern of misconduct."[209] The investigator exhorted his agency to refer the case to the Justice Department so that a grand jury could determine if crimes had been committed. The FDA responded promptly—by reassigning the official, who soon retired. His report was not released until 1994.[210] A prominent specialist in sleep disorders has offered a very critical explanation of why the probe was aborted: "I think that investigation was getting too close to the FDA and eventually they were going to be investigating themselves."[211]

In addition, the physician who managed Upjohn's Drug Experience Unit during the 1980s submitted an alarming report to the company. He warned that Halcion users might "kill somebody without knowing it."[212] He was told by his bosses that he had to "refine" his management techniques and was demoted; he later resigned.[213] His fears proved to be chillingly prophetic, however; for even more disturbing than the claims of amnesia or anxiety were subsequent reports that Halcion could cause bizarre delusions, hostile paranoia, and delirious behavior in some users. "Upjohn may believe such reactions are flukes, no more likely with one benzodiazepine than another, but the company has never convincingly explained Halcion's remarkable ability to generate weird stories."[214] These include the following eruptions of hallucinations, rage, suicide, and murder:

❖ In 1986, a retired New Orleans railroad clerk was prescribed Halcion after surgery for lymphoma. After taking the drug for several months (Upjohn now recommends administration for no more than 7–10 days), he began to undergo a significant personality change. He regularly screamed at his invalid mother and 92-year-old aunt, then quickly forgot each incident. Only after he saw a television feature on the controversy surrounding Halcion did the confused man decide to stop taking it. It reportedly took his doctor 2 months to wean him from the drug, after which his former mild-mannered personality returned.[215]

❖ In 1987, a 65-year-old Texas retiree was prescribed Halcion after complaining of insomnia. During the 8 months he took the drug, "he terrorized his wife, attempted suicide, talked of murder and was twice committed to a mental hospital."[216] Although the man admittedly had a history of psychological instability and problems with alcohol, he maintained that he had never been violent, aggressive, or suicidal until taking Halcion.[217] He filed a suit against Upjohn after watching a news story about Halcion. In 1994, however, a federal jury ruled against him in his litigation, believing that he was already unstable before taking Halcion.[218]

❖ Also in 1987, a partially disabled former Texas police officer placed the barrel of a rifle to the head of a sleeping friend and pulled the trigger, while the two men were away on a hunting trip. After returning home from the cabin a few hours later, the man telephoned the county sheriff's office and reported that he had "had to kill an ol' boy,"[219] whose name he could not even remember. His lawyers later contended that he had been suffering catastrophic side effects from the

(Continued)

extended use of Halcion. At the time of the killing, he had been taking Halcion for about 700 days, "690 days longer than is now recommended."[220] His dose was also double the current maximum.

The man was convicted of murder and sentenced to life in prison. The Halcion issue was never raised at his trial because the drug's alleged effects were still not widely known. In fact, he had continued to take Halcion while in jail awaiting trial and had attempted suicide there twice.

When he appealed for a new trial, one of his allies was Dallas psychiatrist James Grigson. Known as "Dr. Death," Grigson has testified in over 140 capital murder cases, almost always for the *prosecution*. Yet Grigson said he was "100% sure" that the defendant was legally insane when he shot his friend and was equally certain that Halcion was the sole cause of his insanity.[221] Nevertheless, the defendant was denied a new trial because Texas law requires that new trial motions based on newly discovered evidence must be made within 60 days. In a curious twist, a Dallas jury awarded the convicted murderer $2.15 million in a 1992 lawsuit, ruling that Upjohn had been "grossly negligent in marketing a defective product—Halcion."[222] In 1994, however, a Texas appeals court reversed the decision and nullified the award, ruling that Upjohn had caused the plaintiff no injury.[223]

❖ In 1988, a municipal judge in Orange County, California, who had just won re-election, shot himself to death. Friends and acquaintances initially were baffled, but the victim's family later blamed Upjohn, declaring that his 3 years of Halcion use after a 1985 automobile accident had caused the erratic mental state which drove him to suicide.[224]

❖ Also in 1988, a 57-year-old Utah woman pumped eight bullets into the head of her sleeping 83-year-old mother. The woman had been taking Halcion for several months prior to the shooting and had no memory of the killing. In contrast to the Texas shooting, "[c]ourt-ordered psychiatrists found [she] was 'involuntarily intoxicated' on Halcion at the time of the shooting, and [she] was never prosecuted."[225] The woman later settled a multi-million dollar lawsuit against Upjohn shortly before her civil case came to trial in 1991.[226] To make an already tragic story even worse, however, the woman's memory of what she had done gradually began to return, and she took her own life in 1994.[227]

❖ In 1990, a police officer in Kalamazoo, Michigan, who had been convicted and imprisoned for stabbing his estranged wife in the heart 6 years earlier, was acquitted at a retrial. According to new testimony, he had taken a double dose of Halcion 3 hours before the near-fatal attack and claimed no memory of the crime. After seeing a television magazine program describing Halcion's possible side effects, he became convinced that the drug had fueled his assaultive rage. He appealed his conviction and eventually won his freedom.[228]

❖ In 1991, a 37-year-old Colorado businessman, who had been taking Halcion for about 3 weeks, woke up in a psychotic frenzy. He began rolling up the carpets in his home while babbling incoherently to his wife. Later, he went on a rampage, barging into neighbors' houses acting out a "Wild West" fantasy. When he tried to

(Continued)

grab a police officer's gun, he was restrained and taken to a local hospital. Criminal charges were subsequently dismissed, and the man was sent home after the district attorney became convinced that his irrational conduct had been caused by Halcion.[229]

❖ In 1992, a 45-year-old New York advertising executive bludgeoned his father into a coma. He had been visiting his parents' home in Laguna Hills, California, just after his mother's death. He and his father had been drinking into the night, and his father gave him some Halcion to help him sleep. He testified that he awoke during the night and mistook his father for a grotesque intruder, with a face that appeared to have "melted." He called 911 and reported the intruder, but when police arrived they found his father lying in a pool of blood, "his skull split from neck to forehead."[230] The victim later died without ever regaining consciousness. A criminal jury acquitted the defendant, blaming the horrifying act on the combination of alcohol and Halcion.[231]

❖ In 1993, a 56-year-old Houston nurse settled a lawsuit against Upjohn for an undisclosed amount of money. She claimed she had become psychotic after taking the drug for more than 2 years. The suit alleged that she had grown "paranoid, aggressive, suicidal, and totally irrational."[232] As a result, she had been locked up in a mental institution for 2 weeks.

❖ In 1994, two widows from the same small Kentucky town settled separate negligence suits against Upjohn. The women contended that their husbands had each committed suicide while under the influence of Halcion.[233]

❖ Also in 1994, a lawsuit was filed in federal court in Texas charging that Upjohn, along with the FDA and others, had concealed Halcion's dangerous side effects. This was the first case to go beyond specific adverse reactions and allege a full-blown conspiracy among manufacturer, researchers, regulators, and lawyers.[234] One of the plaintiffs claimed he had experienced "personality changes, paranoia, depression, hostility and aggression" while taking Halcion.[235] The other asserted she had suffered "memory loss, mood swings, temperament changes and violent rages" attributable to the drug.[236] She also said that she had contemplated suicide and threatened her husband with a gun.

It remains to be seen how successful this latter case—or any of the other pending Halcion lawsuits[237]—will be. Thus far, Upjohn has fared quite well in court. It has lost only one jury verdict and, as noted, that award was overturned on appeal. It has also made out-of-court settlements in a number of other cases for amounts believed to be relatively modest. Upjohn employs the same high-powered law firm that has represented the tobacco industry with so much ferocity in recent years,[238] so the failure of Halcion litigation is no big surprise.

However, a new FDA report issued in 1996 finally acknowledged what critics have alleged for two decades: that Upjohn had "suppressed, minimized and misrepresented" the lethal dangers posed by Halcion.[239] The report urged the Justice Department to investigate whether Upjohn had suppressed early test results. Upjohn denies any legal or ethical transgressions and has declared

(Continued)

that it "puts nothing ahead of patients' health."[240] Perhaps so, but the head of psychiatry at a major medical school offers a markedly different assessment of Halcion:

> This is a very dangerous drug. . . . No other benzodiazepine has such a narrow margin of safety. The only justification for keeping it on the market is to ensure the company's profitability. From a public-health standpoint, there is no reason at all.[241]

Medical devices constitute a category of consumer products that has come to be recognized as requiring its own form of government regulation. An example of the types of cases included under this category would be that of an Indiana man who sold *used* heart pacemakers. Some had been dropped on the floor during surgery; others had been determined to be faulty and were removed from patients' chests. The pacemakers were sent to Indiana, sterilized, repackaged, and sold as new.[242] The irresponsible entrepreneur, Michael M. Walton, was convicted of fraud in 1994 and received a 6-year sentence.[243] In 1993, a Boston company that made heart catheters agreed in a plea bargain to pay $61 million in fines to settle a case in which it was accused of using patients as "guinea pigs" to test new products. The tests resulted in the death of at least one patient. The company lied to the FDA and covered up malfunctions in the catheters, which sometimes had failed to deflate in patients' arteries and had broken off inside their hearts, necessitating emergency surgeries. The federal prosecutor maintained that the acts were "aimed at enriching the company which made tens of millions of dollars off the sale of adulterated catheters."[244]

The Food, Drug, and Cosmetic Act of 1938 placed medical devices under federal control, and they were first subjected to premarket review under the Medical Device Amendments of 1976.[245] Those amendments were enacted primarily in response to a single case, that of the Dalkon Shield.

The Dalkon Shield was an intrauterine birth control device (IUD) marketed by the A. H. Robins Company, a major pharmaceutical manufacturer. Between 1971 and 1974, 2.2 million American women were fitted with the Dalkon Shield. Robins trumpeted it as "the safest and most satisfying form of contraception."[246] The company had bought the device from a small Connecticut firm owned by its inventor. At a production cost of 35 cents per unit and a wholesale price (to doctors) of around $4, Robins had reason to believe it had struck gold.

The company launched the most aggressive promotional campaign in its history. So eager was Robins to sell the shield that it never took the time to test the device adequately. All its data were based on a single medical study of questionable validity conducted by the inventor, who obviously had a financial stake in the success of the device.[247] With every bogus claim, Robins added another room to its house of lies. The Dalkon Shield turned out to be one of the most immorally misrepresented products ever exposed.

In addition to being unsafe, the shield was not even very effective. Five percent of its wearers became pregnant, a statistic far removed from the 1.1% the company falsely advertised. Many of the women who conceived with the shield in place had a previously rare type of miscarriage known as spontaneous abortion. Still others, in the second trimester, experienced the even rarer infected miscarriage, or septic abortion.[248] The cause of infection was a design defect in the wick used to insert and remove the device; "[I]t served as a pathway for bacteria-laden fluids to travel up into the uterus."[249] Robins became aware of this problem early, but continued fraudulently misrepresenting the shield. When one employee spoke up about his concerns over the safety of the device, he was reprimanded for insubordination and threatened with dismissal.[250]

At least 20 women died as a result of the Dalkon Shield. In addition, hundreds of others who conceived while wearing the shield gave birth prematurely to infants with "grave congenital defects, including blindness, cerebral palsy, and mental retardation."[251] Thousands of women were left with reproductive organs so badly scarred that they would never again be able to conceive children.

A. H. Robins declared bankruptcy in 1986, after paying out more than $378 million to settle 9200 lawsuits. In 1989, a federal judge accepted a plan to reorganize the company that included the creation of a $2.5 billion fund to compensate victims.[252]

Breast Implants

In 1985, a Florida woman discovered that she had been chemically poisoned:

> I looked down at my blouse, meaning to straighten it, and gasped. The blouse was becoming soaked with a foul-smelling liquid. . . . Inside the hospital, I could not stand unaided; I could not sign my name, and I could barely speak.[253]

As this harrowing first-person account attests, the successor to the Dalkon Shield as the medical device most likely to cause innocent women agony is the silicone-gel breast implant. For three decades, 150,000 women received these implants each year. Because they had already been in wide use, the implants had escaped the official scrutiny imposed by the Medical Devices Amendment of 1976. But in 1992, after a review of the industry's safety claims, the FDA called an immediate halt to breast enlargement using silicone implants.

> FDA advisers reviewed evidence submitted by several implant makers and ruled that none really knew whether its product was safe. The devices have been known to leak or rupture, bleeding silicone into the body. But the makers hadn't determined how often that happens or with what possible consequences. Nor could the manufacturers say . . . how often migrating silicone prompts the immune system to attack healthy tissues.[254]

Corporate memos revealed in subsequent litigation have shown that scientists working for Dow Corning, the leading producer of silicone implants, were worried about leaks and ruptures since the 1970s.[255] One of its own engineers had warned the company that it was conducting "experimental surgery on humans."[256] A few months after the moratorium, Dow Corning further disclosed that it had faked the quality control records of some implants it had produced.[257]

In 1993, a consumer research group accused Dow Corning of withholding data from long-term toxicity studies, in which laboratory animals had allegedly suffered negative effects from silicone, including birth defects, nervous system disorders, and death.[258] A preliminary study conducted at a New York medical center hinted that children who were breast-fed by mothers with silicone gel implants may develop symptoms of an autoimmune attack.[259] By that point, the silicone implant industry was effectively out of business. The remainder of the story is a tale of high-stakes consumer litigation and corporate accountability.

A federal jury in Georgia awarded $5.4 million (later reduced by the judge to $2.27 million) to a 31-year-old librarian whose implants, manufactured by Baxter Healthcare, ruptured, leaving her with immune system disorders attributed to silicone.[260] A Texas jury recommended a record award of $25 million to a 45-year-old woman who said she developed an autoimmune disease from ruptured silicone-gel breast implants manufactured by the Medical Engineering Corporation.[261] Another Texas jury awarded three women a total of $27.9 million in damages in a lawsuit charging the 3M Corporation and two smaller companies with the manufacture of leaking implants that caused severe illnesses. A few weeks later, 3M announced that it had agreed to contribute $325 million to a fund to compensate women who had received its implants.[262]

In 1994, Dow Corning agreed to pay $4.25 billion to cover liability claims against its implants.[263] A year later, the company raced into bankruptcy protection after determining that its $4.25 billion settlement fund was inadequate to cover the 300,000 to 400,000 impending claims.[264] In addition to claims of immune system disorders, other victims have charged that their defective implants had caused diseases such as rheumatoid arthritis, scleroderma, and lupus erythematosus.[265]

As a result of the Dow Corning bankruptcy, women who alleged that silicon breast implants had caused them serious health problems began suing Dow Chemical, which (along with Corning, Inc.) owned Dow Corning. Dow previously had been insulated from liability. However, a Nevada jury ordered the corporation to pay $10 million to a 46-year-old woman who had developed skin disorders and tremors from her implants.[266]

The first class action suit regarding silicone implants was filed against Dow in Louisiana on behalf of 1800 women. In 1997 a jury held Dow liable, finding that the company was negligent and intentionally had withheld information from women and their doctors about implant dangers.[267]

Even the newer saline-filled breast implants, which have replaced the silicon ones, are not without serious risks. In 2000, a government advisory board reported that saline implants "break open at 'alarmingly high' rates and require women to undergo repeated surgeries."[268] About 130,000 women receive saline implants each year, and up to 27% are removed within 3 years following implantation. Most of these removed implants have leaked into patients' bodies. Some are blackened with fungus and blamed for infections and excruciating breast pain. The FDA has never declared saline-filled implants safe.[269]

C A S E   S T U D Y

Rely Tampons

Procter & Gamble is one of the largest, best known, and successful corporations in the United States. Its products are found in virtually every American home. But beneath the company's "99 44/100% pure" image, lurks an amoral tale of greed, power, and death: the story of the Rely tampon.

In the 1960s, researchers at Procter & Gamble began working on an ultraabsorbent tampon that was expected to dominate the feminine hygiene industry. Made of super-thirsty synthetics like polyester and a derivative of wood pulp, Rely (as the product would be named) was ballyhooed as the most effective sanitary protection item ever developed.[270] Tampons had been made of cotton since their invention in the 1930s by a Denver barber, who called his product Tampax.[271]

Rely tampons were introduced to the general public in early 1980 after 5 years of test marketing. One of the test sites was Rochester, New York, where free samples were distributed. A local consumer advocate immediately began getting phone calls from women reporting vomiting and diarrhea after using Rely. She asked Procter & Gamble for a copy of its safety records but was refused. The company blamed the adverse reactions on allergies. It failed to mention that it was already receiving more than 100 complaints per month about a product not yet even widely available.[272]

In 1980, *60 million* sample packages of Rely were sent to 80% of U.S. households. By the middle of the year, Rely had captured a quarter of the tampon market and was on the verge of overtaking industry leader Tampax. That same year, however, the CDC began observing a startling phenomenon. It identified 55 fatal cases and 1066 nonfatal case of toxic shock syndrome. This rare disease was beginning to surface primarily in young, menstruating women.[273]

Symptoms of the disease . . . include high fever, a sunburnlike rash, and low blood pressure. After a while, a victim's skin peels off the hands and feet. Breathing becomes difficult, and the lungs fill with fluid until she suffocates or her heart stops. The name is derived from the severe prolonged shock that accompanies the illness.[274]

The CDC informed Procter & Gamble that it was preparing to conduct a study of toxic shock and tampon use. Procter & Gamble's response was the same as

(Continued)

it had been for the 5 years it had known of the danger: say nothing and do nothing. "The company instructed its sales force not to discuss toxic shock. . . . But if asked, the salespeople were given canned answers that denied any link between tampons and toxic shock."[275] The only notable action Procter & Gamble took was to postpone a major high school promotion it had planned.

Women continued to complain that they became ill after using Rely. In July 1980, the death of an Ohio woman—the mother of a 6-month-old infant—was strongly linked to Rely. In September, the CDC concluded its study, in which 70% of the victims of toxic shock syndrome reportedly had used Rely.

On September 21, 1980, Procter & Gamble announced it was pulling Rely from the shelves. "Though Procter & Gamble is often lauded for voluntarily withdrawing Rely . . . it seems clear the company didn't act until the FDA threatened to act for them. And the FDA didn't act until women died."[276]

The day after the announcement, Procter & Gamble met with the FDA.

> P&G spent much of the meeting debating whether the action would be called a withdrawal or a recall. P&G disliked "recall" because it seemed to imply safety violations. Exasperated FDA officials finally said, "If you don't want to call it a recall, we'll call it a *banana*." During the meeting, that's exactly how they referred to it.[277]

Procter & Gamble signed a court agreement, under which it undertook a massive advertising campaign to notify women to stop using Rely tampons. It also agreed to buy back the product from consumers. However, the company adamantly refused to admit that Rely was defective or that the company had done anything wrong.

Procter & Gamble was sued by a Cedar Rapids, Iowa, man whose 24-year-old wife had died of toxic shock syndrome in 1980, 4 days after she began using Rely and 2 weeks before the product was taken off the market. Although the evidence seemed compelling, suing a giant corporation like Proctor & Gamble is never easy. The plaintiff reportedly was bullied by an army of P&G lawyers in his deposition. He was asked irrelevant questions about his late wife's sexual history, e.g., whether she had engaged in oral sex with him, whether she had ever been sexually promiscuous with other men. "The idea was to humiliate and scare him into settling the case before it went to trial."[278]

Procter & Gamble also mobilized its almost limitless financial resources, along with its enormous influence in the scientific community. The plaintiff's attorney found it nearly impossible to enlist physicians as expert witnesses because Procter & Gamble quickly offered lucrative research grants to any doctors researching toxic shock, with the stipulation that all findings be submitted to the company prior to submission for publication.[279] One scientist, whose findings (critical of Rely) had already been reported in the *Wall Street Journal*, renounced them after he had received several hundred thousand dollars in grant money from Procter & Gamble.[280] Another researcher testified for the defense that Rely tampons were *not* to blame for toxic shock. "He too had received P&G grants."[281]

(Continued)

Procter & Gamble conducted several mock trials in Lincoln, Nebraska, a city chosen for its demographic similarity to Cedar Rapids. "Jurors" were questioned about what they liked and disliked in the simulated testimony. "Just as it used focus groups to determine the best way to market toothpaste and detergent, P&G researched how to sell itself in a courtroom. On the third try, its attorneys got the verdict they wanted."[282] The company even distributed free samples of its products throughout Cedar Rapids before the trial in a transparent effort to drum up good will.[283]

However, despite all its legal and public relations clout, Procter & Gamble had left a paper trail. One especially damning memo, written well before the victim's death, disclosed the corporation's decision *not* to release warnings about toxic shock.[284] Unlike the mock jury in Lincoln, the real one in Cedar Rapids ruled in favor of the plaintiff and awarded him $300,000.

At least 38 deaths from toxic shock syndrome have been attributed to Rely tampons. Since Rely was taken off the market, the CDC reports that the number of toxic shock cases has dropped dramatically.[285] Procter & Gamble has long since settled most of the other Rely litigation, including that of a St. Louis girl who became sick and died after using Rely, 2 weeks before her sixteenth birthday.

> By the end of the month, she had trouble breathing and tried to free herself from the hospital respirator. Doctors had to tranquilize her to keep her calm. In late September, she suffered cardiac arrest.[286]

The young victim's attorney, a former Republican state senator, remains bitter at Procter & Gamble to this day: "If this was the socially responsible company that they pretend they are, this little girl would be alive. . . . With all the power the bastards had to get out the word, they could've saved her life."[287]

Quackery

Quackery refers both to medical products that are worthless and to persons who cannot deliver the miraculous cures they promise.[288] There are no swindlers more depraved than those who prey on the ill. Sadly, the United States has a history of tolerance for medical quackery that is perhaps unmatched. The roots of this permissiveness may be traced back to the Colonial era, when such questionable remedies as Daffy's Elixer, Turlington's Balsam of Life, and Bateman's Pectoral Drops were sold by merchants of every stripe.[289]

By the eve of the twentieth century, patent medicines had become an important American industry. A single vendor, such as the maker of the widely popular Pinkham's Vegetable Compound, might spend about $1 million per year on advertising alone.[290] Competition was keen—whether it was Palmer's Hole in the Wall Capsules or Aunt Fanny's Worm Candy, name recognition was considered crucial. The particular formula might change from time to time, and the diseases for which medicines were touted might vary, but the trademark endured.[291]

Then came the Food and Drug Act of 1906. Within 2 years, the first quackery trial under the new statute took place, pitting the federal government against Robert N. Harper, the manufacturer of a favored remedy named Cuforhedake Brane-Fude (pronounced "cure-for-headache brain food"). Harper was convicted, and President Theodore Roosevelt personally urged the prosecutor to seek a prison term for the defendant in order to make an example of him. The judge, however, did not lock Harper up, but instead fined him $700, perhaps initiating a tradition of wrist slapping that remains a feature of many white-collar crime sentences to this day. Because Harper had made $2 million from Cuforhedake Brane-Fude,[292] it seems safe to deduce that he came out substantially ahead.

Present-day quackery is big business, robbing consumers of $25 billion each year.[293] In the words of the FDA, "Difficult to curtail, health frauds, like crab grass, sprout up here, there, and everywhere."[294] Quackery flourishes because it appeals to emotion, rather than reason. An official of the Consumer Health Information Institute has declared, "Quacks provide simple answers to complex problems. The one cause, one cure solution is very comforting."[295]

Teenagers, impatient with the pace of puberty, are one fertile ground for quackery.[296] However, as is the case with most categories of consumer fraud, the elderly are the primary targets, contributing $10 billion (40%) to the total spent.[297] Besides being the fastest-growing segment of the population, the elderly are, understandably, the most ailment prone. The fact that "80% of America's elderly have at least one chronic health problem that restricts them one out of every 12 days"[298] leaves elderly people especially vulnerable to fraudulent gimmicks and concoctions. Sixty percent of those who resort to untested therapies are over age 65.[299]

Quackery can entail more than just fraud; there is also a heavy human and social cost. Quackery can delay timely and appropriate treatment of medical conditions and cause severe illness or death.[300] Some products and services are not only useless, but lethal. One expert has declared that "quackery kills more people than those who die from all crimes of violence put together."[301] Many of these ultimate victims are far from elderly. Consider the example of a 16-year-old diabetic girl in Montana, whose parents were convinced by a mystical quack that her daily insulin injections were unnecessary. "By tapping her chest, he said he could stimulate their daughter's own insulin-making capacity." The girl died in 3 days. A short time later, her parents received a $6325 bill for chest-tapping services rendered.[302]

Quackery at its most venal thrives on persons who are afflicted with life-threatening illnesses for which there are no known cures. This has never been more apparent than in the promotion of bogus AIDS treatments. Desperate consumers spend an estimated $1 billion annually on fraudulent AIDS remedies.[303] Underground "guerrilla clinics" offering homemade treatments have sprung up all over the world.[304] Quacks invent scientific-sounding rationales for their therapies.[305] In 1990, for instance, a California doctor began injecting some of his HIV patients with typhoid vaccine in order to activate the syphilis virus, which he then expected to eradicate, along with the HIV virus. He reportedly had read about this untested and unapproved procedure in a music magazine called *SPIN*.[306] Among other pseudoscientific therapies are herbal tea made from the bark of Brazilian trees,[307] injections of hydrogen peroxide, pills derived from the cells of infected mice, baths in a chlorine bleach solution, and timed exposure of the genitals and rectum to the sun's rays.[308]

The chairman of a health fraud prevention organization observed, "Everything has been converted into an AIDS treatment."[309] Capsules containing poisonous metals are dispensed. Processed algae (nicknamed "pond scum") sells for $20 per bottle. "One man masquerading as a Ph.D. was injecting his patients with a processed byproduct of their own urine at $100 per injection."[310] A European quack reportedly squeezed big profits from the misery of sick and dying people by selling them a costly and potentially dangerous powder based on an extract of human excrement.[311]

Other afflictions also attract their share of quackery. Thalassotherapy, a spa-styled seaweed bath, promises to relieve stress and chronic fatigue syndrome.[312] A magnet placed in men's briefs has been sold as a treatment for impotence, as has an exotic nostrum named "Crocodile Penis Pills."[313]

Snake venom has been peddled to arthritis patients,[314] and shark-cartilage pills have been purported to prevent cancer.[315] This latter claim was the basis of a popular 1993 book, *Sharks Don't Get Cancer*.[316] However, sharks *do* get cancer, so the entire premise of the book is fallacious. Nevertheless, Americans have spent millions of dollars on shark cartilage supplements in the desperate hope of curing their malignancies.[317]

Gerovital, a Romanian dental anesthetic, was brought to the United States illegally and sold as a cure for angina, hypertension, depression, deafness, diabetes, and Parkinson's disease. No health claims have ever been substantiated for Gerovital, and it has caused respiratory difficulties and convulsions in some users.[318] Germanium, a nonessential element marketed as a dietary supplement, has been promoted as a treatment for Alzheimer's disease. Germanium is worse than ineffective; it has caused irreversible kidney damage and death.[319]

In 1998, a Virginia doctor was indicted on charges of fraud for allegedly hastening the death of four cancer patients by treating them with intravenous doses of T-UP, a trade name for an aloe vera solution. Intravenous use of aloe vera is not approved by the FDA and is illegal in the United States. The doctor's assistant, a former automobile mechanic who allegedly administered many of the intravenous treatments, was charged with nursing without a license.[320] Also charged with consumer fraud were the owners of T-UP, Inc., of Maryland. That state's attorney general, Joseph Curran, Jr., called it the most "egregious" fraud he had ever seen: "These men are the 1990's version of snake oil salesmen. They're dealing with a very, very vulnerable group, and the claims they've made to people who are suffering from these terrible diseases border on sinister."[321]

One of the unfortunate patients was a 57-year-old bricklayer with prostate cancer. The Virginia clinic had promised to shrink his grapefruit-sized tumor to the size of a pea.

"Within two days of beginning intravenous aloe vera treatments . . . [his] body turned purple and began to swell. The skin on his toes cracked open. He died a painful death.[322]

Chelation therapy is touted as a cure for arteriosclerosis (hardening of the arteries). Patients receive intravenous infusions of an amino acid, which purportedly flushes plaque from clogged blood vessels. "No one has ever substantiated this claim."[323] Cellular therapy consists of injections of DNA isolated from the fetuses of sheep and cattle. It is promoted for treating heart attacks as well as such conditions as colitis, Down syndrome, acne, radiation damage, senility, and sterility. Not only is this unapproved treatment worthless, it can transmit animal viruses, including the one that causes the deadly type of bovine encephalitis known as "mad cow disease."[324]

For years, metabolic therapy—which allegedly detoxifies the body through the use of unproved drugs and bizarre procedures such as *coffee enemas*—has been promoted as an unorthodox cure for cancer. "The American Cancer Society has not been able to trace a single documented cure of cancer by metabolic therapy, yet thousands of Americans continue to try it—typically at a cost of $6000 (payable in advance) for a three-week session at a clinic."[325] Patients who go to these quack clinics (many of them in Mexico) often abandon legitimate cancer treatments.[326] Actor Steve McQueen died of lung cancer in 1980 while undergoing "treatment" at a metabolic clinic in Tijuana.[327]

There are three basic forms of quackery:

Nutrition.   "Unsound nutrition claims are made on radio, television, in newspapers, books, and magazines, from persons ranging from self-designated 'nutrition experts' to graduates of unaccredited correspondence schools selling nutrition products and services of questionable merit, if any."[328] A 47-year-old Pennsylvania woman, for example, was told she had cervical cancer. Her doctors rated her chance of recovery at 90% if she underwent an immediate hysterectomy. Instead, she visited a macrobiotic diet center where she was told that proper foods would cure her disease. She postponed the needed surgery and embarked on a diet of brown rice and roots, which supposedly could bring her body's opposing forces of yin and yang into balance. A "nutrition consultant" persuaded the wife of a 67-year-old Pennsylvania man with colon cancer that a special diet would bring remission. He prescribed raw vegetables and the juices of wheat grass and watermelon rind.[329]

In addition to their state of residence and their reliance on peculiar dietary regimens, the unfortunate patients in the preceding illustrations share another thing in common. Within a few months of starting their respective "treatments," they were both dead.

Drugs.   The eternal dream of discovering the Fountain of Youth has created a boom market for fake anti-aging drugs. Zumba Forte, derived from the bark of the West African yohimbe tree, is billed as a "sexual tonic" and aphrodisiac for older men. It acts as an alpha-adrenergic receptor blocking agent and can cause dangerously low blood pressure.[330] Another spurious rejuvenator, methyltestosterone, is a chemical derivative of the male sex hormone. It can cause liver and prostate cancer, as well as hepatitis, jaundice, and testicular atrophy.[331]

In the United States, the quest for a slender body is nearly as universal as the search for immortality. For years, the back pages of many popular magazines and supermarket tabloids have contained advertisements for miraculous over-the-counter diet pills. Promises that overweight customers can lose 6 to 10 pounds per week, without exercise, while wolfing down fried chicken, ice cream, and cheeseburgers, are the centerpiece of such ads. The *Healthy Weight Journal* reports that it has never found a single mail order diet pill that could live up to its advertised claims.[332] In the well-chosen words of New York City's commissioner of consumer affairs, those claims are a "fat lie."[333]

One brand of diet pill, known as Cal-Ban 3000, was recalled by the FDA as a health hazard. Cal-Ban contained a vegetable gum that swells when it absorbs moisture. The idea was that the swelling in the user's stomach would make dieters feel more full. The problem was that, when taken with water, the gum could swell up in the throat and cause a dangerous obstruction. In several cases, surgery was required to remove a mass of Cal-Ban. The product was linked to numerous serious injuries and at least one death.[334]

Devices.   There is a labyrinthine array of quack devices currently available to consumers. Some of them are merely incredible, such as the use of gemstones to "cure" a multitude of maladies.[335] Some are truly ridiculous, such as "Chinese Magic Weight-Loss Earrings."[336] Some are even spectacular in their absurdity. Four million women have spent $9.95 for a foot-operated breast enlarger. How this device even functions is barely imaginable. It offers users a choice of three cup sizes—"large, larger, and even larger."[337]

Magnetic therapy has become a hot trend of the early twenty-first century—a trend so lucrative that some professional athletes are adding brand name magnets to their list of endorsements. Americans now spend more than $500 million per year on magnetic mattress pads, back wraps, shoe inserts, seat cushions, and bracelets, although magnetic therapy has never been approved by the FDA.[338] In the interest of full disclosure, it should be noted that one of the authors of this book now regularly wears a magnetic bracelet, much to the chagrin of the other authors.

Because of its painful symptoms and high incidence rate, arthritis particularly has long attracted charlatans hawking weird therapeutic contraptions to desperate sufferers. The most famous of these is the copper bracelet, which has sold for as much as $35 or more. In a single year, 50 million of these pieces of junk were peddled.[339] Countless other elaborate devices have also falsely claimed to cure arthritis. "Among these are the Zerret Applicator, the Spectro-Chrome, Neurocalometer, Oscilloclast, Roto-View, Blender Queen, Relaxacisor, Micro-dynameter, Diapulse, E-meter, and the Detoxacolon, many of which are supposed to benefit the arthritic by using various colored lights to cast 'healing' rays."[340]

An especially outlandish device was the Magic Spike—a small brass tube, the inside of which supposedly was radioactive. (It was not.) For treatment of arthritis, the tube was to be placed over the affected joint. This strange product was marketed as a cure-all and had many other purported uses that were just as senseless. For example, persons with high blood pressure were instructed to wear it low on the body, so it could "pull" their blood pressure down. The Magic Spike sold for $306.[341] When its two promoters were convicted of fraud, they were each sentenced to 1 year in prison. The trial judge denounced them as "despicable quacks" and stated that he regretted that could not hand them longer terms.[342]

One quack who did receive a longer term was British citizen Basil Wainwright, who was sentenced in 1994 to 37 months in a federal prison for selling unapproved ozone generators as a cure for cancer and AIDS. The scheme swindled investors and desperate patients out of hundreds of thousands of dollars. "At least three patients who bought the 'cure' died."[343] Ozone is a toxic form of oxygen with no accepted medical uses in the United States. Wainwright's devices were sold to individuals who were instructed to administer the ozone gas through the rectum or vagina. Ozone reacts with the body to cause several potentially dangerous effects, including damage to the immune system and irritation of tissues lining the respiratory tract.[344] An FDA official described Wainwright as a "'career criminal' who has spent almost his entire adult life perpetrating frauds and [has] left a trail of human misery in his wake."[345]

C A S E   S T U D Y

The King of the Quacks

In 1943, a Louisiana politician named Dudley LeBlanc began selling a tonic he had mixed in barrels behind his barn. He named his elixer Hadacol. Legend has it that when LeBlanc was asked where he found that name he replied, "Hadacol it something!" Hadacol was a blend of B vitamins, some minerals, honey, diluted hydrochloric acid, and plenty of alcohol. (Some Southern druggists dispensed Hadacol in shot glasses.) LeBlanc claimed that Hadacol could relieve an implausible range of ailments: "anemia, arthritis, asthma, diabetes, epilepsy, heart trouble, high and low blood pressure, gallstones, paralysis, and ulcers."[346] Almost immediately, it generated astonishing profits, and LeBlanc would become the most successful quack in American history. One pharmacist recalled, "They came in to buy Hadacol when they didn't have money to buy food. They had holes in their shoes and they paid $3.50 a bottle for Hadacol."[347]

By 1950, LeBlanc was grossing more than $20 million dollars annually, with an advertising budget of a million dollars per month. His spectacular traveling medicine show featured such big-name performers as George Burns and Gracie Allen, Judy Garland, Mickey Rooney, Carmen Miranda, Cesar Romero, Minnie Pearl, and two of the Marx Brothers.

(Continued)

Eventually, LeBlanc caught the attention of the Food and Drug Administration, as well as the Federal Trade Commission and the Bureau of Internal Revenue.[348] Against such formidable opposition, the Hadicol bubble inevitably burst.

Was Hadacol really good for anything? Dudley LeBlanc himself was once asked that question in a television interview. His response: "[I]t was good for five and a half million for me last year."[349]

NOTES

1. This vignette was suggested by the boyhood reminiscences of a former smoker who has become a leading antitobacco crusader (White, Larry C. *Merchants of Death: The American Tobacco Industry*. NY: Beech Tree Books, 1988). According to the World Bank, tobacco-related diseases, such as those that took the lives of Bogart and Murrow, kill about 3 million people per year worldwide, and the annual death toll is expected to climb to 10 million by 2025 ("Toll From Tobacco." *Houston Chronicle*. June 4, 1996: 6A).

2. "Addiction by Design?" *New York Times*. March 6, 1994: E14.

3. Vedantam, Shankar. "Tobacco Industry, Government Debate Researchers' Findings." *Houston Chronicle*. March 30, 1996: 6A.

4. Schwartz, John. "Philip Morris Phrase Could Burn the Firm." *Houston Chronicle*. December 9, 1995: 4A.

5. Freedman, Alix M. "Philip Morris Memo Likens Nicotine to Cocaine." *Wall Street Journal*. December 8, 1995: B1, B14.

6. From "Research Planning Memorandum on the Nature of the Tobacco Business and the Crucial Role of Nicotine Therein," 1972. Quoted in "Tobacco Firm's Documents Note Smoking-Drug Analogy." *USA Today*. October 6, 1995: 4D.

7. Quoted in Shapiro, Eben. "Tobacco Firms May Face New Pressure with Disclosure of Executive's Memo." *Wall Street Journal*. May 9, 1994: A4.

8. Quoted in *Ibid.*, p. A4.

9. Stolberg, Sheryl. "Tobacco Exec Lied to Congress About Nicotine, Scientist Charges." *Houston Chronicle*. January 27, 1996: 4A.

10. Scwartz, John. "Tobacco Files Show Firms Discussed Burying Research." *Houston Chronicle*. September 18, 1996: 2A.

11. "Another Nail in Coffin of Tobacco Firms' Credibility." *USA Today*. October 24, 1996: 12A.

12. Mishra, Raja. "More Fuel for the Fire." *Houston Chronicle*. April 23, 1998: 11A.

13. Quoted in "Mostly Smoke." *Newsweek*. July 4, 1994: 45

14. Shapiro, *op. cit.*

15. Mishra, *op. cit.*, p. 11A.

16. The tobacco industry is often cited as an example of an oligopoly—a market completely controlled by a handful of companies. Philip Morris USA and R. J. Reynolds control about 70% of the market, with the remaining share divided among Brown & Williamson, the American Tobacco Company, Liggett Group, Inc., Lorillard Tobacco, and the United States Tobacco Company.

17. Quoted in Wall, James M. "The market Monster." *Christian Century* 112, August 16, 1995: 763.

18. Marwick, Charles. "Tobacco Hearings: Penetrating the Smoke Screen." *JAMA* 271, 1994: 1562.

19. Friend, Tim. "New Heat on Tobacco Firm." *USA Today*, March 19, 1996: 1A; also: "Tobacco Industry Under Fire." *USA Today*. March 19, 1996: 2B.

20. Quoted in "Nicotine Manipulated, Ex-Officials Say." *Houston Chronicle*. March 19, 1996: 6A.

21. Hohler, Bob. "Firm Admits Nicotine Boost in Cigarettes." *Boston Globe*. January 8, 1998: A3.

22. Levy, Doug. "AMA: Public 'Duped' by Tobacco Firms." *USA Today*. July 14, 1995: 1A.

23. Quoted in Schwartz, John. "Battle Cry Is Sounded on Tobacco." *Houston Chronicle.* July 14, 1995: 1A, 14A.

24. "With Clout Fading, Tobacco Companies Are on the Run." *USA Today.* March 15, 1996: 12A.

25. Cox, Patrick. "Cut Companies Some Slack." *USA Today.* March 15, 1996: 12A.

26. Levin, Myron. "Tobacco Industry Targeted Stop-Smoking Products." *Houston Chronicle.* February 14, 1999: 10A, 11A.

27. Quoted in *Ibid.,* p. 11A.

28. An alleged smoking victim was "successful" in a lower court in a 1983 New Jersey case, but the jury verdict was overturned by a federal judge ("$2 Million Award in Cigarette Asbestos Case." *Houston Chronicle.* September 2, 1995: 11A).

29. Levy, Doug. "Partial Deal Expected in Tobacco Suit." *USA Today.* March 13, 1996: 1A. In 1988, the survivors of a New Jersey woman won $400,000 in a lawsuit against a tobacco company. The award was overturned on appeal, however, and the lawsuit was dropped in 1992. In 1990, a Mississippi jury agreed that cigarettes had killed a longtime smoker but awarded no damages because it found American Tobacco and the victim to be equally at fault (Word, Ron. "Lucky Strike for Ex-Smoker." *Boston Herald.* August 10, 1996: 3).

30. *Ibid.*

31. Word, Ron. "Lucky Strike for Ex-Smoker." *Boston Herald.* August 10, 1996: 3.

32. Zegart, Dan. "Breathing Fire on Tobacco." *Nation* 261, August 28, 1995: 193–196.

33. Levy, March 13, 1996, *op. cit.*

34. Henry, David and Levy, Doug. "Big Tobacco Firms Vow to Fight Suits." *USA Today.* March 14, 1996: 1A.

35. Quoted in Schwartz, John. "Major Tobacco Company Will Settle Claims in Class-Action Lawsuit." *Houston Chronicle.* March 14, 1996: 3A. See also: Levy, Doug. "Settlement Breaches Tobacco's Fortress." *USA Today.* March 14, 1996: 1D, 2S.

36. Wells, Melanie. "Court Ruling Gives Tobacco Stocks a Boost." *USA Today.* May 24, 1996: 1B; "Appeals Court Tosses Out Class-Action Tobacco Suit." *Houston Chronicle.* May 24, 1996: 1A, 18A.

37. "Documents Reveal Tobacco Marketing Strategies." *USA Today.* April 2, 1997: 1D. See also: "Tobacco Firm Reaches Settlement With States." *Houston Chronicle.* March 20, 1997: 21A.

38. Quoted in Kellman, Laurie. "Cigarette Maker Plotted Sweet Snare for Youths." *Houston Chronicle.* February 6, 1998: 4A.

39. *Ibid.*

40. Quoted in "Tobacco Firms: Smoking Risks Well-Known." usatoday.com. October 20, 1998.

41. Quoted in Meckler, Laura. "Teen Gets Pitch to Buy Cigarettes." *Houston Chronicle.* February 2, 1998: 3A.

42. *Ibid.*

43. Stolberg, Sheryl. "Underage Smokers Three Times as Likely to Be Influenced by Ads." *Houston Chronicle.* April 4, 1996: 18A.

44. "Documents Reveal Tobacco Marketing Strategies." *USA Today.* April 2, 1997: 1D.

45. From "Planning Assumptions and Forecast for the Period 1977–1986 for R. J. Reynolds Tobacco Company. Quoted in *USA Today.* September 6, 1995, *op. cit.*: p. 4D.

46. Kellman, *op. cit.*

47. Meier, Barry. "Memos Show Teens Targets for Tobacco." *Houston Chronicle.* January 15, 1998: 2A.

48. Schwartz, John. "Official Made Plan to Draw Teen Smokers." *Houston Chronicle.* October 4, 1995: 2A.

49. Quoted in *Ibid.,* p. 2A.

50. *Ibid.* In 1996, the FDA was empowered by President Clinton to further restrict the promotion and sale of cigarettes to teenagers. The president vowed that his actions would put the Joe Camel advertising icon "out of our children's reach forever" (McDonald, Greg. "New Rules Aimed at Tobacco." *Houston Chronicle.* August 24, 1996: 1A, 16A).

51. "Selling to Children." *Consumer Reports.* August 1990: 518–521.

52. Friend, Tim. "Teen Smoking Rate Highest Since 1970s." *USA Today.* May 24, 1966: 1A.

53. Quoted in Frankel, Bruce. "'Just Like That,' Teens Smoke." *USA Today.* May 24, 1996: 3A.

54. "Clinton, Ex-Lobbyist Hit Tobacco Industry." *Boston Globe.* August 13, 1995: 29.

55. Moss, Desda. "Ex-Tobacco Lobbyist Tried to 'Undo Damage'." *USA Today.* March 5, 1996: 7A.

56. "Tobacco Talks Adjourn: Both Sides Claim Progress Being Made." cnn.com. July 31, 1998.

57. "5 Tobacco Firms Withdraw From Deal." cnn.com. April 8, 1998.

58. Lee, Jessica. "Execs Admit Nicotine's Addictive." *USA Today.* January 30, 1998: 4A.

59. "Big Tobacco Won't Work Toward Settlement." cnn.com. April 8, 1998.

60. Johnson, Kevin V. "Ad Allegations Open Minn. Tobacco Trial." *USA Today.* January 27, 1998: 1D; "Settlement Reached in Minnesota Tobacco Case." cnn.com. May 8, 1998. "Tobacco Industry 'Surrenders' to Minnesota." cnn.com. May 8, 1998. "Settlement Reached in Tobacco Lawsuit." cnn.com. May 8, 1998.

61. "Texas Tobacco Settlement Held Up Over Attorney's Fees." cnn.com May 8, 1998.

62. Levy, Doug. "Florida Settles Tobacco Suit." *USA Today.* August 26, 1997: 1A.

63. cnn.com, July 31, 1998, *op. cit.*

64. "Settlement Reached by States With the Tobacco Industry." cnn.com. May 9, 1998.

65. "Most States Signing on to Tobacco Deal." usatoday.com. November 20, 1998.

66. *Ibid.*

67. Willing, Richard. "Damages Could Be Eye-Popping.'" *USA Today.* July 8, 1999: 3A.

68. Schwartz, John. "Big Tobacco Wins Another Court Victory." *Houston Chronicle.* November 1, 1997: 5A.

69. Willing, *op. cit.*

70. "Tobacco Firms: Smoking Risks Well-Known." usatoday.com. October 20, 1998.

71. Schwartz, John and Torry, Saundra. "Judge Snuffs Out Class-Action Case Against Tobacco." *Houston Chronicle.* October 18, 1997: 2A.

72. Quoted in "Tobacco Industry Says It Won't Settle $200 Billion Lawsuit." cnn.com. July 6, 1998.

73. "Jury Selection Begins in Florida Tobacco Trial." cnn.com. July 6, 1998.

74. Quoted in *Ibid.*

75. *Ibid.*

76. Quoted in usatoday.com. October 20, 1998, *op. cit.*

77. Quoted in "Tobacco Attorney Argues Smokers Knew the Risks." *Houston Chronicle.* October 21, 1998: 9A.

78. *Ibid.*

79. *Ibid.*

80. Sharp, Deborah. "Jury: Tobacco Industry Liable." *USA Today.* July 8, 1999: 1A.

81. Quoted in Meier, Barry. "Florida Jury Awards Damages to Smokers in Class-Action Suit." *Houston Chronicle.* April 8, 2000: 2A.

82. Quoted in *Ibid.,* p. 2A.

83. Sharp, *op. cit.*

84. Quoted in *Ibid.,* p. 1A.

85. *Ibid.*

86. "Record Jury Award Stuns Big Tobacco." *Houston Chronicle.* July 15, 2000: 1A, 14A.

87. *Ibid.*

88. Quoted in *Ibid.,* p. 17A.

89. "Tobacco Verdict in Florida Is Upheld." *Houston Chronicle.* November 7, 2000: 4A.

90. Quoted in Wilson, Catherine. "Smokers May Never Get Money." *Houston Chronicle.* July 16, 2000: 1A, 17A.

91. Meier, Barry. "Tobacco Firm Admits Smoking Causes Cancer." *Houston Chronicle.* October 14, 1999: 5A.

92. "Tobacco Firm Concedes that Cigarettes Are Addictive." *Houston Chronicle.* October 13, 2000: 7A.

93. "Philip Morris Appears to Be Open to Regulation." *Houston Chronicle.* March 3, 2000: 25A.

94. *Ibid.*

95. "Jury's Verdict Gives Smoker $3 Billion." *Houston Chronicle.* June 7, 2001: 5A.

96. Quoted in *Ibid.,* p. 5A.

97. Quoted in *Ibid.,* p. 5A.

98. Thio, *op. cit.*

99. *Ibid.,* p. 424.

100. Quoted in Mintz and Cohen, 260.

101. Dowie, Mark. "Pinto Madness." In Hills, Stuart. *Corporate Violence: Injury and Death for Profit.* Totowa, NJ: Bowman & Littlefield, 1988; 13–29.

102. Thio, *op. cit.,* p. 425.

103. Eitzen and Timmer, *op. cit.,* p. 308.

104. Mintz, Morton. "At Any Cost: Corporate Greed, Women, and the Dalkon Shield." In Hills, Stuart (Ed.). *Corporate Violence: Injury and Death for Profit.* Totowa, NJ: Rowman & Littlefield, 1987; 31.

105. Coleman, James W. *The Criminal Elite: The Sociology of White-Collar Crime* (3rd ed.). NY: St. Martin's, 1994.

106. Dowie, *op. cit.,* p. 29. After moving to Chrysler, Iacocca was once quoted as insisting that "Safety doesn't sell!"

107. Meier, Barry. "Large Recall of School Buses Is Ordered to Fix Fuel Tanks." *New York Times.* July 23, 1992: A16.

108. Kravets, David. "Calif. Judge Orders Ford Recall." schwab-news.excite.com. October 11, 2000. Ford had actually sold about 23 million of the vehicles in question, but the judge's jurisdiction

in the matter did not extend beyond California.

109. *Ibid.*

110. Skrzycki, Cindy. "Firestone to Recall Millions of Tires." *Houston Chronicle.* August 9, 2000: 1A, 14A.

111. Healey, James. R. "Tires to Be Recalled." *USA Today.* August 9, 2000: 1A.

112. Frank and Lynch, *op. cit.*, p. 66.

113. Nathan, Sara. "More People Die Despite Recall." *USA Today.* August 22, 2000: 1B.

114. Healey, James R. and Woodyard, Chris. "Tire Concerns Go Back 1½ Years Before Recall." *USA Today.* September 11, 2000: 1B.

115. "Feds Rebuke Ford Over Lack of Tire Alert." *Houston Chronicle.* August 25, 2000: 3A.

116. Healey and Woodyard, *op. cit.*

117. "Tire Recall Has Trail of Missed Chances." *Houston Chronicle.* September 11, 2000: 2A.

118. *Ibid.*

119. Nye, Peter. "The Faces of Product Liability: Keeping the Courthouse Door Open." *Public Citizen.* November/December 1992: 16–21.

120. "Warning on Leather Spray." *New York Times.* January 10, 1993: 23.

121. Williams, Lena. "Faulty Furnaces Evades Recall." *New York Times.* March 3, 1994: C9.

122. *Ibid.*

123. Applebome, Peter. "Recall Is Ordered for Worm Probes." *New York Times.* June 10, 1993: A18.

124. Swartz, Edward M. "When Products Injure Children." *Trial.* August 1989: 50–54.

125. Berselli, Beth. "Greenpeace Tackles Toy Industry, Warns of Hazardous Vinyl." *Houston Chronicle.* October 11, 1997: 18A.

126. "A Million Auto Child-Safety Seats Recalled." *New York Times.* October 30, 1992: A21. In 1995, Consumers Union tested 25 brands of child safety seats and reported that 3 failed to protect. According to the independent testing organization, the three brands in question broke loose in 30-miles-per-hour test crashes ("3 Child Safety Seats Fail to Protect." *Houston Chronicle.* July 27, 1995: 10A.).

127. "Company Recalls Pacifiers." October 5, 1994: *New York Times.* A19.

128. "420,000 Snuggle Light Dolls Are Recalled by Fisher-Price." *New York Times.* August 15, 1994: 18.

129. O'Donnell, Jayne. "Suffering in Silence." *USA Today.* April 3, 2000: 1B, 2B.

130. *Ibid.*

131. Quoted in *Ibid.*, p. 2B.

132. *Ibid.*

133. "Co. Fined for Flammable Sweaters." October 11, 2000.

134. "Ban Asked on Children's Wear with Flame Retardant." *New York Times.* February 9, 1977: A25.

135. Brozan, Nadine. "U.S. Bans a Flame Retardant Used in Children's Sleepwear." *New York Times.* April 6, 1977: A14.

136. "Supplementary Material from the Associated Press." *New York Times.* October 19, 1978: 77.

137. Dowie, Mark and *Mother Jones.* "The Dumping of Hazardous Products on Foreign Markets." In Hills, Stuart L. *Corporate Violence: Injury and Death for Profit.* Totowa, NJ: Rowman & Littlefield, 1988: 47–58.

138. Sinclair, Upton. *The Jungle.* New York: Harper and Brothers, 1951; 61. (This book was originally published in 1905.)

139. Okun, Mitchell. *Fair Play in the Marketplace: The First Battle for Pure Food and Drugs.* DeKalb, IL: Northern Illinois University Press, 1980.

140. Frank and Lynch, *op. cit.*

141. McCaghy, E. H. *Deviant Behavior, Crime, Conflict, and Interest Groups.* New York: Macmillan, 1976: 215,

142. Eitzen and Timmer, *op. cit.*

143. Wellford, Harrison. *Sowing the Wind: A Report from Ralph Nader's Center for Study of Responsive Laws on Food Safety and the Chemical Harvest.* New York: Grossman, 1972; 69.

144. Snyder, Jean. "About the Meat You Are Buying." *Today's Health* 49, December 1971: 39.

145. Quoted in Ross, Irwin. "How Safe Is Our Food?" *Reader's Digest.* September, 1972: 121.

146. McFarling, Usha L. "Improved Food Safety Advised." *Houston Chronicle.* August 21, 1998: 9A.

147. *Ibid.*

148. Monmaney, Terence. "Tainted Food Has Major Impact." *Houston Chronicle.* September 17, 1998: 14A. See also: Coorsh, Richard. "Modern Meat Infection." *Consumer's Research* 78, 1995: 6.

149. *Ibid.* See also: Williams, Carol J. "Russia's Fowl Play Could Backfire." *Houston Chronicle.* March 17, 1996: 32A.

150. *Ibid.*

151. "Infant Formulas Recalled." *FDA Consumer.* 27, 1993: 3.

152. Cowley, Geoffrey, and McCormick, John. "How Safe Is Our Food?" *Newsweek* 121, 1993: 7–10.

153. Hunter, Beatrice T. "Will Beefed up Inspection Assure Food Safety?" *Consumer's Research* 76, 1993: 17–21.

154. Burros, Marian. "Poultry Bacterium Getting Upper Hand, Health Officials Fear." *Houston Chronicle.* October 20, 1997: 2A.

155. *Ibid.*

156. "Breeders' Ploy Can Lead to *Salmonella.*" *Houston Chronicle.* May 21, 1996: 4C.

157. Kuchler, Fred and MacClelland, John. "The Demand for Food Safety: An Historical Perspective on Recombinant DNA-Derived Animal Growth Hormones." *Policy Studies Journal* 17, 1988: 125–135.

158. Hunter, Beatrice T. "Improving the Fish Inspection Program." *Consumers' Research.* August 1989: 10–15.

159. DeWaal, Caroline S. and Obester, Tricia. "Seafood Safety: Consumers and Manufacturers at Risk." *USA Today Magazine,* July 1994: 24–26.

160. *Ibid.*

161. Schwartz, John. "U.S. Unveils 'Fundamental Shift' in Procedures for Seafood Safety." *Houston Chronicle.* December 6, 1995: 14A.

162. "Largest Food Poison Case." *Houston Chronicle.* May 16, 1996: 10A.

163. "Maker Recalls Granola Bars." *New York Times.* March 16, 1993: A17.

164. Manning, Anita. "Baby Food Has Traces of Pesticide." *USA Today.* July 26, 1995: 1D.

165. Quoted in *Ibid.,* p. 1D.

166. "Heinz Recalls Baby Food Containing Bits of Rubber." *Wall Street Journal.* July 15, 1991: B5.

167. Frank and Lynch, *op. cit.* Lethal problems with nonprescription drugs continue to occur, though with less frequency. Six brands of aerosol cough remedies were recalled after an ingredient was linked to 21 deaths ("The Dangers that Come in Spray Cans." *Changing Times.* August, 1975: 17–19.).

168. Janesh, Barbara J. "How Those Little Pills Went to Market." *Everyday Law.* January 1989: 40–44.

169. Stoll, R. Ryan. "A Question of Competence: The Judicial Role in the Regulation of Pharmaceuticals." *Food, Drug, Cosmetic Law Journal* 45, 1990: 279–299.

170. "Woman Wins $23 Million in Fen-Phen Case." *Houston Chronicle.* August 7, 1999: 1A, 18A.

171. Dowie, Mark and Marshall, Carolyn. "The Bendectin Cover-Up." In Ermann, M. David and Lundman, Richard J. (Eds.). *Corporate and Governmental Deviance: Problems of Organizational Behavior in Contemporary Society.* New York: Oxford University Press, 1982; 262–279.

172. Dowie and Marshall, *op. cit.,* p. 263.

173. A medical researcher, employed by Merrell, wrote an article, defending thalidomide in the prestigious *Am J Obstet Gyne.* This same scientist was also the inventor of Bendectin, another one of Merrell's-Richardson defective drugs, described earlier in this chapter (Dowie and Marshall, *op. cit.*).

174. Dowie and Marshall, *op. cit.*

175. Knightley, Phillip, Evans, Harold, Potter, Elaine, and Wallace, Marjorie. *Suffer the Children: The Story of Thalidomide.* New York: Viking, 1979; 1.

176. *Ibid.*

177. *New York Times.* "3 Babies Born Deformed Here; Thalidomide Taken by Mothers." July 27, 1962: 12.

178. Knightley et al., 69

179. *Ibid.*

180. Schwartz, John. "FDA Warily OKs Use of Thalidomide for Leprosy Lesions." *Houston Chronicle.* July 17, 1998: 2A.

181. Quoted in *Ibid.,* p. 2A.

182. *Ibid.*

183. *Ibid.*

184. Frank and Lynch, *op. cit.*

185. Coleman, *op. cit.*

186. *Ibid.,* p. 86. More recently, a similarly named anti-infection drug, Omniflex, was withdrawn from the market by its manufacturer, Abbott Laboratories, after it was linked to 3 deaths and 50 cases of adverse side effects, including kidney failure ("Drug Is Recalled by Maker After Being Tied to 3 Deaths." *New York Times.* June 6, 1992: 9).

187. Olmos, David R. "3 Plead Guilty in Lab Test Fraud." *Los Angeles Times.* September 27, 1999: A10.

188. *Ibid.*

189. Quoted in Cobb, Kim. "Bush's Halcion Use Divulged After Falling Ill on Japan Trip." *Houston Chronicle.* September 11, 1994: 21A.

190. Cobb, Kim. "FDA Admits Mistake, Urges Probe of Halcion." *Houston Chronicle.* June 1, 1996: 1A.

191. "Dangerous Drug Interactions with the Sleeping Pill Triazolam (Halcion)." *Health Letter.* 11, March 1995: 10; Stephenson, John. "Commercial Confidence: Secrecy or Openness?" *Pharmaceutical Executive* 14, December 1994: 24–26.

192. Reed, Steven R. "Sleep Merchants/The Halcion Story: FDA Ignored Own Halcion Findings." *Houston Chronicle.* September 13, 1994: 1A.

193. O'Donnell, Peter. "Ghosts from the Past." *Pharmaceutical Executive* 15, June, 1995: 36.

194. Cowley, Geoffrey. "Dreams or Nightmare?" *Newsweek* 118, August 19, 1991: 44–51.

195. "Sleep Merchants/Halcion Chronology." *Houston Chronicle.* September 11, 1994: 22A.

196. Cowley, *op. cit.*

197. *Ibid.*

198. *Ibid.*

199. Quoted in Reed, Steven R. "Sleep Merchants/The Halcion Story: Upjohn Paid Heavily to Discredit Critics." *Houston Chronicle.* September 14, 1994: 1A.

200. Quoted in "Sleep Merchants: Upjohn's Paper Trail." *Houston Chronicle.* September 11, 1994: 20A.

201. Reed, Steven R. "Federal Report Targets Upjohn for 'Misconduct.'" *Houston Chronicle.* May 1, 1994: 1A.

202. Cobb, "FDA Admits Mistake," June 1, 1996, *op. cit.*

203. Quoted in Reed, Steven R. "Sleep Merchants/The Halcion Story: Hidden Nightmares." *Houston Chronicle.* September 11, 1994: 1A.

204. Reed, Steven R. "Sleep Merchants/The Halcion Story: Halcion Research Called into Question." *Houston Chronicle.* September 12, 1994: 1A.

205. *Ibid.*

206. Quoted in Cowley, *op. cit.,* p. 49.

207. Quoted in *Ibid.,* p. 47.

208. Reed, "Hidden Nightmares," September 11, 1994, *op. cit.*

209. Quoted in Reed, "FDA Ignored Own Halcion Findings," September 13, 1994, *op. cit.,* p. 1A

210. *Ibid.*

211. Quoted in *Ibid.,* p. 1A.

212. Quoted in Reed, Steven R. "Bearer of Bad News." *Houston Chronicle.* September 14, 1994: 7A.

213. *Ibid.*

214. Cowley, *op. cit.,* p. 49.

215. Cobb, Kim. "Sleep Merchants/Troubled Experiences." *Houston Chronicle.* September 11, 1994: 21A.

216. Tedford, Deborah. "Lawsuit Cites Man's Woes While He Was on Halcion." *Houston Chronicle.* March 9, 1994: 30A.

217. *Ibid.*

218. Urban, Jerry. "Man Loses Lawsuit Against Halcion Maker." *Houston Chronicle.* March 31, 1994: 26A.

219. Quoted in Reed, Steven R. "Through a Halcion Haze." *Houston Chronicle.* January 23, 1994: 1A.

220. *Ibid.,* p. 1A

221. *Ibid.,* p. 1A

222. Reed, Steven R. "Appeals Court Sets Aside Lone Halcion Award." *Houston Chronicle.* August 30, 1994: 9A.

223. *Ibid.*

224. *Ibid.*

225. Cobb, "FDA Admits Mistake, Urges Probe of Halcion," June 1, 1996, *op. cit.*: p. 16A.

226. Cobb, Kim. "Sleep Merchants/Groundbreaking, Heartbreaking Case." *Houston Chronicle.* September 11, 1994: 20A.

227. Cobb, Kim. "Woman in '88 Halcion Case Takes Own Life." *Houston Chronicle.* July 23, 1994: 1A.

228. Cowley, *op. cit.*

229. Cobb, Kim. "Jim Ayers Believes Halcion Triggered Rampage." *Houston Chronicle.* September 11, 1994: 22A.

230. Cobb, Kim. "Sleep Merchants: Troubled Experiences." *Houston Chronicle.* September 11, 1994: 21A.

231. *Ibid.*

232. Quoted in Cobb, "Troubled Experiences," September 11, 1994, *op. cit.,* p. 21A.

233. Cobb, Kim and Reed, Steven R. "Sleep Merchants: The Halcion Story." *Houston Chronicle.* September 15, 1994: 1A.

234. Reed, Steven R. "Halcion Lawsuit Alleges FDA, Upjohn Conspiracy." *Houston Chronicle.* January 7, 1994: 29A.

235. *Ibid.*, p. 29.

236. *Ibid.*, p. 29.

237. Two shareholder class action suits against Upjohn have even been filed in federal court, claiming that Upjohn's directors and officers breached their responsibilities to investors by obscuring potential financial losses posed by product liability. The shareholders charge that Upjohn failed to disclose the severe side effects of Halcion and concealed testing problems and adverse results that occurred in clinical trials of the drug—in violation of the Securities Exchange Act of 1934. Fittingly, one of the lead attorneys representing the shareholders is himself a former Halcion user. In his words: "It nearly destroyed my career. I had terrible, terrible, depression." (Quoted in Cobb, Kim. "Sleep Merchants: Internal Ills." *Houston Chronicle.* September 15, 1994: 15A.)

238. Himelstein, Linda. "Did Big Tobacco's Barrister Set up a Smokescreen?" *Business Week* 3388, September 5, 1994: 68–70.

239. Reed, "Hidden Nightmares," September 11, 1994, *op. cit.*, p. 1A.

240. Quoted in *Ibid.*, p. 1A.

241. Quoted in Cowley, *op. cit.*, p. 45.

242. "Gyps and Frauds Update." *Kiplinger's Personal Finance Magazine.* May, 1994: 11.

243. Ropp, Kevin L. "Selling Used Pacemakers Lands Businessman in Jail." *FDA Consumer* 27, December 1993: 38–40.

244. "Heart Catheter Firm Will Pay $61 Million Fine." *Galveston Daily News.* October 17, 1993: 9B.

245. Hutt, Peter B. "A History of Regulation of Adulteration and Misbranding of Medical Devices." *Food, Drug, Cosmetic Law Journal* 44, 1989: 99–117.

246. Perry, Susan and Dawson, Jim. *Nightmare: Women and the Dalkon Shield.* New York: Macmillan, 1985.

247. *Ibid.*

248. Mintz, *op. cit.*

249. Coleman, *op. cit.*, p. 86.

250. *Ibid.*

251. Mintz, *op. cit.*, p. 31.

252. Coleman, *op. cit.*

253. Kendall, Pamela. *Torn Illusions: One Woman's Tragic Experience with the Silicone Conspiracy.* Far Hills, NJ: Horizon Press, 1994; 24.

254. Cowley, Geoffrey. "Calling a Halt to the Big Business of Silicone Implants." *Newsweek.* January 20, 1992: 56.

255. *Ibid.*

256. Quoted in Smart, Tim. "This Man Sounded the Silicone Alarm—in 1976." *Business Week.* January 27, 1992: 34.

257. Rensberger, Boyce. "Breast Implant Records Were 'Faked'." *Washington Post.* November 3, 1992: A3.

258. Priest, Dana. "Dow Corning Accused of Withholding Silicone Data." *Washington Post.* January 16, 1993: A5.

259. Fackelmann, K. A. "Implants Linked to Disorders in Children." *Science News* 145, 1993: 70.

260. Lewin, Tamar. "As Silicone Issue Grows, Women Take Agony and Anger to Court." *New York Times.* January 19, 1992: 1.

261. "Record $25 Million Awarded in Silicone-Gel Implant Case." *New York Times.* December 24, 1992: A13.

262. "3M Will Pay $325 Million to Settle Implant Suits." *New York Times.* April 12, 1994: B8.

263. "Dow Corning Files for Bankruptcy." *Houston Chronicle.* May 16, 1995: 1C.

264. *Ibid.*

265. "Implant Fiasco: A Case of Putting Safety Last." *USA Today.* May 17, 1995: 12A.

266. Meier, Barry. "Penalties Rise in Breast Implant Case." *Houston Chronicle.* October 31, 1995: 4A.

267. McConnaughey, Janet. "Dow Liable for Implants, Jury Decides." *Orange County Register.* August 19, 1997: 3. "Jury Rules Against Dow Chemical." *Houston Chronicle.* August 19, 1997: 1A. Alexander, Keith. "Jury: Dow Chemical Negligent." *USA Today.* August 19, 1997: 1A.

268. "FDA Advisory Panel Deems One Brand of Breast Implants Safe." *Houston Chronicle.* March 2, 2000: 5A.

269. *Ibid.*

270. Houpert, Karen and Pushkar, Katherine. "Pulling the Plug on the Sanitary Protection Industry." *Village Voice* 40, February 7, 1995: 33–40.

271. Swasy, Alecia. "Rely Tampons and Toxic Shock Syndrome: Procter & Gamble's Responses." In Ermann, M. David and Lundman, Richard J. (Eds.), *Corporate and*

Governmental Deviance (5th Ed.). New York: Oxford University Press, 1996.

272. *Ibid.*

273. Houppert and Pushkar, *op. cit.*

274. Swasy, 1996, pp. 183–184.

275. *Ibid.*, p. 283.

276. Houppert and Pushkar, *op. cit.*, p. 33.

277. Swasy, 1996, *op. cit.*, p. 287.

278. Swasy, Alecia. *Soap Opera: The Inside Story of Procter & Gamble.* New York: Time Books, 1993.

279. *Ibid.*

280. Riley, Tom. *The Price of a Life: One Woman's Death from Toxic Shock.* Bethesda, MD: Adler & Adler, 1986. Upon publication of this book, Riley received numerous offers to appear on television talk shows. All his bookings were mysteriously canceled at the last minute, however. Apparently no one was willing to risk offending Procter & Gamble, the country's largest television advertiser. The book also has had a suspicious history of disappearing from library shelves.

281. Swasy, 1993, *op. cit.*, p. 143.

282. *Ibid.*, p. 144.

283. *Ibid.*

284. Riley, *op. cit.*

285. Swasy, 1993, *op. cit.*

286. *Ibid.*, p. 151.

287. Quoted in *Ibid.*, p. 151.

288. Schaller, Warren E. and Carroll, Charles R. *Health, Quackery & the Consumer.* Philadelphia: W. B. Saunders, 1976.

289. Young, James H. *The Medical Messiahs: A Social History of Health Quackery in Twentieth-Century America.* Princeton, NJ: Princeton University Press, 1967.

290. Waldron, George B. "What America Spends on Advertising." *Chatauquan* 38, 1903: 156.

291. Young, *op. cit.*

292. *Ibid.*

293. Nishiwaki, Robin and Bouchard, Carla. "Combating Nutrition Quackery: The San Bernardino County Experience." *American Journal of Public Health* 79, 1989: 652–653. The $25 billion figure was derived from a 5-year government study headed by former Congressman Claude Pepper.

294. "Top 10 Health Frauds." *FDA Consumer.* October 1989: 29.

295. Quoted in *Ibid.*, p. 82.

296. "Quackery Targets Teens." *Consumers' Research.* 71, April 1988: 24–26.

297. Grossman, Ellie. "Curing the Incurable." *Safety and Health.* February 1992: 51.

298. *Ibid.*, p. 51. The estimate is from the National Center for Health Services Research.

299. Napier, Kristine. "Unproven Medical Treatments Lure Elderly." *FDA Consumer.* March 1994: 32–37.

300. Marvin, *op. cit.*

301. Quoted in Grossman, *op. cit.*, p. 169.

302. Michelmore, Peter. "Beware the Health Hucksters." *Readers Digest* 134, January 1989: 114.

303. Hartigan, Neil F. "Health Quackery: Diet Pills to AIDS Cures." *Journal of State Government* 62, 1989: 102.

304. Pogash, Carol. "Miracle Cure or Snake Oil?" *San Francisco Chronicle Magazine.* July 18, 1993: 6–9.

305. Segal, Marian. "Defrauding the Desperate." *FDA Consumer* 21, October, 1987: 16–19.

306. *FDA Consumer,* 1989, *op. cit.*

307. *Ibid.*

308. Segal, Marian. "Defrauding the Desperate: Quackery and AIDS." *FDA Consumer.* October, 1988: 17–19.

309. *Ibid.*, p. 17.

310. *Ibid.*, p. 17.

311. Campbell, Duncan and Townson, Nigel. "Let Them Eat Shit." *New Statesman & Society* 2, 1989: 10–12.

312. Goldemberg, *op. cit.*

313. Napier, *op. cit.*

314. *Ibid.*

315. Poppy, John. "Bad-Faith Healers." *Men's Health* 9, December 1994: 106–109.

316. Lane, I. William and Comac, Linda. *Sharks Don't Get Cancer.* Garden City Park, NY: Avery, 1992.

317. Rosenfeld, Isadore. "Shark Cartilage to Prevent Cancer? Forget It. *Parade.* January 14, 2001: 16. In 1996, a Connecticut marketing company was fined for advertising pills made from shark parts, which promised "amazing health benefits." ("Ads for Bigger Breasts, etc., Quashed." *Dubuque Telegraph Herald.* May 31, 1996: 7.

318. Napier, *op. cit.*

319. *Ibid.*

320. Smith, Leef. "Md. Businessmen Accused of Fraud in Marketing of Aloe Vera as Cure." *Washington Post.* May 8, 1998: B1.

321. Quoted in *Ibid.*, p. B1.
322. Lipton, Eric and Smith, Leef. "Was Cancer 'Cure' a Painful Lie?" *Washington Post.* February 25, 1998: A1.
323. Michelmore, *op. cit.*, p. 116.
324. Segal, 1992, *op. cit.*
325. *Ibid.*, p. 116.
326. *FDA Consumer, op. cit.*
327. *Ibid.*
328. Nishiwaki and Bouchard, *op. cit.*, p. 652.
329. Michelmore, *op. cit.*
330. Segal, Marian. "Family Indicted for Fountain of Youth Fraud." *FDA Consumer* 26, July 1992: 36–37.
331. *Ibid.*
332. Barrett, Stephen. "Stronger Laws Needed to Stop Mail Fraud." *Healthy Weight Journal* 9, May 1995: 55.
333. Quoted in *Kiplinger's Personal Finance Magazine, op. cit.*, p. 11.
334. Meier, Barry. "Consumer's World: Diet-Pill Death Raises Questions on F.D.A. Role." *New York Times.* August 4, 1990: 48.
335. Thompson, Sharon E. "Gems as Medicine—or—Stone Quackery?" *Lapidary Journal* 49, May 1995: 49–52.
336. *FDA Consumer, op. cit.*
337. Divine, Mary. "The Skeptical Curator." *Minneapolis—St. Paul Magazine.* 22, May 1994: 28.
338. Ruibal, Sal. "Ironclad Cures for Pain?" *USA Today.* August 20, 1997: 3C.
339. Schaller and Carroll, *op. cit.*
340. *Ibid.*, p. 281.
341. *Ibid.*
342. Quoted in *Ibid.*, p. 230.
343. Farley, Dixie. "'Career Criminal' Faces Jail and Possible Deportation." *FDA Consumer* 28, 1994: 30.
344. Farley, Dixie. "'Career Criminal' Faces Jail and Possible Deportation." *FDA Consumer* 28, September 1994: 30–32.
345. Farley, *op. cit.*, p. 30.
346. Young, *op. cit.*, p. 320.
347. *Ibid.*, p. 317.
348. *Ibid.*
349. Quoted in *Ibid.*, p. 328.

Environmental Crime

> *Lawyer:*   In order to build Club Bolt the way you want it, we'd be forced to cut down 6,000 acres of natural Brazilian rain forest.
> *Tycoon:*   So?
> *Lawyer:*   Well, sir, the last 400 Yppi Indians left in the world are still living there.
> *Tycoon:*   So?

From *Life Stinks* (1991). Screenplay by Mel Brooks, Rudy DeLuca, and Steve Haberman.

*C*hapter 3, in its consideration of dangerous and defective consumer products, punctured the prevalent myth that white-collar crimes are nonviolent and carry little in the way of physical costs. In fact, the human cost of white-collar crime is nothing less than devastating. Social activist Ralph Nader has written that "[t]he harm done to human health and safety by business crime should dispel the distinguishing characteristic of 'white-collar crime' as being the absence of physical threat."[1] Testifying before Congress in 1978, the noted criminologist Gilbert Geis observed, "It is quite possible that more people have died from corporate conducted or corporate condoned violence . . . than have been victims of more traditional kinds of murder."[2]

This chapter will consider how pollution of the natural environment and the workplace can be especially deadly examples of what Nader calls "postponed violence."[3] The Environmental Protection Agency (EPA) has urged courts to "view environmental crime for what it really is—a crime of violence and an egregious departure from responsible citizenship."[4]

THE NATURAL ENVIRNOMENT

Sometimes the human costs of environmental negligence are indirect, but tragic nonetheless. An example of indirect physical costs can be found in the aftermath of the disastrous Alaskan oil spill of 1989,[5] for which the Exxon

Corporation received a $900 civil penalty and a $100 million criminal fine.[6] The lifestyle of the Native American population in Kodiak was devastated. Villagers reportedly suffered a 700% increase in emotional problems in the months after the spill. The alcoholism rate soared, and eight suicides occurred in just a 6-week period.[7]

All too often, however, the physical costs of corporate recklessness are brutally direct. The EPA estimates that, of the 100 billion tons of hazardous waste produced each year in the United States, 90% is disposed of in an environmentally unsafe manner.[8] This certainly was the case at the infamous Love Canal, the upstate New York community that has become the symbol of environmental crime.

C A S E   S T U D Y

Love Canal

From 1942 to 1953, the Hooker Chemical Corporation (a subsidiary of Occidental Petroleum) burned more than 20 million pounds of chemical waste in an abandoned waterway near Niagara Falls. The canal was then covered up and sold for $1 to the local board of education, which built an elementary school on the site. A housing development soon followed.[9]

In 1977, melting snow forced contaminated groundwater into residents' basements, where it oozed up in the form of black sludge. Two hundred chemical compounds were identified, including dioxin—"the most toxic synthetic compound ever made"[10]—and benzene—called "the most powerful carcinogen known."[11] When an unusually high number of miscarriages were observed in the vicinity, the New York health commissioner declared an emergency and advised pregnant women to move away.[12] "[A] survey also revealed that in a neighborhood not far from Love Canal only one of the 16 pregnancies in 1979 ended in the birth of a healthy baby, while four ended in miscarriages, two babies were stillborn, and nine were born deformed."[13]

> [A] 1980 study of more than 900 children from the area produced some chilling results. Seizures, learning problems, eye and skin irritations, incontinence, and severe abdominal pains were much more prevalent among Love Canal children than among children from nearby neighborhoods.[14]

A 1987 follow-up study revealed that children born in the Love Canal area had significantly lower birth weight[15] and impaired growth, compared with other children.[16] Although Love Canal eventually was evacuated, it was too late for many prenatal victims. For example, the daughter of one resident was born with bone disease, dental deformities, and learning problems.[17] Another mother, after two miscarriages, gave birth to a daughter whose knee was afflicted with tumors.[18]

(Continued)

Lois Gibbs, the housewife-turned-activist who organized the residents of Love Canal, described the misery of an entire community:

> All around me I saw things happening to my neighbors—multiple miscarriages, birth defects, cancer deaths, epilepsy, central nervous disorders, and more. . . . [W]e were never warned. We had no idea we were living on top of a chemical graveyard.[19]

In 1994, in response to a call from environmentalists to ban the use of chlorine in manufacturing (which produces dioxin as a byproduct, the EPA issued a report that verified what the residents of Love Canal had long suspected. According to the EPA, "Dioxin can cause cancer and other health problems even at very low levels of exposure."[20]

One of the most disturbing aspects of the Love Canal debacle was that much of the attendant pain and anxiety could have been avoided. Internal memoranda from the files of Hooker Chemical indicate that the company knew of the peril as early as 1958, when it investigated the burning of three school children who had come in contact with leaking drums of benzene hexachloride near their school.[21] Hooker failed to notify any authorities and opted to do nothing in order to avoid a $50 million clean-up bill.[22] One of the confidential memos iterated, "We should not do anything unless requested by the school board."[23]

When the U.S. House subcommittee examined hazardous waste practices in 1979, a young Tennessee Congressman (and future vice-president), Albert Gore, condemned Hooker's action—or, more precisely—inaction: "The events we have seen take place at Love Canal could have been avoided if you had heeded these early warnings."[24]

But the company had not heeded those early warnings—nor, apparently, Gore's. In 1990, Hooker was back in court, this time in connection with its waste site in Hyde Park, New York. The Hyde Park landfill contains 80,000 tons of chemical deposits, including over 1 ton of dioxin.[25]

In 1995, after a 16-year dispute, Occidental Petroleum, the parent company of Hooker Chemical, finally agreed to reimburse the federal government $129 million for cleaning up Love Canal.[26]

This chapter will examine similar patterns of corporate malfeasance that have contaminated our environment. In such cases, innocent members of the public become the victims of greed, negligence, and irresponsibility.

Water Pollution

To a tourist standing on a wharf, such famous landmarks as Boston Harbor or San Francisco Bay are like scenic three-dimensional postcards. However, beneath the surface (literally) there is nothing beautiful to behold.

> What is happening underwater . . . is not for the squeamish. Scuba divers talk of swimming through clouds of toilet paper and half-dissolved feces, of bay bottoms covered by a foul and toxic combination of sediment, sewage and petrochemical waste appropriately known as "black mayonnaise."[27]

For years, Boston Harbor served as America's largest cesspool, collecting the waste of three million metropolitan residents. "Local beaches are littered with grease balls, tampon applicators and the occasional condom—all of which are apparently released by the antiquated and overloaded sewage system."[28] Fish, which once abounded in the harbor, virtually disappeared. Those remaining often suffered from fin rot and tumors.

Moreover, the harbor bottom contained high concentrations of pesticides and industrial waste suspected of being carcinogenic. Fortunately, changes in environmental laws appear to have turned things around. In 1990, a Massachusetts firm, Borjohn Optical Technology, became the first company convicted under the new "knowing endangerment" amendment to the federal Water Quality Act. Borjohn had discharged toxic concentrations of nickel and nitric acid into Boston Harbor.[29]

Unfortunately, the resuscitation of Boston Harbor is not typical. Millions of tons of sludge from municipal sewage treatment plants in the metropolitan New York area are dumped each year at a site off the New Jersey coast. This sludge has already entered the oceanic food chain, and the long-term impact remains to be seen.[30]

Beaches from Maine to Texas have been plagued by toxic debris. In the summer of 1988, for example, large amounts of illegally dumped medical waste washed ashore across public beaches along the New York–New Jersey coast. Among the debris were hypodermic needles, intravenous tubing, catheter bags, and vials of blood, some of which tested positive for AIDS.[31] Over nine million people resided in the affected areas.

The culprits in the medical waste debacle are dishonest haulers who contract with hospitals to dispose of their waste at special dumpsites around the country, but who avoid costly transportation expenses by simply tossing infected material into the ocean. Some healthcare facilities themselves also have been implicated in the surreptitious dumping of their own debris in order to save disposal costs, which usually are 10 times higher for medical waste than for other types of waste.[32]

Our harbors and beaches, however, are not the only source of dangerous pollution. Our drinking water sometimes has been contaminated by the illegal dumping or careless storage of toxic waste. In Massachusetts, 28 public water sources were shut down over an 18-month period in 1979–1980.[33] In California, thousands of underground storage tanks containing fuels and industrial solvents currently are leaking into groundwater.[34] Even the community of Lake Arrowhead, long renowned for its pure drinking water, has been affected. Some local residents developed red lumps on their necks after showering.[35]

Without water, of course, there can be no human life; but water also can be directly related to disease and death. According to the World Health

Organization, more than three-quarters of all human disease is waterborne.[36] Because technologically advanced societies like the United States employ modern water treatment practices, nonmalignant waterborne diseases, such as cholera, typhoid, and dysentery, are largely nonexistent. It is the category of malignant waterborne diseases that has created serious health problems in the United States. Three major kinds of contamination have been identified: (1) organic contamination, which has been linked to various forms of cancer; (2) inorganic contamination, most notably from metals such as lead, which are suspected of causing developmental problems in children;[37] and (3) radioactivity, which is believed to cause prenatal damage.[38]

Some water contamination occurs unintentionally, as through the natural corrosion of old pipes or the inadvertent runoff of agricultural chemicals. In 1985, for example, the town of Woodstock, New York, began finding large quantities of asbestos in its water supply. The problem became so acute that clumps of fibers were falling on people in the shower.[39] The source of the contamination was a network of aging pipes built of asbestos-laced cement. Although the carcinogenic properties of asbestos is an area of medical controversy, a number of scientists have related waterborne asbestos to gastrointestinal cancer.[40]

Some of the water contamination problems, however, are hardly unintentional and can be directly attributed to illegal practices at privately owned dumpsites. For example, a disposal firm in Rockland County, New York, whose permit limited it to the handling of construction debris, such as wood, concrete, and plaster, was charging neighboring communities for unlawfully storing their incinerated garbage. As a result of leaching, the water supply in West Nyack, New York, became contaminated by trichloroethylene (TCE), an industrial solvent and degreasing agent "known to have adverse effects on the human nervous system, the cardiovascular system, the liver and the kidney."[41]

Some of the most reckless tales of toxic dumping involve the waste hauling practices of illicit trucking operations. One week before a federal waste monitoring system was to take effect in late 1980, thousands of tons of toxic wastes were hurriedly disposed of in a last-minute rush to circumvent the new law. As the deadline drew nearer, some hazardous materials were even dumped from moving trucks onto interstate highways or abandoned in shopping center parking lots around the country.[42] The proper disposal of hazardous waste is costly: "in some parts of the country averaging $2,000 to $4,000 a truckload."[43] Consequently, certain unscrupulous trucking companies and individual drivers choose to dump dangerous waste illegally and pocket the savings. Other offenders simply abandon dilapidated trucks along with their toxic cargo. "In New York City, for example, authorities routinely impound unattended trucks carrying dangerous waste products."[44]

Truckers, known as "sludge runners," actually open the spigots of their storage tanks and release toxic waste as they drive. A popular venue for sludge runners was the Mianus River Bridge in Connecticut. Gallons of corrosive liquid would drain off the span, not only polluting the river below but eventually weakening the metal support joints of the structure. When the rotting joints finally broke apart in 1983, the bridge collapsed.[45]

Much of our poisoned water is not the result of illegal hauling, however, but is the result of criminal negligence on the part of industrial corporations themselves. This was the case, for example, when the Federal Bureau of Investigation (FBI) raided Colorado's Rocky Flats nuclear weapons plant in 1989. "The facility, which was owned by the Department of Energy and operated by Rockwell International, was the nation's only plant making plutonium triggers used to set off nuclear warheads."[46] The plant had become so contaminated that eventual clean-up costs are projected to be $2 billion.[47] It also has been calculated that the radioactive contamination at Rocky Flats will remain for 24,000 years.[48]

Furthermore, it was discovered that Rocky Flats was dumping radioactive matter into local rivers.[49] A criminal grand jury indicted Rockwell, but in a controversial decision, the Justice Department did not sign the indictments, opting instead for a plea-bargained fine of $18.5 million.[50] Because Rockwell had also received a $22.6 million performance bonus, it actually came out $4.1 million ahead. A report in the *Bulletin of the Atomic Scientists* was titled "The Wages of Sin? About $4.1 Million."[51] A congressional committee decried this arrangement as a miscarriage of justice. When members of the grand jury publicly protested the lack of an indictment, *they* became the subjects of a government investigation.[52] As *US News and World Report* noted, "The Justice Department is supposed to prosecute companies for environmental crimes, not look the other way."[53]

The EPA has estimated that as many as 30,000 waste sites may pose significant health problems related to water contamination.[54] For example, the town of Yellow Creek, Kentucky, had its water supply poisoned when a tannery began disgorging chromium into the local creek. Chromium is a highly toxic metal that is extremely dangerous to human life.[55] It took 7 years of community agitation before the contamination was cleaned up. During that time, children endured chronic diarrhea and vomiting, while adults were stricken with ulcers, kidney problems, and miscarriages. One family, living right along the creek, suffered six cancer deaths in 5 years.[56]

Illegal dumping by the Velsicol chemical company of Memphis had contaminated the wells at a number of farms in Toone, Tennessee. Several families suffered chronic depression for 4 years, "until they discovered chloroform in their drinking water at levels equaling a daily sedative."[57] How potent was Velsicol's waste? Consider the following repercussions:

> The truck driver who hauled Velsicol's leaking barrels of chemical wastes from Memphis to Toone lost his sight after continued exposure to the corrosive fumes. His 29-year-old son, who worked alongside him, developed nerve damage. Although formerly a keen athlete, the young man's once-powerful legs began to tremor uncontrollably; one summer, he drowned while swimming.[58]

Of all the waste site-related health hazards, the contamination of drinking water probably represents the most serious threat because of its potential to affect the greatest number of people.[59] Nearly half the people in America, including about one-third of those residing in our largest cities and most of the rural population, depend on groundwater for their drinking supplies.[60] "When poisonous materials are dumped or seep into the earth, they mix with precipitation, percolate through the soil . . . and then become part of the water supply."[61] Once a water supply is contaminated, it can remain so for decades or even centuries or millennia.

So persistent are the effects of water contamination that, in 1990, families in Ponca City, Oklahoma, were paid $40,000 to abandon their homes and leave their neighborhood. The Conoco Oil Company, which had contaminated the community's drinking water, had opted to minimize its exposure to litigation by surrounding its refinery with a ring of deserted houses.[62]

Toxic water has been linked to a variety of ailments, including kidney disorder, digestive problems, chronic headaches, blurred vision, and peeling skin.[63] In addition, water contamination also has been connected to a virtual catalogue of birth defects. For example, after the Fairchild Camera and Instrument Company of San Jose, California, leaked an industrial solvent into one neighborhood's drinking supply, the number of babies born with congenital heart deformities rose sharply. Although the state health department was equivocal in its conclusions, the company agreed to a financial settlement in a lawsuit filed on behalf of 117 affected children.[64]

The most serious health problem related to water contamination undoubtedly is cancer, especially when it afflicts children. Children seem to be more vulnerable to the effects of chemical exposures than adults.[65] "Their behavior, diet, developing physiology, and growth needs all contribute to children's unique susceptibility to toxic harm."[66]

C A S E   S T U D Y

The Woburn Leukemia Cluster

Woburn, Massachusetts is a lower middle-class community 12 miles north of Boston. Since the nineteenth century, Woburn has been an industrial town, first as a leather-tanning center and later as a popular venue for the chemical and plastic industries. The source of Woburn's water supply is Lake Mishawum.

In the 1930s, townspeople began noticing that Lake Mishawum often took on a red coloring and emitted a nauseating odor.[67] Residents continued to complain about discoloration, bad smell, and bad taste in their water through the 1970s. In 1978, Woburn was forced to close two wells because of a high concentration of carbon-chloroform extract (CCE) far in excess of the accepted limits for public safety.[68] The problem was attributed to the town's chlorination method. The real source of the toxic pollution, as well as its full extent and tragic consequences, had not yet been recognized.

(Continued)

There was, however, at least one resident who had become obsessed with the danger of Woburn's contaminated water. Annie Anderson, a housewife whose son Jimmy was diagnosed with acute lymphocytic leukemia in 1972, learned of other such cases and met families of other victims at stores and at the hospital where Jimmy was being treated. "In 1973, she began to suspect that the growing number of leukemia cases might have been caused by something carried in the water."[69] She asked the state to test Woburn's water supply, but her request was denied. Anderson's suspicions initially were dismissed as the displaced anger of a distraught parent.[70] Her husband asked the family pastor to try to get her mind off what he felt was an erroneous obsession. The pastor would later recall, "I set out to prove her wrong, that cancer and leukemia don't run in neighborhoods, but she was right."[71]

Annie Anderson's claims received a more official measure of validation in June 1979, when scientists from the EPA tested the wetlands surrounding the two closed wells and found "dangerous levels of lead, arsenic, and chromium."[72] Anderson soon produced a map of Woburn plotted with the homes of children who had been diagnosed with childhood leukemia. Twelve such cases were identified, six of them closely clustered within blocks of the Anderson home.

On January 18, 1981, 12-year-old Jimmy Anderson died of leukemia. Five days after the boy's death, the Massachusetts Department of Public Health (DPH) released a report confirming a statistically improbable incidence of childhood leukemia in Woburn, as well as an elevated incidence of kidney cancer. Although the DPH was somewhat vague in its findings, eight families of young leukemia victims, relying on additional data generated by the Harvard School of Public Health, filed a $100 million lawsuit in 1982 against the alleged sources of the carcinogenic water. The main defendant was the Cryovac Division of the giant W. R. Grace Corporation. Grace was accused of negligent waste disposal practices leading to groundwater contamination and its resultant diseases.[73] The suit sought damages for wrongful death, pain and suffering, medical expenses, and mental anguish, including a legally untested claim of anticipatory distress concerning potential future illness.[74]

The trial was held in 1986. Expert witnesses presented evidence of a "chemical causeway" from the Grace plant to the victims' water supply. The company denied that it was the primary source of the contamination. In response to evidence of the presence of CCE on its property, it contended that trespassers had dumped it there, even though a number of eyewitnesses, including workers and executives, testified that they had seen the firm dump toxic wastes.[75] A contractor testified that he had been asked in 1974 by the manager of the Cryovac facility "to build a pit in which to bury chemical wastes."[76] In the face of such compelling evidence, Grace changed its strategy. It argued that, even if its chemicals were present in the town's water supply, none had been shown to be carcinogenic.

After 77 days of the trial, the jury ruled that W. R. Grace negligently had dumped chemicals on its property. The judge, whom most observers had perceived as sympathetic to the defense, set aside the verdict on the grounds that the jury had not understood the highly technical data upon which the case had been based. He

(Continued)

ordered a new trial, but a few days later Grace reached an out-of-court settlement with the families for $8 million.

But Grace's troubles were not over. Annie Anderson's long-sought moment of vindication likely came when Grace admitted in U.S. District Court that it had provided false information to the EPA in 1982 in response to questions about its toxic waste disposal practices. A criminal indictment was handed down in 1988.[77] The company entered a plea bargain in which it agreed to plead guilty to one of the 12 charges and pay the maximum fine of $10,000.[78]

As a grim postscript, it can be noted that, in the period between the filing of the original lawsuit in 1982 and the termination of the trial in 1986, seven more Woburn children were diagnosed with leukemia, nearly four times the state average.[79]

Air Pollution

Many of the same toxic chemicals that have poisoned the water we drink also have contaminated the air we breathe. The term air pollution usually brings to mind images of belching smokestacks, noxious smog, and acid rain. Certainly, all these phenomena are serious threats to public health. For example, a 1973 government survey discovered that the Bunker Hill smelting complex was exposing the neighboring community of Kellogg, Idaho, to dangerous levels of arsenic air pollution.[80] Two years later, airborne emissions from the Asarco lead smelting plant in El Paso, Texas, was cited by the CDC as a cause of neuropsychological dysfunction in local children.[81]

A study of nine major cities conducted by the American Lung Association between 1981 and 1990 attributed 3% of all deaths to outdoor air pollution.[82] In New York City, hundreds of deaths have been attributed to huge quantities of particles and gases that are produced by power and industrial plants and held in place by occasional stagnant air masses.[83] Californians have grown accustomed to periodic smog alerts. In the Rust Belt, urbanites have become almost as aware of their city's air quality index as its daily temperature.

Respiratory disease has, in fact, become the most rapidly increasing cause of death in America.[84] Every day massive amounts of toxic particles and gases are emitted into the air. Many citizens literally are choking to death on the "treacherous residues [of a] small-minded, money-blinded, out of control technology."[85]

Although the term "air pollution" probably suggests an outdoor risk to most citizens, this perception is dangerously false. "[A] flurry of reports in the popular and scientific literature call attention to a greater variety of potentially harmful pollutants indoors than had ever been of concern outdoors."[86] The best documented example is asbestos, which is at the center of one of the most egregious of all environmental crimes.

Asbestos is a mineral found in rocks, and it has been used in construction since the time of ancient Rome.[87] It does not occur naturally in homes. It has been added purposely to many types of building materials, including textured paint, pipe wrap, boarded and spray-on insulation, ceiling and floor tiles, roofing shingles, wall plaster, and cement. In many respects, it lives up to its modern nickname, the "magic mineral."[88] "The mineral acts as an insulator and fire retardant; it strengthens concrete and sound-proofs; it allows for high traction and resists chemical breakdown."[89]

Unfortunately, asbestos fibers, particularly in older homes and buildings, can crumble and become airborne. When inhaled, these fibers can cause a potentially lethal illness called asbestosis, which scars the lungs, stifles breathing, and impedes the flow of oxygen to the blood. One writer contends that 25 million Americans could be victims of asbestos-related diseases[90] such as asbestosis and mesothelioma, a cancer of the linings of the lungs. Many of the victims are not succumbing to occupational exposure but to the asbestos inside their homes and schools. Approximately 10,000 deaths each year are attributed to asbestos.[91] Little wonder the "magic mineral" also has been called "the most widespread toxic substance in the nation."[92]

Researchers at the University of Texas Medical Branch have even suggested a link between asbestos and the mysterious sudden infant death syndrome (SIDS). They performed autopsies on 17 SIDS victims and found that 6 had asbestos in their lungs at levels comparable to adults with lung cancer.[93]

The health dangers of asbestos have been recognized for many decades. The first report directly linking asbestos exposure to disease was published in the *British Medical Journal* in 1924.[94] Internal memoranda have revealed that Johns-Manville, the giant firm which has dominated the asbestos industry for over 100 years, has been aware of reported asbestos hazards since at least 1930.[95] In 1965, its own confidential findings reported that 44% of its workers exposed to asbestos for 10 to 19 years had asbestosis. The company's public position remained that no scientific proof existed that working with asbestos causes asbestosis.[96] This contention seemed as illogical as denying that food poisoning is caused by food.

In 1992, Johns-Manville, one of the nation's largest corporations and the world's biggest asbestos producer, filed for bankruptcy protection, despite 1991 sales of $2.2 billion. The company's strategy was intended to halt the threat of inevitable asbestosis lawsuits by minimizing its liability. Manville's attorneys promised that the company would conduct "business as usual" during the reorganization.[97]

More recently, as asbestos litigation has proliferated, victims' attorneys have used the legal discovery process to unearth thousands of incriminating corporate documents detailing an escalating cycle of denial and cover-up for nearly a half century. Some of the correspondence reveals a pattern of suppression of information. For example, Johns-Manville and Raybestos-Manhattan conspired to distort the results of a 1935 study of the health effects of asbestos sponsored by the industry.

> In effect, the documents reveal the smoking gun of corporate
> irresponsibility . . . [They] also allow us a much clearer picture—

unique in the annals of industrial health in the U.S.—of how one industry established a corporate policy of covering up its products' hazards. The result has been needless loss of tens of thousands of lives over several decades with many thousands more expected, as well as profound human suffering by the victims of asbestos diseases and their families.[98]

The second half of this chapter examines more of these documents in conjuction with the contamination of the work environment. For now, it can be observed that the obvious failure of the asbestos industry to take any meaningful remedial action for over a half century was spurred solely by the profit motive. As one criminologist has lamented, "The priority of profits over human life sometimes leads to corporate actions that look like premeditated murder."[99]

C A S E   S T U D Y

The Hemlock Horrors

Midland, Michigan, is a company town, and the company is Dow Chemical. Indeed, a sign at the nearest airport reads "Welcome to Dow Country." A few miles from Midland, there is a small community with the chillingly prophetic name of Hemlock. Since the late 1970s, things reportedly have been happening in Hemlock for which the term "strange" would be an understatement.[100]

Local hunters claim to have shot deer whose meat was green. Farmers describe three-legged chickens, epileptic mice, bald cows, and geese born with their wings on backward. "[N]ot a few eyes in Hemlock were turning in search of an answer to that historical benefactor in Midland, the Dow Chemical Company."[101]

Midland's version of Annie Anderson was Diane Herbert, who resided near the mammoth Dow Complex. Like her Woburn counterpart, Mrs. Herbert became obsessed with explaining unusual reports of neighborhood illnesses, including chloracne (a serious skin condition), beltline hives, and even the development of hard lumps on her own back. Mrs. Herbert worked nearly alone for years, conducting a quiet letter-writing campaign. However, by 1983, she was making occasional television appearances and receiving modest financial support from the environmental group Greenpeace. It was becoming evident to her that the sorts of biological anomalies plaguing tiny Hemlock were also present in Midland. Witnesses described hawks that could not fly, squirrels with no tails, even a female peacock born with fancy male feathers. Dogs seemed to be contracting cancer and suffering heart attacks at an accelerated rate; some reportedly developed swollen glands the size of grapefruits. More alarming still, the human population was beset by nosebleeds, headaches, and thyroid problems. Saginaw

(Continued)

County, where Hemlock is situated, had an infant mortality rate 67% above the state average.

When Michael Brown, the journalist who earlier had illuminated the Love Canal story, investigated conditions in Midland, his chief suspect was airborne dioxin—the same chemical compound that (in a waterborne form) had wreaked havoc at Love Canal. Researchers at the EPA have concluded that dioxin affects fetal development and the immune system.[102] Other scientists have linked dioxin to "digestive disorders, effects on some essential enzyme systems, aches and pains of muscles and joints, effects on the nervous system, and psychiatric effects."[103] The effects of dioxin on laboratory animals has been reported to be even more debilitating, including several forms of cancer, liver disease, and birth defects.[104] And after decades of debate, an EPA report drafted in 2000 finally concluded that dioxin does cause cancer and other health problems in humans.[105] Tiny amounts of dioxin are known to become part of the food chain.[106] Brown had become something of an authority on dioxin. He knew that dioxin had been associated with soft-tissue sarcomas, a rare form of cancer that afflict muscles, cartilage, nerves, blood vessels, fat, and tendons.

Clearly, if dioxin was causing cancers in Midland, it seemed likely that soft-tissue sarcoma would be among them. When it showed up at abnormal levels, it was rather like spotting a ripple in the water that could be the head of the Loch Ness monster.[107]

Brown described a graph depicting birth defects in Midland during the 1970s: "[T]he line during that period had risen to a craggy peak that put one in mind of Mount Everest."[108] Midland's rate of birth defects seemed irrefutably excessive: three times the expected number of cleft palates; nearly five times the expected cases of urogenital defects. Brown also observed disproportionate incidence of congenital heart defects and mental retardation. In his words, "Something seemed to be very wrong, and it carried the ring of dioxin."[109]

Among Brown's most compelling Midland reports were stories of entire families afflicted with oral pus sacs, of farmers falling off their tractors from seizures, of a young girl born with deformed black teeth shaped like rabbit ears, of people losing chunks of their memories—one woman suddenly forgot how to play the piano after 11 years of lessons.[110]

Dow, one of America's most powerful corporations—whose slogan boasts that "Dow Let's You Do Great Things," and whose diverse menu of products ranges from Styrofoam and Saran Wrap to Napalm and Agent Orange—denied any connection with the bizarre health problems afflicting the Midland-Hemlock vicinity. Dow's researchers maintained that their own dioxin experiments had yielded no abnormal cancer rates in laboratory rats.

Yet when the EPA tested the soil at the Dow complex for dioxin, it found levels *six times higher* than at Love Canal. "[T]he EPA was finally concluding what so many had guessed and feared all along: 'Air emissions from the Dow Chemical plant are the likely source of contamination in the Midland area.'"[111]

Regulation and Enforcement

Uniontown, Ohio, was the site of the aptly named Industrial Excess Landfill, a 30-acre dump containing 750,000 metric tons of toxic waste. Methane gas regularly wafted from the dump, and one day in 1984, it collected inside a local home. The house promptly exploded.[112]

In 1982, residents of Times Beach, Missouri, discovered that their whole community had been poisoned. A decade earlier, the town had hired a firm to spray a slick coat of oil on 10 miles of unpaved streets to reduce a dust problem. Unfortunately, that firm was also in the business of hauling toxic waste from a downstate chemical factory, and it recognized an opportunity to collect two fees for the same job. Consequently, Times Beach unknowingly became a toxic dump.

> Incredible as it might sound, dioxin had been sprayed, dumped or used as grading fill near a home for the aged, near a Methodist church, at calf farms, and in horse arenas, where birds literally fell from their roosts and horses died in droves.[113]

Because of pervasive dioxin contamination, the government bought all the homes in Times Beach. In a chilling replay of Love Canal, the community was evacuated and an entire town ceased to exist.[114] Among those forced to abandon their town, an all too familiar roll call of strange illnesses developed. Four sisters, who evacuated as teenagers, all developed serious reproductive problems. The last mayor of Times Beach has reported that one of her daughters has epilepsy and another has thyroid problems, her son is afflicted with Grave's disease, and her ex-husband suffers from immune system disorders.[115]

A dozen years later, the EPA issued a report, which finally verified what former residents of Love Canal and Times Beach long had feared. Dioxin is one of the most toxic substances ever produced and "can cause cancer and other health problems even at very low levels of exposure."[116]

These stories are vivid, but appropriate, representations of the 1980s—surely a golden age of environmental crime. When the Reagan administration assumed power in 1981, it brought to Washington a clear antiregulation agenda. It is difficult to find any evidence of compatibility between deregulation and environmental safety. To a president with no environmentalist constituency, environmental crime simply was not an important priority. Indeed, according to an EPA estimate, about 90% of chemical wastes were disposed illegally in the early 1980s.[117]

> If the Carter administration reluctantly implemented the complex and expensive laws meant to guard the public from toxic harm, the Reagan administration robustly set about demolishing them. "Government is not the solution to our problem," the new president declared in his first inaugural address. "Government is the problem." Accordingly, the Reagan administration softened the bite of environmental regulators by extracting crucial staff and funding as though they were impacted wisdom teeth.[118]

Rita Lavelle, the new assistant administrator of the EPA, articulated some of the revised goals of the agency:[119]

1. Change perception (local and national) of Love Canal from dangerous to benign.
2. Obtain credible data that 50 of the nation's most dangerous hazardous waste sites have been rendered benign.
3. Provide credible proof that industries operating today are not dangerous to the public health.

Lavelle would later go to prison for perjury, but she was not lying about her objectives. "Her view that the nation's environmental problems could be resolved through the magic of public relations reflected the perverse fantasy life that separated Reagan administration deregulators from the growing number of ordinary citizens who now feared for the health of their communities."[120]

The indifference to environmental crimes which characterized the 1980s spawned a number of insidious by-products. Two of the more appalling ones are "environmental racism"[121] and "toxic terrorism."[122]

Environmental Racism

Toxic waste dumps are not randomly distributed across America. They often are located in communities with high percentages of minority residents.[123] In the words of one black newspaper publisher, "These dangerous facilities are put in communities of people considered to be marginal, not as important or valuable as white people."[124]

In 1987, for example, one-third of the total hazardous waste landfills operating in the 48 contiguous states were located in just five Southern states and represented well over 50% of the nation's hazardous waste landfill capacity. Four of those nine sites, representing about 60% of the landfill total for the Southern region, were in three zip code areas composed predominantly of African Americans, although African Americans make up only about 20% of the South's total population.[125]

One of those sites was in the town of Emelle, Alabama, with a 79% black population. Emelle was the home of the world's largest toxic waste dump, owned and operated by Chemwaste, a company that "had been repeatedly sued for millions of dollars by the EPA and various state regulatory agencies for numerous violations of standard safety practices at its waste disposal sites throughout the country."[126] Chemwaste dubbed the Emelle dump the "Cadillac of Landfills."[127] The town's residents could not have disagreed more. A local activist charged that Chemwaste was turning his community into "the pay toilet of America."[128]

Another of the most problematic dumps is one in predominantly black Warren County, North Carolina, which was selected in 1982 as the burial site for more than 32,000 cubic yards of soil contaminated with highly toxic polychlorinated biphenyls (PCBs).[129] The residents of Warren County demonstrated in opposition to their unsolicited selection, but they were unable to halt the landfill construction. As is generally the case with the disenfranchised, their protests went largely unheard. Public opposition to the siting of noxious facilities has been taken far more seriously in middle- and upper-income localities.

> The NIMBY (not in my backyard) syndrome has been the usual reaction in these communities. As affluent communities became more active in opposing a certain facility, the siting effort shifted toward more powerless communities. Opposition groups often called for the facilities to be sited "somewhere else." The Somewhere, U.S.A., was often in poor, powerless, and minority communities.[130]

In a similar vein, the children of McFarland, California, a small town whose residents are mostly Latino farm workers, are dying from cancer at a rate four times the national average. This harrowing statistic has been attributed to exposure to toxic chemical pesticides. Like the residents of Warren County and Emelle, Alabama, the people of McFarland have sought help from the federal government but have yet to receive it.[131]

In 1994, a group of 20 utility companies started negotiations aimed at burying highly radioactive nuclear waste under an Apache reservation in Mescalero, New Mexico.[132] This facility, one of several being proposed for tribal reservations nationwide, is being touted by proponents as a much needed source of jobs and income. Critics have voiced grave concerns over health and safety issues.

Toxic Terrorism

One of President Carter's *last* official acts was the issuance of an executive order toughening the notification requirements for companies wishing to export products whose use is restricted in the United States. One of President Reagan's *first* official acts was the immediate revocation of the month-old Carter order.[133] America could "now expand its program of poisoning the world"[134] by engaging in what has been termed "toxic terrorism." Toxic terrorism can assume any of three forms.

The Sale of Dangerous Chemicals.   American companies have developed "a multi-billion dollar toxic chemical trade which includes the global peddling of millions of pounds of pesticides—including some so dangerous that they wouldn't even be allowed to be used in America under the EPA's weak standards."[135] The president of the National Agricultural Chemicals Association defended this practice in 1981: "We should not impose on these countries a standard that we have imposed on ourselves."[136] That same year, the White House deputy adviser for consumer affairs reiterated the new spirit of deregulation: "We can't be the world's nanny."[137]

One such pesticide, for example, has been sold regularly to the Philippines. "Unaware of the chemical's harmful effects, three rural tribesmen once turned hoses on each other as a joke. They all died."[138] Velsicol Chemical Company used to manufacture a nerve-attacking pesticide called leptophos, which is so lethal that when it was used in Egyptian cotton fields, 2000-pound water buffalo began dropping dead.[139]

   To compound the offense, hundreds of tons of pesticides, too lethal for domestic use, have been included in American foreign aid programs.[140] Many of these lethal pesticides later come back to threaten the health of the American public in the form of imported produce and other food. In 1975, traces of leptophos were found in nearly half the imported Mexican tomatoes sampled by federal food and drug inspectors.[141] This seems frighteningly reminiscent of Rachel Carson's dire prophecies in her famous book, *Silent Spring*, in which she warned of "sinister" pesticides and their power to alter the very nature of life on earth.[142] It was surely not by caprice that Velsicol, the manufacturer of leptophos, had tried to block the publication of *Silent Spring* in 1962.[143] Since *Silent Spring* was published, "at least 136 active ingredients in pesticides have been found to cause cancer in humans or animals."[144]

The Export of Hazardous Waste.   The 1980s also witnessed the emergence of a "shadow industry" involving the export of toxic waste from the United States to other nations.[145] The search for foreign markets for hazardous residues and contaminated sludge was spurred by the closing of many domestic landfills owing to public health problems and the shrinking capacity. In addition, the economics of foreign dumping undoubtedly were attractive. When the cost of legitimately disposing of toxic waste in the United States was about $2500 per ton, some impoverished countries, burdened by massive foreign debts, were accepting as little as $3.00 per ton to dispose of toxins within their borders.[146] In 1987, for example, it actually was cheaper to ship waste by barge to the Caribbean than to move it overland just 40 miles.[147]

   Surprisingly, the majority of the legally exported waste of that period ended up in Canada, where restrictions were far less stringent than in the United States.[148] However, it soon was recognized that the future of foreign dumping rested in Third World countries. "Since 1980, thirty-five of the seventy-five approved destinations for these exports have been underdeveloped nations, including the Philippines, Mexico, and many in Central America and the Middle East."[149] A 1988 report also listed the African nations of Zaire, Guinea, Gabon, and Sierra Leone as favorite dumping grounds for exported waste.[150]

   Little concern was demonstrated regarding the health and environmental repercussions of toxic exports. A U.S. Commerce Department official summed up the American "hands off" policy: "After [it] gets there, the country can do whatever it wants with it. I assume it gets tossed out."[151] Of course, "tossing out" hazardous waste is precisely the practice that produced Love Canal, Times Beach, and so many other domestic environmental horror stories described in this chapter.

The American government not only permitted the hazardous waste trade, certain agencies encouraged it. Among the contaminated material shipped to such countries as India, South Korea, Nigeria, and Zimbabwe during the 1980s were wastes from the U.S. Army and Navy, the Department of Defense, and the Department of Agriculture. One entrepreneur even attempted to buy lead-tainted paper from the Treasury Department's Bureau of Engraving and ship it to Africa to be resold as toilet paper.[152]

In 1987, an official in the EPA's Office of International Activities defended the Reagan administration's "buyer beware" philosophy: "At EPA, we're not in a position to say, 'That's a bad deal,' or 'They don't know what they're doing.' If the receiving country says yes, there's nothing we can do about the shipments."[153]

The Construction of Polluting Factories.   In the Mexican border town of Matamoros, they are called *masquiladores*.[154] They are American-owned factories that have crossed the Rio Grande for two very profitable reasons. First of all, the labor is cheap. Indeed, in the 1980s real wages in Mexico fell by 50%. Most *masquila* workers are young, many only 13 or 14 years old. "Some of the proudest names of U.S. business are riding on the backs of Mexican children—from General Electric and Westinghouse to Ford, General Motors, and Chrysler."[155]

Second, environmental regulation is lax. These plants have filled the sky and the water with a staggering amount of chemical pollution. With this contamination have come all the accompanying human miseries. A disturbing pattern of deformities and mental retardation has been observed among the children of the area. Their mothers had all worked in the *masquiladores* zone and had been exposed to toxic chemicals.[156] "Just over the border in the South Texas Rio Grande Valley, eighty babies were born with fatally underdeveloped brains during a five-year period—more than double the national average."[157] It has been said that the U.S.–Mexico border has become "a two-thousand mile Love Canal."[158]

Among the wastes generated are the known carcinogen TCE, deadly PCPs, copper cyanide (a derivative of electroplating), methylene chloride, and sundry other toxic substances.[159] Many company officials claim they return their wastes to the United States. However, in 1988 a director of the U.S. Customs Service declared that he had never seen a single barrel of chemical waste enter the United States from Mexico.[160] So where does all that toxic waste really go?

Some wastes are put in drums and stored right at the factories. As these containers get old, they often begin to leak. In 1987, dozens of chemical drums were observed outside the Zenith plant in Agua Prieta. They were marked *sucios*—Spanish for "dirty."[161] Some are dumped unscrupulously at regular city dumps in border towns. Numerous clandestine dumps also proliferate in the Mexican desert.[162] For example, in 1988 General Motors (GM) contracted with a Mexican firm to dispose of several hundred

barrels of paint sludge at a hazardous waste site n
never arrived; instead they had been dumped in th
discovered, the Mexican firm claimed that the de
temporary open-air dump. Worse yet, GM would
that the sludge was dangerous. A spokeswoman i
paint sludge was nonhazardous material in container.
ardous waste."[163]

Because of its proximity—and because *masquila*
lowest in the world—Mexico has become a haven for Am
luters; but it is hardly unique. In December 1984, for exam   ..um
city of Bhopal suffered the worst industrial accident in his   .,. A storage tank
containing the dangerous chemical methyl isocyanate gas (MIC) began to leak
at a pesticide plant owned by the giant American corporation Union Carbide.
What followed that night was a virtual kaleidoscope of death.

> People were choking and gasping for breath. Some fell as they ran, and
> some lay on the roadside vomiting and defecating. Others, too weak to run,
> tried to clutch onto people passing them in the hope of being carried
> forward.[164]

Before the week was over, nearly 3000 people had died, and more than
300,000 had been injured.[165] "Union Carbide's standard reply to all queries
that night remained: 'Everything is under control.'"[166] Eight years later, an average of five Bhopal victims per week were still dying.[167]

The Superfund

In 1980, Congress passed the Comprehensive Environmental Response, Compensation, and Liability Act (CERCLA), better known as Superfund.[168] The
legislation, which provided remedies for uncontrolled and abandoned hazardous waste sites, was a political response to the public outcry over the Love
Canal scandal.[169]

Under CERCLA, the parties responsible for the hazardous conditions
are supposed to do the cleanup themselves or reimburse the government for
doing it. Unfortunately, in the words of the environmental consultant who
turned in a blistering report to Congress in 1988, "This is a program that
hardly ever gets anything right."[170] Superfund is widely regarded as one of
the most ineffective pieces of legislation ever enacted in the United States. It is
not supportable through its original scheme of fines and industry fees, and the
final cleanup bill almost certainly will be handed to taxpayers. Some experts
predict that Superfund's eventual cost may even exceed that of the S & L
bailout (Chapter 7).[171]

Superfund is the epitome of all the environmental half-measures to
emerge from the 1980s. CERCLA was designed ostensibly to please many environmentalists by throwing an unprecedented amount of money ($1.6 bil-
lion) at its clean-up task. However, its true beneficiary was the waste disposal
industry, which was delighted at the prospect of enormous future profits.

In effect, all that Superfund generally does is take waste from one landfill and move it to another. In some cases, disposal firms, which are the very targets of Superfund sanctions, receive lucrative contracts to move their own illegally dumped toxins. In 1982, an outspoken EPA official summed up the Superfund fiasco: "[W]hat they're doing is buying more iron lungs instead of investing in the vaccine."[172]

The deficiencies of Superfund may be exemplified by briefly reviewing the story of one contaminated site: Brio, a 50-acre abandoned refinery located 18 miles south of Houston.

C A S E   S T U D Y

Brio

1957–1982

The Brio facility was operated as an oil refinery by a succession of owners, until finally declaring bankruptcy. During that period, waste material was deposited in unlined pits and covered with soil. Between 500,000 and 700,000 cubic yards of soil was contaminated with fuel oil residues, styrene tars, heavy metals, and volatile organic compounds (VOCs). Groundwater under the site also was contaminated with vinyl chloride and benzene.[173]

1984

Brio was designated a federally controlled Superfund site.[174]

January 1988

The EPA finally proposed cleanup plans for Brio. It recommended that contaminated soil and sludge be excavated and destroyed in an on site mobile incinerator.[175]

September 1988

More than 200 homeowners from the nearby 500-acre South Bend subdivision filed suit against the companies allegedly responsible for the contamination of Brio. Several doctors and scientists insisted that the site posed significant health risks. The EPA maintained that Brio represented no threat to the community.[176]

1989

The residents of South Bend conducted an informal health survey of their community. According to their findings, "10 of 12 mothers who were pregnant at

(Continued)

the time chemical pits were disturbed in early 1987 gave birth to children with physical defects."[177] The parents of one pair of siblings who had grown up in South Bend described their children's ongoing medical problems. The daughter suffered from chronic nosebleeds and ovarian cysts; the son suffered upper respiratory infections that had left him with a speech impediment.[178] Another set of anguished parents reported serious medical conditions in all three of their children. One daughter was born without reproductive organs; another daughter had autoimmune and hearing problems; the son suffered from strabismus, an eye coordination defect.[179] Stories of children stricken with spinal bifida, as well as congenital heart, lung, and brain defects, were also collected.

March 1992

The elementary school in South Bend closed.[180]

June 1992

The buyout of homes in South Bend began.[181]

September 1993

A Brio investigation in *Time* reported: "Virtually nothing has been done."[182]

October 1993

Brio task force officials acknowledged that chemical emissions from the site were draining into nearby Clear Creek. Levels of TCE were termed "dangerously high."[183] The EPA assured area residents that the fish in the creek were safe to eat. The EPA, however, did issue a stop-work order at the Brio site when inspectors noticed a chemical release problem involving the carcinogens vinyl chloride and methylene chloride.[184] One public health official went as far as to recommend the evacuation of South Bend, but the EPA decided against it. It also was revealed that the site contractor, Chemical Waste Management (the owners of the controversial Emelle, Alabama, landfill, discussed earlier), had waited almost a month before releasing the toxicity report on Brio's poisoned air.[185]

November 1993

The Texas state health commissioner warned against eating fish from Clear Creek, saying that the Brio facility had contaminated them.[186]

January 1994

Construction of the on-site incinerator was completed at a cost of $18 million.[187]

(Continued)

April 1994

Work was halted at Brio before the incinerator was ever used.[188] Ten years had elapsed since Brio was designated a Superfund site, and the EPA admitted that "the cleanup was still in its infancy."[189] Under orders from the EPA, hazardous material was no longer even being handled at Brio, pending the formulation of a new plan.[190]

May 1994

The EPA acknowledged that it was considering paying for the relocation of South Bend's remaining residents, because the Brio task force had refused to do so.[191]

October 1994

A medical study was released on the health risks of living next to Brio. The report backed away from suggestions that the numerous illnesses found in adjacent neighborhoods were linked to the Superfund dump. Interestingly, however, when the co-author of the report was asked by reporters whether he personally would feel comfortable living next to Brio, he replied: "Ah, well, I'm not going to get into that. I have no comment."[192]

February 5, 1995

The Brio Site Task Force reported to the Friendswood City Council that only 9 families remained in the 687 homes in the South Bend subdivision.[193]

August 25, 1995

Only two homes in South Bend were now occupied. The Brio Site Task Force released three new proposals for the much-delayed cleanup effort. Each plan carried a price tag of at least $40 million. A spokesperson for the task force surprised absolutely no one when she declared, "We still have a long road ahead of us."[194]

The torpid tale of Brio underscores the failure of Superfund. For over a decade, bureaucratic red tape and wholesale litigation have combined to thwart any meaningful remediation. It has been said of Superfund that "the only people who have cleaned up have been lawyers."[195] Since the Superfund program began, private companies have spent $4.7 billion on legal fees, more than a third of the total expenditures for toxic cleanups.[196] Indeed, despite numerous financial settlements over the years, at least 18 lawsuits were still pending by 1994 against the chemical companies comprising the Brio task force, including such corporate giants as Monsanto, Arco, and Chevron,[197] and the clean-up remained in limbo. Meanwhile, the city of Pearland, Texas, sitting in the shadow of Brio, is said to have developed the highest cancer rate in the nation.[198]

Regrettably, there is little reason for optimism regarding CERCLA in the years to come. Originally, Superfund listed over 1200 priority projects, representing "only a fraction of the sites anticipated to become future disasters."[199] The actual number of contaminated waste sites eventually could exceed 10,000.[200] A single company—General Motors—has been linked to 200 Superfund sites.[201] In its first 13 years, Superfund managed to redeem a total of 33 hazardous sites. At that rate, the original 1200 sites should be cleaned up in about 500 years.

There were, on the other hand, some encouraging indications that the criminal justice system's routinized wrist-slapping of the 1980s appeared to give way to tougher sanctioning policies in the 1990s. One significant change in enforcement policy has been an increased determination on the part of prosecutors to pursue convictions of individual managers, rather than corporations.[202] Through most of the 1980s, the sanctioning of environmental criminals had been most remarkable for its inconsistency. "The courts had so much discretion that individuals convicted of the same offense could receive widely disparate sentences; one could receive 20 years in prison and another simply be placed on probation."[203] However, in 1987 new federal sentencing guidelines were established, and objective numerical formulas largely replaced judicial subjectivity.[204]

Five categories of sanctions exist for environmental crime. They may be imposed individually or in combination.

Fines.   Prescribed financial penalties are increased and decreased according to a mathematical weighting of specific aggravating or mitigating factors.[205] Chief among those factors is whether an environmental offense is deemed simple negligence or "willful" negligence. Under the simple negligence standard, "it must be shown that the violation resulted from a lack of due care."[206] Actual knowledge of the violation need not be shown. For example, in 1992, the PureGro pesticide company was fined $100,000 for illegally dumping dirt contaminated with toxic substances in an undeveloped area of California's Imperial County.[207] Willful negligence requires actual knowledge of illegality or a reckless intent to further an illegal objective.[208] An example of willful negligence occurred in 1993, when Bethlehem Steel was fined $6 million for its "*willful* failure to comply with environmental laws."[209]

Other examples of fines levied against corporate polluters include the following cases:

> Texaco was fined $750,000 for failing to conduct important tests on a California offshore oil rig.[210]
>
> Ocean Spray was fined $400,000 for discharging acidic waste water from its Massachusetts plant.[211]
>
> Ashland Oil was fined $2.5 million for a collapsed storage tank in Pennsylvania that discharged more than 700,000 gallons of diesel fuel into the Ohio and Monongahela Rivers.[212]

Chevron agreed in 2000 to pay a $6 million fine for violations of the Clean Air Act at its offshore loading terminal in El Segundo, California.[213]

Also in 2000, Koch Industries, one of the largest privately held companies in the United States, agreed to pay a $30 million fine from spilling an estimated 3 million gallons of oil, over an 8-year period, from its pipeline system in 6 states.[214]

Restitution. Court-ordered restitution involves offenders paying victims for any loss caused by the offense or the performance of remedial measures to eliminate present or future harm associated with the offenses, such as a mandatory clean-up.[215] For example, the government took the large Sherwin-Williams paint company to court in 1993, seeking to force the firm to clean up contamination at its Chicago factory.[216] That same year, Sbicca, a California shoe company, admitted attempting to smuggle toxic waste into Mexico and was ordered to pay all expenses incurred by the California Department of Toxic Substance Control and the U.S. Customs Service in their investigations of the case, in addition to a heavy fine.[217]

Probation. Supervised probation entails the imposition of "environmental audits" on offending companies.[218] For example, the Pratt and Whitney jet engine division of United Technologies Corporation was fined $5.3 million in 1993 and then placed on probation for abuses in handling and discharging hazardous wastes. Under the settlement, the company agreed to undergo extensive audits of its environmental practices until the year 2000.[219]

Nontraditional Sanctions. Some judges have ordered offending firms to give money to various state or local environmental programs. "For example, when the Transit Mix Concrete Company pleaded guilty to knowingly discharging pollutants into a tributary of the Arkansas River without a permit, the court . . . ordered the firm to spend $55,000 on a community service project, with the 'suggestion' that the money be spent on improving hiking trails near the river."[220] There also have been cases in which companies were ordered to place advertisements in local newspapers publicly apologizing for their actions. Two such cases were those of Vermont Industries and the General Wood Preserving Company of North Carolina.[221]

In 1996, Dow Chemical was fined $192,000 by Texas environmental officials for 25 different air quality violations. Under a novel arrangement, the company was ordered to pay $100,000 of that fine to help protect and restore the prairie chicken, one of the most critically endangered of all native bird species of which less than 50 remain in the wild.[222]

Incarceration. In the 1980s, the government often treated environmental cheaters like minor tax cheaters, assessing fines but seldom locking up offenders. In 1985, federal courts handed out less than 2 years of total prison terms for environmental crimes. Five years later, the total had jumped to 37 years and the trend continues upward.[223] The EPA now recognizes criminal sanctions as its most powerful tool. According to the Department of Justice, more than half the individuals convicted of environmental crimes since 1990 have gone to prison.[224] For example, in 1993 the two top executives of Allied Applicators, a Texas spray-painting company, received 3-year sentences for ordering the dumping of 13 barrels of lead solvents at a dead-end street in Houston. The district attorney had asked for probation, "[b]ut the judge apparently wanted to send a message to polluters by sending the president and vice-president to prison."[225]

Criminal law is a relatively new tool for enforcing environmental statutes.[226] Advocates of criminal prosecution argue that incarceration provides a greater deterrence effect than civil penalties, because it "discourages corporate willingness to view environmental misconduct as a mere economic risk."[227] Moreover, even stronger criminal enforcement efforts are predicted for future cases of what has been called "toxic turpitude."[228] "[C]orporate officials who disregarded their responsibilities under the environmental laws will find that there truly is nowhere to run and nowhere to hide."[229]

THE WORKPLACE ENVIRNOMENT

Years ago, coal miners took caged canaries underground with them as a primitive early warning detection system for lethal carbon monoxide gas. If the bird collapsed and died, the miners knew to evacuate. An investigative report on occupational health hazards, written in 1976, offered a morbid analogy: "Today . . . American workers have themselves become canaries."[230]

As many as 20% of all cancer cases are believed to stem from carcinogens in the workplace.[231] It has been estimated that at least 5% of deaths from heart disease result from occupational causes. Indeed, about one-third of all diagnosed medical conditions are said to be job-related.[232] When one factors in the injuries and deaths caused by industrial accidents, the grand total is a sad reflection of institutionalized negligence.

One of the most shocking accidents occurred in 1968 when a coal mine blew up in Farmington, West Virginia, killing 78 men.[233] This was by no means the deadliest mine accident in American history, but it was the first major one of the television era. A horrified nation heard the calamitous roar of incendiary eruptions and saw immense clouds of black smoke drifting across their screens like a funereal pall.

This tragic incident, more than any other event, likely prompted the enactment of the Occupational Safety and Health Act of 1970. The language of the Act contained a clear statement of its purpose and statutory mandate: "[T]o assure as far as possible every working man and woman in the Nation safe and healthful working conditions."[234] In the Act's first decade, the two best-known employee endangerment cases probably were the Kepone debacle in Virginia and the Scotia mine disasters in Kentucky.

Kepone is a highly toxic pesticide developed by Allied Chemical Corporation in the 1950s. It was sold mainly to banana growers in Latin America, Africa, and Asia. By the early 1960s, several studies, including one by Allied itself, revealed the tendency of Kepone to induce tremors. Other research noted liver abnormalities and possible cancer links. In addition, laboratory tests on rats produced kidney lesions in females and atrophy of the testes and sterility or impaired reproductive performance in males.[235]

None of these findings, however, slowed down the commercial production of Kepone. In 1973, Allied, perhaps concerned about its liability for such a dangerous substance, set up a new corporation, ironically named Life Science Products (LSP), to process Kepone exclusively for it. LSP was housed in an abandoned filling station near the Allied plant in Hopewell, Virginia. The facility was an environmental nightmare come true. Neighbors complained that the plant's airborne emissions sometimes were so thick that traffic in the area was halted.[236] Toxic dust saturated workers' clothing and hair and even the sandwiches they brought from home.[237] Workers at LSP began to develop the "Kepone shakes," sometimes within 2 weeks of starting work.[238] "One man later recalled that when he stopped off for a beer after work, friends had to help him hold the glass."[239] Local doctors, who allegedly had "informal agreements" with the company, diagnosed workers' problems as hypertension and prescribed tranquilizers and psychotherapy.[240]

In 1975, one worker, who could not stop trembling, saw a specialist, who in turn contacted the state epidemiologist. When that official began examining workers coming off their shifts at LSP, he quickly realized that a major industrial scandal was unraveling. The first man he saw was "a 23-year-old who was so sick he was unable to stand up due to unsteadiness."[241] Within days, Life Science Products was shut down.

Federal criminal indictments were brought against Allied and LSP, citing 1096 violations.[242] Two former Allied executives, who had gone to work for LSP when it was created, were tried on charges involving the pollution of a local waterway in the years when Allied had manufactured Kepone. They were acquitted and, consequently, charges were dropped against a group of their subordinates, even though they had already pleaded guilty. LSP was convicted, however, and fined $3.8 million. This was merely symbolic, because LSP was by that time long defunct and had no assets. Because, technically speaking, LSP was not a subsidiary of Allied Chemical, but an independent contractor, Allied was never sanctioned for its role in the damage done to the Kepone workers, although it was fined for violating federal water pollution control laws when it dumped quantities of Kepone in the James River.[243] Virginia had been forced to prohibit the consumption of fish from the James River,[244] and unacceptable amounts of Kepone had even appeared in some Chesapeake Bay bluefish.[245]

The state epidemiologist who uncovered the so-called Kepone mob, warned at the time that the disaster could well be repeated elsewhere.[246] His words proved prophetic because in 1976, workers at the Bayport, Texas, chemical plant where Velsicol manufactured leptophos (the pesticide that would kill over 1200 water buffalo in Egypt), suffered an outbreak of nervous disorders described by one official as "another Kepone case."[247] Employees were stricken with "partial paralysis, failure of muscular coordination, blurred vision, choking sensations, and dizziness."[248] In addition, two workers were diagnosed with multiple sclerosis and three others contracted encephalitis.[249] One ex-employee, a 33-year-old former Army paratrooper who was exposed to leptophos for only 10 months, became almost completely disabled from nervous system damage. Doctors called his condition "spastic paralysis of the lower extremities," but he offered a less clinically detached description: "My spine is deteriorating. It's dissolving."[250]

When Velsicol finally halted the production of leptophos in 1976, it told the government that it was not motivated by concerns about safety, but by a "softening of the market."[251] Besides, Velsicol had already developed a successor to leptophos, a pesticide brand-named EPN, which was twice as poisonous as leptophos and, unlike its predecessor, licensed for domestic use. Studies at the Duke University medical school have reported that it takes only half as much EPN as leptophos to kill a laboratory animal.[252]

At the same time the Texas workers were being debilitated, the Scotia case was unfolding at a coal mine in Kentucky. The Scotia mine was owned by the Blue Diamond Coal Company which, in 1976 (the worst economic year since the Great Depression) was generating record profits.[253] Blue Diamond was typical of many of the nation's coal producers. "No one connected in any way with the management of the company displayed any visible concern for land, air, or water. They regarded environmentalists as nuts."[254]

Scotia's overriding goal was to dig coal and make money. Many of the miners probably agreed. As a nonunionized mine, Scotia was paying relatively high wages in an effort to discourage any interest in the United Mineworkers of America. In a good year, a man willing to work 7 days per week, including holidays, might earn $30,000.[255]

Unfortunately, 1976 was anything but a good year. On March 9, 15 miners died in an explosion at an uninspected section of the mine. Mechanical equipment had set off accumulated gases for which no one had bothered to test. Two days later, 11 more men were killed by a second explosion.[256]

Coal mining, of course, is a tough job and, even under the best of conditions, a dangerous one.[257] The shame is that many of America's mines do not approach any semblance of the "best of conditions," as the Scotia explosions graphically demonstrate.

> The gritty work of running the pits [rests with] low-echelon foremen and superintendents of mediocre competence. . . . Top management avoids the tipples and tunnels and knows little about the guts of the operation. [It] delegates responsibility ever downward.[258]

Despite lengthy investigative hearings, no indictments, corporative or individual, ever were handed down relating to Scotia. Despite 26 deaths and a long record of serious violations, no sanctions for negligence ever were levied against the owners of the mine.

As the Kepone and Scotia cases illustrate, employees may be victimized either in terms of health or safety. Both these areas warrant further exploration.

Employee Health: Hazardous Substances

Asbestos. The adverse effects of asbestos (discussed earlier in this chapter) have been well-documented. In 1978, the U.S. Department of Health, Education and Welfare concluded that "as many as half of the 8 to 11 million Americans who worked with asbestos during and after World War II might die of lung cancer as a result of their exposure."[259] A 20-year follow-up study of former workers at a New Jersey asbestos insulation plant, which had moved to Texas in 1954,[260] reported an excessive incidence of fatal lung cancer, even in those workers who had been employed there for 1 month or less.[261] Many Americans said to be at risk worked with asbestos in wartime shipyards. A medical survey of a sample of 360 persons exposed to asbestos at a northern California shipyard revealed that 59% had lung abnormalities.[262] A study of over 6000 former workers at the Long Beach Naval Shipyard in southern California reported that at least 31% of those who had worked there 17 years or longer had asbestosis.[263]

Numerous victims later sued major companies such as Johns-Manville and Raybestos-Manhattan. Lawyers representing asbestos victims have produced reams of long-suppressed corporate minutes and correspondence indicating that these firms knew of the hazards to their workers many years before they would later claim awareness. For example, the minutes of two 1933 Johns-Manville board of directors meetings state that the company voted to settle 11 pending asbestosis cases for $35,000 in exchange for a written agreement that the afflicted employees would drop all present and future claims. According to one federal judge who has examined some of these documents, they reflect "a conscious effort by the industry in the 1930s to downplay, or arguably suppress, the dissemination of information to employees and the public for fear of the promotion of lawsuits."[264]

Perhaps most disturbing of all is a confidential 1949 report written by the medical director of Johns-Manville, recommending that workers who likely had asbestosis, but who had not yet developed symptoms, should not be informed of their illness. According to the report, "As long as the man feels well, is happy at home and at work and his physical condition remains good, he should be permitted to live and work in peace."[265]

In keeping with its policy of suppression, the industry did not warn workers of the dangers of asbestos exposure until 1964. That delay was critical to millions of workers, because asbestos-related diseases generally take at least 15 years to develop.[266] Thus, by the time an entire generation of asbestos workers was informed of the health risks, it was too late to arrest their diseases.

In 1972, Johns-Manville decided against the installation of a dust-control system to protect its workers. The company's executives had calculated that, given the system's $12-million price tag and its $5-million-per-year operating cost, it was more economical to pay $1 million per year in workers' compensation for employees who were disabled or killed by asbestos dust.[267]

In 1994, it was reported that dozens of teachers at a Bronx, New York, high school had contracted cancer since the school opened in 1976; 16 had died. The school had been shut down in 1993 for asbestos clean-up.[268]

In 1995, a Texas court found three asbestos makers—Owens Corning, Pittsburgh Corning, and Fuller-Austin Insulation—liable for $42.6 million in damages for causing disease or death in 11 former workers. After the trial, the foreman of the jury declared, "The evidence was overwhelming."[269]

Another Texas jury awarded $115 million in 1998 to 21 steelworkers because they developed asbestosis while working at an Alabama steel mill. The case was tried in Texas because Alabama law requires that asbestos lawsuits be filed within a year of exposure—a classic "Catch 22," because "[s]ymptoms of asbestosis may not become evident until 15 to 20 years after exposure."[270] The jury found the Carborundum Company acted with "gross negligence and malice"[271] and the award included $100 million in punitive damages. The jury reached a verdict in only 30 minutes. Carborundum is the manufacturer of an asbestos-containing grinding wheel that was used to cut pipe at a U.S. Steel plant in Birmingham, Alabama. Testimony revealed that Carborundum had failed to warn workers of health dangers they faced when using the tool. The steelworkers were not even given masks to wear while wielding the tool inches from their faces. The plaintiffs, although appreciative of the verdict, said that the judgment would not compensate them for their failing health. One of them lamented, "This is great, but I've got to walk around with it in my lungs the rest of my life. . . . I feel like justice has been done, but money's no good to a dead man."[272] Indeed, two of the original defendants had already died before the case even made it to court.[273]

A growing number of people without any direct or long-term connection to asbestos production are now being identified. At least one litigant contracted asbestosis from exposure to fibers over just three working summers during his college years.[274] Also, there are countless victims of what is called secondary or nonoccupational exposure.[275] A number of wives are believed to have contracted lung cancer "simply by washing the asbestos-laden clothes of their husbands."[276] A 50-year-old Maine woman attributes her terminal mesothelioma (a cancer of the cells that comprise the lining surrounding the lungs and inside of the ribs) to exposure to her husband's work clothes when he worked at a local iron works and regularly came in contact with asbestos. Her husband adds:

> "The whole issue of take-home toxins doesn't get enough education. Workers aren't generally aware of the concerns of bringing it home. . . . People need to know."[277]

An investigative report published in 1999 charged that a closed vermiculite mine had killed at least 192 people in Libby, Montana, over the preceeding 40 years. The mine had released more than two tons of asbestos per day into the air, 6 days per week.[278] To put the extent of this tragedy into perspective, 192 deaths represents nearly 8% of the population in this town of 2500, which is the equivalent of over 600,000 deaths in New York City. It is no surprise, then, that Libby is considered one of the nation's worst public health disasters in years.

Mining for vermiculite, a mineral used for insulation and gardening, releases tremolite asbestos, a rare and extremely toxic form of asbestos. In addition to the miners who contracted asbestosis, lung cancer, and mesothelioma, relatives also have contracted asbestos-related diseases due to exposure to contaminated work clothes.[279] One woman lost her miner husband to asbestosis; now four of her five grown children have the disease. Yet none of her children had ever worked in the mine.[280] Another Libby resident was diagnosed with asbestosis 34 years after he quit working at the mine. His wife and two of his children have also developed the disease.[281]

Finally, in a case horrifying in its callousness, three men were indicted by the Justice Department in 1998 for allegedly recruiting 20 homeless workers to remove nearly 2 miles of asbestos insulation from a manufacturing plant in Marshfield, Wisconsin. According to federal prosecutors, the three defendants recruited the homeless men in a soup kitchen in Chattanooga, Tennessee. They gave them fake identification, promised them work, then put them on a bus bound for Wisconsin.[282] In the words of Attorney General Janet Reno, "Knowingly removing asbestos improperly is criminal. Exploiting the homeless to do this work is cruel."[283]

Cotton Dust.   Cotton dust contains certain particulate materials which produce a serious and, in its later stages, irreversible respiratory disease called byssinosis,[284] or brown lung. The story of brown lung is yet another tale of powerful and greedy corporations willing to sacrifice workers' lives on the altar of maximum profits.

In 1980, the number of textile workers in North and South Carolina with byssinosis was estimated to be as high as 35,000. Nevertheless, from their inception until 1980, the workers' compensation boards of these two states granted only 320 disability awards for brown lung. The average award to these "lucky" recipients was less than $15,000, a sum which was supposed to pay medical bills and then provide for the remaining years of the victim's life. In reality, after deducting medical and legal fees, this compensation for a shortened, more painful life span seldom amounted to a single year's wages.[285]

Such inadequate treatment reflects how ferociously the textile mills have fought workers' compensation claims over the years. "While only two percent of all other compensation cases are contested by employers in the Carolinas, until 1980, eighty percent of the North Carolina and one hundred percent of the South Carolina brown lung cases were litigated by the textile companies."[286]

Since then, owing in large part to the slow but dogged expansion of unionization, the companies have softened their resistance, but only moderately. The southern textile industry, after all, was built on a traditional foundation of "authoritarian and often illegal rule in the workplace."[287] For example,

J. P. Stevens, the country's second largest textile manufacturer, has been singled out by the National Labor Relations Board as the greatest labor law violator in America. Many Stevens workers who have complained of unhealthy conditions or have tried to organize protests on behalf of employee safety have been intimidated or fired.[288]

Often, local doctors are in the employ of the textile companies. Until fairly recently, many of these doctors denied the very existence of byssinosis, although it has been a widely recognized medical condition since the 1940s. Thus, many cases went unreported because they were recorded as bronchitis or emphysema, with no designated occupational cause. One investigator describes a company doctor who once made the "mistake" of properly diagnosing byssinosis in a worker and was summarily dismissed by the textile firm.[289] One can only wonder how many unsophisticated textile workers have grown old before their time and gone to premature graves unaware of their industry's long pattern of criminal negligence.

Over a 7-year period, over 60% of the mills in North Carolina and nearly 80% of those in South Carolina that were inspected by the Occupational Safety and Health Administration (OSHA), the Labor Department agency charged with enforcing the Occupational Safety and Health Act, were found to exceed mandated cotton dust limits. In 75% of these cases, the dust levels were three times the permissible standard. Until 1980, the typical fine for noncompliance was $50, and most fines were never paid.[290]

In 1977, OSHA actually lowered its standard in a compromise with President Carter's Council on Wage and Price Stability, which was concerned that increasing the textile industry's dust reduction costs would fuel inflation. OSHA, which had feared being made a scapegoat for the spiraling inflation of that decade, later acknowledged that the price of their "cost effectiveness consideration" was an estimated 5200 additional cases of byssinosis. These 5200 victims saved the cotton processors about $600 million dollars.[291] It was, to say the least, a very cynical trade. Since 1981, OSHA has improved its record slightly, but major enforcement problems remain.[292]

Richard Guarasci, in his landmark article *Death by Cotton Dust*, documents the refusal of the textile industry to recognize byssinosis as well as that industry's resolve to fight all byssinosis claims and fiercely resist OSHA regulation.[293] Guarasci quotes one victim's description of his plight: "My bossman . . . said to me: 'You don't have no brown lung. There is no such thing.'"[294]

The last word here goes to a man whose 40 years working in a South Carolina cotton mill had left him with 57% of his lung capacity and a monthly pension of $22:

> The good Lord gives man the breath to breathe and I don't think the textile mills have the right to take it away . . . I want my lungs back.[295]

Radioactivity. There is a cluster of shoddy little homes in Cove, Arizona, where uranium once was mined for atomic bombs. These shanties formerly housed Navajo miners. Many of them died young from lung cancer; many others are still dying from the effects of radioactive exposure decades ago. In the 1940s, the U.S. government recruited young Navajos away from their fields and flocks, promising them high wages to dig for uranium ore. The government neglected to warn them, however, of the excessive levels of radiation in the mines and the terrible health dangers posed by radiation.[296] Former Interior Secretary Stewart Udall, who represented the Navajos in their claims against the federal government argued, "The case of the Navajo uranium miners is one of egregious government malfeasance."[297]

In 1990, Congress passed a bill officially acknowledging that the government had exposed about 220,000 military personnel and 150,000 civilians to harmful radiation between 1945 and 1953. Included in the Radiation Exposure Compensation Act was a provision for monetary compensation to victims of radiation sickness.[298] According to a longitudinal OSHA study 4200 uranium miners, 400 died of lung cancer, which is five times the national average.[299]

Radiation may be less visible than cotton dust, but it can be no less lethal. For example, a nuclear weapons factory in Fernald, Ohio, for years released radioactive wastes through faulty filters or unfiltered vents.[300] In 1994, the University of Cincinnati released a mortality study of over 1000 workers at the Fernald plant between 1953 and 1991. Analyses of medical records revealed that those workers "died at a significantly younger age and suffered a higher incidence of lung, intestinal, and blood cancers than the American population as a whole."[301]

The causal link between radiation and cancer has been acknowledged for over a century. Indeed, as early as the sixth century, miners of pitchblende (a form of uranium ore) in Germany and Czechoslovakia were known to almost invariable develop fatal lung diseases.[302] More recently, dentists' chronic exposure to x-rays is said to contribute to their abnormally high rates of leukemia, Hodgkin's disease—and suicide.[303]

In 1979, an incinerator worker at the controversial Rocky Flats Nuclear Weapons Complex began developing odd-shaped bruises on her upper torso and painful red sores on her skin. She also suffered periods of nausea and diarrhea and debilitating fatigue.[304] She would later learn that these are classic symptoms of radiation sickness. When she complained to the Rockwell Corporation, which managed the facility, she was told that her problems were a common reaction to the caustic solution in which her work clothes were washed. Her union representative interceded on her behalf and was told that "Rockwell does not recognize the skin as an organ."[305]

According to the afflicted employee, when she announced her intention to testify before the grand jury which had convened in the wake of the FBI raid on Rocky Flats, she was warned that "whistleblowers would be dealt with 'surely and completely.'"[306] Shortly thereafter, she discovered that a hole had been punched in the work gloves she used to handle plutonium ore. As a result, her hair, face, neck, arms, and mouth became contaminated. Although the monitor alarm that detects airborne radiation sounded immediately, she was left unattended for 15 minutes. She would later describe the steep price of whistleblowing:

"I was chased on the highway by a private investigator hired by Rockwell. There were incidents of vandalism at my home. My mail was tampered with."[307]

Former Energy Secretary Hazel O'Leary has acknowledged that workers who expose flaws at nuclear weapons plants and laboratories are harassed regularly by their bosses,[308] and their careers are sometimes ruined by the Department of Energy.[309] In a videotaped deposition on behalf of a whistleblower, whose lawsuit alleged that he was punished by the Department of Energy for raising safety concerns about the Oak Ridge nuclear weapons site in Tennessee, O'Leary said, "[There] has been a practice of repeated and long-term reprisal."[310]

An example of such alleged reprisals is the case of an engineer who was employed by the Tennessee Valley Authority for nearly 20 years. In 1997, he found some broken sheet metal screws, which he saw as evidence of a safety risk in the cooling system of the Watts Bar Nuclear Plant.[311] "He . . . lost his job and his security clearance. He . . . endured harassing late-night calls and threatening notes."[312] A fake bomb was planted in his pickup truck when he parked it at a shopping mall. One of the threatening notes he received contained a single word: Silkwood.[313]

Indeed, the ultimate price for nuclear whistleblowing may have been paid by Karen Silkwood. Silkwood, whose story has been depicted in a popular movie, was a 29-year-old laboratory worker at the Kerr-McGee Corporation's Cimarron Facility in Oklahoma, a plant that manufactured highly radioactive plutonium fuel for nuclear reactors.

In its first 4 years of operation, Kerr-McGee's plutonium plant had suffered 17 contaminating incidents involving 77 employees. In one incident, seven workers were exposed to levels of airborne plutonium exceeding the standards set by the Atomic Energy Commission (AEC)—standards which many scientists believe are already too lenient to protect human health.[314] In another incident, an employee had, in the words of a report to the AEC, "a small portion of skin excised to remove plutonium in a wound."[315] The toxicity of plutonium is well-known, and "laboratory tests indicate that, like other radioactive materials, it is carcinogenic."[316]

By the time Karen Silkwood had been elected to her union's governing committee, Kerr-McGee had a history of carelessness with an extremely hazardous substance.

Twice Kerr-McGee shipped radioactive wastes in improper containers. In another incident, some drums of waste being stored on a flatbed truck leaked. The truck bed, axle, and tires had to be cut up, the ground underneath it dug up, and everything put in barrels for burial at a nuclear dump.[317]

Silkwood herself had twice been contaminated, once by airborne radioactivity which had escaped into the laboratory where she worked, and once when she had been performing some operations in a glove box (a sealed box in which radioactive substances are handled with built-in gloves). In November 1974, Silkwood contacted a *New York Times* reporter about conditions at the Cimarron plant, along with allegations of record falsification by Kerr-McGee. According to witnesses, she had put together her purported evidence in a large manila folder which she had intended to give to the reporter. While driving to a scheduled meeting, however, her car went off the road, and she was killed instantly.[318] The official finding stated that Silkwood had fallen asleep at the wheel. No manila folder was ever found.

An autopsy revealed that there was plutonium in her lungs and clinging to her bones. She was buried in a new dress, because the clothes in her closet were contaminated and had to be sealed in drums.[319]

Some journalists later portrayed Silkwood as an unstable young woman with a history of drug problems and unconventional sexual proclivities, who had become a posthumous pawn in the antinuclear movement.[320] Others, however, called her America's first nuclear martyr, arguing that her allegations were sufficiently credible for a 1978 jury to order Kerr-McGee to pay $10.5 million in personal and punitive damages to the Silkwood estate.[321]

So many mysteries persisted that the case was investigated by a congressional committee. In 1977, the House Subcommittee on Energy and Environment concluded that Silkwood's death had indeed been an accident.[322] On the other hand, investigative journalist Jack Anderson reported that "there was considerable evidence that her car was run off the road and the incriminating evidence stolen."[323] It seems that the life and death of Karen Silkwood are destined to remain a source of controversy.

Even Karen Silkwood's most ardent champions would be hard-pressed to argue that her well-publicized warnings have resulted in the elimination of perilous negligence in the nuclear industry. In 1993, the Westinghouse Hanford Company, the Energy Department contractor that oversees operation at America's largest nuclear waste site, acknowledged major health and safety problems. Westinghouse Hanford blamed the problems on carelessness and errors on the part of workers, just as Kerr-McGee had earlier blamed Karen Silkwood. The Hanford Nuclear Reservation houses 177 underground tanks containing 61 million gallons of radioactive wastes left over from 40 years of plutonium production for the manufacture of nuclear weapons. Many of these tanks have leaked and are considered to be at risk for explosion. More than 17,000 people are employed at the site.[324]

In 2000, federal nuclear regulators began investigating the burial of as much as 1600 tons of nuclear weapons hardware on a 3000-acre Energy Department site near Paducah, Kentucky. The material is located under a leased portion of the site, known as the Paducah Gaseous Diffusion Plant, which is operated by U. S. Enrichment Corporation (USEC). USEC is a private company that processes uranium for use in commercial nuclear power plants. A health and safety specialist employed by USEC had requested the investigation in order to determine if USEC employees were at risk.[325] In a memo to the Nuclear Regulatory Commission, he wrote:

I am deeply concerned for the safety of personnel working at the plant. . . . Some sanity needs to be put back into the system and personal safety needs to have commensurate emphasis with national security.[326]

For years, Paducah employees have complained about an increased number of cancers they believe are linked to exposure between the 1950s and 1970s to uranium dust, which they did not know was laced with plutonium.[327] Plutonium is highly radioactive and "can cause cancer if ingested, even in minute amounts."[328]

Beryllium.   In 1999, an investigative report in an Ohio newspaper charged that since 1950, the U.S. government has risked the lives of thousands of workers by knowingly exposing them to dangerous levels of beryllium, a metal critical to the military.[329] Beryllium is a strong, lightweight metal used to encase nuclear weapons. It creates a dust which, when breathed, can cause berylliosis, an incurable disease marked by lung inflammation and ulceration. Berylliosis can be fatal if not treated, and symptoms may not appear for 15 to 30 years.[330]

Workers at private weapons plants in Ohio and Pennsylvania allegedly were exposed to levels of beryllium dust 100 times federal safety limits. An estimated 1200 cases of berylliosis are confirmed nationwide, but it is believed that many other cases have been misdiagnosed or not yet detected.[331] "At the nation's largest beryllium plant at Emore, just outside Toledo, at least 39 workers have contracted the disease and 6 have died."[332] The investigative report also alleged that the plant has never consistently met federal safety standards.[333]

The Rocky Flats nuclear weapons plant in Colorado (discussed earlier in this chapter) is another facility that has left a legacy of disease, debilitation, and death. For years, workers who built triggers for nuclear weapons during the Cold War were exposed to beryllium dust. Many experts believe that this nonradioactive disease will turn out to be more deadly to former Rocky Flats workers than the radioactive plutonium handled there. At lease 26 former workers have been diagnosed with berylliosis, a number expected to grow dramatically.

Workers at Rocky Flats were supposed to be protected against beryllium dust by an elaborate ventilation system. Since Rocky Flats was shut down, serious questions have arisen about the safety of the air filters utilized as well as the airways that linked buildings.[334] The worker who changed those filters between 1970 and 1977 now suffers from berylliosis. Although he never worked on any weapons, the fine particles trapped in filters destroyed his health. In his words, "I've coughed 'til it feels like my head is going to explode."[335]

Employee Safety: Industrial Accidents

More than 6000 fatal work injuries occur in the United States each year,[336] including approximately 70 adolescent deaths annually from work-related injuries. We already have observed what a dangerous job coal mining is.

According to OSHA, two other occupations rank as similarly hazardous: construction and steel making.

Texas recorded 1436 construction deaths during the 1980s, more than any other state, despite a huge economic decline in the latter part of the decade.[337] On October 31, 1988, for example, a crane operator for the Baytown Construction Company of Texas was electrocuted when his cable came in contact with an overhead power line. The operator, who had been employed by Baytown for only a week, had been unloading pipe with the crane. The electrified cable energized an attached pipe, which in turn transmitted 7620 volts of electricity into the employee's body.

When Baytown was cited by OSHA for violating the requirement that cranes be operated with a minimum 10 feet of clearance between any crane part and power lines, the company blamed the accident on the deceased operator, calling it "unavoidable employee misconduct."[338] The federal courts, however, ruled that Baytown was responsible, because it had neglected to train its employee properly regarding job safety and had failed to provide adequate protection for him. Similarly, several fatal electrocution cases have been filed in California involving undertrained tree trimmers.[339]

The 10-feet standard had been affirmed earlier in a 1979 case, when a federal court had ruled that the Georgia Electric Company had permitted employees to erect a steel light pole within 10 feet of an energized power line. "The Court found that the indifference of an employer, who was aware of its duty to conform and had ample opportunity to acquaint itself with the requirements of OSHA but never did, coupled with its disregard for safety of its employees, supported a finding of willful violation."[340]

The number of deaths caused by contact of mechanical equipment with uninsulated power lines appears to be increasing. This trend is particularly disturbing because the technology to avoid most of these fatalities has been commercially available since the 1950s.

> Most hoisting equipment can be fitted with a proximity warning device similar to a radar detector. As the boom approaches the energy field, the warning device senses the electro- magnetic signals emitted by power lines and sounds an alarm inside the operating cabin.[341]

Cranes also can easily be equipped with insulated cages that surround the boom and prevent the conduction of electricity into the crane, even if power line contact is made.[342] Unfortunately, many construction companies do not provide these safety features, alleging that proximity warning devices and boom cages give operators a false sense of security. Apparently, they believe that the risk for impending death helps keep employees more alert. Some construction companies also question the reliability of the two devices, although in about 40 years, "there have been no reported deaths or injuries caused by their failure to perform."[343]

Inadequate hoisting equipment poses a threat to more than just the operator; anyone in the vicinity is at risk. In 1992, a 3000-pound water tank was being hoisted at the Oak Ridge nuclear plant in Tennessee when one of its two straps snapped. A worker named David Wickes was killed. In a chilling postscript to this tragedy, Wickes' sister found a piece of notebook paper in his wallet on which he had been scribbling a list of safety problems he was documenting. All the factors that had contributed to her brother's death—incorrect straps, improper forklift, untrained personnel, negligent safety standards—were on his list.[344]

In 1990, a construction worker plunged to his death from a Manhattan building as he stepped backwards to avoid being hit by a steel brace that had suddenly snapped free. A few weeks later, the victims' employer, American Steel, was cited by OSHA for violating safety standards requiring fall prevention devices. OSHA proposed a fine of $720.[345]

Congressional testimony in 1992 revealed that a number of other employees of American Steel had died as a result of similar safety violations. "In each case, a single OSHA citation had been issued along with a fine of a few hundred dollars."[346] Congressman Charles Schumer declared that more than 200,000 American workers had died in work-related accidents since the passage of the Occupational Safety and Health Act 22 years earlier. He decried the absence of serious sanctions in the overwhelming majority of these cases. In Schumer's words, "The penalty for removing a tag from a mattress is higher than the penalties for creating worksite conditions that kill."[347]

Steel making is another industry that has a questionable record regarding worker safety and generates a high injury rate—probably even higher than what is officially recorded owing to self-serving record-keeping deficiencies on the part of employers.[348]

A 1980 investigative report on the large Bethlehem Steel plant in Sparrows Point, Maryland, revealed a long-standing pattern of injuries and fatalities. "In numerous cases, management neglected to take elementary safety precautions, failed to maintain hazardous equipment and ignored patently dangerous conditions."[349]

In a single year, workers at the plant suffered 6 deaths and a total of 5304 accident-related injuries, including 1 coma and 7 amputations. These data translate into an average of one injury for every 3.3 workers.[350] Among those workers killed was a member of a blast furnace repair crew who died from deadly carbon monoxide fumes. Bethlehem labeled the accident a "mystery" and issued a public statement saying, "Concern for employee safety is paramount at Sparrows Point."[351]

What the "concerned" company failed to reveal was that this was the second carbon monoxide fatality that year, the first having occurred only 200 yards from where the second victim had succumbed. In both cases, the gas had seeped from a dilapidated furnace system that had been scheduled to be shut down 2 years earlier but had been kept in operation to save money. When OSHA had investigated the first death, it determined that the company had committed flagrant safety violations and levied a $24,000 fine against Bethlehem.[352]

The following year saw six more deaths at Sparrows Point. One of these victims was a 29-year-old worker whose gloved hand had become entwined in a wire machine he was operating. "He was swept off his feet and flung headfirst into an unshielded metal spool";[353] he was killed instantly. OSHA concluded that a shield would have prevented the worker's horrible death, and Bethlehem was fined $27,000 for neglecting to place shields around its wire machine. The Maryland Occupational Safety and Health Agency had demanded shields the previous year, but later backed down "after company executives protested at a private meeting with agency officials."[354]

The Sparrows Point tragedies underscore what has been termed the "invisible risk" that can permeate an ailing industry such as American steel making.[355] From troubled management's point of view, one of the most tempting cost-cutting areas appears to be maintenance. The general manager of the Sparrows Point plant summed up the moral and fiscal dilemma: "When production levels are down and we are not making money, we cannot spend it. . . . [O]bviously this is not the best situation for maintenance."[356]

Thus, in tough economic times, management is more apt to tolerate hazardous equipment, neglect safety precautions, ignore dangerous conditions, and disregard the welfare of workers. Safety, it seems, does not necessarily pay. After all, workers' compensation benefits are relatively inexpensive, and fines for fatal accidents are insignificant for big corporations like Bethlehem Steel. At Sparrows Point, it was "cheaper for Bethlehem to pay safety fines and workmen's compensation than to fix its machinery and change its production system."[357]

Exporting Occupational Disease

As the Sparrows Point example illustrates, many of America's most dangerous industries are housed in old plants that require major renovations to meet state and federal safety standards. "Faced with this reality, some manufacturers find it economically attractive to move hazardous manufacturing plants to less restrictive locales rather than stay where they are and meet tough regulations."[358]

Not surprisingly, one of the industries relying increasingly on "runaway shops" is that pacesetter of environmental crime, asbestos manufacturing. High American wages, combined with federal regulations requiring that workers be informed of the mortal hazards of asbestos and be provided with regular medical examinations and mandatory on-site monitoring to ensure that exposure does not exceed the legal standard, have spurred a mass exodus.[359] For example, one American firm, Amatex, closed its asbestos yarn mill in Pennsylvania in 1972 and moved to the small *masquila* towns of Agua Pieta (across the Arizona border) and Ciudad Juarez (across the Texas border). Five years later, a prominent American industrial health specialist visited the Agua Pieta plant and gave a somber account of conditions there. He described machinery caked with asbestos waste and floors covered with asbestos debris. "Asbestos waste clings to the fence that encloses the brick plant and is strewn across the dirt road behind the plant where children walk to school."[360] Likewise, Amatex failed to warn workers at the Juarez plant of the health risks of asbestos, nor were workers given respiratory protection or even a change of clothes for work.

Asbestos textile plants have been built by American companies in Taiwan, South Korea, Venezuela, and Brazil. Brazil offers an especially hospitable environment because of a perverse policy under which pay increments for certain hazardous industries serve as disincentives for worker health and safety. Small wage premiums are allotted to dangerous occupations, but the pay increases are discontinued if the hazard is eliminated. In effect, by making workers suffer pay cuts in exchange for improved working conditions, Brazil has made unsafe work environments economically attractive and undermined any efforts to improve conditions. "Management has the choice of taking steps to protect workers or paying them extra for losing their health, and presumably does whichever costs less."[361]

Another fugitive industry is the mining and refining of mineral ores. Once again, lax environmental and workplace regulations present an obvious temptation to American firms unwilling to comply with all the domestic air and water pollution standards, worker health and safety laws, and waste disposal requirements. In addition, many cash-poor, mineral-rich foreign nations have been willing, even eager, to "accept or ignore substantial worker health hazards and pollution as the price of economic development."[362] An entry in the *Congressional Record* (June 29, 1978) contains the following indictment of this shameless form of quasi-colonial exploitation:

> A starving man might accept a polluting factory even at great peril to future generations of man and other living things. He could hardly be blamed for that, but can the same be said for those who wish to profit from his misery?[363]

Regulation and Enforcement

The same commitment to deregulation that undermined the EPA in the 1980s dramatically changed the orientation of OSHA under the Reagan administration. While still a presidential candidate, Reagan had expressed a general disdain for OSHA and its punitive enforcement policies. Consequently, he appointed the owner of a construction company that had been cited by OSHA for a number of safety and health violations as OSHA's new chief administrator.[364]

In addition, President Reagan's first secretary of labor almost immediately withdrew a series of safety and health standards promulgated near the end of the Carter administration.[365] These rules had been established to address some of the most serious issues regarding the protection of American workers, including imposing more stringent cotton dust[366] and airborne lead[367] standards, as well as the mandatory labeling of all toxic chemicals used in the workplace[368] and the publication of an annual list of suspected industrial carcinogens.[369] The effect of rescinding these "midnight rules" (so named because of their creation in the waning hours of the Carter presidency) was literally a matter of life and death. The tougher cotton dust standard alone reportedly would have prevented 21,000 cases of byssinosis per year.[370]

The biggest change occurred in the relationship between OSHA and industry. During the Reagan years, OSHA inspectors were inclined to interpret violations as the result of good faith mistakes, unless there was compelling evidence to the contrary.

> This would explain the dramatic decrease in the number of willful violations after the Reagan administration took office. These declined from 1,009 in 1980 to 269 in 1981, 100 in 1982, and 164 in 1983.[371]

In addition, the number of follow-up inspections conducted to determine if cited conditions had been corrected was substantially reduced. In many cases, a letter from an employer stipulating that the problems had been corrected was considered sufficient verification.[372]

Morale at OSHA became dispirited, especially during the second Reagan term. Following the 1984 election, it was reported that "purges reminiscent of the McCarthy era were being conducted at OSHA."[373] Administrators were quoted as "urging subordinates to get rid of the 'communists' in the agency."[374] One OSHA inspector in the agency's Baltimore area office resigned in disgust over OSHA's failure to listen to its own inspectors. While driving on a family trip, he had observed workers on Maryland's Kent Narrows Bridge standing on 65-foot concrete pier caps and jumping to and from crane-suspended platforms without any fall protection. When he reported what he had seen to his superiors, his concerns allegedly were ignored. Eleven days later, a worker at the bridge died from a fall under the very circumstances the inspector had described.[375]

In the 1990s, OSHA, like the EPA, appeared to begin moving from its unaggressive posture of the 1980s back to its more traditional adversarial stance. In the area of administrative sanctions, however, the overall effectiveness of OSHA remained less than exemplary. One reason for this is the continued presence of deregulation advocates. A shocking illustration of residual indifference to health and safety in the workplace is a 1992 letter from the Office of Management and Budget (OMB) to the Labor Department. In this letter, OMB puts forth the curious argument that more lives would be saved if the protection given to workers was *reduced*. OMB argues that the costs of compliance could force employers to lower wages. "[H]igher paid workers tend to take better care of themselves and if they can no longer afford to do so, more may be killed than saved."[376] A Labor Department spokesperson has characterized OMB's logic as "bizarre" and "ridiculous."[377] The then executive director of the National Safe Workplace Institute asserted, "When government is less than tough, it unwittingly encourages marginal actors to take risks they would not take if government sanctions were appropriately severe."[378]

The president of a large labor union has observed dismissively that, to a wealthy corporation, civil penalties, even substantial ones, are merely another "cost of doing business."[379] Because most major OSHA cases are settled out of court—usually for less than the penalty originally proposed—trials have been rare.[380] Thus, for administrative sanctions to be a more effective deterrent, the size of allowable fines probably would have to be markedly increased. Presumably, this would generate an echo effect on negotiated settlements and increase the "cost of doing business" to a level where compliance with health and safety regulations would become a more economical alternative to paying out mega fines.

To that end, OSHA began utilizing two aggressive enforcement tactics in the 1990s: (1) the "egregious multiplier" policy and (2) the "repeated" policy. The egregious multiplier policy, also known as the instance-by-instance policy, is the "policy under which OSHA proposes a separate penalty for each instance of a violation or, in some cases, for each employee exposed to a particular hazard."[381] This power has been in the OSHA arsenal for some time, but was seldom exercised during the Reagan years.

The deterrence value of the egregious multiplier was iterated in 1992 by a federal judge deliberating the case of the Interstate Lead Company, a secondary lead smelter located in Alabama. "A secondary lead smelter typically reclaims lead from used automobile batteries by busting them apart to get the lead plates out, then melting down the lead and removing the impurities. It is usually a dirty, messy job."[382] The toxic effect of lead, of course, "has been well known for a very long time, and it was one of the first substances for which OSHA chose to develop a comprehensive standard,"[383] which requires protective clothing, exposure monitoring, and regular blood tests for employees. Interstate Lead was a chronic violator, having been cited seven times between 1976 and 1989. The first six citations were settled out of court or through the uncontested payment of OSHA fines. The judge in the seventh case, however, characterized the company's compliance record as "stonewalling." In his view, Interstate Lead willfully had failed to obey almost every relevant section of the lead standard.[384]

Consequently, the judge determined that there was sufficient justification for the egregious multiplier policy and he imposed instance-by-instance penalties totaling over $1.7 million. He explained his actions as an affirmation of competitive fairness:

> If the penalties assessed are substantially less than the money saved by correcting the condition, the economic consideration provides a strong incentive to those employers to ignore the standards. A violator of the standards in such circumstances tends to enjoy an unfair economic benefit over competitors who have complied with the standards. The employer who proceeds to act in good faith should not suffer from unethical competition.[385]

The repeated policy was a product of a series of enforcement changes made by OSHA in 1992. Previously, violations had been classified as repeated only when they had occurred at a fixed or permanent facility within a single OSHA area office's geographical jurisdiction.[386] Under the revised policy, OSHA could cite as repeated any violation evaluated as "high gravity serious," based on the previous citations at any facility of the same employer, regardless of location. Later, OSHA went even further and eliminated the gravity requirement, determining that any violations could be cited as repeated.[387]

The repeated policy represents a very significant development in administrative enforcement and could increase considerably the protection of workers endangered by chronically negligent employers. However, the strongest deterrent effect in the area of worker health and safety probably rests in the criminal courts.

OSHA is something of a paper tiger when it comes to criminal prosecution. First of all, the agency has no direct enforcement powers; it must convince the Justice Department to bring charges. Second, for all its renascent vigor regarding administrative sanctions and civil penalties, many of OSHA's teeth were pulled during the deregulatory years (1980–1992) "in the name of getting government off the back of business."[388] Thus, many states have assumed the initiative and have sought to apply their own more stringent criminal laws. They are no longer persuaded by the stale claim that corporate officers are isolated by the bureaucratic layers of complex organizations and therefore seldom know about criminal activity.[389] This clumsy and self-serving argument is nothing more than the corporate version of the long-discredited Nuremberg defense.

Obviously, one cannot incarcerate a corporation nor easily "kill" it, but some states seem to have shown a greater willingness to hold corporate officers and managers criminally liable for decisions which endanger employees.[390] For example, in California, the Los Angeles County District Attorney's office created a special section in 1985 to investigate workplace accidents and fatalities. This innovation has directly led to the prosecution of more than 50 criminal cases.[391] The first prosecution resulting from the new section was a 1986 involuntary manslaughter case filed against Michael Maggio, the president of a small company that was drilling an elevator shaft. At about 33 feet, an obstacle was hit. Maggio ordered an employee to descend the shaft and remove the obstacle. The employee was lowered by cable to the bottom of the hole with his foot inserted in a sling.

> The air was not tested, the walls or sides of the hole were not encased or shored, and the victim was not placed in a safety harness. Almost immediately, the victim went into convulsions. . . . By the time the victim was removed, he was dead.[392]

Maggio pleaded no contest and was sentenced to 60 days in the county jail and, as a condition of probation, was required to implement a comprehensive accident prevention plan for his company.[393]

Probably the best-known of the Los Angeles cases involving alleged crimes against employees was the 1986–1987 trial of the director of the motion picture *The Twilight Zone* and four of his associates. They were charged with manslaughter in the decapitation of actor Vic Morrow and the deaths of two child actors during the filming of a battle scene involving a helicopter that crashed accidentally. The defendants were acquitted after a stormy 10-month trial,[394] but Los Angeles County had sent out a strong message that workplace fatalities would not be dismissed lightly, even in its most cherished and glamorous industry. Former District Attorney Ira Reiner, who established the occupational safety and health enforcement section has written: "[T]he program has made a substantial difference in convincing corporate managers and supervisors that safety in the workplace should be given high priority. . . . The number of prosecutions may be small, but, like a barking dog, their very presence may deter thousands of violations."[395] Other jurisdictions have since followed Reiner's lead.

Incarcerating corporate officials whose decisions or neglect endanger workers is predicated on the belief that this is a far more effective deterrent than fines,[396] because corporations may "simply pass on the costs of the fines to employees as lower wages, to consumers as higher prices, and to shareholders as lower dividends."[397] If individual corporate officers and managers know that they could face criminal prosecution, they would be more likely to spend money on necessary improvements, rather than opt for short-term profit maximization at the expense of health and safety.[398] "The possibility of a jail sentence may significantly alter an individual decision-maker's calculus when facing the decision of what resources to expend on worker safety."[399]

Criminologist Gilbert Geis contends that society will not view corporate crime in the same light as other crimes until white-collar criminals are punished in the same manner as other criminals. Geis reports that even convicted corporate officers agree that being held criminally liable is a very effective deterrent.[400] Furthermore, at the organizational level, when one attaches a criminal stigma to a corporation, the corporation's likely response will be to attempt to regain public confidence by repairing its image, presumably by correcting or modifying its behavior.[401]

In addition to its deterrence effect, retribution theorists would argue that criminal prosecution is appropriate because corporate recklessness and irresponsibility regarding health and safety are morally intolerable to the community.[402] Thus, from a "just deserts" perspective, the incarceration of environmental criminals—with the attendant loss of liberty and employment, as well as the acute embarrassment—has become increasingly attractive.[403]

A number of landmark cases of employee endangerment have been prosecuted as common law offenses, ranging from battery to homicide. Let us examine briefly four of the more striking examples.

Commonwealth v. Godin (1977).   In this case, the president of Pyro Products, a Massachusetts fireworks manufacturer, was convicted of manslaughter following an explosion in which three employees were killed. The structure that exploded was one of 21 buildings in the Pyro complex. Historically, it had been used for the drying of fireworks and the completion of their manufacture by inserting charges. However, at the time of the explosion the building was being used abnormally for the storage of large quantities of fireworks owing to a prolonged labor strike which had backed up production. According to testimony, employees had warned the defendant on a number of occasions about the dangers of excess accumulation. According to the jurors, failure to consider the potential dangers constituted reckless behavior and caused the needless loss of three lives.[404]

People v. Pymm (1989).   In 1981, a worker at the Pymm Thermometer plant in Brooklyn wrote to OSHA asking for an inspector to examine conditions there. His brief letter concluded: "We only make the minimum wage, so at least we will know our health is okay."[405] What OSHA found at Pymm was deplorable.

> No protective gear was being used to reduce workers' exposure to mercury—no respirator masks, no aprons, and no gloves. Work surfaces were covered with mercury, and even the area where workers ate their lunch was contaminated with mercury.[406]

OSHA fined the company and set up a deadline for cleaning up the factory. In true 1980s fashion, however, one deadline after another came and went without any evidence of compliance. Moreover, in 1984, acting on a tip from a former Pymm employee, OSHA discovered a mercury salvage operation hidden in a cellar at the Pymm plant—"a cellar virtually without ventilation, filled with broken thermometers, with pools of mercury on the floor, and noxious vapors in the air, which produced permanent brain damage in one employee."[407] In all, 42 employees were injured by Pymm's appallingly wanton conduct.[408] Pymm, its owners, and its managers were indicted for criminal assault and reckless endangerment and were quickly convicted by a New York jury.

North Carolina v. Roe (1992).   On September 3, 1992, a fire started near some huge grease-filled vats in the frying room at the Imperial Food Products poultry plant in Hamlet, North Carolina. Twenty-five employees were killed,[409] and 56 more were injured.[410] It was the most deadly industrial fire since the infamous 1911 Triangle Shirtwaist Fire in New York City, in which 145 workers lost their lives.[411] The Imperial plant had no fire alarm or sprinkler system, in violation of occupational safety laws. But the most shocking discovery was that fire exits had been padlocked to prevent employees from stealing chickens.[412] The plant had never had a single safety inspection in its 11 years of operation, however, so this practice was not revealed until after the fire, when charred bodies were found at the sealed doors in poses of escape.[413] A witness later testified, "They were screaming 'Let me out!' . . . They were beating on the door."[414]

One year later, the owner of the plant entered a plea bargain with the state and pleaded guilty to 25 counts of involuntary manslaughter. He was sentenced to nearly 20 years in prison.[415]

Illinois v. O'Neil (1985).   Film Recovery Systems was a small Chicago-area corporation engaged in the salvage extraction of silver from used x-ray plates. At its peak, the company generated annual revenues of $13 million to 20 million. It used a recycling process that included soaking the plates in a cyanide solution. Pure silver was then recovered by electrolysis. Employees manually added and removed the plates from the plant's 140 cyanide tanks.[416] Most of these employees were illegal aliens from Mexico and Poland who could not speak or read much English. To them, "CYANIDE" was just another mysterious word on a label.

Cyanide, however, is so highly poisonous when swallowed, inhaled, or absorbed through the skin that "workers must be protected with rubber gloves, boots, aprons, respirators, and effective ventilation."[417] At the Film Recovery plant, none of these normal precautions were taken. On February 10, 1983, one employee, a 59-year-old Polish immigrant named Stefan Golab, staggered from the cyanide tank where he was working and collapsed in an adjacent lunchroom. "His fellow workers dragged him outside and called an ambulance while Golab went into convulsions, frothed at the mouth, and passed out. When the ambulance arrived at the hospital, Golab was dead."[418] An autopsy revealed that Golab had succumbed to a lethal dose of cyanide.

A week after Golab's death, OSHA visited the plant and cited the company for 17 violations. Among other findings, employees were given unapproved cloth gloves and *paper* respirators, both of which were ineffective against cyanide fumes. When the inspector asked the president of the firm why employees were not trained or educated regarding the hazards of cyanide, the president replied that he did not want to scare his workers away.[419]

That same week, the director of the County Department of Environmental Control visited the plant. He reported his findings to the county prosecutor, who began considering the idea of filing involuntary manslaughter charges. Over the next 8 months, the story became increasingly more horrible. The prosecutor would later call Film Recovery "a huge gas chamber."[420]

Investigators encountered a worker who had lost 80% of his vision in one eye from a cyanide splash at his tank. They learned of workers who vomited regularly and suffered recurring headaches and dizziness. They heard that when workers would complain, they were told simply to step outside for some fresh air. They saw that the plant had no vents to shunt the deadly fumes from the building. Even the first aid kit was found to be filthy and held only an empty aspirin box.[421]

Slowly, the prosecutor was being drawn to a radical but inescapable conclusion: What happened to Stefan Golab was more than involuntary manslaughter. Accordingly, the president of Film Recovery Systems, along with his plant manager and plant foreman, were indicted for murder—an unprecedented charge. There had been occasional manslaughter convictions relating to the death of workers through reckless negligence on the part of employers (such as the Pyro Fireworks case), but never had an employer been charged with murder in such a case. To the prosecutor, however, murder seemed a reasonable charge under the circumstances. In his words:

> People talk about this case extending the law and being so unusual. That's not really so. We were just applying the old, basic law in a different area. Firing a gun into a crowd is murder. We had the crowd—the workers. The cyanide was the gun.[422]

At the close of the trial, the three defendants were convicted, and the judge handed them each a 25-year prison sentence. It was a stunning conclusion to an extraordinary case. Regarding the company president, the judge noted that the defendant had testified that he knew cyanide gas was present in the plant and that it could be fatal if inhaled. Regarding the plant manager, the judge observed that the defendant was sufficiently aware of the dangers of cyanide to wear the appropriate equipment denied to the workers.[423] And regarding the plant foreman, the judge recounted that the defendant had painted over the skull-and-crossbones symbol on the cyanide labels, even though he knew that workers were getting sick.[424]

The Film Recovery convictions were overturned in 1990 on technical grounds—the corporation (found guilty of involuntary manslaughter) and the individual defendants (found guilty of murder) had been convicted of mutually inconsistent offenses.[425] Nevertheless, the case represents a legal landmark, despite its eventual reversal. Although corporate criminal liability has been recognized in the United States for well over a century, until *Film Recovery Systems,* courts had hesitated to convict corporations of crimes such as homicide, which require a specific criminal intent *(mens rea)* or a malicious spirit *(malus animus).* This reluctance also rested on the general use of the term "person" in homicide statutes and the impossibility of imposing the legally prescribed punishment of incarceration on a corporation.[426]

Film Recovery Systems, however, marked a new trend in corporate homicide prosecutions. The courts now recognize that criminal prosecution can be a strong deterrent against work-related deaths. The stigma of such a conviction, for example, can make it difficult for a company to hire and maintain an adequate labor force. As the number of corporate homicide prosecutions increases, more and more companies are likely to realize that the effects of criminal stigmatization are potentially far more devastating than civil penalties or administrative sanctions.[427] In addition, corporate homicide prosecutions can have an incapacitation effect, as convicted companies like Film Recovery Systems are forced out of business.[428]

Film Recovery Systems undoubtedly inspired prosecutors in later cases; indeed, it is doubtful if there ever would have been a *Pymm Thermometer* case, for example, if not for the former. The *Film Recovery* case also may have sensitized some corporations to the issue of worker safety. The man who prosecuted the case wrote: "To save a life is as important as it is to redress a wrong which takes a life."[429] If this is so, then the *Film Recovery* case was surely not a wasted effort.

Common Law for Uncommon Crimes?

Despite some successful common law prosecutions of environmental criminals at the state level, this trend has not been unqualifiedly embraced. The general counsel of the U.S. Chamber of Commerce has argued that Congress, through the Occupational Safety and Health Act, has given the federal government jurisdiction in this area, and "there is, therefore, no rationale for states to regulate safety through enforcement of their general criminal laws."[430] Such a contention is based on the Supremacy Clause of the Constitution, which invalidates state laws that interfere with or are contrary to federal law—a principle known as the *preemption doctrine*.[431]

Although preemption has been interpreted by its advocates to preclude state prosecutions for crimes by employers, other jurists see no fundamental conflict in concurrent (as opposed to exclusively federal) supervision of workplace safety. In the landmark case, *People v. Chicago Magnet Wire Corporation* (1989), the Illinois Supreme Court ruled that the state was *not* preempted from prosecuting officials of a wire manufacturing company for aggravated battery in the injury of dozens of employees who had been exposed to highly toxic substances, even though such conduct was also regulated by federal health and safety standards.[432] Subsequently, "every other state supreme court which has addressed this issue has followed the Illinois holding."[433]

However, in *Gade v. National Solid Wastes Management Association* (1992), the U.S. Supreme Court determined that Illinois laws regulating the training and licensing of hazardous waste site workers *were* preempted by federal safety and health standards. Although the Court did not directly address whether federal statute also preempts states from criminal prosecution in this area, earlier assumptions clearly have been challenged by the Court's reasoning in *Gade*.[434]

The flaw in applying the preemption doctrine to crimes in the workplace is that preemption would require states to afford less protection to one class of persons—employees—than to others. For example, consider the *Pyro Fireworks* case. Under the preemption doctrine, the state would not have had the jurisdiction to prosecute the president of the company under common law for the deaths of the three workers; that responsibility would fall to the Department of Justice. Yet, if a neighbor or passerby also had been killed in the same explosion, then the state could have prosecuted—for that death only. In other words, all four deaths would have been the result of the same criminal negligence, but only one would not be preempted from state criminal prosecution. This would seem to be an illogical and unjustifiable inequity, at odds with the residual legislative authority ("reserved powers") granted to the states by the Tenth Amendment.

Another argument against common law prosecutions for crimes by employers is offered by a former EPA counsel. She contends that "criminal poisoning" and workplace poisoning are distinctly different, with only the former involving *mens rea*—that is, an "evil" or criminal state of mind.[435] In other words, incarceration would reduce "decent and respectable employers"[436] to the level of common criminals. One of the defendants in *Pymm Thermometer* employed this rationale before the court after he was sentenced to serve weekends in the city jail for 6 months: "I've always done my best—if my best wasn't good enough, please do not send me to jail for that."[437] Likewise, the attorney representing one of the convicted defendants in *Film Recovery Systems* told the judge at the sentencing hearing:

> The man who is standing before you about to be sentenced is a classic example of middle-class America. . . . The story of his background is probably similar to the story of millions of other men and women in this country . . . who have attempted through their labors to provide their families with a decent home.[438]

This familiar "illegal but not criminal" rationale also fails to hold up under scrutiny. It is a long-standing statutory principle that any person who causes the death of another person, however unintentionally, while engaged in the violation of any law is guilty of homicide.[439] The equation is a simple one: "Since the days of the common law . . . certain actions, while not taken with intent to kill, have been deemed equivalent to murder when they caused a death."[440] In recent years, this principle has been applied with a *jihad*-like vengeance to unintentional deaths caused by drunk drivers. Why not to white-collar criminals? Is an indifferent employer who is aware of safety regulations but chooses not to comply, and thus endangers the lives of employees, any less reckless or negligent than a drunk driver?

"[T]he public, prosecutors, and judges have begun to identify some kinds of risks taken by corporations as intolerable."[441] In the *Film Recovery* case, for example, the judge found that the defendants were well aware of the substantial risk of cyanide poisoning. When such outrageous risks actually cause death, a charge of homicide is wholly consistent with the moral tradition of American criminal law. In all the aforementioned common law convictions, each defendant violated his "duty of care to another human being."[442] The consequent "accidents" were not really accidents at all—they were crimes.

Common law prosecutions can serve an auxiliary purpose as well, by heightening popular recognition of the violent side of white-collar crime. The common law approach seems an appropriate attempt to raise public consciousness and help achieve the essential societal goal of workplace safety. Until white-collar crime is punished like street crime, it will not be perceived as comparably serious. Many members of the public nevertheless remain uncomfortable with the idea of sending businesspersons, however negligent or callous, to prison as if they were "real" criminals. The Citizen's Clearinghouse for Hazardous Wastes argues that these offenders *are* real criminals. That organization has campaigned passionately for common law prosecutions: "Rich people's money is not more important than employees' lives, and the laws need to recognize that."[443]

NOTES

1. Nader, Ralph. "Business Crime." *New Republic* 157, July 1, 1967: 7.
2. Quoted in Anderson, George M. "White-Collar Crime." *America* 144, March 30, 1981: 446.
3. Quoted in Thio, Alex. *Deviant Behavior* (3rd ed.). New York: Harper & Row, 1988; 424.
4. Quoted in Parker, Patricia. "Crime and Punishment." *Buzzworm: The Environmental Journal.* March/April 1992: 35.
5. Badger, T. A. "Jury: Exxon, Hazelwood Both Reckless." *Houston Post.* June 14, 1994: A1, A8.
6. Parker, *op. cit.*

7. Davidson, Art. *In the Wake of the Exxon Valdez: The Devastating Impact of the Alaska Oil Spill.* San Francisco: Sierra Club Books, 1990.

8. Humphreys, Steven L. "An Enemy of the People: Prosecuting the Corporate Polluter as a Common Law Criminal." *American University Law Review* 39, Winter 1990: 311–354.

9. Griffin, Melanie L. "The Legacy of Love Canal." *Sierra* 73, 1988: 26–30.

10. Tallmer, Matt. "Chemical Dumping as a Corporate Way of Life." In Hills, Stuart L. (Ed.). *Corporate Violence: Injury and Death for Profit.* Totowa, New Jersey: Rowman & Littlefield, 1988; 114.

11. *Ibid.*

12. Danzo, Andrew. "The Big Sleazy: Love Canal Ten Years Later." *The Washington Monthly* 20, September, 1988: 11–17.

13. Thio, *op. cit.* p. 434.

14. Griffen, *op. cit.*, p. 27.

15. Paigen, Beverly and Goldman, Lynn R. "Lessons from Love Canal: The Role of the Public and the Use of Birth Weight, Growth, and Indigenous Wildlife to Evaluate Health Risk." In Andelman, Julian B. and Underhill, Dwight W. (Eds.). *Health Effects From Hazardous Waste Sites.* Chelsea, Michigan: Lewis; 1987.

16. Paigen, Beverly, Goldman, Lynn R., Magnant, Mary M., Highland, Joseph H., and Steegmann, A. T., Jr. "Growth of Children Living Near the Hazardous Waste Site, Love Canal." *Human Biology* 59, 1987: 489–508.

17. Cunningham, Miles. "The Return to Love Canal: Signs of Life over Stillness." *Insight* 4, October 24, 1988: 20–22.

18. Griffen, *op. cit.*

19. Quoted in Kraus, Celene. "Grass-Root Consumer Protests and Toxic Wastes: Developing a Critical Political View." *Community Development Journal* 23, 1988: 258–265. See also Gibbs, Lois. *Love Canal: My Story.* Albany, New York: State University of New York Press, 1982.

20. Howlett, Debbie and Tyson, Rae. "Toxicity of Times Beach 'No Longer in Doubt.'" *USA Today.* September 13, 1994: 10A.

21. Mitchell, Grayson. "Firm Knew of Peril in Love Canal Chemical Waste 20 Years Ago, Investigators Say." *Los Angeles Times.* April 11, 1979: 4, 8.

22. Thio, *op. cit.*

23. Mitchell, *op. cit.*, p. 4.

24. Quoted in Mitchell, *op. cit.*, p. 4.

25. Humphreys, *op. cit.*

26. Johnson, Kevin. "Firm to Pay $129 Million for Love Canal Cleanup."*USA Today.* December 22, 1995: 1A.

27. Morganthau, Tom. "Don't Go Near the Water." *Newsweek* 112, August 1, 1988: 43.

28. *Ibid.*, p. 44.

29. Schwartz, Jr., Robert G. "Criminalizing Occupational Safety Violations: The Use of 'Knowing Endangerment' Statutes to Punish Employers Who Maintain Toxic Working Conditions." *Harvard Environmental Law Review* 14, 1990: 487–507.

30. Kenworthy, Tom. "Researchers Chart Impact of Dumping Sludge at Sea." *Washington Post.* November 12, 1992: A13.

31. *Ibid.*, p. 43.

32. *Ibid.*, p. 44.

33. Knight, *op. cit.*

34. Kelley, Darryl. "Tests of Buried Tanks Lag: Leaks into Water Feared." *Los Angeles Times.* August 28, 1988: A1, A3, A24, A25.

35. Kelley, Darryl. "Lake Arrowhead Community Gets Taste of Underground Pollution: Gas Odor Poisons Faith in Mountain Drinking Water." *Los Angeles Times.* August 28, 1988: A3, A22.

36. Guest, Ian. "The Water Decade 1981–1990." *World Health.* January 1979: 2–5.

37. Landrigan, Philip J., Whitworth, Randolph, H., Baloh, Robert W., Staehling, Norman W., Barthel, William F., and Rosenblum, Bernard F. "Neuropsychological Dysfunction in Children with Chronic Low-Level Lead Absorption." *Lancet* 1, March 29, 1974: 708–712.

38. Guest, *Ibid.*

39. Prose, Francine. "Woodstock: A Town Afraid to Drink Water." *New York Times Magazine.* April 13, 1986: 42.

40. Gay, Kathlyn. *Silent Killers: Radon and Other Hazards.* New York: Franklin Watts, 1988.

41. Block, Alan A. and Scarpitti, Frank R. *Poisoning For Profit: The Mafia and Toxic Waste in America.* New York: William Morrow, 1985; 29.

42. Knight, Michael. "Toxic Wastes Hurriedly Dumped Before New Law Goes into Effect." *New York Times.* 1980: 1, 28.

43. Salzano, Julienne. "Sludge Runners Keep on Trucking." *FBI Law Enforcement Bulletin* 64, May 1995: 23.

44. *Ibid.*, p. 24.

45. *Ibid.*

46. Sachs, Andrea. "Rebellious Grand Jurors Hire Lawyer." *ABA Journal* 79, February 1993: 31.

47. *Ibid.*

48. Brever, Jacqueline. "Nuclear Whistle-blower." *The Progressive* 57, July 1993: 36.

49. "The Rocky Flats Cover-Up, Continued." *Harper's*, 285, December 1992: 19–23.

50. Schneider, Keith. "U.S. Shares Blame in Abuses at A-Plant." *New York Times.* March 27, 1992: A12. Wald, Mathew. "Rockwell to Plead Guilty and Pay Large Fine for Dumping Waste." *New York Times.* March 26, 1992: A1, A21.

51. Rothstein, Linda. "The Wages of Sin? About $4.1 Million." *Bulletin of the Atomic Scientists* 49, January 1993: 5.

52. Sachs, *op. cit.*

53. "Miscarriage of Justice at Rocky Flats." *U.S. News & World Report*, 114, January 18, 1993: 14.

54. Department of Health, Education, and Welfare. *Report of the Subcommittee on the Potential Health Effects of Toxic Chemical Dumps on the DHEW Committee to Coordinate Environmental and Related Problems.* Washington, DC: U.S. Department of Health, Education, and Welfare, May 1980.

55. Setterberg, Fred and Shavelson, Lonny. *Toxic Nation: The Fight to Save Our Communities from Chemical Contamination.* New York: Wiley, 1993.

56. *Ibid.*

57. *Ibid.*, p. 95.

58. *Ibid.*, p. 95–96.

59. Marsh, Gary M. and Caplan, Richard J. "Evaluating Health Effects of Exposure at Hazardous Waste Sites: A Review of the State-of-the-Art, with Recommendations for Future Research." In Andelman, Julian B. and Underhill, Dwight W. (Eds.). *Health Effects From Hazardous Waste Sites.* Chelsea, Michigan: Lewis, 1987; 3–80.

60. Gay, *op. cit.*

61. *Ibid.*, p. 74.

62. Suro, Robert. "Refinery's Neighbors Count Sorrows as Well as Riches." *New York Times.* April 4, 1990: A14.

63. *Ibid.*

64. Setterberg and Shavelson, *op. cit.*

65. *Ibid.*

66. *Ibid.*, p. 50.

67. Brown, Phil and Mikkelsen, Edwin J. *No Safe Place: Toxic Waste, Leukemia, and Community Action.* Berkeley: University of California Press, 1990.

68. *Ibid.*

69. *Ibid.*, p. 11.

70. DiPerna, Paula. *Cluster Mystery: Epidemic and the Children of Woburn.* St. Louis: Mosby, 1985.

71. Knight, Michael. "Pollution Is an Old Neighbor in Massachusetts." *New York Times.* May 16, 1980: A16.

72. Brown, Phil. "Popular Epidemiology: Community Response to Toxic Waste-Induced Disease in Woburn, Massachusetts." *Science, Technology, & Human Values* 12, 1987: 79.

73. Brown, *op. cit.*

74. Brown and Mikkelsen, *op. cit.*

75. Doherty, William F. "Jury: Firm Fouled Wells in Woburn." *Boston Globe*, July 29, 1986: 1.

76. Brown and Mikkelsen, *op. cit.*, p. 28.

77. Brown and Mikkelsen, *op. cit.*

78. The Federal Code was later amended to increase the maximum fine in future cases like Woburn's to $500,000.

79. Brown and Mikkelsen, *op. cit.*

80. Castleman, Barry I. "The Export of Hazardous Factories to Developing Nations." *International Journal of Health Services* 9, 1979: 569–606.

81. Landrigan, Phillip J. "Neuropsychological Dysfunction in Children with Chronic Low-Level Lead Absorption." *Lancet* 1, 1975: 708–712.

82. Levy, Doug. "Dirty Air Kills in Clean Cities." *USA Today.* May 23, 1995: 1A.

83. Glasser, Marvin, Greenberg, Leonard, and Field, Franklyn. "Mortality and Morbidity During a Period of High Levels of Air Pollution." *Archives of Environmental Health* 15, 584–594. Bach, Wilfred. *Atmospheric Pollution.* New York: McGraw-Hill, 1972.

84. *Ibid.*

85. *Ibid.*, p. 5.

86. Ziegenfus, Robert C. "Air Quality and Health." In Greenberg, Michael R. (Ed.) *Public Health and the Environment: The United States Experience.* New York: Guilford, 1987; 139–172.

87. Gay, *op. cit.*

88. Kotelchuck, David. "Asbestos: 'The Funeral Dress of Kings'—and Others." In

Rosner, David and Markowitz, Gerald (Eds.) *Dying for Work: Workers' Safety and Health in Twentieth-Century America.* Bloomington, Indiana: Indiana University Press, 1987; 193.

89. Gay, *op. cit.*, p. 29.
90. Brodeur, Paul. *Outrageous Misconduct: The Asbestos Industry on Trial.* New York: Pantheon Books, 1985.
91. Gay, *op. cit.*
92. *Ibid.*, p. 29.
93. Gay, *op. cit.*
94. Cooke, W. E. "Fibrosis of the Lungs Due to the Inhalation of Asbestos Dust." *BMJ* 2, 1924: 147.
95. Castleman, Barry T. *Asbestos: Medical and Legal Aspects.* New York: Harcourt Brace Jovanovich, 1984.
96. Lavelle, Michael J. "Business Ethics: Tone Set at the Top." *Richmond Times-Dispatch.* April 16, 1989: F3.
97. Feder, Barnaby J. "Manville Submits Bankruptcy Filing to Halt Lawsuits." *New York Times.* August 27, 1982: A1, D4.
98. Kotelchuck, *op. cit.*, p. 192.
99. Thio, *op. cit.*, p. 424.
100. The description of the Midland/Hemlock environmental phenomena is taken largely from a vivid—and very frightening—account in Michael Brown's *The Toxic Cloud: The Poisoning of America's Air.*
101. *Ibid.*, p. 24.
102. "Dioxin Threat to Fetuses." *Houston Post.* May 11, 1994: A16.
103. Tschirley, Fred H. "Dioxin." *Scientific American.* February 1986: 29–35.
104. Gay, *op, cit.*
105. Watson, Traci. "Dioxin Draft Stops Short of Calling for More Cuts." *USA Today.* May 18, 2000: 15A.
106. *Houston Post,* May 11, 1994, A16.
107. Brown, *op. cit.*, p. 34–35.
108. *Ibid.*, p. 36.
109. *Ibid.*, p. 41.
110. *Ibid.*
111. *Ibid.*, p. 48.
112. Setterberg and Shavelson, *op. cit.*
113. Brown, *op. cit.*, p. 128.
114. "Our Toxic-Waste Time Bomb." *Readers Digest.* March 1986: 181–86.
115. Howlett and Tyson, *op. cit.*
116. Howlett, Debbie and Tyson, Rae. "Toxicity of Times Beach 'No Longer in Doubt.'" *USA Today.* September 13, 1994: 10A.
117. Cohen, Jessica. "Environmental Crime: Polluters in One Community Are Learning that Crime Doesn't Pay." *Omni* 15, January 1993: 24.
118. *Ibid.*, p. 121
119. Lash, Jonathan, Gillman, Katherine, and Sheridan, David. *A Season of Spoils: The Story of the Reagan Administration's Assault on the Environment.* New York: Random House, 1984.
120. Setterberg and Shavelson, *op. cit.*, p. 122.
121. *Ibid.*, p. 216.
122. Ruffins, Paul. "'Toxic Terrorism' Invades Third World Nations." *Black Enterprise* 19, November, 1988: 31.
123. Bullard, Robert D. and Wright, Beverly H. "Toxic Waste and the African American Community." *Urban League Review* 13, 1989–1990: 67–75.
124. Setterberg and Shavelson. *op. cit.*, p. 229.
125. Bullard and Wright, *op. cit.*
126. Setterberg and Shavelson, *op. cit.*, p. 234.
127. *Ibid.*
128. *Ibid.*, p. 238.
129. Bullard and Wright, *op. cit.*
130. *Ibid.*, p. 71.
131. Setterberg and Shavelson, *op. cit.*
132. Montes, Eduardo. "Tempers Flare over Tribe's Talks to Store Nuclear Waste." *Houston Chronicle.* July 10, 1994: 25A.
133. Grossman, Karl. *The Poison Conspiracy.* Sag Harbor, NY: Permanent Press, 1983.
134. *Ibid.*, p. 218.
135. *Ibid.*, p. 210.
136. Quoted in *Ibid.*, p. 211.
137. Quoted in *Ibid.*, p. 211.
138. *Ibid.*, p. 211.
139. Castleman, *op. cit.*
140. Milius, Peter and Morgan, Dan. "Hazardous Pesticides Sent as Aid." *Washington Post.* December 8, 1976: A1; Milius, Peter. "Leptophos Handled at 9 Plants in U.S." *Washington Post.* December 4, 1976: A1; Morgan, Dan and Milius, Peter. "U.S. Is Pesticide Arsenal for World." *Washington Post,* December 26, 1976: A1, A6, A7.
141. Milius, Peter and Morgan, Dan. "Leptophos Found on Imported Tomatoes." *Washington Post.* December 9, 1976: A1, A6, A7.
142. Carson, Rachel. *Silent Spring.* Boston: Houghton Mifflin, 1962.
143. Milius, Peter and Morgan, Dan. "EPA Challenging 4 Velsicol Pesticides." *Washington Post.* December 14, 1976: A1, A6.

144. Honey, Martha. "Pesticides: Nowhere to Hide." *Ms.* 6, July, 1995: 20.

145. Porterfield, Andrew and Weir, David. "The Export of U.S. Toxic Wastes." *The Nation* 245, October 3, 1987: 325, 341–344.

146. Ruffins, *op. cit.*

147. *Ibid.*

148. *Ibid.*

149. *Ibid.*, p. 343.

150. "The North's Garbage Goes South: The Third World Fears It Will Become the Global Dump." *World Press Review,* 35, November 1988: 30–32.

151. Quoted in Porterfield and Weir, *op. cit.,* p. 343.

152. *Ibid.*

153. Quoted in *Ibid.,* p. 344.

154. Setterberg and Shavelson, *op. cit.*

155. Greider, William. "Across the Border." *Utne Reader* 55, January/February 1993: 84.

156. *Ibid.*

157. Setterberg and Shavelson, *op. cit.,* p. 98.

158. Greider, William. "How We Export Jobs and Disease." *Rolling Stone.* September 3, 1992: 32–33.

159. Juffer, Jane. "Dump at the Border: U.S. Firms Make a Mexican Wasteland." *The Progressive* 52, October, 1988: 24–29.

160. *Ibid.*

161. *Ibid.*

162. *Ibid.*

163. Quoted in *Ibid.,* p. 36.

164. Shrivastava, Paul. *Bhopal: Anatomy of a Crisis.* Cambridge, MA: Ballinger, 1987; 2.

165. Hazarika, Sanjoy. "Bhopal Payments by Union Carbide Set at $470 Million." *New York Times.* February 15, 1989: A1, D3.

166. Nanda, Meera. "Secrecy Was Bhopal's Real Disaster: Why Was Information Hidden from the Public?" *Science for the People.* November/December 1985: 13.

167. Kumar, Sanjay. "India: The Second Bhopal Tragedy." *Lancet* 341, May 8, 1993: 1205–1206.

168. Greeberg, Michael R. and Anderson, Richard F. *Hazardous Waste Sites: The Credibility Gap.* New Brunswick, NJ: Center for Urban Policy Research, 1984.

169. Landers, Robert K. "Living with Hazardous Wastes." *Editorial Research Reports* 2, 1988: 378–387.

170. Setterberg and Shavelson, *op. cit.,* p. 123.

171. Viviano, Frank. "Superfund Costs May Top S & L Bailout." *San Francisco Chronicle.* May 29, 1991: A1.

172. Quoted in Grossman, *op. cit.,* p. 128.

173. *United States Environmental Protection Agency—Region 6: "Progress at Superfund Sites in Texas."* Dallas: EPA, Winter 1993/1994: 5.

174. Harper, Scott. "Industries Cleaning up Brio Site Balk at Tougher EPA Guidelines." *Houston Post.* April 15, 1994: A15.

175. Dawson, Bill. "EPA Proposes Cleanup Plans for Four Houston-Area 'Superfund' Sites." *Houston Chronicle.* January 22, 1988: A22.

176. Kreps, Mary Ann. "EPA Downplays Brio Health Risks, Some Say." *Houston Chronicle.* September 29, 1988: A25.

177. Harper, Scott. "Brio Site's Remaining Neighbors Feel Trapped." *Houston Post.* May 8, 1994: A1, A21.

178. Deaton, Rebecca. "Neighborhood in Transition." *Houston Chronicle.* July 15, 1992: A31.

179. "Driven from Home." *Dallas Morning News.* October 4, 1992: A45.

180. Rendon, Ruth. "3 Brio Cleanup Proposals Carry $40 Million Tags." *Houston Chronicle.* August 25, 1995: 1A. 8A.

181. *Ibid.*

182. Van Voorst, Bruce. "Toxic Dumps: The Lawyers' Money Pit." *Time.* September 13, 1993: 63.

183. Greene, Andrea D. "Resident Urges Warning Signs Near Toxic Spill." *Houston Chronicle.* October 8, 1993: A25.

184. "EPA Halts Work at Brio." *Houston Chronicle.* October 9, 1993: A36.

185. Rendon, Ruth. "Chemical Release at Brio Cleanup Spurs List of Evacuation Standards." *Houston Chronicle.* October 15, 1993: A29.

186. Rendon, Ruth. "State Warning: Don't Eat Clear Creek Fish." *Houston Chronicle.* November 19, 1993: A33.

187. Rendon, August 25, 1995, *op. cit.*

188. *Ibid.*

189. Harper, April 15, 1994, *op. cit.,* p. A15.

190. Harper, Scott. "Brio—It's a Dirty Job, and Nobody's Able to Do It." *Houston Post.* April 19, 1994: A1, A24.

191. Harper, May 8, 1994, *op. cit.*

192. Harper, Scott. "'No Comment' on Toxic Dump." *Houston Post.* October 9, 1994: A33.

193. Lutz, Heidi. "10% HL&P Cut Possible." *Galveston Daily News.* February 6, 1995: 14.

194. Rendon, August 25, 1995, *op. cit.*, p. 8A.

195. Carney, Dan. "Nation's Leaders Having Hard Time Cleaning up Superfund Legislation." *Houston Post*. April 24, 1994: A14.

196. Sablatura, Bob. "With Superfund, Lawyers Clean Up." *Houston Chronicle*. October 23, 1995: 1A, 6A.

197. Harper, May 8, 1994, *op. cit.*

198. Setterberg and Shavelson, *op. cit.*

199. *Ibid.*, p. 123.

200. *Ibid.*

201. "Toxic Ten: America's Truant Corporations." *Mother Jones* 18, January, 1993: 39–42; "America's Worst Toxic Polluters." *Business & Society Review* 84, Winter 1993: 21–23.

202. Litvan, Laura M. "The Growing Ranks of Enviro-Cops." *Nations Business* 82, June 1994: 129–132.

203. Dreux, Mark S. and Zimmerman, Craig H. "The Proposed Federal Sentencing Guidelines for Environmental Crimes." *Occupational Hazards*. July 1993: 46.

204. Kafin, Robert J. and Port, Gail. "Criminal Sanctions Lead to Higher Fines and Jail." *National Law Journal*. July 23, 1990: 20–23.

205. Dreux and Zimmerman, *op. cit.*

206. Riesel, Daniel. "Criminal Prosecution and Defense of Environmental Wrongs." *Environmental Law Reporter* 15, March 1985: 10071.

207. "Firm Pleads Guilty in Toxic Dumping." *Los Angeles Times*. January 15, 1993: A30.

208. Riesel, *op. cit.*

209. "Bethlehem Steel Fined for Waste Violations at Indiana Facility." *Wall Street Journal*. September 7, 1993: B5.

210. Sanders, Alain L. "Battling Crimes Against Nature." *Time* 135, March 12, 1990: 54.

211. *Ibid.*

212. *Ibid.*

213. "Chevron to Pay Pollution Fine." *Houston Chronicle*. August 24, 2000: 2C.

214. Ivanovich, David. "Pipeline Firm Fined by EPA." *Houston Chronicle*. January 14, 2000: 1A, 10A.

215. Dreux and Zimmerman, *op. cit.*

216. "EPA Sues Sherwin-Williams; Pattern of Pollution at Paint Factory is Alleged." *Wall Street Journal*. July 19, 1993: B4.

217. Abrahamson, Alan. "Firm Fined for Smuggling Toxic Waste." *Los Angeles Times*. January 15, 1993: A3, A41.

218. Cohen, Mark. "Environmental Crime and Punishment: Legal/Economic Theory and Empirical Evidence on Enforcement of Federal Environmental Statutes." *Environmental Crime* 82, 1992: 1082.

219. Naj, Amal K. "United Technologies Fined $5.3 Million for Series of Environmental Violations." *Wall Street Journal*. August 24, 1993: B6.

220. *Ibid.*, p. 1083.

221. *Ibid.*

222. Dawson, Bill. "Dow Fine to Benefit Rare Fowl." *Houston Chronicle*. June 13, 1996: 37A, 42A.

223. Stipp, David. "Toxic Turpitude: Environmental Crime Can Land Executives in Prison These Days." *Wall Street Journal*. September 10, 1990: A1.

224. Parker, *op. cit.*

225. Zuniga, Jo Ann. "Pair Convicted of Hazardous Dumping." *Houston Chronicle*. December 8, 1993: 1.

226. Brewer, Wayne. "Traditional Policing and Environmental Enforcement." *FBI Law Enforcement Bulletin* 64, May 1995: 6–13.

227. Humphreys, *op. cit.*, p. 325.

228. Stipp, *op. cit.*

229. Marzulla, Roger J. and Kappel, Brett G. "Nowhere to Run, Nowhere to Hide: Criminal Liability for Violations of Environmental Statutes in the 1990s." *Columbia Journal of Environmental Law* 16, 1991: 203.

230. Cooper, Richard T. and Steiger, Paul E. "Occupational Health Hazards—A National Crisis." *Los Angeles Times* June 27, 1976: A1.

231. Clay, Thomas R. *Combating Cancer in the Workplace: Implementation of the California Occupational Carcinogens Control Act*. University of California—Irvine: Unpublished doctoral dissertation, 1984.

232. *Ibid.*

233. Wokutch, Richard E. *Cooperation and Conflict in Occupational Safety and Health*. New York: Praeger, 1990.

234. Ashford, Nicholas A. and Caldart, Charles C. *Technology, Law, and the Working Environment*. New York: Van Nostrand Reinhold, 1991; 88.

235. Stone, Christopher D. "A Slap on the Wrist for the Kepone Mob." *Business and Society Review*. Summer 1977: 4–11.

236. Bray, Thomas. "Health Hazard: Chemical Firm's Story Underscores Problems of

Cleaning up Plants." *Wall Street Journal.* December 2, 1975: 1, 38.

237. Stone, *op. cit.*

238. *Ibid.*

239. Cooper, *op. cit.*, p. A24.

240. Stone, *op. cit.*

241. *Ibid.*, p. 6.

242. Kiernan, Laura. "Kepone Indictments Cit 1,096 Violations: Manufacturing Firms, Hopewell Face Charges." *Washington Post.* May 8, 1976: A1, A6.

243. "Paying the Costs of Kepone." *Washington Post.* February 4, 1977: A20.

244. Kiernan, Laura. "Key Kepone Case Figure Pleads Guilty." *Washington Post.* August 11, 1976: C1, C4.

245. "Coping with Kepone." *Washington Post.* July 16, 1976: A26.

246. Smith, J. Y. "Kepone Indictments Cite 1,096 Violations: Contamination Problems Still Plague Va. Area." *Washington Post.* May 8, 1976: A1, A6.

247. Milius, Peter. "Kepone-Like Case at Texas Pesticide Plant Probe." *Washington Post.* December 1, 1976: A1, A4.

248. *Ibid.*, p. A1.

249. *Ibid.*

250. Milius, Peter. "2nd Plant Linked to Pesticide." *Washington Post.* December 3, 1976: A1, A7.

251. Milius, Peter. "Pesticide Sales Halt Laid to Economics, Not Safety." *Washington Post.* December 2, 1976: A13.

252. *Ibid.*

253. Caudill, Harry M. "Manslaughter in a Coal Mine." *The Nation* 224, April 23, 1977: 492–497.

254. *Ibid.*, p. 494.

255. *Ibid.*

256. *Ibid.*

257. Mullins, Vicki. "A Day in the Life of a Coal Mine Inspector." *Women & Work: News from the United States Department of Labor* 7, November 1992: 1–3.

258. Caudill, *op. cit.*, p. 496.

259. Weinstein, Henry. "Did Industry Suppress Asbestos Data?" *Los Angeles Times.* October 23, 1978: 3.

260. Brodeur, Paul. *Expendable Americans.* New York: Viking Press, 1974.

261. Castleman, *op. cit.*

262. *Ibid.*

263. *Ibid.*

264. *Ibid.*, p. 3.

265. *Ibid.*, p. 27.

266. *Ibid.*

267. Thio, *op. cit.*

268. Stone, Andrea. "String of Teachers' Cancers Sounds Alarm at NYC School." *USA Today.* September 30, 1994: 2A.

269. Flynn, George. "Jurors Award $42 Million in Asbestos Cases." *Houston Chronicle.* November 23, 1995: 1A.

270. Olafson, Steve. "21 Steelworkers Who Contracted Asbestos Disease Win $115 Million." *Houston Chronicle.* February 20, 1998: 1A, 14A.

271. *Ibid.*, p. 1A.

272. Quoted in *Ibid.*, p. 1A.

273. *Ibid.*

274. Weinstein, *op. cit.*

275. Ritter, John. "Town Clenched in Suffocating Grip of Asbestos." *USA Today.* February 1, 2000: 8A.

276. *Ibid.*, p. 3.

277. Armour, Stephanie. "Workers Unwittingly Take Home Toxins." *USA Today.* October 5, 2000: 1A, 4A, 6A.

278. "192 Asbestos Deaths in Small Town Over Last 40 years, Paper Reports." *Houston Chronicle.* November 21, 1999: 26A.

279. *Ibid.*

280. Ritter, February 1, 2000, *op. cit.*

281. "House Action Is Delayed on Bill to Streamline Asbestos Claims." *Houston Chronicle.* March 15, 2000: 9A.

282. Cannon, Angie. "Homeless Recruited as Asbestos Workers." *Houston Chronicle.* April 25, 1998: 2A.

283. Quoted in *Ibid.*, p. 2A.

284. McCaffrey, *op. cit.*

285. Guarasci, Richard. "Death by Cotton Dust." In Hills, Stuart L. (Ed.) *Corporate Violence: Injury and Death for Profit*, Totowa, NJ: Rowman & Littlefield, 1987; 76–92.

286. *Ibid.*, p. 79.

287. *Ibid.*, p. 79.

288. "Stevens Mill Workers Protest Their Lack of a Contract." *New York Times.* August 8, 1979: A13.

289. Guarasci, *op. cit.*

290. *Ibid.*

291. McCaffrey, *op. cit.*, p. 114–115.

292. Guarasci, *op. cit.*

293. *Ibid.*

294. *Ibid.*, p. 88.

295. Quoted in *Ibid.*, pp. 78, 86.

296. Schneider, Keith. "A Valley of Death for the Navajo Uranium Miners." *New York Times.* May 3, 1993: A1; "Uranium Miners Tell Panel Radiation Caused Ailments." *New York Times.* May 14, 1990: 20.

297. Dumas, Kitty. "House OKs Radiation Payments for Miners and 'Downwinders.'" *Congressional Quarterly.* June 9, 1990: 1794.

298. "House Votes Funds for Western Victims of Radiation Illness." *New York Times.* June 6, 1990: A22.

299. Schneider, Keith. "Uranium Miners Inherit Dispute's Sad Legacy." *New York Times.* January 9, 1990: A1.

300. Wald, Mathew. "Court Says Ohio Can Penalize U.S." *New York Times.* June 12, 1990: A17.

301. Schneider, Keith. "Study of Nuclear Workers Finds High Cancer Rates." *New York Times.* April 13, 1994: A16.

302. Phillips, B. J. "The Case of Karen Silkwood." *Ms.* April 1975: 61.

303. Cooper and Steiger, *op. cit.*

304. Brever, *op. cit.*

305. *Ibid.*, p. 35.

306. *Ibid.*

307. *Ibid.*, p. 35.

308. Eisler, Peter. "O'Leary Admits Whistle-Blowers Face Reprisal." *USA Today.* May 21, 1998: 1A.

309. Eisler, Peter. "Whistle-Blowers Finally Getting Back at DOE." *USA Today.* May 21, 1998: 7A.

310. Quoted in *Ibid.*, p. 1A.

311. Mansfield, Duncan. "Whistle-Blower Plagued by Threats After Reporting Nuclear Safety Risks." *Houston Chronicle.* January 31, 1999: 2A.

312. *Ibid.*, p. 2A.

313. *Ibid.*

314. Phillips, *op. cit.*

315. Quoted in *Ibid.*, p. 61.

316. *Ibid.*, p. 61.

317. *Ibid.*, p. 61.

318. Rashke, Richard. *The Killing of Karen Silkwood.* New York: Houghton Mifflin, 1981.

319. *Ibid.*

320. Thimmesch, Nick. "Karen Silkwood Without Tears" (Part I). *The Saturday Evening Post* 251, November 1979: 14–35, 119.

321. Thimmesch, Nick. "Karen Silkwood Without Tears" (Part II). *The Saturday Evening Post* 251, November 1979: 26–35, 83.

322. Fossett, Judy. "Hill Unit Lawyers Call Death of Karen Silkwood Accidental." *Washington Post.* February 4, 1977: A2.

323. Anderson, Jack. "FBI Smear Tactics in Silkwood Case." *Washington Post.* February 4, 1980: C25.

324. "Mishap Casts Pall Over Big Atomic Waste Site." *New York Times.* August 15, 1993: 18.

325. "Latest Find at Kentucky Plant." *Houston Chronicle.* February 16, 2000: 10A.

326. Quoted in *Ibid.*

327. "Compensation Proposed for Workers Sickened by Plutonium." *Houston Chronicle.* September 17, 1999: 15A.

328. *Ibid.*

329. *Houston Chronicle.* "U.S. Reportedly Knew About Metal that Put Workers Lives at Risk." March 29, 1999: 2A.

330. Scanlon, Bill. "Beryllium Disease Hits 26th Rocky Flats Worker." archives.insidedenver.com. November 7, 1992; *Rocky Mountain News.* "Database Provides Information on Flats Radiation Research." archives.insidedenver.com. April, 7, 1994; *Rocky Mountain News.* "Flats Workers Sue over Ailment." archives.insidedenver.com. November 10, 1996.

331. *Houston Chronicle,* March 29, 1999, *op. cit.*

332. *Ibid.*

333. *Ibid.*

334. Scanlon, Bill. "Flats Restart Gets Mixed Blessing if Various Panels Vouch for Safety." archives.insidedenver.com. August 26, 1991.

335. Quoted in Morson, Bernie. "Rocky Future: Ex-Workers at Rocky Flats Believe Health Hazards That Lurked There Years Ago Still Linger." archives.insidedenver.com. December 21, 1997.

336. Bureau of Labor Statistics. "National Census of Fatal Occupational Injuries, 1996." August 7, 1997.

337. Morris, Jim. "OSHA Drops 'Numbers' Emphasis in Its Work." *Houston Chronicle.* October 23, 1994: 1A, 20A.

338. "Contested Cases." *Occupational Hazards.* June, 1993: 57.

339. Reiner, Ira and Chatten-Brown, Jan. "When It Is Not an Accident, but a Crime: Prosecutors Get Tough With OSHA." *Northern Kentucky Law Review* 17, Fall 1989: 83–103.

340. Rabassa, Santiago C. "Employment Related Crimes." *American Criminal Law Review* 30, Spring 1993: 545–563.

341. Mongeluzzi, Robert J. "Electrocution Accidents on the Job: Heavy-Equipment Workers Put Their Lives on the Line." *Trial* 25, March 1989: 69.

342. *Ibid.*

343. *Ibid.*, p. 69.

344. Pasternak, Douglas and Cary, Peter. "Department of Horrors: America's Energy Agency and Its Appalling Record of Worker Safety." *U.S. News & World Report*. January 24, 1994: 47–49.

345. Spayd, Liz. "Fines for Work Safety Violations Under Fire." *Washington Post*. May 29, 1992: A21.

346. *Ibid.*, p. A21.

347. Quoted in *Ibid.*, p. A21.

348. Reutter, Mark. "The Invisible Risk: Why Sparrows Point Workers Should Be Congratulated for Making It Through a Day Without Injury." *Mother Jones* 5, August 1980: 49–60.

349. Reutter, *op. cit*, p. 50.

350. *Ibid.*

351. *Ibid.*, p. 49.

352. *Ibid.*

353. *Ibid.*, p. 59.

354. *Ibid.*, p. 59.

355. *Ibid.*

356. *Ibid.*, p. 57.

357. *Ibid.*, p. 60.

358. Castleman, *op. cit.*, p. 569–570.

359. *Ibid.*

360. Quoted in *Ibid.*, p. 576.

361. *Ibid.*, p. 578.

362. *Ibid.*, p. 589.

363. Quoted in *Ibid.*, p. 599.

364. Wokutch, *op. cit.*

365. Calavita, Kitty. "The Demise of the Occupational Safety and Health Administration: A Case Study in Symbolic Action." *Social Problems* 30, April 1983: 437–448.

366. Palisano, Peg. "Reagan's OSHA team—They Hit the Ground Running." *Occupational Hazards* 43, 1981: 67–74.

367. "OSHA Communiqué." *Occupational Hazards* 44, 1982: 39–40.

368. Engel, Paul. "Close-up on OSHA's Proposed New Chemical Labeling Standard." *Occupational Hazards* 44, 1982: 35–39.

369. "Showdown Looms Over OSHA's Cancer Policy." *Occupational Hazards* 44, 1982: 60–63.

370. Verespe, Michael A. "Has OSHA Improved?" *Industry Week*. August 4, 1980: 48–56.

371. Wokutch, *op. cit.*, p. 45

372. *Ibid.*

373. *Ibid.*, p. 41.

374. *Ibid.*

375. Morris, Jim. "Dangerous Bridge Led to OSHA Official's Resignation." *Houston Chronicle*. October 23, 1994: 20A.

376. Swoboda, Frank. "OMB's Logic: Less Protection Saves Lives." *Washington Post*. March 17, 1992: A15.

377. *Ibid.*

378. Kinney, Joseph A. "Foreword: Justice and the Problem of Unsafe Work." *Northern Kentucky Law Review* 17, Fall 1989: 1–7.

379. Quoted in Rabassa, *op. cit.*, p. 551.

380. Tyson, Patrick R. "Court Favors Huge OSHA Penalties." *Safety and Health* 146, November 1992: 19–24.

381. *Ibid.*, p. 19.

382. *Ibid.*, p. 21.

383. *Ibid.*

384. *Ibid.*

385. *Ibid.*, p. 23.

386. Gombar, Robert C. and Yohay, Stephen C. "OSHA 'Repeated' Violations—It's Time for Reexamination." *Employee Relations Law Journal* 18, Fall 1992: 315–324.

387. *Ibid.*

388. Jefferson, Jon. "Dying For Work." *ABA Journal*. February 1993: 48.

389. Dunmire, Thea D. "The Problems With Using Common Law Criminal Statutes to Deter Exposure to Chemical Substances in the Workplace. *Northern Kentucky Law Review* 17, Fall 1989: 53–81.

390. Humphreys, *op. cit.*

391. Jefferson, Jon. "L.A. Law: Prosecuting Workplace Killers." *ABA Journal*. January 1993: 48.

392. Reiner and Chatten-Brown, *op. cit.*, p. 97.

393. *Ibid.*

394. Feldman, Paul. "All 'Twilight Zone' Figures Acquitted." *Los Angeles Times*. May 30, 1987: 1, 28, 29.

395. Reiner and Chatten-Brown, *op. cit.*, p. 103.

396. Dutzman, Joleane. "State Criminal Prosecutions: Putting Teeth in the Occupa-

tional Safety and Health Act." *George Mason University Law Review* 12, Summer 1990: 737–755.

397. Uelmen, Amelia J. "Trashing State Criminal Sanctions? OSHA Preemption Jurisprudence in Light of *Gade v. National Solid Wastes Management Association.*" *American Criminal Law Review* 30, Winter 1993: 373–415.

398. Orland, Leonard. "Reflections on Corporate Crime: Law in Search of Theory and Scholarship." *American Criminal Law Review* 17, 1980: 501–520.

399. Uelmen, *op. cit.*, p. 379.

400. Geis, Gilbert. "Criminal Penalties for Corporate Criminals." *Criminal Law Bulletin* 8, 1972: 377–380.

401. Koprowicz, Kenneth M. "Corporate Criminal Liability for Workplace Hazards: A Viable Option for Enforcing Workplace Safety?" *Brooklyn Law Review* 52, 1986: 183–227.

402. Bennett, Steven C. "Developments in the Movement Against Corporate Crimes." *New York University Law Review* 65, 1990: 871–874.

403. Dutzman, *op. cit.*

404. Koprowicz, *op. cit.*

405. Quoted in Reiner and Chatten-Brown, *op. cit.*, p. 89.

406. *Ibid.*, p. 89.

407. *Ibid.*, p. 89.

408. Uelmen, *op. cit.*

409. Smothers, Ronald. "25 Die, Many Reported Trapped, as Blaze Engulfs Carolina Plant." *New York Times.* September 4, 1991: A1, B7.

410. Miller, Lenore. "Revisiting the 'Jungle.'" *Washington Post.* October 20, 1992: A20.

411. Jefferson, *op. cit.*

412. *Ibid.*

413. Smothers, *op. cit.*

414. Quoted in *Ibid.*, p. A1.

415. "Meat-Plant Owner Pleads Guilty in a Blaze That Killed 25 People." *New York Times.* September 15, 1992: A6.

416. Wang, Charleston C. K. "How to Manage Workplace Derived Hazards and Avoid Liability." Park Ridge, NJ: Noyes Publications, 1987.

417. Frank, Nancy K. and Lynch, Michael J. *Corporate Crime: Corporate Violence.* New York: Harrow and Heston, 1992.

418. *Ibid.*, p. 43.

419. Siegel, Barry. "Murder Case a Corporate Landmark." *Los Angeles Times.* September 15, 1985: 1, 8, 9.

420. Wang, *op. cit.*, p. 183.

421. Siegel, *op. cit.*

422. *Ibid.*, p. 8.

423. Frank, *op. cit.*

424. Siegel, *op. cit.*

425. Rabassa, Santiago C. "Employment Related Crimes." *American Criminal Law Review* 30, 1993: 545–563.

426. Koprowicz, *op. cit.*

427. Helverson, Alana L. "Can a Corporation Commit Murder?" *Washington University Law Quarterly* 64, 1986: 967–984.

428. *Ibid.*

429. Magnuson, Jay C. and Leviton, Gareth C. "Policy Considerations in Corporate Criminal Prosecutions After *People v. Film Recovery Systems, Inc. Notre Dame Law Review* 62, 1987: 939.

430. Bokat, Stephen A. "Criminal Enforcement of OSHA: Employers' Rights at Risk." *Northern Kentucky Law Review* 17, Fall 1989: 135–151.

431. Ducat, Craig R. and Chase, Harold W. *Constitutional Interpretation: Powers of Government* (5th ed.). New York: West Publishing, 1992.

432. Uelmen, *op. cit.*

433. *Ibid.*, p. 387.

434. *Ibid.*

435. Dunmire, *op. cit.*

436. Uelmen, *op. cit.*, p. 375.

437. Quoted in *Ibid.*, p. 375.

438. Siegel, Barry. "Cyanide Trial in Illinois Makes History, Headlines." *Los Angeles Times,* September 16, 1985: 8.

439. Rodella, Patricia. "Corporate Criminal Liability For Homicide: Has the Fiction Been Extended Too Far?" *Journal of Law and Commerce* 4, 1984: 95–125.

440. Michael, Alan C. "Defining Unintended Murder." *Columbia Law Review* 85, May 1985: 786.

441. Frank, Nancy. "Unintended Murder and Corporate Risk-Taking: Defining the Concept Justiciability." *Journal of Criminal Justice* 16, 1988: 24.

442. Reiner and Chatten-Brown, *op. cit.*, p. 103.

443. Quoted in Parker, *op. cit.*, p. 35.

CHAPTER 5

Institutional Corruption: Mass Media and Religion

Assistant: Y'know, there's gonna be some really sick people out there tonight.
Phony Faith Healer: Seat 'em in the back. It's harder for them to get onstage.

From *Leap of Faith* (1992). Screenplay by Janus Cercone.

*I*n preceding chapters, we have examined the consequences of white-collar crime in terms of physical or financial costs. There is, however, another type of cost—perhaps less obvious or directly measurable, but far more pervasive: the social cost. Here, the victims are not limited to endangered employees or exploited consumers, but include all of society. As Sutherland observed many years ago, "White-collar crimes violate trust and therefore create distrust; this lowers social morale and produces social disorganization."[1]

To understand the notion of social disorganization in Sutherland's context, one must first consider its opposite—social organization. Social organization usually is seen by sociologists as a synthesis of culture and institutional structure.[2] Although both these components are implicated in white-collar crime, culture seems to be more *cause* and institutional structure more *effect*, although there is clearly a reciprocal relationship.

White-collar crime mirrors American culture, with its strong emphasis on achievement and what has been termed the "fetishism of money."[3] Robert Merton, who has proposed a link between crime and culture since the 1930s, argues that money is the yardstick by which achievement is measured in the United States.[4] In other words, money is how we "keep score" in our materialistic culture. To theorists like Merton, there can be little doubt that the quest for financial success and competitive superiority makes our culture relatively hospitable to white-collar crime. For example, research reports that unethical behavior is often determined by situational competition,[5] and illegal conduct becomes increasingly likely as the corporate environment becomes more competitive.[6]

But it is the other component of social organization, institutional structure, in which the effects—that is, the social costs—of white-collar crime are more visible. Institutions have been called "the lengthened shadows of men."[7] They are defined as "relatively stable sets of norms and values, statuses and roles, and groups and organizations."[8] As such, institutions regulate human conduct and interaction in order to meet society's basic needs.[9] They allow a society to "endure over time despite the constant 'coming and going' of individual members."[10]

Another influential social theorist, Talcott Parsons, referred to institutions as "the 'backbone' of the social system."[11] To extend Parsons' metaphor, a weakening of important social institutions is like the progressive degeneration of a backbone; it can incapacitate or even kill a society. And this is the crux of Sutherland's thesis: that the erosion of the public's confidence in its social institutions can tear apart the fabric of American society by attacking our most fundamental beliefs.

It would be difficult to identify a significant social or cultural institution uncontaminated by white-collar crime. In this chapter, we will consider two important examples: the mass media and religion. It must be acknowledged, however, that a case could be made easily that *every* category of white-collar crime depicted in this book manifests a deleterious effect on some social institution, and thereby inflicts damage on society as a whole. To cite one obvious example, crimes of the government described in Chapter 8 have devalued the democratic process.

THE MASS MEDIA

The mass media have been identified as among the most influential sources for the "social construction of reality."[12] In other words, each person constructs his or her perception of the world through a socialization process resting heavily on shared knowledge, much of which is derived from the mass media. Because almost all Americans have access to the same media, we tend to construct similar social realities,[13] a process that communication theorist George Gerbner has termed *worldview cultivation*.[14] Consequently, corruption of the mass media can change the very way we think about the world.[15]

Television, the most dominant and pervasive of all modern mass media, generated a major corruption scandal in its first decade of preeminence. By 1955, television's most popular and highest-rated entertainment genre was the big money quiz show. Programs like *The $64,000 Question* and *Twenty-One* awarded millions of dollars in prizes to contestants who seemed to demonstrate an encyclopedic range of knowledge. After a sensational Congressional investigation in 1959, however, it was revealed that these "geniuses" were fakes and that the programs had been "fixed." Those contestants, whom the producers, sponsors, and networks had deemed appealing, had been routinely given the correct answers in advance.[16]

Some apologists have characterized the quiz show fraud as a "victimless crime." But was it? The passage of time allows for a less myopic assessment of the social consequences of television's first white-collar crime scandal. Decades have elapsed since contestants were taught by producers to lie and cheat in order to sell sponsors' lipstick and iron tonic. In their hunger for higher ratings, the networks had demonstrated at the very least a willingness to tolerate an endemic fraud and to abet its subsequent cover-up. With the benefit of hindsight, it now could be argued that those who rigged the quiz shows were engaged in a criminal conspiracy to rob the American people of their idealism and promote in its place a dispiriting national cynicism. It has been said that "[t]he worst part of a scandal is that is actually scandalizes."[17] Perhaps so, but the worst part of the quiz show scandal may have been its *failure* to scandalize. Instead, like so many white-collar crimes, it helped make dishonesty more respectable. After the Congressional hearings had adjourned, a "man on the street" interview asked passers-by, "Would you have any qualms about appearing on a TV quiz show if it were rigged and you knew you would win a large sum of money?" Two-thirds of those queried responded that they would have no qualms and would appear.[18]

National cynicism no doubt also was fueled by the selective nature of the prosecutions resulting from the quiz show fraud. Almost all of those who were indicted, arrested, convicted, and sentenced were former contestants. The privileged few who owned or controlled the quiz programs and who reaped enormous profits from them seemed to be beyond the reach of the criminal justice system. It is reasonable to wonder how much less cynically the public might have reacted if it had been the engine that derailed, rather than the caboose.

The most serious effect of the quiz show scandal, however was the long-term corruption of our preeminent mass medium. The scandal occurred when the television industry was barely out of its infancy, still forming the moral codes and conduct norms it would carry into its adulthood.[19] If the child truly is the father of the man, then whatever ethical shortcomings television has since displayed—everything from fraudulent advertising practices to dissembled news reports to "dramatized" documentaries to the perfidious televangelists—may be a product of its misspent youth.

C A S E   S T U D Y

Payola

A few weeks after the House Commerce Subcommittee had concluded its examination of the quiz shows in 1959, it reconvened to investigate another systemic scandal, this one involving the music industry. "The U.S. was becoming familiar with a new word, 'payola', trade jargon for bribes to promote certain

(Continued)

records over the air."[20] These bribes came from music publishers or record manufacturers and distributors, and were paid to both disk jockeys and station managers.

What seemed to outside observers to be an insidious new form of corruption really was just an extension of a longstanding tradition of bribery in the music industry. At least as early as the 1890s, "gifts and money were given to performers [by music publishers] as an inducement to sing particular songs."[21] For example, the composer of "After the Ball" originally helped popularize that classic tune by paying the star of a lavish musical review $500 and a percentage of future royalties in exchange for placing the song in the show.[22]

By the 1920s, the surest way to launch a new song successfully was to induce a vaudeville headliner to use it in his or her act. The most charismatic entertainer of that period was Al Jolson, and it became commonly acknowledged as a show business truism that "to get Jolson to sing a song was to have a big hit on your hands."[23] Jolson often received a percentage of a song's royalties by being given undeserved collaborating credit as the song's lyricist or composer. One publisher even gave Jolson an expensive racehorse as a "gift."[24]

Likewise, by the 1930s, dance band leaders routinely were bribed by music publishers to induce them to include certain songs in their radio programs.[25] The most prominent band leaders sometimes were even given a financial interest in the publishing house or in the copyright of a song.[26] It was during this period that the term "payola" was coined by the show business periodical, *Variety*, which reported that payola had become accepted within the music industry as a normal business practice. A writer who chronicled radio's "big band" era observed, "There is little philanthropy in Tin Pan Alley. If you scratch my back, I must scratch yours—or your palm."[27]

By the 1950s, radio was providing an even more hospitable climate for bribery, because many more recordings were produced than could be played on the air, creating a fierce level of competition.[28] By that time, the nature of payola had changed radically. Record companies had replaced music publishers as the primary source of illicit payoffs, and disk jockeys had replaced singers and musicians as the primary recipients. A Detroit disk jockey, in his congressional testimony, described the new mechanics of payola in 1959:

> I was often approached by small companies who were having a tough time getting their stuff on the air. They would say, "Well, how much do you want to ride this record for the next three weeks?" They might offer $100 for a one-week ride, which would have meant playing the record several times a day to make it popular. Many disk jockeys are on the weekly payroll of five to 10 record companies, which can mean a side income of $25,000 to $50,000 a year. The payment is by cash in an envelope.[29]

Congress heard testimony from an array of disk jockeys working in the major radio markets. "[T]he hearings demonstrated the enormous moral confusion which [existed] over payola."[30] Almost all the disk jockeys admitted they had

(Continued)

accepted large sums of money, but most denied that the money had bought airtime for records; they maintained it was a legitimate fee system for "auditioning" records.[31] A former Boston disk jockey, who had accepted about $10,000 in payola over a 3-year period,[32] was an unapologetic exception, offering his own candid analysis: "This seems to be the American way of life . . . I'll do for you. What would you do for me?"[33] The effect of such testimony "was to suggest that payola was widespread."[34] Furthermore there seemed to be an almost total lack of any serious effort on the part of the broadcasting industry to prevent payola.[35]

Many who testified lost their jobs. Among them was one of the country's best-known radio personalities, Alan Freed, the self-proclaimed "King of Rock 'n Roll." Freed denied that he had received payola, but admitted accepting gifts from companies after playing their records. He characterized such payments as "consultant fees."[36] Freed added a trenchant observation: "What they call payola in the disk-jockey business, they call lobbying in Washington."[37]

Other testimony described a disk-jockey convention held in Miami Beach in 1959, at which 18 record companies reportedly picked up a $118,000 tab for hotel rooms, meals, liquor, and call girls. The hearings further revealed that major figures in the broadcasting industry sometimes were given as much as a 50% interest in a singer's contract or a record's profits in exchange for promoting the artist or the song.[38] This complex practice was especially evident when the subcommittee turned its attention to television in May 1960. A subpoena was issued to one of the most influential figures in the music business, Dick Clark, the host of ABC-TV's *American Bandstand,* a televised "record hop" viewed daily by millions of loyal teenage fans.

Clark told the subcommittee, "I have never agreed to play a record in return for payment or any other consideration."[39] However, he had amassed a personal fortune in the previous 3 years, which left many members skeptical. One Congressman coined the term "Clarkola."[40]

Actually, in a literal sense, Clark's denial probably was true. His stature in the music industry transcended conventional payola. He did not need to rely on crude cash bribes in surreptitious envelopes. Like Jolson 40 years earlier, Clark had developed a far more profitable system.

> It hinged on his numerous corporate holdings which included financial interests in three record companies, six music publishing houses, a record pressing plant, a record distributing firm and a company which manages singers. The music, the records and the singers involved with these companies gained a special place in Clark's programs, which the committee said gave them systematic preference.[41]

For example, over a 2-year period Clark had given far less airtime to Elvis Presley, the sovereign "rock 'n roll" star, than to newcomer Duane Eddy. Clark had no financial stake in Presley, but "firms in which he held stock both managed and recorded Eddy."[42] Clark was accused by one committee member of exploiting his

(Continued)

position: "By almost any reasonable test, records you had an interest in were played more than the ones you didn't."[43] Clark's incredible reply: "I did not consciously favor such records. Maybe I did so without realizing it."[44]

In addition, Clark acknowledged owning the copyrights to 160 songs, 143 of which had been given to him as "gifts":

> A shining example was a record called *16 Candles*. Before getting the copyright, Clark spun it only four times in 10 weeks, and it got nowhere. Once he owned it, Clark played it 27 times in less than three months and it went up like a rocket. Each time the record was purchased Clark shared in the profits to the merry tune of $12,000.[45]

Clark, of course, deflected the payola scandal and went on to become one of television's wealthiest and most successful producers. Moreover—as Chapter 2 details—he still finds the time to shill for a disreputable sweepstakes promotion that at best straddles the cusp between deception and outright fraud.

As a result of the Congressional hearings, the Communications Act of 1934 was amended in 1960 to prohibit cash payments and other favors given to disk jockeys by record producers and distributors. However, more than a decade later, it was widely reported that payola continued to flourish.[46] Payments in cash[47] or in illegal drugs[48] allegedly still were being made. Hearings by the Federal Communications Commission (FCC) "left little doubt that payola had not been stopped by the change in the law."[49]

In 1973, the Department of Justice and the IRS began a new round of payola investigations,[50] which concluded that payola had been received by radio station employees in at least 16 American cities. By 1975, 16 individuals and 6 corporations had been indicted by grand juries in Newark, Philadelphia, and Los Angeles for violating the amended Communications Act, as well as for bribery, mail fraud, tax evasion, and perjury.[51]

In 1976, a New York grand jury indicted the former president of CBS Records and another CBS executive for engaging in payola.[52] That same year, four executives of the Brunswick Record Company were fined and given prisons terms after radio station music directors (who had been granted immunity) testified that they had received cash payments from Brunswick representatives.[53] "The lawyers for the executives had argued that 'cash payments were a way of life in the record industry and part of the promotion end of the business,' to which the judge replied, 'If this is true, then the record business is a dirty business indeed.'"[54]

The broadcasting industry has never seemed willing to acknowledge the inherent corruption of payola, which is why the problem still persists decades after the first scandal. When new allegations surfaced in the press in 1998. The radio journal *M Street Daily* declared, "It's not improper to accept payments for things you put on the air."[55]

Although the electronic media are clearly the most dominant form of mass communication, the print media have not been without their share of duplicity. In 1981, for example, the Pulitzer Prize for feature writing[56] was awarded to *Washington Post* reporter Janet Cooke for her gut-wrenching account of an 8-year-old heroin addict named Jimmy.[57] Two days later, the prize was withdrawn and Cooke resigned from her job after admitting that her "Jimmy" story was a fabrication.[58] Executive editor Ben Bradlee acknowledged, "The credibility of a newspaper is its most precious asset. . . . When that integrity is questioned and found wanting, the wounds are grievous."[59] In its contrite *apologia*, the *Post* took a hard look at itself and the news media in general: "How could this have happened? What does it say . . . about the reliability of other stories?"[60]

In 1998, an eye-catching story appeared in the respected weekly journal, *The New Republic,* describing the exploits of Ian Restil, a 15-year-old computer hacker, who broke into the database of a large software firm named Jukt Micronics and then demanded money, a sports car, and lifetime subscriptions to pornographic magazines when he was offered a job by the victimized company. According to the article, teenage hackers are in such demand in the new economy that some have actually hired agents. It was later discovered that the story by writer Stephen Glass was wholly fictitious. Neither Restil or Jukt Micronics even exist.[61]

Perhaps the most intriguing American literary fraud of our times was *The Autobiography of Howard Hughes.* In 1971, publishing giant McGraw-Hill announced the purchase of Hughes' memoirs, as narrated to writer Clifford Irving. Irving had produced a stack of personal correspondence from the legendary billionaire recluse in which Hughes expressed his approval for the project. On that basis, H. R. Hughes was paid an advance of $750,000 for what was considered the publishing coup of the century. Hughes, after all, had built Trans-World Airlines, had himself set many speed records as a pilot, had been awarded a rare Presidential Medal of Honor, had run a major movie studio, had owned virtually every big hotel-casino in Las Vegas, had been linked romantically with some of the most glamorous women in the world and—if all that were not enough—he was widely believed to be insane.

The finished product was a detailed first-person account of Hughes' extraordinary business career, as well as his remarkable personal escapades. The problem was that Hughes had not dictated his life story, had never met Irving, and had not even known of the book until McGraw-Hill's announcement. Irving, a meticulous researcher, had created a fantastic literary hoax. He had endorsed the publisher's checks by forging "H. R. Hughes," and his wife had deposited them in a Swiss bank under the name Helga Renate Hughes. The fraud was exposed dramatically when Hughes, who had not been seen or heard in public in years, held a press conference (via speaker phone) to denounce the mendacious memoirs. Many observers still doubt that the vigorous and rational-sounding voice on the speaker was actually Howard Hughes. They believe it was more likely an imposter hired by Hughes or his business associates to expose Irving's brazen hoax.

Clifford Irving was convicted of grand larceny in federal court and was sentenced to $2\frac{1}{2}$ years' imprisonment.[62] Although Irving became a successful novelist after his parole, his fictional masterpiece, *The Autobiography of Howard Hughes*, has never been published.[63]

More recently in 1999, Lawrence X. Cusack III was sentenced to 6 to 8 years in prison for forging love letters between President John F. Kennedy and movie star Marilyn Monroe. Cusack had cheated investors out of nearly $7 million between 1993 and 1997 by selling documents bearing Kennedy's forged signature. The judge excoriated Cusack for his "nearly sociopathic disregard for the impact his actions would have on others."[64]

RELIGION

When Dick Clark became the focus of the payola investigation in 1960, one of his most vigorous defenders was pop singer Bobby Darin, who said of Clark, "He is as innocent of doing harm as any clergyman I know."[65] Although Darin surely did not intend to be facetious, his "clergyman" analogy may not have been the best way to verify Clark's integrity, as we shall see when we examine another battered cultural institution: religion.

Religion is one of the most fundamental cultural institutions. It arose from our perception of a power outside ourselves, which provides moral constraint, behavioral reinforcement, and attitudinal support. To the great sociologist, Emile Durkheim, religion is society's consciousness of itself.[66] Religion helps to hold a society together, "enabling both the group and the individual to cope with the problems of everyday life."[67] Because faith is, by definition, the very essence of religion, an erosion of public trust probably damages religion more than most other social institutions. Betrayals of faith seem to be occurring with alarming regularity in the United States, which has experienced a series of highly publicized white-collar crimes involving religious figures since the 1980s.

C A S E   S T U D Y

Sun Myung Moon

One of the best known of the religious cases was that of the Reverend Sun Myung Moon, the leader of a neo-Christian sect named the Unification Church. Like many self-proclaimed prophets, Moon's background is something of a mystery. It is known that he was born in 1920 in North Korea.[68] It is also known that he was arrested several times as a young man. Moon insists that those arrests were the result of his religious beliefs and anti-Communist fervor; however, some early acquaintances maintain that the arrests stemmed from accusations of sexual promiscuity and bigamy.[69]

(Continued)

Some time prior to 1954, Moon had moved to South Korea, ordained himself, and chartered his church. He also had become a successful businessman, and by the age of 34 he was "board chairman of South Korean concerns as diverse as a pharmaceutical company specializing in ginseng tea and a corporation that manufactured shotguns."[70]

In 1959, Moon sent his first missionaries to the United States, but the Unification Church attracted few followers until Moon personally arrived in 1971 to take charge of his American organization. Because anti-communism was a major aspect of Moon's distinctive interpretation of Christian doctrine, he soon became a vocal supporter and financial contributor to conservative political causes. He was especially visible during the Watergate investigations (Chapter 8), when he organized a media campaign to save the beleaguered Nixon presidency. One of his advertisements announced that, "[A]t this moment in history, God has chosen Richard Nixon to be President of the United States."[71]

The Unification Church attracted thousands of young Americans, although the exact number is indeterminable. However, by the late 1970s, public hostility toward religious cults was mounting, particularly following the murders and mass suicides at the People's Temple in Jonestown in 1978. The Unification Church's finances began to generate increasing public attention and official scrutiny. Moon's followers—known derisively as "Moonies"—traveled across the country raising money in public places from the sale of such items as flowers or tea. "Hundreds of members brought in from one to five hundred dollars on an average day, usually not revealing their affiliation."[72] These funds then were channeled into lavish real estate acquisitions and sizable business investments.

Public concern over the "Moonies" led to a Congressional investigation of the Unification Church and its charismatic leader. The House Subcommittee on International Organizations reported that it "had found evidence that Reverend Moon . . . had systematically violated the United States tax, immigration, banking, currency, and foreign-agent registration laws, as well as state and local laws on charity fraud."[73]

In 1981, Sun Myung Moon was indicted for tax fraud. He had failed to report the interest on $1.6 million he had deposited in his own name in several New York bank accounts.[74] Moon eventually served 11 months in federal prison, but the Unification Church apparently suffered no significant decline in the commitment of its members, and Moon resumed active leadership on his release in 1985.

"Lyin'" Henry Lyons

The National Baptist Convention, USA, one of the largest and most influential African American Protestant denominations, with nearly 1 million members, was rocked in 1999 by the conviction of its president Henry J. Lyons. Rev. Lyons, once an advisor to President Clinton on racial policies, was found guilty in a Florida criminal court of swindling millions of dollars from companies that sought to do business with his followers and grand theft in the disappearance of almost $250,000 from the Anti-Defamation League of B'nai Brith (a large national Jewish organization)—money donated to help rebuild firebombed Black churches in the South.[75]

Lyons stole more than $4 million from corporations that wanted to sell everything from cemetery plots to insurance policies to credit cards to the church's members. He duped these companies by promising them access to non-existent membership mailing lists. Lyons created his phony lists using a computerized telephone directory. The Loewen Group, the world's second-largest funeral home company, was the biggest victim, shelling out nearly $3 million. Another company, Globe Life Insurance, paid Lyons $1 million for a fabricated list. The company realized it had been duped when it received a complaint from a Grand Dragon of the Ku Klux Klan, who had received a sales letter from Globe with Lyons' endorsement.[76]

Lyons diverted the money to a secret bank account and used it to support an opulent lifestyle for himself and his mistress. He purchased a waterfront home, a 20-carat diamond (said to be "the size of a dime"), and two Mercedes and a Rolls-Royce.[77] Lyons' problems began when his wife, allegedly in a jealous rage, set fire to the $700,000 home he owned with his mistress. The fire led to closer scrutiny of his lavish finances.[78]

Lyons' attorneys argued that "the personal use of church money is the way that black churches in the U.S. 'do business.'"[79] It is difficult to determine how much of this assertion is neutralizing rhetoric and how much is a statement of fact. It is noteworthy, however, that most of the leaders of the National Baptist Convention, USA, as well as many of its rank and file members stood firmly behind Rev. Lyons. The pastor of an affiliated Houston church portrayed Lyons as the victim, a victim of having too much power and too little accountability. "What Dr. Lyons did is what many of us would have done if given the same opportunities and the same almost unlimited access to money and power."[80]

A sobbing Henry J. Lyons pleaded for mercy as he was sentenced to $5\frac{1}{2}$ years in prison and was ordered to repay $2.5 million. He belabored the obvious when he told the presiding judge, "I cannot shake the feeling that I have let so many people down."[81] He apologized tearfully for the theft of the B'nai Brith money intended to restore burned churches: "It stinks in God's nostrils and I know it stinks in the law's nostrils and it stinks to me."[82] The judge's reply was terse: "It's time to pay the piper, Dr. Lyons."[83]

Phony Faith Healers

Another way in which white-collar crime has insinuated itself into the religious arena is through the practice of fraudulent faith healing.[84] Faith healing is probably as old as religion itself. The traditional Christian notion that certain people can heal sickness by means of special divine gifts is derived from the New Testament.[85] The present-day American belief in this practice originated in Indiana in the 1940s with the Reverend William Branham, a former game warden whose fire-and-brimstone tent revivals included "miraculous" cures. "Branham was so convincing a preacher that, when he died in a 1965 automobile accident, he wasn't buried for four months because his flock expected him to rise from the dead at Easter. He didn't."[86]

Branham's success inspired dozens of imitators, and traveling tent revivals began criss-crossing the country, spreading the gospel and passing the collection plate. Some religious entrepreneurs, such as Oral Roberts and Rex Humbard, discovered the enormous potential of radio to enlarge their congregations. Later, the popularization of television in the 1950s made media stars out of some preachers and turned faith healing into a multimillion dollar industry.

One of those early stars was A. A. Allen, who founded his own community of Miracle Valley, Arizona, in 1958. From there Allen broadcast a daily 1-hour radio program to 58 stations across the United States and several other countries, and a weekly television program to 43 states. Miracle Valley also contained a private airstrip, a 3000 seat church, a recording studio, a publishing plant, and a "telephone prayer center." Allen's ministry soon was generating revenues of nearly $4 million per year.[87]

Like many faith healers, Allen had a life history at odds with his pious stage persona:

> A. A. Allen began his career as a minister of the Assemblies of God in his twenties. He worked at it successfully until 1955, when he jumped bail on a drunken driving charge and was defrocked. . . . In typical fashion, he immediately re-ordained himself and started up his big moneymaker, the Miracle Revival Fellowship. He went "under canvass" and began touring with his big tent show.[88]

When Allen discovered radio and television, he abandoned his tent shows and switched to the electronic media. Allen had a galvanizing stage presence. *Look* magazine praised his "purity" and "nobility."[89] Nevertheless, Allen's ascribed virtues did not prevent him from resorting to the shabbiest sorts of fraud. He peddled jars of water and containers of dirt from Miracle Valley over the airwaves, claiming these products could heal the afflicted. Allen himself eventually joined the ranks of the afflicted and died in 1970 of liver disease brought on by acute alcoholism.[90]

The most dramatic exposé of fraudulent faith healing occurred in 1986 and involved the Reverend Peter Popoff and his Miracle and Blessing Crusade, which was aired at that time on over 50 television stations in the

United States.[91] The Bulgarian-born Popoff[92] and his California-based organization reportedly had a computerized mailing list containing the names of over 100,000 contributors, who were solicited for donations relentlessly every 2 weeks.[93]

> In 1986, he *admitted* to an operating cost of $550,000 a month; his actual grossed income can only be guessed. Because Popoff—like all evangelists— is not required by any government agency to account to anyone for any of the money that is taken in, except whatever he decides to pay himself as personal income, it is difficult to know just how much is collected.[94]

Popoff's written appeals for money were masterfully created to convey a sense of dire urgency. For example, one elderly woman sent Popoff her entire life savings of $21,000 for a bizarre plan to float Russian Bibles into the Soviet Union attached to balloons. Popoff's proposed airlift—which was of course physically impossible (as well as a violation of international law)—reportedly generated a wave of contributions so immense that it arrived daily in 100-pound mail sacks. It also has been reported that these donations yielded only "three-hundred ordinary party balloons and two small tanks of helium."[95]

Another outrageous scheme involved sending out plastic shower caps to Popoff's mailing list. Each of these cheap items was represented as a "Holy Shower Cap." Recipients were instructed to wear the cap once, then wrap it around a check or some cash and send it back to Popoff. Reportedly, a single mailing of "Holy Shower Caps" netted $100,000 in contributions, which, incredibly, was considered a failure by Popoff's usual standards.[96]

Popoff's reputation among his followers was built on his purported healing ability. Faith healers are a prime target of James Randi ("The Amazing Randi"), a veteran magician who has emerged over the years as America's foremost debunker of paranormal claims. By the mid-1980s, Popoff had moved to the top of Randi's "hit list." At a 1986 news conference, Randi issued an angry denouncement:

> He excoriated Popoff for urging people to throw their pills up on stage during crusades. Although Popoff later insisted he wanted only illegal drugs discarded, Randi reported finding diabetes medication, nitroglycerine tablets, and digitalis prescriptions among the litter on Popoff's stage.[97]

The Popoff-Randi showdown occurred in a Detroit auditorium in April 1986. Randi and a group of allies had prepared a trap for the greedy charlatan. Among those confederates was Don Henvick, who had been following the Popoff crusade around for months. Donning disguises, he already had been "cured" twice by Popoff—of alcoholism in San Francisco and arthritis in Anaheim, California. This time the 38-year-old, 260-pound mailman posed as a woman suffering from uterine cancer, a notion so absurd that Popoff could not possibly be fooled if he was receiving messages from God.[98]

One of Popoff's most impressive feats was his apparent ability to run around a revival hall and quickly call out the names of afflicted persons, along with their respective afflictions.[99] This was an old mentalist's trick that Randi had recognized at a previous Popoff revival in Houston. Popoff's wife, Elizabeth, toured the audience before the service engaging members in seemingly casual conversation, which was carried backstage to her husband by a radio transmitter hidden in her oversized purse. Popoff would transcribe all the relevant information.

> When the evangelist later made his rounds of the audience, he had in his left ear a hidden miniature receiver that enabled Elizabeth, now backstage, to direct him to those members of the audience she had already pumped for information.[100]

Earlier, Randi had elicited the help of an electronics expert, who identified the frequency of the signal that was broadcast by Elizabeth Popoff to her husband. That evening, Randi placed eavesdropping equipment in a trash bag by some bushes next to the trailer where Mrs. Popoff was seated in front of a microphone and a bank of closed-circuit monitors. She was relaying information to her husband inside the auditorium.[101] Throughout the afternoon, Mrs. Popoff was secretly taped while she transmitted names, addresses, and diseases, mixed with snide comments about audience members, such as, "Oh, look at that butt."[102]

When "Bernice Manicoff," a.k.a. Don Henvick, arrived at the auditorium, "she" was escorted to a wheelchair and placed in it by one of Popoff's employees. As planned, Henvick said he (she) was suffering from uterine cancer. Midway through the revival, Popoff approached Henvick, while receiving a radio message from his wife:

> There's one there, looks like she has a beard. Her name is Bernice Manicoff. The doctors think she has cancer of the uterus.[103]

Popoff placed his hands on "Bernice," and went into his act:

> Dr. Jesus is going to burn all those cancer cells out of your body. . . . I tell you, you're going to feel new strength. It's going to surge through you— THERE IT IS![104]

Suddenly, back in the control room, Elizabeth Popoff recognized Henvick and panicked:

> That's not a woman. . . . Hey, isn't that the guy who was in Anaheim? Pete, that's the man who was in Anaheim you said had arthritis. . . . Get rid of him.[105]

A short time later, Randi appeared on the *Tonight Show* television program and played a videotaped segment of Popoff's performance overlaid with an audio track of Mrs. Popoff's transmissions. The studio audience was flabbergasted, and even host Johnny Carson was visibly shocked at such blatant fakery. As a result of this exposure, donations to Popoff's ministry fell so sharply that he soon declared bankruptcy.[106]

Some persons perhaps are persuaded to ridicule Popoff's flock as gullible fools, all but asking to be bilked. However, this would be an overly harsh and shortsighted judgment. Swindlers, masquerading as respectable clergy, prey on desperate, vulnerable people. Many of their victims no doubt are gravely ill; most are prompted by a devout religious faith. It is difficult to find a suitable word to characterize phony faith healers—"contemptible" hardly seems adequate.

The Televangelists

Another category of religious crime—the one that probably has received the most public attention in recent years—is the misappropriation of funds by televangelists. Religious broadcasting has been part of American culture since the invention of electronic media. For example, radio provided an effective vehicle for the flamboyant revivalist Aimee Semple McPherson in the 1920s[107] and the vituperative priest Charles E. Coughlin in the 1930s.[108] Over the decades, religious broadcasters periodically have generated controversy as they have used the airwaves to transmit unorthodox spiritual and political messages.

When television eclipsed radio, evangelists, perhaps owing to their tradition of theatricality, seemed to have little trouble making the transition. The real turning point, however, came with the introduction of satellite broadcasting and cable reception, which spurred an unprecedented growth of religious television. From the late 1960s through the early 1980s, the average number of Americans viewing religious television programs soared from 5 million to 25 million.[109] "The ancillary projects of the televangelists, including cathedrals, colleges and universities, religious theme parks, and total-living communities, also grew at a phenomenal rate."[110]

As the audiences grew, so too did the revenues. By 1986, the most successful televangelists were presiding over financial empires. Pat Robertson, who would run for president of the United States in 1988, was earning a reported $183 million annually from his Virginia-based Christian Broadcasting Network (CBN) and from contributions to his daily *700 Club* program. In fact, Robertson agreed in 1998, after a 10-year legal battle, to pay what was termed a "significant" fine to the Internal Revenue Service for using CBN money to finance his presidential campaign. The network also agreed to accept retroactive loss of tax-exempt status for 1986 and 1987.[111]

In Tulsa, Oklahoma, Oral Roberts was overseeing a $500 million complex, containing Oral Roberts University and the City of Faith Hospital. Roberts' annual budget was about $120 million, most of it raised through donations.

In Garden Grove, California, Robert Schuller was syndicating his weekly *Hour of Power* broadcast from his $20 million Crystal Cathedral. Schuller's contributions were reported at about $42 million per year.

Jerry Falwell's Virginia ministry, including Liberty University and a 22,000 member church, was generating about $84 million annually, mainly from contributions solicited on Falwell's 1.5 million-subscriber cable television system.

And in Baton Rouge, Louisiana, singer-turned-preacher Jimmy Swaggert was raking in an estimated $142 million a year from his daily and weekly television programs, Bible college, and elaborate tours.[112]

Although most of these televangelists were earning salaries that could have been considered modest, relative to the size of their respective operations (e.g., Robertson, $60,000; Schuller, $80,000; Swaggert, $86,000; Falwell, $100,000),[113] their opulent lifestyles seemed far in excess of their reported personal incomes.

One of the most conspicuous salary-lifestyle discrepancies belonged to Jimmy Swaggert. A 1987 *Time* article analyzed Swaggert's personal finances:

> In 1985, the Swaggerts borrowed $2 million from the ministry to build three luxurious homes in a wealthy Baton Rouge subdivision. They have the use of a $250,000 ministry "retreat" in California and say that such luxury items as twin Lincoln Town Cars and handsomely furnished offices come from donors.[114]

Also in 1987, some of his former associates charged that Swaggert had raised $20 million for a children's fund, but had spent less than 10% on needy children.

Swaggert, whose spellbinding oratory usually featured harangues against sexual immorality, was disgraced in 1988 when stories of his own moral turpitude were reported by the press. He was forced to admit long-standing obsessions with prostitutes, voyeurism, and pornography. Before millions of riveted television viewers, he verbally fell on his sword with a tearful, histrionic apology, delivered in his inimitable style. Swaggert's flock, however, so conditioned by his intolerant tirades against Catholics, Jews, secular humanists, mental health professionals, intellectuals, liberals, gays, and so many other species of social scapegoats, were ill-disposed to forgive sin— even their shepherd's. Swaggert was dismissed from his Assemblies of God denomination and expelled from the National Religious Broadcasters association.[115] Although he quickly established his own denomination and continued to preach and plead for money, his impetuous sermons virtually disappeared from the airwaves.

The most sensational of the televangelist scandals involved the PTL (Praise the Lord) ministry led by the husband-and-wife team of Jim and Tammy Faye Bakker. Like Jimmy Swaggert, the Bakkers were members of the Assemblies of God denomination, a Pentecostal sect holding evangelical or fundamentalist views and stressing miraculous "gifts," such as prophecy and glossolalia (speaking in tongues).[116] Also like Swaggert, the Bakkers would become very rich.

After several years as traveling revivalists, the Bakkers had entered the public spotlight in 1965, when they were invited to join Pat Robertson's Christian Broadcasting Network. Jim Bakker proved to be a gifted preacher, and he was soon doing a morning radio program and hosting the *700 Club* at night.

Jim Bakker reportedly became angered when he was told by CBN management that he would receive no salary while he was recuperating at home from what Tammy Faye called a "nervous breakdown)." Bakker became anxious to leave Robertson's organization. In November, 1972, the two charismatics parted after a 7-year association.

A few months later, the Bakkers started the *Praise the Lord* show for Paul Crouch's Trinity Broadcasting Network in southern California. By 1974, however, they were back on the traveling evangelical circuit. After 6 more months, they began a new television ministry in Charlotte, North Carolina. "From California, they brought with them the initials 'PTL.'"[117] From the very beginning, the PTL ministry was characterized by questionable financial practices. This ignited a ferocious enmity between Bakker and the FCC that would continue for years to come.

By 1976, the PTL show was aired on 70 stations and 28 cable systems in North America. Jim Bakker had built Heritage Village in Charlotte and, on his thirtieth birthday in 1978, he broke ground for the new PTL complex in Fort Mill, South Carolina, 20 miles south of Charlotte:[118]

> By then Bakker had developed the habit of speaking less than truthfully about his financial operations. In the summer of 1978 he announced that Tammy and he had given "every penny" of their life savings to PTL. Only days later he made a $6,000 payment on a houseboat.[119]

The first major PTL scandal erupted in 1979, when it was reported that $350,000 raised by PTL for the stated purpose of upgrading its overseas television capacity had been diverted to pay bills at the Bakker home.[120] In 1982, three members of the FCC voted to prosecute Jim Bakker for using the airwaves to solicit funds fraudulently. They were barely overruled by a four-member majority, who opted for administrative sanctions.

For the Bakkers, 1984 would prove to be both the best and worst of times. The year began auspiciously, when Jim Bakker announced the formation of the Lifetime Partnership Plan, which sought to persuade 100,000 PTL supporters to donate at least $1000 apiece in exchange for 3 free nights at the planned Heritage Grand Hotel every year of their lives.[121] In May, Bakker was commended by President Reagan for his efforts on behalf of a proposed School Prayer Amendment.[122]

At about the same time, however, a 21-year-old church secretary named Jessica Hahn began accusing Bakker and members of his inner circle of sexual misconduct.[123] Ms. Hahn eventually received a payment from PTL—reportedly $115,000.[124] Whether this was "hush money," as the press implied, or an out-of-court settlement for emotional trauma, as Hahn claimed, is a matter of opinion. It has been alleged, however, that Hahn's money was funneled through the building contractor at Heritage Park under the guise of construction invoices.[125] One British journalist offered a tongue-in-cheek suggestion that PTL now stood for "Pay The Lady."[126]

In November 1985, Bakker was hit by a double-barreled assault. The IRS, which had been examining PTL's tax returns, threatened to revoke the ministry's tax-exempt status, because of the excessive pay and perquisites the Bakkers were receiving.[127] At the same time, the FCC released a 4500-page report on its 5-year investigation of PTL. Both of these attacks encouraged closer media scrutiny and by the following year, the gaudy extravagance of the Bakkers was widely reported: 47 bank accounts,[128] 6 luxurious homes, complete with gold-plated bathroom fixtures,[129] a $1.9 million annual salary, a Rolls-Royce and a Mercedes-Benz, "and for the lacquered Tammy, a wardrobe worthy of Imelda Marcos."[130] Perhaps the most prodigal symbols of the Bakkers' conspicuous consumption were the $5900 multistory playhouse constructed for the Bakker children[131] and the huge air-conditioned doghouse built for Tammy's Saint Bernard.[132]

As the negative publicity grew, PTL tried to lower its profile. In December 1986, PTL withdrew from the Evangelical Council for Financial Responsibility. A few months later, Jim Bakker announced that he had "temporarily" entrusted his ministry to Jerry Falwell. By the end of April 1987, however, Falwell publicly was vilifying Bakker as a liar, an embezzler, and a sexual deviate, declaring that Bakker would never return to PTL as long as he, Falwell, remained in charge. To demonstrate his intentions, Falwell fired Bakker's entire inner circle. What may have begun as a rescue mission quickly had become a hostile takeover.[133]

Bakker reportedly was enraged. Falwell, after all, was a former ally. Furthermore, Falwell's ministry, The Old Time Gospel Hour, had itself been the target of allegations of misappropriation. A former Falwell employee recently had charged that the ministry had "raised more than $4 million in a 1979 appeal for Cambodian Refugees but had sent a mere $100,000 to aid the victims."[134]

Falwell announced that PTL was $72 million in debt and in imminent danger of shutting down. He emphasized that the greed of the Bakkers had driven PTL to the brink of bankruptcy.[135] When Falwell had taken over PTL, he had promised that one thing he would not do was "beg for money on the air."[136] Within 2 months, however, he was doing just that.

In May 1987, Jim Bakker was defrocked by the Assemblies of God for his self-confessed adultery and for alleged homosexual activity. A few weeks later, Bakker appeared on ABC-TV's *Nightline*, generating the highest ratings in the history of that program. He described Falwell as a thief who had stolen PTL from him. Asked about the large bonuses he and his wife had collected from PTL, Bakker acknowledged, "We should have said no."[137]

On September 21, 1987, a federal grand jury convened in Charlotte to hear testimony in a criminal investigation of Bakker and PTL. Two weeks later, "Falwell and his board of directors abruptly resigned."[138] Falwell's efforts to keep PTL afloat had failed. In a hyperbolic parting shot, Falwell contended that Bakker had created "probably the greatest scab and cancer on the face of Christianity in two thousand years of church history."[139]

Meanwhile, the Bakkers announced plans for a $2 billion religious retreat in California's Mojave Desert. "Nothing came of the plan. As the summer heat descended on the desert, the Bakkers moved back to Charlotte and into a house paid for by the Bring Bakker Back Club."[140]

In April 1988, the bankruptcy court ordered the 2300-acre Heritage U.S.A. put up for sale. Jim Bakker made a $172 million offer, but could not raise the $3 million down payment.[141] His proposed 26-city "Farewell for Now" tour had to be canceled because of slow ticket sales.[142] "The IRS told the court PTL could owe as much as $82 million in back taxes, depending on how much of the organization's operations are determined to be tax exempt."[143] In December, PTL's assets were sold to a Toronto real estate developer (ironically, an ordained rabbi) for $65 million.[144]

In December 1988, the federal government handed down a 28-page indictment of Jim Bakker, including 24 counts of fraud and conspiracy. Bakker was charged with taking huge bonuses "out of the PTL trough."[145] He also was accused of vastly overselling his Lifetime Partnership Plan. "[S]ome 9,700 hapless 'partners' were offered the right to stay regularly in what turned out to be a single bunkhouse with 48 beds."[146]

Incredibly, Jim and Tammy Bakker returned to television on January 2, 1989—just 3 weeks after Jim's indictment—with an hour-long weekday program broadcast from the home of a wealthy Charlotte Amway distributor. The show was carried by only a handful of stations, and was soon taken off the air because of zoning restrictions against the use of a private home for television broadcasting. Time clearly was running out for the Bakkers and the peripatetic remains of their ministry.

> In April 1989, they moved to Orlando, Florida. In May, they resumed their broadcast from a little-used shopping center. On June 1, 1989, the Bakkers learned that the IRS had filed a lien claiming the Bakkers owed $666,492 in back taxes for 1981 and $565,434 for 1982.[147]

Jim Bakker stood trial in February 1989 and was convicted in federal court of fraudulently raising more than $158 million in contributions. Many observers within the legal community anticipated a short sentence or perhaps even probation. After all, the government had been investigating PTL seemingly for forever, but had shown little inclination to press charges. Years earlier, Bakker had denied responsibility for a $13 million accounting discrepancy by suggesting that "the devil got into the computer."[148] Even then, the government had declined to prosecute.

However, the judge in Bakker's case was Robert Potter, who was known as "Maximum Bob" because of his penchant for stiff sentences. Potter handed Bakker a stunning 45-year prison term, declaring, "Those of us who do have a religion are sick of being saps for money-grubbing preachers and priests."[149] Although Bakker's sentence was later reduced to 18 years, it was still an unexpectedly severe punishment. Jim Bakker, who already had lost PTL and most of his personal wealth, now had lost his freedom. Moreover, he would soon lose Tammy Faye; in 1992, the Bakkers were divorced,[150] and Tammy remarried while her ex-husband served his sentence. Jim Bakker was paroled in the summer of 1994. He returned to Charlotte, but not to his once-luxurious lifestyle. The preacher whose PTL ministry had collected over $150 million was released to a halfway house operated by the Salvation Army.[151]

Jim Bakker was far from the only loser, however. The final report of the court-appointed bankruptcy trustees overseeing the liquidation of Bakker's religious empire revealed that, although $40 million had been paid to PTL creditors, "the many thousands of small contributors whom Mr. Bakker defrauded got nothing."[152] After his release, Bakker announced that he planned to write inspirational books in order to help people who have suffered great personal losses in their lives. Perhaps he could start with his former contributors, although they would be well-advised to hold their wallets, rather than their breath.

The religious scandals of the 1980s have generated a number of effects. First, and most apparent, has been the decline of the teleministries. Long gone, of course, are the days when the Bakkers could draw 6000 ardent followers at their Heritage U.S.A. services. In 1991, the remnants of the Praise the Lord Club had been reduced to some leased space in an industrial complex on the outskirts of Fort Mill. On a "good" Sunday, PTL would attract perhaps 150 worshippers. Notably absent were any television cameras. The Jim and Tammy show, which once reached millions of viewers each day, had become a fading memory.

Jimmy Swaggert lost over 80% of his former audience of 2.2 million viewers.[153] Oral Roberts, who created a furor in 1987 when he threatened that God would kill him if he did not raise $4.5 million, reportedly lost half his viewers along with half his former revenues.[154] Jerry Falwell's television ministry was downsized substantially as well. By the 1990s, his *Old Time Gospel Hour* was carried on only a few stations.[155]

The second consequence of the religious scandals is the damage inflicted on those electronic ministries not directly tainted by ecclesiastic crimes. An editorial in *Christianity Today*, an evangelical journal, laments this "bad apple" effect: "[Q]uestions about one minister's morals impute suspicions to others."[156] A time-series study reports that the percentage of people attributing trustworthiness to *all* televangelists as a group "fell from 41% in 1980 to 23% in 1987 (after the first scandals broke), to 16% in 1989 near the end of the disclosures."[157] The major exception appears to be Billy Graham, whose occasional prime-time crusades still garner high television ratings. Graham's viewership remains at record levels, suggesting the continuing presence of "a faithful group of hard-core viewers whose donations are shifting but not declining."[158] Graham's revenues are especially impressive, given that his crusades are "notable in their lack of appeals for money."[159]

The third effect is an overall weakening of organized religion. Another *Christianity Today* editorial decries the legacy of what it terms "religious hucksters" and notes that "when prominent representatives of the faith are discredited . . . all Christians suffer."[160] Indeed, overall church membership declined in 1988, after the PTL scandal.[161] Pharmacists now rate higher than ministers in polls of occupational esteem.[162] A more subtle problem also has been detected. In the wake of the scandals, the core mission of televangelism—the winning of converts—seems to have been lost. Surveys of viewers report that almost all are already believers; studies of recent converts reveal that less than 1% became Christians through a televised ministry.[163] This suggests that televangelists—even those with untarnished reputations—may now simply be "preaching to the choir." As the dean of one Baptist seminary observed in 1992:

> "Televangelism is no longer the 'anointed method' it was in the 1970s and early 1980s. People on both sides of the camera have lost confidence in it. Its prime time has passed."[164]

The control of all the categories of white-collar crime examined in this book depends largely on vigorous enforcement on the part government agencies—*except* in the area of religious fraud. Here, the government generally has been reluctant to involve itself in the policing of religious commerce because of the First Amendment's protection regarding the free exercise of religion. Thus, a considerable reliance has been put on self-regulation.

In 1988, when the religious broadcasting industry was shaken by the PTL debacle, the National Religious Broadcasters (NRB) approved a stronger code of ethics in order to restore credibility in its financial and fund raising activities. Among other things, the code requires members to submit audited reports annually, disclosing all financial information except salaries.[165] In addition, the NRB established restrictive guidelines concerning the placement of family members on payrolls. Nepotism has been a long-standing problem with the electronic churches. Jimmy Swaggert, for example, once kept 17 relatives on his payroll.[166]

The new code also stressed a tougher stance regarding religious broadcasters whose integrity is compromised. As one writer has observed, "Integrity is at the heart and core of what it means to be a minister."[167] In the past, fallen church leaders had resorted to hand-wringing confessions and teary pleas for forgiveness, followed by aggressive efforts to reclaim their thrones. This strategy had enabled preachers like Swaggert and Bakker to accomplish the improbable feat of appearing to be simultaneously arrogant and contrite. The NRB code, while acknowledging that forgiveness is a central aspect of Christianity, implied that forgiveness need not necessarily entail restoration to leadership.[168]

Unfortunately, good intentions do not always yield good outcomes. Although the NRB code was approved nearly unanimously, little subsequent progress has been made in the area of enforcement, and compliance has moved at a snail's pace. For example, since enactment of the code, Paul Crouch's Trinity Broadcasting Network, the largest producer of religious programming in the world, has come under fire. The FCC is investigating allegations of financial improprieties. Crouch is being sued by his former personnel director, who claims she was fired for failing to "go along with allegedly illegal and unethical practices."[169] One of the practices in question is Crouch's policy of ordaining the managers of his chain of television stations as ministers, "which allows them to deduct their housing expenses as parsonages."[170] This permits Crouch to pay them less money. Another allegation is that "Crouch and his wife supplement their combined annual salaries of $150,000 by charging almost everything they use—their three homes, living expenses, fleet of cars and a corporate jet—to their not-for-profit ministry."[171]

Moreover, in 1993—5 years after approval of the NRB code—a judge fined Dallas evangelist Robert Tilton more than $80,000 for "refusing to provide records related to the healing miracles about which he had boasted in his television ministry."[172] This fine was levied in response to a $50-million lawsuit filed against Tilton by a woman accusing him of fraud stemming from the solicitation of donations in exchange for praying for her husband's health. The woman claimed that "The miracles-for-money offers arrived by mail for months after her husband's death."[173] The lawsuit further alleged that Tilton had defrauded at least 500 contributors through false claims that he could heal sick and injured people. A Texas court, however, disallowed most of the woman's claims.

Tilton had earlier been the subject of a 1991 ABC-TV report which charged that prayer requests received by Tilton's ministry were thrown away after the enclosed contributions were removed.[174] "In the wake of the ABC report, Tilton canceled his Success-N-Life television program."[175] Tilton's teleministry, which once appeared on 200 stations and netted $80 million per year, had become mired in a morass of litigation. By 1995, Tilton's church membership had shrunk from 10,000 to less than 1000.[176] The first case against Tilton to make it to trial was a lawsuit filed by a Florida couple who had donated $3500 toward a proposed crisis center. According to the couple's attorney, his clients' contribution was "nothing more than fuel for Tilton's lavish lifestyle."[177] A Dallas jury agreed, and in 1994, the couple was awarded $1.5 million in actual and punitive damages. This verdict prompted the judge who had rejected the earlier fraud suit against Tilton to reinstate the plaintiff's claim.[178]

Tilton's avarice is rivaled by the excesses of evangelist Tony Alamo, who was convicted and jailed in 1994 for understating his large personal income and failing to file tax returns from 1986 to 1988. Alamo's California-based ministry is a multimillion dollar enterprise with business interests in several other states. Alamo also had married *eight* different women from his congregation. Some of his brides were as young as 15 years old; others already had husbands, whom he expelled from his church after claiming their wives.[179]

The conduct of religious entrepreneurs like Crouch, Tilton, and Alamo would seem to cast doubt on the efficacy of any self-regulating code of ethics. Why has self-regulation not been a more successful antidote to religious fraud? The reason is the same basic inadequacy that has caused it to come up short in every other milieu susceptible to white-collar crime—business, banking, investing, politics, healthcare, and so on. Self-regulation may be a useful control mechanism, but it obviously is not a sufficient one.

A number of critics have contended that the self-regulation of religious broadcasting must be supplemented with some measure of external control. For Constitutional reasons already noted, this is not a comfortable role for the government.[180] Perhaps the solution lies in placing external control over television ministries in the hands of the large evangelical denominations themselves, rather than individual ministers. Although Jim Bakker and Jimmy Swaggert were both members of the Assemblies of God, they were largely independent operators. "Both had their own local churches . . . partly to ensure nonprofit status in the eyes of the Internal Revenue Service."[181] If the televangelists were more accountable to denomination officials and, indeed, to local pastors, the fund-raising ethics and personal lifestyles of the electronic preachers would be of day-to-day concern, rather than of concern only when exposed by the news media.

An even more stringent alternative would be to make television ministries accountable to a board of directors composed of respected business leaders from outside the ministry. This has long been the approach favored by the Reverend Billy Graham. In 1987, Graham's salary was $59,000 plus a housing allowance and a limited number of expenses—remarkably modest for a ministry that had collected donations of over $66 million the previous year.[182] Graham allows himself no access to unaudited gifts. Decades ago, he turned over financial control of his ministry to an independent board of directors. This governing board publicly issues audited financial statements regularly. By contrast, Oral Roberts, for example, reportedly *never* issues financial statements. Only a handful of close associates know how much money he collects or how the donations are used.[183] It is understandable that Graham's public standing has remained consistently favorable,[184] even as so many other clerical reputations have crumbled. In 1995, an annual nationwide poll reported that Billy Graham was the "most admired" American for the fourth year in a row.[185] Between 1963 and 1999, Graham also made the Gallup Poll's top 10 list of admired Americans an incredible 35 years in a row.[186]

Helping the Needy . . . or the Greedy?

Finally, there may be another less direct but very troubling consequence of religious fraud that warrants consideration: the possibility of a contagion effect on the secular fund-raising community. In 1992, United Way, one of America's foremost charitable organizations, was rocked by a series of revelations strikingly reminiscent of the gross excesses of the televangelists. United Way president, William Aramony, was forced to resign when stories were reported in the press concerning his annual salary of nearly a half million dollars and his placement of numerous friends and relatives on the United Way payroll. At the local level, flagrant extravagance also was reported. The head of the United Way of New York, for example, reportedly maintained a $4700-per-month apartment and a membership in an exclusive private club, both paid for by the charity.[187]

In 1994, Aramony was the principal target of a 71-count criminal indictment, alleging that he misappropriated $1.5 million. Among the specific charges were that: (1) he spent $383,000 of United Way money to buy a New York apartment and $72,000 to furnish it; (2) he authorized a $10,000 payment for a European vacation for his girlfriend and himself; (3) he routed a $60,000 bogus "consulting fee" to his girlfriend for renovating her Florida home and paying off her taxes; and (4) he diverted $325,000 to a dummy company he had created and used some of the funds to purchase a plush Florida condominium.[188] At the trial, Aramony's girlfriend testified that United Way paid her a salary of $80,000 for working "an hour or so."[189] By the time she left the witness stand, she had spent far longer testifying than she had ever spent earning her "no show" salary.[190]

Aramony was convicted of fraud, conspiracy, and money laundering and was given a 7-year prison sentence.[191] Like the teleministries, the United Way experienced a public backlash. One-third of United Way's local chapters dropped out of the organization;[192] contributions for 1992 were reported to be down significantly—as much as 15% in some chapters,[193] more than $100 million overall.[194] Five years later, donations for social service charities were still down 5% from pre-Aramony levels.[195] Moreover, a new controversy erupted in 1996 over $292,000 in severance pay promised to Aramony's successor after she resigned.[196] The charity once more appeared to be testing the fragility of the public trust in 1998 when a federal judge ruled that Aramony was owed a $2.38 million pension by the United Way. The president of United Way reacted angrily:

> "I was stunned. . . . All of us were amazed that he could bring this suit to begin with. How could he, given the damage he's done to this organization?"[197]

Given the vital social services provided by the United Way, the dissipation of confidence among its donors is a disturbing development, with implications clearly more important than a deserted cathedral or a fleet of empty tour buses. The building of fewer child-care centers, job-training facilities, and substance abuse clinics seems far more problematic for society in the long run than the construction of fewer Biblical theme parks.

In 2000, Daniel Wiant, an executive of the American Cancer Society, pleaded guilty to embezzling nearly $8 million from that charity. Wiant admitted to bank fraud, money laundering, and mail fraud in the thefts that began in 1997.[198] He used some of the money to pay for an addition to his home, plush landscaping, and two all-terrain vehicles. The balance was secretly transferred from the Cancer Society to a bank in Austria.[199]

The federal prosecutor's warning in the United Way case that, "[S]ociety won't tolerate individuals who are charged with protecting the precious assets of charity diverting those assets for their own personal use,"[200] was directed at the sort of secular mendacity displayed by Daniel Wiant. But it could just as easily have been aimed at all the faithless purveyors of faith who have turned their ministries into shabby confidence games.

NOTES

1. Sutherland, Edwin H. *White-Collar Crime.* New York: Dryden, 1949: 9.

2. Messner, Steven F. and Rosenfeld, Richard. *Crime and the American Dream.* Belmont, Calif.: Wadsworth, 1994.

3. Taylor, Ian, Walton, Paul, and Young, Jock. *The New Criminology: For a Social Theory of Deviance.* New York: Harper and Row, 1973: 94.

4. Merton, Robert K. "Social Structure and Anomie." *American Sociological Review* 3, 1938: 672–682.

5. Trevino, Linda K. "Ethical Decision Making in Organizations: A Person-Situation Interactionist Model." *Academy of Management Review* 11, 1986: 601–617.

6. Staw, Barry M. and Szwajkowski, Eugene. "The Scarcity-Munificence Component of Organizational Environments and the Commission of Illegal Acts." *Administrative Science Quarterly* 20, 1975: 345–354.

7. Mann, Arthur. "When Tammany Was Supreme." Introduction to Riordan, William L. *Plunkitt of Tammany Hall.* New York: E. P. Dutton, 1963: xv.

8. Bassis, Michael S., Gelles, Richard J., and Levine, Ann. *Sociology: An Introduction* (4th Ed.). New York: McGraw-Hill, 1991: 142.

9. Messner and Rosenfeld, *op. cit.,* p. 72.

10. *Ibid.,* p. 72.

11. Parsons, Talcott. *Essays in Sociological Theory.* New York: Free Press, 1964: 239.

12. Quinney, Richard. *The Social Reality of Crime.* Boston: Little, Brown, 1970.

13. Surette, *op. cit.*

14. Gerbner, George. "Television and Its Viewers: What Social Science Sees." *Rand Paper Series.* Santa Monica, Calif.: Rand Corporation, 1976.

15. Even the venerated oceanographer and television star Jacques Cousteau was accused in 1998 by his own film team of faking scenes in his popular documentaries. In one case it was alleged the an octopus was "encouraged" to scramble out of a tank and hop overboard by having assistants pour bleach into the tank. ("Something Fishy?" *Houston Chronicle.* May 11, 1998: 2A.)

16. Anderson, Kent. *Television Fraud: The History and Implications of the Quiz Show Scandals.* Westport, Connecticut: Greenwood Press, 1978; Karp, Walter. "The Quiz-Show Scandal." *American Heritage* 40, May/June 1989: 77–88; Stone, Joseph and Yohn, Tim. *Prime Time and Misdemeanors: Investigating the 1950s TV Quiz Scandal: D.A.'s Account.* New Brunswick, NJ: Rutgers University Press, 1992.

17. *America: A Catholic Review, op. cit.,* p. 98.

18. Allen, James E., Jr. "The TV 'Fixes' and Teacher Responsibility." *School and Society.* April 23, 1960: 202.

19. After a conspicuous absence of 40 years, big-money quiz shows returned to prime time television in 1999 with the debut of *Who Wants to Be a Millionaire.* This program dwarfed its predecessors with a top prize $1 million. It immediately became one of the highest rated programs on network television. (Bauder, David. "Hot Game Show Boosts ABC to Its First Sweeps Victory in Five Years." *Houston Chronicle.* December 1, 1999: 5D.)

20. "Gimme, Gimme, Gimme on the Old Payola." *Life.* November 23, 1959: 45.

21. Coase, *op. cit.,* p. 272.

22. Ewen, David. *The Life and Death of Tin Pan Alley.* New York: Funk and Wagnall's, 1964.

23. Coase, *op. cit.,* p. 273.

24. *Ibid.*

25. "Bribery to Get Song Plugs Rampant, Despite Pledges and Grandstanding." *Variety.* February 9, 1938: 1.

26. "Coercion Widely Used on Pubs [publishers]." *Variety.* February 23, 1938: 1, 43.

27. Goldberg, Isaac. *Tin Pan Alley: A Chronicle of the American Popular Music Racket.* New York: John Day, 1930: 210.

28. *Ibid.*

29. McKenzie, Ed. "A Deejay's Expose—and Views of the Trade." *Life* 47, November 23, 1959: 46.

30. "Good-by, Ookie Dookie." *Newsweek.* February 22, 1960: 60.

31. *Ibid.*

32. Coase, *op. cit.*

33. *Ibid.,* p. 60.

34. Coase, *op. cit.,* p. 293.

35. Denisoff, Serge. *Solid Gold: The Popular Record Industry.* Brunswick, NJ: Transaction Books, 1975.

36. "Jockeys on a Rough Ride." *Newsweek.* December 7, 1959: 98.

37. *Ibid.,* p. 98.

38. McKenzie, *op. cit.*

39. "Music Biz Goes Round and Round: It Comes Out Clarkola." *Life.* May 16, 1960: 118.

40. *Ibid.,* p. 120.

41. *Ibid.,* p. 120.

42. *Ibid.,* p. 120.

43. *Ibid.,* p. 120.

44. *Ibid.*, p. 120.

45. *Ibid.*, p. 120.

46. Passman, Arnold. *The Deejays.* New York: MacMillan, 1971.

47. Anderson, Jack. "New Disc Jockey Payola Uncovered." *Washington Post.* March 31, 1972: C23.

48. Anderson, Jack. "Disc Jockey Play-for-Drugs Outlined." *Washington Post.* April 21, 1972: C21.

49. Coase, *op. cit.*, p. 304.

50. *Ibid.*

51. Coase, *op. cit.*

52. *Ibid.*

53. *Ibid.*

54. *Ibid.*, p. 305

55. Johnson, Dean. "WXKS Parent Denies Payola." *Boston Herald.* December 18, 1998: S16.

56. Peterson, Cass. "Post Writer Wins Pulitzer for Story on Child Addict." Washington Post April 14, 1981: A1, A5. Although the Pulitzer carries a cash prize of only $1000, it is considered the most prestigious award in journalism and can "make" a career, particularly for a young reporter like Cooke.

57. Cooke, Janet. "Jimmy's World: 8-Year-Old Heroin Addict Lives for a Fix." *Washington Post.* April 14, 1981 (originally published September 28, 1981): C6.

58. Maraniss, David A. "Post Reporter's Pulitzer Prize Is Withdrawn." *Washington Post.* April 16, 1981: A1, A25. It was further revealed that Cooke had also falsified her autobiography to the Pulitzer Advisory Board.

59. Quoted in *Ibid.*, p. A1. In 1996, Janet Cooke resurfaced after 15 years of professional exile, publicly seeking a "second chance." The president of a national association of African American journalists offered no hope of forgiveness: "Making up the news has long been considered the worst crime in journalism. . . . If she deserves a second chance, let her write fiction" (Quoted in Neuharth, Al. "Why You Deserve a Second Chance." *USA Today.* May 17, 1996: 13A).

60. "The End of the 'Jimmy' Story." *Washington Post.* April 16, 1981: A18.

61. "'Incredible' but Fictitious: New Republic Writer Fired After Fabricating Story." *Houston Chronicle.* May 12, 1998: 5A.

62. Irving, Clifford. *The Hoax.* Sagaponack, NY: The Permanent Press, 1981.

63. Dwarfing even the prodigious Hughes deception, the most lucrative literary hoax ever perpetrated was the fake 62-volume "Hitler Diaries" for which the West German magazine *Stern* paid $3.75 million to journalist and Nazi aficionado Gerd Heidemann in 1983. In addition to the many factual and stylistic errors in the diaries, the labels on the individual volumes contained polyester threads, and some pages were written with a mechanical pencil. Polyester and mechanical pencils were both not even invented until after the War. With eyes apparently tightly shut, *Stern* sold the foreign serialization rights for over $3 million to such major publications as *Newsweek* and *Life.* After the error-riddled forgery was unmasked, Heidemann was convicted of fraud by a German court and given a 4½-year sentence. Most of the payoff money was never recovered. Calling the diaries "the most expensive waste-paper collection in the world," the publisher of *Stern* stated tersely: "We have reason to be ashamed."

64. "Judge Won't Write Off JFK Forgeries." *Houston Chronicle.* September 17, 1999: 25A.

65. *Ibid.*, p. 121.

66. Durkheim, Emile. *The Elementary Forms of Religious Life.* New York: Free Press, 1965. This book was originally published in 1915.

67. Greeley, Andrew M. *Unsecular Man.* New York: Schocken Books, 1972.

68. Galanter, Marc. *Cults: Faith, Healing, and Coercion.* London: Oxford University Press, 1989.

69. Blau, Eleanor. "Sun Myung Moon a Prophet to Thousands." *New York Times.* September 16, 1974: 1, 26.

70. Galanter, *op. cit.*, p. 130.

71. Thomas, Jo. "Some in Congress Seek Inquiries on Cult Activities." *New York Times.* January 2, 1979: A1, A14.

72. Galanter, *op. cit.*, p. 132.

73. *Ibid.*, p. 132–133.

74. Austin, Charles. "Sun Myung Moon Still an Elusive Figure." *New York Times.* October 19, 1981: B4.

75. "Rev. Henry Lyons Found Guilty of Racketeering, Grand Theft." *Jet.* March 15, 1999: 16–18.

76. *Ibid.*

77. "Trial Begins for Rev. Henry Lyons, Head of National Baptist Convention." *Jet.* February 1, 1999: 24.

78. Leisner, Pat. "Baptist Leader Sentenced to Prison." *Washington Post* Search Archives. March 31, 1999.

79. "Lyons Found Guilty." *The Christian Century.* March 1999: 302.

80. Quoted in "Lyons Says He's 'Truly Repentant,' Resigns National Baptist Position." *Houston Chronicle.* March 17, 1999: 7A.

81. Quoted in *Ibid.*

82. Quoted in *Ibid.*

83. Quoted in "Minister gets $5\frac{1}{2}$ Year Prison Term in Swindling Case." *Houston Chronicle.* April 1, 1999: 12A. When Henry Lyons went to prison, a number of leaders from the National Baptist Convention, USA, had hoped to convince political activist Rev. Jesse Jackson, a member of the denomination, to serve out the balance of Lyon's term. Jackson declined the offer. Ironically, a little over a year later Jackson himself would become embroiled in a controversy involving his own long-time mistress, with whom it was revealed he had a daughter out of wedlock. The Rainbow-PUSH Coalition, headed by Jackson, acknowledged that it had paid the woman a $15,000 advance on a contract to do consulting for the organization and $20,000 in "moving expenses." ("Coalition Gave 'Severance Pay' to Mother of Jackson's Child." *Houston Chronicle.* January 20, 2001: 17A.)

84. Much of the background and case materials described in this section are derived from James Randi's remarkable expose' of phony faith healers, *The Faith Healers* (Rev. Ed.; Buffalo, NY: Prometheus Books, 1989).

85. "Now the manifestations of the Spirit is given to everyone for profit. To one through the Spirit is given the utterance of wisdom; and to another the utterance of knowledge, according to the same Spirit; to another the *gift of healing* [italics added], in the one Spirit; to another the working of miracles; to another prophecy; to another the distinguishing of spirits; to another various kinds of tongues; to another interpretation of tongues." *I Corinthians 12: 7–10.*

86. Randi, James. *The Faith Healers* (Revised Edition). Buffalo, NY: Prometheus Books, 1989: 31.

87. *Ibid.*

88. *Ibid.,* p. 85.

89. Hedgepeth, William. "Brother A. A. Allen on the Gospel Trail: He Feels, He Heels, & He Turns You on with God." *Look* 33, 1969: 31.

90. *Ibid.*

91. Tierney, John. "Fleecing the Flock." *Discover* 11, November 1987: 50–58.

92. Dart, John. "Skeptics' Revelations." *Los Angeles Times.* May 11, 1986: D1, D2.

93. Randi, *op. cit.*

94. *Ibid.,* p. 139.

95. *Ibid.,* p. 175.

96. *Ibid.*

97. Tierney, *op. cit.,* p. 53.

98. *Ibid.,* p. 53.

99. Jaroff, Leon. "Fighting Against Flimflam." *Time* 131, June 13, 1988: 70–72.

100. Jaroff, *op. cit.,* p. 72.

101. Randi, *op. cit.*

102. Tierney, *op. cit.,* p. 56.

103. *Ibid.,* p. 56.

104. *Ibid.,* p. 56.

105. Randi, *op. cit.,* p. 151.

106. "Duping the Faithful: Charlatans in the Church." *U.S. News & World Report.* March 29, 1993: 51.

107. Schultze, Quentin J. *Televangelism and American Culture: The Business of Popular Religion.* Grand Rapids, Mich: Baker Book House, 1991.

108. Bruce, Steve. *Pray TV: Televangelism in America.* New York: Routledge, 1990.

109. Hadden, Jeffrey K. and Shupe, Anson. *Televangelism: Power and Politics on God's Frontier.* New York: Henry Holt, 1988.

110. Hadden, Jeffrey K. "The Rise and Fall of American Televangelism." *Annals of the American Academy of Political and Social Science* 527, 1993: 120.

111. Edsall, Thomas B. "Robertson Network Agrees to 'Significant' Fine by IRS." *Houston Chronicle.* March 21, 1998: 10A.

112. Income estimates for the Robertson, Roberts, Schuller, Falwell, and Swaggert ministries are derived from: Ostling, Richard. "TV's Unholy Row." *Time* 129, April 6, 1987: 60–67.

113. Ostling, *op. cit.*

114. Ostling, Richard N. "Enterprising Evangelism." *Time* 130, August 3, 1987: 53.

115. Woodward, Kenneth. "What Profits a Preacher?" *Newsweek* 109, May 4, 1987: 68; Steinfels, Peter. "The Swaggert Case: When a Religious Leader Strays, What Path Should Be Followed?" *New York Times.* February 28, 1988: E7.
116. Ostling, April 6, 1987, *op. cit.*
117. *Ibid.,* p. 45.
118. Shepard, Charles. *Forgiven: The Rise and Fall of Jim Bakker and the PTL Ministry.* New York: Atlantic Monthly Press, 1989.
119. Barnhart, *op. cit.,* pp. 4–5.
120. Shepard, *op. cit.*
121. *Ibid.*
122. Barnhart, *op. cit.*
123. Hackett, George. "Paying the Wages of Sin: Sexual Mischief and a Payoff Disgrace a Preacher. "*Newsweek* 109, March 30,1987: 28.
124. Ostling, Richard N. "A Really Bad Day at Fort Mill." *Time* 129, March 30, 1987: 70.
125. Barnhart, *op. cit.*
126. *The Economist.* "Pity the Lot." June 6, 1987: 26.
127. Ostling, Richard N. "Taking Command at Fort Mill." *Time* 129, May 11, 1987: 60.
128. Barnhart, *op. cit.*
129. Barnhart, *op. cit.*
130. Watson, Russell. "Fresh Out of Miracles." *Newsweek* 109, May 11, 1987: 70.
131. Tidwell, Gary L. "The Anatomy of a Fraud." *Fund Raising Management* 24, May 1993: 58–62.
132. Shepard, *op. cit.*
133. Martz, *op. cit.*
134. Woodward, May 4, 1987, *op. cit.*
135. Ostling, Richard N. "Of God and Greed." *Time* 129, June 8, 1987: 70–74.
136. Gates, David. "Falwell and the PTL: 'Send Money.'" *Newsweek* 109, May 25, 1987: 6.
137. Shepard, *op. cit.,* p. 70.
138. Shepard, *op. cit.,* p. 548.
139. *Ibid.,* p. 548.
140. *Ibid.,* p. 549.
141. Barnhart, *op. cit.*
142. "The Televangelist Fiasco: Top '87 Religion Story." *Christian Century.* December 23, 1987: 1163–1165.
143. "Rendering Unto Caesar." *Christianity Today.* January 15, 1988: 54.
144. Barnhart, *op. cit.*
145. Ostling, Richard N. "Jim Bakker's Crumbling World." *Time* 132, December 19, 1988: 72.
146. *Ibid.,* p. 72.
147. Shepard, *op. cit.,* p. 552.
148. Hackett, *op. cit.,* p. 28.
149. Sanders, Alain L. "The Wrath of 'Maximum Bob.'" *Time* 134, November 6, 1989: 62.
150. Frank, Jeffrey A. "Tammy & Jim, Together no More." *Washington Post.* March 13, 1992: F1, F3.
151. "Jim Bakker Arrives at Halfway House." *Houston Post.* July 2, 1994: A4.
152. "Donors to Bakker Get Nothing." *New York Times.* November 15, 1992: 31.
153. Shipp, E. R. "Scandals Emptied Pews of Electronic Churches." *New York Times,* March 3, 1991: 24.
154. *The Economist.* "To Err Is Human." March 28, 1987: 26–32.
155. *Ibid.*
156. Muck, Terry C. "The Bakker Tragedy." *Christianity Today* 31, May 15, 1987: 14.
157. Smith, Tom W. "The Polls: Poll Trends— Religious Beliefs and Behaviors and the Televangelist Scandals of 1987–1988." *Public Opinion Quarterly* 56, 1992: 361.
158. "TV Preachers Still Rake It In." *Psychology Today.* November 1988: 6.
159. Sidey, Ken. "Addicted to Broadcasting." *Christianity Today* 36, February 10, 1992: 12.
160. *Ibid.,* p. 12.
161. Smith, *op. cit.*
162. Plagenz, George R. "Clergy Mistakenly Steps off Pedestal to Be 'Like the Rest of Us.'" *Houston Post,* January 22, 1994: E4.
163. Sidey, *op. cit.*
164. *Ibid.,* p. 12.
165. "Religious Broadcasters Adopt Stiffer Ethics Code." *New York Times.* February 4, 1988: 14.
166. Ostling, August 3, 1987, *op. cit.*
167. Stenfels, *op. cit.,* p. E7.
168. *Ibid.*
169. Woodward, Kenneth L. "The T Stands for Trouble." *Newsweek* 119, March 30, 1992: 60.
170. *Ibid.,* p. 61.
171. *Ibid.,* p. 61.
172. Reed, Steven R. "Evangelist Tilton Told to Pay $81,742 Fine for Files Delay." *Houston Chronicle.* September 4, 1993: 38A.
173. *Ibid.,* p. 38A.
174. Brown, Rich. "Trouble in Paradise?" *Broadcasting* 121, December 2, 1991: 28–30.

175. "Jury: Tilton Defrauded Fla. Couple." *Houston Post*. April 22, 1994: A22.

176. "Lawsuit Thrown Out." *Houston Chronicle*. December 16, 1995: 36A.

177. *Ibid.*, p. A21.

178. "Tilton Sees Fraud Suit Reinstated." *Houston Post*. April 24, 1994: A26.

179. "Jury Convicts an Evangelist of Tax Evasion." *New York Times*. June 12, 1994: 30.

180. Oden, Thomas C. "Full Disclosure: Broadcast Ministries Can No Longer Have Financial Secrets." *Christianity Today* 32, 1988: 40–41.

181. Schultze, *op. cit.*, p. 228.

182. Ostling, Richard N. "Enterprising Evangelism." *Time* 130, August 3, 1987: 50–53.

183. *Ibid.*

184. *Washington Post*. "Billy Graham's Star on Walk of Fame." October 21, 1989: B6.

185. *Houston Chronicle*. "Write-Ins Get Him 2nd." December 14, 1995: 2A.

186. *USA Today*. "Billy Graham: 35 Years in a Row." December 15, 1999: 8A.

187. Stodghill, Ron II. "United They Stand?" *Business Week* 3288, October 19, 1992: 40.

188. *Houston Post*. "Ex-United Way Head Indicted for Misusing Funds." September 14, 1994: A11.

189. Quoted in *Galveston Daily News, op. cit.*, p. 3A.

190. *Ibid.*

191. *Galveston Daily News*. "United Way Ex-President Guilty." April 4, 1995. 3A; *Houston Chronicle*. "United Way Ex-President Gets 7 Years." June 23, 1995: 16A.

192. Gartner, Michael. "Aborted United Way Deal Failed Smell Test." *USA Today*, June 18, 1996: 13A.

193. Segal, Troy. "They Didn't Even Give at the Office." *Business Week* 3302, January 25, 1993: 68–69.

194. Gartner, *op. cit.*

195. Johnston, David C. "Neediest Suffer as Donations to United Way Dwindle." *Houston Chronicle*. November 9, 1997: 16A.

196. *Ibid.*

197. Quoted in: Wee, Eric L. "Judge Upholds $2 Million Pension for Convicted Ex-United Way Leader." *Houston Chronicle*. October 26, 1998: 8A.

198. Gillespie, Charley. "Former Cancer Society Official Pleads Guilty to Embezzlement." *Houston Chronicle*. August 26, 2000: 25A.

199. *Ibid.*

200. *Ibid.*, p. 3A.

CHAPTER 6

Securities Fraud

First Investment Banker: We want Drexel Burnham to sell the bonds on this one. . . . They work cheap and they're the best.
Second Investment Banker: They're also about to go before a grand jury because of their Milken-Boesky connection.
Corporate CEO: Just what we need—stationary from Alcatraz.

From *Barbarians at the Gate* (1993). Screenplay by Larry Gelbart.

*I*n the preceding chapter we have seen how white-collar crime inflicts serious damage on vital social institutions such as the mass media and religion. But perhaps no institution is damaged more by fraud and other illicit activities than the economy. Economy refers to activities organized around the production and distribution of goods and services. Simply put, the economy functions to satisfy people's basic material requirements. Many scholars have suggested that in the United States the economy is the most dominant of all social institutions. As such, the importance of the American people maintaining a trust in their economy cannot be overstated.

A recent example of how such trust can be betrayed occurred in 2000 when the three top financial officers of a newly merged corporation pled guilty to accounting fraud that resulted in a $2.83 billion settlement with shareholders—the largest settlement of its kind ever.[1]

Since the Industrial Revolution crossed the Atlantic—but especially since the 1980s—white-collar crime has sapped the American economy and undermined the public interest. Specifically, we will look at securities fraud, because the honest trading of securities is the "soul" of a successful capitalist economy.

Paper Entrepreneurism

If the American economy has weakened as a social institution, one factor may be the emergence of a newer, less productive, brand of capitalism, known pejoratively as "paper entrepreneurism."[2] It has been lamented that the best financial minds in America are now wasted on computer-generated models which produce nothing but enormous paper profits and zero-sum games of dubious value to the overall economy.[3] There has been a growing public perception since the early 1980s that the nucleus of the American economy has shifted from investing to trading, from industrial production to deal making. During the 1980s, fully one-third of the Fortune 500 companies were either taken over or went private.[4]

Indeed, the 1980s have been viewed retrospectively as the decade when greed came out of the closet. The love of money, which once "dared not speak its name," refused to shut up. Nowhere was the new signification of greed more pronounced or the spiraling decline of public trust more problematic than on Wall Street, which grew more and more estranged from Main Street.

Public confidence in the honesty of its financial markets—without which they hardly could exist—was shaken in the 1980s by a seemingly endless chain of scandals. For example, Prudential Securities defrauded thousands of customers when its brokers lured them into risky investments by deliberately making false statements about the financial returns investors could expect. After it was sued by the Securities and Exchange Commission (SEC), Prudential was forced to repay more than $700 million to its victimized clients.[5]

One of most repercussive cases involved the giant brokerage house, E. F. Hutton. Like many investment firms, Hutton had suffered during the recession of the 1970s and was experiencing financial difficulty. The company began writing huge overdrafts in order to profit from the "float," that is, the interest that banks can earn on funds they hold while waiting for a check to clear.[6] Con-artists refer to this scheme as "check kiting."

> Hutton would pay its bills with a check that was covered by another check that was written on a different bank, which was covered by a check written on still another bank and so on. While all the banks were waiting for these various checks to clear, Hutton was getting a kind of interest-free loan. In 1980, the first year the scheme got into full swing, Hutton saved about $27 million in interest, which accounted for about a third of its profits.[7]

The scheme unraveled in 1982 and, after lengthy negotiations, Hutton agreed in 1985 to pay a $2 million fine.[8] For a company as wealthy as Hutton, this penalty was little more than a slap on the wrist. Moreover, no individuals were ever prosecuted. But in an industry built on trust and reputation, Hutton was finished as a major player. Not too long after the settlement, Hutton was sold to another firm and lost its corporate identity forever. As we shall see shortly, an even more lethal fate was awaiting the firm of Drexel Burnham

Lambert at the end of the decade; for the demise of E. F. Hutton was just a pro-logue to the immensely, scaled crimes that were to follow.

In this chapter two categories of securities fraud will be considered: *insider trading* and *stock manipulation*. Clearly the distinction between these two crimes is blurred. The former will be detailed as a traditional offense committed, as the term suggests, by corporate and brokerage insiders. The latter will be examined as a more inclusive arena for fraud, incorporating the technology of the so-called new economy and creating unprecedented illegal opportunities to market outsiders as well, from teenage cyberpunks to sleazy swindlers to Mafia racketeers.

Insider Trading

Insider trading was criminalized under the Securities Exchange Act of 1934. As defined by the SEC, insider traders are stockholders, directors, officers, or any recipients of information not publicly available who take advantage of such limited disclosure for their own benefit.[9] The SEC has determined that insiders have a "fiduciary duty" not only to refrain from trading on their private information but to disclose it as well.[10]

A typical example of insider trading occurred in 1981 when the fugitive owner of a Swiss brokerage house, an Italian national named Giuseppe Tome, was convicted of violating American securities laws. Tome had cultivated a personal friendship with the chairman of the multinational Seagram conglomerate, which was then seeking to make a number of corporate acquisitions. This friendship made Tome "privy to a stream of proprietary information,"[11] which he and his associates exploited by investing heavily in an eventual takeover target of Seagram's. They netted an illegal profit of $3.5 million in just 2 days.

In the first half of the decade—before Boesky and Milken became household names—a pair of cases shocked the business world and raised the crime of insider trading to public consciousness. The first case involved Paul Thayer, the former CEO of LTV Corporation, a large steel and aerospace company based in Dallas. Thayer was serving as deputy secretary of defense in 1984, a post to which he had been appointed by his friend Ronald Reagan, when he was charged by the SEC with being the linchpin of an insider trading ring.[12]

In 1981, LTV was exploring the possibility of making a takeover offer for the Grumman Corporation, another big aerospace contractor. During the pre-takeover negotiations, Thayer allegedly leaked word of LTV's impending bid for Grumman to his Dallas stockbroker and close friend, Billy Bob Harris, who in turn passed the word to a circle of his friends, lovers, and business associates. One of the recipients of this inside information was a stockbroker at the Atlanta office of Bear Stearns, and he relayed it to a New York colleague, who agreed to split the profits earned through the purchase of Grumman stock. Another of Harris' friends made the same deal with two Boston associates. Thayer's leak was barely hours old and already its ripple effects were eddying widely.

When the news of LTV's offer of $45 per share for Grumman stock was announced publicly less than a week later, the Thayer-Harris network had purchased over 100,000 shares at around $25. The stock jumped more than 10 points the day of the announcement, generating profits of about $800,000 to Harris and his cronies.

Later that year, Thayer leaked word of an imminent financial turn-around for the slumping LTV to his girlfriend and to Harris. Acting on this in-side information, Harris bought LTV stock on margin for his own account and through the accounts of his father and three friends. The following day, LTV announced its earnings had tripled for the year and raised its dividend sub-stantially. The stock of course increased in value almost immediately. Harris and his group cashed in and took their quick profits.

Thayer, who reportedly never conducted insider trading on his own behalf and did not personally profit from his friends' transactions, seemed to relish the role of "Texas-sized sugar daddy,"[13] and soon began leaking in-side information from other companies on whose boards he sat—notably Anheuser-Busch and Allied Corporation. When he learned that Busch was considering a takeover bid for a Texas baking company, he again gave this in-formation to his girlfriend and to the ubiquitous Harris. Once more, the "good old boy" network (or more correctly, the "good old person" network, because it included a female flight attendant and a female aerobics instructor) grabbed more than 100,000 shares of the target firm. When the takeover was an-nounced, the group walked away with over $200,000 in profits.

When the Allied Corporation was preparing a takeover offer for the Bendix Corporation, the scenario was repeated on an even grander scale, and the illegal profits exceeded $750,000. This was to be Thayer's final betrayal of trust. The SEC had detected the pre-announcement run-up in price of Bendix shares and charged Thayer with leaking inside information. Thayer and Har-ris were indicted by the U.S. Department of Justice. Thayer, who initially had denied all charges, pleaded guilty in 1985 and, despite requests for mercy from such illustrious friends as Gerald Ford and Barry Goldwater,[14] he was given a 4-year prison sentence. This punishment stunned many observers, but the government had "hooked a big fish" and apparently was intent on filleting Thayer as an example to others.[15]

The other sensational insider trading scandal of the early 1980s began in 1983, when R. Foster Winans, a journalist who co-authored the daily "Heard on the Street" column for the *Wall Street Journal*, was asked a fateful question by Peter Brant, a prominent stockbroker from the firm of Kidder Peabody: "Wouldn't you like to be a millionaire?" The reply was immediate: "Sure."[16] And with that, a criminal conspiracy was spawned.

That a reporter earning $575 per week could have possessed the po-tential to greatly enrich an already wealthy man and perhaps generate a per-sonal fortune as well may seem strange; but the "Heard" column exerts a powerful influence on market professionals, who read it ritually every work-day morning. By cultivating a network of market analysts and expert sources, the column serves as an early signal of a company's imminent growth or failure. A positive or negative story can elevate the price of a stock significantly—or sink it. Knowing the contents of a "Heard" column prior to its publication could be an invaluable tool to an investor skilled in the intricacies of buying short or going long on a stock. Such inside information has been compared to "having your own time machine . . . of knowing the winning horse in the fifth race at Belmont before post time."[17] Indeed, insider trading has been termed "the financial equivalent of fixing a race."[18]

This conspiracy lasted little over a year, with Brant regularly receiving advance information about "Heard" columns. Winans never did become a millionaire—his share of the illegal profits came to only about $30,000. When an investigation by the American Stock Exchange revealed a link between "Heard" columns and the trading patterns of one of the Brant's "clients," it all came crashing down in a pile of shattered careers and ruined lives. The conspirators and their accomplices were convicted in 1985, receiving tough sentences and heavy fines. It was, in the words of the man who then headed the SEC Enforcement Division, a "celebrity hanging."[19]

Unfortunately, if the high-profile prosecutions in the Thayer and *Wall Street Journal* cases were meant to deter future violations by unscrupulous insiders, their effects seem to have been minimal. As evidence, consider the career of Dennis Levine, a man so thoroughly dishonest that his biographer calls him "Wall Street's worst nightmare come true."[20]

C A S E   S T U D Y

Dennis Levine

In the rarified atmosphere of the investment banking community, where the plushest offices often are reserved for aristocratic scions with Ivy League MBAs, Dennis Levine was an anomaly. Born to a middle-class family in the Bayside section of Queens and educated at a tuition-free public university, he was hardly an obvious candidate for dazzling success in his chosen arena; but dazzle he did. Fueled by the ever-dangerous mixture of ambition and amorality, he elbowed his way up the Wall Street food chain. Dennis Levine was determined to swim with the sharks; it was his own perverse facsimile of the American dream.

By 1980, Levine had taken an entry-level position in the mergers and acquisitions (M & A) department of Smith Barney. Talented and only 28 years old, he could have proceeded up a linear path toward an honorable and lucrative career; but that was to be the proverbial road not taken. The ink was barely dry on his new business cards when he began testing the mechanics of insider trading. "In June, 1980 he made a profit of about $4000 by buying—and then selling after the price

(Continued)

climbed—1500 shares of Dart Industries, Inc., one day before the public announcement of a merger offer by Kraft."[21] The proceeds from this first transaction were deposited in the Bahamian branch of a Swiss bank, where Levine had set up a dummy account earlier that year with the help of two accomplices, a corporate attorney from a prominent New York law firm[22] and an international banker from the investment firm of Lazard Freres.[23] From that point on, it was simply a matter of progressively raising the stakes, which Dennis Levine fully intended to do.

In 1981, Levine became a vice-president in the M & A department of Lehman Brothers. There he continued making illegal insider trades and carrying suitcases filled with money to and from Nassau. He was accumulating a substantial cash reserve in his secret account, which now was controlled by a virtually untraceable Panamanian holding company he had set up for himself. By 1984, he was ready, and eager, for a big score.

Lehman Brothers represented American Stores, a Utah-based retail conglomerate that was secretly planning an attempted acquisition of Jewel Companies, a Chicago-based supermarket and drugstore chain. Levine, of course, was privy to this inside information, and Diamond Holdings (his Panamanian company) purchased 75,000 shares of Jewel for $3.7 million. He even leaked the merger story to the press anonymously to drive up the value of his Jewel stock more quickly. When the two companies eventually merged, Levine sold his shares for a $1.2 million profit.[24]

In January, 1985 Levine went to work for Drexel Burnham as a managing director of M & A. He was given a base salary of $140,000 and a minimum guaranteed annual bonus of $750,000 along with 1000 shares of Drexel stock worth about $100,000.[25] Obviously, 1985 would be a very good year for the public Dennis Levine. And for the private Dennis Levine, it would be spectacular. Just four illegal trades in a 4-month period would generate profits of nearly $6 million:[26]

February 1985

Ten days after starting at Drexel, Levine learned of a confidential plan by Drexel client Coastal Corporation to acquire American Natural Resources (ANR), a gas pipeline company. From a pay phone he called his Swiss broker in Nassau and bought 145,000 shares of ANR for $7 million, almost his entire "Panamanian" holdings. When ANR agreed to accept Coastal's offer 2 months later, Levine made nearly $1.4 million in profits.[27]

March 1985

A confederate at the firm of Goldman Sachs informed Levine that Goldman Sachs had been hired by McGraw-Edison Company in connection with a proposed buy-out by Forstman Little & Company. Levine bought 80,000 shares for $3.4 million. A week later, the buy-out was announced, and Levine sold his stock at a profit of over $900,000.[28]

(Continued)

April 1985

Levine learned from his confederate at Lazard Freres that Houston Natural Gas Corporation (HNG) was in secret merger talks with InterNorth, another energy company. Levine bought 75,000 shares of HNG for $4 million. Two weeks later, the merger was announced, and another $900,000 was added to his Bahamian account.[29]

May 1985

Yet another confederate, this one at Shearson Lehman Brothers, leaked details to Levine of a proposed merger between R. J. Reynolds, the big tobacco firm, and Nabisco Brands, the giant food company. Levine, sensing a huge opportunity, dumped his entire Diamond account into Nabisco stock—over $9 million. A few weeks later, Nabisco went public regarding its merger talks with Reynolds, and its stock took a sizable jump. Levine cashed in at a profit of $2.7 million.[30] This was to be his biggest single coup among the estimated $12.6 million in illegal trades Levine made in his career.[31]

By the fall of 1985, however, the Enforcement Division of the SEC had become increasingly concerned about the apparent proliferation of insider trading. Every announcement of a proposed merger, acquisition, or leveraged buy-out seemed to be preceded by heavier-than-usual sales in the stock of the target company. A major investigation had been undertaken, and the name of a certain Swiss bank in the Bahamas kept cropping up again and again.[32]

Levine's bankers were being pressured to explain 28 suspicious transactions extending from 1983 through 1985. In 1986, "Mr. Diamond" finally was identified as Dennis Levine. He was arrested in May 1986, convicted in February 1987, fined $11.6 million, and sentenced to 2 years in prison—of which he served 17 months. After Levine's arrest, a long-time Wall Street luminary wrote, "The cancer is greed. Too much money is coming together with too many young people who have little or no institutional memory, or sense of tradition."[33]

Following his release, Levine became president of a financial consulting firm in New York.[34] He announced his intention to start a $100 million offshore investment fund.[35] Rumors had abounded since his arrest that he still had a great deal of "Diamond" money left, carefully hidden away.[36] In 1990, the Ethics Club at the Columbia Business School initiated a lecture series by white-collar felons. The first speaker invited was Dennis Levine.[37]

If Levine's punishment seems remarkably light compared with that of Thayer, who was by any standard far less corrupt, it is because Levine was a deal-maker to the very end. He plea-bargained his relatively lenient sentence in exchange for testifying as a government witness against his co-conspirators.[38] He would not be the last convicted insider to cut such a deal.

Levine's cooperation was considered important because the SEC recognized that he did not commit his crimes in unabetted isolation. About 30 of his alleged 54 illegal trades involved stocks in companies whose takeover deals were not handled by Levine or the firm for which he worked.[39] In fact, the Levine investigation had already paid a big dividend a few months earlier in the form of one of the richest and most visible figures on Wall Street: Ivan Boesky.

C A S E S T U D Y

Ivan Boesky

Boesky was born in Detroit in 1938. Beyond that, the details of his biography often vary considerably from source to source.[40] Some writers depict his childhood as one of poverty—this is the version favored by Boesky himself. Other sources portray his early life as one of upper-middle class comfort. Boesky claimed to have graduated from Cranwood, an elite prep school whose tuition he financed by selling ice cream from a truck. Although he apparently did attend Cranwood for a while, he graduated from an innercity Detroit high school. Boesky reportedly liked to give others the impression that he was a Harvard graduate as well, when, in fact, he never had attended that university. He did, however, donate a large sum of money, which garnered him an honorary position on the advisory board of the Harvard School of Public Health. This position enabled him to join the prestigious New York branch of the Harvard Club, and he often conducted business there. In sum, depending on what one chooses to believe, Boesky was either a self-made man, or a self-invented one.

Boesky graduated from the Detroit School of Law, but was unable to land a job with any of that city's big law firms. While in school, however, he had met and married a wealthy woman whose father owned (among other things) the famous Beverly Hills Hotel. His new father-in-law reportedly did not think much of Boesky, nicknaming him "Ivan the Bum."[41]

Boesky moved his family to New York in 1966 to seek his fortune. Although he was at times unemployed, the Boeskys lived in a luxurious Park Avenue apartment, compliments of his father-in-law. Boesky moved through a series of positions with various Wall Street firms. He was fired from one job on the first day after losing $20,000 on a deal.[42]

Finally, in 1972, Boesky was hired by the small brokerage house of Edwards & Hanly. Surprisingly, given his checkered employment history, he was put in charge of the company's modest arbitrage department and given a free hand to develop it. It was here that the Boesky legend first took root. He had found his niche in the esoteric domain of arbitrage, where he was quickly skirting rules and outmaneuvering peers. On one occasion, he was censured and fined by the New York Stock Exchange. Along the way, "Ivan the Bum" had picked up a new nickname that would endure for the rest of his Wall Street career: "Ivan the Terrible."[43]

(Continued)

Arbitragers (alternatively known as arbitrageurs) are investment specialists who speculate in so-called deal stocks, on behalf of a brokerage house, an investment bank, or a limited partnership. It is not a new concept; arbitrage has existed for well over 100 years,[44] but for most of that time it occupied a relatively obscure position in the Wall Street milieu.

The basic dynamics of arbitrage are not especially complicated. Boesky himself explained the process in his 1985 book.[45] Company A and Company B are negotiating a merger, which if consummated would result in the exchange of one share of Company A stock (currently valued at $50; for each share of Company B stock (currently valued at $30). It is the task of the arbitrager to assess the likelihood that the proposed deal will be made. If his assessment is positive, he will then offer to buy the outstanding stock of Company B at a price somewhere between the current value of $30 and the potential takeover value of $50—for example, $43. The Company B shareholders would be faced with a choice of waiting several months to reap a potential profit of $20 per share on a deal that may or may not happen, or to accept the arbitrager's offer for an immediate guaranteed profit of $13 a share. Many times, Company B's shareholders opt not to wait and instead choose to settle for the certain (although smaller) profit. The arbitrager then buys the Company B stock and immediately sells Company A stock short at $50, which locks in a sure profit—if the deal goes through. Let us say the merger is completed 3 months later, as the arbitrager had predicted. He would then exchange his $43 Company B stock for $50 Company A stock and, after covering his short sales, he would net a 3-month profit of 16.3%, for an annualized return of over 65%.

Eventually, the undercapitalized Edwards & Hanly went bankrupt, and in 1975 Boesky started his own firm. He proved to be a brilliant investor, and his limited partnership accumulated holdings of $90 million in just 5 years.

> Boesky's investors had trounced the stock market average. Someone who invested $1 with Boesky in April 1975 would have had $7.54 at the end of 1980 compared with $2.19 if the money had been invested in the stock market.[46]

In 1980, Boesky sold his company, but started another one the following year. At its height, his investment fund was returning a "staggering 142 percent."[47] However, by 1984 the wheels seemed to be coming off the Boesky machine. He was now underperforming the market with a yield of only 7.7%. More important, unlike many of his peers who cultivated a preferred anonymity, Boesky craved personal fame. His reputation and considerable ego clearly were in jeopardy. This made him an ideal candidate for recruitment into Dennis Levine's insider network.[48]

Predictably, those who have chronicled the Boesky-Levine nexus differ as to who first approached whom. It is acknowledged, however, that the money-hungry investment banker had long admired, almost to the point of obsession, the larger-than-life arbitrager. However it was initiated, the relationship began shortly after Levine had moved to Drexel from Lehman in early 1985. Levine began doling out inside information to Boesky on such imminent deals as the ANC-Coastal and

(Continued)

HNG-InterNorth mergers.[49] Some accounts speculate that Boesky's initially toll-free hotline to Levine exploited Levine's urge to ingratiate himself with his "idol," but this explanation probably underestimates Levine's cunning. Boesky could serve as a kind of "insurance policy" to Levine. Many traders still followed Boesky's lead, and if he committed his vast financial resources to Levine's "deal stocks," other buyers would pour in, thus assuring a run-up in price and a profit for Levine.[50] Moreover, by April 1985, the two men had struck a new deal. Levine's inside information would no longer be toll-free. He was to receive 5% of Boesky's profits.[51] For Boesky, too, it was an attractive arrangement. He could use Levine's illegal network to restore his sagging legend.

> It was a marriage made in heaven—or, in the terminology Wall Street prefers, a "perfect synergy." Each party brought a rich dowry to the union: Levine airtight information and Boesky enormous capital to put this information to maximum advantage.[52]

Boesky went on to make far more money from Levine's deals, such as the R.J.R.-Nabisco takeover, than Levine himself. Furthermore, he never paid Levine one nickel of the promised 5% commission."[53] Levine, the young man who had wanted to swim with the sharks, was chewed up and spit out by one of the most carnivorous.

But once the SEC had "bought" Levine's services as a friendly witness, Boesky's days were numbered, and he knew it. Although arbitragers as an investor class are the most insulated against charges of insider trading because rumors and market intelligence are their everyday tools,[54] they are, of course, forbidden to trade on "tips they know come from a tainted source."[55] Because no source was more tainted than Levine, Boesky realized he was going to prison. In desperation, he took a page from the Levine playbook and agreed to help apprehend and testify against other insiders in order to avoid a longer sentence. Thus, in September 1986, Boesky was officially enrolled as a government agent.[56] Two months later he faced a federal judge, who was made aware of his ongoing cooperation. Accordingly, Boesky was fined a "mere" $100 million ($50 million in restitution, $50 million in penalties).[57] Several weeks later he received a sentence of 3 years, not nearly as severe as it could have been had he chosen to protect his associates.

If "mere" seems like a strange description of a $100 million fine, consider that Boesky had been permitted by the prosecution to liquidate his current holdings of an estimated $1 billion in "deal stocks" on the open market *prior* to the announcement of his co-optation by the government.[58] In effect, the SEC allowed Boesky to trade on and profit from inside information about *his own arrest.*[59] This controversial dispensation enabled him to avoid the panic that was sure to ensue when it was revealed that "Agent" Boesky had been recording his conversations with some of the most influential figures in the investment community.[60] As one veteran reporter observed at the time, "It's something like capturing the whorehouse madam: now the cops have her date-book."[61]

(Continued)

As feared, the Dow Jones Industrial Average plummeted the day the Boesky scandal was confirmed.[62] "Deal stocks" were hit especially hard, of course; it was estimated that arbitragers lost somewhere between $1 billion and $2 billion in the week following the Boesky hearing.[63] The arbitrage department at a single firm, Merrill Lynch, reportedly "lost $40 million in the trading dip after Boesky's plea."[64] It further has been estimated that Boesky had made at least $203 million in illegal trades—more than four times the SEC's $50 million claim.[65] It is little wonder that *Fortune* magazine dubbed him "Crook of the Year."[66] Despite the magnitude of his fines, Boesky was permitted to walk out of prison a very rich man. Indeed, when he was released at the end of 1989, he left his wife after suing *her* for $50 million in alimony,[67] purchased two homes in France, and reportedly lived like a maharajah.

Given all the repercussions, did the SEC made a good bargain with Ivan Boesky? They clearly thought so. By February 1987, Boesky had already helped them build a case against one of the reigning "whiz kids" of Wall Street, Martin Siegel, the talented young investment banker with the firm of Kidder Peabody.

C A S E   S T U D Y

Martin Siegel

Martin Siegel was yet another product of a middle-class urban environment. His father had co-owned three shoe stores in the Boston area, but had gone bankrupt when Siegel was 20 years old. The elder Siegel never recovered financially or emotionally from the failure of his business.[68] The bankruptcy left also an indelible impression on the son, who became haunted by the fear of failure and reportedly was a compulsive saver even after he became rich.

Because Kidder had no arbitrage department in the early 1980s, Siegel had begun utilizing Ivan Boesky as a source for takeover valuations. Siegel and Boesky soon developed a close professional and later personal relationship. Like so many others, Siegel was awed by Boesky's vast wealth and opulent lifestyle. One evening in 1982, the two men met by chance at the Harvard Club (Siegel, a Harvard Business School graduate, was also a member). In the course of their impromptu meeting, Siegel complained to Boesky about his personal financial worries. This conversation would prove to be a judgmental error that ultimately would wreck Siegel's life; but Siegel was no innocent dupe. He surely realized that for an M & A insider to cry poverty to an unprincipled arbitrager is "like placing red meat before a lion."[69] By the end of the evening, Siegel had been seduced. He had agreed to provide Boesky with inside information in exchange for a percentage of the profits Boesky would derive from that information.

Siegel went to work on Boesky's behalf almost immediately. One of his clients, the Martin Marietta Corporation, was fighting a takeover bid by Bendix.

(Continued)

Siegel had devised a so-called Pac-Man defense, in which the target company, Martin Marietta, would make a counteroffer to buy the suitor company, Bendix—for $1.5 billion. Siegel leaked this top-secret plan to Boesky, who then accumulated Bendix shares and made a handsome profit when those shares jumped in value after Siegel's strategy was made pubic. Siegel was paid $125,000 by Boesky. The payoff had all the trimmings of a cloak-and-dagger operation, which in a sense it was. The money was delivered in a suitcase to a public location by a courier who exchanged secret passwords with Siegel. Future dealings were to be initiated by Siegel, who would call Boesky from a pay phone and simply say, "Let's have coffee." The two would then meet at a predetermined time and place.[70]

By the end of 1984, Siegel had received a total of something between $575,000[71] and $700,000[72] from Boesky, depending on which source one chooses. However, Siegel was becoming increasingly nervous (and perhaps even guilt-ridden) about his participation in a criminal conspiracy. When Boesky suggested that Siegel should open a foreign bank account to handle the illegal payments, this was the last straw. "Throughout 1985, [Siegel] resisted Boesky's efforts to obtain more information and refused to accept any more money."[73] When Siegel moved to Drexel in 1986 to become the co-head of M & A, this reportedly infuriated Boesky. What did he need another source at Drexel for? He already had Dennis Levine.

In November 1986, the Boesky fine was announced, along with the news that Boesky had been cooperating in an ongoing undercover investigation. Siegel reacted much the same as Boesky had when Levine's conscription had been announced months earlier. He, too, rushed to cut a deal and agreed to become a government witness against his former confederates. By December, a plea bargain had been finalized. The government would seize all of Siegel's assets except his two homes and his pension plan contributions.[74] Siegel's longstanding fear of ruination had become a self-fulfilled prophecy. He would, however, receive a prison sentence of only 2 months. In exchange, Siegel would finger other insider traders and testify for the government in any cases where his testimony was deemed relevant.

Siegel's first catch would be Robert Freeman, the head of arbitrage at Goldman Sachs and a partner at that powerful investment banking firm. Siegel had entered an arrangement with Freeman to swap inside information.[75] For example, Freeman was accused of giving Siegel confidential information about Unocal, a Goldman Sachs client, concerning Unocal's plans to buy back 50 million shares of its own stock as a defense against a takeover attempt by Mesa Petroleum. At about the same time, a Kidder client, Kohlberg, Kravis, Roberts & Company (KKR), was bidding for Storer Communications. Siegel, in similar fashion, had informed Freeman of KKR's plans.[76] Both men, and their firms, allegedly had profited from this unlawful symbiosis.

Freeman eventually pleaded guilty and ended up serving 4 months in jail in 1990.[77] He also paid two fines totaling $2.1 million.[78] Unlike Levine, Boesky, and Siegel, Freeman generally was viewed with sympathy by his peers.[79] In contrast to his accuser, he was not denounced as a venal "yuppie," recklessly careening along

(Continued)

the fast track. He had been with Goldman Sachs for 22 years and was regarded as a member of the establishment.[80] Perhaps even more important, he was the *rara avis* of insider traders; he never agreed to testify against former associates to save his own skin. Apparently, even in a corrupted environment, loyalty sometimes begets loyalty. After his release, Freeman was soon back in the market, reportedly running "very big money" for himself out of his suburban New York home.[81]

Fortunately for the government, it had little need for Freeman. It was Boesky who mattered most. He had agreed to help the SEC stalk the biggest quarry of all, a man who effectively had reinvented the leveraged buyout and almost single-handedly elevated high-yield junk bonds from the ridiculous to the sublime: Michael Milken.

C A S E   S T U D Y

Michael Milken

Milken was born in 1946 in the city of Encino in southern California's San Fernando Valley. His father was a successful accountant. Milkin graduated Phi Beta Kappa from University of California, Berkeley and attended the Wharton business school at the University of Pennsylvania. While at Wharton, he worked part-time for 2 years in the Philadelphia office of what was then called Drexel Harriman Ripley. After leaving Wharton in 1970, he was offered a full-time position in the research department at the Wall Street office of the firm (which had just been renamed Drexel Firestone).[82]

Milken soon gravitated to the company's bond-trading department. Since his undergraduate days, he had been entranced by a small, arcane corner of the bond market—high-yield, low-grade bonds, or what one Drexel executive derisively labeled "crap."[83] These would later be renamed (reportedly by Milken himself, much to his everlasting regret) "junk bonds." The story goes that Milken was meeting with one of his early clients, Meshulam Riklis. Riklis was the force behind a number of major acquisitions such as the liquor distributor Schenley and several well-known department store chains. After studying Riklis's portfolio, Milken reportedly remarked: "Rik, this is 'junk.'"[84]

Most of the bonds being traded at the time Milken landed on Wall Street were investment-grade and rated AAA. They were virtually risk-free, but barely yielded more than U.S. Treasury bonds. Milken's specialty, however, became the sub-investment-grade, deep-discount bonds, rated BB+ or lower.[85] One of his professors at Berkeley had published a 20-year study maintaining that a portfolio of low-grade bonds—if sufficiently large and diversified—consistently would outperform a higher-grade portfolio. Even though some of the low-grade bonds inevitably would default, the greater overall yield of the nondefaulting bonds would more than compensate, or so the theory went.

(Continued)

In the mid-1970s, there was little market demand for junk bonds, and not much trading was being conducted. Investors were reluctant to go near unrated debt. In addition to the intrinsic risk, many of the bonds were issued by relatively obscure companies, about whom comprehensive financial research was seldom available. Junk bonds were thus trapped in a spiral, in which light trading would translate into low liquidity, which would then retranslate into light trading, and so on. But Michael Milken, a "workaholic" of seemingly limitless energy, began to find a niche for junk bonds. "Starting with $2 million in capital in 1973, he was generating astounding 100 percent rates of return, earning bonus pools for himself and his people that were approaching $1 million a year."[86]

In 1975, Milken was allowed to set up a semiautonomous bond trading unit with a remarkable bonus arrangement giving Milken and his team 35% of the profits they generated. By 1977, his organization controlled 25% of Wall Street's entire high-yield bond market. Milken promoted his wares with an almost evangelical zeal, and this was to change the very dynamics of capitalism. Junk bonds could enable corporate raiders "to make multibillion-dollar acquisitions, even if they had relatively few assets to begin with."[87] Often, these raiders would soon begin stripping assets from their new acquisitions in order to service the debt.

In addition to his flair for the creative non-use of cash, Milken's success in reshaping the junk bond market can be credited to that market's almost complete lack of regulation. In 1977, Milken convinced his firm (now renamed Drexel Burnham) to underwrite new issues of high-yield bonds from heavily leveraged companies and market them directly to the public. Because few formal rules existed, Drexel took a commission of 3% to 4% for underwriting these issues, an astonishing figure compared with the customary 0.875% in the high-grade bond arena. Milken, in turn, was given 30% of Drexel's commissions. Milken often would give his salesperson a miserly cut of 1% and pocket the remaining 29% for himself.[88] Later that year, Milken created the idea for the first junk bond mutual fund.[89] Junk bonds were now being traded with increasing regularity, and with that came the long-missing element of liquidity.

In 1978, Milken decided to move his operation to his native Los Angeles. This would remove him from any day-to-day control by Drexel management and allow him to expand his domain from trading and underwriting into investment banking and mergers and acquisitions. Drexel was not thrilled at the prospect of putting Milken on a 3000-mile leash, but "[i]t was already obvious that Milken's success had little to do with Drexel, and that Drexel's success had everything to do with Milken."[90] Indeed, by this time Milken was generating almost *100%* of Drexel's profits.

Milken's first West Coast client was Steve Wynn. Five years earlier, Wynn had taken control of a seedy downtown Las Vegas casino called the Golden Nugget, spruced it up, added a hotel, and increased annual profits from $1.1 million in 1973 to $7.7 million in 1978. Wynn was yearning to open a Golden Nugget in Atlantic City, which was beginning to dwarf Las Vegas in revenues. Investment bankers long had eschewed the gaming industry because of its unsavory

(Continued)

reputation and because it was not considered a growth industry at that time. So how does a company worth $10 million raise $100 million? Steve Wynn's answer was a fellow Wharton alumnus named Michael Milken. Over the next 2 years, Drexel raised $160 million for Wynn's project. Six years later, Wynn would sell his Atlantic City casino for $440 million.[91] In countless interviews over the years, Wynn has been quick to credit his stunning success to Milken. It was also Wynn who perhaps best described the secret of Milken's operation: "Venture capital masquerading as debt finance."[92]

When the 1980 recession hit, Milken took a characteristically contrarious position; when other investment bankers were bailing out, he was increasing Drexel's hegemony in the junk bond market. Milken had devised creative ways to restructure debt, so that while some underwriters were suffering default rates as high as 17%, Drexel's defaults never exceeded 2% during that period.[93] Some prophets of doom may have warned that Drexel merely was postponing the day of reckoning, but few were listening, least of all Milken. In fact, by 1983 the junk bond business was bigger than ever. Drexel (now renamed Drexel Burnham Lambert) was entrenched firmly on top, and Michael Milken was hailed as The King.

Let us now jump ahead momentarily to the fall of 1987. "Agent" Boesky had been enrolled in what some were deriding as the SEC's "Frequent Liars Program"[94] and was preparing to help build prosecutable cases against some of his associates at five major brokerage houses.[95] He was instructed to place phone calls to everyone he had implicated and arrange meetings. The plan was to "wire" him at those meetings and tape-record incriminating evidence. One call, for example, went to Martin Siegel; another to Michael Milken. Milken agreed to meet with Boesky, and in mid-October they dined in Boesky's sumptuous Beverly Hills hotel suite.[96]

The Milken-Boesky relationship had begun in 1981 when Boesky was seeking sufficient capital to become a "merchant broker," Boesky's preferred term for corporate raider.[97] Drexel seemed the perfect source, so Boesky made a West Coast pilgrimage to see The King. Boesky was after Vanguard, his late father-in-law's company, whose holdings included the Beverly Hills Hotel where Boesky was staying (and where Boesky would secretly tape-record Milken years later). Boesky, so accustomed to mesmerizing others, was himself awed by Milken.

From Boesky's perspective, the meeting had been a glorious success, for in 1983 Milken arranged $100 million for the Vanguard (now known as Northview) deal. Boesky began traveling regularly to Beverly Hills to oversee his interest in the hotel, so he and Milken became ever closer. It is no quirk that of the six charges of which Milken eventually would be convicted, four involved dealings with Boesky. The two men engaged in a number of reciprocal "parking" arrangements. Parking refers to one investor buying and holding stock for another in order to conceal the true owner's identity. The titular buyer typically is guaranteed against loss by the true owner.[98] For Boesky, parking stock with Milken would allow him to circumvent SEC regulations requiring public notification of the acquisition of a 5% or

(Continued)

greater stake in a company. In other words, Boesky could buy just under 5% himself and then buy more through Milken. For Milken, parking a stock with Boesky would be useful if the purchase involved a Drexel client, restricting Milken (or anyone at Drexel) from buying it.[99] Either way, the practice of parking stock is illegal.

In 1985, plans were drawn up for the largest arbitrage organization in history. Boesky would dissolve his corporation and raise $220 million from a new group of limited partners. Then Milken would raise $660 million with junk bonds. This would provide Boesky with the resources to mount a raid on almost any company. Boesky, as usual, had little trouble attracting partners to put up $220 million. Milken, on the other hand, was hard pressed to sell investors on a $660 million arbitrage fund. Eventually, however, the money was raised. It is worth noting that $100 million of the debt was purchased by Charles Keating's Lincoln Savings,[100] which was to figure so prominently in the S & L debacle a few years later (Chapter 5). In effect, Milken now owned Boesky's soul. One of Boesky's close associates observed: "It is obvious that Boesky wouldn't pee without Milken's consent."[101]

A subsequent example of the parking arrangement involved Wickes Corporation, the Los Angeles-based home-building products company, which was emerging from bankruptcy in the spring of 1986. The Wickes chairman was eager to acquire National Gypsum, so Milken and Drexel raised hundreds of millions of dollars for that purpose by issuing junk bonds and preferred stock. The preferred stock was an expensive proposition, because it paid a walloping 10% dividend, which was necessary to attract investors. There was, however, an unusual provision written into the preferred offering: If the price of Wickes stock rose to a certain level, the company could redeem its preferred stock and give investors common stock, which paid no dividends. Milken had Boesky manipulate the price of Wickes stock by purchasing 2.8 million shares over a relatively short period of time. This naturally inflated the price, which allowed Drexel's client to eliminate its preferred dividend and save $15 million per year.[102]

Thus, when Milken and Boesky met in Boesky's hotel suite in 1987, they brought to the dinner table a tangled history of collusion. Boesky had been coached by prosecutors on where to direct the conversation, but Milken had heard rumors of Boesky's impending hearing and behaved circumspectly. For instance, when Boesky mentioned an illegal $3.5 million kickback that he owed Milken from the arbitrage fund deal, Milken told him to keep it. At one point Milken even warned Boesky, who was wearing a hidden recording device taped to his body, to be wary of electronic surveillance.[103]

When the news of Boesky's ongoing cooperation was announced a few weeks later, Milken's caution seemed justified. Although Boesky had been involved in enough crooked deals to put dozens of careers at risk, most of Wall Street realized that the primary targets of the Boesky arrangement had to be Milken and Drexel.

By mid-1988, however, Boesky was in prison and the Milken case seemingly had stalled. Milken, moreover, had hired an aggressive public relations firm

(Continued)

which had begun packaging him to the American people as a "national treasure."[104] Milken, who had always been a very private man, started giving self-serving interviews to selected journalists. He even took a group of 1700 underprivileged children to a baseball game. The public was seeing a philanthropic Michael Milken at his carefully orchestrated best.

That same public saw a very different picture when Milken was subpoenaed to testify before a Congressional investigation subcommittee later that year. He immediately invoked the Fifth Amendment and refused to answer a single question. After adjournment, the chairman held an angry press conference in which he excoriated Milken, flatly accusing him of insider trading and market manipulation.

In September 1988, Milken's top salesman defected to the government in exchange for immunity from prosecution.[105] This "triggered a stampede of other "friendly" witnesses eager to cooperate."[106] That same month, the government filed a lawsuit against Milken and Drexel. In November, federal racketeering (RICO) charges were filed, a clear precursor to a criminal indictment. Drexel had had enough. It entered a plea bargain in which it agreed to acknowledge wrong doing, pay a $650 million fine (an all-time record), and suspend Milken, withholding his enormous annual bonus.[107] On March 29, 1989, Milken was indicted by a federal grand jury on 98 felony counts and RICO charges. Six months later, the junk bond market collapsed.

In February 1990, Drexel filed for bankruptcy. There was a grim symmetry to it all. The "greed" decade had opened with the downfall of E. F. Hutton and had closed with the implosion of Drexel Burnham Lambert. The road between had become strewn with the professional remains of Paul Thayer, Peter Brant, Dennis Levine, Ivan Boesky, Martin Siegel, Robert Freeman, and a cast of supporting players. Only Milken remained. Like a tontine in reverse, the harshest punishment had been saved for the last survivor. Milken agreed to plead guilty to six counts and to pay a fine of *$600 million*. On November 21, 1990, Michael Milken received a 10-year prison sentence.

> Milken broke down completely. He began to shriek and wail so loudly that it attracted the attention of people throughout the courthouse. Fearing that he would faint, federal marshals rushed in with an oxygen tank. Milken's hysteria had subsided only slightly by the time he got to the airport for his chartered flight back to Los Angeles: During the entire trip, he lay in his wife's arms sobbing. At 44, Milken had seen his carefully constructed edifice definitively collapse.[108]

Milken's sentence was later reduced to 2 years. After his parole in 1993, he began teaching a business course at University of California, Los Angeles under the oversight of Professor Bradford Cornell. The class consisted mainly of case studies of Milken's deals. One student has described the class and Milken's input:

> He had to win every point. . . . He would debate Cornell and to make sure he'd won, he'd make some dig like: "Now that kind of thinking is why Bradford is a professor." The implication was, *I made a billion dollars. Who are you going to listen to?*[109]

(Continued)

At the end of the term, Milken held a dinner for his students and presented each of them with a plaque embossed with 12 "Milken Maxims." Number 6 stated: "The 1980s was a time for giving."[110] Milken's academic role was satirized by Gary Trudeau in his popular "Doonesbury" comic strip. A student at the first class meeting was shown asking his instructor, "Professor Milken? Can we cheat in this class?"[111]

"Professor" Milken probably never addressed the issue of motivation in his lectures. Many people still may wonder why persons earning incomes of seven, eight, or even nine figures would cheat and steal. Jaded respondents likely would counter that the question answers itself: Cheating and stealing are precisely why these individuals accumulated so much money. Greed no doubt is a reasonable explanation of insider trading. To Milken and his fellow travelers—indeed to so many white-collar criminals—the question of "How much is enough?" is not only unanswerable, it is unworthy of consideration. One might just as well ask, "How high is up?"

Greed, however, may not be the only explanation. Egomania cannot be overlooked. For example, the noted economist Paul Samuelson has written of Ivan Boesky, "His need was not simply to be rich, but to be seen as richer and smarter than anyone else."[112]

One writer even has compared the criminogenic Wall Street subculture with a male bonding group—a kind of postgraduate college fraternity. "As in all fraternities, the values that draw praise are male values: bigness, wealth, and, most of all, being on the inside."[113] In such a hypermasculine environment, insider trading can be a means of demonstrating wealth, connections, and bigness simultaneously.

There is a certain appeal to the masculinity contest hypothesis. However, dismissing insider trading as merely an elaboration of locker-room braggadocio is not nearly adequate. Perhaps the best explanation is also the most parsimonious. Why did insider traders do it? Because they could. Because for years we let them. Because at some level we may even have admired them.

A society that is unwilling to equate white-collar crime to street crime, in terms of seriousness and social cost, cannot effectively inhibit insider traders. A culture that extols the often conflicting values of acquisitiveness and probity creates the sort of ambivalence that can motivate insider trading, then excuse it.

One of Dennis Levine's former professors has defended his protégé: "Dennis wasn't taking money from orphans and widows. His was a victimless crime."[114] This is a careless argument, but not an unexpected one. Because insider trading does not leave a chalk outline on the sidewalk or put bloodstains on the walls, it can be mistaken for a victimless crime. Nevertheless, insider trading is very much a predatory crime. "The victim is the investing public, individually or institutionally."[115]

Some economists, however, have maintained that although the morality of insider trading may be questionable, its effects have been distorted by the mass media. Such critics contend that the financial markets actually would benefit from a more relaxed regulatory attitude regarding insider trading.[116]

> When an insider knows something the stock market doesn't and acts on the strength of that knowledge, he moves share prices closer to where they will be when the news eventually gets out. In this view, insider dealing acts as an economic lubricant.[117]

This point of view seemingly rejects the "fixed race" and "level playing field" analogies in favor of a pure *laissez-faire* model. Financial markets are not gambling casinos, it is argued; so the overriding issue is not fairness, but efficiency. This argument would be more compelling if the economy were meant, in fact, to achieve homeostasis within a moral vacuum; but as we stressed at the beginning of this chapter, the economy is a *social* institution. Efficiency alone will not sustain it. It must be perceived as fair; it must be trusted by the public.

Thus, from a social perspective, insider traders have "tainted the free enterprise system,"[118] by subverting the very essence of capitalism—the notion that there ought to be a positive correlation between risk and potential return to investors. "Those willing to accept higher levels of risk should be rewarded with potentially higher levels of return."[119] But the insider trader collects the highest returns with little risk at all, while the ordinary investor, who assumes most of the risk, is exploited like some naive bumpkin lured into a rigged game of chance. The lawyer who prosecuted Ivan Boesky took note of this in his opening statement:

> [I]nvestors' worst fears that they are playing against a stacked deck on Wall Street are true. . . . Mr. Boesky has committed very great crimes. He has, in effect, stolen great sums of money from an investing public that believed that everyone started the game with the same chance of winning.[120]

Although many people have reviled Ivan Boesky in similar or even stronger terms, the brunt of public hostility has been reserved for Michael Milken. Milken has become the personification of Wall Street corruption. A sizable percentage of Americans blame Milken and his junk bonds for the rise of paper entrepreneurism and the erosion of traditional industrial productivity. By the mid-1980s, even Fortune 500 companies had become actual or potential targets of leveraged buyouts, financed in large measure by high-yield bonds. Some of these companies were forced to submit to so-called greenmail, where they would be compelled to buy back a raider's stock at a huge premium to make him go away.[121] This, of course, diverted corporate assets, which could have been used for research and development or job creation.

Moreover, the fraud which accompanied so many leveraged buyouts has been linked to the bankruptcy of a number of corporations.[122] This was particularly the case with smaller businesses that had raised cash through junk bonds. It has been reported that "[o]f the 104 small firms involved in public issues of nonconvertible Drexel junk bonds since 1977, 24 percent had defaulted on their debt or were bankrupt by mid-1990—five times the default rate of comparable firms."[123] And even if the price of a corporate takeover is not outright bankruptcy, it invariably is reduced productivity—and a significant loss of jobs. "Research indicates that firms subjected to protracted takeover battles do very little work, and experience little growth during and immediately after the takeover period."[124]

Corporate restructuring generally means "downsizing," which is essentially a euphemism for large-scale layoffs and firings. A recent editorial cartoon captures the harsh reality of downsizing. Three anguished-looking men are reading identical newspapers headlined "Dow Jones Hits 5000!" The first man declares: "I missed the rally. I wonder if there's still time to get in." The second says: "I caught the rally. I wonder if it's time to get out." The third man, however, laments: "I got laid off in order that there could be a rally."[125] The title of this book is more than a mild play on words. Profit "earned" not as the result of increased productivity but at the expense of discarded employees truly is "profit without honor."

Many employees who lose their jobs as a result of leveraged buyouts cannot find another. Furthermore, displaced workers who find other employment usually do so at a lower salary level.[126] Thus, the merger mania of the 1980s not only expanded the ranks of the unemployed, but contributed to a reduced standard of living among the re-employed. And even among those employees fortunate enough to survive mass layoffs, fear and anger can limit their risk-taking and often hurt productivity.[127] Historian Kevin Starr has analyzed the social effects of restructuring: "Americans never used to be envious of wealth, since rich people also created jobs—but now people don't get rich by putting people to work, but by putting people out of work."[128] It has become an economic fact of life that stock prices generally jump when companies terminate workers.[129] Again, because restructuring usually is necessitated by the heavy debt service created by leveraged deals, some critics have singled out Michael Milken for blame for the woeful human cost of downsizing.

The true extent of Milken's culpability, however, remains a subject of debate. Milken's defenders argue that all he did is popularize a product—the junk bond[130]—that was neither intrinsically good nor bad. The same instrument that helped bankrupt Bloomingdale's and 7-Eleven also helped create MCI and Turner Broadcasting. Milken himself denies that he did anything wrong. Reportedly, he now regrets his decision to plead guilty.[131] "As with so many ex-cons, the vision of himself as a victim is one that Milken still harbors."[132]

The pro-Milken arguments are not entirely devoid of merit. Financial affairs journalist James Glassman has written, "For all their faults, Michael Milken . . . and other wheeler dealers of the 1980s found real money that went into real businesses."[133] But it is difficult to separate Milken from the collapse of the junk bond market and the consequent aftershocks. Indeed, some of Milken's harshest critics contend that his "product" was a fraud sustained mainly through Milken's gift for "hype." They point out how he routinely overfunded his issuers, so they, in turn, could buy the bonds of other issuers.[134] This type of fraud, resembling a gigantic chain-letter, is a variation of the classic Ponzi swindle. One critic has characterized Milken as the central figure in the "biggest scam ever."[135]

The widely respected financier, Felix Rohatyn, senior partner at Lazard Freres, was an early and outspoken critic of mega deals financed with junk bonds. Testifying before Congress in 1985, he emphasized the social cost of market manipulation: "It completely fails to take into account the fact that a large corporation is an entity with responsibilities to employees, customers, and communities."[136] Years before the collapse, Rohatyn was warning anyone who would listen that junk bonds were not secure and that their high rates of interest would inflict stifling debt upon corporations that could be serviced only through the divestiture of assets.[137] Where others saw The King, Rohatyn saw a naked emperor.

If Milken's ascribed "genius" was genius at all, it was not in recognizing the value of junk bonds, but in recognizing their lack of value—and creating a high demand for them nonetheless. Indeed, one of the indicators of Milken's inflated reputation is the surprisingly mediocre performance of junk bonds. The 10-year return for "high-yield" bond funds in the 1980s was 145%. This return was considerably lower than that for A-rated corporate bonds (+202%) or even conservative treasury bonds (+177%).[138] One is tempted to conclude that the "genius" label bestowed on Michael Milken may have been hyperbolic.

Of all the consequences brought on by the downfall of the junk market, none has received more attention than the ensuing decline of the S & L industry (Chapter 7). Some of the most criminally mismanaged of these institutions were clients of Milken, including the now-defunct Columbia Savings & Loan of Beverly Hills[139] and the notorious Lincoln Savings & Loan of Irvine, California. Lincoln became the largest bank failure in American history,[140] and its chairman, Charles Keating, Jr., was handed a 10-year prison sentence in 1992 for defrauding customers by selling them $250 million in unsecured bonds that were falsely represented as secure.[141]

Milken's defenders have argued that those S & L's which got into trouble by over investing in junk were headed for bankruptcy regardless.[142] It could be counter argued that absolving Milken from complicity in the S&L scandal on such questionable grounds is somewhat akin to exonerating the murderer of a 90-year-old invalid because she was sure to die soon anyway.

When Federal Judge Kimba Wood sentenced Milken, she noted how a decade of insider trading, corporate raiding, and market manipulation had hurt the confidence of individual investors, upon whom the American economy ultimately depends.[143] The corrupted image of that economy had led many small investors to abandon the stock market and conclude that "the Wall Street game is best played by the well-connected."[144] Judge Wood acknowledged that Milken's heavy fine and forced removal from the securities industry represented a substantial penalty, but she also felt a responsibility to send a stern warning to the next generation of ambitious MBAs by locking up Milken: "I believe that a prison term is required for the purposes of general deterrence; that is, the need to deter others from violating the law."[145]

At least two basic approaches have been advocated to eliminate or at least reduce the incidence of insider trading: decrease the profit or increase the risk. Diminishing the profit is the aim of a proposal from the legendary investor Warren Buffett, one of the most successful capitalists in history, who, in 1993, was proclaimed the richest man in America.[146] Buffett is a long-term investor, who has always believed that the rewards of capitalism should emanate from business building, not from paper shuffling—or to paraphrase columnist George Will, from pie producing, not pie dividing.[147] Testifying before a congressional subcommittee in 1991, Buffett declared, "I have no trouble with there being very tough penalties administered by very tough people for anybody who messes around with this market."[148]

Buffett's cure for insider trading is to impose a tax of *100%* on all profits earned from the sale of any stocks owned for less than 1 year. In Buffett's words, "The most enticing category of inside information—that relating to takeovers—would become useless."[149] Because radical ideas, especially those entailing tax increases, seldom come from unradical multibillionaires, Buffett's proposal merits thoughtful assessment, although Buffett may be too wealthy to appreciate the average investor's need for liquidity.

The other approach to controlling insider trading—escalating the risk—is reflected in Judge Wood's deterrence strategy. How successful has that strategy been? Consider the following cases of nondeterrence:

❖ The very week that Ivan Boesky was paying out his $100 million fine, a young analyst with Morgan Stanley allegedly was conspiring with a Taiwanese investor to generate profits of $19 million from inside information about pending mergers to which the analyst was privy.[150]

❖ In 1987, a broker with a prestigious regional firm in Florida was fined for leaking confidential information about several corporations to selected clients. He contended that he was just following company policy.[151]

❖ In 1988, fast-food magnate Carl Karcher and his son were accused by the SEC of passing confidential information to relatives, which allowed the relatives to "dump" their shares of CKE (the Carl's Jr. chain headed by the Karchers) just 4 days before a public report of seriously declining profits. This information enabled the relatives to avoid $310,000 in losses.[152] The case eventually was settled out of court and the Karchers were fined.

❖ Also in 1988, a consultant employed by game-show producer Merv Griffen passed inside information about Griffen's planned buyout offer for the hotel/casino company Resorts International to reputed organized crime figures, who used it to turn illegal profits when the stock later soared from $22 per share to $35 per share after Griffen's bid was announced.[153]

❖ In 1989, an employee at a pharmaceutical firm relayed insider information through her aunt to a pair of Hollywood film producers, who netted profits of over $400,000.[154]

❖ In 1991, the head of the bond trading desk at Salomon Brothers was accused of manipulating the bidding at government auctions of Treasury securities

(Chapter 1), thus allowing his firm—and himself—to reap millions of dollars in illegal profits.[155] Shortly before this new scandal erupted, he sold $1.7 million worth of his personal shares of Salomon stock. When the disclosure came, the value of those shares decreased by about $500,000. It was alleged in the financial press that, like Ivan Boesky before him, the so-called Salomon cowboy[156] appeared to profit by inside information concerning his own impending arrest.[157]

❖ Just weeks before Michael Milken received his prison sentence in 1990, an employee of AT&T illegally traded on sensitive information he possessed regarding AT&T's intentions to acquire the NCR and Teradata Corporations. He later was fined more than $550,000.[158]

❖ A few weeks after Milken went to prison in 1991, two employees of Vista Chemical, a large Texas company, used confidential information about Vista's impending merger with a German firm to reap profits of nearly $900,000. In 1993, they were convicted in a Houston court, in one of the few insider-trading prosecutions ever to take place outside of New York.[159]

❖ Shortly after Milken was released from prison in 1993, Harvard Business School withheld an MBA degree from a student indicted on insider trading charges which involved alleged profits of $500,000.[160]

❖ In late 1992, a young financial analyst for a large New York law firm discovered the identity of two companies that were about to be acquired by clients of that firm. According to the SEC, she passed this inside information to her father, who bought stock in the target companies, sold it immediately after the deals were announced, pocketed $60,000 in quick profits, then gave his daughter two gifts totaling $4000.[161]

❖ In January 1993, a former director of the Foxboro Company, a Massachusetts-based high-tech manufacturer, was fined $2.1 million for insider trading in connection with the 1990 acquisition of that firm by a British company.[162]

❖ In March 1993, criminal indictments were filed against an insider-trading ring, which allegedly had garnered illegal profits of $4.5 million in 1990 from non-public information about a proposed buyout of a French economy hotel chain by Motel 6.[163]

❖ In July, 1993, a paralegal at a prominent New York law firm was convicted of stealing information about the firm's takeover clients and relaying it to an insider-trading ring.[164]

❖ One of the oddest insider trading cases also occurred in July 1993. A judge ruled that a New York stockbroker had violated insider-trading laws by receiving nonpublic information from the psychiatrist of the wife of a noted financier. The broker was fined more than $160,000 to offset profits he had made.[165]

❖ In 1994, a major investor was convicted of insider trading after he paid a Keystone mutual fund analyst $700,000 for advance information regarding the fund's planned investments.[166]

❖ Also in 1994, the Grumman corporation, which had figured so prominently in the early Paul Thayer–Billy Bob Harris insider trading case, again became linked to an SEC investigation. On the Friday before a Monday announcement that Grumman would be acquired by Martin Marietta for nearly $2 billion, Grumman stock rose 8.5%, a strong sign of possible insider trading. Even more suspicious was that heavy buying had taken place in Grumman call options (contracts giving buyers the right to purchase Grumman shares at fixed prices) just 4 days before the deal was publicized. "After the announcement, Grumman shares jumped 36 percent, locking in big profits for options buyers."[167] One buyer reportedly made $400,000 on just two trades.[168]

❖ In February 1995, Oded Aboodi, one of Wall Street's master deal-makers, agreed to pay $1 million in penalties to settle insider trading charges brought by the SEC. Aboodi had helped structure a $2.7 billion stock offering for Time Warner, which was struggling to ease its postmerger debt. Aboodi knew, of course, that the new stock would cause existing stock to fall in value. On the day of the planned stock offering, Aboodi sold 20,000 shares of Time Warner and avoided $413,700 in losses.[169]

❖ In June 1995, two brothers, Richard and John Woodward, pleaded guilty to charges related to insider trading. Over a 4-year period, Richard, a lawyer with a large Wall Street firm, gave his brother information regarding companies targeted for takeover by the firm's clients. John would then purchase stock. The pair netted over $250,000 in profits.[170]

❖ In 1993, a 62-year-old former broker with Oppenheimer & Company was sentenced to 10 months in jail for insider trading. The presiding judge lectured the defendant in words that echoed those delivered to Michael Milken 2 years earlier: "When a guy in your position commits a crime that undermines the financial and justice systems, society demands a sentence of general deterrence."[171]

Despite the assertions of the judge in the preceding vignette, it is difficult to measure the deterrent effect of the prison sentences given to Milken, Boesky, or anyone else. The number of potential insider traders dissuaded by the incarceration of others is, by its nature, indeterminable. However, all the aforementioned cases suggest that insider trading continued to occur even as some of Wall Street's biggest stars were being arrested and locked up. And there is plenty of reason to believe that it continues to proliferate.[172] The 1990s—supposedly the decade for rethinking the excesses of the 1980s—has seen a discouraging continuance of securities fraud. According to a 1994 report by *Business Week*, "[I]nsider trading is alive and well—and growing."[173]

Corporate takeovers totaled $339.4 billion in 1994, easily topping the previous record set in the 1988 heyday of junk-financed mergers. Also setting a record that same year were the 45 insider trading cases brought by the SEC.[174] In its investigation, *Business Week* analyzed the 100 largest stock deals of 1994 and came to a stunning conclusion: "One out of every three of the merger deals or tender offers was proceeded by stock-price runups or abnormal volume that couldn't be explained by publicly available information."[175] To cite just one of many suspicious examples, stock in American Cyanamid jumped 60% in value the day before American Home Products launched a hostile takeover bid.[176]

Furthermore, fund managers, brokers, and big traders have come under increasing attack since the 1990s for "front running," a smaller, harder-to-detect, and increasingly pervasive form of insider trading. Front running refers to managers buying stock for themselves *before* buying it for their funds, or one broker tipping off another trader of an impending transaction in return for some kind of kickback. In either case, a quick profit is usually made, since stocks almost always rise following a large institutional purchase.[177] The practice is, of course, unethical and completely illegal.

Describing front running as "just another of the schemes that invariably arise when aggressive young men and lots of money are in close proximity,"[178] *Fortune* magazine has detailed the mechanics of this crime using an unidentified but very real young trader:

> Less than an hour before the closing bell, a wealthy young Manhattan day trader we'll call "Billy" got a call from the trading desk of a major brokerage firm. A big client was buying a million shares of Network Associates. Did Billy want to sell? The caller knew quite well that Billy did not have a million shares of Network Associates lying around. And Billy knew perfectly well that the call was not really about filling the client's order. . . . Billy quickly bought 40,000 [shares of] Network Associates, anticipating that the client's million-share buy order would cause the stock to rise. It did. Billy had unloaded his shares at a profit of around $80,000. Not bad for less than an hour's work—as long as you're willing to ignore that Billy and his pal had just committed a crime.[179]

As always, the insider's (in this case "Billy's") profits came at the expense of the legitimate investor (in this case his confederate's institutional client), "which paid a higher price than it would have had its confidential trading intentions not been betrayed."[180] Anyone who owns shares in a mutual fund or a 401(k) has probably been cheated by a front-runner. "At its basic level, an inside tip on an institution's trading plans amounts to stealing from an institution. While the theft may be small on any given trade, the constant nibbling at the margins of trades can reduce a fund's annual rate of return."[181]

C A S E   S T U D Y

The Great "Chat Room" Conspiracy

On March 14, 2000, 19 people were arrested by federal authorities in the largest criminal insider trading case ever, in terms of the number of people who allegedly made illegal trades and the number of business deals for which inside information was stolen.[182] The case was also notable because it was the first in which the Internet had been the center of an insider-trading scheme. Four broker-dealers were among those charged,[183] but most of those accused were amateur profiteers, including a waiter, a retired schoolteacher, and a dentist.[184] The

(Continued)

criminal conspiracy revolved around John Freeman, a 34-year-old ex-waiter, aspiring actor, and part-time computer graphics worker, who was employed as a late night "temp" at two major Wall Street investment bankers, Goldman Sachs and Credit Suisse First Boston. His job entailed creating or revising graphics, flow charts, spreadsheets, and other documents. His "unofficial" duties consisted of pilfering documents before they were shredded, stealing papers from printers, ransacking garbage pails, and rummaging through the desks of employees to uncover confidential information about mergers and acquisitions.[185]

In mid-1997 Freeman was in an American Online (AOL) chat room where a group of investors was bemoaning money they had lost on a company that manufactures helmets. He connected with two of the chatters, James Cooper, a Kentucky insurance agent, and Benton Erskine, vice-president of a West Virginia laser printing company. The three men formed an anonymous online relationship, and a few months later Freeman told the other two that he could get them inside information. They agreed to pay Freeman a percentage of their profits in return.[186]

Cooper passed the material to his brother Benjamin, part-owner of a day-trading website, and stockbroker Chad Conner. Conner helped the "tippees" (as prosecutors would later call them) get an unsecured bank loan to finance their trading.[187] The list of co-conspirators grew longer as time went on and included an assortment of friends, relatives, and associates.[188]

Over a 3-year period, Freeman passed on stolen information involving Regal Cinemas, Illinois Central Railroad, Baker Hughes, Ciena, and many other corporations involved in sensitive negotiations.[189] The "Chat Room Gang" bought stock in the targeted companies before the mergers and quickly sold it when the stock soared afterward.[190]

The renegade chatters made a total of 23 illegal trades,[191] netting a combined profit of $8.4 million.[192] Some of the "tipees" kicked back fees to Freeman, who had complained over the Internet that he was "too broke to invest."[193] Usually his "commissions" arrived in the form of birthday cards stuffed with cash.[194] Despite his "birthday presents," Freeman never staked any of his own money, believing the stock market to be too risky.[195] His share of the illegal profits came to "only" $110,000. That may be a lot of money in absolute terms but just one of his beneficiaries, a Manhattan waiter and former co-worker, allegedly made $285,000 and, in a "man bites dog" story of a waiter tipping a customer, a regular patron at the restaurant where that waiter was employed netted a profit of $445,000.[196] The waiter reportedly paid off Freeman with cases of wine.[197]

The plot began to unravel in early 1998 when computers monitoring trades at the American Stock Exchange (Amex) flagged unusual trading in three firms.

> Amex analysts checked to see who was doing the trading and found many of the same names popping up for each of the far-flung firms—Oregon Metalurgical, DSC Communications of Plano, Texas, and Coherent Communications of Ashburn, Va. Analysts also noted that several traders were from Bowling Green, Ky. and Tennessee—not exactly the hotbed of investment in the United States. . . . And in each case the trades had taken place before news reports about the firms.[198]

(Continued)

John Coffee, a Columbia Law School professor who specializes in corporate securities law has observed, "This is *The Gang That Couldn't Shoot Straight* of insider-trading. . . . [It] is one of the dumber schemes I've encountered, because they left too much information on their trail."[199] The Amex turned that information over to the SEC, which contacted a U.S. attorney in March 1999. The U.S. attorney then brought in the FBI to find the source of the inside information. Because Goldman Sachs and Credit Suisse First Boston had handled all the deals in question, investigators quickly zeroed in on Freeman as someone who had access to information at both banks.[200] When telephone records revealed calls between Freeman and other suspects, the "Great Chat Room Conspiracy" was finished.

Freeman was arrested on January 6, 2000. He pleaded guilty to 12 felony counts of insider trading and 1 count of conspiracy and agreed to help the government pursue the case. Cooper was arrested on February 20, 2000. He pleaded guilty to 7 counts of insider trading and 1 count of conspiracy and also agreed to cooperate. Remarkably, Freeman and Cooper had never even met in person.[201]

At this writing, the remaining cases have yet to be adjudicated. But whatever fate awaits the other defendants, the "Great Chat Room Conspiracy" signals the emergence of a significantly new public arena for a crime once largely restricted to the private world of the Wall Street elite. In the 1980s, when the term "insider trading" entered the popular lexicon, it was a crime committed by the Boeskys and Levines of the world, professionals who exchanged secret information in person or via the telephone. But a decade later, insider trading clearly had moved well beyond its traditional boundaries and into cyberspace. The U.S. Attorney in charge of the case called it a good example of "insider trading, millennium style."[202]

> She said it showed how the nature of insider trading had changed as the public's captivation with the stock markets, and the explosion of financial information on the Internet, had led to a culture in which more people are searching desperately for the latest edge or hot tip. . . . "This is a case of Wall Street meeting Main Street and coming back again—over the Internet."[203]

The "Chat Room" case even had a little touch of Hollywood thrown in. One of the defendants traded in an account he named Blue Horseshoe Investments. In the movie *Wall Street*, Blue Horseshoe is a code name for the ruthless corporate raider Gordon Gekko (played by Michael Douglas). When Gekko says in the film, "Blue Horseshoe loves Anacott Steel," he means that he is buying Anacott stock on the basis of inside information.[204] An investigator for the Amex, who helped break the case did not find this homage to pop culture at all amusing: "A lot of us saw that movie. . . . With Blue Horseshoe it was like they were trying to rub our face in it."[205]

The Internet also played a role, albeit less conspicuously, in one of the most unusual insider trading cases to hit Wall Street. One month after the Chat Room defendants were charged, the trial of James J. McDermott, Jr., began in a New York federal court. McDermott, the former chairman of the investment bank Keefe Bruyette & Woods (KBW), stood accused of violating his fiduciary duties when he was chief executive of KBW by passing confidential nonpublic information to two confederates, who in turn traded on these illicit tips through Internet accounts.[206]

McDermott's accomplices were Anthony Pomponio, a New Jersey businessman and McDermott's mistress, Kathryn B. Gannon. What drew media and public attention to what otherwise might have been just another routine insider trading case was the revelation that Gannon, under her stage name Marilyn Star, was a porno actress and adult-film star. Indeed, co-accessory Pomponio was seldom even mentioned by name in the press; he was usually simply dubbed "one other man."[207] Most of the media attention was reserved for Ms. Gannon.

McDermott, a married man with a $4 million annual income, began his relationship with Gannon in 1997. Over a 2-year period he supplemented Gannon's $100,000 income with $80,000 in checks[208] *and* secret information about six KBW clients—mainly smaller or regional banks—which were the targets of merger or acquisition efforts.[209] Gannon shared the inside information with Pomponio, with whom she was also having an affair. Together they reaped an illegal profit of $170,000.[210]

McDermott was convicted of six counts of insider trading and one count of conspiracy. On August 3, 2000, he was sentenced to 8 months in prison. He was also fined $25,000 and ordered to perform 300 hours of community service. The trial judge, Kimba Wood, who had sentenced so many other white-collar defendants including Michael Milken, commented once again that securities fraud carries a heavy social cost by undermining investor confidence in the economy. Judge Wood, however, displayed some mercy in this case. McDermott's prison term was less than half of what federal sentencing guidelines recommend. Wood believed that McDermott was needed at home to care for a daughter with special needs.[211]

Before his sentence was handed down, McDermott turned toward the spectators inside the courtroom and apologized in a firm voice, "I was called a stud stock picker, a master of the universe. Those things couldn't be further from the truth."[212]

On December 13, 2000, Anthony Pomponio was convicted of insider trading, conspiracy, and perjury and sentenced to 21 months in prison.[213] As of this writing, the X-rated defendant Kathryn Gannon, a.k.a. Marilyn Star, remains in her native Canada as the United States seeks her extradition.[214]

A 1996 SEC report noted, in surprisingly gentle language, that traders regularly share clients' secrets: "Market makers may at times be tempted to overlook their obligations to deal fairly with their customers."[215] Finance professor Nasser Arshadi, an authority on insider trading, is more blunt in his conclusion that "the law has not been effective" in deterring insider trading.[216]

Why has deterrence apparently not been more successful? Perhaps because the risk/reward ratio of white-collar crime remains a bargain in the minds of some market insiders. At first glance, the heavily publicized sentences that culminated in 1990 may appear to qualify as examples of what social theorist Harold Garfinkle termed "successful degradation ceremonies."[217]

Just how "successful" they actually were, however, is open to interpretation, especially when one considers the post-release lifestyles of the most visibly sanctioned offenders. Dennis Levine became the head of his own firm; Ivan Boesky retired to a European estate; and Michael Milken lectured at a major university while sitting atop a fortune estimated at $500 million, which was carefully hidden in a maze of partnerships, junk bonds, and hugely valuable stock warrants from the 1980s. One former associate has compared Milken's personal finances to "the lost city of Atlantis."[218] It seems as though degradation ceremonies have been devalued almost as much as Drexel's bonds.

In fact, Milken, although beset by health problems, staged a remarkable business comeback. In 1994, he helped arrange media mogul Rupert Murdoch's $500 million investment in New World Communications Group. In 1995, he reportedly was paid $40 million by Murdoch to arrange a $2 billion deal, the largest fee ever paid to a "consultant." In 1996, Milken was promised $50 million for helping to facilitate the proposed merger between Turner Communications and Time Warner.[219] The consensus on Wall Street is that Milken has nimbly violated the spirit of his 1990 consent agreement with the government, under which he was banned from the securities business. One analyst has declared, "I think what he's doing makes a mockery of the SEC."[220] There is an old Wall Street adage that sometimes the bulls win, sometimes the bears—but never the pigs. If it were only so.

Stock Manipulation

Insider trading is an obvious example of illegal stock manipulation, but it is not the only form this crime can take. During the frenzied bull market of the 1990s, people who never before would have dared buy a common stock were rushing into the market trying to grab their share of the unprecedented boom. If the 1980s were the golden age of insider trading, the 1990s became the securities fraud decade. The reason for this is that nothing is more valuable to a swindler than credibility, and never before had phony claims of exploding profits seemed so plausible. At a time when the legitimate markets were rising 30% per year (with many blue chip stocks recording gains of 70% or more) and some new issues were doubling in value on their first day of trading, promises of instant riches, once the "dead giveaway"[221] of a scam, did not seem so outlandish. In 1998 the chairman of the SEC lamented, "The best markets bring out the worst elements."[222]

From hundreds of boiler rooms nationwide, con artists stalked trusting but inexperienced investors, trying to lure them onto the prosperity bandwagon. A single Long Island operation was making an astonishing 1 million telephone calls a month.[223] According to a report by the New York attorney general, "Regulators close a firm one day, only to find the operation reopen the next day in the same building under a different name."[224]

Like insider trading, securities fraud has moved to the Internet. The mass audience, low costs, and perceived anonymity of cyberspace is obviously attractive to crooks. In 15 seconds a computer literate stock hustler can send out an e-mail that can reach a million people. A federal prosecutor has observed, "We're seeing more of the alumni of these notorious boiler rooms migrating to the Internet."[225]

Cyberspace is stuffed with hundreds of exotic investment scams—everything from wireless cable television to ostrich farming.[226] Con artists have masqueraded as financial advisers or licensed brokers on the Internet and solicited investments in fictitious mutual funds. One Michigan scam artist talked a New York investor into sending him $91,000 and cheated a Texas victim out of $10,000. Six months later, the Texan ruefully acknowledged his gullibility: "I was terribly embarrassed. I knew I'd been screwed."[227]

The most publicized of these Internet investment schemes, however, involve microcap fraud. Often called "penny stocks" or "over the counter" stocks, microcap companies are often not even required to file periodic reports with the SEC. Thus, public information about these inexpensive, lightly traded, and thinly capitalized enterprises generally is limited. Moreover, they are unlisted on major exchanges, so only a relatively few brokers control the market.

Microcap stock swindlers post messages on "investors" bulletin boards, which abound on the Internet, about supposedly major developments at small companies. The object is to build interest in and increase the buying of the stock so that the price will shoot up. The people behind the fabricated messages then sell their shares on the run-up at a hefty profit and leave other stockholders with near-worthless paper when the stock inevitably plummets. This technique is known as *pump and dump*. For example, an Oklahoma con artist pumped and dumped to drive up the shares of Bagels and Buns, a publicly traded company with no assets, from 38 cents to $7.50 in just 4 months.[228] More recently, shares of Broadband Wireless International rose a spectacular *10,000%* when they were pumped from 12 cents per share in late 1999 to $12 per share in early 2000, and then dumped.[229]

Pumping and Dumping "Goodfellas"-Style

With huge amounts of money being invested in securities during the biggest and longest bull market in American history, it was only a matter of time before the sharks of organized crime joined the feeding frenzy. According to a U.S. attorney, "Mobsters go wherever the money is, and obviously the stock market is one of those places."[230] Another federal prosecutor echoes this claim: "Stock manipulation is seen by the mob as an easy way to make money without much effort or risk."[231]

In one of the first cases linking Wall Street to organized crime, Louis Malpeso, an alleged associate of the Columbo crime family and son of alleged Columbo soldier "Bobo" Malpeso, pleaded guilty in 1998 to working with two brokers to pump and dump the stock of a Utah hotel supplies company. Prosecutors also charged Malpeso with attempted bribery of an FBI agent in an effort to "fix" the case.[232]

In March 2000, 19 people were indicted for running a large-scale pump and dump operation over a nearly 3-year period that cheated unsuspecting investors out of nearly $40 million. "In predawn raids 100 federal agents arrested 11 of the 19 people charged in the stock fraud scheme, including the brother-in-law of Salvatore Gravano, the Mafia hit man turned informer better known as Sammy the Bull."[233]

The defendants represented an interesting blend, including the heads of two Manhattan brokerage firms, an alleged capo in the Bonanno crime family, and two members of the Russian Mafia who allegedly laundered the illicit profits through overseas accounts. Thousands of investors were fleeced. "In some cases the stocks these investors held plunged from being worth tens of thousands of dollars to being worthless within seconds."[234]

But cases like the two just described were only the warm-up for the largest security fraud bust in American history. On June 14, 2000, 600 FBI agents began arresting 120 suspects across the country in the endgame of a 1-year undercover investigation code-named "Uptick."[235] Operation Uptick was a coordinated effort by the FBI, the SEC, and the National Association of Securities Dealers (NASD).[236] Uptick used wiretaps and undercover witnesses to penetrate the labyrinthine scam.[237]

Caught in the sting were 57 stockbrokers, 12 stock promoters, 30 officers and directors of companies issuing securities, 5 pension fund officials, 2 accountants, a lawyer, a hedge-fund manager, and a New York City police detective who was also treasurer of the Detective's Endowment Association. The remaining 11 indictees were alleged organized crime figures. "Authorities said the five crime families of New York—the Gambinos, Lucheses, Genoveses, Bonannos, and Columbos—had infiltrated [Wall] Street by taking over a Manhattan investment firm, DMN Capital Investments, using it as a lever to defraud investors."[238] "The charges ranged from racketeering and securities fraud to solicitation of murder, money laundering and extortion."[239]

Investors, many of them elderly, were promised returns of 100% on microcap stocks. "These investors were defrauded of at least $50 million in schemes involving stock manipulation, boiler-room sales and using the Internet to fraudulently hype stocks."[240]

The Mafia has brought an element of violence to Wall Street seldom seen in the world of securities fraud. An assistant director of the FBI notes, "From the fish market to the stock market, the methods [the Mob] uses are always the same: violence and the threat of violence."[241] The indictment charged that the DMN used its organized crime ties to terrorize or beat brokers and other market participants who did not agree to cooperate in the pump and dump scam in return for bribes.[242]

A former member of the New York State Police task force on organized crime offers a pithy postscript: "In the mirror image of Wall Street businessmen who become criminals, now you have criminals becoming Wall Street businessmen."[243]

C A S E   S T U D Y

I Was a Teenage Wheeler-Dealer

In 2000, a New Jersey teenager became the youngest person ever charged with illegal stock dealing. In fact, the 15-year-old high school student became the only minor ever sanctioned by the SEC. Jonathan Lebed was accused of buying large blocks of cheap microcap stocks, then pumping them on the Internet using financial message boards and hundreds of phony names. His investments included an importer of Italian cheese, a computer reseller, and a manufacturer of bendable toy figures based on World Wrestling Federation characters. "Within hours of Lebed's stock purchases, he would use aliases to send false or misleading e-mails, saying the stock was about to 'take off' and would be the 'next stock to gain 1,000%,'"[244] and was the "most undervalued stock ever."[245] He would then dump the stock—within 24 hours—and cash in his profits. "In some instances Lebed placed a sell limit order before the market closed on the day he purchased the stock to ensure that he would not miss the price spike while he was in school the next day."[246]

The SEC brought civil fraud charges against the teenage wheeler-dealer for 11 alleged manipulations between August 1999 and February 2000. A settlement was reached in September 2000, under which Lebed neither admitted nor denied the charges and agreed to return $285,000 he had made.[247]

According to the Lebed family's attorney, "The Lebeds feel this is a very fair settlement."[248] That sentiment became even more understandable when an investigation by the television news program *60 Minutes* reported that Lebed's actual profits were about $800,000. The SEC allegedly had ignored 16 other questionable trades Lebed had made, opting to bring charges only on those cases for which the evidence was most abundant.[249] So despite a $285,000 settlement, the precocious trader cleared a profit of about a half-million dollars.[250]

As of this writing, the U.S. attorney's office in New Jersey is still investigating whether Lebed violated federal securities fraud laws and should be charged with juvenile delinquency.[251] The Justice Department has *never* prosecuted a minor in a stock fraud case. But Lebed's remarkable escapades underscore how problematic it is becoming to apply traditional criminological theories to a new breed of middle-class, computer-savvy teenagers who are reinventing juvenile delinquency.

On one hand, it could be argued that juveniles charged with federal crimes typically are afforded special protections such as sealed charges, closed proceedings, and sealed outcomes; thus any deterrent value of bringing a case like Lebed's to the courts would be questionable. Moreover, a former U.S. attorney has characterized any Lebed prosecution as a "grotesque overreaction."[252] He asserts, "It's one thing to pile on to John Gotti. It's another thing to pile on to a kid carried away by his ability to use the Internet."[253]

On the other hand, Lebed's conduct seems a lot more serious than puerile mischief. Every honest, if naïve, investor who went down the drain after Lebed

(Continued)

dumped his holdings was a victim. The stock market is often a zero-sum game. For every "Abbott" who makes an $800,000 profit, a bunch of "Costellos" can suffer an $800,000 loss. The chairman of the SEC characterizes Lebed's pump and dump scheme as "a wholesale effort at deceiving many investors,"[254] and points out that "[Lebed's] purpose . . . was not to help investors . . . but rather to line his own pockets as soon as he hyped the price of the stock."[255] The district administrator of the Philadelphia office of the SEC that handled the case maintains that Lebed broke securities laws in a number of ways: "He lied, he did anonymous false postings, he purchased cheap stocks knowing that he planned to lie to move the price and then sold in light of the price movement his lies created."[256]

Lebed himself displayed no remorse when interviewed on *60 Minutes*, insisting that he did nothing wrong. He professed, "I'm not aware of one investor that exists that I cheated."[257] In an interview with the *New York Times* his father declared, "I'm proud of my son."[258] He maintains that at least Jonathan "didn't sit behind a garage smoking pot, or stealing wheels off a car."[259] The senior Lebed may have been trying to help differentiate between traditional juvenile delinquency and the newer phenomenon of *"white-collar delinquency."* Or perhaps he simply was reminded of garages and wheels and cars by the new Mercedes his son had bought for the family.

Whatever the final outcome of the case, the boy's lawyer predicts, "I think you can expect to see Jonathan Lebed in lots of entrepreneurial activities."[260] Would anyone bet against that?

NOTES

1. "Ex-Executives Admit Guilt." CNNfn. June 14, 2000.
2. Sheets, Kenneth R. "How the Market Is Rigged Against You." *U.S. News & World Report* 101, December 1, 1986: 44–51.
3. *Ibid.*
4. Durham, Brad. "Party's Over in the U.S.: End of the Greedy '80s." *WORLDPAPER.* January 26, 1992: 6.
5. Lewis, Anthony. "Maintain Laws Against Securities Fraud." *Houston Chronicle.* May 23, 1995: 16A. See also: Keenan, William, Jr. "On the Trail of the Serpent." *Sales & Marketing Management* 147, September 1995: 84–85.
6. Sterngold, James. *Burning Down the House: How Greed, Deceit, and Bitter Revenge Destroyed E. F. Hutton.* New York: Summit Books, 1990.
7. Coleman, James W. *The Criminal Elite* (3rd ed.). New York: St. Martin's Press, 1994: 89.
8. Thio, Alex. *Deviant Behavior* (3rd ed.). New York: Harper & Row, 1988.
9. Cho, Jang Y. and Shaub, Michael K. "The Consequences of Insider Trading and the Role of Academic Research." *Business & Professional Ethics Journal* 10 1988: 83–98.
10. "SEC: Next Please." *The Economist:* January 24, 1987: 74.
11. Stevens, Mark. *The Insiders: The Truth Behind the Scandal Rocking Wall Street.* New York: G.P. Putnam's Sons, 1987: 27.
12. In our description of the Thayer case, we rely heavily on Mark Stevens's (1987) excellent account.
13. Stevens, *op. cit.,* p. 18.
14. Thio, *op. cit.*
15. Stevens, *op. cit.,* p. 21.
16. Winans, R. Foster. *Trading Secrets: Seduction and Scandal at The Wall Street Journal.* New York: St. Martin's Press, 1986: 13.
17. *Ibid.,* p. 12.

18. Francis, Diane. "Business as Usual in the Greed Game." *Maclean's* 101, November 7, 1988: 11.

19. Winans, *op. cit.*, p. 303.

20. *The Economist*: 20. Frantz, Douglas. *Levine & Co.: Wall Street's Insider Trading Scandal.* New York: Henry Holt, 1987: 352.

21. Dentzer, Susan. "Greed on Wall Street: A Spectacular Insider-Trading Case Scandalizes the Investment Community." *Newsweek*, 107 May 26, 1986: 46.

22. Brill, Steven. "The Rise and Fall of an Insider." *U.S. News & World Report* 101, December 1, 1986: 52–54.

23. DeMott, John S. "Finger Pointing: Wall Street's Scandal Grows." *Time* 128, July 14, 1986: 46.

24. Stewart, James B. *Den of Thieves*. New York: Simon & Schuster, 1991.

25. Frantz, *op. cit.*

26. The numbers are taken from a chart constructed by Dentzer and colleagues (1986), p. 45.

27. Stewart, *op. cit.*

28. Frantz, *op. cit.*

29. *Ibid.*

30. Stewart, *op. cit.*

31. Dentzer, *op. cit.*

32. Welles, Chris. "The Mysterious 'Coincidences' in Insider Trading Cases." *Business Week*, September 8, 1986: 76–77.

33. Quoted in Taylor, John. "The Insiders." *New York* 26, April 19, 1993: 183.

34. Levine, Dennis. "The Insider." *New York Magazine*. September 16, 1991: 38–49.

35. Reese, Jennifer. "Boy, Have I Got a Deal for You." *Fortune* 127, March 8, 1993: 135.

36. Stewart, *op. cit.*

37. Marks, Peter. "Ethics and the Bottom Line." *Chicago Tribune Magazine.* May 6, 1990: 26.

38. Powell, Bill. "The Levine Case: New Names." *Newsweek* 108, July 14, 1986: 55.

39. Labich, Kenneth. "The Fast Track Ends for One Baby Boomer." *Fortune* 113, June 9, 1986: 101.

40. The confusing and at times contradictory details of Ivan Boesky's youth and early career have been gleaned from a variety of sources, most notably Frantz (1987), Stevens (1987), and Stewart (1991).

41. Frantz, *op. cit.*, p. 146.

42. *Ibid.*

43. *Ibid.*

44. Wyser-Pratte, Guy. *Risk Arbitrage II*. New York: New York University Press, 1982. Wyser-Pratte relates an early example of classic risk arbitrage involving the famous Rothschild bank of London. When Wellington defeated Napoleon at Waterloo, Rothschild received the news first— via carrier pigeon. In a bold strategy, the bank began *unloading* its British holdings, which unleashed a selling panic on the London Stock Exchange. Rothschild then secretly began buying back the now-undervalued British government bonds. By the time the Waterloo news finally arrived by more conventional (and much slower) means, the bank had made a financial killing.

45. Boesky, Ivan F. *Merger Mania*. New York: Holt, Rinehart & Winston, 1985.

46. Frantz, *op. cit.*, p. 148.

47. *Ibid.*, p. 149.

48. *Ibid.*

49. Stevens, *op. cit.*

50. Frantz, *op. cit.*

51. *Ibid.*

52. Stevens, *op. cit.*, p. 125.

53. *Ibid.*

54. "Insider Trading." *The Economist*. November 22, 1986: 15–16.

55. Tell, Lawrence J. "Inside Information: It Isn't Always Easy to Define." *Barron's* 66, November 24, 1986: 56–57.

56. Stewart, *op. cit.*

57. Quinn, Jane B. "Stocks: The Inside Story." *Newsweek* 109, March 16, 1987: 54. See also "Boesky Payout to Investors." *New York Times.* July 12, 1993: 5.

58. Edgerton, Jerry. "What the Boesky Scandal Means to You and Your Money." *Money* 16, January, 1987: 64–67.

59. Stein, Benjamin J. "The Reasons Why: What Motivated the Insiders." *Barron's,* 67, February, 23, 1987: 16, 22.

60. Tabb, William. "What the Boesky Case Means: The Apple Falls Near the Tree." *The Nation* 243, December 13, 1986: 668–672.

61. Rowan, Hobart. "White Knuckles on Wall Street." *Washington Post.* November 20, 1986: A27.

62. Tabb, *op. cit.*

63. Russell, George. "A Raid on Wall Street: Agents Put the Cuffs on Insider

Traders." *Time* 129, February 23, 1987: 64–66.

64. Baer, Donald. "Handcuffs on Wall Street." *U.S. News & World Report* 102, February 23, 1987: 38–39.

65. *Ibid.*

66. Kinkead, Gwen. "Ivan Boesky: Crook of the Year." *Fortune* 115, January 5, 1987: 48–49.

67. Dickerson, John F. "Battling Boeskys." *Time* 141, May 3, 1993: 57.

68. Stewart, *op. cit.*

69. Stewart, James B. and Hertzberg, Daniel. "Unhappy Ending: The Wall Street Career of Martin Siegel Was a Dream Gone Wrong." *Wall Street Journal*, February 17, 1987: 1, 30.

70. *Ibid.*

71. *Ibid.*

72. Baer, *op. cit.*

73. Frantz, *op. cit.*, p. 161.

74. Stewart, *op. cit.*

75. Henriques, Diana. "Handcuffing the Street? Effects of the Inside-Trading Scandal Will Be Severe." *Barron's* 67, February 16, 1987: 18–24.

76. Pauly, David. "New Arrests on Wall Street: Who's Next in the Insider-Trading Scandal?" *Newsweek* 109, February 23, 1987: 48–50.

77. Stolley, Richard B. "The End of an Ordeal." *Fortune* 128, October 1993: 138–146.

78. Quint, Michael. "Repayment and Ban Set in Insider-Trading Case." *New York Times.* July 8, 1993: 4. See also Moses, Jonathan N. "SEC Suit Settled by Ex-Partner of Goldman Sachs." *Wall Street Journal.* June 8, 1993: 14.

79. "Insider Trading Cases: A Bridge Too Far?" *The Economist.* April 18, 1987: 76–77.

80. Russell, *op. cit.*

81. Byron, Christopher. "Happily Ever After." *Esquire* 123, April 1995: 60.

82. Bruck, Connie. *The Predator's Ball: The Junk Bond Raiders and the Man Who Staked Them.* New York: Simon and Schuster, 1988.

83. *Ibid.*, p. 29.

84. Alcaley, Roger E. "The Golden Age of Junk." *New York Review of Books* 41, May 26, 1994: 32.

85. Bruck, *op. cit.*

86. Stewart, *op. cit.*, p. 43.

87. Norris, Floyd. "The Breakdown of 'Junk': Drexel's Innovations Built Some Fortunes but the Costs May Hurt the Nation Badly." *New York Times.* November 22, 1990: A1, D4.

88. Bruck, *op. cit.*

89. *Ibid.*

90. *Ibid.*, p. 49.

91. Bruck, *op. cit.*

92. *Ibid.*, p. 60.

93. *Ibid.*

94. Schwartz, Steven F. "The Frequent Liars Program: Providing Incentive for Wall Street's Snitches." *Barron's* 68, March 7, 1988: 72.

95. "Ivan Boesky: Ever So Helpful." *The Economist.* December 26, 1987: 33–34.

96. Stewart, *op. cit.*

97. *Ibid.*

98. Stewart and Hertzberg, *op, cit.*

99. Bruck, *op. cit.*

100. Stewart, *op. cit.*

101. *Ibid.*, p. 201.

102. Zey, Mary. *Banking on Fraud.* New York: Aldine De Gruyter, 1993.

103. *Ibid.*

104. *Ibid.*

105. Taub, Stephen. "From Rats to Riches." *Financial World* 163, April 26, 1994: 22–26.

106. *Ibid.*, p. 391.

107. "Drexel: Prosecution and Fall." *Wall Street Journal.* February 15, 1990: A14.

108. Andrews, Suzanna. "Michael Milken Just Wants to Be Loved." *New York.* June 10, 1996: 26.

109. *Ibid.*, p. 28.

110. *Ibid.*, p. 28.

111. Trudeau, Gary. "Doonesbury." *Houston Post.* November 15, 1993: A12.

112. Samuelson, Robert J. "The Super Bowl of Scandal." *Newsweek* 108, December 1, 1986: 64.

113. *Ibid.*, p. 16.

114. Stevens, *op. cit.*, p. 254.

115. Francis, *op. cit.*, p. 11.

116. Meulbroek, Lisa K. "An Empirical Analysis of Illegal Insider Trading." *Journal of Finance* 47, 1992: 1661–1699. See also, "Inside Out." *The Economist.* May 22, 1993: 86.

117. "Cheating Is Wrong . . . Isn't It?" *The Economist.* May 7, 1988: 73. See also, Leland, Hayne E. "Insider Trading: Should

It Be Prohibited?" *Journal of Political Economy* 100, August 1992: 839–857.

118. Fuhrman, Peter. "The Securities Act of 1988?" *Forbes* 139, March 9, 1987: 40–41.

119. Cho and Shaub, *op. cit.*

120. Alpert, William M. "Judgment Day: Ivan Boesky Draws Three-Year Jail Term." *Barron's* 67, December 21, 1987: 24–25.

121. "The Other Scandal." *The New Republic.* May 23, 1987: 6.

122. Anders, George and Mitchell, Constance. "Junk King's Legacy." *Wall Street Journal,* November 20, 1990: 1.

123. Stewart, *op. cit.*, p. 430.

124. Zey, *op. cit.*, p. 55.

125. Editorial cartoon by Toles. *Houston Chronicle.* November 30, 1995: 42A.

126. *Ibid.*

127. Noer, David M. *Healing the Wounds: Overcoming the Trauma of Layoffs and Revitalizing Downsized Organizations.* San Francisco: Jossey-Bass, 1993.

128. Quoted in Martz, Larry. "True Greed." *Newsweek* 108, December 1, 1986: 48–50.

129. Associated Press. "Downsizing Proving Costly, Strategists Say." *Houston Post,* July 6, 1994: C1, C4.

130. Powell, Bill and Friday, Carolyn. "The Feds Finger the King of Junk." *Newsweek,* September 19, 1988: 42–44.

131. Stewart, *op. cit.*

132. Andrews, *op. cit.*, p. 25.

133. Glassman, *op. cit.*, p. 27A.

134. Stein, Benjamin J. "The Biggest Scam Ever?" *Barron's,* February 19, 1990: 8–9, 30–32.

135. *Ibid.*, p. 8.

136. Bruck, *op. cit.*, p. 206–207. See also, Hylton, Richard D. "On Wall St., New Stress on Morality." *New York Times,* September 11, 1991: D1, D3.

137. *Ibid.*

138. Anders and Mitchell, *op. cit.*

139. Heins, John. "Tom Spiegel's (Dubious) Claim to Fame." *Forbes* 142, November 14, 1988: 153–156.

140. Salwen, Kevin G. "Three Ex-Officials of Lincoln Savings State Fraud Charges with the SEC." *Wall Street Journal.* September 25, 1991: A5.

141. Salwen, *op. cit.*

142. "Too Much Milken Moralizing." *New York Times.* November 27, 1990: A22.

143. "Stunning Justice in the Milken Case." *New York Times.* November 22, 1990: A26.

144. Rudolph, *op. cit.*, p. 54.

145. Eichenwald, Kurt. "Milken Gets 10 Years for Wall St. Crimes: Term is Longest of Any Given in Scandal." *New York Times.* November 22, 1990: A1, D5.

146. Lenzner, Robert. "Warren Buffett's Idea of Heaven: 'I Don't Have to Work with People I Don't Like.'" *Forbes 400,* October 18, 1993: 40–48.

147. Will, George. "Keep Your Eye on Giuliani: Handcuffs on Wall Street Wrists Stress that Crimes Can Be Committed in Genteel Surroundings." *Newsweek* 109, March 3, 1987: 84.

148. Henriques, Diana B. "House Panel Assails Treasury Regulation." *New York Times.* September 5, 1991: D1, D26.

149. *Ibid.*, p. 84.

150. Work, Clemens P. "A 'Chinese Wall' that's Less than Great at Stopping Secrets." *U.S. News & World Report* 105, July 11, 1988: 42. See also, Collingwood, Harris. "Was Morgan Stanley Asleep at the Switch?" *Business Week,* July 11, 1988: 26–27; and "The Littlest Insider." *Time* 132. July, 11, 1988: 45.

151. Antilla, Susan. "Stock Picks Plagued by Leaks." *New York Times.* January 22, 1993: D1.

152. Szockyj, Elizabeth. "Insider Trading: The SEC Meets Carl Karcher." *Annals of the American Academy of Political and Social Science* 525, 1993: 46–58.

153. Mahar, Maggie. "Wheel of Misfortune." *Barron's,* May 6, 1991: 18.

154. "Insider Cases Are Settled." *New York Times.* February 13, 1993: 11.

155. Fuerbringer, Jonathan. "Solomon Brothers Admits Violations at Treasury Sales." *New York Times.* August 10, 1991: 1, 37.

156. Bartlett, Sarah. "Solomon's Errant Cowboy." *New York Times.* August 25, 1991: 1, 10.

157. Fuerbringer, Jonathan. "Dismissed Solomon Trader Sold Stock Before Scandal." *New York Times.* August 29, 1991: D1, D6.

158. "Insider Case Is Settled." *New York Times.* March 11, 1993: D5.

159. Harlan, Christi. "Two Are Convicted of Insider Trading by Houston Jury." *Wall Street Journal.* July 7, 1993: 8B.

160. "An M.B.A. Is Withheld." *New York Times.* May 21, 1993: D18.

161. France, Mike. "Insider Traitors." *New York* 28, May 1, 1995: 15–16.

162. "S.E.C. Suit Is Settled." *New York Times.* January 14, 1993: D16.

163. Moses, Jonathan M. "More Are Named In Probe of Motel 6 Insider Trading." *Wall Street Journal.* March 5, 1993: B4. See also, "Insider Case Is Expanded." *New York Times.* March 5, 1993: D9.

164. "Insider Case Sentencing." *New York Times.* July 20, 1993: 16D.

165. "Insider-Trading Ruling." *Wall Street Journal.* July 1, 1993: B5.

166. Hass, Nancy. "New Games, New Rules." *Newsweek.* March 14, 1994: 43.

167. "Grumman's Suspicious Rise." *U.S. News & World Report,* 116, March 21, 1994: 14.

168. *Ibid.*

169. Pogrebin, Robin. "Aboodi Who?" *New York* 28, February 6, 1995: 23–25.

170. Jensen, Rita H. "Cravath Lawyer Admits to Insider Trading." *ABA Journal* 81, September 1995: 26.

171. "Former Trader Sentenced." *Wall Street Journal.* February 25, 1993: B12.

172. Antilla, Susan. "The Murky World of Front-Running." *New York Times.* February 7, 1993: 15.

173. Barrett, Amy. "Insider Trading." *Business Week.* December 12, 1994: 70.

174. "17 Implicated in AT&T Insider Trading." *Houston Post.* February 10, 1995: C1, C3.

175. Barrett, *op. cit.*, p. 71.

176. *Ibid.*

177. Baldo, Anthony. "Sweeping the Street." *Financial World.* August 16, 1994: 61–63.

178. Vinzant, Carol. "The New Improved Game of Insider Trading." *Fortune* 139, June 1999: 115.

179. *Ibid.*

180. *Ibid.*, p. 116.

181. *Ibid.*, p. 116.

182. Drew, Christopher. "The Markets." *New York Times.* March 15, 2000: C1. See also: McMorris, Francis A., Smith, Randall, and Schroeder, Michael. "Insider Case Involves a Temp at Two Brokers and Web Ring." *Wall Street Journal.* March 15, 2000: C1, C13; Witheridge, Annette. "Wall Street Hit by Cyber Scam." *The Scotsman.* March 16, 2000: 13.

183. Freeman, John. J. and Labate, John. "19 Charged in Dollars 8.4m Insider Trading Case." *Financial Times.* March 15, 2000: 23.

184. "Temp Allegedly Leads Insider Trading Ring." *Cleveland Plain Dealer.* March 15, 2000: 4C.

185. Walsh, Sharon. "Office Temp Gave Out Merger Secrets Online." *Washington Post.* March 15, 2000: A01.

186. O'Donnell, Jayne. "Inside Trading with a Net Connection." *USA Today.* March 27, 2000: 1B.

187. *Ibid.*

188. Valdmanis, Thor. "Internet Played Role in Inside-Trading Case." *USA Today.* March 15, 2000: 1B.

189. Valdmanis, *op. cit.*

190. Smith, Greg B. "Nab Temp in Stock Scam." *Daily News.* March 15, 2000: 7.

191. Tompkins, Wayne. "Six in State Accused of Insider Trading." *Louisville Courier-Journal.* March 15, 2000: 1.

192. O'Donnell, *op. cit.*

193. *Ibid.*

194. *Ibid.*

195. *The Guardian.* "Chat Room Trades Result in Charges." March 16, 2000: 28.

196. Smith, *op. cit.*

197. *Ibid.*

198. O'Donnell, *op. cit.*, p. 1B.

199. Quoted in Farrell, Greg. "Net Snags Inside Trading Suspects." *USA Today.* March 16, 2000: 3B.

200. O'Donnell, *op. cit.*

201. *Ibid.*

202. Quoted in Drew, *op. cit.*, p. C1.

203. *Ibid.*, p. C1.

204. O'Donnell, *op. cit.*, p. 1B.

205. Quoted in *Ibid.*, p. 1B.

206. Labate, John. "Wall St. Braced for Unusual Insider Trading Case." *Financial Times.* April 10, 2000: 8.

207. *Ibid.*

208. Neumeisier, Larry. "'Marilyn Star' a No Show." ABC News.com. April 10, 2000.

209. Labate, *op. cit.*

210. Neumeisier, *op. cit.*

211. *Ibid.*

212. Quoted in *Ibid.*

213. Reuters. "Businessman Gets Jail for Using Trade Tips from Porn Star." Yahoo!. Finance. December 14, 2000.

214. Neumeisier, *op. cit.*

215. Quoted in *Ibid.*, p. 116.

216. Quoted in *Ibid.*, p. 119.

217. Garfinkle, Harold. "Conditions of Successful Degradation Ceremonies." *American Journal of Sociology* 50 1956: 353–359.

218. Quoted in Andrews, *op. cit.*, p. 29.

219. Andrews, *op. cit.*

220. Quoted in Scott, Walter. "Personality Parade." *Parade,* May 12, 1996: 2.

221. Henry, David. "Bull Market Brings Rush of Con Artists." *USA Today.* February 12, 1998: 3B.

222. Quoted in *Ibid.*, p. 3B.

223. *Ibid.*

224. Quoted in *Ibid.*, p. 3B.

225. Quoted in Lowry, Tom. "Stock Hustlers Creep Out of Boiler Room and Onto Internet." *USA Today.* August 23, 1999: 1B.

226. "On-Line Investment Schemes: Fraud in Cyberspace." *Consumers' Research,* 77, August 1994: 19–22.

227. *Ibid.*, p. 56.

228. Spears, Gregory. "Cops and Robbers on the Net." *Kiplinger's Personal Finance Magazine,* February 1995: 56–59.

229. Andrejczak, Matt and O'Brien, Stephanie. "SEC Brings Charges in Fraud Sweep." CBS.MarketWatch.com. September 6, 2000.

230. Quoted in Mulligan, Thomas S. "120 Charged in FBI Probe of Mafia Securities Scams." *Los Angeles Times.* June 15, 2000: 1A.

231. Quoted in Lowry, Tom. "Mob Linked to Stock Fraud." *USA Today.* February 6, 1998: 1B.

232. *Ibid.*

233. Feuer, Alan. "19 Charged in Stock Scheme Tied to Mob." *New York Times.* March 3, 2000: B3.

234. *Ibid.*

235. Knox, Noelle. "FBI Swoops Down on Wall Street Mob Authorities Arrest 120 in Farthest-Reaching Securities Fraud Yet." *USA Today.* June 15, 2000: 1B. See also, McNair, James. "9 in Area Accused of Stock Fraud." *Miami Herald.* June 15, 2000: 1A.

236. Anderson, Lisa. "Feds Charge 120 in Stock Fraud Scheme." *Chicago Tribune.* June 15, 2000: 1A.

237. Mulligan, *op. cit.*

238. Kaul, Donald. "Seems Like the Mob Got a Bit Exuberant, Too." *Houston Chronicle.* June 22, 2000: 24A.

239. Walsh, Sharon. "120 Charged in Probe of Mob on Wall St." *Washington Post.* June 15, 2000: A1.

240. *Ibid.*, p. A1.

241. Quoted in Knox, *op. cit.*, p. 1B.

242. Knox, Noelle. "Mob Linked to Stock Scam." *USA Today.* June 15, 2000: 1A.

243. Quoted in O'Harrow, Robert, Jr. "On Wall Street Families Cooperated." *Washington Post.* June 15, 2000: A21.

244. Knox, Noelle. "Teen Settles Stock-Manipulation Case." USA Today.com. September 21, 2000.

245. "Teen Stock Tout to Pay $285,000 for 'Pump and Dump' Scheme." CNN.com. September 21, 2000.

246. "Precocious 'Pump and Dumper'?" ABCNEWS.com. September 21, 2000.

247. *Ibid.*

248. Quoted in Knox, *op. cit.*

249. Associated Press. "Manipulating a Profit." ABCNEWS.com. October 20, 2000.

250. Associated Press. "Stock Manipulator's Crime Did Pay." USA Today.com. October 20, 2000.

251. Bloomberg. "Teen Stock Manipulator Not Out of Woods." USA Today.com. October 5, 2000.

252. Quoted in *Ibid.*

253. Quoted in *Ibid.*

254. Quoted in Associated Press, ABCNEWS.com, *op. cit.*

255. Quoted in *Ibid.*

256. Quoted in CNN.com, *op. cit.*

257. Quoted in Associated Press, ABCNEWS.com, *op. cit.*

258. Quoted in Bloomberg, *op. cit.*

259. Gelsi, Steve. "Teen Defends Stock-Promotion Actions." CBSMarketWatch.com. October 19, 2000.

260. Quoted in ABCNEWS.com, September 21, 2000, *op. cit.*

CHAPTER 7

Fiduciary Fraud:
Crime in the Banking, Insurance, and Pension Fund Industries

> *Teacher:*   What's the capital of Nebraska?
> *First Student:*   Lincoln.
> *Teacher:*   Right. Who freed the slaves?
> *Second Student:*   Lincoln.
> *Teacher:*   Right. Charles Keating cooked the books at what S & L?
> *Third Student:*   Lincoln?

From *High School High* (1996). Screenplay by David Zucker, Robert Locash, and Pat Proft.

*I*n the classic 1946 movie, *It's a Wonderful Life,* a young man named George Bailey (portrayed by James Stewart) inherits the leadership of a small S & L institution from his late father.[1] Honest and selfless, George barely makes a living from the family business; indeed, he seems to be the lowest-paid bank president in the country. The Bailey Bros. Building & Loan Association is conspicuously unobsessed with extravagant salaries and escalating profits. Its funds are reserved to help the working-class families of Bedford Falls obtain mortgages for the modest little homes of their dreams. But through an unfortunate set of circumstances, culminating in the theft of a large deposit by a villainous slumlord, the Building and Loan becomes insolvent, just as a state bank examiner unexpectedly arrives to audit its books. Believing that his business and personal reputation are about to crumble and that he will probably go to prison, Bailey jumps off an icy bridge on Christmas Eve in a desperate suicide attempt and is rescued by a guardian angel dispatched from heaven to restore his shattered idealism. Ultimately, the Building and Loan is saved by the loyalty of its depositors, and George Bailey lives to lend another day.

In the wake of the calamitous S & L crisis, it seems natural to speculate about how George Bailey might have reacted if *It's a Wonderful Life* had been set in the 1980s instead of the 1940s. Would he be renamed George Bailout? Suppose his unworldly "guardian" had come from a less celestial and more sulfuric venue. Might he have tried to keep his bank afloat by making risky, unlawful investments in the hope of striking it rich? Might he have juggled the books, then bribed the auditor? Might he simply have looted the remaining funds and sailed off to Bora Bora, leaving his depositors holding an empty bag? Would the film's familiar penultimate line—"Every time a bell rings, an angel gets his wings"—be replaced by a more up-to-date piece of doggerel: "Every time a bell peals, a banker lies and steals?" Luckily for Bedford Falls, George Bailey was not Charles Keating, but the product of a more virtuous era; because the most expensive white-collar crime epidemic in history occurred as the result of fraud in financial institutions during the 1980s. The S & L debacle of that decade resulted in almost $200 billion in short-term losses to taxpayers, with the eventual cost predicted to be over twice that much, as it accumulates—with interest—over the next several decades. A significant portion of this cost is believed to be the result of criminal fraud on the part of S & L operators, borrowers, and other entrepreneurs.

Financial institutions (banks, S & L or "thrifts," financial service companies, pension funds, and insurance companies) handle "other people's money." They are entrusted to properly invest and oversee large amounts of funds that are deposited with them. The traditional crime of embezzlement by lower-level employees has become overshadowed by concerns with upper-level management—sometimes with the help of outsiders—mismanaging and looting their own companies. As this chapter will examine, these crimes result in massive losses to investors, shareholders, beneficiaries, consumers, and taxpayers. Consider the following "whirlwind tour" of financial crimes:

❖ In 1997, Philip S. Zanghi II was found guilty of securities fraud, tax evasion, and money laundering in a scheme that bilked investors out of $830,000, which he claimed was used to help revive production of America's first motorcycle, the Indian. Zanghi promoted the idea of resurrecting Indian in 1990, but the government was able to prove that he did little but license T-shirts. He used proceeds from stock sales and licensing agreements to finance a luxurious lifestyle that included expensive cars, furs, jewelry, and international travel.[2]

❖ In 1998, BankAmerica Corporation agreed to pay $187.5 million to the State of California and 300 local governments to settle charges that it mishandled hundreds of millions of dollars of bond payments from 1978 through 1995. The case was originally filed as a whistleblower suit by a former employee, who was later joined in the action by the state and local governments. Prior to the settlement, the bank had made a $10.6 million payment, contending that was all it owed. In the suit the largest U.S. bank was accused of "systematically pocketing unclaimed bondholder payments that should have been returned to help build schools, hospitals and roads."[3]

❖ In 1998 the General Accounting Office reported that employees of the IRS embezzled over $5 million in taxpayer checks and cash between 1995 and 1997. In one case, a check for $590,000 was stolen from a tax-return processing center, and the bank and account numbers on it were used to clone multiple fraudulent blank checks, which were then made out for smaller amounts to avoid raising suspicion. In another scheme, an IRS employee and his conspirators altered a check to change the payee from "I.R.S." to "I. R. Smith" and deposited it into a personal account.[4]

❖ In another southern California case, Douglas P. Blankenship was convicted of masterminding a $25 million fraud against financial institutions, companies, and private investors in 17 states. Blankenship posed as a wealthy real estate developer and was able to secure funds through phony loan applications. He and 13 accomplices pleaded guilty to defrauding Puget Sound National Bank of $4.5 million and stealing millions more from other institutions and investors. The federal judge who sentenced him to the maximum term of 9 years for his crimes characterized Blankenship as a "danger to the public."[5]

❖ In 1992, a federal judge in Los Angeles sentenced Westley Scher to almost 6 years in prison and ordered him to pay $26.7 million to defrauded investors. Scher was a principal of FSG Financial Services, Inc. of Beverly Hills and other related companies which marketed phony municipal bonds. Investors thought they were buying tax-free securities that were issued and backed by local government. Prosecutors found that there were in fact no bonds, and hundreds of investors were defrauded over a 6-year period.[6]

❖ In a New Jersey case, Louis Angelo, former president of an airplane charter service, was found guilty and sentenced to 18 months in federal prison, 3 years supervised release, and 200 hours of community service for participating in a scheme to defraud banks in Georgia, Indiana, New Jersey, and Massachusetts of more than $6 million. Angelo and his associates had financed executive aircraft purchases for more than their actual prices, skimming the excess money for themselves. He reportedly received more than $700,000 from his serial frauds.[7]

❖ In Miami, a former financial planner, Henry Gherman, was convicted on federal embezzlement and mail fraud charges. In the early 1980s, Gherman embezzled close to $10 million from clients of Financial and Investment Planning, Inc. of North Miami Beach and later fled to Asia. In 1988, he was arrested in Tokyo and extradited to Florida to face criminal charges.[8]

❖ In a 1984 Chicago case, a former chairman and president of a defunct Des Plaines, Illinois, bank received a 5-year prison term and 5 years probation after agreeing to plead guilty to two counts of fraud. He had been indicted on 23 charges, including wire fraud, receiving stolen securities, transporting fraudulently obtained money, and bribing a county official. In imposing the maximum allowable sentence, the judge said that Angelos, "breached a very sacred trust that bankers and the banking community impose on every banker."[9]

❖ In 1988, a federal judge in Austin, Texas, sentenced the former president of National Bank of Texas to the maximum term of 12 years in prison for engaging in fraud that contributed to the bank's failure. Richard Homer Taylor had pleaded guilty to charges related to a scheme in which designated individuals obtained so-called nominee loans under his approval and then transferred the funds to him.[10]

❖ In Orange County, California, two stockbrokers were sentenced to 15 months in prison for diverting $2.9 million bequeathed to Guide Dogs for the Blind. William Clark II and Gibrahn Verdult were convicted of money laundering in a scheme which put the money under their control after they cooked up a "fake will." The two were hired by Leland Parker shortly before he died in 1994. Parker had directed that his estate go to Guide Dogs for the Blind. Instead, prosecutors found that the men had used the money to buy a $500,000 home, a $130,000 lot, and a $35,000 Corvette. They then hired a firm to invest the remaining ill-gotten funds.[11]

❖ In Boston, William J. Lilly, who was convicted of defrauding two failed banks of more than $9 million, was sentenced to 5 years imprisonment and ordered to pay $5.7 million in restitution. Lilly had directed buyers of condominiums in Massachusetts to sign purchase agreements on which he had misstated their assets and down payments. He used those meretricious documents to obtain a $7 million loan from First Mutual Bank for Savings in Boston. He then sold the fraudulent mortgages for $9 million to a thrift in Florida. Both financial institutions were subsequently seized by government regulators, and many of the mortgages went into default.[12]

❖ In 1994, a federal judge in Baltimore sentenced Tom Billman to 40 years in prison and ordered him to pay $25 million in restitution for looting his failed S & L institution years earlier.[13] After his thrift collapsed in the mid 1980s, Billman fled the country and led investigators on a 4-year international manhunt. After using his two yachts to sail the Mediterranean and traveling the world under false passports, the posse finally caught up with Billman in Paris in 1993 and returned him to Baltimore to stand trial.[14] The captive fugitive was convicted on 11 counts related to his stealing at least $28 million from his depositors. At Billman's sentencing, the judge commented, "Society is finally saying that this conduct is intolerable and unacceptable."[15]

❖ In Little Rock, Arkansas, the former chairman of failed First South F.A., at one time the largest S & L in the state, was sentenced to 4 years in prison and fined $75,000 for looting his financial institution. Howard Weichern, Jr., was convicted in 1990 of loan fraud for concealing from both regulators and shareholders an agreement that two borrowers would not be liable for paying back their loans.[16]

❖ In 1998, Robert Colgin Wilson, a Palm Beach investment promoter, was sentenced to 57 months in prison for conspiracy to commit wire fraud in Florida. In

California, he was sentenced to 46 months on charges of wire fraud and tax evasion. The cases resulted from the activities of his company, Debenture Guaranty Corp., which supposedly invested in U.S. Treasury securities. Instead it was found that the company was a Ponzi scheme that bilked investors out of millions of dollars. One of the investors, U.S. Employer Consumer Self-Insurance Fund of Sarasota, Florida, lost $3.9 million and was declared insolvent by the state Department of Insurance.[17]

❖ In Los Angeles, the former head of Family Savings and Loan was convicted on charges related to his illegal purchase of the financial institution. Oliver Trigg, Jr., was sentenced to more than 7 years in prison for perpetrating "an elaborate scheme" to buy the thrift with its own funds.[18] While serving on the thrift's board, Trigg had utilized a dummy company he controlled to sell land in Whittier, California to Family Savings at an inflated price. Trigg then used some of the profit from the sale (about $1.7 million of the total $2.7 million he had "earned") to buy a controlling interest in the thrift. A jury decided that he had illegally exploited his position on the board of directors to arrange the transaction. He was found guilty of conspiracy, bank fraud, money laundering, and tax fraud.[19]

❖ In 1999 the former chief executive of the failed Bank of San Pedro was sentenced to more than 7 years in federal prison for his role in defrauding the bank out of $2.3 million. Lance Darrell Oak was convicted of bank fraud, tax fraud, and conspiracy to launder money in a scheme in which he and three others created a sham mortgage company that sold inflated loans to the bank in the early 1990s. As a result, the bank failed and was seized by regulators in 1994. After Oak apologized for his actions in court, the judge who sentenced him labeled his conduct "a disgrace."[20]

These cases represent just a small sample of the financial frauds perpetrated in the recent past. Their vast monetary cost is incontrovertible and their effects resonate broadly throughout all segments of the economy and society as a whole. This chapter considers some of the major forms of financial frauds in various institutions, including pension funds, insurance companies, financial service companies, and last, but certainly not least, the blighted S & L industry.

PENSION FUND FRAUD

One of the most callous forms of white-collar predation entails the looting of money from retirees and workers who have deposited their savings in pension funds. Pension funds are loosely regulated in the United States and can take many forms, but their mission is inviolate: to provide sound and profitable investments for individuals and companies. Many persons rely on such institutions to manage their money for retirement. As the following case illustrates, that trust can easily be broken—with devastating results.

C A S E   S T U D Y

First Pension = "Worst" Pension

One of the largest pension fund scams occurred in California. In 1994, First Pension Corporation of Irvine was charged with stealing or misappropriating up to $124 million from its investors. The company was set up as a pension fund administrator to help clients create various retirement accounts, including IRAs, and Keoughs (401[K]). It was also alleged that the corporation, through its "direct participation program," enticed investors into buying trust deeds offered by other companies owned by the same individuals who owned First Pension. As much as $100 million was never invested at all, but utilized in a Ponzi scheme, whereby new investor money was used to pay dividends and interest on older investments, until the pyramid collapsed and First Pension declared bankruptcy.[21]

First Pension, which was run by businessman William E. Cooper, had purportedly invested $350 million for about 8000 individuals, mostly from the southern California region. The company filed for bankruptcy in 1994 after another company, Summit Trust Company, which served as the custodian for First Pension investors' money, was seized by regulators. The president of Summit, which was also controlled by Cooper, told regulators that $10 million in funds had been transferred without his authority. Summit was soon taken over by the government.[22] By May 1994, the FBI and SEC were engaged in ongoing investigations of First Pension, Cooper, and two other owners, Robert Lindley and Valerie Jensen.[23] The government estimated that as much as $124 million could have been lost to fraud, forgery, and outright theft through an "elaborate pyramid scheme that misled clients into thinking they were investing in mortgages that in fact did not exist."[24]

Despite their lawyers' proclamations that their clients were cooperating with authorities, none of the three principals appeared at a hearing in June 1994, where they were to be questioned under oath as to the whereabouts of the missing investor funds. Their absence certainly did little to ease the fears of investors, one of whom, an unemployed man who had given Cooper's firm $120,000 from a pension and inheritance, verbalized the unmistakable pain of financial ruination: "I feel sick . . . I just want to get out a razor blade. This is all the money I've scrimped and saved in the world."[25]

The U.S. attorney's office in Los Angeles filed formal charges against Cooper, Lindley, and Jensen in July 1994. The defendants had earlier signed agreements to plead guilty and cooperate with the investigation. An assistant U.S. attorney commented, "This is one of the longest-running and most elaborate schemes I have ever seen. To a certain extent, they had to fool their own employees as well as investors."[26] The three operators of First Pension faced maximum prison terms of 10 years and fines up to $500,000 each for their crimes.

One example of the extraordinary level of deceit at First Pension involved Cooper's hiring of an actress to portray a state auditor after he was confronted by

(Continued)

an employee about the fact that no trust deeds existed in the mortgage pools.[27] The actress, who was given a forged California Corporations Department business card, sat in the offices of Vestcorp Securities, a First Pension-related firm, and pretended to review files for 3 weeks. Later, a letter was drafted on phony official stationery stating that the business records were in order.[28]

Although Cooper and his associates pleaded guilty to mail fraud, their explanations provided little relief to the investors they had swindled. Showing little emotion, Cooper declared, "It's something you can't live with. . . . I feel incredibly bad."[29] After First Pension's first year of operation, Cooper claimed he knew that he was breaking the law but continued in an attempt to recoup substantial losses: "It was clear we had violated laws and were violating laws, and at that point we invested in other businesses in an attempt to bring money back into the business."[30] Lindley's excuse for his behavior was similarly flimsy. He also invoked the inveterate vow of white-collar plea bargainers: "I'm sorry I did it."[31] Jensen claimed that she did not initially understand that what she was doing was illegal, but was "swept away by events and willingly participated."[32] Cooper was sentenced to a 10-year prison term, while Lindley and Jensen were sentenced to 9 years and 4 years, respectively.

In 1995, investors filed a class action lawsuit against the California Corporations Department, which regulates businesses in that state, charging negligence in handling First Pension. The suit alleged that the Department and its commissioner knew about the illegal pension administration but refused to conduct an examination or warn investors.[33] The state had never investigated First Pension, even though it admittedly had received a written complaint regarding the bogus audit conducted by Cooper's "actress."[34]

In July 2000, 6 years after investors lost $136 million in fraud-ridden First Pension Corp., they finally received some good news. In a civil suit brought against accounting firms involved in certifying First Pensions financial status, an Orange County jury ruled against accounting giant Coopers & Lybrand and one of its partners, finding them liable for both general and punitive damages.[35] They found that Coopers, which had since merged to become Pricewaterhouse Coopers, and partner Hal Hurwitz misrepresented First Pension's financial condition and concealed material information. The following month, investors settled with the former accounting giant for an undisclosed sum.[36] Finally, in October 2000, lawyers for investors announced that the California Department of Corporations had agreed to a nonmonetary settlement of claims against it.[37]

INVESTMENT AND FINANCIAL SERVICES FRAUD

Southern California was the headquarters of another extremely large Ponzi scheme, involving the Irvine-based investment firm, Institutional Treasury Management, headed by Steven Wymer. In 1992, Wymer pleaded guilty to numerous federal fraud charges and was ordered to refund $209 million to clients, although authorities doubted that they would be able to recoup even half of that sum. Wymer had lured clients to his investment firm by promising spectacular returns, and then used the money for illegal securities speculation and exorbitant personal spending. His investors were mostly municipalities and government agencies that lost about $174 million.[38] The fraud was uncovered when SEC examiners noticed "irregularities" in the account of the city of Marshalltown, Iowa.

Wymer began diverting clients' funds in 1986. He later claimed to have done so because he was "embarrassed to admit" that the firm that preceded Institutional Treasury Management, Denman & Co., had incurred huge losses on accounts.[39] Wymer told a federal judge, "Convinced that I could recover these lost funds, I concealed the losses by sending out false account statements. . . . I began taking money from other clients to make up the losses and sending false statements, audit confirmations, and other documents to those clients to cover up the diversion of their funds."[40]

Wymer's justification for his behavior is virtually identical to the "official" explanation of how huge financial losses occurred during the S & L crisis. Proponents of this purely economics-based view discount the role of cupidity in financial institution fraud. They typically claim that owners, pushed to the brink of insolvency by various market conditions, "gambled for resurrection" by making risky investments that could produce a high return. In reality, this "desperation" excuse falls apart when one examines the actual portfolios of the worst thrift failures, which reveal that their investments were not only unsafe and illegal, but usually involved substantial fraud as well.[41]

Moreover, Wymer's "altruistic" alibi might appear more reasonable had he not squandered his clients' remaining funds on expensive personal luxury items. If he had been *making* money for clients, such symbols of success could be more readily justified. But by *losing* other peoples' money, while amassing real and personal property totaling $10 million to $15 million, including houses in Newport Beach, New York City, Sun Valley, Idaho, and Palm Beach, Florida, as well as 13 cars, Wymer was just another greedy crook caught looting the cash drawer.

Standing before the court, his voice cracking, Wymer recited the customary white-collar pledge of contrition: "I am deeply sorry for and ashamed of what I have done. Unfortunately, my illegal activities have greatly hurt some of my clients, my wife, my daughter and my family."[42] One of his prosecutors resolved that Wymer would spend considerable time behind bars: "He was robbing Peter to pay Paul. He acted out of greed and he certainly lived a very lavish lifestyle as a result."[43] Wymer was sentenced to serve nearly 15 years in prison and to forfeit $9 million in assets. Prosecutors noted, however, that Wymer had spent more than $29 million on himself, "far more than he says he earned and far more than he has agreed to forfeit."[44]

Wymer's crimes, as destructive as they were, told only part of the story of the extent of illegal activities in the financial services industry. Before his sentencing, Wymer appeared before a congressional committee and told the members that broker-dealers had helped him defraud investors. He did not name the firms he alleged had abetted his crimes but stated, "The principal reason I was able to get away with diverting money from one client to another was that the broker-dealers with whom I dealt agreed not to send confirmations and monthly statements to my clients. As a result, some of my clients never learned the real status of their accounts."[45] Although Wymer's certainly could be taken as an attempt to diffuse his own culpability in the matter, an SEC investigatory official concurred that Wymer had in fact escaped attention through the complicity of broker-dealer employees, who falsified documents and allowed him access to clients' money. The official further declared, "I'm not sure if we had given his firm the equivalent of a proctological exam we would have found something unless this [broker] employee told us the truth."[46] Wymer also commented that investment fraud is "common," that regulatory ineptitude aided his crimes, and that federal reform measures were necessary to curb abuses.[47]

The Institutional Treasury Management case illustrates a number of important points about financial crime, its extent, and the need for better control mechanisms. As a postscript to this massive swindle, it should be emphasized that the biggest losers were taxpayers. Most of the money stolen and squandered by Wymer belonged to municipalities and government agencies, which were enticed into investing because of the lure of high returns. If there is a moral to the story, it is simply this: In times of fiscal constraint in government, officials must be extremely wary of lavish entrepreneurial claims. The Orange County bankruptcy (detailed in Chapter 12) has demonstrated the folly of gambling away public funds on high-risk, high-return investments in the hope of increasing revenues without raising taxes. Getting something for nothing may be a universal aspiration, but it is seldom a realistic one.

INSURANCE COMPANY FRAUDS

Insurance is one of the most pervasive businesses in America; almost everyone comes into contact with this industry at some point in their lives. Insurance companies sell over $400 billion of new policies every year to businesses and individuals.[48] Although the major insurers are generally conservative and reputable, a smaller number of rogue companies have the potential to wreak havoc on the entire industry. Insolvencies have increased dramatically since the early 1980s. Between 1982 and 1992, approximately 100 life insurers were declared insolvent, 73 of them between 1990 and 1992.[49] Officials note that fraud has played a major role in 30% to 50% of those failures.[50]

Federal oversight is woefully deficient in the largely unregulated insurance industry, which comprises more than 5000 companies and controls more than $2 trillion in assets.[51] States do regulate insurers operating within their jurisdiction and require that many of them contribute to a "guaranty fund," which is supposed to pay claims against a failed company. In practice, however, it has been reported that many claimants in such circumstances receive no benefits. Moreover, increases in guaranty fund assessments resulting from claims are passed along to consumers in the form of higher premiums.[52]

When the mass media and, for that matter, the general public discuss insurance fraud, they generally refer to beneficiary frauds perpetrated by customers who send in false claims to their carriers for payment. This emphasis is understandable, because beneficiary fraud is a significant problem for the industry and incurs great financial loss. It is nevertheless arguable whether beneficiary frauds—as draining and annoying as they are—really contribute the bulk of losses within the industry. The fact is that insurers themselves are in a much better position to reap immense illicit profits than beneficiaries, however dishonest. They are also in a much better position to settle their cases once unscrupulous practices are uncovered. For example, in what was believed in 1998 to be the largest settlement of its kind in California, an insurance company agreed to refund as much as $115 million to elderly customers who were deceived into buying inappropriate investments aimed at avoiding the high costs of the state's probate system. Great American Life Insurance Company of Cincinnati admitted no wrongdoing, but sold the investments through a southern California company, Alliance for Mature Americans. Investigators found that salespeople often sold investment instruments to seriously ill people, or to those with Alzheimer's disease who were not able to understand the transactions, the tax ramifications, or the potential risks involved. Officials noted that Alliance was one of several "trust" mills in the state that lured senior citizens by offering reasonably priced living trusts, which are legal devices for avoiding costly probate proceedings. Once their financial information was collected, high-pressure sales tactics were employed to force them to buy investments without adequately informing them of the risks. Officials suspect that former Alliance salespeople have now started living-trust mills of their own.[53] In what could be considered an ironic footnote to this case, former California Attorney General Dan Lungren praised Great American for "voluntarily coming forward and cooperating" after his office had begun investigating Alliance's deceptive sales tactics in 1996. Had there been no investigation, however, it is highly doubtful that Great American would have come forward at all.

Deceptive sales tactics are not confined to lesser-known companies, but involve some of the nation's largest firms who, by virtue of their size, are able to settle such cases for enormous sums of money. In 1998, for example, State Farm Mutual Automobile Insurance agreed to pay $200 million to settle a class action lawsuit charging that it misled customers in selling 4.4 million insurance polices over a 15-year period. The company admitted no wrong doing, but said it was settling to avoid a "costly legal fight."[54]

Similarly, giants Prudential, New York Life Insurance, and Metropolitan Life Insurance have spent billions of dollars in the last few years to settle lawsuits over their sales of life insurance. In 1999, for example, Metropolitan Life, the nation's second largest life insurance company, agreed to pay at least $1.7 billion to settle allegations that policyholders were victims of deceptive sales practices. Policyholders who sued the company claimed that its agents encouraged them to trade in old policies for new ones in order to generate commissions in a practice known as "churning."[55] Other allegations included the sale of policies with so-called vanishing premiums, where the premium would not have to be paid after a certain number of years. In some cases, the premiums never "disappeared." Insurance policies were also sold as "investment products" but did not earn the returns that customers were led to believe they would.[56] Nevertheless, insurers, including Met Life, claimed no wrongdoing in these settlements. Indeed, according to current laws, insurance companies are not required to and often refuse to provide basic information about the policies they sell. As Joseph M. Belth, professor emeritus at Indiana University and an expert on life insurance notes, "As long as there are no requirements for disclosure, this whole area is ripe for all kinds of deceptive practices to go on."[57] Let us consider some of the frauds committed by unscrupulous insurance companies.

One common form of fraud is known as "premium diversion," whereby funds intended to cover claims are diverted for other purposes. Small "fly-by-night" companies have been known to do this, then simply "disappear" after collecting premiums or after complaints about claims begin to pour in. More sophisticated schemes rely on creating a network of service and affiliate companies, which fraudulently bill larger companies for ambiguous items such as "operating costs."[58] William Shackelford, the former head of an automobile insurance company in North Carolina, was once known as a very generous man. The problem was, as a federal prosecutor put it, "his generosity was with other people's money."[59] Shackelford, an auto racing fan, gave away almost $16 million in premiums to friends, family, and stock-car drivers before he was convicted and imprisoned for fraud.

Another way that insurers can cheat customers is by creating phony assets. Insurers must show that they have sufficient assets to meet capitalization requirements to pay potential claims. Given lax regulation, spurious insurers can often pretend to have more assets than they actually do—and get away with it. Regulators, who are vastly understaffed for serious financial examinations, jokingly refer to their annual audits of companies as "one second solvency tests."[60] Some companies temporarily "rent" assets for the requisite "one second" to place them on their books as genuine corporate holdings when regulators examine them. One company, for example claimed it owned $20 million in Texas real estate; the property had been condemned by the city of San Antonio and had a value nowhere near $20 million.[61] Another company claimed $72 million in Indonesian war bonds. Because these dubious bonds are not traded anywhere, it is impossible to determine what they are worth, if anything.[62] Although these may be unusually creative examples, companies can also simply lie about, borrow, or rent more reasonable sounding assets.

Yet another form of insurance fraud, involving small business scams, has also been quite common.[63] Because it can be difficult for employees in small companies to obtain low-cost health insurance, a new organizational form has emerged to meet their needs—and sometimes clean out their wallets. The Multiple Employer Welfare Arrangement (MEWA) was created by Congress to help small businesses obtain reasonably-priced health care coverage for their employees. A MEWA is usually organized through industry associations and consists of several small companies that pool their funds to provide health coverage for all employees. Once cited as a "godsend," the Insurance Commissioner of Massachusetts now complains that MEWAs "have turned out to be a major-league disaster."[64] Investigators have found that some firms that administer MEWAs are fraudulent enterprises—"virtual money machines for the unscrupulous."[65]

Crooks have had a field day with MEWAs because of even looser regulatory oversight than that which exists for the insurance industry as a whole. Licensed insurers must abide by state regulations regarding minimum assets and contributions to state guaranty funds. A federal law exempts MEWAs from these requirements.[66] Thus, unlike traditional health insurers, practically anyone can start a MEWA with virtually no capital, paying off tomorrows claims with today's premiums, thus making them "ticking time bombs for consumers."[67] Government reports indicate that, between January 1988 and June 1989 alone, MEWAs did not pay at least $123 million in claims to almost 400,000 covered workers and their beneficiaries.[68]

In addition to fraudulent MEWAs, crooks have used similar regulatory ambiguities to defraud employees of health insurance benefits through companies known as "employee leasing organizations."[69] Small companies would "fire" their employees, who were then "hired" by the leasing firm which would provide insurance, payroll, and other services to the companies. Through such pooling of employees, the leasing firm, would be able to qualify for lower group rates.[70] Although some of these arrangements were legitimate, many were simply fraudulent operations with the leasing company obtaining unsound or nonexistent employee insurance, where Ponzi schemes were used to pay old claims with new premiums. When these schemes ultimately collapsed, thousands of workers were left without health or compensation benefits.[71]

Crooks also have used bogus labor unions that are exempt from numerous regulations in order to perpetrate massive insurance scams on unsuspecting members. In some instances, control was gained over dormant unions which were then used to market fraudulent insurance plans. Bolder crooks have simply "created" labor unions which, as it turns out, is easily accomplished by filing several documents with the Department of Labor.[72] Once established, these sham unions can readily defraud members by convincing them to join bogus health plans, and laws protecting unions from state intervention make them very difficult to shut down when they are discovered by authorities.[73]

The failure of Transit Casualty Company—which has been called the "Titanic" of insurance company failures, with a cost of over $3 billion—illustrates yet another significant and very expensive mechanism for fraud in the insurance industry. According to a congressional committee, the causes of Transit's insolvency were "management incompetence, excessive reinsurance, and reckless expansion."[74] Reinsurance is a legitimate practice in the industry, which allows companies to sell their policies to other companies ("reinsurers"), so that they can write additional policies and are not "wiped out" in the event of a disaster precipitating a deluge of expensive claims. It is crudely analogous to one bookmaker "laying off" sizable bets with another to protect himself from potentially unaffordable losses. In the insurance industry, this practice generally is beneficial to all concerned, unless the reinsurer is under-capitalized or, worse yet, fraudulent.

Reinsurance companies function outside of the formal regulatory system because they do not directly affect consumers. In the recent past many have operated offshore, where they can be protected by bank secrecy laws of other countries. Firms looking to expand quickly (as in Transit's case) frequently turn to reinsurance companies.

As is the case with other types of financial institutions, the reinsurance system is flawed by avarice. Although technically reducing their liabilities through the sale of their policies, insurers remain liable for claims that the reinsurer cannot pay. In other words, if the reinsurer is insolvent, undercapitalized, or simply fraudulent, then the insurer (and the state guaranty fund) is left holding the bag. This explains why reinsurance has been called the "'black hole' of solvency regulation."[75]

But the villain is not always the reinsurer. Mendacious primary insurers can use reinsurers to inflate their net worth artificially by reducing their required reserves by the amount of risk supposedly transferred to the reinsurer. The federal government's General Accounting Office found that four large insurance company failures were attributable to questionable reinsurance transactions.[76]

Sometimes official reactions to insurance scams are pitifully slow. California Pacific Bankers and Insurance Ltd., which was purportedly based in the "Dominion of Melchizedek"—*a country which does not exit*—openly operated in the state for months before regulators closed its doors.[77] In Maryland, the case of fugitive Martin Bramson's International Bahamian Insurance Company brought an even slower response, despite an insider's tip to regulators *10 years* before authorities moved on the case.[78] Bramson and some family members used a complex and sophisticated web of offshore companies to sell fake malpractice insurance to thousands of doctors and healthcare professionals at below-market rates. The Bramsons operated 53 companies, some of which were registered in Micronesia, the British Virgin Islands, and the Bahamas.[79]

There are a number of reasons for such foot-dragging which allows this kind of criminal activity to flourish. First, regulators and investigators are outgunned by their small numbers relative to the mammoth size of the insurance industry. Second, state insurance commissioners are known for their coziness with the industry, which sometimes results in official corruption or appointees to the job who are inept or unmotivated to confront their friends or benefactors. In Wyoming and Louisiana, for example, insurance commissioners have been convicted of taking bribes from those under their watch.[80] The good news is that things appear to be changing in this area, albeit slowly. Commissioners in some states have beefed up regulations and the FBI has increased investigations. On the other hand, needed federal legislation has met with substantial opposition—from certain state commissioners and from much of the insurance industry itself.[81]

Teale—as in "Steal"

Congressional investigators looking into insurance company fraud have concluded:

> There is strong evidence to suggest that the insurance fraud that we have identified is global in nature. We have merely exposed the tip of a number of international white-collar criminal syndicates.[82]

On the roster of criminal insurance syndicates, one name is legendary: Alan Teale. In a few short years starting in the early 1980s, Teale and his associates were able to create a far-flung empire of insurance companies both within and outside U.S. borders that bilked thousands of unsuspecting individuals out of millions of dollars they thought was going to provide them with insurance coverage. Teale's story reveals just how easy it is for clever con men (and women) to stay one step ahead of regulators, who are hamstrung by a crazy-quilt of insurance laws and regulations that limit their ability to pursue these financial pirates.

Teale, a native of England, got his start working for the legendary Lloyds of London, where he learned the insurance trade. In the early 1980s, he emigrated to south Florida where he eventually became director of the Miami-based Insurance Exchange of the Americas (IEA), an ambitious company that sold reinsurance plans worldwide and whose founders saw it as the new Lloyds. The Exchange attracted an interesting group of investors that included Michael Milken and his brother. IEA was known for its flashy investments and underwriting. In one case, the syndicate underwrote 50% of a New Jersey racetrack's offer to pay $2 million to the owners of a Kentucky Derby winner if their horse continued its winning streak in New Jersey. When the horse crossed the finish line ahead of the field, IEA lost $1 million.[83] After the Exchange eventually failed, regulators were left to settle $200 million in claims for about 5 cents on the dollar.[84]

In the mid-1980s Teale, moved to Georgia where he established the new headquarters for his fraudulent insurance empire. Teale's flagship was the Victoria Insurance Company, a property and casualty insurer based in Atlanta. Victoria was in operation only 18 months before it was shut down by regulators; but in that short period it collected $16 million in premiums and, when it was closed, left $20 million in unpaid claims. One of the specialty lines offered by Victoria was disability coverage to professional athletes, particularly football players. Such well-known NFL stars as Jim Kelly, Bo Jackson, and Joe Montana paid as much as $115,000 for policies that would pay off in the event of a career-ending injury, only to find out later that their policies were bogus. In one case, a former running back

(Continued)

for the Atlanta Falcons testified that after a knee injury put an end to his career, he thought he would receive the $320,000 provided for by his policy. Instead, he found that Victoria was bankrupt and he would receive nothing. He eventually went to work as a hospital aide earning $6.35 an hour.[85]

In a variation on this scheme, another Teale-backed company sold liability policies to high school athletic programs. When the company went under in 1992, it left 60 catastrophically injured teenagers without any financial support; some were quadriplegics, others were in nursing homes.[86]

Teale and his associates were able to fool regulators into thinking that their companies were financially sound by ceding much of their insurance business to Teale-owned reinsurers operating offshore where it was difficult for regulators to verify their assets. The principal assets for one of these offshore companies was $25 million in "treasury notes" issued by an entity that called itself the Sovereign Cherokee Nation Tejas. This "sovereign nation" turned out to be a sandbar in the middle of the Rio Grande River whose "chief" did business out of an office building in Dallas. When investigators called the office, they spoke to a representative who referred to himself as Wise Otter, but who "spoke with a very distinct British accent."[87] Inquiries into the financial holdings of the Nation revealed that among them was a plaster-of-paris facemask of Marlon Brando, valued (by the owners) at $1.5 million.[88]

Teale's spectacular career in insurance fraud came to an end in 1993, when he was arrested by federal authorities. He died in prison while serving a 17-year sentence. Curiously, Wise Otter has not been heard from since.

THE S & L IMPLOSION

The devastation of the S & L (or "thrift") industry in the 1980s will cost the American taxpayer hundreds of billions of dollars. Estimates range from a "mere" $200 billion to a mind-boggling $1.4 trillion by the year 2021.[89] This latter figure translates into about $5500 for every man, woman, and child in America.[90] A private investigator hired by the federal government to uncover swindled thrifts put the projected cost in perspective: "Every family in America is going to make the equivalent of car payments for the savings and loan fiasco. The only question is whether it's going to be a Chevrolet or a Cadillac."[91]

One industry consultant claims that only 3% of the total bailout costs are directly due to crime.[92] Likewise, a number of economists have downplayed the role of crime in the S & L crisis.[93] However, there is extensive evidence that white-collar crime *was* a key ingredient in the debacle. The National Commission on Financial Institution Reform, Recovery and Enforcement speculates that losses due directly to criminal fraud "probably amount[ed] to 10 to 15 percent of total net losses."[94] Long-time thrift regulator, William Black, former Senior Deputy Chief Counsel of the Office of Thrift Supervision and chief legal officer for the western region, maintains that "fraud and insider abuse caused on a *lower* bound estimate, 25 percent of total

S & L failure losses."[95] A Resolution Trust Corporation (RTC) report estimates that about 51% of insolvent thrifts had suspected criminal misconduct referred to the FBI.[96] Finally, a General Accounting Office study of 26 of the most costly thrift failures found that *every one* of these institutions was a victim of major insider fraud and abuse.[97] The General Accounting Office further suggests that criminal activity was a central factor in as many as 70% to 80% of thrift failures.[98] Thus, there appears to be ample support for the contention that material fraud played a significant role in the S & L debacle, despite the claims of detractors, most of whom have produced no empirical data to support their position that fraud was minimal. Thus, although there may be little consensus as to the exact amount of fraud and deliberate insider abuse involved, there is substantial agreement that these swindles constitute the most costly series of white-collar crimes in American history.[99]

Origins of a Financial Disaster

Economic conditions of the late 1970s substantially undermined the health of the S & L industry and ultimately contributed to the dismantling of the traditional boundaries within which they operated. Perhaps most important, high interest rates and slow growth squeezed the industry at both ends. Locked into low-interest mortgages from previous eras and precluded from offering adjustable rate mortgages (ARMS), prohibited by Regulation Q from paying more than 5.5% interest on new deposits despite inflation reaching 13.3% by 1979, the industry suffered steep losses. Compounding the problem (so to speak) was the development of money market mutual funds by Wall Street, which allowed middle-income investors to buy shares in large denomination securities at high money-market rates, which triggered "disintermediation"—that is, mass withdrawals of deposits from savings and loans.

Confronted with rising defaults and foreclosures as the recession deepened, and increasing competition from new high-yield investments, S & L seemed doomed to extinction. The industry's net worth fell from $16.7 billion in 1972 to a *negative* net worth of $17.5 billion in 1980, with 85% of the country's S & Ls losing money.[100]

Although policymakers had gradually loosened the restraints on S & L since the early 1970s, it was not until the *laissez-faire* fervor of the early Reagan administration that this approach gained widespread political acceptance as a solution to the rapidly escalating S & L crisis. In a few strokes, Washington dismantled most of the regulatory infrastructure that had kept the thrift industry together for four decades.[101] These deregulators were convinced that the free enterprise system works best if left alone, unhampered by perhaps well-meaning but ultimately counterproductive government controls. Many knowledgeable onlookers passionately disagreed and pointed the finger of blame for the subsequent gush of S & L abuses directly at deregulation. One critic said of deregulation, "[It] allowed the real estate developers, with a borrower's mentality, to own banks, replacing the sober, conservative bankers. It's like giving the fattest kid on the block the keys to the candy store."[102]

Two major laws were passed in the early 1980s which opened the doors to the impending disaster. In 1980, the Depository Institutions Deregulation and Monetary Control Act was signed into law,[103] followed in 1982 by the Garn-St. Germain Act.[104] These laws provided for a loosening of government control over the industry, which both dramatically expanded their investment powers and moved them farther away from their traditional role as providers of home mortgages for the working class, a role idealized so memorably in *It's a Wonderful Life.*

Deregulatory changes included: a phasing out of limits on deposit interest rates; permitting thrifts to make commercial real estate loans, business and consumer loans, and direct investments in their own properties; authorization to issue credit cards; and increasing federal deposit insurance from $40,000 to $100,000 per savings account. Moreover, the Garn-St. Germain Act allowed thrifts to provide 100% financing, requiring no down-payment from the borrower, in an effort to attract new business to the desperate industry.

Industry regulators quickly jumped on the *laissez-faire* bandwagon. The elimination of the 5% limit on brokered deposits in 1980 gave thrifts access to unprecedented amounts of cash. "Brokered deposits" were placed by middlemen who aggregated individual investments as "jumbo" certificates of deposit (CDs). Because the maximum insured deposit was $100,000, these brokered deposits were packaged as $100,000 CDs commanding high interest rates. So attractive was this system to all concerned—brokers who made hefty commissions, individual investors who received high interest for their money, and thrift operators who now had almost unlimited access to these funds— that between 1982 and 1984, brokered deposits as a percentage of total thrift assets increased 400%.[105]

By 1984, federally insured thrifts had access to $34 billion in brokered deposits.[106] The National Commission on Financial Institution Reform, Recovery and Enforcement points out that, even without brokered deposits, thrifts would have been able to grow rapidly through the combination of insured deposits and risky capital ventures. Nonetheless, as they observe, "Brokered deposits proved to be a convenient and low cost means of raising vast sums."[107]

Regulators also abandoned the requirement established in 1974 that thrifts have at least 400 stockholders, with no one individual owning more than 25% of the stock. This effectively allowed a single entrepreneur to operate a federally insured S & L. Furthermore, single investors could now start thrifts backed up by noncash assets, such as land or real estate. Presumably hoping that this move would attract innovative entrepreneurs who would rescue the industry, the regulators seemed oblivious to the disastrous potential of virtually unlimited charters in a vulnerable industry.

Following deregulation, losses continued to escalate. In 1982, the Federal Savings and Loan Insurance Corporation (FSLIC) spent over $2.4 billion to close or merge insolvent S & L, and by 1986 the federal insurance agency was itself declared insolvent.[108] With the number of insolvent thrifts climbing steadily, the FSLIC, knowing that it had insufficient funds to cope with the disaster, slowed the pace of closures, allowing technically insolvent institutions to stay open. Not surprisingly, the "Zombie" thrifts,[109] as they came to be known, continued to hemorrhage. In the first half of 1988, the thrift industry reported that it had lost an unprecedented $7.5 billion.[110] It is now known, of course, that the actual losses were much higher.

Unfortunately, the effect of deregulation (or "unregulation" as some call it) was to attract an unsavory breed of entrepreneur to an already troubled industry. These hustlers did not see an opportunity to help rebuild the industry, but a chance to plunder it through various get-rich-quick schemes. S & Ls became "money machines" or mere shell organizations by which unscrupulous individuals could enrich themselves. After the thrift had served its purpose and was insolvent—that is, bankrupt—it could be left for dead. Government regulators then had to act as undertakers, "cleaning up" the remains by reimbursing depositors whose funds had been squandered and stolen, and attempting to sell off the remaining assets of the thrift for whatever price they could get.

"Insider" Thrift Frauds

Although the list of potential frauds open to thrift operators and related outsiders is a long one, researchers have classified them into three distinct categories of white-collar crime: (1) "desperation dealing"; (2) "collective embezzlement"; and (3) "covering up."[111] The categories often overlap in actual cases, because one individual may commit several types of fraud and because the same business transaction may involve more than one type. Each type of offense is considered in turn.

Desperation Dealing. After lengthy hearings and testimony, the House Committee on Government Operations concluded:

> [N]ormally honest bankers (including thrift insiders) . . . resorted to fraud or unsafe practices in efforts to save a battered institution. In those cases an incentive existed to turn an unhealthy financial institution around by garnering more deposits and then making even more speculative investments, hoping to "make it big."[112]

In his testimony, former Federal Home Loan Bank Board (FHLBB) Chair M. Danny Wall described the bind of thrift operators: "[They were] on a slippery slope of a failing institution trying to save probably their institution first and trying to save themselves and their career."[113] It is this "slippery slope" of fraud that constitutes "desperation dealing."

The factors that triggered this effect in the thrift industry are similar in some ways to those described in other white-collar crime studies. In an overview and synthesis of white-collar crime theory, Coleman points out that the "demand for profit is one of the most important economic influences on the opportunity structure for organizational crime."[114] Geis' famous study of the electrical equipment price-fixing conspiracy (Chapter 2) reveals the central role played by the corporate emphasis on profit-maximization and the consequent corporate subculture conducive to, or at least tolerant of, illegal behavior.[115]

Similarly, Farberman argues that the necessity to maximize profits within the context of intense competition produced a "criminogenic market structure" in the automobile industry.[116]

Desperation dealing by thrift operators is akin to these other white-collar crimes in that it too is motivated by the profit imperative. In the case of an insolvent S & L, the profit imperative takes on special urgency as managers struggle to turn the failing institution around. But desperation dealing is also distinct in a number of ways from these traditional white-collar crimes. Although the corporate crime previously described resulted in increased profits and long-term liquidity for the company, desperation dealing in the thrift industry was a gamble with very bad odds. Unlike corporate crimes in the industrial sector, these financial crimes usually contribute further to the *bankruptcy* of the institution.

Examples include violations of loans-to-one-borrower limits, inadequate underwriting, and other unsafe practices. Although the specific type of violation may vary, their common good is that they are motivated by a desperate effort to save a failing enterprise. Like a gambler with dwindling funds, desperation dealers "go for broke." More often than not, they end up "broke."

Collective Embezzlement.   Although much attention has been paid in congressional testimony and elsewhere to the desperation dealing just described,[117] research has shown that self-interested fraud was the more frequent and costly form of misconduct.[118] Most S & L crimes were not committed by desperate entrepreneurs trapped by economic forces. "They were perpetrated by crooks who funneled investors' money into dummy corporations, hid assets in their wives' maiden names and performed other acts of larcenous legerdemain."[119] Such premeditated fraud for personal gain on the part of thrift management has been referred to as "collective embezzlement."[120]

The Commissioner of the California Department of Savings and Loans stated in 1987, "The best way to rob a bank is to own one."[121] Collective embezzlement, or "looting," entails the siphoning off of funds from a S & L institution for personal gain, at the expense of the institution itself and with the implicit or explicit sanction of its management. This "robbing of one's own bank" has been estimated to be the single most costly category of crime in the S & L debacle, having precipitated a significant number of the largest insolvencies to date.[122] The General Accounting Office concludes that, of the S & Ls it studied, "almost all of the 26 failed thrifts made transactions that were not in the thrift's best interest. Rather, the transactions often personally benefited directors, officers, and other related parties."[123]

Embezzlement is by no means an isolated or uncommon form of white-collar crime. The advent of computers and their proliferation in business makes access to "other people's money" easier than ever (Chapter 11). Not surprisingly, the toll from such crime is considerable. Conklin notes that between 1950 and 1971, at least 100 banks were made insolvent as a result of embezzlement.[124] Moreover, in the mid-1970s, commercial banks lost almost five times as much money to embezzlers as they did to armed robbers.[125]

The traditional embezzler is usually seen as a lower-level employee working alone to steal from a large organization. Sutherland noted, "[T]he ordinary case of embezzlement is a crime by a single individual in a subordinate position against a strong corporation."[126] Similarly, Cressey, in his landmark study, Other People's Money, examined the motivations of the lone embezzler (discussed in Chapter 11).[127] The collective embezzlement, however, differs in important ways from this traditional model.[128]

Collective embezzlement constitutes not only deviance in an organization,[129] but deviance by the organization. Not only are the perpetrators themselves in management positions, but the very goals of the institution are to provide a money machine for owners and other insiders. The formal goals of the organization thus comprise a "front" for the real goals of management, who not infrequently purchased the institution in order to loot it, then discard it after it serves its purpose. It is a prime example of what Wheeler and Rothman have called "the organization as weapon": "[T]he organization . . . is for white-collar criminals what the gun or knife is for the common criminal—a tool to obtain money from victims."[130] The principal difference between Wheeler and Rothman's profile of the organization as weapon and the case of collective embezzlement in the S & L industry is that the latter is an organizational crime against the organization's own best interests. That is, the organization is both weapon and victim. This form of financial crime is referred to repeatedly in government documents[131] and was highlighted by informants in a major research study as the most egregious form of thrift fraud.[132]

Covering Up.   A considerable proportion of the criminal charges leveled against S & L institutions involved attempts to cover up or hide both the thrift's insolvency and the fraud that contributed to that insolvency.[133] "Covering up" is usually accomplished through a manipulation of S & L books and records. This form of fraud may have been the most pervasive criminal activity of thrift operators. Of the alleged 179 violations of criminal law reported in the 26 failed thrifts studied by the General Accounting Office, 42 were for covering up, constituting the single largest category.[134] The same study found that *every one* of those thrifts had been cited by regulatory examiners for "deficiencies in accounting."[135]

Covering up has been employed to a variety of ends by S & L operators. First, it is used to produce a misleading picture of the institution's state of health or, more specifically, to misrepresent the thrift's amount of capital reserves, as well as its capital-to-assets ratio. Second, deals may be arranged which include covering up as part of the scheme itself. For example, in cases of risky insider loans, a reserve account may be created to pay off the first few months (or years) of a development loan to make it look current, whether or not the project has failed or was phony in the first place. Third, covering up may be used after the fact to disguise illegal investment activity. Previously honest bankers, responding to the competitive pressures of the 1980s and the deregulated thrift environment, may have stepped over the line into unlawful risk-taking or other illicit attempts to save their ailing institutions and their own reputations. In such cases, covering up became an essential part of the fraud.[136]

One of the most devious ways to disguise unlawful income is through money laundering. Money laundering refers to taking the proceeds from illicit operations and running them through banks and other institutions which, in turn, issue them back in the form of "clean" paper that can be accounted for as legitimate income.[137] The practice is most often associated with the illegal drug trade, but it also became an element of the S & L scandal. For example, a former executive of Community Savings of Maryland was indicted on charges of looting $28 million from that thrift and laundering those funds in Swiss banks.[138]

Although S & L frauds occurred nationwide, California and Texas accounted for a preponderance of the worst thrift failures and frauds. Southern California, which federal authorities have long dubbed the "fraud capital of the United States," was home to numerous insolvencies in which financial crimes played a significant role. The notorious case of Charles Keating's Lincoln Savings and Loan of Irvine, which will be (analyzed later in this chapter) is perhaps the best-known illustration.

Another major southern California case involved North America Savings and Loan of Santa Ana. A federal grand jury returned a 40-count indictment against former executive consultant, Janet F. McKinzie, and five business associates. The indictment charged that the failed financial institution had operated as a fraudulent enterprise almost since its inception in 1983. The North America Savings case was the first on the West Coast to use racketeering laws (the Racketeer-Influenced and Corrupt Organization Act, or RICO statute) to bring charges against thrift executives. The defendants were accused of looting more than $16 million from depositors in a systematic attempt to use the institution as a front for bogus real-estate transactions, then utilizing part of the fraudulent earnings to make the thrift appear to have adequate capital long after it was insolvent. The remainder of the looted funds was siphoned off to purchase expensive Newport Beach homes, Rolls Royces, and other luxury items. A 15-month FBI investigation concluded that the failed thrift represented the worst case of insider fraud uncovered at a California S & L at that time and could be directly traced to the fraudulent activities of the institution's management.

One scheme used by the looters of North America Savings involved the creation of a series of phony real-estate escrows into which $11 million in thrift funds were deposited and then diverted back to the thrift's operators. Another $5.6 million was stolen through the creation of false billings for fictitious construction costs related to two real-estate projects, payments for which were diverted to a company owned by Janet McKinzie.[139]

McKinzie's co-conspirator, Dr. Duayne Christensen, a Westminster, California, dentist, had invested $6 million to open North America Savings in 1983. He was killed in a single-car freeway crash just hours before state regulators seized the thrift.[140] On March 29, 1990, Janet McKinzie was convicted of looting the S & L. After an 8-week trial, a jury found her guilty of 22 of 26 counts, including racketeering, conspiracy, bank fraud, and interstate transportation of stolen property. Her creative defense had centered around her self-portrayal as a "helpless victim" duped into carrying out the fraud because she was being pumped full of prescription drugs by the thrift's chairman, Dr. Christensen.[141] But prosecutors painted a dramatically different picture of the pair. They charged that the couple was a "modern day Bonnie and Clyde, stealing millions of dollars to enrich themselves."[142] McKinzie was sentenced to 20 years in prison and ordered to pay $13 million in fines. Numerous thrift outsiders were also convicted in related schemes.[143] The collapse of North America Savings and Loan cost taxpayers more than $120 million.[144]

In another infamous southern California case of S & L fraud, two former owners of Ramona Savings and Loan, Donald Mangano (who ran a construction company) and John Molinaro (a rug salesman), were handed sentences of 15 years and 12 years, respectively, as a result of looting their thrift between 1984 and 1986. The pair had used the thrift as a money machine for pumping up their other businesses, making loans to projects being built by Mangano and Sons Construction Company and carpeting the projects' floors with rugs purchased from Molinaro. The collapse of Ramona cost taxpayers approximately $70 million.[145] To their presumable relief, at least no one compared Mangano and Molinaro with Bonnie and Clyde.

"Outsider" Thrift Frauds

S & L fraud was not confined to insiders. Thrift officers were often joined in the largest scams by "outsiders" from various occupations and professional groups. Industry regulators and FBI investigators have reported that appraisers, lawyers, and accountants were among the most frequent co-conspirators; indeed, their compromised services made many of the S & L scams possible. Perhaps foremost in this regard were accountants, whose audits allowed many fraudulent transactions to go unnoticed. Professional accounting firms were highly paid for their services, and thus could easily turn a blind eye when evidence of wrongdoing surfaced. One study conducted by the General Accounting Office reports that of 11 failed thrifts in Texas, 6 involved such laxity on the part of auditors that investigators referred them to professional and regulatory agencies for formal action.[146]

Appraisers were central players in the epidemic of fraud as well. As assessors of property values, appraisers are essential to the real estate and banking systems. In some states where the thrift industry was particularly hard hit, such as Texas, the appraisal business is entirely unregulated. Like many other professionals involved in the thrift crisis, appraisers were susceptible to designing their results to meet clients' wishes, because they are particularly dependent on repeat business and referrals. Thrift regulators have reported that inaccurate and inflated appraisals were found in the wreckage of failed thrifts throughout the country.[147]

Accountants, lawyers, and appraisers interested in retaining lucrative contracts with S & Ls in the 1980s were confronted with the tension between safe banking procedures, legal statutes and fiduciary regulations, and professional standards on one hand, and the demands of their clients on the other. Periodically the line was crossed, or even erased, as these "outsiders" violated not only professional codes of conduct but, in some cases, the law. Much as the criminogenic environment of the S & Ls triggered insider abuse and fraud, the very structure of the relationship between insiders and professionals on the outside assured that some segment of those outsiders would become accomplices to fraud.

Criminal Networks

Another consistent theme in the S & L debacle is the degree to which the financial resources of the thrift industry and individual thrift executives enabled troubled S & Ls to secure the support of influential policymakers.[148] Regarding the collapse of thrifts in Texas, a staff member of the Senate Banking Committee predicted: "What you're going to find in these thrifts is a sort of mafia behind them. I don't mean Italians, but I'm using it in a generic sense: a fraudulent mutual support."[149]

The nature of many of the crimes permeating the thrift industry depended on this "mutual support." A Senate Banking Committee memo delineates the four most common forms of fraudulent transactions: land flips, nominee loans, reciprocal lending arrangements, and linked financing.

Land Flips.   In a land flip, a piece of property, usually commercial real estate, is sold back and forth between two or more partners, inflating the sales price each time and refinancing the property with each sale until the value had increased several times over. In one of the most infamous cases, a Dallas developer and his partner purchased a parcel of land outside of Dallas. They then sold it to each other inflating the price from $5 million to $47 million in less than a month.[150] The final loan was defaulted on, leaving the partners with hefty profits and the lending institutions with short-term points and fees. A flip scam requires an organized network of participants—at a minimum, two corrupt borrowers (who are often affiliated with the lending thrift) and a corrupt appraiser.

Nominee Loans.   Nominee loan schemes involve loans to a "straw borrower" outside the thrift who is indirectly connected to the thrift. Nominee loans are used to circumvent regulations limiting the permissible level of unsecured commercial loans made to thrift insiders. Don Dixon, the owner and operator of the infamous Vernon Savings and Loan in Texas, provides an extreme example of how nominee loans can be used in a fraudulent manner. Dixon established a network of over 30 subsidiary companies for the sole purpose of making loans to himself and other insiders.

Reciprocal Lending.   Reciprocal lending arrangements are similarly designed to evade restrictions on insider loans. These arrangements were used extensively in the mid-1980s by thrift officers and directors who, instead of making loans directly to themselves (which would have sounded an alarm among regulators), agreed to make loans to *each other*, with each loan contingent on receiving a comparable loan in return. One 1987 investigation in Wyoming revealed a "daisy chain" of reciprocal loans among four thrifts, which resulted in a $26 million loss to taxpayers.[151]

Linked Financing.   Finally, linked financing is "the practice of depositing money into a financial institution with the understanding that the financial institution will make a loan conditioned upon receipt of the deposits."[152] These transactions usually involved brokered deposits in packages of $100,000, the limit on FSLIC insurance. Deposit brokers often received a generous nonrecourse loan, which was frequently defaulted on, in return for these deposits.

Investigators and regulators report finding variations of these four basic "mutual support" scams over and over in their autopsies of insolvent S & L. In each of these schemes a network of participants is absolutely essential. Arthur Leiser, an examiner with the Texas Savings and Loan Department for 35 years, kept a diary and noted the relationships among S & L operators, developers, brokers, and a variety of borrowers. One network recorded by Leiser included 74 participants. According to Leiser's calculations, practically all the insolvent thrifts in Texas were involved in such networks.[153]

The conspiratorial quality of thrift frauds was not confined to Texas or the southwest. In a speech to the American Bar Association in 1987, William Weld, Assistant Attorney General and Chief of the Criminal Division at the Justice Department (later Governor of Massachusetts), declared, "We now have evidence to suggest a nationwide scheme linking numerous failures of banks and savings and loan institutions throughout the country."[154] That same year, the General Accounting Office reported that 85 criminal referrals had been made to the Department of Justice relating to the 26 insolvent thrifts in its study, involving 182 suspects and 179 violations of criminal law.[155]

These crimes were sometimes facilitated by connections between perpetrators and those in a position to shield them from prosecution. At the lowest level of field inspectors and examiners, evidence has surfaced of collusion with fraudulent thrift operators. One strategy of thrift executives was to woo examiners and regulators with job offers at salaries several times higher than their modest government wages. When "Erv" Hansen, owner of Centennial Savings and Loan in Santa Rosa, California, was questioned by examiners about his extravagant parties, excessive compensation schemes, and frequent land flips, he hired the Deputy Commissioner of the California Department of Savings and Loans, making him an executive vice-president and doubling his $40,000-per-year state salary. According to an interview with Hansen's partner, the new employee's chief assignment was to "calm the regulators down."[156] Similarly, Don Dixon at Vernon Savings hired two senior officials from the Texas Savings and Loan Department and, according to one official, "provided prostitutes along the way."[157]

Even more important than these relatively infrequent forms of explicit collusion were connections between thrift industry executives and elected officials. Not only was the powerful U.S. League of Savings and Loans, with its generous campaign contributions and lobbying efforts, a significant force behind the deregulation that provided the opportunities for fraud in the first place, but financial pressure was brought to bear by the operators of fraudulent institutions in order to avoid regulatory scrutiny. Although the "Keating Five" case is by far the most well-publicized instance of political influence-peddling to stave off official actions in response to thrift violations, it was only one card in a sinister deck. The repercussions of bribery and political corruption in the S & L tragedy go far beyond one or two institutions. The connections between former House Speaker Jim Wright, Congressman Tony Coelho, and thrift executives illustrate this pattern.[158] Such ties were replicated throughout the country, most notably in California, Texas, Arkansas, and Florida, where failures proliferated and losses soared. One senior official in Florida reported that to his knowledge, *all* the Florida thrifts that managed to stay open after insolvency did so with the help of their owners' and operators' well-placed political connections.[159]

Reflecting on Fraud

Representative Henry Gonzalez, Chair of the House Committee on Banking, warned FBI Director William Sessions of the urgency of dealing with thrift crime:

> The issue is very, very serious. We cannot allow . . . a loss of faith in the deposit insurance system. . . . Confidence is at the root of everything because if we lose the confidence of the people, no system will stand up to that.[160]

General Accounting Office Director Harold Valentine called thrift fraud and the financial collapse to which it contributed "perhaps the most significant financial crisis in this nation's history."[161] The Department of Justice referred to it as "the unconscionable plundering of America's financial institutions."[162] A senior staff member of the Senate Banking Committee explained the attention being given to thrift fraud:

> This industry is very close to the heart of the American economy! We teetered on the edge of a major, major problem here. Well . . . we got a major problem, but we teetered on the edge of a major collapse. . . . You know, all these [financial] industries could bring down the whole economy.[163]

In summary, the major federally funded study on S & L fraud and the response of the government to the ensuing debacle concluded the following:[164]

❖ Crime and deliberate fraud were extensive in the thrift industry during the 1980s, thereby contributing to the collapse of hundreds of institutions and increasing the cost of the taxpayer bailout.

❖ Deregulation of the thrift industry in the early 1980s, combined with continued deposit insurance, were key elements of a criminogenic industry environment. In particular, these policy changes increased the opportunities for fraud while decreasing the risks associated with fraud.

❖ Although there were numerous variations of fraudulent thrift deals, four basic types of transactions provided the vehicle for the most egregious frauds: land flips, nominee loan schemes, linked financing, and reciprocal lending. Further, frauds consisted generally of three types of misconduct: "desperation dealing," "collective embezzlement," and "covering-up."

❖ Thrift crimes typically involved networks of insiders, often in association with affiliated outsiders.

❖ Fraud was correlated with specific organizational characteristics at failed S & Ls. Institutions that were stock-owned, were less involved in the home mortgage market, and undertook strategies that led to dramatic growth in assets were the sites and vehicles for the most frequent, most costly, and most complex white-collar crime.

❖ The government response to thrift fraud focused on containing the financial crisis, rather than punishing wrongdoing per se.

❖ Despite the urgency of this response and its unprecedented scale, its effectiveness is limited by the complex nature of these frauds, resource constraints, interagency coordination difficulties, and inherent structural dilemmas related to financial regulation.

❖ A relatively high proportion of those formally charged in major thrift cases were convicted (91%), and of those, a significant proportion (78%) received prison sentences.

❖ Thrift offenders received relatively short prison sentences compared with those convicted of other federal offenses.

❖ Significant amounts of fraud will go undetected and a large proportion of individuals suspected of major thrift offenses will never be prosecuted.

One high official put the S & L crisis in particularly graphic terms when he compared the damage with a major environmental disaster, too enormous to be cleaned up effectively:

> I feel like it's the Alaskan oil spill. I feel like I'm out there with a roll of paper towels. The task is so huge, and what I'm worrying about is where can I get some more paper towels? I stand out there with my roll and I look at the sea of oil coming at me, and it's so colossal![165]

Given the best available evidence, at least one thing is certain from this sad chapter in American history—which makes it all the sadder: The incredible financial losses directly attributable to white-collar crimes that were discovered and recorded in official statistics on the S & L crisis represent only "the tip of the iceberg."[166]

Charles Keating—"A Not-So-Wonderful Life"

The collapse of Lincoln Savings and Loan of Irvine, California, the most expensive thrift failure (costing taxpayers more than $3 billion) is notorious not only because of its massive losses, but because it serves as a prime example of all the excesses and corruption which plagued the industry. The case of Lincoln Savings and its flamboyant owner, Charles H. Keating, Jr., was characterized by Congressman Gonzalez as nothing less than a "mini-Watergate."[167] Keating, a Phoenix real-estate developer, had an eclectic past. Once a national champion swimmer, Keating became a major antipornography crusader who traveled the country battling smut for Republican administrations. In 1980, he served as campaign manager for John Connally's ill-fated run for the Republican presidential nomination.[168] There was another side to Keating, however, which was conveniently forgotten when he was allowed to purchase Lincoln with junk bonds sold by Michael Milken and the now-defunct firm of Drexel Burnham Lambert. In 1979, Keating had settled charges brought by the SEC which alleged illegal and fraudulent transactions regarding his loans from a bank in his home state of Ohio.[169]

Keating bought Lincoln Savings and Loan in 1984 and quickly transformed it from a traditional small thrift that made home mortgage loans into his own (and his family's) personal money machine. Lincoln traded in junk bonds, huge tracts of undeveloped real estate, and Keating's "masterpiece"—the Phoenician Hotel in Scottsdale, Arizona. The resort was financially doomed from the start because of Keating's lavish spending on all aspects of the project; Keating embarked on a $260 million spending spree, which was made that much easier because it involved other people's money. Given its staggering cost, government regulators estimated that to turn a profit, the Phoenician would need to have a 70% occupancy rate with an average room cost of $500 per night.[170]

The preposterous Phoenician Hotel was not Keating's only questionable business practice, however. He used Lincoln to provide a steady source of funding to his real estate company, American Continental Corporation. The thrift became involved in a series of fraudulent real estate deals designed to pump money into Americian Continental. He named his son, a 28-year-old college drop-out and former busboy, chairman of the board of Lincoln and paid him nearly $1 million. Keating took nearly $2 million. In total, nearly $34 million was paid to the Keating family from the thrift and parent company.[171]

As government regulators discovered what was happening at Lincoln and other thrifts that were "flying high" (and blind) with reckless investments, Keating fought back using his political clout. Keating's lawyer, Lee Henkel, was appointed to the federal bank board and was soon embroiled in scandal after proposing a rule that directly favored Lincoln and only one other S & L. He resigned soon thereafter.[172]

(Continued)

Keating hired a slew of prestigious law firms, as well as an accountant from one of the country's largest firms, which for years had attested to the soundness of Lincoln's books, and paid him over $900,000 per year. He paid Alan Greenspan, who was to become the Chairman of the Federal Reserve Board, to prepare an economic report declaring that Lincoln was on sound financial footing. As writer Michael Waldman notes, "Greenspan's letter said that Lincoln was as sound as seventeen other 'thriving' thrifts. Within three years, sixteen of them would be bankrupt."[173] Keating also offered lucrative employment to his nemesis, Ed Gray, who was then chief S & L regulator, leading the charge against direct investments such as those that Lincoln recklessly had made. Gray refused Keating's offer.

Finally, and most ignominiously, Keating contributed $1.4 million to the campaigns and causes of five U.S. Senators who would later become known as the "Keating Five": Alan Cranston, Democrat from California; Dennis DeConcini, Democrat from Arizona; Don Riegle, Democrat from Michigan and chair of the Senate Banking Committee; John McCain, Republican from Arizona; and John Glenn, Democrat from Ohio and former astronaut. In 1987, Gray was called to a meeting in DeConcini's office, where he found Senators DeConcini, McCain, Cranston, and Glenn. In arguing for their "friend," DeConcini offered a deal which consisted of Lincoln making more traditional home loans if Gray would ease up on the direct investment rule and leave Lincoln alone.

Another meeting took place a week later with the full Keating Five, which also included the San Francisco regulators who were putting together the case against Lincoln. One of the regulators, Bill Black, took meticulous notes at the meeting which clearly indicate that the senators were attempting to thwart the government agency's actions regarding Lincoln. The regulators informed the senators that they were going to file a criminal referral with the Justice Department. Gray later stated that the Keating Five meetings "were exercises in naked political power on behalf of a major political contributor."[174]

When Ed Gray's term as Bank Board Chairman expired, M. Danny Wall, a self-described "child of the Senate," was appointed as his replacement. Wall had reportedly met with Keating several times and later took the San Francisco regulators off the Lincoln case. This was a curious move given the evidence they had amassed against the thrift. Lincoln remained in operation for 2 more years, during which time it continued to hemorrhage big losses.[175] In testimony before the House Banking Committee in 1989, before which Keating had refused to testify by invoking the Fifth Amendment, Wall admitted that he had bungled the Lincoln case: "We have all learned some tough lessons from this case. We made some mistakes."[176] This weak concession seemed to take the matter rather lightly. In testimony given by the two chief regulators in San Francisco whom Wall had removed from the Lincoln case, Wall and other top officials were accused of undercutting regulatory actions against Lincoln, despite strong evidence of wrongdoing.

William Black, who was one of the San Francisco regulators, was unequivocal about the stench of influence peddling hanging over the Lincoln investigation:

(Continued)

"Chairman Wall's instructions . . . to achieve a 'peaceful' resolution with Lincoln assured the outcome. All that remained was to negotiate the terms of the bank board's surrender."[177] Black further maintained that Lincoln was given effective veto power over which government officials would negotiate the case, which accountants would audit its books, and which officials would supervise its day-to-day activities.[178]

In April 1989, Keating's wild ride on the backs of taxpayers came to an end. The government seized Lincoln and uncovered what was described as "a web of fraud and deceit with few parallels in the history of finance."[179] New accountants, after careful review, concluded that Lincoln, through a series of phony real estate transactions, had been showing "profits" by giving its money away.[180] In 1989, the government filed a $1.1 billion racketeering lawsuit against Lincoln.

The Senate Ethics Committee held lengthy hearings on the actions of the Keating Five but found no impeachable offenses, although Cranston received the strongest reprimand. At the hearings, Gray responded indignantly to Cranston's accusations that he, Gray, had mischaracterized the nature of the meetings: "Your continuing efforts to, yes, intervene with regulators in behalf of Lincoln has occurred at the expense of taxpayers and perhaps even thousands of debt holders. I would hope that in the future, the taxpayers' interests—rather than political contributors—would be given the priority."[181] DeConcini boldly told the committee that his intervention on behalf of contributor Keating "was not only a right but an obligation."[182] Moreover, he accused the committee's counsel of "manufacturing" a case against the Keating Five.[183] In a deposition given to investigators, Cranston, a liberal Democrat, stated that Keating, a conservative Republican, had donated nearly $1 million to his political activities because Keating was a "patriot who believes in democracy."[184] In 1991, the Senate Ethics Committee found Cranston to have violated Senate rules by intervening on Keating's behalf while soliciting large campaign contributions from him.[185]

M. Danny Wall was later forced to resign as a result of the Lincoln mess. Calling for Wall's removal as chief S & L regulator, Congressman Gonzalez blamed Wall and other federal regulators for not stopping the looting of Lincoln by officials of American Continental and for allowing Lincoln to become Charles Keating's personal "cash machine."[186] Just days before Lincoln was seized by the government, Wall was still expressing confidence in Keating and arguing for alternatives to a federal takeover.[187]

In that same year, another more disturbing scam perpetrated by Keating came to light. It involved the illegal sale of junk bonds in Lincoln's parent real estate company, American Continental Corporation, also controlled by Keating. Over 20,000 customers, mostly elderly or poor, were tricked into buying the bonds at Lincoln branch offices through high pressure sales tactics, which had led them to believe that the bonds were government-insured. One company sales memo sounded like it had been cribbed from the sleaziest boiler room operation: "[T]he weak, meek and ignorant are always good targets."[188] Some of the victims had

(Continued)

invested their life's savings, thinking that the soon-to-be-worthless bonds were a safe haven for their retirement funds. One elderly man, who was distraught over losing his $200,000 life's savings in the Lincoln collapse, killed himself.[189]

In the meantime, Keating not only offered no apologies but went on the offensive, campaigning against the "injustice" which government regulators had perpetrated against him. Claiming that overzealous regulators had left him impoverished, Keating denied claims that he had hidden funds in foreign bank accounts.[190] Regarding his namesake senators, he said that they "had done darn well and should be congratulated."[191] Despite his cry of indigence, a few months later regulators filed a $40.9 million claim for restitution against Keating, charging him and his associates with using phony tax shelters and shady land deals to plunder Lincoln Savings.[192]

Keating legally challenged the government's takeover of his thrift. In denying Keating's claims, U.S. District Judge Stanley Sporkin ruled that the government was "fully justified" in seizing Lincoln, and noted that the thrift was "in an unsafe and unsound condition to transact business."[193] Judge Sporkin added that Keating and his accomplices had "abused their positions through actions that amounted to a looting of Lincoln."[194]

Finally, in September 1990, Keating and three others were indicted by a grand jury in Los Angeles on charges of securities fraud regarding the sale of almost $200 million in American Continental bonds at Lincoln branches.[195] A superior court judge refused to reduce Keating's $5 million bail, arguing that given his pursuit by regulators, creditors and prosecutors, "he has significant reasons not to stay around."[196] Bail was reduced, however, for Keating's co-conspirators, Judy J. Wischer, former American Continental president, and Robin S. Symes and Ray C. Fidel, both former Lincoln presidents.[197] After a month-long stay at the Los Angeles County Jail, Keating finally was released when a federal judge lowered his bail to $300,000.[198]

Keating was convicted on December 4, 1991, his sixty-eighth birthday. Still strongly proclaiming that the regulators were to blame for the demise of his financial empire, Keating was found guilty on 17 of 18 counts related to the sale of junk bonds at Lincoln Savings branches.[199]

Just 8 days after his conviction on state charges, Keating again pleaded innocent after a federal grand jury indicted him and 4 associates on 77 counts of racketeering, bank fraud, and other charges, culminating a $2\frac{1}{2}$-year investigation into the failure of Lincoln Savings and Loan.[200] Facing numerous investor and government lawsuits, Keating, the champion swimmer, was in way over his head and sinking fast. His insurance carrier refused to pay any additional legal bills, claiming that he had reached the $5 million limit on his policy.[201]

On April 10, 1992, Keating remained emotionless in court as he was sentenced to the maximum term of 10 years in prison by Judge Lance Ito[202] for duping Lincoln depositors into buying his uninsured bonds.[203] Keating's children and grandchildren wept as he was hauled off to jail after Ito denied his lawyer's request that he be set free on bail pending his appeal.[204]

(Continued)

In the biggest fraud trial ever, federal prosecutors rested their case against Keating in December 1992,[205] and in January, he and his son were found guilty of racketeering, conspiracy, and fraud.[206] Keating was convicted on 73 counts, while his son was found guilty on 64. The verdict exposed Keating, who was already incarcerated at the time on his state conviction, to a maximum of 525 years in prison.[207] The younger Keating was slightly less vulnerable—facing only 475 years.

Although the prospect of having the Keatings locked up for the rest of their lives no doubt gratified some of their defrauded investors, Keating's victims, who lost much or all of their life savings, had more immediate concerns. As one investor in Lincoln's worthless bonds put it, "The thing is now, where do we find his money?"[208] Government efforts to recoup Keating's loot were largely fruitless, however. Keating's 20,000-acre dream community, Estrella, the single largest real estate venture of Lincoln, was valued at less than 10 cents on the dollar.[209]

Before his sentencing on the federal charges, prosecutors had asked for a relatively stiff term of 25 to 30 years in prison, claiming that Keating had shown no remorse, despite convictions in two trials, and that he had perjured himself repeatedly and thus deserved extra punishment for obstructing justice.[210] As one assistant U.S. attorney explained: "Despite the findings of two criminal juries that he is guilty of fraud beyond a reasonable doubt, defendant Keating still refuses to shoulder any of the blame for the devastation his conduct caused. . . . Instead, he continues to blame everyone but himself."[211] In calling Keating's fraud "staggering in its proportion," a U.S. district judge sentenced him to 12 years and 7 months in prison for looting Lincoln Savings and Loan and defrauding investors in American Continental of more than $250 million.[212]

The state and federal convictions did little to make Keating repentant. In fact, he remained steadfast in his refusal to deliver the standard *mea culpa* declaration. That defiance set Keating apart from most of his upperworld criminal counterparts. Not only was he not sorry, he would not even pretend that he was. He again asserted that Lincoln's failure and his own legal and financial demise were caused by vindictive regulators who were out to get him.

In late 1993, the cost of liquidating the remaining assets of Lincoln Savings was raised to over $3.4 billion,[213] and subsequent estimates have gone even higher. In 1996, Keating won his appeal on the state securities fraud conviction, which meant that he had to serve "only" his 12-year federal sentence.[214] In overturning the state conviction, a federal appeals judge ruled that Keating's constitutional due process rights were denied because his state conviction was based on "nonexistent legal theory" and erroneous jury instructions from Judge Ito.[215]

Three years later, Charles Keating received more good news. On December 2, 1996, an appellate court overturned his federal convictions, finding that jurors in the case had improperly learned about his prior state court conviction. On November 9, 2000, the decade-long criminal case against Keating finally ended quietly as prosecutors formally withdrew fraud charges, representing the final act among state and federal cases and civil and government lawsuits against him. Still

(Continued)

unrepentant, he said he had learned his lesson: "Stay . . . out of the government's way. . . . Don't mess with the regulators."[216] It was reported that prosecutors dropped the case for practical reasons, including the deaths and old age of witnesses, the $4\frac{1}{2}$ years Keating had already served in federal prison, and his guilty plea in federal court.[217]

Whether a bank or thrift failure and investor loss of the magnitude of Lincoln Savings and Loan could happen again is doubtful. Observers were stunned at the scale of the losses. One thing is certain, however. As Michael Manning, a lawyer involved in unraveling Keatings "deals" noted, "[N]o thrift operator rivaled Keating's combination of risky investments, political influence, multimillion-dollar payments to family and friends and sheer, bold arrogance."[218] Charles Keating indeed earned the title of "poster boy" of the savings and loan debacle.

Financial institution fraud is, unfortunately, a very real and very costly part of American life. It takes many forms and exacts a gigantic social toll. Its victims are from all segments of society: corporations and employees, governments and taxpayers, young and old, rich and poor, professionals and blue-collar workers.

In a competitive marketplace, individuals and businesses are always hungry for higher returns on their investments. This can have a positive effect on financial services, keeping such companies efficient and opening new investment opportunities, as well as benefiting the entire economy. The same conditions, however, with too little regulation or enforcement oversight, can invite scam artists whose phantom organizations are designed only to bilk investors. The number of such fake institutions has risen dramatically according to federal banking authorities.[219] Swindlers play on human greed—the eternal quest for the "quick buck"—and lure their prey with promises of guaranteed high returns, typically much higher than more legitimate enterprises offer. The best advice to investors is also the oldest: If a deal sounds too good to be true, it probably is.

Shortly before Christmas in 1990, the *Wall Street Journal* held a private screening of *It's a Wonderful Life* for a panel of S & L experts. During the movie's stirring finale, as George Bailey's depositors bring him their hats and bowls and cookie jars filled with enough hard-earned cash to save his S & L, one of the panelists declared, "It's just what the taxpayers will do."[220]

NOTES

1. See: Fretts, Bruce. "Everybody's Favorite S & L Movie." *American Heritage.* February/March 1991: 62–63.
2. "O.C. Man Found Guilty of Indian Motorcyle Scam." *Los Angeles Times.* August 13, 1997: D6.
3. "BankAmerica Will Pay $187.5 Million to Settle Municipal-Bond Allegations." *Orange County Register.* November 13, 1998: B2.

4. "IRS Workers Embezzled $5.3 Million in Checks and Cash. *Washington Post.* November 16, 1998: 1.

5. "Blankenship Sentenced to Prison." *Los Angeles Times.* September 28, 1991: D2.

6. "Former High Official With FSG Financial Sentenced to Fraud." *Wall Street Journal,* May 27, 1992: B2.

7. "Ex-Air-Charter Official in New Jersey Gets 18-Month Sentence." *Wall Street Journal.* June 13, 1995: B4.

8. "Ex-Financial Planner Pleads Guilty." *New York Times.* February 9, 1995: D16.

9. "Ex-Chairman of Bank in Des Plaines, Ill., Gets Prison Sentence." *Wall Street Journal.* March 22, 1984: E18.

10. "Ex-Texas Bank Aide Gets 12-Year Sentence for Committing Fraud." *Wall Street Journal.* June 14, 1990: B8.

11. "Brokers Get Prison for Cheating Charity." *Los Angeles Times.* October 26, 2000: B7.

12. "Massachusetts Man Gets Prison Sentence in Bank-Fraud Case." *Wall Street Journal.* November 5, 1991: C22.

13. "Prison Term in S & L Case." *New York Times.* June 22, 1994: D8.

14. *Ibid.*

15. *Ibid.*

16. "Arkansas S & L Head Sentenced to Prison and Fined $75,000." *Wall Street Journal.* March 18, 1991: A9G.

17. Buettner, Michael. "Promoter Goes to Prison for Ponzi Scheme." *Tampa Bay Business Journal.* February 2, 1998: 5.

18. White, George. "Former Family S & L Chief Gets 7-Year Sentence." *Los Angeles Times,* April 23, 1991: D2.

19. *Ibid.*

20. Sanders, Edmund. "Bank of San Pedro Ex-CEO Gets Prison Term." *Los Angeles Times.* August 10, 1999: B3.

21. Myers, David W. "First Pension Allegations Spark 'Direct Participation' Concern." *Los Angeles Times.* May 18, 1994: D1.

22. Gomez, James M. "SEC Joins Hunt for $10 Million Missing From Investment Firm." *Los Angeles Times.* April 29, 1994: D2.

23. Hiltzik, Michael A. "Millions May Be Missing From First Pension Corp." *Los Angeles Times.* May 11, 1994: A1.

24. Hiltzik, Michael A. "SEC Says First Pension Ran Pyramid Scam." *Los Angeles Times.* May 14, 1994: D1.

25. Quoted in Vrana, Debora. "Investors Demand Answers on First Pension, Get None." *Los Angeles Times.* June 1, 1994: D1.

26. Quoted in Vrana, Debora. "Fraud Charges Filed in First Pension Scam." *Los Angeles Times.* July 26, 1994: D2.

27. *Ibid.*

28. *Ibid.*

29. Quoted in Vrana, Debora. "First Pension Chairman, 2 Partners Plead Guilty to Fraud." *Los Angeles Times.* August 2, 1994: D2.

30. Quoted in *Ibid.,* p. D2.

31. Quoted in *Ibid.,* p. D2.

32. Quoted in *Ibid.,* p. D2.

33. Granelli, James S. "First Pension Investors Sue State for $17 Million." *Los Angeles Times.* October 27, 1995: D6.

34. *Ibid.*

34. Hernandez, Greg. "O.C. Jury Finds Accounting Firm Liable for Fraud." *Los Angeles Times.* July 29, 2000: A1.

35. Ballon, Marc. "First Pension Investors Reach Settlement." *Los Angeles Times.* August 29, 2000: B1.

36. "First Pension Settlement Reached." *Los Angeles Times.* October 10, 2000: B2.

38. Stevens, Amy. "Wymer Pleads Guilty to Charges of Fraud Scheme." *Wall Street Journal.* September 30, 1992: B10.

39. *Ibid.,* p. B10.

40. Quoted in *Ibid.,* p. B10.

41. Black, William K., Kitty Calavita, and Henry N. Pontell. "The Savings and Loan Debacle of the 1980s: White Collar Crime or Risky Business?" *Law and Policy* 17, 1995: 23–55.

42. Gomez, James M. "Wymer is Guilty in Huge Fraud." *Los Angeles Times.* September 30, 1992: D1.

43. Quoted in *Ibid.,* p. D5.

44. "Money Manager Sentenced to 15-Year Term for Fraud." *New York Times.* May 13, 1993: D6.

45. Shiver Jube, Jr. "Wymer to Lawmakers: Collusion is Common." *Los Angeles Times.* March 5, 1993: D1.

46. Quoted in *Ibid.,* p. D4.

47. *Ibid.*

48. Headden, Susan, Witkin, Gordon, and Lord, Mary. "Preying on the Helpless," *U.S. World and News Report.* May 24, 1993: 48–52.

49. Hoge, Nettie. "Cracks in the Rock." *Dollars & Sense,* June 1992: 6–8.

50. Headden et al., *op. cit.*

51. *Ibid.*

52. *Ibid.*

52. Pulliam, Liz. "Seniors to Get Millions in Insurance Settlement." *Los Angeles Times.* December 30, 1998: A1.

53. "State Farm to Pay $200 Million to Settle Class-Action Lawsuit." *Los Angeles Times.* August 29, 1998: D3.

54. Pulliam, Liz. "Met Life to Pay $1.7 billion to Settle Lawsuits on Policy Sales." *Los Angeles Times.* August 19, 1999: C1.

55. *Ibid.*

56. *Ibid.*

58. Headden, et al., *op. cit.*

59. *Ibid.*, p. 48.

60. *Ibid.*, p. 50.

61. *Ibid.*

62. *Ibid.*

63. *Ibid.*

64. Quoted in *Ibid.*, p. 50.

65. *Ibid.*, p. 51.

66. Employment Retirement Security Act of 1974. P.L. 93–406.

67. U.S. Congress, Senate, Permanent Subcommittee on Investigations, Committee on Governmental Affairs, "Fraud and Abuse in Employer Sponsored Health Benefit Plans." 100 Congress, 2nd Session, May 15, 1990: 122. In the early 1990s, a number of states began to change their laws, with federal approval, so that MEWAs could be more closely regulated by state insurance commissions.

68. *Ibid.*, p. 51.

69. Tillman, Robert. *Broken Promises: Fraud by Small Business Health Insurers.* Boston: Northeastern University Press, 1998.

70. *Ibid.*

71. *Ibid.*

72. *Ibid.*

73. *Ibid.*

74. U.S. Congress. House, Committee on Energy and Commerce, Subcommittee on Oversight and Investigations. "Failed Promises: Insurance Company Insolvencies," February 1990. Washington, DC: Government Printing Office: 31.

75. *Ibid.*, p. 60.

76. Headden, Witkin, and Lord, *op. cit.*

77. *Ibid.*, p. 52.

78. *Ibid.*

79. *Ibid.*

80. *Ibid.*

81. *Ibid.*

82. *Ibid.*, p. 112.

83. Dannen, Frederic. "Miami vice." *Institutional Investor* 20, 1986: 170–174.

84. U.S. Congress, Senate, Permanent Subcommittee on Investigations, Committee on Governmental Affairs, "Efforts to Combat Fraud and Abuse in the Insurance Industry: Part II." 102nd Congress, First Session, June 26, 1991: 33.

85. U.S. Congress, Senate, Permanent Subcommittee on Investigations, Committee on Governmental Affairs, "Efforts to Combat Fraud and Abuse in the Insurance Industry: Part I." 102nd Congress, First Session, April 24, 1991: 22–53.

86. Ridenhour, Ron. "Plundered Lives." *Penthouse,* December, 1993: 58.

87. U.S. Congress, Senate, Permanent Subcommittee on Investigations, Committee on Governmental Affairs, "Efforts to Combat Fraud and Abuse in the Insurance Industry: Part III." 102nd Congress, 1st Session, July 19, 1991: 79.

88. *Ibid.*, p. 90.

89. U.S. Congress. House Committee on Ways and Means. 1989. Budget Implications and Current Tax Rules Relating to Troubled Savings and Loan Institutions: Hearings Before the Committee. 101st Cong., 1st sess. Washington, DC: Government Printing Office, 22 February, 2 and 15 March: 2; U.S. Congress. Senate Committee on Banking, Housing, and Urban Affairs. 1989. Problems of the Federal Savings and Loan Insurance Corporation (FSLIC): Hearings before the Committee: Part 3. S. Hrg. 101–127, 101st Cong. Washington, DC: Government Printing Office, 3, 7–10 March, 9; Hill, G. Christian. 1990. The Never Ending Story: An Introduction to the S & L Symposium. *Stanford Law & Policy Review* 2 (Spring):21–24.

90. Meigs, A. James and Goodman, John C. "What's Wrong with Our Banking System?" *Consumers' Research.* March 1991: 11–17.

91. Quoted in Sheehy, Sandy. "Super Sleuth—White-Collar Criminals Beware: Ed Pankau Is Looking for You." *Profiles.* July, 1992: 38.

92. Ely, Bert. "Crime Accounts for Only 3% of the Cost of the S & L Mess." Alexandria, Va.: Ely. Unpublished report, July 19, 1990.

93. See for example, Ely, 1990; White, Lawrence J. *The S & L Debacle.* New York: Oxford University Press 1991; Litan,

Robert E. Deposit Insurance, Gas on S & L Fire." *Wall Street Journal.* July 29, 1993, A10.

94. National Commission on Financial Institution Reform, Recovery and Enforcement. *Origins and Causes of the S & L Debacle: A Blueprint for Reform.* A Report for the President and Congress of the United States. Washington DC: Government Printing Office, July, 1993.

95. Black, William. "The Incidence and Cost of Fraud and Insider Abuse." Staff Report No. 13, National Commission on Financial Institution Reform, Recovery and Enforcement, 1993: 75 (emphasis in the original).

96. Resolution Trust Corporation. *Report on Investigations to Date.* Office of Investigations, Resolutions, and Operations Division, December 31, 1990.

97. U.S. General Accounting Office. *Thrift Failures: Costly Failures Resulted From Regulatory Violations and Unsafe Practices: Report to Congress.* GAO/AFMD-89-62. Washington DC: Government Printing Office, June, 1989.

98. U.S. General Accounting Office. *Failed Thrifts. Internal Control Weaknesses Create an Environment Conducive to Fraud, Insider Abuse and Related Unsafe Practices.* Statement of Frederick D. Wolf, Assistant Comptroller General, Before the Subcommittee on Criminal Justice, Committee on the Judiciary, House of Representatives. GAO/T-AFMD-89-4. Washington DC: Government Printing Office, March 22, 1989; United States Congress. House Committee on Government Operations. *Combating Fraud, Abuse, and Misconduct in the Nation's Financial Institutions: Current Federal Reports are Inadequate: 72d Report by the Committee on Government Operations.* H.Rpt No. 100-1088. 100d Cong., 2d sess. Washington DC: Government Printing Office, 13 October 13, 1988.

99. U.S. General Accounting Office. *Bank and Thrift Fraud: Statement of Harold Valentine, Associate Director, Administration of Justice Issues. Testimony Before the Subcommittee on Consumer and Regulatory Affairs. Committee on Banking, Housing, and Urban Affairs. U. S. Senate. Washington DC:* Government Printing Office, 6 February, 1992, 1.

100. Pizzo, Stephen, Mary Fricker, and Paul Muolo. *Inside Job: The Looting of America's Savings and Loans.* New York: McGraw-Hill, 1989.

101. Mayer, Martin. *The Greatest Bank Robbery Ever: The Collapse of the Savings and Loan Industry.* New York: Charles Scribner's Sons, 1990.

102. Quoted in Sheehy, *op. cit.,* p. 39.

103. DIDMCA; P.L. 92–221.

104. P.L. 97–320.

105. U.S. General Accounting Office. *Thrift Industry Restructuring and the Net Worth Certificate Program: Report to Congress.* GAO/GGD-85–79. Washington DC: Government Printing Office, 1985. 7.

106. Pizzo, et al., *op. cit.*

107. National Commission on Financial Institution Reform, Recovery and Enforcement, *op. cit.,* p. 47.

108. U.S. Congress. House. Subcommittee on Financial Institutions Supervision, Regulation and Insurance, Committee on Banking, Finance, and Urban Affairs. *Financial Institutions Reform, Recovery, and Enforcement Act of 1989 (H.R.1278): Hearings before the Subcommittee, Part 1.* Serial No. 101–12. 101st Cong., 1st sess. Washington DC: Government Printing Office, March 8, 9, 14, 1989, 286.

109. Meigs and Goodman, *op. cit.*

110. Eichler, Ned. The Thrift Debacle. Berkeley: University of California Press, 1989.

111. Calavita, Kitty, and Pontell, Henry N. "'Heads I Win, Tails You Lose': Deregulation, Crime and Crisis in the Savings and Loan Industry." *Crime & Delinquency* 36, 1990: 309–341.

112. House Committee on Government Operations, 1988, *op. cit.,* p. 34.

113. *Ibid.,* p. 46.

114. Coleman, James. Towards an Integrated Theory of White Collar Crime. *American Journal of Sociology* 93, 1987: 427.

115. Geis, Gilbert. "White Collar Crime: The Heavy Electrical Equipment Antitrust Cases of 1961." In Marshall Clinard and Quinney Richard (Eds.). *Criminal Behavior Systems: A Typology.* New York: Holt, Rinehart & Winston, 1967.

116. Farberman, Harvey A. "A Criminogenic Market Structure: The Automobile Industry." *Sociological Quarterly* 16, 1975: 438–457.

117. Lowy, Martin. *High Rollers: Inside the Savings and Loan Debacle.* New York: Praeger, 1991; Pilzer, Paul Z. and Dietz,

Robert. *Other People's Money: The Inside Story of the S & L Mess.* New York: Simon and Schuster, 1989; O'Shea, James. *The Daisy Chain: How Borrowed Billions Sank a Texas S & L.* New York: Pocket Books, 1991.

118. Pontell, Henry, Calavita, Kitty, and Tillman, Robert. "Fraud in the Savings and Loan Industry: White-Collar Crime and Government Response." Final Report of Grant #90-IJ-CX-0059 submitted to the National Institute of Justice, Office of Justice Programs, U.S. Department of Justice, October 1994.

119. Sheehy, *op. cit.,* p. 39.

120. Calavita and Pontell, 1990, p. *op. cit.*

121. Quoted in U.S. Congress. House Committee on Government Operations 1988, *op. cit.,* p. 34 (emphasis in the original).

122. U.S. Congress. House Committee on Government Operations 1988, *op. cit.,* p. 41; U.S. General Accounting Office, *Thrift Failures: Costly Failures Resulted From Regulatory Violations and Unsafe Practices: Report to Congress.* 1989, *op. cit.,* p. 19.

123. U.S. General Accounting Office, *Thrift Failures: Costly Failures Resulted From Regulatory Violations and Unsafe Practices: Report to Congress.* 1989, *op cit.,* p. 19.

124. Conklin, John E. *Illegal, But Not Criminal: Business Crime in America.* New York: Spectrum Books, 1977.

125. *Ibid.,* p. 7.

126. Sutherland, Edwin. *White Collar Crime: The Uncut Version.* New Haven: Yale University Press, 1983: 231.

127. Cressey, Donald R. *Other People's Money: A Study of the Social Psychology of Embezzlement.* Glencoe, Ill.: Free Press, 1953.

128. Calavita and Pontell, 1990, *op. cit.*

129. Sherman, Lawrence. *Scandal and Reform.* Berkeley: University of California Press, 1978.

130. Wheeler, Stanton and Rothman, Mitchell L. "The Organization as Weapon in White Collar Crime." *Michigan Law Review* 80, 1982: 1406.

131. U.S. Congress. House Committee on Government Operations 1988, *op. cit.;* U.S. General Accounting Office, *Thrift Failures: Costly Failures Resulted From Regulatory Violations and Unsafe Practices: Report to Congress.* 1989, *op. cit.*

132. Pontell, et al., 1994, *op. cit.*

133. *Ibid.*

134. U.S. General Accounting Office, *Thrift Failures: Costly Failures Resulted From Regulatory Violations and Unsafe Practices: Report to Congress.* 1989, *op. cit.*

135. *Ibid.,* p. 40.

136. Pontell et al., 1994, *op. cit.*

137. Kerry, John. "Where Is the S & L Money?" *USA Today Magazine.* September 1991: 20–21.

138. *Ibid.*

139. Murphy, Kim. "Racketeering Charged by U.S. in S & L Failure," *Los Angeles Times.* April 12, 1989: 1.

140. It may be worth noting that David Phillips speculates that many fatal single-vehicle "accidents" might be disguised suicides (Phillips, David P. "Suicide, Motor Vehicle Fatalities, and the Mass Media: Evidence Toward a Theory of Suggestion." *American Journal of Sociology* 84, 1979: 1150–1174).

141. Crouch, Gregory. "McKinzie Found Guilty in North America S & L Case." *Los Angeles Times.* March 30, 1990: D1.

142. *Ibid.,* p, D1.

143. Crouch, Gregory. "Santa Ana Thrift Figure Gets 20 Years." *Los Angeles Times.* July 21, 1990: A1.

144. *Ibid.*

145. Pizzo, et al., *op cit.*

146. U.S. General Accounting Office. CPA Audit Quality: Failures of CPA Audits to Identify and Report Significant Savings and Loan Problems: Report to the Chairman, Committee on Banking, Finance and Urban Affairs, House of Representatives. GAO/AFMD-89-45. Washington DC: Government Printing Office, February, 1989.

147. Calavita, Kitty, Pontell, Henry N., and Tillman, Robert H. *Big Money Crime: Fraud and Politics in the Savings and Loan Crisis.* Berkeley: University of California Press, 1997.

148. Pizzo, et al., *op cit.;* Adams, James R. *The Big Fix: Inside the Savings and Loan Scandal.* New York: John Wiley and Sons, 1990; United States Congress. House Committee on Standards of Official Conduct. *Report of the Special Outside Counsel in the Matter of Speaker James C.Wright, Jr.* Richard J. Phelan, Special Outside Counsel. 101st Cong., 1st sess. Washington DC: Government Printing Office, February 21, 1989.

149. Quoted in Calavita, Kitty, and Pontell, Henry N. "Savings and Loan Fraud as Organized Crime: Toward A Conceptual Typology of Corporate Illegality." *Criminology* 31, 1993: 534.

150. *New York Times.* "4 Convicted of Defrauding Texas Savings And Loan," November 7, 1991, C16; Pizzo, et al., *op. cit.*

151. United States Congress. House Subcommittee on Commerce, Consumer, and Monetary Affairs. Committee on Government Operations. *Adequacy of Federal Efforts to Combat Fraud, Abuse, and Misconduct in Federally Insured Financial Institutions: Hearing Before the Subcommittee.* 100st Cong., 1st sess. Washington DC: Government Printing Office, November 19, 1987: 79–80, 129–130.

152. U.S. Congress. House Committee on Government Operations 1988, *op cit.*, p. 42.

153. U.S. Congress. House Committee on Banking, Finance, and Urban Affairs. *Effectiveness of Law Enforcement Against Financial Crime (Part I): Field Hearing before the Committee, Dallas, Texas.* Serial No. 101–111. 101st Cong., 2d sess. Washington DC: Government Printing Office, April 11, 1990: 804–872.

154. Quoted in Pizzo, et al., *op. cit.*, p. 279.

155. U.S. General Accounting Office, 1989, *Thrift Failures, op. cit.*

156. Quoted in Pizzo, et al., *op. cit.*, p. 47.

157. Personal interview with Henry Pontell, Kitty Calavita, and Robert Tillman.

158. Jackson, Brooks. *Honest Graft: Big Money and the American Political Process.* New York: Alfred A. Knopf, 1988; U.S. Congress. House Committee on Standards of Official Conduct, 1989, *op cit.*

159. Pontell, et al., 1994., *op. cit.*

160. U.S. Congress. House Committee on Banking, Finance and Urban Affairs, 1990, *op. cit.*, p. 15.

161. U.S. General Accounting Office, 1992, *op. cit.*, p. 19.

162. U.S. Department of Justice. *Attacking Savings and Loan Institution Fraud: Department of Justice Report to the President.* Washington DC: Government Printing Office, 1990.

163. Personal interview with Henry Pontell, Kitty Calavita and Robert Tillman.

164. Pontell, Henry N., Calavita, Kitty and Tillman, Robert. "Fraud in the Savings and Loan Industry: White-Collar Crime and Government Response." Executive Summary of Grant #90-IJ-CX-0059, National Institute of Justice, Office of Justice Programs, U.S. Department of Justice, October, 1994: 42–45.

165. Quoted in Pontell, Henry N., Calavita, Kitty and Tillman, Robert. "Corporate Crime and Criminal Justice System Capacity: Government Response to Financial Institution Fraud." *Justice Quarterly* 11, September, 1994: 400.

166. *Ibid*, p. 395.

167. Waldman, Michael, *Who Robbed America?: A Citizen's Guide to the Savings & Loan Scandal.* New York: Random House, 1990: 92.

168. *Ibid.*

169. *Ibid.*

170. *Ibid*

171. *Ibid.*

172. *Ibid.*

173. *Ibid.*, pp. 94–95.

174. *Ibid.*, p. 97.

175. *Ibid.*

176. Quoted in Weir, Jeff. "Keating Takes the Fifth." *Orange County Register.* November 22, 1989: 1.

177. Quoted in Eaton, William J. "Top Regulator Blocked S & L Seizure, Panel Told." *Los Angeles Times.* October 27, 1989: A1.

178. *Ibid.*

179. Waldman, *op. cit.*, p. 97.

180. *Ibid.*

181. Quoted in Granelli, James S. "Senators, Ex-Regulator Waging War of Letters." *Los Angeles Times.* November 8, 1989: A15.

182. Quoted in Berke, Richard L. "DeConcini is Adamant on his Help for Keating." *New York Times.* January 10, 1991: A16.

183. Rosenblatt, Robert A. "DeConcini Lashes Out at Ethics Panel Counsel." *Los Angeles Times.* November 20, 1990: A1.

184. Quoted in Fritz, Sara and Rosenblatt, Robert A. "Keating Contributed as 'Patriot' Cranston Says." *Los Angeles Times.* November 30, 1990: A4.

185. Fritz, Sara. "Ethics Panel Says Cranston Broke Rules in Keating Ties." *Los Angeles Times.* February 28, 1991: A1.

186. Quoted in Fritz, Sara. "House Panel Assails Wall's Policy to 'Trust Keating.'" *Los Angeles Times.* November 22, 1989: A1.

187. *Ibid.*

188. Quoted in Waldman, *op. cit.*, p. 98.

189. Connelly, Michael. "Elderly Victim of Lincoln S & L Loss Takes Own Life." *Los Angeles Times*. November 29, 1990: A1.

190. Rosenblatt, Robert A. "Keating Vows to Keep Fighting to Regain S & L." *Los Angeles Times*. May 10, 1990: D3.

191. Quoted in *Ibid.*, p. D3.

192. Rosenblatt, Robert A. and Granelli, James S. "Keating, 5 Others Ordered to Pay $40.9 million." *Los Angeles Times*. August 10, 1990: D1.

193. Quoted in Jackson, Robert L. "U.S. Judge Denies Keating Challenge to Seizure of S&L." *Los Angeles Times*. August 24, 1990: D1.

194. Quoted in *Ibid.*, p. D1.

195. Granelli, James S. "Sealed Indictments Reportedly Name Keating, 3 Others." *Los Angeles Times*. September 18, 1990: D1.

196. Quoted in Granelli, James S. "Judge Refuses to Lower $5-Million Bail for Keating." *Los Angeles Times*. September 22, 1990: D1.

197. *Ibid.*

198. White, George. "Keating Got Star Treatment During Stay in County Jail." *Los Angeles Times*. October 20, 1990: D1.

199. Granelli, James S. and Bates, James. "Keating Guilty of Fraud; Faces 10-Year Term." *Los Angeles Times*. December 5, 1991: A1.

200. Granelli, James S. "Keating Indicted on New Charges of Bank Fraud." *Los Angeles Times*. December 13, 1991: A1.

201. Granelli, James S. "Keating Insurer Stops Paying His Legal Bills." *Los Angeles Times*. February 26, 1992: D1.

202. Ito, of course, would become the most famous judge in America 3 years later when he presided at the sensational O. J. Simpson murder trial.

203. "Keating is Sentenced to 10 Years for Defrauding S & L. Customers." *New York Times*. April 11, 1992: A1.

204. *Ibid.*

205. Granelli, James S. "Prosecutors Rest Case Against Keating." *Los Angeles Times*. December 2, 1992: D2.

206. Granelli, James S. "Keating, Son Guilty of U.S. Fraud Charges." *Los Angeles Times*. January 7, 1993: A1.

207. *Ibid.*

208. Quoted in *Ibid.*, p. A1.

209. Granelli, James S. "Keating's Dream is Devalued." *Los Angeles Times*. June 2, 1993: D1.

210. Granelli, James S. "U.S. Atty. Seeks 25 - to 30 -Year Keating Term." *Los Angeles Times*. July 3, 1993: D1.

211. Quoted in *Ibid.*, p. D2.

212. Quoted in Granelli, James S. "Keating Gets 12 Years in Federal Fraud Case." *Los Angeles Times*. July 9, 1993: A1.

213. Granelli, James S. "Forecast is Now $3.4 Billion to Liquidate Lincoln Savings." *Los Angeles Times*. October 31, 1993: D1.

214. Granelli, James S. "Keating's U.S. Appeal Takes on New Import." *Los Angeles Times*. April 5, 1996: D1.

215. *Ibid.*, p. D5.

216. Recard, Scott E. "Prosecutors Withdraw Charges Against Keating." *Los Angeles Times*. November 10, 2000: C1.

217. *Ibid.*, p. 2.

218. *Ibid.*

219. "Phantom Banks Bilk Investors Out of Millions." *Los Angeles Times*. September 12, 1994: D6.

220. Quoted in Suskind, Ron. "Help Me, Clarence! The Building & Loan Has Lost Billions!" *Wall Street Journal*. December 14, 1990: A1, A11.

Crimes by the Government

Reporter: What kind of stuff did you guys do?
Watergate Conspirator: Nickel and dime stuff.
Reporter: You mean when you sent out on Muskie stationary that Senator Hubert Humphrey was going out with call girls?
Watergate Conspirator: . . . So sometimes it got up to a quarter.

From *All the President's Men* (1975). Screenplay by William Goldman.

No area of white-collar crime is more infectious than crimes by the government. A government that breaks the law encourages emulation by other elite institutions. In 1928, Supreme Court Justice Louis Brandeis wrote a famous dissent in an early case involving the domestic surveillance of citizens, in which he warned that governmental lawlessness was "contagious." Brandeis further noted that persons in power who disregard or violate the Constitutional tenets upon which the United States was built place our political contract in jeopardy: "In a government of laws, the existence of the government will be imperiled if it fails to observe the law scrupulously."[1]

In this chapter, we will examine how some officials of the American government have discarded fundamental principles of democracy, civil liberty, and morality in the name of expedience. Three illustrative topics will be considered: (1) the use of human "guinea pigs;" (2) the violation of sovereignty; and (3) the abuse of power.

USE OF HUMAN GUINEA PIGS

Officially condoned abuses of unknowing or unwilling human subjects immediately suggest the crimes of the Third Reich, where military doctors performed hideous medical experiments on concentration camp prisoners. Without a doubt, no other society ever carried human experimentation to such a monstrous extreme; but the United States does have a shameful history of its own.

At the core of the Nazi atrocities was the concept of eugenics—the "improvement" of the human race through such practices as selective breeding and compulsory sterilization. Even before this perverted synthesis of social Darwinism and Mendelian biology was tried in Germany, the eugenics movement thrived in the United States. In fact, the United States and Germany remain the only "civilized" Western nations in which sterilization laws were ever enforced. By the time the infamous Nuremberg Laws were enacted in Germany in 1935, providing for sterilization of those who were considered genetically unfit to propagate the species, an estimated 20,000 Americans who were deemed feeble-minded or morally degenerate already had been sterilized—12,000 in California alone.[2]

In 1933, the *Journal of the American Medical Association (JAMA)* published a report entitled "Sterilization to Improve the Race." Although the subject of the report was Germany's new sterilization laws, the uncritical language helped provide American eugenics statutes with a veneer of scientific respectability:

> Countless individuals of inferior type and possessing serious hereditary defects are propagating unchecked with the result that their diseased progeny becomes a burden to society and is threatening within three generations to overwhelm completely the valuable strata. . . . [S]terilization is the only sure means of preventing the further hereditary transmission of mental disease and serious defects.[3]

Between 1924 and 1972, the state of Virginia sterilized over 8300 mentally retarded citizens.[4] This practice, rooted in what has been called the "biology of stupidity,"[5] was upheld by the U.S. Supreme Court in a landmark 1927 ruling in *Buck v. Bell.*[6] This case involved the first victim of Virginia's Compulsory Sterilization Law, a teenage girl named Carrie Buck, who had been committed to the notorious Lynchburg Colony for Epileptics and the Feeble-minded and subsequently was sterilized without her agreement or understanding.[7] Writing for the Court, Justice Oliver Wendell Holmes declared, "Three generations of imbeciles is enough."[8]

Lamentably, the fate of Carrie Buck was no aberration. The total number of Americans sterilized under eugenics statutes has been estimated at 63,000.[9] Although many of these laws have been repealed, sterilization without a subject's consent still was permitted in 14 states as recently as 1985.[10] In a more modern variation on this theme, a mother who was charged in 1991 with beating her children after she caught them smoking, was sentenced by a California court to a year in prison. A condition of her release on probation at the end of that period was that she be given the contraceptive drug Norplant, which must be implanted *surgically* in a woman's forearm.[11] Civil libertarians have expressed concern that such compulsory contraception violates medical ethics by involving doctors in operations that have nothing to do with medicine per se, and abrogates women's rights to control their procreative capacity.

As one observer has noted, "Far from being part of a new trend, these cases hark back to old-fashioned eugenics plans to 'improve' society by ensuring that 'undesirables' do not reproduce."[12]

It also is worth noting that one of the most widely discussed books in recent years is *The Bell Curve*[13] (1994), a pseudo-scientific affirmation of racially-based theories of intellectual inferiority. This book has been attacked by some critics as a harbinger of a potential revival of the eugenics movement in the twenty-first century.

C A S E   S T U D Y

The Tuskegee Syphilis Experiment

The best-documented human guinea pig case in American history is the Tuskegee Study of Untreated Syphilis in the Negro Male.[14] For 40 years, between 1932 and 1972, the United States Public Health Service (PHS), in cooperation with local health officials, withheld all treatment from more than 400 syphilitic men in an economically depressed, predominantly black county in rural Alabama. The purpose of the Tuskegee study was to compare the incidence of death and debilitation among untreated subjects with a sample of treated syphilitic men, as well as a healthy control group. "[S]yphilis is a highly contagious infection spread by sexual contact, and . . . if untreated, it can lead to blindness; deafness; deterioration of the bones, teeth, and the central nervous system; heart disease; insanity; and even death."[15] Syphilis may be transmitted to a fetus by an infected mother.[16]

All the untreated subjects were uneducated black sharecroppers and laborers. The Tuskegee study thus has to be viewed within the context of the ingrained racist beliefs permeating the American medical establishment of the time. The social Darwinism that had spurred the eugenics movement had generated a fallacious agreement "that the health of blacks had to be considered separately from the health of whites."[17] Many doctors thought that Africans were genetically predisposed toward sexual promiscuity. "In this atmosphere it was not surprising that physicians depicted syphilis as the quintessential black disease."[18]

The Tuskegee study emerged from a syphilis control survey that had been carried out by Alabama health officials in 1930 at the instigation of a local white plantation owner who had noticed a decline in the live birth rate among his 700 black tenants and had attributed it to syphilis. A curious feature of the program was its avoidance of the word "syphilis." Instead, the health officials told subjects that they had come to test people for "bad blood," a catchall phrase from the rural black argot, used for everything from indigestion to pellagra.[19]

The survey revealed even a higher incidence of syphilis than had been expected, so when the program was terminated in 1932, some doctors from the U.S. PHS perceived what one termed a "ready-made opportunity"[20] to study untreated syphilis in a living outside the world of modern medicine.

(Continued)

The afflicted men identified by the survey were sent an imposing letter, which invoked the authority of the Macon County Health Department, the Alabama State Board of Health, the U.S. PHS, and even Tuskegee Institute, the eminent college known as the "black Harvard."[21] The opening paragraph read:

> Some time ago you were given a thorough examination and since that time we hope you have gotten a great deal of treatment for bad blood. You will now be given your last chance to get a second examination. This examination is a very special one and after it is finished you will be given a special treatment if it is believed you are in a condition to stand it.[22]

The letter closed with an ominous exhortation, written in capital letters that jumped off the page: "REMEMBER THIS IS YOUR LAST CHANCE FOR SPECIAL TREATMENT."[23] In its skillful exploitation of the subjects' ignorance and desire for medical care, the letter was a "masterpiece of guileful deceit."[24] Among the "special treatments" in store were spinal taps performed without anesthesia.[25]

Participants were not told about the true nature of the experiment. The idea of the study was to observe the subjects over the course of their lives and eventually bring them to autopsy. Burial stipends would be provided to the families of the deceased. Over the next four decades, 161 autopsies were performed.

No therapeutic intervention was ever provided for the subjects, nor for their wives who invariably contracted the disease, nor for their children who subsequently were born with congenital syphilis. Even when antibiotics became available in 1946 and penicillin emerged as an effective drug for syphilis, treatment still was denied.[26] This is particularly troubling, because the advent of penicillin seemingly obviated any rational purpose to the experiment. As one PHS officer finally would acknowledge, 38 years too late: "Nothing learned will prevent, find, or cure a single case of infectious syphilis or bring us closer to our basic mission of controlling venereal disease in the United States."[27] Indeed, the only contribution the Tuskegee study ever made to medical science was keeping laboratories supplied with syphilitic blood samples for testing purposes. "The benefit seems small when one remembers that some of the blood donors later died from syphilis."[28]

In 1965, a young venereal disease investigator employed by the PHS, first heard about the ongoing Tuskegee study from co-workers; "He had difficulty believing the stories."[29] After reviewing all the articles and official documents on the experiment, he was horrified and began warning his superiors that the ethical and racial aspects of the study were potentially explosive: "The excuses and justifications that might have been offered for starting the study in 1932 were no longer relevant. . . . [Subjects] were nothing more than dupes and were being used as human substitutes for guinea pigs."[30]

Two years after joining the PHS, the investigator resigned. The following year he wrote a letter to the director of the Division of Venereal Diseases, reexpressing grave moral concerns about the experiment. In 1972, he finally told the "bad blood" story to the press. The outrage was predictable. Senator Abraham

(Continued)

Ribicoff labeled the Tuskegee study a "frightening instance of bureaucratic arrogance and insensitivity."[31]

Seventy surviving subjects sued the government, and in 1974 an Alabama court awarded each $37,500. When divided by 40 years, that sum worked out to $2.50 per day.[32]

The "bad blood" study was by no means the government's only 40-year excursion into human experimentation. From 1938 to at least 1978, "there was an effort made by the agencies of the U.S. government to develop sophisticated techniques of psycho-politics and mind control."[33] This dangerous research involved tens of thousands of subjects—many of them involuntary.[34] These unwitting human guinea pigs were victimized by an amoral cadre of psychiatrists, psychologists, and chemists under contract to various government agencies, most notably the CIA.[35]

Among the areas under study were: (1) the use of hypnosis to induce amnesia or elicit false confessions;[36] and (2) the refinement of powerful conditioning techniques, such as sensory deprivation, desensitization, and aversion therapy, to control human behavior.[37] In the words of one journalist, these and other methods "were eventually developed and used to reduce some of our own citizens to a zombie state in which they would blindly serve the government."[38] In 1958, the Central Intelligence Agency (CIA) even prepared a report which suggested that intelligence agencies might control people through drug addiction. "The report went so far as to recommend that wounded GIs who had become addicts to pain-killing drugs be recruited from hospitals."[39]

One of the most chilling examples of mind control research was that of Dr. David Cameron at the Allen Memorial Institute in Montreal, Canada. The "brainwashing" experiments Cameron conducted between 1957 and 1963 were funded by the CIA. A Canadian facility was utilized because Cameron's work was so repulsive in nature that, for once, the CIA was apparently unwilling to violate the proscription against the conducting of domestic operations by the agency.

Cameron specialized in two mind-control techniques: *depatterning* and *psychic driving*. The objective of depatterning is the disintegration of a subject's personality. This was accomplished through: (1) repeated electroconvulsive shock treatment—at levels up to 40 times the intensity considered safe; (2) massive doses of hallucinogenic drugs, including LSD; and (3) lengthy periods of drug-induced sleep, lasting as long as 90 days.[40] Psychic driving is aimed at breaking down a subject's free will. Individuals were locked in a darkened cell and bombarded incessantly with selected messages. These unfortunate subjects were the hospitalized mental patients at Allen Memorial. Cameron's work destroyed the minds, bodies, and lives of his victims.[41] That it was financed and supported by the American government compounds the outrage.

The CIA, in fact, has a long history of complicity in medical abuse. Its immediate predecessor, the Office of Strategic Services (OSS), once tested the effects of concentrated marijuana on suspected communists.[42] When the CIA began experimenting with LSD in the early 1950s, it determined that members of the borderline underworld would make the best subjects, because even if they realized that they had been drugged, they would not go to the police. LSD was administered covertly to prostitutes, addicts, and petty criminals. One agent even slipped some LSD to a lieutenant of mob boss Lucky Luciano.[43] "[The CIA] reasoned that if they had to violate the civil rights of anyone, they might as well choose marginal people."[44]

In 1953, the agency decided to test LSD on a group of unsuspecting scientists from the Army Chemical Corps; the drug was mixed into their after-dinner drinks. "The dose pushed one of its victims—Frank Olson—into a psychotic confusion; several days later . . . Olson [apparently] leapt to his death from a New York hotel window."[45] For 26 years, the cause of Olson's death had been concealed from his family, who had been led to believe that he had committed suicide because of an unexplained mental breakdown.[46] When Olson's family finally were told the circumstances of his death, they questioned that he had jumped. On June 2, 1994, more than 40 years after Frank Olson's purported leap, his body was exhumed. Forensic remains revealed that "[s]kull injuries and the lack of cuts on the body were inconsistent with the CIA's description of events surrounding his death."[47] Whatever really happened to Frank Olson seems destined to remain a mystery.

The first Director of the CIA, Allen Dulles, had approved another early method of testing mind-altering drugs on unwitting subjects. "[A]n arrangement had been made with the Bureau of Narcotics whereby the CIA financed and established 'safe houses' in which federal narcotics agents could dispense the drugs and record the reactions of those who took them."[48] The San Francisco "safe house" even employed prostitutes,[49] who would drug their customers, whose behavior then would be observed by agents through two-way mirrors.[50] The victims were chosen randomly in bars and off the street. Many of these unwary "johns" subsequently required hospitalization.[51]

During the Cold War, the CIA also tested knockout drugs and incapacitating substances at Georgetown University. These experiments were disguised as legitimate "anticancer" research. "[T]he pool of subjects consisted of terminal cancer patients who had no idea they were being used as guinea pigs in a CIA drug project."[52]

The CIA is not the only branch of the government with a record of questionable involvement in human experimentation. The military had engaged in unethical medical practices at least since 1900, when Dr. Walter Reed used Army volunteers to test his theory that deadly yellow fever was transmitted by mosquitoes. Reed's soldiers permitted themselves to be bitten by infected insects. Medical historians now wonder how much the Army had pressured these "volunteers" to risk contracting a disease for which there was no known treatment.[53] Researchers funded by the U.S. Army once fed hepatitis viruses to retarded infants at New York's Willowbrook State School.[54]

Moreover, the Army itself conducted covert germ warfare tests over a 20-year period. In 1950, the Army blanketed the San Francisco region with a microorganism called *Serratia marcescens*. "Worried about the effects of lethal germs that might be sprayed by the Soviet Union on an unsuspecting American public, the Pentagon had decided to unleash its own, supposedly harmless, bacteria into the air and trace the germs along their windblown journeys until they settled into the lungs of American citizens."[55] Although the Army still maintains that *S. marcescens* is harmless, there is considerable evidence that it can be lethal. "In the late 1970s, doctors in the San Francisco area reported a surge of infections and death caused by *Serratia marcescens*."[56]

One of the Army's most brazen experiments took place over a 4-day period in 1966. Another microorganism, *Bacillus subtilis*, was dumped into the heart of the New York City subway system. A report on this test, released later under the Freedom of Information Act, described the scene:

> "When the cloud engulfed people," the report says, "they brushed their clothing, looked up at the grating apron and walked on." . . . The experiment was a huge success. Everyone was breathing the bacteria and no one was ever aware of it.[57]

> *B. subtilis* is nearly indestructible, and most of the bacteria dropped in 1966 may remain throughout the twenty-first century.[58]

> [H]ow dangerous is *Bacillus subtilis?* It is dangerous indeed if one happens to be allergic to it, or is very old, very young, very ill or very anything that classifies a person as a compromised host. Might such people have been riding the subways? Of course. But beyond that, the exposed commuters became carriers, and took the bacteria with them as they traveled to their homes, to their offices or to hospitals to visit elderly relatives.[59]

A spokesperson for the Army's scientific division defended its simulated biological warfare tests by characterizing them as less hazardous than an urban bus ride:

> "[W]hen you get on the bus in Philadelphia or New York, you're going to be riding with a bunch of people—the Chinese, the Vietnamese, the blacks, the lower-class Irish and all these people—that may have tuberculosis and never know it, and be coughing in your face, and end up exposing you to a far more serious type of organism than what was being sprayed into the air."[60]

The bigotry and contempt for humanity that oozes out of every crack in the preceding statement goes a long way toward answering the inevitable "How could they do that?" question.

The use of unsuspecting human guinea pigs is not unique to the Army, however. In the late 1950s, doctors working for the Air Force fed about 100 Alaskan Eskimos radioactive drugs to test nuclear survival in Arctic Climates.[61] As recently as 1972, the Air Force was supporting LSD research at the Universities of Missouri and Minnesota. One misled subject, an 18-year-old girl, went into a catatonic state for 3 days.[62]

The U.S. Navy has the distinction of overseeing perhaps the most sickening of all the military experiments. The Navy earned this dubious honor between 1943 and 1945 because the research in question was so gruesome that even the Army was reluctant to participate. At a time when the horrors of Auschwitz were still hidden from the world, the Navy was building its own gas chamber, not in Eastern Europe but in Washington, DC and Maryland.

> [Y]oung Navy men were sealed in cinder block chambers behind steel doors and were doused with mustard gas, one of the most insidious chemical weapons ever devised. . . . The researchers wanted to know just how much chemical exposure a man could take under various conditions. But the sailors were told neither the nature of the experiments nor the likely consequences.[63]

As always, military secrecy provided a permissive environment for cruelty and abuse. Wartime documents reveal that the sailors were ordered into the chambers and threatened with court-martial if they refused.[64] "By all accounts, the U.S. military researchers who sent young 'volunteers' into gas chambers . . . stood by dispassionately, writing reports, while mustard gas burned the men's skin and seared their lungs."[65] One experimental report concluded:

> The scrotal region was the most vulnerable area of the body to H vapor [mustard gas] and would be the most important area in the production of casualties. It was found that ulcerated and crusted lesions of the ponoscrotal region required from three to four weeks to heal.[66]

Some of the experiments were termed "man break tests," meaning the exposure to mustard gas continued until the subject was "broken."[67] One of those "broken" was a 17-year-old sailor, who had just completed his basic training in mid-winter. He was asked to volunteer to test clothing under tropical conditions. Thinking he would be sent to a warmer climate, he put his name on the list. In fact, he traveled only 25 miles, and the "tropical clothing" consisted of a gas mask. His memory of that day remains vivid:

> I passed out in the chamber. When I came to I was lying beside the road on a pile of snow. I had thrown up in my gas mask. . . . I thought they had left me there for dead.[68]

Today, 50 years later, he is totally disabled. "He has had two open-heart operations, skin cancer, brain hemorrhages, chronic bronchitis and blood clots in his legs."[69]

Unfortunately, philosopher George Santayana's familiar warning about the consequences of failing to learn from the past[70] was punctuated during the Persian Gulf War in 1990. An unapproved pretreatment drug for nerve gas attacks, which had never undergone clinical testing, was administered to American soldiers without their consent. Members of the armed forces who were ordered to take the drug "have begun coming forward to say they are suffering serious long-term side effects."[71]

Radiation Experiments

In November 1993, a newspaper in Albuquerque, New Mexico, uncovered documents revealing that the government had injected 18 civilians with highly radioactive plutonium during the 1940s to determine to what doses workers could be exposed safely. Rumors of widespread secret radiation testing, which had been circulating for decades, could no longer be officially dismissed. A week after the Albuquerque story broke, the government acknowledged that it had conducted 800 radiation tests on humans, some of whom were unaware of the risks. As the scandal unfolded over the following year, it became apparent that there was plenty of blame to go around.

The now-defunct Atomic Energy Commission (AEC), for example, sanctioned research at the University of Chicago in the 1950s involving the cremation of 44 newly deceased infants and the chemical analysis of residual radioactive material in their ashes.[72] This designated "Chicago Baby Project" was meant to determine the fallout effects from the nuclear weapons tests of that period. Official reports indicated that parents probably were not notified or asked permission for the use of their children's corpses in the experiments.[73] In another AEC-sponsored study at Massachusetts General Hospital, researchers injected pregnant women with radioactive iodine 24 hours before scheduled therapeutic abortions. A day later, the doctors then removed the fetuses intact to measure how much radiation was absorbed in the thyroid glands.[74]

The AEC also practiced human experimentation on live subjects at least through the late 1960s, when 14 workers at the Hanford nuclear weapons plant in Washington State were purposefully exposed to promethium, a substance used in the manufacture of atomic bombs.[75]

Mentally retarded teenaged boys at the Fernald State School in Massachusetts were used as guinea pigs in radiation studies sponsored by the AEC and conducted by Harvard University and the Massachusetts Institute of Technology (MIT) between 1946 and 1956. The boys were fed radioactive milk and breakfast cereal in order to study the body's digestive ability.[76] These innocent "volunteers" were told that they were joining a "science club."[77]

In late 1997, MIT and Quaker Oats agreed to pay $1.85 million to 15 former residents of the Fernald School who were fed radiation-spiked breakfast cereal in nutrition experiments conducted in the 1940s and 1950s. This research, designed to give Quaker Oats a competitive advantage in the cereal market, was conducted without the informed consent of the children's parents.[78]

Researchers from Harvard and Boston University fed radioactive iodine to 60 mentally retarded children at the Wrentham State School, also in Massachusetts, in the early 1960s in order to test a possible antidote to fallout from nuclear blasts.[79] In 1994, a state panel condemned this research in unmistakable terms: "For government researchers concerned about radioactive fallout to use institutionalized children is an insult to the children, their families and to everyone concerned with individual rights and dignities."[80]

The Defense Department, too, has engaged in questionable radiation experiments on humans. During the 1950s, substantial amounts of radiation were released into the environment as a part of a secret military program aimed at developing a weapon that would kill enemy soldiers with radioactive fallout. In at least 12 underground tests, conducted at the Los Alamos Laboratory in New Mexico, the Army detonated conventional bombs containing large concentrations of nuclear materials. In some cases, the ensuing radioactive cloud of particles was detectible in communities 70 miles away.[81]

To medical researchers, who were more interested in obtaining federal funds and winning academic honors than in maintaining ethical standards, the poor were an especially appealing target for human experimentation. One scientist defended the use of "charity" patients as an economically fair exchange of services: "We were taking care of them, and felt we had a right to get some return from them."[82] For example, a team of researchers from Tulane University conducted a series of radiation experiments at New Orleans' Charity Hospital in 1946, under a grant from the U.S. War Department (the forerunner of the Defense Department). These experiments involved at least 300 patients.

> For more than a decade, mostly black female patients swallowed or were injected with the radiation equivalent of up to 100 chest x-rays in one experiment as researchers studied how quickly the human body could process radioactivity. The research could be unpleasant, sometimes requiring test subjects to endure 118-degree heat, intestinal blisters or diarrhea.[83]

At the time, Charity Hospital was a manifestation of an overtly racist society. The facility was woefully overcrowded and underfunded; 25 patients might share a single toilet, "and the bedridden could suffer malnutrition if family members did not feed them."[84] In a 1994 interview, a former member of the Tulane research team portrayed the radiation experiments as a blessing to the "lucky" subjects:

> The patients that we used for research really loved us. They really did. . . . They got the most attention. We saw them several times a day. We cared about their diets.[85]

However, a less philanthropic retrospective was provided by the vice-chancellor for research at Tulane Medical Center:

> "The whole population of the hospital was used for guinea pigs. You could pick anyone you wanted and do any tests you wanted to. No one would ask any questions."[86]

Between 1942 and 1946, the U.S. Army conducted research in which dying patients were exposed to powerful x-rays in order to examine the effect of radiation on the body. One subject was a California house painter believed to be suffering from terminal stomach cancer. He was injected with plutonium at a level "many times the so-called lethal textbook dose."[87] He was never told the nature of the experiment and, in a gruesome good news/bad news scenario, a biopsy performed the next day revealed that he had an ulcer, not cancer.

Another experimental subject abused by the Army was a 17-year-old soldier who, in 1957, was ordered to stand up a few thousand yards from ground zero and watch the detonation of a hydrogen bomb.[88] "In 1988, at the age of 49, he had already suffered two strokes, deterioration of the spine and muscle weakness so severe he was confined to a wheelchair."[89]

Between 1960 and 1972, the Defense Department sponsored research at the University of Cincinnati Medical School in order to discover how much radiation a soldier could endure before becoming disoriented.[90] A total of 86 cancer patients, ranging from 9 to 84 years of age, were exposed to intense doses of radiation at levels "that were known to make people acutely ill."[91] Most of these hapless patients were indigent; 60% were black.[92] Nine of the first 40 subjects died within 38 days.[93]

When the Cincinnati researchers first published their findings in 1969 in the *Archives of General Psychiatry*, they insisted that informed consent had been obtained from each subject.[94] According to the Nuremberg Code of 1947—a statement of internationally recognized bioethical principles composed by the War Crimes Tribunal—informed consent is an absolutely inviolable requirement for human experimentation.[95] However, the Cincinnati researchers also reported that their 16 initial subjects had a mean educational level of 4.2 years, a low-functioning mean IQ, and strong evidence of cerebral organic deficit.[96] It is highly questionable if the notion of "informed consent" can be applied to such subjects in any meaningful way. Moreover, the very title of the article, "Total and Half Body Irradiation: *Effect on Cognitive and Emotional Processes* [italics added]," suggests that "cancer therapy was *not* the true purpose of the research."[97]

In 1994, Dr. David Egilman of Brown University analyzed the Cincinnati study and came to a disturbing conclusion: The "terminal" subjects were not even terminally ill. Egilman contends that most of the subjects were in relatively good health prior to irradiation, and that at least 8 and probably more than 20 of them died as a result of the experiment.[98]

Following an exhaustive 2-year archival study of classified documents undertaken by the Department of Energy at the request of President Clinton, the federal government admitted in 1995 that 4000 radiation experiments had been conducted between 1945 and 1974.[99] Most of the subjects were infants, pregnant women, terminally ill patients, poor people, or other vulnerable targets.[100] As one professor of medicine has observed: "That's the history of human experimentation. It's always using the poor or women, never white middle-class men."[101] Among the more exploitative examples of such studies are the following:

❖ Washington University researchers injected about 140 children, most of them healthy newborns or premature infants, with radioactive sodium. Likewise, researchers at the Beth Israel Hospital in Boston injected tracer doses of radioactive sodium into terminally ill patients.[102]

❖ Columbia University researchers also gave 880 pregnant women tracer doses of radioactive sodium. Today, of course, doctors "strongly urge pregnant women to avoid radiation exposure."[103]

❖ Researchers at Vanderbilt University gave 819 pregnant women radioactive iron to determine its effect on fetal development.[104] "A follow-up study of children born to the women found a higher-than-normal cancer rate."[105]

❖ A research team from the Massachusetts General Hospital injected or fed radium to 20 elderly residents of a nursing home to measure the passage of that substance through their bodies. This same hospital also injected 12 terminal brain tumor patients with uranium to determine the dose at which kidney damage begins to occur.[106]

❖ Researchers at Boston's Brigham and Women's Hospital injected subjects with radioactive sodium, then removed a section of rib to see how much had been absorbed into the bones.

❖ Doctors from Harvard Medical School gave kidney transplant patients the equivalent of 65 chest x-rays to see how the exposure would affect the risk of organ rejection. The study ended abruptly when the radiation killed 1 patient within 28 days.[107]

The principal objectives of these studies was "to determine how quickly the radioactivity was digested or absorbed by the human body and how much damage it caused."[108] In 1994, the chair of the congressional subcommittee that had investigated the propriety of the radiation experiments stated, "The appalling truth is that in some cases American citizens were used as nuclear calibration instruments."[109]

Finally, it is worth pondering that in the United States, *no one* has ever been convicted of a crime involving the violation of the right to informed consent in a medical experiment that has caused harm.[110]

Prison Experiments: Who Gives a Damn?

Another controversial form of human experimentation is the use of American prisoners as subjects for medical research. In a 1950 memorandum to the Atomic Energy Commission, Dr. Joseph Hamilton of Livermore National Laboratory in California expressed his concern that "tests aimed at discovering at what level radiation would injure soldiers would conjure up images of Nazi concentration camp experiments if performed on humans."[111] Indeed, after World War II, the issue of experimentation on prisoners was stressed at the Nuremberg War Crimes trials.

Obviously, informed consent had no relevance to the Nazis, but in the United States participation usually is "voluntary," in the technical sense that prisoners must sign consent forms and waivers. However, the psychological defenselessness of a captive role makes genuine consent illusory. "[B]ecause a prisoner has limited choices, his consent to such experimentation cannot be obtained without at least the appearance of coercion."[112] The American Civil Liberties Union has estimated that approximately 10% of the American prison population participates in medical and drug experiments.[113]

In 1961, some Harvard University scientists gave a group of inmates at the Concord State Prison in Massachusetts between two and five doses of pellocybin, a dangerous hallucinogenic drug. This research was directed by the flamboyant psychopharmacologist, Timothy Leary.

> He once used Harvard students in some of his drug experiments, and Harvard fired him two years after the Concord experiment when his own drug usage became public. . . . Later on, he was imprisoned for smuggling hashish from Afghanistan. President Nixon once described him as "the most dangerous man in America."[114]

The purpose of the Concord prison study was to test whether pellocybin could reduce the high recidivism rate among parolees. All of the participating inmates were chosen because they were scheduled for parole within 3 months. By 1965, 4 years after receiving the drug, 59% of the subjects were back behind bars.[115]

Between 1963 and 1971, 131 inmates in Washington and Oregon agreed to have their testicles exposed to very high levels of x-rays. This experiment was designed by the government to determine the minimum dose that would cause healthy men to become sterile. Although consent forms did indicate some of the risks, no mention was made that radiation could cause testicular cancer. Furthermore, no follow-up studies were ever conducted on the prisoners after the conclusion of the study.[116] A 23-year-old convict, for example, had his testicles bombarded with a dose of radiation equivalent to 20 x-rays in 1965. He had received a stipend of $5 for his participation. Thirty years later, he complained of lumps on his body, along with testicular pain and chronic rashes. Other ex-convicts from similar studies have voiced the same complaints.[117]

At some prisons, pharmaceutical corporations have competed vigorously to purchase exclusive rights to conduct drug toxicity tests on inmates.[118] In 1975, some prisoners testified at a U.S. Senate hearing concerned with human experimentation. One was James Downey, who had been a state prisoner in Oklahoma:

> He told of having participated in a planned thirty-day program to test a potent new drug intended to cure liver ailments. Downey said he was told it was a new "wonder" drug, and was assured it would have no adverse effects.[119]

After receiving the "wonder" drug for 11 days, Downey became very sick. He was denied any medical attention for several days and then was told he had measles. He was assured that his illness was unrelated to the drug; but Downey later learned that he was suffering from drug-induced hepatitis.[120]

From the experimenters' point of view, there are two reasons why prisoners make convenient human subjects. First, because the studies take place in an outcast environment, if prisoners such as James Downey become seriously ill—or even if they happen to die—it is unlikely to generate much public concern.[121] Second, prison studies are economical. Downey told the Senate that he had volunteered in order to earn money for cigarettes. One doctor has remarked that prisoners are ideal for medical experimentation because they are "cheaper than chimpanzees."[122]

VIOLATION OF SOVEREIGNTY

In Chapters 4 and 5, we examined how American corporations have exported environmental crime and crimes against employees. There is, unfortunately, nothing unique about this pattern; most domestic varieties of white-collar crime also have been committed abroad, either by American companies or by the United States government itself. These offenses range from bribery and covert manipulation to outright interference in the affairs of other nations.

Bribery of government officials is commonly used to obtain business contracts in many foreign countries. This practice is often concealed in company books under such euphemistic entries as "facilitating payments."[123] Although bribery violates both American and international law, it has continued for many decades because the penalties seldom exceed the gains.[124] During the 1970s, nearly 400 American corporations admitted making payments totaling $750 million to foreign officials.[125] Among the more notorious examples were the following:

❖ Mobil Oil contributed nearly $2 million to Italian political parties, concealing this information from its own stockholders. Exxon later admitted to a Senate subcommittee that it had given over $50 to Italian politicians, including some communists.[126]

❖ The Northrup Corporation passed on cash "gifts" of $450,000 to two Saudi Air Force generals, who in turn helped Northrup close a massive arms deal with the Saudi Arabian government.[127]

❖ Lockheed admitted that it had spent more than $22 million on payments to foreign officials and political organizations, in such places as Indonesia, Iran, and the Philippines. Lockheed also had paid Prince Bernhard of the Netherlands $1 million to arrange the sale of its planes to the Dutch government. Moreover, Lockheed's bribery of Japanese government officials led to the worst political scandal in that nation's postwar history.[128]

❖ Two units of Litton industries pleaded guilty in 1999 to fraud and conspiracy involving illegal payments the company made to obtain defense business in Greece and Taiwan. The company agreed to a fine of $16.5 million and an additional $2 million to reimburse the Justice Department for the cost of its investigation.[129]

American corporations long have insisted that political bribery is a traditional and necessary cost of doing business overseas.[130] This self-serving argument ignores the considerable damage that corporate bribery inflicts on our national image abroad. It also disrespects the principle of national sovereignty, which is the cornerstone of global order. For example, a single corporation— Lockheed—effectively toppled a government in Japan, nearly destroyed the Dutch monarchy, corrupted national elections in Germany, Portugal, and Brazil, and caused the arrest of a former Italian prime minister.[131]

Agencies of the American government have disregarded the sovereignty of other nations even more recklessly than have corporations. It is ironic that the United States, which was founded upon the sanctity of self-determination, has such a sorry record of denying that right to others. For example, when the Iranian government attempted to nationalize the properties of American oil companies in the early 1950s, the CIA engineered a coup that restored the dictatorial Shah to the throne.[132] In the 1960s, the CIA financed the overthrow of the left-wing government of Ecuador[133] and played a pivotal role in an Indonesian revolution in which at least 500,000 people were killed.[134]

In fact, it is now acknowledged that the CIA participated in the overthrow or attempted overthrow of numerous regimes around the world, including those in Syria, Somalia, the Sudan, Angola, Ghana, Guatemala, and Guyana.[135] In each of these countries, "CIA intrusion has left a trail of poverty, social chaos, and political repression."[136]

During the Vietnam War, Congress had by law forbidden the hiring of mercenaries from neighboring countries or the deployment of American troops in those countries. Nevertheless, the CIA organized unlawful secret armies composed of ethnic minorities from Laos and Thailand to fight along the borders of North and South Vietnam.[137] Even more dismaying, when American troops illegally invaded Cambodia, soldiers' death certificates were falsified to read that they had died elsewhere.[138]

One of the best-known cases of illegal foreign intervention occurred in Chile in the 1970s. This case represented an unsavory alliance between the governmental and corporate establishments. Since the 1920s, a giant conglomerate, International Telephone and Telegraph (ITT), had built or purchased telephone companies throughout Latin America. Over time, however, the rise of nationalization policies in that region had left ITT with only one remaining South American telephone company in Chile, a nation conspicuously lacking a strong nationalist movement. This enterprise was worth $150 million, and ITT was determined to hold on to it.

The CIA, too, had an interest in Chile. In the 1966 Chilean election, the agency had contributed $20 million in American taxpayers' money to a victorious pro-American presidential candidate. When Chile expanded its telephone service shortly after the election, ITT received the contract, despite a lower bid from a Swedish company.[139]

During the next election in 1970, the CIA and ITT worked in tandem against the popular socialist candidate, Salvador Allende. An estimated $13 million was spent to thwart Allende's candidacy, including the bribery of Chilean legislators to cast electoral votes against Allende.[140] Despite these concerted efforts, Allende was elected. ITT then began an intensive lobbying campaign in Congress and the State Department aimed at preventing the expropriation of American holdings in Chile. As a result, the White House stopped all loans and foreign aid to Chile, which fomented discontent in the Chilean army and provoked disruptive labor strikes.[141] Furthermore, the CIA spent millions of dollars—much of it contributed by ITT—to destabilize the Allende government. Allende was assassinated in 1973 and replaced by an oppressive military junta that was friendly to American corporate and political interests.[142]

Although only circumstantial evidence exists that the CIA was actively involved in the Allende assassination, that ubiquitous agency has been implicated more clearly in the murders of several other foreign leaders, such as Dominican dictator Rafael Trujillo and South Vietnamese president Ngo Din Diem.[143] The Senate Select Subcommittee on Intelligence uncovered evidence that the CIA had planned the assassination of Congolese leader Patrice Lumumba, under orders from President Eisenhower.[144] The Committee also has reported at least eight separate death plots against Cuban president Fidel Castro, ranging from lacing a box of Castro's cigars with lethal botulinium toxin to attempting to give him a poisoned wet suit for scuba diving.[145]

In 1997, a newly declassified memorandum revealed that in 1960 the CIA approached Chicago crime boss Sam Giancana and offered him $150,000 to arrange a Mafia "hit" on Castro. Giancana, who would later himself be a victim of a mob hit, turned the offer down.[146]

Recently, it was also revealed that a Salvadoran "death squad" had been trained in the United States in 1981, with the knowledge of the Reagan administration. These troops later massacred dozens of peasants in El Salvador.[147]

In 1984, *Psychological Operations in Guerrilla Warfare*, a book attributed to the CIA, was distributed widely in Nicaragua.

> While not concerned with killing for direct military purposes, the book takes a generous attitude to killings that may be done for propaganda effect. There is a lot about "armed propaganda," and page 32 has useful hints on what to tell the population if, while proselytizing a village, you find it necessary to shoot a citizen who is trying to leave.[148]

The book also contains a primer on the selection of appropriate targets for "neutralization" (i.e., assassination), such as judges or police officers.[149] It is not by caprice that the CIA's Clandestine Services division has been labeled "the President's personal 'Saturday Night Special.'"[150]

C A S E   S T U D Y

The Iran-Contra Affair

The Iran-Contra Affair is a tale of an "invisible government"[151] sustained through deceit and contempt for the rule of law. The roots of this maze of crimes and cover-ups may be traced back to the foreign policy agenda of the new Reagan administration in 1981. It was President Reagan's announced intention to encourage the removal of the Marxist Sandinista government in Nicaragua. Initially, there was nothing furtive about this policy. The president had publicly supported aid to the Contras, a pro-American rebel army engaged in a guerrilla war against the Sandinistas.

(Continued)

Congress, however, was less willing to authorize funding for an interventionist policy and passed a series of amendments between 1982 and 1986 (known as the Boland Amendments, after their principal author, a Massachusetts congressman), severely limiting or prohibiting the appropriation of funds on behalf of the Contras. By that time, however, the White House had committed itself to backing the Contras at all costs.

This policy could not be carried out without defying Congress. Open defiance was politically unfeasible. The only other way was to do it covertly.[152]

The Administration formulated two types of schemes for circumventing the legally imposed restraints. The first method was to give the task of arming the Contras to the National Security Council (NSC). Congress explicitly had proscribed the use of funds by the Defense Department and the CIA or any other intelligence agency on behalf of the Contras. The NSC was not technically an intelligence agency, so its utilization provided the administration with a way of evading the spirit of the law, if not the letter. The second method was to employ "private" or "third-party" funds, on the assumption that only official United States funds had been prohibited.[153] This plan also would be implemented by the NSC. The NSC was headed by national security adviser Robert McFarlane, who had been instructed by President Reagan to keep the Contras together "body and soul."[154] McFarlane assigned this task to his chief "action officer," Marine Lieutenant Colonel Oliver North.

North, a decorated Vietnam veteran, who reportedly once had suffered a 2-year emotional breakdown after the war, became the designated "contact" between the NSC and the Contras. He was appointed Deputy Director for Political Military Affairs, a vague title that removed him from the NSC chain-of-command and made him answerable only to McFarlane. In effect, an obscure soldier became a one-man operation. His job was to recruit others to help fund the Contras.

Foremost among the "others" to whom North turned were a pair of international arms dealers, retired Air Force Major General Richard Secord and his business partner, an Iranian-born American citizen named Albert Hakim. Ultimately, Secord and Hakim sold about $11 million worth of weapons to the Contras.[155] Much of their proceeds were stashed away in Swiss bank accounts. Secord later told Congress that he had been motivated solely by patriotism and would gladly give his share of the profits to the Contras.[156] He never did.

Obviously, the Contras required a large influx of cash in order to pay for weapons and equipment. In order to deceive Congress, millions of dollars had to be raised privately. This was accomplished in part through nonprofit conservative foundations. Although private citizens were entitled to raise money for the Contras on their own, official cooperation by the administration entailed a criminal conspiracy, especially when donations were disguised as humanitarian assistance.

The "third-country" strategy began in 1983 when overtures were made to Israel and South Africa regarding aid to the Contras. In 1984, Saudi Arabia agreed

(Continued)

to contribute $1 million per month, ostensibly from private funds, to help the Contras survive. The following year, the Saudis' monthly contribution was raised to $2 million. The total Saudi contribution eventually exceeded $30 million.[157] The Reagan administration realized that Nicaragua was of no real interest to Saudi Arabia (the two countries did not even have diplomatic relations); thus, the money was solicited as an opportunity for the Saudis to curry personal favor with President Reagan.

The government of Taiwan also contributed $2 million after North promised that Nicaragua would recognize the Taiwanese regime once the Sandanistas were ousted. In addition, President Reagan vetoed a bill which would have placed restrictions on imported Taiwanese textiles.[158]

The "private" and "third-country" contributions enabled the Contras to survive well into 1985. That year, the American ambassador to Costa Rica, Lewis Tambs, was instructed by North to obtain permission from the Costa Rican government for the construction of a "private" airstrip to be used to supply the Contras. When he subsequently was asked if he thought that building a secret pro-Contra military installation in a neutral country violated the Boland Amendments, Tambs replied that he had never read those amendments because, in his words, "I have difficulty reading a contract for a refrigerator."[159]

The governments of Guatemala, El Salvador, and Honduras also were pressured into cooperation. Honduras was particularly important, because the main Contra force was based there; all supplies had to be brought there for distribution.[160] For example, another arms dealer, retired Major General John Singlaub, purchased weapons from Eastern Europe for $4.8 million, shipped them to Honduras, and sold them to the Contras for $5.3 million.[161]

Concurrent, although seemingly unrelated, events on the other side of the globe were to further complicate an already Byzantine enterprise. Another item on the Reagan foreign policy agenda was the punishment of the Iranian regime led by the ferociously anti-American Ayotollah Khomeini. Khomeini had overthrown the despised Shah in early 1979. The following November, a group of Iranian students had stormed the United States embassy in Tehran on Khomeini's behalf and kidnapped a group of innocent Americans, holding them hostage for 444 days. In 1982, the White House accused Iran of supporting international terrorism and launched a vigorous campaign to block the sale of arms to that nation.

By 1984, however, another group of hostages was being held in Lebanon by Islamic extremists under Khomeini's control. President Reagan looked the American people in the eye and stated his position in resolute terms: "The United States gives terrorists no rewards. . . . We make no deals."[162] These words later would come back to haunt the president like Marley's ghost.

On August 6, 1985, McFarlane met with Reagan to discuss a proposal to use Israel for the sale of 100 TOWs (Tube-launched Optically-tracked Wire-guided missiles) to Iran, with the deal to be followed by the release of the American hostages. The President later acknowledged that he had authorized the sale, then said that he

(Continued)

had *not* authorized the sale, and finally claimed that he had no recollection one way or the other.[163] In any case, 2 weeks later 96 TOWs were transferred by Israel to Iran. No hostages were released.[164]

Israeli and Iranian negotiators met again in September. The Iranians indicated that 1 hostage would be released in exchange for an additional 400 TOWs. On September 15, 408 missiles arrived in Tehran, and the first hostage, Presbyterian minister Benjamin Weir, was released.[165] In November, 19 Hawk missiles were delivered from Israel to Iran aboard a CIA plane; no hostages were released.

As 1985 drew to a close, an emotionally exhausted McFarlane resigned as National Security Adviser and was replaced by his deputy, Vice-Admiral John Poindexter.[166] In one of his first acts, Poindexter presented a "finding" to President Reagan. (A finding is a written document describing the need for and nature of covert operations and requires the President's signature.[167]) Reagan signed that finding, which retroactively authorized the Hawk shipment.[168] A year later, Poindexter destroyed the finding on the ground that it would be politically embarrassing if it ever were revealed publicly. "He could not have realized what a good prophet he was going to be."[169]

Of all the documents written during this period, however, the most notorious was undoubtedly the so-called diversion memorandum. Drafted by North in April 1986 and forwarded to Reagan and Poindexter, it summarized the Iranian operations and indicated the use of arms sale profits for the Contras in Nicaragua.[170] "Those few lines created more future trouble for North than anything else he ever said or wrote."[171]

On July 26, a second hostage, Father Lawrence Jenko, director of Catholic Relief Services in Beirut, was released. Two weeks later, 240 Hawk missile parts were shipped to Iran.[172]

🔵 By the middle of 1986, however, reports were beginning to appear in the press connecting North to fund-raising activities on behalf of the Contras. When a supply plane linked to a CIA "front" was shot down over Nicaragua in October, that incident provided an unmistakable disclosure of an illegal, covert American policy. "As might have been expected, a denial reflex took over in official circles."[173] CIA Director William Casey nervously advised North to shut down the operations. North began shredding incriminating documents and destroying ledgers and address books. The spool was starting to unravel. "North was now a man in a hurry."[174]

The news of North's secret role in the arms-for-hostages deals with Iran burst onto the front pages on November 6. When the story broke, North reportedly sat at a computer terminal in his office at the NSC and tapped out a weirdly, coded confidential computer memo to a colleague:

> Oh, Lord. I lost the slip and broke one of the high heels. Forgive please. Will return the wig on Monday.[175]

As of this writing, more than 15 years later, it is still not clear to anybody what this cryptic message means.

(Continued)

On November 13, in a speech drafted by North and polished by White House writers, President Reagan addressed the nation and stated, "We did not—repeat—did not trade weapons or anything else for hostages nor will we."[176] A poll in the *Los Angeles Times* reported that only 14% of the public believed the president.[177] Even Republican icon Barry Goldwater was skeptical. In his words, "I think President Reagan has gotten his butt in a crack on this Iran thing."[178]

Reagan, unaccustomed to harsh rejection, was shaken.[179] He held a press conference on November 19, which would be remembered as the worst public performance of his presidency. He conceded that a small amount of arms had been sold to Iran, but that he was terminating all such sales. He claimed that he had the legal right not to have informed Congress. When he described the TOW missile as a "shoulder-mounted" weapon, he was corrected by a reporter, who explained to the commander-in-chief that TOWs were ground-to-ground weapons fired from tripods.[180]

Reagan's worst blunder occurred when he categorically denied any "third country" involvement. Secretary of State George Schultz already had disclosed to the press that the United States *had* condoned the Israeli shipment of arms to Iran the previous year. Schultz had to meet with Reagan and correct him the day after the press conference. Schultz later testified, "[I]t was not the kind of discussion I ever thought I would have with the President of the United States."[181]

For Reagan, the time had come for damage control. He decided to fire Poindexter and transfer North out of the NSC. But damage control is a two-way street: On November 21, North instructed his young secretary, former fashion model Fawn Hall, to alter a series of NSC documents from his files. She and North also shredded documents until 4:15 A.M.[182] When she later testified before Congress, the intensely loyal Hall was asked whether she had realized that altering these documents was wrong. "Sometimes," she said, "you have to go above the written law."[183]

The next presidential press conference must have been a painful experience for a politician whose brilliantly successful career had been built on superb communicative talent. After a few brief remarks, in which he claimed that he had not been fully informed of the Iranian activities, Reagan turned the microphone over to Attorney General Edwin Meese. "After his fiasco on November 19, he could not be trusted—or could not trust himself—to go on the stage and face a disbelieving, tumultuous press conference alone."[184]

Meese acknowledged the diversion of funds from Iranian arms sales to the Contras. He implied that North may have been guilty of violating the law—without presidential authorization. North reportedly was stunned by what he perceived as abandonment by his superiors. He realized that he was in real danger of being convicted of criminal acts. When his office was sealed by NSC security, Hall smuggled documents out inside her clothing. But surreptitiously removing a few documents, as well as shredding or altering a handful of others, was not going to save Oliver North. "Like many other things North did, this effort to hide the traces

(Continued)

of his activity was marked as much by ineptitude as by anything else."[185] A paper trail connecting three continents could not be erased one page at a time.

> So many hundreds of incriminating documents and memoranda were left or recovered that it was possible to reconstruct the course of the Iran and contra affairs in extraordinary detail. Even the diversion, "the deepest, darkest secret of the whole activity," as [North] called it, came to light.[186]

The Iran-Contra Affair effectively was finished. North was not the only figure to be racing ahead of the posse, however. Reagan's friends were urging him to hire a criminal lawyer to defend his position. "[S]ome of those close to Reagan expected him to be one of the prime victims of the scandal."[187] The president immediately appointed a Special Review Board, headed by former Senator John Tower, to study the conduct of the NSC staff. Both houses of Congress created select committees to investigate Iran-Contra. An Independent Counsel also was appointed to prosecute any criminal offenses.[188]

In May 1987, the House and Senate began rare joint hearings on the Iran-Contra Affair. All the major figures testified, with the exception of the president and CIA Director Casey, who died on the second day of the hearings. America heard the feisty Secord explain the logistics of the operation; the contrite McFarlane, 3 months after a failed suicide attempt, implicate the president in a robotic monotone; and the unrepentant Poindexter blame Congress and the press for distorting the importance of Iran-Contra. Witnesses—from the unscrupulous Hakim, to the glamorous Hall, to the pugnacious leader of the Contras, Adolfo Calero, to a roll call of supporting players—appeared on millions of American television screens.[189] This cast, however, had to settle for roles in the chorus—center-stage belonged to Oliver North.

North strode into the hearing room in full Marine uniform, complete with six rows of medals. Although he had not worn his uniform in 5 years at the NSC, it was an effective strategy. North's lawyers had packaged him for the American public as a persecuted patriot. By the time the hearings had concluded, the press had coined the term "Olliemania."

> There were Ollie T-shirts, Ollie bumper stickers, Ollie dolls, Ollie haircuts, Ollieburgers (shredded beef topped with shredded American cheese and shredded lettuce), Ollie recipes, and even Ollie-for-President boomlets.[190]

North presented himself as a defiant hero, an obedient soldier, a blameless scapegoat whose conduct had been dictated or approved by his superiors. He defended the need for covertness and deception, and made clear his low opinion of Congress. With moist eyes, he even spoke of his widowed mother who scrubbed floors to feed her children. It was bathos of Nixonian proportions, executed with far more skill.

> In an astonishing role reversal, North succeeded in transforming the pre-hearings public perception of him as mysterious cowboy run amok—a lone

(Continued)

ranger whose horse jumped the fence for a romp through Indian Country without authorization—to persecuted patriotic victim, just following orders . . . He was the Marlboro Man without the Marlboro. The Rebel With a Cause.[191]

The television critic in *The Washington Post* compared North's performance to James Stewart's in the classic movie *Mr. Smith Goes to Washington*. The critic offered a piquant metaphor: "[L]ike they say in pro wrestling, Ollie North is the 'television champion.'"[192] Unlike the wrestling arena, however, it was not left to vociferous fans to designate the villains; that responsibility belongs to the courts.

On March 11, 1987, Robert McFarlane pleaded guilty to four misdemeanor counts of withholding information from Congress. He was placed on 2 years probation and fined $20,000. He had avoided a prison sentence by agreeing to cooperate with the government in its prosecution of the other Iran-Contra cases.[193]

On March 16, a federal grand jury returned criminal indictments against Oliver North, John Poindexter, Richard Secord, and Albert Hakim.[194] In November, Secord made an agreement with the prosecutor, under which he pleaded guilty to one felony count and agreed to testify against North and Poindexter in exchange for the dropping of 11 other charges.[195] Like McFarlane, Secord was sentenced to 2 years probation.[196] Hakim also received 2 years probation and a $5000 fine. In an unusual agreement, however, Hakim was allowed to keep a share of the $1.7 million surplus from the arms sales, which was still sitting in Swiss banks.[197] Poindexter became the only Iran-Contra figure to receive a prison term; he received a 6-month sentence in 1990 for lying to Congress, making him the highest ranking White House official since Watergate to be incarcerated for illegal acts committed in office.[198]

As for North, he worked out an agreement under which he pleaded guilty to 3 of 12 felony counts, thus avoiding the ignominy of a prison sentence. He was, however, fined $178,785 and ordered to perform 1200 hours of community service.[199] Many observers considered this a surprisingly light sentence. Not only had North participated in the Iran-Contra cover-up by lying to Congress and shredding key documents, he also had acknowledged using $13,000 of Iran-Contra proceeds to purchase a security system for his home.[200] Moreover, North was accused of cashing $2000 worth of traveler's checks, part of a $90,000 donation by Contra leader Adolfo Calero meant to help retrieve the hostages from Lebanon. This represented something of a "reverse diversion," with funds going from the Contras to Iran. Thus, North's alleged embezzlement was akin to a "diversion of a diversion." North used the siphoned funds to pay for such things as dry-cleaning, groceries, hosiery, and snow tires. When Calero was shown a chart during the congressional hearings documenting the dozens of traveler's checks cashed by North, he staunchly defended North's integrity. "He conceded to Senator Rudman that it did not snow in Nicaragua, but he was sure that North could explain the expenditures."[201] On September 16, 1991, a divided appeals court overturned North's conviction on technical grounds regarding the immunity which had been granted to his congressional testimony. A few weeks later, Poindexter's conviction was

(Continued)

reversed on the same grounds.[202] North pronounced himself "totally exonerated."[203] Most journalists rejected this claim as a "wild overstatement,"[204] noting that the reversal had nothing to do with the facts of the case.[205] Ironically, North had wriggled off the hook using the very sort of legal loophole which his hard-line supporters habitually berate in their "law and order" and "soft on crime" rhetoric.

North became a luminary on the lecture circuit, commanding $30,000 for an appearance. He was the Republican nominee for a U.S. Senate seat in Virginia in 1994, but was defeated in a very costly and bitterly fought election—the most conspicuous exception to a national Republican landslide. A short time later, he became the host of a nationally syndicated daily radio program.

ABUSE OF POWER

More than 150 years ago, political philosopher John Stuart Mill wrote, "A governing class not accountable to the people are sure, in the main, to sacrifice the people to the pursuit of separate interests and inclinations of their own."[206] Mill's message about the need for accountability has lost none of its timeliness. Even the government of the United States, democratically elected and Constitutionally restrained, has at times been willing to "sacrifice" the rights of its citizens on behalf of some extralegal "higher" purpose. Most of these abuses of power have occurred under the guise of national security.[207]

Consider the ignominious example of the internment of Japanese American citizens during World War II. In 1942, President Roosevelt issued an Executive Order evacuating over 100,000 Japanese American residents of California, Oregon, and Washington and herding them into barbed wire enclosures under military guard.[208] Victims of racial prejudice and war hysteria, they were branded as traitors and robbed of their businesses and farms. Virtually every one of them, as far as is known, were loyal citizens; most were too young or too old to pose any plausible threat.[209] Moreover, citizens of Japanese ancestry in Central and South American countries were rounded up, handed over to American authorities, transported to the United States, and thrown into concentration camps as well.[210] It is difficult to characterize that abuse of power in any terms other than kidnapping.

In this section, we will focus on the records of several federal agencies in the area of unlawful surveillance and persecution, and then analyze the most resonant example in American history of government divorced from accountability—the crimes of Watergate.

The CIA

From 1953 to 1973, the CIA intercepted, opened, and photographed 250,000 personal letters, generating an index of 1.5 million names.[211] It also collected arrest reports from state and local police forces, including "the names of 300,000 persons arrested for homosexual acts."[212]

Beginning in the 1960s, the agency regularly monitored the overseas activities of so-called domestic dissidents. Although it purportedly was interested only in Americans believed to be foreign agents, the CIA spied on a vast range of traveling citizens with no apparent foreign intelligence value.[213] For example, singer Eartha Kitt was put under surveillance for at least 10 years while living and working in Paris.[214] Under this program, known as Operation CHAOS, the CIA reported on many anti-war activists, as well as expatriates like Kitt. Agents "burglarized their hotel rooms and their homes, eavesdropped on their conversations, and bugged their phones."[215]

As part of CHAOS, the CIA also spied on political radicals *inside* the United States, in violation of its 1947 charter. It created detailed files on 7000 American citizens and 1000 groups, including peace and civil rights organizations.[216] Operation CHAOS officially ended in 1974, but by then the ban on domestic CIA activity had become effectively inoperative. In 1981, President Reagan issued an Executive Order formally rescinding that prohibition, thus enabling the CIA to conduct covert domestic operations.[217]

The Defense Department

During the social upheaval of the late 1960s, military intelligence agencies collected vast amounts of information about the activities, financial affairs, sex lives, and psychiatric histories of persons engaged in "domestic unrest," a term the Army applied to anyone seeking to change government policy. By 1971, the Army possessed over 80,000 biographical dossiers and over 211,000 "subversive files" on organizations. None of those targeted individuals was affiliated with the armed forces; nor were any of the targeted organizations, such as Americans for Democratic Action and the Urban League.[218]

> Army agents infiltrated Resurrection City during the 1968 Poor People's March on Washington. Agents also posed as students to monitor classes in Black Studies at New York University. The army infiltrated the October and November 1969 moratorium marches around the country. Military personnel even posed as newspaper reporters and television newsmen during the 1968 Democratic National Convention in Chicago to tape interviews with demonstration leaders.[219]

The NSA

Between 1952 and 1974, the National Security Agency (NSA), the most secretive of all American intelligence agencies,[220] compiled files on 75,000 American citizens. The first NSA surveillance program was called SHAMROCK and involved the interception of all private cables leaving the United States. Eventually, "the NSA was intercepting some 150,000 messages per month . . . dwarfing the CIA's mail-opening program."[221]

The second NSA domestic intelligence program was called MINARET and involved the monitoring of international telephone communications of individuals and organizations on a designated "watch list," ranging from political groups to celebrities to ordinary citizens. "[T]he names on the list included the peaceful, nonviolent, and totally legal."[222]

The FBI

Of all government agencies, the FBI has conducted the most vindictive domestic intelligence campaigns.[223] The Bureau of Investigation (forerunner of the FBI) began intelligence-gathering operations just before World War I. Its General Intelligence Division (GID), headed by an ambitious J. Edgar Hoover, a young former cataloguer for the Library of Congress, "spied on citizens who criticized the war, opposed the draft, or participated in militant labor organizing efforts."[224] By the end of the war, the energetic Hoover already had created a substantial index and file system covering suspected political radicals, including such prominent liberals as Fiorello LaGuardia, who later would become mayor of New York City. When Hoover was put in command of the renamed Federal Bureau of Investigation in 1924, he was ordered to abolish the GID; the mission of the new FBI was to investigate crimes, not engage in political activities. For over a decade, the bureau observed this restriction.[225] During this period, Hoover, a master publicist, cultivated the FBI's "gangbuster" image in a series of sensational cases.

However, as World War II approached, Hoover was called on to supervise domestic intelligence operations. President Roosevelt issued a series of secret instructions to Hoover, authorizing the bureau to conduct broad surveillance programs aimed at American citizens. Hoover was empowered to engage in warrantless searches, wiretapping, and bugging against persons suspected of communist or fascist sympathies.[226]

A few days after the war began in Europe in 1939, Roosevelt issued a proclamation officially placing the FBI in charge of all investigations of espionage, sabotage, and subversive activities.[227] This document has come to be known as the Magna Carta of the bureau's intelligence mission.[228] Hoover seized on the statement as an authorization for virtually unlimited investigative powers. Espionage and sabotage were clearly defined statutory offenses; subversion was not. Congress had never said what specific kinds of "subversive activities" were crimes, so Hoover took this task upon himself.[229]

Hoover personally supervised the surveillance of such "dangerous" radicals as blind and deaf author Helen Keller, who must have been the easiest target in the history of surveillance, and Justice Felix Frankfurter, one of the more conservative jurists ever to sit on the modern Supreme Court. Such excesses underscored the danger of police power limited only through self-regulation. At what point does a permissible law enforcement technique like surveillance begin to encroach on the Constitutional rights of citizens regarding free speech, free assembly, or security against unreasonable search and seizure? To Hoover, such a question was better suited to high school civics classes; it had no relevance to the real world of national security.

The vagueness of domestic intelligence laws gave the FBI such latitude that abuses by agents were inevitable. "And once they had moved into the gray area—say, by tailing someone they mistrusted but had no evidence against—it was a short step into the black area of clear illegality."[230] When a powerful agency turns its resources against persons who have committed no crimes, prosecution becomes persecution.

> [N]o federal judge would give permission to the F.B.I. to install a wiretap or search an office when there was no probable cause to believe that the target had done anything wrong. Stymied by the law and yet firm in the belief that subversives were out to bring down the Republic, the F.B.I. began pursuing them in the only way left to it; by breaking the law.[231]

The sedition provisions of the Alien Registration Act of 1940, known as the Smith Act,[232] as well as postwar measures such as the Loyalty Program of 1947,[233] the Internal Security Act of 1950,[234] and the Communist Control Act of 1954,[235] expanded the FBI's authority to spy on American citizens. Hoover even had a 300-page file on Richard J. Daley, who would become the scourge of the New Left in the 1960s. The dossier spans Daley's political career from state senator in the 1940s to his election as mayor of Chicago in the 1950s up to his death in 1976. A writer who has chronicled the FBI explains, "It was typical of Hoover to try to just gather any information he could about powerful politicians as a way of making sure he maintained his own seat of power."[236]

Two programs, COMINFIL and COINTELPRO, were directed at communist infiltration. In addition to the Communist Party, however, agents also penetrated liberal organizations like the American Civil Liberties Union, civil rights groups like the NAACP, peace organizations like SANE, and professional coalitions like the National Lawyers Guild. "Any group or organization that advocated social change or reform was fair game for the bureau."[237]

During the "Red Scare" decade, the American Communist Party, by the FBI's own estimate, never exceeded 80,000 members, but the FBI opened about 500,000 files on "subversive" organizations.[238] A favorite target was the tiny and completely legal Socialist Workers Party (SWP), whose membership was estimated at 1000.[239] As even the bureau admitted, the SWP was not under the control or influence of any foreign power and was "in active opposition to the Communist party."[240] Yet, the FBI kept the SWP under surveillance for 34 years, burglarized the party's offices on 94 different occasions in just one 6-week period,[241] and sent anonymous letters to members' employers.[242] The FBI expended tens of thousands of man hours to generate an 8-million page dossier on a "small, peaceable, and wholly ineffectual political party."[243]

The FBI also conducted checks on over 6 million government employees for possible disloyalty. Thousands of individuals were subjected to adversarial hearings on vague charges of membership, or even "sympathetic association" with allegedly subversive organizations.[244] According to the Center for National Security Studies, not a single case of espionage was uncovered by those investigations.[245]

The FBI likewise engaged in "smear" campaigns against selected citizens by leaking derogatory information to friendly media contacts.

> FBI agents conducted anonymous-letter operations to have "subversives" fired from their jobs. The bureau also recruited other organizations, such as the American Legion, to launch similar actions. The bureau brought pressure on universities and schools to have professors and teachers fired. Many of these initiatives were successful.[246]

Apparently, no occupational position was beyond the bureau's reach. Documents obtained under the Freedom of Information Act[247] revealed over 2000 pages of FBI files on members of the Supreme Court[248] who were deemed politically suspect during the Cold War years. Chief Justice Earl Warren and Associate Justices Hugo Black and Abe Fortas were among those listed.[249] Particular attention was paid to liberal Justice William O. Douglas, whose file encompassed 1937 to 1978.[250] In 1969, President Nixon, who despised Douglas,[251] arranged for some FBI material to be passed to then-Representative Gerald Ford, who was requested to move to impeach Douglas. Ford complied, but when he bitterly denounced Douglas on the floor of the House in 1970, his speech was so riddled with errors that even a Nixon ally in the Department of Justice observed, "Ford really blew it. . . . You don't start down that road without having the facts."[252] In the end, the Douglas impeachment attempt vaporized.

A new kind of political activism emerged in the 1960s. A nonviolent civil rights movement, along with a more aggressive "black power" movement, converged with an anti-Vietnam War movement, a student protest movement, and a woman's liberation movement to ignite one of the most turbulent periods in modern American history. Hoover, predictably, viewed the new politics of dissent as subversive. Over the course of the decade, the FBI files expanded to encompass over one million Americans. "The FBI went after the whole spectrum of political dissent":[253] from the American Nazi Party to the Jewish Defense League; from the Ku Klux Klan to the Black Panther Party; from the Southern Christian Leadership Conference to the Nation of Islam; from the John Birch Society to Vietnam Veterans Against the War; from the idealistic militancy of the Students for a Democratic Society to the anarchist rage of the Weathermen; from Malcolm X to Jane Fonda. The 1960's, it is said, "brought roses to the cheeks"[254] of political intelligence units.

In 1968, the FBI began an operation dubbed "New Left"—a program of covert persecutions under the pretext of counterintelligence. For example, an attack was orchestrated against Antioch College, a small school in Ohio noted for its involvement in social causes. The bureau traced the postgraduate careers of a number of former student leaders, hoping to uncover a consistent record of low achievement. The plan was to publicize that information and discredit Antioch as an educational institution. To the FBI's regret, it discovered that the Antioch graduates were leading successful lives.[255]

Many other examples of the New Left program related to the alleged sexual licentiousness of young political radicals. The "eroticizing of the New

Left"[256] reflected the institutionalized prudery of the FBI, fueled by the Director's well-known puritanical attitudes about sex. In one case, a white woman who belonged to ACTION, a biracial St. Louis civil rights organization, married a man who did not share her political agenda. The FBI sent an anonymous letter to the husband, hoping to foment marital discord and distract the wife from her activism:

> Look man, I guess your old lady doesn't get enough at home or she wouldn't be shucking and jiving with our black men in ACTION, you dig? Like all she wants to integrate is the bedroom and we black sisters ain't gonna take no second best from our men.[257]

To the bureau's delight, the couple's marriage did indeed break up.[258]

Movie actress Jean Seberg was another victim of New Left. Seberg was a financial supporter of the Black Panther Party. In a sordid ploy to embarrass her publicly, the FBI sent a letter to Hollywood gossip columnists, alleging that the father of Seberg's unborn child was a prominent Black Panther leader:

> I was in Paris last week and ran into Jean Seberg who was heavy with baby. I thought she and Romain had gotten together again but she confided the child belonged to [name deleted] of the Black Panthers. The dear girl is getting around. Anyway, I thought you might get a scoop on the others.[259]

The *Los Angeles Times* printed this "blind" item—which was completely untrue—and it subsequently was reported throughout the print media. When *Newsweek* published the story, Seberg and her husband, author Romain Gary, successfully sued for libel. Seberg, however, suffered a miscarriage and a mental breakdown, and eventually committed suicide.[260]

It is well-documented that the American civil rights movement has been subjected to intense FBI scrutiny for more than 50 years. When President Roosevelt empowered the bureau to gather information on the activities of subversive groups and organizations in the late 1930s, Hoover used that mandate to link the struggle for racial equality with communist infiltration. Hoover had no personal sympathy for the egalitarian goals of the civil rights movement. "At worst he was a 'primitive racist' and, at best, someone with the racist instincts of a white man who had grown up in Washington when it was still a southern city."[261]

Hoover warned that a communist-inspired "messiah" would one day attempt to indoctrinate Afro-Americans. After the Supreme Court rejected the "separate but equal" doctrine in 1954, a number of civil rights leaders and organizations found new prominence: Roy Wilkens and the NAACP; James Farmer and the Congress of Racial Equality; John Lewis and the Voter Education Project. "But it was the Reverend Martin Luther King, Jr. and the Southern Christian Leadership Conference that came to symbolize the nonviolent movement."[262] Hoover saw King as the sinister black messiah he had long feared.

Hoover's view of King filtered through the entire bureau. Following King's memorable "I have a dream" speech in Washington, the FBI's Intelligence

Division denounced King in a memo to the director: "We must mark him now as the most dangerous Negro of the future in this nation from the standpoint of Communism, the Negro, and national security."[263]

The vendetta against King has been characterized as the "most ignoble chapter in the history of FBI spying and manipulation."[264]

> All of the arbitrary power and lawless tactics were marshaled to destroy King's reputation and the movement he led. The FBI relied on its vague authority to investigate "subversives" to spy on King and SCLC; its vague authority to conduct warrantless wiretapping and microphonic surveillance to tap and bug him. The campaign began with his rise to leadership and grew more vicious as he reached the height of his power; it continued even after his assassination.[265]

The investigation of King began in earnest in 1962 with the knowledge and tacit approval of President John F. Kennedy, who publicly claimed to be a King supporter. In 1963, Attorney General Robert Kennedy, another self-professed King ally, approved Hoover's request for wiretaps on King.

Less than 2 weeks after the Kennedy assassination, while the country still mourned, the FBI held an all-day conference to plan the destruction of King and the civil rights movement. Among the proposals discussed were "using ministers, 'disgruntled' acquaintances, 'aggressive' newsmen, 'colored' agents, Dr. King's housekeeper, and even Dr. King's wife or 'placing a good looking female plant in King's office' to develop discrediting information and to take action that would lead to his disgrace."[266]

Early in 1964, an electronic "bug" placed in King's Washington hotel room apparently picked up information about King's extramarital sexual activities. Throughout that year, the FBI offered this and other King tapes to journalists around the country.[267] This vicious "smear" campaign was known to President Johnson and many of his closest advisers, such as Special Presidential Assistant Bill Moyers, yet another King "admirer"; but not one official, including the president, was willing to risk a confrontation with Hoover.[268]

The most infamous episode occurred in 1968, 34 days before King was to be awarded the Nobel Peace Prize. King received a tape, allegedly made while he was in a hotel room with a woman. Accompanying the tape was an astonishing unsigned note from the FBI, which seemingly urged King to commit suicide:

> King, there is only one thing left for you to do. You know what it is. You have just 34 days in which to do it. (This exact number has been selected for a specific reason.) It has definite practical significance. You are done. There is but one way out for you. You better take it before your filthy fraudulent self is bared to the nation.[269]

Although a subsequent meeting between Hoover and King averted a public scandal, the FBI's war on King took a toll, both on the civil rights leader personally and on the movement he had come to represent.

> [T]he smear campaign caused donors to turn away from SCLC and created factionalism in the civil rights movement over whether King should continue to lead. The FBI did "expose" and "disrupt" the movement. And the anguish this caused for King is incalculable."[270]

In 1988, 20 years after King's death and 16 years after Hoover's, the SCLC still was protesting harassment by the FBI.[271]

As a further illustration that the bureau's disdain for civil liberties and intolerance of political dissent have survived Hoover, declassified documents reveal that Ronald Reagan used the FBI in the 1980s to conduct covert surveillance and infiltration of groups of Americans opposed to the his policies in Central America, including Amnesty International and the American Federation of Teachers. Despite an intensive intelligence campaign, no evidence of criminal wrongdoing ever was produced.

In his classic *Olmstead* dissent (discussed at the outset of this chapter), Justice Brandeis further observed, "The right to be left alone is the most comprehensive of rights and the right most valued by civilized men."[272] Regrettably, the FBI has never fully grasped this fundamental truth. The inexorable expansion of electronic eavesdropping, that so troubled Justice Brandeis in 1928 approached critical mass in 1995, when the Bureau proposed a national wiretapping system to monitor simultaneously 1 out of every 100 telephone lines in some parts of the country.[273]

The IRS

"No agency of the federal government retains more information on American citizens than the IRS."[274] Its files contain financial records of all working Americans, corporations, and organizations, which makes agency records a formidable tool in government campaigns against political targets. "Most likely under pressure from the FBI, the IRS focused its selective enforcement capabilities throughout the 1950s on dissident organizations and individuals."[275] During the 1960s, the IRS served as the Kennedy administration's "hired gun" against chosen targets, mainly right-wing extremist groups. In 1963, President Kennedy used the IRS to develop an aggressive plan, called the Ideological Organizations Project, to examine the tax-exempt status of 10,000 political organizations.[276] That project was abandoned after Kennedy's assassination.

Between 1966 and 1974, the IRS and the FBI engaged in a persecutive alliance, which even a high-ranking IRS official termed "probably illegal."[277] Tax records were used to "disrupt and neutralize the political threat of the New Left."[278] The idea was that prosecutions and convictions of any kind, such as for tax evasion, could remove the leaders of dissident movements—by putting them in prison. For example, of the 90 individuals designated as "Key Black Extremists" by the FBI, the tax files on 72 were passed to the bureau by the IRS. The FBI also used IRS-released contribution lists of political organizations, including the SCLC led by Martin Luther King, Jr. It was hoped that a publicized tax investigation would raise doubts about King and his group among donors and thereby reduce contributions.[279]

In 1969, the IRS created a Special Service Staff (SSS) to examine what it termed "ideological organizations." "Its purpose was to gather information on political groups and individuals . . . and to stimulate audits by local and district IRS offices based upon this information."[280] Like Hoover, Paul Wright, who headed the SSS, justified any improprieties on the ground "that he was participating in an effort to save the country from dissidents and extremists."[281] The SSS did not even pick its own targets; they were provided by outside agencies, primarily the FBI. By 1973, the SSS possessed surveillance files on over 8500 Americans, including Mayor John Lindsay of New York City and Nobel Prize-winning scientist Linus Pauling, and over 2800 organizations, such as the Americans for Democratic Action and the California Migrant Ministry.[282]

No president ever used the IRS as a punitive weapon more than Richard Nixon. Nixon pressured the IRS to audit selected persons on his notorious "enemies list." Nowhere in American political history did John Stuart Mill's warning of unaccountability, abuse of power, and the sacrifice of constitutionality to some dubious higher purpose (in this case, Nixon's re-election) ever ring truer than in Watergate.

C A S E   S T U D Y

Watergate

The cluster of crimes known collectively as "Watergate" has come to symbolize the abuse of political power in America. Richard Nixon, who had won re-election by a huge majority, had to jettison the core of his administrative staff; then, facing certain impeachment, conviction, and removal from office, he himself was forced to resign.[283]

Watergate lies on the cusp between the two types of political crime differentiated by political scientist Theodore Lowi: "Little Corruption," the bribery and individual malfeasance examined in Chapter 9; and "Big Corruption," in which governmental deviance is normalized through political authority.[284] Clearly, Watergate abounded with "Little Corruption." Consider the following examples:

❖ The Committee to Re-elect the President (known as derisively as CREEP) was indicted for campaign spending violations following an investigation by the General Accounting Office.[285] It was later revealed that CREEP also had failed to report a secret fund of millions of dollars in campaign contributions.[286]

❖ The House Banking and Currency Committee reported that CREEP had channeled money through a Luxembourg bank in order to circumvent campaign spending laws.[287]

❖ John Mitchell and Maurice Stans, former cabinet members, solicited an illegal $200,000 cash contribution to CREEP from Robert Vesco, a financier accused by

(Continued)

the SEC of a $244 million stock fraud. Mitchell later arranged a meeting between Vesco and SEC Chairman William Casey after the $200,000 was delivered.[288]

❖ Illegal campaign contributions were solicited from some of the biggest corporations in America, such as Chrysler, American Airlines, and Ashland Oil. One company, American Motors, was asked for an illegal contribution of $100,000, but rejected the request. It later was given a second chance, at the "bargain" rate of only $50,000.[289] Some corporate executives testified that they were blackmailed by CREEP into giving large donations. For example, the vice-president of Gulf Oil maintained that he had been led to believe that a refusal to contribute would have placed his company on a "blacklist" with respect to government contracts.[290]

❖ "The *Wall Street Journal* [published] documents revealing that President Nixon had been told of the dairy industry's huge campaign contributions, had expressed his gratitude, and two days later had given them highly profitable price-support increases."[291]

❖ Republican officials donated $50,000 from campaign funds to pay for a 1972 dinner honoring Vice-President Spiro Agnew, who would later resign in disgrace.[292]

❖ The brother-in-law of White House Chief of Staff H. R. Haldeman received $50,000 in diverted campaign contributions for helping to arrange the purchase of President Nixon's California home.[293]

❖ Nixon's close friend, banker "Bebe" Rebozo, channeled $50,000 from laundered campaign funds for Nixon's private use. The money had paid for a swimming pool, putting green, and pool table at Nixon's Florida home. "Another $4,562 had gone into the purchase of diamond earrings for the President's wife."[294]

❖ "[T]he Joint Committee on Internal Revenue Taxation . . . disclosed that [Nixon] used every tax dodge and loophole to escape paying $432,787 in income taxes."[295] The report revealed that the president had grossly underestimated his income and had deducted nearly a half-million dollars for donating some of his presidential papers, a vastly inflated figure. Nixon also had charged the government for nearly $100,000 in personal expenses, including $5000 to throw a lavish party for his daughter.[296]

Outrageous as these offenses were, a review of American history makes clear (and as Chapter 9 will underscore) that corrupt politicians have never been in short supply. Why, then, has the stain of Watergate been so indelible? The naked dishonesty it revealed at the highest level of government is not easily forgotten: campaign contributions illegally donated or extorted, the "skimming" of these funds for gifts to the President's friends and relatives, the purchase of political favors, the sale of ambassadorships, the president's own questionable tax returns.

Beyond all this, however, Watergate was "Big Corruption," a constitutional crisis of the first magnitude, perhaps America's closest brush with despotism. It revealed the creation of a "shadow government, a secret 'state within a state.'"[297] It

(Continued)

signified an attempt to replace a traditional "rule of law" morality with a kind of "new Machiavellianism,"[298] layered with psychopathy and marbled with paranoia.

In the midst of the Senate hearings in 1973, a national poll reported that a majority of the public rated Watergate as the *worst* scandal in American history.[299] Decades later, Watergate remains our transcendent political crime. In perpetual motion, it glides on tightropes of our consciousness; often drifting away, but always coming back.

The scandal began inauspiciously with what President Nixon's press secretary dismissed as a "third rate burglary."[300] Early on the morning of June 17, 1972, five men were arrested in national headquarters of the Democratic Party on sixth floor of the swank Watergate Complex in Washington, DC. The burglars were carrying electronic surveillance equipment.

"Incredulity, sometimes accompanied by cynical laughter, typified the initial public reaction to the bungled break-in."[301] After all, President Nixon's reelection was a virtual certainty; polls put him far ahead of any Democratic rival. Nixon was already on his way to the most smashing presidential landslide in American political history.[302] "One had to suspend logic and belief to link the president or the president's men with the transgressions of Watergate."[303]

Even when it was revealed that the burglars worked for a special "plumber's unit" of CREEP, the press and public paid scant attention to the incipient scandal. However, from the summer of 1972 through the spring of 1973, a federal grand jury heard testimony in connection with the Watergate burglary. Before too long, the public was not laughing anymore. Stories began to surface about great sums of money allegedly funneled into Republican intelligence operations. "Bit by bit, the stone wall erected by the White House began to crumble, and the American people learned, not just about the Watergate break-in itself, but about a whole series of related crimes."[304]

On August 1, 1972, journalists Carl Bernstein and Bob Woodward reported in the *Washington Post* that a $25,000 check intended for Nixon's campaign had been deposited in the bank account of one of the Watergate burglars.[305] Later, CREEP admitted that a $30,000 campaign contribution from the Philippine sugar industry, solicited on behalf of an "urgent White House project,"[306] had also helped pay for the Watergate cover-up.

The FBI reportedly was thwarted in its Watergate investigation by CREEP officials. Acting FBI Director L. Patrick Gray III turned over the bureau's Watergate file to White House Counsel John Dean. On April 27, 1973, the *New York Daily News* further revealed that Gray had destroyed documents belonging to Watergate conspirator E. Howard Hunt. Gray reportedly had been acting under orders from Nixon's chief of domestic affairs, John Ehrlichman.[307] Gray resigned that same day.

A month later, a memorandum was disclosed in which the deputy director of the CIA said that powerful White House Chief of Staff H. R. Haldeman told him, "It is the President's wish that the CIA help block an FBI investigation of Nixon

(Continued)

campaign money."[308] The money in question had been "laundered" in a Mexican bank. When former CIA Director Richard Helms appeared before the Senate Foreign Relations Committee, he was asked why he had never informed the president of White House efforts to enlist the CIA in a Watergate cover-up. Helms replied, "Frankly, I wanted to stay as head of the agency."[309]

During this same time, all charges were dismissed in the "Pentagon Papers" trial of former Defense Department analyst, Daniel Ellsberg, who had been accused of leaking to the press classified documents that concerned efforts by the Pentagon to deceive Congress into supporting the corrupt regime in South Vietnam. The judge in the Ellsberg case declared that the government had "incurably infected the prosecution."[310] Specifically, it had been revealed that Watergate conspirators E. Howard Hunt and G. Gordon Liddy had burglarized the office of Eilsberg's former psychiatrist in an effort to uncover discrediting information. In addition, Helms' successor as CIA director, James Schlessinger, conceded that the CIA had cooperated in the burglary at the instigation of Ehrlichman.[311] Later, when testifying before the Watergate Committee, Ehrlichman defended the practice of political espionage and argued that the president had the power to break the law if he believed national security was endangered.[312]

Incredibly, it was also revealed that the judge in the Ellsberg case had been invited to President Nixon's California home where he was asked if he would be interested in becoming the new director of the FBI. This brazen overture later would be characterized by members of the Senate Watergate Committee as attempted bribery.[313]

CREEP used a secret fund to finance intelligence-gathering operations against the Democrats. Democratic presidential contenders and their families were followed and dossiers were assembled on their personal lives. For example, probes were ordered on close associates of Senator Edward Kennedy, including his mother, Rose.[314] False and defamatory stories about Democratic candidates were leaked to the press and letters were forged in the name of prominent Democrats. In addition, Republican saboteurs stole Democratic campaign files and hired provocateurs to disrupt the Democratic National Convention.[315] When Haldeman, who controlled the espionage fund, later appeared before the Senate Watergate Committee, he set a new standard for evasive testimony. He responded "I can't remember" or "I don't know" to more than 150 questions.[316]

One of the ringleaders of the Republican political sabotage conspiracy was the president's appointments secretary, Dwight Chapin. He employed a former Treasury Department attorney, Donald Segretti, to engage in a series of "dirty tricks" against the Democrats. In 1972, Segretti distributed a phony letter on the stationery of then Democratic presidential front-runner, Senator Edmund Muskie, accusing rival presidential aspirants Senators Henry Jackson and Hubert Humphrey of sexual misconduct.[317] Segretti later testified before the Senate Committee concerning "all the acts of forgery, libel, burglary, and character assassination he performed to get Nixon re-elected."[318] Patrick Buchanan, Nixon's caustic speechwriter,

(Continued)

also testified before the Committee and admitted participating in the sabotage of the Muskie presidential campaign. Buchanan further admitted to having urged the White House "to use the IRS against . . . Nixon's enemies list."[319]

Nixon, however, did not limit the use of illegal surveillance to his enemies. He had once ordered the Secret Service to wiretap the phone of his brother Donald, out of fear that Donald's financial dealings might embarrass the re-election campaign.[320] Likewise, on the same day the Senate Watergate Committee began its televised hearings in May 1973, the *New York Times* reported that National Security Adviser Henry Kissinger had ordered the wiretapping of some of his own aides between 1969 and 1971.[321]

In June 1973, the *Washington Post* printed a summary that Woodward and Bernstein had obtained of John Dean's testimony at a closed meeting of the Senate Watergate Committee. According to this report, Dean said that Nixon had requested the IRS to stop tax audits of his friends. Dean reportedly also testified that Nixon had ordered him to keep a list of troublesome reporters, so that they could be punished after the 1972 election.[322] In his public testimony, Dean revealed that Nixon's "enemies list" contained hundreds of names singled out for persecution.[323] For example, Daniel Schorr, the CBS White House correspondent and one of the most respected journalists in Washington, had been subjected to an intense FBI investigation.[324]

Dean also maintained that President Nixon had been aware of the Watergate cover-up from the beginning. Nixon denied this and suggested that he had been misled by the unscrupulous Dean. On November 17, 1973, at a televised question-and-answer session before an audience of newspaper editors, Nixon delivered the most memorable line of his long political career: "I am not a crook."[325]

During the Watergate hearings, Alexander Butterfield, head of the Federal Aviation Administration and a former Nixon aide, stunned the Committee when he revealed that Nixon had secretly tape-recorded all White House conversations, including those relating to Watergate.[326] For the first time in 166 years, a president of the United States was subpoenaed.[327] Nixon refused to cooperate. For months thereafter, the president disobeyed a court order to surrender eight Watergate tapes. Instead he offered special Watergate prosecutor Archibald Cox sanitized written "summaries" of the subpoenaed conversations. When Cox rejected that deal, Nixon ordered Attorney General Elliot Richardson to fire Cox. When Richardson refused, he was fired by Nixon. When Deputy Attorney General William Ruckelshaus also refused, he too was fired by Nixon. Finally, Solicitor General Robert Bork agreed to dismiss Cox. An indignant press quickly labeled this remarkable sequence of events the "Saturday Night Massacre."[328] The "third-rate burglary" had become what John Dean would call a "cancer on the Presidency."[329]

While the tapes were being transcribed, Nixon's attorney informed the Watergate court about an unexplainable $18\frac{1}{2}$ minute buzz that "blots out a crucial discussion about Watergate between Nixon and Haldeman on a key tape."[330] The angry judge, John Sirica, demanded an explanation. Rose Mary Woods, the president's longtime secretary, testified that she had been transcribing the tape for the

(Continued)

president and accidentally had erased it while answering the telephone. According to her story, while "reaching for [the phone] with one hand, with the other she mistakenly pushed the 'record' instead of the 'stop' button on her recorder, while keeping her foot on the operating treadle."[331] When Woods attempted to demonstrate what allegedly had happened, she resembled a side-show contortionist as she twisted her body into a grotesque posture. Her ludicrous explanation was met with almost universal scorn. In fact, months later a panel of technical experts reported that someone had "made at least five separate, deliberate *hand* erasures on the tape."[332]

On July 24, 1974, the American people discovered incontrovertibly that their president was indeed a crook. In *United States v. Richard M. Nixon*, the Supreme Court unanimously ordered that the president surrender the subpoenaed tapes. The most damaging tape turned out to be a conversation between Nixon and Haldeman recorded less than a week after the Watergate break-in. On that tape, Haldeman informs Nixon that the burglars had been financed by CREEP campaign funds, and Nixon orders Haldeman to use the CIA to impede the FBI investigation. This tape has become known as the "smoking gun";[333] it effectively ended the Nixon presidency. Three days after the tapes were released, the House Judiciary Committee approved a Bill of Impeachment against the president of the United States; 12 days later, Nixon resigned.

Watergate proved to be a mucilaginous trap; the harder Nixon had tried to extricate himself, the more entangled he became in crimes, cover-ups, and cover-ups of cover-ups. And like some prehistoric tar pit, Watergate has left a legacy of remains that begs for explanation. Although it obviously was a seminal event, the fundamental meaning of Watergate can be understood in various ways. Interpretation, of course, depends on the perspective of the interpreter.

To many journalists, for example, Watergate was about money. The investigative reports of Bernstein and Woodward, which first revealed the dimensions of the scandal, focused on the illegal contributions, the secret funds, the payoffs and influence peddling. Watergate, however—as we already have observed—transcended "Little Corruption." It must be examined more broadly to grasp its full significance.

To many social psychologists, Watergate was about destructive obedience to a malevolent authority figure, Richard Nixon. Indeed, any retrospective consideration of Watergate must begin with Nixon. Three generations of armchair psychoanalysts have feasted on the Nixon psyche and its web of contradictions. He has been characterized as a man admired by millions of citizens, who chose to obsess over a relative handful of enemies, real and imagined; a man renowned for his political cunning, yet capable of committing acts of almost unfathomable stupidity; a man seized by a grandiose need for praise, yet filled with petty spite and primal hatred. Columnist Stewart Alsop once said of Nixon, "He behaved as if he were waging war, not politics."[334]

One of Richard Nixon's most striking contradictions was that he could inspire such fierce loyalty in his staff. Given the history of his career, that loyalty

(Continued)

could not have been based on any reasonable expectation of reciprocity. His instinct for survival had always been intensely selfish. It was vintage Nixon that he tried to make a scapegoat of the young sycophant, John Dean; or that he retired to opulent exile, pardoned by President Ford for any crimes he might have committed while in office, whereas some of his closest associates and oldest friends, such as Haldeman, Ehrlichman, and Mitchell, went to prison for crimes committed on his behalf. Nixon's character flaws were nearly as familiar a part of the American landscape as the McDonald's arches, so Watergate seems more likely to have been inspired by Nixon the authority figure than by Nixon the inspirational leader.

Whether Nixon personally ordered the burglaries or the extortion of campaign contributions is largely irrelevant. Those acts "were consistent with an operating style that the President himself had followed in the past and was clearly sanctioning, even if he was not familiar with all of the details."[335] It is characteristic of an authoritarian environment that the moral principles which generally govern human relationships cease to apply.

> [W]hen immoral, criminal, or corrupt acts are explicitly ordered, implicitly encouraged, tacitly approved, or at least permitted by legitimate authorities, people's readiness to commit or condone them is considerably enhanced. The fact that such acts are authorized seems to carry automatic justification for them.[336]

"[S]ituational pressures to 'win at all costs' were particularly appealing to the . . . persons who comprised the leadership of the Nixon administration."[337] One merely has to scrutinize the testimony and demeanor of most of the witnesses before the Senate Watergate Committee to discern "an orientation to authority based on unquestioning obedience to superior orders."[338] When one Senator asked John Ehrlichman, for example, whether the president's power to protect national security extended to the commission of murder, Ehrlichman coolly replied: "I do not know where the line is."[339]

To many political sociologists, Watergate was about power.

> Watergate was a scandal motivated by the quest for political power. Although Richard Nixon left the office of the President a far wealthier man than when he entered it, Watergate is not a tale of personal aggrandizement. For the most part, money was simply a means to an end.[340]

Max Weber's early concept of *legitimacy* seems particularly germane to Watergate. A "legitimate" political system is "generally accepted by the populace as ruling in accord with consensual values and norms."[341] In Weber's view, a regime forfeits its legitimacy when it no longer enjoys that acceptance. In other words, "political authorities are [only] legitimate to the extent that the citizens perceive them as holding their positions by right."[342]

When it subverted the 1972 presidential election, the Nixon administration lost its legitimacy. "Voters who had voted for President Nixon considered their vote

(Continued)

to have been fraudulently claimed and felt betrayed."[343] Nixon's "power disease"[344] and its symptomatic intolerance for opposition pulled an unwary nation ever closer to a police state: "The illegal wiretaps [and] political espionage represented, in large part, an attempt to weed out government officials who could not be relied upon to be absolutely loyal to the President."[345]

Also, in the inevitable manner of a police state, the pretext of national security was used to justify every illegal act. Nixon always had both the capacity and the inclination to relegate his opponents to a "less-than-human category, outside of the bounds of human sympathy, and fair game for whatever forms of suppression might be required."[346] Dissenters were persecuted; those citizens consigned to Nixon's "enemies list"—that is, those who opposed the president—were harassed by federal agencies from the IRS to the FBI to the Secret Service to the Post Office.

> There were the "Harvards," the Kennedys, the "upper intellectual types," the "establishment," the Jews, the Italians. The famous "enemies list" . . . included such dangerous folk as Carol Channing, Steve McQueen, Barbara Streisand, Gregory Peck, Bill Cosby, Tony Randall, and Joe Namath.[347]

Logic decrees that the hypocrisy of an amoral president carried to power on the shoulders of "law and order" rhetoric would generate profound effects upon a deceived electorate. A president's responsibility, after all, reaches far beyond his role as commander-in-chief of the armed forces or administrator of the executive branch. The White House is first and foremost a place of moral leadership. Richard Nixon poisoned the well of political rectitude. His abdication of moral leadership, through his routinization of "Big Corruption," was the ultimate crime of Watergate.

Applying classical sociological theories to Watergate yields some disturbing predictions. For example, the loss of political legitimacy engendered by the scandal might be expected to have produced a general state of normlessness (what Durkheim termed "anomie") or a weakening of the social bonds that tie citizens to critical institutions (what Marx called "alienation"). Did this actually occur? The answer appears to be yes. As one analysis concluded at the time, "Watergate may affect the maintenance of supportive attitudes toward the political system."[348]

A 1976 study reported, "There was a clear and general loss of confidence . . . in the executive branch of the federal government concomitant with the unfolding of the Watergate scandal, and this loss was dispersed or extended to political leaders in general."[349] A 1979 survey revealed that those voters who had misplaced their trust in Richard Nixon, and thus felt most betrayed, became significantly more cynical about people in general than those who had not voted for Nixon.[350]

It is not difficult to understand why Watergate exacerbated public cynicism. For instance, of the 21 business executives who were sanctioned for illegal presidential campaign contributions uncovered by the Watergate Special Prosecutor, only 5 were convicted of "willful violations" (a felony). Of these, only three officials of the Associated Milk Producers Cooperative received short prison terms. The remaining two, Thomas Jones, CEO of the Northrup Corporation, and

(Continued)

shipbuilder/sports mogul George Steinbrenner, were slapped with financially in-consequential fines.[351] Moreover, "with the one exception of campaign financing, no major reforms have been enacted as a direct response to Watergate."[352]

Perhaps most disturbing of all is the effect of Watergate on young Ameri-cans of that period. Research on political socialization suggests that "instead of being uninterested in and insulated from political events, children may be one of the more affected segments of the population."[353] Comparative studies of grade-school children's political attitudes in the pre- and post-Watergate era report that children of the post-Watergate era were much more cynical about politics[354] and less respectful of the presidency.[355]

Among college undergraduates, evidence has been presented that Water-gate reduced political interest.[356] Moreover, a 1976 study of young voters revealed a negative correlation between support for Nixon and subsequent scores on a moral judgment scale. One implication of this finding is that the cognitive disso-nance produced by having voted for a disgraced president may have depressed moral judgment among some young voters.[357] Indeed, CREEP regularly hired un-dergraduate interns to infiltrate Democratic campaigns and spy for Republicans in exchange for college credits.[358]

Ironically, 1972 was the first presidential election in which 18- to 20-year-old voters were allowed to participate. Instead of those new voters making the elec-toral process more idealistic, the electoral process may have made those new voters less idealistic. One researcher reports that in the wake of the Watergate scandal, po-litical attitudes of first-time voters became almost indistinguishable from those of their parents.[359] The young subjects of the post-Watergate studies now comprise the dominant demographic segment in the United States. If they are less idealistic, less trusting, and more cynical than they might otherwise have turned out to be, this is indeed a sad legacy of Watergate.

Finally, it is chilling to ponder the "what ifs" of Watergate. What if a night watchman had not accidentally stumbled upon the burglars? What if an obscure White House aide had not off-handedly revealed the existence of the White House tapes? Such questions can only be answered subjunctively, but the crisis of legiti-macy created by Nixon's imperious assault on the Constitution may not have oc-curred without these turns of fate. Democracy often rests at the top and tyranny at the bottom of a slippery slope. Could a second-term Nixon, unable to run again, have shucked any lingering pretense of moral restraint? It is surely fortunate that we will never know.

NOTES

1. *Olmstead v. United States*, 277 U.S. 438 (1928).

2. Allen, Garland E. "The Misuse of Biologi-cal Hierarchies: The American Eugenics Movement, 1900–1940." *History and Phi-losophy of the Life Sciences* 5, 1983: 105–128.

3. "Sterilization to Improve the Race." *JAMA* September 9, 1933: 866.

4. Reinhold, Robert. "Some Unfortunate Verdicts on Writing Science into the Law." *New York Times*. March 9, 1980: 8E. For a historical review of the American eugen-ics movement, see also: Rafter, Nicole H.

"Claims-Making and Socio-Cultural Context in the First U.S. Eugenics Campaign." *Social Problems* 39, 1992: 17–35.

5. Barker, David. "The Biology of Stupidity: Genetics, Eugenics and Mental Deficiency in the Inter-War Years." *British Journal of Health Science* 22, 1989: 347–375.

6. Leonard, Arthur S. *Sexuality and the Law: An Encyclopedia of Major Legal Cases.* New York: Garland, 1993.

7. Smith, J. David, and Nelson, K. Ray. *The Sterilization of Carrie Buck.* Far Hills, NJ: New Horizon Press, 1989.

8. *Buck v. Bell,* 274 U.S. 200 (1927).

9. Reinhold, Robert. "Virginia Hospital's Chief Traces 50 Years of Sterilizing the 'Retarded.'" *New York Times.* February 23, 1980: 6.

10. Stroman, Duane F. *Mental Retardation in Social Context.* Lanham, Md: University Press of America, 1989.

11. Platt, Steve. "Fertility Control." *New Statesman and Society* 4, 1991: 11.

12. *Ibid.* p. 7

13. Herrnstein, Richard J. and Murray, Charles. *The Bell Curve.* New York: Free Press, 1994.

14. Jones, James H. *Bad Blood: The Tuskegee Syphilis Experiment—A Tragedy of Race and Medicine.* New York: Free Press, 1981: 91.

15. Mintz, Morton and Cohen, Jerry. *Power, Inc.: Public and Private Rulers and How to Make Them Accountable.* New York: Viking, 1976: 477.

16. Jones, *op. cit.*

17. *Ibid.*, p. 16.

18. *Ibid.*, p. 24.

19. *Ibid.*

20. Quoted in *Ibid.*, p. 44.

21. *Ibid.*

22. *Ibid.*, p. 127.

23. *Ibid.*, p. 127.

24. *Ibid.*, p. 126.

25. Stolberg, *op. cit.*

26. Mintz and Cohen, *op. cit.*

27. Jones, *op. cit.*, p. 202.

28. *Ibid.*, p. 202.

29. *Ibid.*, p. 191.

30. *Ibid.*, pp. 193, 192.

31. Quoted in Mintz and Cohen, *op. cit.*, p. 478.

32. Cohn, Victor. "Experiment Settlement is Faulted." *Washington Post.* December 16, 1974: A24.

33. Bowart, Walter. *Operation Mind Control.* New York: Dell, 1978: 23.

34. Eitzen, D. Stanley and Timmer, Doug A. *Criminology: Crime and Criminal Justice.* New York: John Wiley & Sons, 1985.

35. Bowart, *op. cit.*

36. *Ibid.*

37. *Ibid.*

38. *Ibid.*, p. 73.

39. *Ibid.*, p. 81.

40. Thomas, Gordon. *Journey into Madness: The True Story of Secret CIA Mind Control and Medical Abuse.* New York: Bantam Books, 1989.

41. *Ibid.*

42. Marks, John. "Sex, Drugs, and the CIA: The Shocking Search for an 'Ultimate Weapon.'" *Saturday Review.* February, 3, 1970: 12–16.

43. *Ibid.*

44. *Ibid.*, p. 14.

45. *Ibid.*, p. 13.

46. Bowart, *op. cit.*

47. "LSD Death Inquiry." *Houston Post.* July 13, 1994: A16.

48. Bowart, *op. cit.* p. 107.

49. Marks, *op. cit.*

50. Eitzen and Timmer, *op. cit.*

51. Halperin, Morton H., Berman, Jerry J., Borosage, Robert L., and Marwick, Christine M. *The Lawless State: The Crimes of the U.S. Intelligence Agencies.* New York: Penguin Books, 1977.

52. Lee, Martin A. "C.I.A.: Carcinogen." *The Nation.* June 5, 1982: 675.

53. Stolberg, *op. cit.*

54. Rothman, David J. "Government Guinea Pigs." *New York Times,* January 9, 1994: 21.

55. Cole, Leonard A. "Americans as Guinea Pigs: The Army's Secret Germ-War Testing." *The Nation.* October 23, 1982: 397.

56. *Ibid.*, p. 399.

57. *Ibid.*, p. 398.

58. *Ibid.*

59. *Ibid.*, p. 398–399.

60. Quoted in *Ibid.*, p. 399.

61. Jones, October 18, 1993, *op. cit.*

62. Budiansky, Stephen. "The Cold War Experiments." *U.S. News & World Report.* January 24, 1994: 34.

63. Jones, Daniel P. "Without Consent: The Government's Secret Experiments on Humans—Wartime Tests Leave Scars, Ethical Concerns." *Hartford Courant.* October 17, 1993: A1.

64. Jones, October 18, 1993, *op. cit.*

65. *Ibid.*, p. A1.

66. Quoted in *Ibid.*, p. A1.

67. *Ibid.*, p. 1A.

68. Quoted in Jones, October 18, 1993, *op. cit.*, p. 1A.

69. *Ibid.*, p. 1A.

70. "Those who cannot remember the past are condemned to repeat it." (Santayana, George. *Reason in Common Sense,* Volume One in "The Life of Reason." New York: Dover, 1980. This work was first published in 1905.)

71. Jones, October 18, 1993, *op. cit.*, p. A1.

72. Schneider, Keith. "Stillborns' Ashes Used in Studies of Radiation, Documents Show." *New York Times.* May 5, 1994: B12.

73. Lee, Gary. "Stillborn Babies Used in '50s Radiation Test: Energy Dept. Widens Disclosure of Experiments." *Washington Post.* May 3, 1995: A3.

74. Allen, Scott. "43 Given Radiation in Mass. Research." *Boston Globe.* August 18, 1995: 27, 31.

75. Schneider, Keith. "A Spreading Light on Radiation Tests." *New York Times.* January 14, 1994: A14.

76. "Paper Says Experiment Exposed 19 Retarded Youths to Radiation." *New York Times.* December 27, 1993: A17.

77. "2 Recall 1949 Radiation Tests on Them." *New York Times.* January 14, 1994: A14.

78. Yemma, John. "Ex-Fernald Residents Awarded $1.85m" *Boston Globe.* December 31, 1997: B1, B7.

79. Allen, Scott. "Radiation Test Used Retarded Children at Wrentham." *Boston Globe.* February 9, 1994: 20.

80. Quoted in *Ibid.*, p. 20.

81. Schneider, Keith. "Trying to Build Secret Weapons, U.S. Spread Radiation in 1950s." *New York Times.* December 16, 1993: A1.

82. MacPherson, Karen. "40's Ethics Policies Ignored in Human Radiation Testing." *Houston Chronicle.* January 23, 1995: 2A.

83. Allen, Scott. "Free Care Came with a Price." *Boston Globe.* February 28, 1994: 25–26.

84. *Ibid.*, p. 25.

85. *Ibid.*, p. 25.

86. *Ibid.*, p. 26.

87. Herken, Gregg and David, James. "Doctors of Death." *New York Times.* January 13, 1994: 21.

88. Gallagher, Carole. *American Ground Zero: The Secret Nuclear War.* Cambridge, Mass.: MIT Press, 1993.

89. Watkins, T. H. "Under the Mushroom Cloud." *Washington Post.* May 2, 1993: 7.

90. Schneider, Keith. "Cold War Radiation Test on Humans to Undergo a Congressional Review." *New York Times.* April 11, 1994: D9.

91. Schneider, Keith. "Energy Official Seeks to Assist Victims of Tests." *New York Times.* December 29, 1993: 1.

92. Schneider, April 11, 1994, *op. cit.*

93. Schneider, December 29, 1993, *op. cit.*

94. Gottschalk, Louis A., Kunkel, Robert, Wohl, Theodore, Saenger, Eugene L., Winget, and Carolyn N. "Total and Half Body Irradiation: Effect on Cognitive and Emotional Processes." *Arch Gen Psychiatry* 21, 1989: 574–580.

95. Howard-Jones, Norman. "Human Experimentation in Historical and Ethical Perspectives." *Social Science & Medicine* 16, 1982: 1429–1448.

96. Gottschalk et al., *op cit.*

97. Egilman, David S. and Reinert, Alexander. "What Is Informed Consent?" *Washington Post.* January 14, 1994: 23.

98. *Ibid.*

99. Hoversten, Paul. "Clinton Apologizes for Radiation Tests." *USA Today.* October 4, 1995: 10A.

100. Kong, Dolores. "1800 Tested in Radiation Experiments." *Boston Globe.* February 20, 1994: 1, 22.

101. *Ibid.*, p. 22.

102. *Ibid.*, p. 22.

103. Allen, Scott. "MIT Records Show Wider Radioactive Testing at Fernald." *Boston Globe.* December 31, 1993: 1.

104. Schneider, Keith. "Scientists Share in Pain of Experiment Debates." *New York Times.* March 3, 1994: A12.

105. Schneider, Keith. "Secret Nuclear Research on People; Comes to Light." *New York Times.* December 17, 1993: A1.

106. Markey, Edward J. "Compensating America's Nuclear Guinea Pigs." *Boston Globe.* January 13, 1994: 15.

107. Allen, August 18, 1995, *op. cit.*

108. Markey, *op. cit.*, p. 15.

109. Markey, *op. cit.*, p. 15.

110. Jones, October 17, 1993, *op. cit.*

111. Allen, Scott and Kong, Dolores. "50 Memo Warned Radiation Tests Would Suggest Nazism." *Boston Globe.* December 28, 1993: 1.

112. Mintz and Cohen, *op. cit.*, p. 480.

113. Mitford, Jessica. *Kind and Usual Punishment: The Prison Business.* New York: Knopf, 1973.

114. McGrory, Brian and Murphy, Sean. "Inmates Used in '60s Drug Tests." *Boston Globe.* January 1, 1994: 16.

115. *Ibid.*

116. Schneider, December 17, 1993, *op. cit.*

117. Hoversten, *op. cit.*, p. 10A.

118. Mitford, *op. cit.*

119. Mintz and Cohen, *op. cit.*, p. 479.

120. *Ibid.*

121. Mitford, *op. cit.*

122. *Ibid.*, pp. 139–140.

123. Rakstis, Ted J. "The Business Challenge: Confronting the Ethics Issue." *Kiwanis Magazine.* September 1990: 30.

124. Beck, Paul J. and Maher, Michael W. "Competition, Regulation and Bribery." *Managerial and Decision Economics* 10, 1989: 1–12.

125. Roebuck, Julian, and Weeber, Stanley C. *Political Crime in the U.S.: Analyzing Crime By and Against Government.* New York: Praeger, 1978.

126. *Ibid.*

127. *Ibid.*

128. *Ibid.*

129. "Litton Units to Pay $18.5 Million in Fraud Case." *Houston Chronicle.* July 1, 1999: 3C.

130. Hershey, Robert D. "Payoffs: Are They Stopped or Just Better Hidden?" *New York Times.* January 29, 1978: 23.

131. Sampson, Anthony T. *The Arms Bazaar.* New York: Viking, 1977.

132. Eitzen and Timmer, *op. cit.*

133. Roebuck and Weeber, *op. cit.*

134. Agee, Phillip. *Inside the Company: CIA Diary.* New York: Stonehill, 1975.

135. Roebuck and Weeber, *op. cit.*

136. *Ibid.*

137. Halperin, *op. cit.*

138. Wise, David. *The Politics of Lying.* New York: Vantage, 1973.

139. Sampson, Anthony T. *The Sovereign State of ITT.* New York: Stein and Day, 1973.

140. Eitzen and Timmer, *op. cit.*

141. Roebuck and Weber, *op cit.*

142. Agee, *op. cit.*

143. Eitzen and Timmer, *op. cit.*

144. "CIA Murder Plots—Weighing the Damage to U.S." *U.S. News & World Report.* December 1, 1975: 13–15.

145. Powers, Thomas. "Inside the Department

146. Myers, Laura. "CIA Asked Mafia to Kill Castro, Newly Declassified Memo Reveals." *Houston Chronicle.* July 2, 1997: 9A.

147. Krauss, Clifford. "How U.S. Actions Helped Hide Salvador Human Rights Abuses." *New York Times.* March 21, 1993: 1, 10.

148. "America and Nicaragua: Read (Almost) All About It." *The Economist.* October 27, 1984: 25.

149. *Ibid.*

150. Borosage, Robert L. "What to Do With Intelligence Agencies." *Working Papers* 4, 1977: 41.

151. Bradlee, Jr., Ben. *Guts and Glory: The Rise and Fall of Oliver North.* New York: Donald Fine, 1988.

152. Draper, Theodore. *A Very Thin Line: The Iran-Contra Affairs.* New York: Hill and Wang, 1991: 27.

153. *Ibid.*

154. Bradlee, *op. cit.*

155. Draper, *op. cit.*

156. Magnuson, Ed. "Patriots Pursuing Profits." *Time.* June 8, 1987: 24–25.

157. Draper, *op. cit.*

158. Bradlee, *op. cit.*

159. Quoted by Draper, *op. cit.*, p. 98.

160. Draper, *op. cit.*

161. *Ibid.*

162. "Transcript of Reagan's Remarks on the Hostages." *New York Times.* July 1, 1985: A7.

163. Cohen, William S. and Mitchell, George J. *Men of Zeal: A Candid Inside Story of the Iran-Contra Hearings.* New York: Viking, 1988.

164. *Ibid.*

165. *Ibid.*

166. Bradlee, *op. cit.*

167. Draper, *op. cit.*

168. Cohen and Mitchell, *op. cit.*

169. Draper, *op. cit.*, p. 216.

170. Cohen and Mitchell, *op. cit.*

171. Draper, *op. cit.*, p. 302.

172. Cohen and Mitchell, *op. cit.*

173. Draper, *op. cit.*, p. 355.

174. *Ibid.*, p. 417.

175. Quoted in Wine, Michael. "White House E-Mail Gives Peek at Hi-Jinks During Iran-Contra." *Houston Chronicle.* November 26, 1995: 2A.

176. "Transcript of Remarks by Reagan About

Iran." *New York Times*. November 14, 1986: A8.

177. Reagan, Ronald. *An American Life*. New York: Simon and Schuster, 1990.

178. Draper, *op. cit.*, p. 475.

179. *Op. cit.*

180. Draper, *op. cit.*

181. Cohen and Mitchell, *op. cit.*, p. xxviii.

182. *Ibid.*

183. Bradlee, *op. cit.*, p. 491.

184. Draper, *op. cit.*, pp. 541–542.

185. *Ibid.*, p. 551.

186. *Ibid.*, p. 551.

187. *Ibid.*, p. 552.

188. Morganthau, Tom. "Ollie North's Secret Network." *Newsweek*. March 9, 1987: 32–37.

189. Bradlee, *op. cit.*

190. *Ibid.*, p. 538.

191. *Ibid.*, p. 538.

192. Shales, Tom. "On the Air: The High Drama of a Duel." *Washington Post*. July 8, 1987: B2.

193. Kaplan, Fred. "Judge Gives McFarlane $20K Fine." *Boston Globe*. March 4, 1989: 1, 4.

194. Dellinger, Walter. "Case Closed." *The New Republic*, January 9 & 16, 1989: 15–16.

195. Kaplan, Fred. "Secord Guilty Plea Avoids Trial." *Boston Globe*. November 5, 1989: 3.

196. Yost, Peter. "Secord, Iran-Contra Figure, Gets 2 Years' Probation." *Boston Globe*. January 26, 1990: 5.

197. Wines, Michael. "Hakim on Probation in Iran-Contra Deal but Shares Proceeds." *New York Times*. February 2, 1990: A1, A18.

198. Johnston, David. "Iran-Contra Role Brings Pondexter 6 Months in Prison." *New York Times*. June 12, 1990: A1, A19.

199. Lowther, William. "A Forgiving Sentence." *Maclean's*. July 17, 1989: 23.

200. Lamar, *op. cit.*

201. Cohen and Mitchell, *op. cit.*, p. 97.

202. Johnston, September 17, 1991, *op. cit.*

203. Johnston, David. "Judge in Iran-Contra Trial Drops Case Against North After Prosecutor Gives Up." *New York Times*. September 17, 1991: A1, A19.

204. "Oliver North Beats the Rap."[Editorial], *New York Times*. September 17, 1991: A20.

205. Gartner, Michael. "Oliver North's Disloyalty." *USA Today*. October 18, 1994: 11A.

206. Mill, John Stuart. *Dissertations and Discussions: Political, Philosophical, and Historical*. New York: Haskell House, 1975.

207. Eitzen and Timmer, *op. cit.*

208. Daniels, Roger. *Concentration Camps USA: Japanese-Americans and World War II*. New York: Holt, Rinehart, and Winston, 1972.

209. Girdner, Audrie and Loftis, Anne. *The Great Betrayal: The Evacuation of the Japanese-Americans During World War II*. London: MacMillan, 1969.

210. Weglyn, Micki. *Years of Infamy: The Untold Story of American Concentration Camps*. New York: William Morrow, 1976.

211. Borosage, Robert L. "What to Do With the Intelligence Agencies." *Working Papers* 4, 1977: 38–45.

212. Halperin, et al., *op. cit.*, p. 148.

213. *Ibid.*

214. Hersh, Seymour M. "CIA Keeps Eartha Kitt File." *Washington Star News*. January 3, 1975: 7.

215. Halperin, et al., p. 149.

216. *Ibid.*

217. Cannon, Terence. "The CIA under Reagan." *World Marxist Review*. August 1983: 69–72.

218. Halperin, et al., *op. cit.*

219. *Ibid.*, p. 165.

220. Donner, Frank J. *The Age of Surveillance: The Aims and Methods of America's Political Intelligence System*. New York: Knopf, 1980.

221. Halperin, et al., *op. cit.*, p. 175.

222. *Ibid.*, p. 176.

223. Roebuck and Weeber, *op. cit.*

224. Halperin, et al., *op cit.*, p. 94.

225. Donner, *op. cit.*

226. Halperin, et al., *op. cit.*

227. Harris, Richard. "Reflections: Crime in the F.B.I." *The New Yorker*. August 8, 1977: 30–42.

228. Donner, *op. cit.*

229. Harris, *op. cit.*

230. Harris, *op. cit.*, p. 39.

231. *Ibid.*, p. 39.

232. Donner, *op. cit.*

233. Halperin, et al., *op. cit.*

234. Donner, *op. cit.*

235. Halperin, et al., *op. cit.*

236. Quoted in "Hoover's FBI Targeted Chicago's Daley." *Houston Chronicle*. August 31, 1997: 11A.

237. *Ibid.*, p. 107.

238. *Ibid.*

239. Donner, *op. cit.*

240. Halperin, et al., *op. cit.*, p. 117.

241. Harris, *op. cit.*

242. Eitzen and Timmer, *op. cit.*

243. Harris, *op. cit.*, p. 40.

244. Donner, *op. cit.*

245. Halperin, et al., *op. cit.*

246. *Ibid.*, p. 113.

247. Mauro, Tony. "Striking Gold with the FOIA: How FBI's Court Files Came to Light." *Legal Times.* September 12, 1988: 22.

248. Charas, Alexander. "How the FBI Spied on the High Court." *Washington Post.* December 3, 1989: C1, C4.

249. Charns, Alexander. *Cloak and Gavel: FBI Wiretaps, Bugs, Informers, and the Supreme Court.* Urbana, Ill.: University of Chicago Press, 1992.

250. "F.B.I. Kept Close Watch on Douglas." *New York Times.* July 22, 1984: 42.

251. Ehrlichman, John. *Witness to Power: The Nixon years* New york: Simon and Schuster, 1982.

252. Charns, 1992, *op. cit.*, p. 113.

253. Halperin, et al., *op. cit.*, p. 117.

254. Donner, *op. cit.*, p. 28.

255. *Ibid.*

256. *Ibid.*, p. 235.

257. Eitzen and Timmer, *op. cit.*, p. 346.

258. Harris, *op. cit.*

259. Rawls, Wendell, Jr. "F.B.I. Admits Planting a Rumor to Discredit Jean Seberg in 1970." *New York Times.* September 15, 1979: 1, 6.

260. Eitzen and Timmer, *op. cit.*

261. O'Reilly, Kenneth. "The FBI and the Civil Rights Movement During the Kennedy Years—From the Freedom Rides to Albany." *Journal of Southern History* 54, 1988: 202.

262. Halperin, et al., *op, cit.*, p. 62.

263. Quoted in *Ibid.*, p. 78.

264. *Ibid.*, p. 63.

265. *Ibid.*, p. 64.

266. *Ibid.*, p. 80.

267. Navasky, Victor. *Kennedy Justice.* New York: Athenium, 1971.

268. *Ibid.*

269. Harris, *op. cit.*, p. 40.

270. *Ibid.*, p. 89.

271. "Lowery Blasts FBI for Spying on SCLC, Others." *Jet.* February 15, 1988: 4.

272. *Olmstead v. United States, op. cit.*

273. Markoff, John. "FBI Seeks Massive Wiretap Capabilities." *Houston Chronicle.* November 2, 1995: 11A.

274. Halperin, et al., *op cit.*, p. 187.

275. *Ibid.*, p. 190.

276. *Ibid.*

277. *Ibid.*, p. 194.

278. *Ibid.*, p. 195.

279. *Ibid.*

280. *Ibid.*, p. 199.

281. *Ibid.*, p. 299.

282. *Ibid.*

283. Archer, Jules. *Watergate: America in Crisis.* New York: Thomas Y. Crowell, 1975: 270.

284. Lowi, Theodore. "The Intelligent Person's Guide to Political Corruption." *Public Affairs* 82, 1981: 1–8.

285. Congressional Quarterly. *Watergate: Chronology of a Crisis.* Washington, DC: Congressional Quarterly, Inc., 1974.

286. *Ibid.*

287. *Ibid.*

288. *Ibid.*

289. *Ibid.*

290. Cook, Fred J. *The Crimes of Watergate.* New York: Franklin Watts, 1981.

291. *Ibid.*, p. 112.

292. Congressional Quarterly, *op. cit.*

293. Archer, Jules. *Watergate: America in Crisis.* New York: Thomas Y. Crowell, 1975.

294. *Ibid.*, p. 236.

295. *Ibid.*, p. 224.

296. *Ibid.*

297. Wrong, Dennis H. "Watergate: Symptom of What Sickness?" *Dissent* 23, 1974: 502.

298. Brown, Bruce. "Watergate: Business as Usual." *Liberation* July/August: 1974, 22.

299. Erskine, Hazel. "The Polls: Corruption in Government." *Public Opinion Quarterly* 37, 1973: 628–644.

300. Quoted in Silverstein, Mark. "Watergate and the American Political System." In Markovits, Andrei S. and Silverstein, Mark (Eds.), *The Politics of Scandal: Power and Process in Liberal Democracies.* New York: Holmes & Meier, 1988: 15–37.

301. Cook, *op. cit.*, p. 2.

302. *Ibid.*

303. Silverstein, *op. cit.*, p. 15.

304. Cook, *op. cit.*, p. 2.

305. Bernstein, Carl and Woodward, Bob. *All the President's Men.* New York: Simon and Schuster, 1974.

306. Congressional Quarterly, *op. cit.*, p. 139.

307. Wieghart, James. "FBI Chief to Tell of Burning Hunt File." *New York Daily News*, April 27, 1973: 1, 81.

308. Congressional Quarterly, *op. cit.*, p. 149.

309. *Ibid.*, p. 150.

310. Bernstein and Woodward, *op. cit.*, p. 313.

311. Congressional Quarterly, *op. cit.*

312. Ehrlichman, John. *Witness to Power*. New York: Simon and Schuster, 1982.

313. *Ibid.*

314. Congressional Quarterly, *op. cit.*

315. Bernstein and Woodward, *op. cit.*

316. Archer, *op. cit.*

317. Congressional Quarterly, *op. cit.*

318. Archer, *op. cit.*, p. 200.

319. *Ibid.*, p. 200.

320. Archer, *op. cit.*

321. Hersh, Seymour M. "Kissinger Said to Have Asked F.B.I. to Wiretap a Number of His Aides." *New York Times*. May 17, 1973: 1, 35.

322. Woodward, Bob and Bernstein, Carl. "Dean: Nixon Asked IRS to Stop Audits." *Washington Post*. June 20, 1973: A1, A7.

323. Dean, John. *Blind Ambition: The White House Years*. New York: Simon and Schuster, 1976.

324. Cook, *op. cit.*

325. Feinberg, Barbara S. *Watergate: Scandal in the White House*. New York: Franklin Watts, 1990.

326. Congressional Quarterly, *op. cit.*

327. Barker, Karlyn and Pincus, Walter. "Watergate Revisited." *Washington Post*. June 14, 1992: A1.

328. Cook, *op. cit.*

329. *Ibid.*, p. 112.

330. Feinberg, *op. cit.*, p. 216.

331. Archer, *op. cit.*, p. 216.

332. *Ibid.*, p. 216.

333. Archer, *op. cit.*

334. Quoted in *Ibid.*, p. 271.

335. Kelman, *op. cit.*, p. 307.

336. Kelman, Herbert C. "Some Reflections on Authority, Corruption, and Punishment: The Social-Psychological Context of Watergate." *Psychiatry* 39, 1976: 303–317.

337. Candee, Dan. "The Moral Psychology of Watergate." *Journal of Social Issues* 21, 1975: 183.

338. Kelman, *op. cit.*, p. 307.

339. Cook, *op. cit.*, p. 139.

340. Silverstein, *op. cit.*, p. 33.

341. Dunham, Roger G. and Mauss, Armand L. "Waves from Watergate: Evidence Concerning the Impact of the Watergate Scandal Upon Political Legitimacy and Social Control." *Pacific Sociological Review* 19, 1976: 470.

342. Kelman, *op. cit.*, p. 304.

343. Vidich, Arthur J. "Political Legitimacy in Bureaucratic Society: An Analysis of Watergate." *Social Research* 42, 1975: 793.

344. Barber, James D. "The Nixon Brush with Tyranny." *Political Science Quarterly* 92, 1977: 594.

345. Archer, *op. cit.*, p. 274.

346. Kelman, *op. cit.*, p. 311.

347. *Ibid.*, p. 603.

348. Hershey, Marjorie R. and Hill, David B. "Watergate and Preadults' Attitudes Toward the President." *American Journal of Political Science* 19, 1975: 703–726.

349. Dunham and Mauss, *op. cit.*, p. 485.

350. Zimmer, Troy. "The Impact of Watergate on the Public's Trust in People and Confidence in the Mass Media." *Social Science Quarterly* 59, 1979: 743–751.

351. Jensen, Michael C. "Watergate Donors Still Riding High." *New York Times*. August 24, 1978: 1, 7.

352. Hedlo, Hugh, Brown, Fred R., and Dillon, Conley. "Watergate in Retrospect: The Forgotten Agenda." *Public Administration Review* 36, 1976: 306.

353. Hawkins, Robert P., Pingree, Suzanne, and Roberts, Donald F. "Watergate and Political Socialization: The Inescapable Event." *American Politics Quarterly* 3, 1975: 406.

354. Arterton, F. Christopher. "The Impact of Watergate on Children's Attitudes Toward Political Authority." *Political Science Quarterly* 89, 1974: 269–288.

355. Dennis, Jack and Webster, Carol. "Children's Images of the President and of Government in 1962 and 1974." *American Politics Quarterly* 3, 1974: 386–405.

356. Fowlkes, Diane L. "Realpolitik and Play Politics: The Effects of Watergate and Political Gaming on Undergraduate Students' Political Interest and Political Trust." *Simulation & Games* 8, 1977: 419–438.

357. Garrett, James B. and Wallace, Benjamin. "Cognitive Consistency, Repression-Sensitization, and Level of Moral Judgment: Reactions of College Students to the Watergate Scandals." *Journal of Social Psychology* 98, 1976: 69–76.

358. Congressional Quarterly, *op. cit.*

359. Chaffee, Steven H. and Becker, Lee B. "Young Voters' Reactions to Early Watergate Issues." *American Politics Quarterly* 3, 1975: 360–386.

Corruption of Public Officials

Prosecutor: I saw you take that bribe, and tamper with evidence,
and resist arrest, and perjure yourself under oath.
Cop: Don't forget I ran a red light, too.

From *The Big Easy* (1993). Screenplay by Daniel Petrie, Jr.

At the beginning of the eighteenth century, the governor-general of colonial New York was Edward Hyde (Lord Cornbury), a first cousin of the Queen of England. Among other things, Governor Hyde was a drunkard and an unabashed transvestite, with a penchant for addressing the New York Assembly while wearing one of his wife's hooped gowns. Hyde was also a crook,[1] as thoroughly dishonest in his public role as he was outlandish in his private life. He routinely accepted kickbacks and bribes, and gave large, illegal land grants to his friends in exchange for cash.[2] In 1707, he claimed to have received secret information that the French were preparing to invade New York by sea. He taxed the citizenry 1500 pounds, ostensibly for the construction of protective batteries around the harbor. The French invasion was, of course, a fabrication, and Hyde used the funds to build a lavish new home for himself.

Hyde's behavior prompted so many complaints from the Assembly that he was removed from office and briefly imprisoned.[3] This may have been the first major political corruption scandal in American history. It would not be the last.

Indeed, the misuse of public authority for private gain has been a persistent phenomenon throughout American history. If the abuses of power described in Chapter 8 conform to Lowi's notion of "Big Corruption," then bribery and misappropriation represent "Little Corruption." In this context, the "Little" sobriquet does not mean trivial or uncostly; it merely distinguishes the crimes of renegade individuals from organizational deviance.

In the first section of this chapter, we will examine how officials within various branches of the government have violated the public trust and breached the public interest. In the second section, we will focus on police corruption as a distinct but closely related form of white-collar crime.

POLITICAL CORRUPTION

The simplest explanation of political corruption is that it reflects the frailty of human nature.[4] Political scientist James Q. Wilson has offered a pithy rule-of-thumb: "[M]en steal when there is a lot of money lying around loose and no one is watching."[5] More complex (although not necessarily more valid) explanations of corruption generally are rooted in the interaction between the individual and the social structure. Thus, corruption has been attributed variously to ambivalence toward behavioral norms,[6] the existence of wealthy elites denied direct formal influence on political policy,[7] as well the intrinsic flaws in organizational arrangements and bureaucratic procedures.[8]

At its most basic, official behavior can be considered corrupt when it "deviates from the formal duties of a public role" for personal gain.[9] This is a useful little definition, because "all illegal acts are not necessarily corrupt and all corrupt acts are not necessarily illegal."[10] For example, former Congressman Allan Howe was plainly guilty of an unlawful act when he was convicted in 1976 of soliciting two undercover policewomen posing as prostitutes.[11] However, his behavior might not be construed as truly corrupt, because he did not betray his official position. But when former Congressman Wayne Hays put his mistress on the federal payroll as a secretary that same year—despite her admitted inability to type, file, or even answer the telephone[12]—that would meet the corruption criterion, because Hays' conduct involved a misuse of public office. Conversely, the craterous loopholes in campaign finance laws may encourage conduct that is technically legal yet inevitably corrupting.

In earlier generations, some functionalists suggested that corruption may not be inherently evil because it serves as a "lubricant which eases the rigid wheels of a bureaucracy."[13] It was argued that government cannot be carried on efficiently without corruption.[14] Most modern scholars, however, perceive the social effects of political corruption as unmistakably dysfunctional.[15]

The Executive Branch

In the United States, access to power and resources permits incumbents to buy political support by selling political favors. Corruption is further perpetuated because elected officials "can often engage in illegal activities without being reprimanded at the polls."[16] Of course, there are only two elected officials in the entire executive branch of the federal government, a president and a vice-president. Thus, despite occasional anomalies like Spiro Agnew, known instances of "Little" corruption at this highest level of elective office have been relatively rare. More typically, when presidential (or vice-presidential) malfeasance has occurred, it has taken the form of "Big" corruption aimed at promoting an administration's organizational goals, as was the case with Watergate, the Iran-Contra affair, and other such abuses of executive power.

An exception to this thesis would be some of the well-documented fundraising excesses of the Clinton administration. From dispensing overnight stays in the White House's fabled Lincoln Bedroom in exchange for hefty campaign contributions,[17] to the illegal Democratic National Committee (DNC) fundraiser at the Hsi Lai Buddhist monastery in California,[18] to the suspicious contributions made by South Korean and Chinese companies,[19] President Clinton and the DNC seemed to engage in a level of alleged influence peddling not seen since Watergate.

Year by year, scandal by scandal, the corruption of American politics only seems to get worse. Writing in 1999, the veteran political reporter Elizabeth Drew ruefully observed:

> Indisputably, the greatest change in Washington over the past twenty-five years . . . has been the preoccupation with money. . . . The culture of money dominates Washington as never before; money now rivals or even exceeds power as the preeminent goal.[20]

"Little" corruption, however, has never been a stranger to the myriad federal agencies which comprise the executive branch. Unelected administrators and government agents often have the same value to the buyers of influence and special favors as do elected officials.[21] Bureaucrats cannot make laws, but they can determine the way laws are carried out through their administrative authority and regulatory powers. "The mere structural availability of the opportunity for illicit gain is sufficient motivation for some corrupt employees."[22]

Structural facilitation of corruption can be illustrated by the experiences of two large federal agencies: the U.S. Department of Agriculture (USDA) and the Department of Defense.

The Department of Agriculture.   The USDA was rocked in the 1970s by revelations that government grain inspectors were being bribed to misgrade substandard or adulterated grain and to overlook the short weighting of grain shipments.[23] The Bunge Corporation, one of the world's largest grain exporters, admitted that it had bribed an inspector to ignore a shipment infested with insects. "In a case brought against the Archer-Daniels-Midland Company and the Garnac Grain Company, a government investigator indicated that the two companies saved about $450,000 worth of grain annually through short-weighting, and that misgrading added another $1.2 million to company coffers."[24]

While corrupt USDA inspectors have allowed adulterated grain to leave the country, inspectors from the FDA have been convicted of accepting bribes to allow adulterated food into the country. Four such officials knowingly approved more than 20 tons of contaminated seafood in 1988.[25]

More recently, in 1995, the head of the USDA's Cooperative State Research Service was removed from his job after investigators found that he had lobbied Congress illegally in order to steer $1.8 million in research contracts to friends.[26]

The Department of Defense.   "One of the most common forms of government corruption involves the purchasing agents who decide which firms are to supply the government with various products and services."[27] In 1776, the Continental Congress granted a gunpowder contract to the firm of Willing, Morris & Company.[28] Both Willing and Morris were members of the Congressional committee that had issued the contract. They cleared a profit of 12,000 pounds.[29]

Today, because government purchases total hundreds of billions of dollars annually and make up nearly one-quarter of our gross national product,[30] the incentives for corruption are obvious. Pentagon bid-rigging scandals involving $700 toilet seats[31] and platinum-coated hammers[32] have underscored the great potential for abuse within the military-industrial complex. This was never more evident than in the case of Melvyn Paisley.

Paisley served as Assistant Secretary of the Navy for Research and Development between 1981 and 1987 and was largely responsible for procurement. "[W]hile in office, he corrupted the bidding process on hundreds of millions of dollars of weapons systems in order to divert contracts to those who secretly bought his services."[33] Consider just two examples of Paisley's gross misconduct.

In 1985, Paisley and his partner, defense consultant William Galvin, conspired to induce the Navy to select the big industrial firm Martin Marietta as the prime contractor on a classified government research program. The complicated scheme involved Paisley and Galvin forming a company named Saphire Systems, which would become a subcontractor on the program in collusion with Martin Marietta. Paisley's financial interest in Saphire was, of course, carefully concealed. Seven months later, Paisley awarded a $900,000 contract to Martin Marietta and $300,000 to Saphire Systems—his own company.[34]

That same year, Paisley also conspired with the Sperry Corporation (now Unisys) to rig the bidding to supply the Navy with a sophisticated airport surveillance system. "He went to extraordinary lengths to persuade his Pentagon colleagues to alter the terms of the competition in ways that would favor Sperry."[35] Paisley also passed secret information to Sperry concerning rival bids, which allowed Sperry to come in as the low bidder and win the $45-million contract.[36]

Even after Paisley left the Pentagon in 1987, he continued to collect large deferred "consulting" fees from companies with whom he earlier had conspired. Over just a 15-month period, he was paid more than $500,000.[37]

Paisley was arrested as part of Operation Ill Wind, the biggest federal investigation of defense procurement fraud ever conducted. In addition to

Paisley, this operation led to the convictions of 8 other government employees, 42 corporate executives and defense consultants, and 7 major corporations.[38] As the highest-ranking official uncovered by Ill Wind, Paisley received the stiffest sentence, 4 years in prison. Ironically, he once had been asked by a Congressional committee what should be done about corrupt defense contractors. Paisley's prophetic reply: "[Y]ou have to hang them from a tree where everyone can see them."[39]

The Legislative Branch

For the first half-century of American independence, members of Congress commonly sold their influence to private interests, as if that practice were part of their job description. In an 1833 letter to the president of the National Bank, Senator Daniel Webster complained indignantly that his retainer had not been *"refreshed* as usual."[40] Webster threatened to discontinue his legislative services to the bank if it failed to send him his customary payment. Understandably, public resentment over such corruption of their legislators grew and in 1853, Congress passed its first "conflict of interest" statute.

Over the years, like a malarial fever in perennial relapse, the problem of Congressional influence peddling has refused to go away. In 1996, for example, Dan Rostenkowski, the former Illinois congressman, who for years had chaired the powerful House Ways and Means Committee, was handed a 17-month prison sentence in federal court after agreeing to plead guilty to two felony counts. He had engaged in a "pattern of corrupt activities spanning three decades."[41] Rostenkowski stole more than $640,000 from the government in a string of schemes including the conversion for personal use of House post office funds intended for official mailings.[42] In late 2000, during the waning days of his administration, Bill Clinton granted a presidental pardon to Dan Rostenkowski.

Most critics contend that at the heart of Congressional corruption is the manner by which American political campaigns are funded. "The overwhelming majority of voters believe the current system for financing campaigns is basically unsound."[43] Such a national consensus is not hard to explain. The cost of running for office has increased exponentially since the days of Daniel Webster. (In fact, senators were not even popularly elected in Webster's time.) After the Supreme Court ruled in 1976 that statutory limits upon Congressional election expenditures were unconstitutional,[44] members (and would-be members) of Congress came to depend increasingly on special interest groups for campaign contributions.[45] The result has been "a parasitic symbiosis between the public and private sectors."[46] In 1986, the deputy solicitor of the Department of Labor articulated this disheartening conclusion:

> Virtually every member of Congress has been compelled to become a crook. Most of them, we can hope, regret the necessity of having had to accept a life of crime as the price of holding office, but crooks they certainly are.[47]

Political action committees (PACs) are one very convenient source of campaign money. Although federal law limits direct PAC contributions to $5000, the law can be circumvented easily through the use of so-called soft money—legally unrestricted donations to political parties, as opposed to restricted donations to individual candidates. During the 1992 presidential election, for example, the Republican National Committee collected $70 million in soft money. A Republican group known as "Team 100" consisted of 270 donors of $100,000 or more. The Democrats also had an elite group of their own, "The Managing Trustees," for donors of over $200,000.[48] A 1995 study by the nonpartisan Center for Public Integrity, titled "The Buying of the President," concluded that the American political system resembles "a giant auction."[49]

The proliferation of soft money in the 1996 presidential campaign dwarfed the 1992 figures. The Republican and Democratic parties amassed a record-breaking $170 million in unregulated contributions.[50] It was a short-lived record, however. In 2000 the two major parties received over $226 million in soft money.[51]

An analysis of the spending for the 1986 Congressional elections proclaimed that "[t]he statistical evidence staggers the mind."[52] PACs contributed $132.2 million to Congressional candidates, 28% of total receipts. Incumbents in the Senate and the House received $89.5 million, challengers received $19.2 million, and the balance went to open-seat candidates.[53] It has been quipped that the United States produces "the best politicians money can buy."[54]

Although the explicit quid pro quo arrangements of the Webster era may now be relatively rare, PACs unquestionably extract an implicit price for their financial support. One lobbyist openly acknowledges that PAC funds represent "a civilized approach to vote-buying."[55] Another lobbyist admits: "We're skirting the edge of felonious conduct."[56]

Lobbying and political fundraising have fundamentally distorted our democratic system.[57] In 1996, a retiring congressman described a system of institutionalized corruption in remarkably blunt terms:

> No lobbyist ever made a contribution without expecting something in return. . . . The only reason it's not bribery is that Congress gets to say what's bribery.[58]

The power of PAC money was made apparent, for example, in 1982, when Congress was debating a Federal Trade Commission regulation requiring the disclosure of known defects in used cars. One unnamed Congressman was quoted as declaring, "I got a $10,000 check from the National Auto Dealers Association. I can't change my vote now."[59] Apparently, he was not alone; Congress overturned the regulation, even though it clearly served the public interest.

An illustration of a well-heeled lobbying blitzkrieg was provided when baby food was not included in a 1993 bill authorizing an aid package for the former Soviet Union. Immediately, the Gerber Company pulled out its checkbook.

For Gerber, the stakes were high. Someday the republics would buy their own baby food; they would probably choose the brand they had come to know through U.S. aid. So the company started spending big bucks in Washington. It hired a lobbying firm to press its case, and a Gerber executive traveled to Washington weekly. The result: a second aid bill . . . paving the way for U.S. taxpayers to send Gerber products to Russia.[60]

Some lawmakers argue that lobbyists perform a valuable service by providing them with important information on critical issues. In 1995, the House Majority Whip, Representative Tom DeLay of Texas, attacked a proposal to limit lobbyists' gifts to members of Congress as a "leftist plot."[61] Defenders of the current system also contend that campaign contributions do not dictate Congressional votes. This position espouses an "investment theory" of politics.[62] From this perspectives, campaign contributions are viewed not as covert bribes, but as investments in candidates who are likely to share a donor's point of view. As one critic has noted, "Congressmen don't have to chase money with their votes; there's so much around they can cop all they want no matter what their stance on a specific issue."[63]

We have thus far looked at Congressional corruption as an institutional phenomenon. We now turn our attention to an individual level of analysis.

In recent times, most of the offenses involved in most of the successful prosecutions of corrupt federal legislators have fallen into three general categories: (1) violations of election laws; (2) payroll fraud; and (3) bribery. Each of these areas reflects the sort of betrayal that moved one federal judge to ponder aloud while passing sentence on a convicted Congressman, "If people who make the laws can't obey them, who can we expect to?"[64]

Violation of Election Laws.   In 1975, The SEC revealed that the Gulf Oil Corporation had maintained a multimillion dollar secret fund from which it had made illegal corporate campaign contributions, clumsily disguised as personal donations.[65] The money had been funneled into Gulf's Bahamian subsidiary and then dispersed to selected political candidates, mostly influential incumbents. Gulf's gift list read like a "Who's Who" of the U.S. Senate, containing such prominent names as Hubert Humphrey, Henry Jackson, Howard Baker, and Russell Long.[66] The biggest contribution, $100,000, reportedly was given to Minority Leader Hugh Scott, who announced his retirement shortly after the Gulf story was reported by the media.[67] When the scandal was uncovered, Gulf acted as if *it* were the victim; its chairman called it a "tragic chapter in the history of Gulf Oil."[68] Gulf even sent letters to its powerful donees, requesting that they return the illegal gifts.[69] It seemed as though Gulf believed that the Senate could be purchased with a money-back guarantee.

Also in 1975, Representative George Hansen of Idaho was sentenced to 2 months in prison for lying about his campaign financing. Hansen would have been the first sitting congressman to be locked up since Representative Lane Smith of Massachusetts served a 4-month sentence in 1956 and was re-elected while in prison. However, the judge in Hansen's case opted for leniency and revoked the sentence in favor of a small fine.[70]

Smith's dubious record was threatened again 2 years later, when freshman Representative Richard Tonry of Louisiana went to prison for receiving and conspiring to receive illegal campaign contributions. However, Tonry resigned from office. In his farewell message to the House, he vowed to return and urged his fellow legislators to "Keep my seat warm."[71] Except perhaps on C-SPAN, Tonry never saw that seat again.

In 1994, nine-term Representative Carroll Hubbard, Jr., of Kentucky was sentenced to 3 years in prison after pleading guilty to conspiracy to file false campaign finance reports. The presiding judge called the case a "sad and sorry tale" of official misconduct.[72] In what may have been an oblique reference to the light sentence in the earlier Hansen case, the judge further noted the he had received a deluge of letters from Hubbard's embittered constituents urging *against* leniency.[73]

As of this writing, the most recent sitting member of the House of Representatives to be convicted of campaign fraud is Jay Kim of California, the nation's first Korean-born congressman. Kim pleaded guilty in 1997 to federal charges of accepting and hiding more than $200,000 in illegal contributions.[74] He later received a sentence of 2 months house arrest and 1 year probation, along with a $5000 fine.[75] Despite pleas from his own party, Kim refused to resign his House seat, but was easily defeated in the 1998 Republican primary.[76]

Payroll Fraud.   In addition to campaign funds, another tempting source of ready cash which some unscrupulous members of Congress have tapped illegally is their generous budget allowance. A number of legislators have been convicted of diverting money from their payrolls to their pockets. Representative J. Irving Walley of Pennsylvania received a suspended prison term and 3 years probation after admitting that he had forced kickbacks from his staff and used the funds for his own expenses.[77] Less fortunate was Representative James Hastings of New York, who received a 2- to 5-year sentence for a similar offense. Hastings had extorted kickbacks from two of his Congressional employees and used the money to buy cars and snowmobiles.[78]

Representative Charles Diggs of Michigan was given a 3-year prison term for carrying out a fraudulent scheme in which he increased the pay of employees in his Washington and Detroit offices and kept the surplus to help pay mounting alimony costs and to inject needed cash into a struggling Detroit funeral parlor he owned.[79] A somewhat different strategy was utilized by Representative Frank Clark of Pennsylvania. Instead of diverting employees' paychecks to help pay his household expenses, Clark put his entire household staff on the Congressional payroll.[80] After pleading guilty, Clark was sentenced to 2 years in prison.[81]

Bribery.   Bribery is the offense most likely to lead to the criminal prosecution of legislative officeholders. Congressional influence peddling can range from overt acts, such as the buying of a member's vote on a particular piece of legislation or the introduction of a bill aimed at benefiting some generous special interest group, to more subtle behaviors, such as providing help in securing government contracts or intervening in the federal bureaucracy on a benefactor's behalf.[82]

For instance, when Representative John Dowdy of Texas walked into an Atlanta airport in 1971, he was handed a bag containing $25,000. The money was to buy his influence in halting a federal probe of a Maryland construction company.[83] Dowdy was convicted and received an 18-month prison sentence. Special prosecutor Stephen Sachs had argued that it was important that Dowdy serve time, both as a deterrent to other public officials and as an affirmation that the war on crime must transcend social and occupational boundaries. As Sachs noted, "There are an awful lot of people in jail and in prisons who have done far less than Mr. Dowdy and have had far less opportunity."[84]

Another typical case is that of Representative Bertram Podell of New York, who was jailed for selling favors to a Florida air taxi company trying to obtain a Caribbean route from the government.[85] A more insidious example is Representative Frank Brasco, also of New York, who was bribed to obtain lucrative post office hauling contracts for a trucking firm headed by a reputed mobster.[86] Brasco received a 3-month sentence for what the prosecutor termed an "extraordinary sequence of corruption."[87]

Representative Richard Hanna of California became a key figure in the notorious "Koreagate" scandal of the late 1970s.[88] A prominent Korean businessman named Tongsun Park, who represented the Korean rice industry in America, testified that he had given a total of $850,000 to 31 members of Congress in order to advance his business interests and the interests of the South Korean government. Hanna was one of Park's biggest beneficiaries, collecting $246,000.[89] In 1978, Hanna pleaded guilty to conspiring with Park to defraud the United States.[90] Park, however, denied any wrongdoing. In his words, "I thought I was taking part in the American political process. So far as I was concerned, I was helping Congressional friends who were loyal to me."[91] Missing from this defense, of course, is any recognition that members of the United States Congress are not supposed to be "loyal" to foreign lobbyists.

If one had to choose a single model of the corrupting effects of entrenched legislative power, one could hardly do better than Representative Daniel Flood of Pennsylvania. A former Shakespearean actor known for his mellifluous oratory and distinctive waxed mustache, Flood parlayed his seniority and great popularity with voters into one of the most influential power bases in Congress. True to his name, he "flooded" his home district with federal funds. "His constituents could be born at the Daniel J. Flood Rural Health Center, be educated at the Daniel J. Flood Elementary School, be employed in the Daniel J. Flood Industrial Park, and retire in the Daniel J. Flood Elderly Center."[92]

But Flood's agenda was not limited to the life span of his constituents; he also used his considerable influence and well-honed political skills for personal profit. He took so many bribes it was hard to keep track of them all. He pocketed $5000 from a businessman trying to sell disaster housing to the government for victims of Hurricane Agnes. He was paid $50,000 to obtain new certification for a chain of California trade schools about to lose its accreditation.[93] Flood collected regular payoffs, totaling $89,000, from a Washington conference center in exchange for channeling funds from the government's family planning program.[94] A banker gave him $4000 worth of stock for using his influence to persuade the Treasury Department to approve a merger.[95] A New York rabbi paid Flood $5000 to help his religious school receive millions of dollars in federal grants.[96] Flood once joked, "Little birdies fly by and drop these goodies on my desk."[97]

After his indictment, Flood struck a very generous plea bargain with the government, under which he agreed to plead guilty to one misdemeanor charge in exchange for the dropping of 11 felony counts.[98] Because of his advanced age, he received no prison time and was placed on short-term probation.[99] He died 15 years later at the age of 90.

Finally, it should be noted that the tripartite division of Congressional misconduct employed in this chapter is merely a convenient device for expositive purposes. The three categories are by no means mutually exclusive. Consider, for example, the sordid case of Representative Frederick Richmond of New York, who managed to blend all three varieties of corruption, in addition to a drug charge,[100] a securities violation,[101] and the solicitation of a male prostitute.[102] Richmond once even obtained a clerical job in the House of Representatives for an escaped convict.[103]

Richmond hid illegal corporate campaign contributions by converting them to traveler's checks or by swapping equivalent amounts of cash for unaddressed personal checks from district residents, who were then listed as individual contributors. Most of them did not even know the destination of their checks.[104]

Richmond's payroll practices also raised serious ethical questions. His Congressional aides received paychecks from private companies owned or controlled by Richmond, in violation of federal statutes. The assistant treasurer of Richmond's campaign committee testified that she made regular deposits into the account of the Richmond Corporation, but had no idea what that company did.[105]

Worst of all, Richmond reportedly accepted large bribes from a Brooklyn shipbuilding firm for his help in securing $310 million in Navy repair contracts.[106] In 1982, Richmond pleaded guilty to federal charges and resigned from Congress.[107] He was sentenced to a year and a day in prison.[108]

Operation ABSCAM

In 1987, Melvin Weinberg, international con artist and convicted swindler, was facing a prison sentence for fraud after pleading guilty in a Pittsburgh federal court. The FBI's New York office, which had been looking for informants involved in white-collar crimes to help the bureau make some criminal cases, decided to conscript Weinberg in exchange for probation. Thus, Operation ABSCAM, the most depraved scandal in Congressional history, was born.[109]

With the FBI's cooperation, Weinberg set up a phony company known as Abdul Enterprises, purportedly owned by a fictitious Arab sheikh. The cover story claimed that "Abdul" was a multimillionaire who wanted to pull his money out of Muslim banks (which paid no interest in accordance with Islamic proscriptions against usury) and invest it in profitable American business ventures.

Among the first notable figures snared in the ABSCAM net was Angelo Errichetti, the colorful mayor of Camden, New Jersey, and one of the most influential politicians in that state. Errichetti accepted payoffs from Abdul's representative (Weinberg) in exchange for helping the sheikh obtain an Atlantic City casino license. "Abdul" was so grateful for the mayor's assistance that he even presented him with an impressive gift. a "priceless" tribal dagger that Weinberg had bought for $2.75 at a Greek flea market.[110] Erichetti was delighted.

In his Runyonesque style, Weinberg would later say, "I never met a straight politician the whole time I was in New Jersey. They must hafta screw 'em in the ground when they die."[111] As if to prove Weinberg's point, Mayor Errichetti introduced him to New Jersey's best-known political figure, Senior U.S. Senator Harrison Arlington Williams, Jr., who turned out to be incredibly greedy, even by ABSCAM standards. Williams and three partners (including a close associate of aged mob boss Meyer Lansky) proposed a lucrative investment opportunity for the sheikh's money. The Williams group would borrow $100 million from Abdul and purchase the country's largest titanium mine in Virginia.

> This deal, they claimed, would give them a virtual monopoly on titanium in the U.S. The Senator, himself, had said that the rare metal was vitally needed by the government for the construction of submarines and other defense projects. With the titanium monopoly, they predicted, they would make a fortune.[112]

Williams, as one of the highest-ranking Democrats in the Senate, could channel government and defense contracts to his partners.[113] Obviously, he knew his participation in the deal had to be as subterranean as the mine, because using his office to help secure titanium contracts would be a blatant federal crime. What he did not know was that his meetings with Weinberg were being tape-recorded. In another of Weinberg's inimitable phrases, Senator Williams "had been left standing bare-assed in Macy's window."[114]

(Continued)

In July 1979, Errichetti was told that "Abdul" and an ersatz emir named "Yassir" were concerned about political unrest in their homeland and would like to remain in the United States.

> Errichetti eagerly replied that he had the political connections to handle the Arabs' residency problems. After all, he winked, Abdul and Yassir had plenty of money to cover the expenses. He'd go to work on the problem.[115]

Within days, the mayor had arranged meetings between the Abdul organization and two Congressmen from Philadelphia, Michael ("Ozzie") Myers and Raymond Lederer, with additional meetings in the works. Errichetti told Weinberg that the Congressmen would pledge the use of their offices to help Abdul and Yassir obtain asylum. The price would be $100,000 per Congressmen (later "marked down" to $50,000). The FBI rented a three-room suite in a hotel at New York's Kennedy Airport and set up hidden cameras and microphones. It recalled the old tale of the spider and the fly.

On August 22, 1979, Mel Weinberg welcomed Erichetti and Myers into the web. Myers, a hard-drinking former longshoreman with a ninth-grade education, who once had been arrested for punching a waitress in the mouth hours before his swearing-in ceremony, was steered to the couch in direct view of the camera.

The scene would become familiar to tens of millions of television viewers. When Myers was asked directly if he could guarantee that the Arabs would have no problems getting asylum in the United States, he boasted of his Congressional power:

> [W]ithout someone in my position . . . you're in deep trouble. People wouldn't even want to deal with you. You gotta use connections to make connections. . . . I gotta lotta guys who is willing to do business—you know, work with you. Different states. Guys right off the Judiciary Committee. You, know, key people, key staff guys, show you how to stall things, how to lay things out.[116]

Myers was given a briefcase containing the $50,000 payoff. He left the meeting alone through the hotel's rear exit, reportedly at a dead run.

> It had been perfect. All the criminal elements. A Congressman had accepted cash to perform specific official acts. He had frosted the cake by offering to make similar deals with his colleagues and Congressional staffers. The video and sound had been on the button. Myers had minced no words. He was a flat-out crook.[117]

Congressman Lederer's performance mirrored that of Myers. He promised to push a bill on behalf of Abdul and Yassir. The man who had once headed Philadelphia's Criminal Probation Department calmly took a $50,000 bribe. One of the highlights of the Lederer tape was his memorable understatement: "I'm no Boy Scout."[118]

(Continued)

In addition to Erichetti, another key middleman in ABSCAM was Philadelphia attorney and veteran influence peddler Howard Criden. Criden had assured Weinberg that bribable Congressmen were in plentiful supply. He bragged, "I can get you about anyone you want."[119]

True to his boast, Criden produced Representative Frank Thompson of New Jersey, chairman of the powerful House Administration Committee. Thompson accepted the usual $50,000 and promised to recruit more Congressmen, particularly his friend John Murphy of New York. ABSCAM was becoming a rogues' parade.

When Murphy arrived 11 days later for his session before the ABSCAM camera, he was asked if he could help with Abdul's immigration difficulties. He replied, "I don't think that there will be any problem."[120] Murphy was given the now-customary suitcase full of cash, most of which reportedly went to Thompson and Criden as "finders fees." It seemed that Murphy's greed transcended a five-figure payoff; he had a far more ambitious, nine-figure scheme in mind. He made a pitch for a $100-million loan so that he secretly could buy a Puerto Rican shipping line. Murphy chaired the House Merchant Marine and Fisheries Committee, a position from which he said he could guarantee passage of legislation to make his shipping enterprise highly profitable.[121]

The next Congressman to snap at the bait was John Jenrette, Jr. of South Carolina. Jenrette was a member of the important House Appropriations Committee—and a chronic alcoholic. He was deeply involved in a failing real estate venture that was under federal investigation, and he needed money. When he was asked by an undercover agent if he would accept the sheikh's bribe, he declared, "I've got larceny in my blood. I'd take it in a goddamn minute."[122]

The final ABSCAM catch was Representative Richard Kelly, a former judge who recently had gained national attention when he urged Congress to let New York City go broke and "sink" into the ocean after a financial crisis. Kelly was delivered by three more intermediaries: attorney William Rosenberg, who reportedly was "drooling over Weinberg's stories about the money grabbed by middlemen as their cut of the Congressional bribes"[123]; wealthy Long Island accountant Stanley Weisz, who claimed he also could get Abdul forged gold certificates[124]; and convicted gangster and former Mafia bodyguard Gino Ciuzio, who bragged that he "owned" Kelly.[125]

Kelly provided the most visually compelling moment captured in the ABSCAM tapes when, in order to double-cross Rosenberg, Weisz, and Ciuzio, he refused the suitcase and feverishly stuffed 250 one hundred-dollar bills into all his pockets.[126] His whiny lament was a sharp contrast to the bluff self-assurance of Myers and Lederer: "I'm so damned poor, you wouldn't believe it; I mean if I told you how poor I was, you'd cry—I mean, tears would roll down your eyes."[127]

The unprecedented sting operation ended a short time later. In an interview conducted the following year, Mel Weinberg expressed his disappointment: "I wish we coulda done more. . . . I think we coulda got at least a third of the whole Congress."[128]

(Continued)

When the ABSCAM tapes were shown publicly, seven members of Congress—"distinguished gentlemen," as they like to call each other—had disgraced themselves in full view of a disgusted nation. One by one, they would pay a heavy price for their cupidity.

Myers offered a curious "I may be greedy but I'm not corrupt" brand of defense, in which he claimed that the money was not a bribe because he had no real intention of lifting a finger on behalf of the expatriate Arabs. "[I] saw it as a way to pick up some easy money for doing absolutely nothing."[129]

Myers also testified that he had spent all the money in just 2 weeks "to pay tuition at his children's private schools, buy appliances at Sears, and finance construction at his hunting club in upstate Pennsylvania."[130] He further claimed that he was drunk at the meeting. At one point during the trial, his lawyer rewound the tape and gave the jury an "instant replay" of Myers "dribbling bourbon down his chin."[131] The former Congressman presumably was quite sober when a federal jury convicted him of bribery. He was sentenced to three concurrent 3-year prison terms.

Raymond Lederer was the only one of the six indicted House members who was re-elected in 1980. In fact, his jury was being selected while he was being sworn in.[132] Lederer was convicted of bribery and, like Myers, received three concurrent 3-year sentences. He resigned his seat after the House Ethics Committee recommended his expulsion.[133] While appealing his conviction (which would not be overturned[134]), he reportedly worked at various times as a bartender, doorman, and carpet cutter.[135]

Williams, the would-be titanium magnate, stood trial in 1981. He combatively dismissed his recorded statements to Mel Weinberg as what he called meaningless "baloney," meant only to impress Abdul's organization into giving his friends a $100-million loan.[136] He denied any financial stake in the mining venture. He asserted that the one interest he had was to make it the safest mine in the country.[137] Williams' claims were ridiculed by the prosecutor,[138] who denounced him as "a corrupt public official."[139] Williams was found guilty, the first incumbent senator to be convicted of a crime since 1905.[140] In February 1982, he received a 3-year prison term.[141] A month later, facing certain expulsion, he resigned from the Senate.[142]

Thompson, who had bragged to Abdul's bagmen (bribe collectors) that he was the most important Democrat in New Jersey,[143] was convicted of conspiracy and received the familiar 3-year sentence.[144] The fleet of ships that Murphy had dreamed of owning sank into the sea of oblivion when he, too, was handed a 3-year prison term.[145]

Like so many politicians caught up in scandal, when Jenrette stood trial he claimed that his judgment had been clouded by excessive drinking.[146] This defense proved no more successful for Jenrette than it had been for Myers. He was convicted by a federal jury after only $4\frac{1}{2}$ hours of deliberation.[147] He later was given a 2-year prison sentence.[148] In an odd postscript, a few months after the trial Jenrette's estranged wife announced that she had found $25,000 stashed in a brown

(Continued)

suede shoe in her husband's closet.[149] Some of the one hundred-dollar bills were traced to ABSCAM.[150]

Of all the dubious defenses employed by the ABSCAM defendants, none was greeted with more journalistic scorn and public hilarity than that of pocket-stuffing Kelly, the last to stand trial. At a pretrial news conference, Kelly self-righteously maintained that he had only *pretended* to take the $25,000 bribe as part of a one-man investigation of corruption that he was conducting. He blamed the FBI for "blowing his cover."[151] One sardonic reporter asked Kelly if he was planning to plead insanity.[152] Kelly, nevertheless, still managed to earn the lightest of the Congressional sentences—6 to 18 months confinement at Elgin Air Force Base in his home state of Florida.

Despite its success, ABSCAM remains one of the most controversial law enforcement operations in modern American history. At least two problematic issues deserve consideration. First, the central role of Melvin Weinberg, a career criminal, represented a troubling strategy on the part of the FBI. According to Weinberg, "There's only one difference between me and the Congressmen I met on this case. The public pays them a salary for stealing."[153] But the public also paid Weinberg's salary and, according to at least one witness, he was stealing too. In a sworn statement made in 1982, Weinberg's wife alleged that he had perjured himself and had siphoned some of the ABSCAM bribe money into his own pocket.[154] If proved, Marie Weinberg's charges might have compelled the courts to throw out all the ABSCAM convictions. In a dramatic and mysterious turn, however, she committed suicide 2 weeks later, hanging herself in a vacant condominium near her Florida home.[155]

The second and more fundamental issue is whether enticed bribery is an appropriate law enforcement technique for apprehending white-collar criminals[156] or whether it constitutes unlawful entrapment, that is, "the covert facilitation of crime by or on behalf of government agents,"[157] In the past, when entrapment usually was reserved for prostitutes, homosexuals, or drug dealers, it generated little critical attention, except among a handful of scholars and civil libertarians.[158] ABSCAM, however, changed the dynamics of entrapment; the targets were not denizens of the social fringe, but high elected officials—"distinguished gentlemen" of Congress. Suddenly, the fairness of undercover tactics and the moral acceptability of enticed bribery had become fodder for mass debate. Was it justifiable to solicit crimes which otherwise might not have been committed? Is vulnerability to theatrically contrived temptation equivalent to true corruption?[159] Many persons argued—including, of course, the defendants—that the mission of the FBI is to catch criminals, not create them.

Yet, however much the ABSCAM defendants were tricked or beguiled, the conduct they exhibited is wholly indefensible. These were men to whom we had entrusted the integrity of our government, and they behaved like pigs at a trough. A treatise on political ethics written 2 years before ABSCAM asked the rhetorical question: When can a gift become a bribe?[160] Maybe a warning was etched in the ashes of seven incinerated careers that, for Congress, the safest answer is "always."

The Judiciary

Judicial corruption may occur less frequently than legislative corruption, but it is hardly unknown. A number of state and local jurists have been convicted of official corruption. Consider the following examples:

❖ In 1985, New York state Judge William C. Brennan was found guilty of federal racketeering charges.[161] Brennan accepted nearly $50,000 in bribes to fix criminal cases involving gambling, narcotics, organized crime, and attempted murder.[162] He received a 5-year prison term and a $209,000 fine. In pronouncing sentence, the trial judge declared that "[n]o crime is more corrosive of our institutions than bribery of our judges."[163]

❖ A New York Civil Court Judge, Samuel Weinberg, pleaded guilty in 1987 to racketeering charges. Judge Weinberg owned several rent-controlled buildings in Brooklyn and Queens and had harassed elderly, low-paying residents with fraudulent eviction notices. He had also hired arsonists to torch his property.[164] Weinberg, whose callous treatment of his aged tenants brought new definition to the word "heartless," begged for mercy on the grounds that he was too old to go to prison.

❖ Francis X. Smith, a New York City administrative judge, was sentenced to a year in prison in 1987 for committing perjury before a grand jury. Smith lied about his offer to help a cable television company obtain a franchise. In his defense, he claimed he had been interested only in helping "honest businessmen"[165] by putting in a "good word" with friends.[166]

❖ Roy Gelber, a judge in Florida's Dade County, pleaded guilty in 1991 to racketeering charges related to the taking of bribes from drug-trafficking defendants.[167] Gelber implicated several of his judicial colleagues, two of whom later were convicted of accepting a total of $266,000 in payoffs.[168]

❖ In 1993, Judge Jose Luis Guevara of Zapata County, Texas, was convicted of six drug counts. A videotape played at his trial showed Guevara at a local airstrip rushing to welcome the pilot of a plane loaded with cocaine. Guevara was arrested as part of Operation Prickly Pear, a federal narcotics sting that decimated local government in Zapata County. In addition to the judge, the sheriff and county clerk were sent to prison.[169]

Between 1984 and 1989, 15 judges from Chicago's Cook County courts were convicted of assorted bribery, extortion, racketeering, and conspiracy charges. Two other implicated jurists committed suicide before facing certain indictments.[170] They all had been targets of Operation Greylord,[171] an aggressive FBI crackdown on flagrant corruption inside the country's largest municipal court system, where more than 6 million cases are filed each year.[172] For $3\frac{1}{2}$ years, FBI agents, carrying concealed recorders, worked undercover posing as defendants, defense attorneys, prosecutors, and crime victims. They created phony cases and participated in numerous bribery schemes.[173] A Chicago lawyer, when asked later how many judges he had bribed over a 10-year period, offered this memorable reply:

I didn't count them. I just bribed them. It was kind of like brushing your teeth. I did it every day.[174]

One of the convicted judges, Thomas Maloney, had accepted bribes to fix murder cases.[175] Perhaps equally troubling, it has been alleged that Maloney, who was handed a 16-year prison sentence, was unduly harsh in nonbribed cases to deflect attention from his leniency in the bribed cases.[176]

The centerpiece of the Greylord probe was Senior Cook County Judge Richard LeFevour, who, according to a federal prosecutor, had "peddled justice like it was apples."[177] LeFevour was found guilty on all 59 counts lodged against him[178]—including the acceptance of eight automobiles and $400,000 in cash payoffs in return for dismissing countless drunken driving cases over more than a decade.[179] He received a 12-year prison sentence.[180]

Many state and local judges must run for office and are thus as dependent as any other politicians on campaign contributions. Consequently, even the caretakers of American justice are not immune to conflicts of interest. For example, the Houston-based conglomerate Tenneco has admitted that it made illegal cash contributions to a state district judge in Louisiana who was running for an appellate court seat. That judge later rendered a decision involving a labor dispute injunction that was highly favorable to Tenneco.[181]

A statewide race for the Texas Supreme Court costs hundreds of thousands of dollars, and "contributions of $10,000 and up from lawyers who practice before the court are not uncommon."[182] The danger of placing judges on the auction block was demonstrated in 1984 in the largest civil suit in American history. The Texas-based Pennzoil Company had agreed orally to buy a 40% interest in the Getty Oil Company for $110 per share. Subsequently, New York-based Texaco tendered a written offer to buy 100% of Getty stock at $128 per share, an agreement quickly accepted by Getty. Pennzoil sued, accusing Texaco of unlawful interference with a binding contract.[183]

One of the half-dozen lawyers representing Pennzoil was Houston attorney Joe Jamail, a star litigator known as the "king of torts." Jamail donated $10,000 to the campaign fund of the judge assigned to the case and solicited thousands of dollars in additional contributions from members of the Houston bar, even though that judge was facing no real opposition. As things turned out, it was probably one of the best $10,000 investments ever made.

> When Texaco attorneys suggested [the judge] disqualify himself from the case, he claimed that "mere bias or prejudice" was no ground for disqualification. On nearly every motion, he ruled against Texaco.[184]

The jury awarded Pennzoil $10.53 *billion*, forcing Texaco, then the fifth-largest corporation in the United States, into bankruptcy. Texaco appealed to the Texas Supreme Court, whose nine justices had already received $238,000 in contributions from Jamail and $117,000 more from other Pennzoil attorneys. "The justices refused even to allow Texaco to present oral arguments."[185] Pennzoil and Texaco eventually agreed to settle for $3 billion. "Jamail made at least $200 million out of the case."[186]

In a blistering editorial, the *New York Times* declared, "The behavior of the Texas courts has been reminiscent of what passes for justice in small countries run by colonels in mirrored sunglasses."[187] A San Antonio newspaper was even more colorful in its denunciation: "The Texas Supreme Court resembles a dead fish that has been in the refrigerator far too long. People as far away as New York can smell it."[188]

In contrast to Texas judges, federal jurists are appointed for life. Thus, campaign contributions are not a consideration to members of the federal bench, but a few have nonetheless managed to disgrace themselves in other ways. Since the Constitution was written, only seven federal officials have been impeached and removed from office. All of them were judges.

In 1986, Federal District Judge Harry Claiborne of Nevada became the first such case in 50 years when the U.S. Senate convicted him of the requisite "high crimes and misdemeanors" and stripped him of his judicial position.[189] A federal jury earlier had found Claiborne guilty of tax evasion for his failure to report more than $100,000 in personal income.[190] He was handed a 2-year prison sentence.[191]

Although Claiborne was convicted by both the Senate and the courts, it should be noted that these were independent events. This separation of criminal and political sanctions was underscored in 1989, when District Judge Alcee Hastings of Florida became the only federal official ever to be impeached and removed from office despite a jury *acquittal*.[192] Hastings had been found not guilty in 1983 of conspiracy to commit bribery, even though his alleged co-conspirator, a disbarred Washington lawyer, was convicted of the same crimes in a separate trial.[193] "A panel of federal judges, following their own three-year investigation, concluded that Hastings was guilty of the crimes and recommended impeachment."[194] The Senate found that Hastings had solicited a $100,000 bribe from an undercover FBI agent posing as a defendant in a racketeering case before him.[195]

Also in 1989, the familiar words of "Impeach" and "Nixon" were paired in headlines for the first time since Watergate. The Nixon in question, however, was not the former president, but Federal District Judge Walter Nixon of Mississippi, who had been convicted of perjury in 1986. Nixon had lied to a federal grand jury investigating drug smuggling.[196] The case involved the son of a business associate who had given Nixon a "sweetheart deal" on oil and gas royalties. "The businessman was trying to win leniency for his son, who had been indicted on drug charges."[197] Nixon began serving a 5-year prison sentence in 1988 and was removed from office by the Senate the following year.[198]

In a similar case, Federal District Judge Robert Collins of Louisiana was convicted in 1991 of bribery, conspiracy, and obstruction of justice. Collins was paid $16,500 by a convicted drug dealer to obtain a lighter sentence in a case that was pending in federal court. Collins later sentenced that defendant to $3\frac{1}{2}$ years in prison—considerably less than the 8 years recommended by the government. Collins may have been a competent jurist, but he was a bungling crook. Two days after the trial, FBI agents found most of the bribe money in a cabinet in Collins' courthouse chambers; the balance was found in the judge's wallet.[199] Collins received a prison term of 6 years 10 months,[200] nearly twice as long as the sentence he had "sold." Mercifully, he resigned from the bench, sparing a weary Senate from yet another judicial impeachment trial.

From the ceremonial robes they wear to the solemnity of the rituals they command, everything about judges reflects the exalted station to which the public has elevated them.

> When a judge enters a courtroom, men rise. Rarely is another civil officer addressed as "Your Honor," in the ordinary course of his functions. This is not in specific tribute to the man but to acknowledge what the man, as judge, symbolizes. Regardless of the level at which a judge serves—from magistrate's court to the Supreme Court—the office is customarily, legally, and almost instinctively regarded as sacrosanct.[201]

It is difficult, then, to overstate the social cost of judicial corruption. To citizens, judges are the trustees of due process, the guardians of equal protection. Therefore, no profession demands more unswerving honesty. Judges who descend into the iniquitous realm of white-collar crime do more than shame themselves; they skew the scales of justice. A judge who is suborned by one side in a legal confrontation renders the other side unequal under the law; the rule of law then becomes the rule of fraud.[202]

State and Local Government

In 1986, Attorney General Edwin Meese announced a Justice Department crackdown on state and local political corruption: "We've got a full court press on this stuff. . . . We intend to go on knocking such corrupt heads—that's our business, that's our job."[203] Meese's crusade may seem a bit sanctimonious in retrospect, given that at least 225 Reagan appointees,[204] including Meese himself, have faced allegations of ethical or criminal wrongdoing[205]—an unprecedented number. Nevertheless, the attorney general was quite correct in his assertion of widespread corruption at the nonfederal levels of our political system. "Political corruption in state and local governments is an old and abiding phenomenon."[206] In fact, the same year Meese articulated the government's "get-tough" policy, a survey of the 93 U.S. attorneys reported that over 100 state and local officials had been indicted for corruption, with many more under investigation by federal grand juries.[207]

Between 1970 and 1985, criminal indictments were brought against 7 governors or former governors,[208] more than 60 state legislators,[209] nearly 50 mayors,[210] as well as a considerable assortment of county officials. A striking aspect of most of these cases is how correspondent they are to the various forms of federal corruption previously described in this chapter.

❖ When prosecutors charged New York legislators with padding the state payroll with "no show" jobs doled out to friends, relatives, and campaign workers in 1987,[211] it was reminiscent of the Congressman Hays scandal.

❖ The corrupt USDA meat inspectors of the 1970s could have been the prototypes for the 11 building inspectors in Boston who were convicted in 1986 of accepting payoffs in exchange for overlooking code violations.[212]

❖ Melvyn Paisley's crimes within the Defense Department had their counterpart in those of Atlanta aviation commissioner Ira Jackson, who received a 3-year prison sentence in 1994 for using his influence to win favorable contracts for airport businesses in which he held secret interests.[213]

❖ The dark side of presidential and congressional campaign funding was mirrored when the New York City Investigations Department reported in 1993 that the City Comptroller, Elizabeth Holtzman, was "grossly negligent"[214] in receiving a $450,000 campaign loan from a bank she had selected to underwrite millions of dollars in city bonds.[215]

❖ Even Senator Williams' naked conflict of interest, uncovered in Operation AB-SCAM, was echoed (albeit on a much less grand scale) when the John Harwood, Speaker of the Rhode Island House of Representatives was fined in 1994 for introducing numerous pieces of legislation designed to enrich himself and his clients.[216]

❖ And finally, the most treacherous Congressional bribery cases are more than matched in shock voltage by the 1974 conviction of Spiro T. Agnew, who had resigned as vice-president when it was revealed that he had taken large kickbacks from contractors in exchange for construction projects during his terms as Baltimore County executive and governor of Maryland.[217]

State Corruption.   Agnew was not the first former governor to be sanctioned for corruption. He was not even the first one that year. Federal Judge Otto Kerner became federal prisoner Number 00037-123 in 1974.[218] following his conviction for bribery, fraud, conspiracy, and tax evasion. During Kerner's term as governor of Illinois a few years earlier, he had accepted stock in a local racetrack in exchange for the assignment of lucrative racing dates. The tax charges stemmed from Kerner's declaration of his illicit racetrack profits as capital gains. According to the IRS, *bribes must be treated as regular income* .[219]

Agnew's successor as governor of Maryland, Marvin Mandel, apparently was undeterred by Number 00037-123's fall from grace. Mandell was convicted of fraud and racketeering charges in 1977. Like Otto Kerner, he took bribes from racetrack owners in exchange for special favors.[220] He was handed a 4-year prison sentence[221]—one year more than Kerner had received. Afterward, an unremorseful Mandel stood on the steps of the federal courthouse and told the public that he did not regret his actions.

> He said it calmly, almost proudly. . . . He admitted to a feeling of "satisfaction" with his 25-year career in politics. He said he started with nothing and was back to nothing. Then he shrugged.[222]

In 1978, a Tennessee Chancery Court, citing evidence collected by the FBI, accused Governor Ray Blanton of participation in a scheme to sell paroles and sentence commutations to state prisoners.[223] In one instance, investigators alleged that relatives of a convict who was serving a 60-year term for armed robbery and murder paid $85,000 in bribes to aides of the governor so that the man could be released on parole.[224]

A week before his term expired, Governor Blanton held what might be described as a "Going Out of Business Sale" when he granted executive clemency to 52 inmates, nearly half of whom were convicted murderers. Blanton claimed that his actions were meant solely to help relieve prison overcrowding in the state. Among those whose sentences were commuted was Roger Humphreys, the son of one of Blanton's political allies, who was serving a lengthy term for the murders of his ex-wife and her lover. Humphreys had shot the couple 18 times, stopping to reload frequently. The treatment Humphreys had received while locked up had already generated cries of cronyism. Within only 2 months of entering prison, Humphreys had been made a trustee and had been assigned employment as a photographer for the state tourist department. He had been given the use of a state car and had been sent on photographic assignments throughout Tennessee.[225]

Blanton's successor was sworn in 3 days early, after federal prosecutors warned that the lame duck governor might free all potential witnesses in the parole-selling investigation.[226] Even after he was summarily ousted from office, Blanton continued trying to pardon 30 additional convicts, insisting unsuccessfully that he was still the rightful governor.[227]

"As an outgrowth of the pardons and paroles investigation, Governor Ray Blanton was indicted and convicted of conspiring to take kickbacks for liquor-store licenses."[228] Because it was a federal case, Blanton would miss the opportunity to serve in one of the state prisons he had made less crowded. His conviction later was reversed "reluctantly" by a U.S. Appeals Court, not on the merits of the evidence, but on the technical grounds that the trial judge had not questioned jurors sufficiently about their biases.[229]

The next governor to earn a criminal conviction was Guy Hunt of Alabama in 1993. Hunt looted his 1987 inauguration funds and diverted them for his personal use.[230] He was placed on 5 years probation, fined $200,000, and ordered to perform 1000 hours of community service.[231] An argument can be made that the time he spent vacating his office should have counted as community service hours.

Then came Governor Jim Guy Tucker of Arkansas, who was convicted of fraud and conspiracy by a federal jury in 1996.[232] Tucker was involved in a deal with co-defendants James and Susan McDougal, operators of the failed Madison Guaranty Savings and Loan, to arrange a $3 million loan backed by fraudulently overvalued real estate appraisals. In addition, Tucker had received a $150,000 loan from Madison Guaranty used as a down payment for a $1.2 million water and sewer utility. This transaction was also overvalued, producing a bogus profit for Madison's books at a time when it was under heavy scrutiny by examiners.[233] Following the verdict, Tucker announced his resignation from office to work on his appeals. Arkansas Lieutenant Governor Mike Huckabee replaced Tucker, calling the conviction "a sad day for the state."[234]

What separated this case from the dozens of sleazy S&L scams that have proliferated since the 1980s (Chapter 7) is that the McDougals were former business partners of Bill Clinton and Hilary Rodham Clinton in an unsuccessful land development venture known as Whitewater. Clinton was Tucker's predecessor as governor of Arkansas. Although he was not formally implicated in any of the criminal charges, Clinton had a visible role in the trial, when he was subpoenaed during his presidency by the defense to testify via videotape.[235]

Arizona long has had the reputation as one of the most hard-nosed states when it comes to law enforcement and punishment. In the early 1990s, Governor Fife Symington was the embodiment of tough-talking law-and-order rhetoric. He once declared, "Crime is not traced through the lack of material things. It happens through loss of values."[236] In 1997, Symington proved how right he was when he was convicted in federal court of seven counts of fraud.

The Symington administration was "tainted almost from the start."[237] Soon after taking office he was sued by the Resolution Trust Corporation for his role in directing a failed Phoenix S & L institution. Despite his troubles he won re-election in 1994; but the scandals just kept coming. A year into his second term a court ruled that Symington was personally liable for a $10 million loan from six pension funds to his defunct real estate company. He declared personal bankruptcy.[238]

When he was indicted on 23 felony counts, Symington insisted he had never tried to defraud creditors. He blamed it all on "sloppy accountants."[239]

> But 40 prosecution witnesses and 1,400 documents were enough for the jury to find him guilty. Assistant U.S. Attorney David Schindler called Symington a classic con man, who falsely inflated his net worth when he wanted to borrow and pleaded poverty when he wanted to refinance a loan on more favorable terms. Between 1989 and 1991, for instance, his declared net worth swung between $12 million and minus $23 million.[240]

The disgraced governor was sentenced to $2\frac{1}{2}$ years in prison and resigned from office; although that conviction was later overturned on appeal, prosecutors continued to pursue the case and were preparing to retry him. In 2001, it was reported that Symington was within days of striking a bargain with prosecutors under which he would agree to plead guilty to one felony count in exchange for avoiding any prison time. During the negotiations, however, Symington received a presidential pardon from Bill Clinton in the final days of his administration and walked away.[241]

When Symington resigned from office in 1997, he became the second Arizona governor in a decade to step down as a result of a corruption scandal. Governor Evan Meacham had been impeached and removed from office in 1988 on charges of obstructing justice and misusing state money, although he was acquitted of those charges in a criminal trial.[242]

Next in the docket was former Rhode Island governor Edward DiPrete, who pleaded guilty in 1998 to charges of bribery, extortion, and racketeering, admitting that he had accepted $250,000 in exchange for state contracts while in office. As part of his plea bargain agreement, DiPetre was sentenced to 1 year in a prison work release program in exchange for having the remaining charges dropped. DiPrete had accepted numerous kickbacks from architects, engineers, and others in search of state business in exchange for construction contracts during his tenure as governor between 1985 and 1991.[243]

C A S E   S T U D Y

Edwin Edwards

As of this writing, the most recent governor or ex-governor to be convicted of corruption charges is Edwin Edwards, the boisterous, flamboyant former four-term governor of Louisiana. The 73-year-old Edwards was no stranger to the criminal justice system. His on-again off-again gubernatorial career spanned three decades, during which he had been the subject of 22 grand jury investigations.[244] These earlier probes included such issues as cattle sales to state prisons and an attempt to relocate the Minnesota Timberwolves of the National Basketball Association to New Orleans.[245] Edwards had been tried twice before, in 1985 and 1986, on racketeering charges related to questionable hospital and nursing home deals, from which he had made $2 million. The first jury deadlocked and the second acquitted him.[246] An admitted high-stakes gambler who once won $220,000 on one of his frequent trips to Atlantic City, he had earned a colorful reputation for legal invincibility. He always seemed able to wisecrack his way out of one scrape after another.

But Edwards' fabled luck ran out in 2000, when a federal jury in Baton Rouge convicted him on 17 counts of extortion and racketeering. Both while in office and later, he had extorted hundreds of thousands of dollars from wealthy businessmen seeking licenses to operate riverboat casinos.

The case came to light in 1997 when FBI agents raided Edwards' home and office, seizing records and more than $400,000 in cash. Unlike Edwards' previous trials, however, much of the evidence was electronic. This time jurors would see and hear Edwards in action. Prosecutors built their case on 24,000 hours of secretly recorded telephone conversations and videotapes made by a camera that agents had hidden inside the office Edwin Edwards shared with his son and co-defendant, Stephen Edwards.[247]

The government's star witness was businessman Edward DeBartolo, Jr., owner of the San Francisco 49ers, one of the crown jewels of the National Football League. In 1998 he pleaded guilty to concealing Edwards' extortion plot. In exchange for 2 years probation, DeBartolo agreed to testify against Edwards. DeBartolo had won a license in 1997 for a floating casino along Shreveport's Red River. Edwards, out of office at this time but still politically influential, had demanded and received $400,000.[248] DeBartolo handed Edwards his payoff in a briefcase stuffed with cash at the San Francisco Airport.[249] According to DeBartolo, Edwards had also wanted a $50,000-per-month consulting fee, a per-head commission on every customer entering the casino, and 1% of the gross revenues.[250] Flanked by

(Continued)

his 50-year-old daughter and 33-year-old wife, Edwards denounced his longtime friend DeBartolo to reporters as "the Linda Tripp of Louisiana."[251] Edwards added, "I hope the 49ers lose this Sunday."[252]

Prosecutors also paraded in contractors and designers who testified Edwards paid in cash when he was building a home. In all, Edwards paid $733,567 in cash for his $1.4 million house. A delivery man said Candy Edwards [the defendant's wife] paid him $4,500 in $100 bills. When he stepped inside to collect the money, he said he saw $100 bills lying on the floor.[253]

In his closing argument, a federal prosecutor pointed to Edwards and told jurors, "Look him straight in the eye and tell him he's guilty."[254] Three weeks later, those jurors did exactly that.

On January 8, 2001, Edwin Edwards, who had been the most dominant Louisiana politician since the legendary Huey Long, was handed a stiff 10-year prison sentence. His son was also convicted and sentenced to 7 years. Colorful and unrepentant to the end, Edwards has compared his fate to a Chinese proverb: "If you sit by a river long enough, the dead bodies of your enemies will float by you. I suppose the feds sat by the river long enough, and here comes my dead body.[255]

County Corruption. Numerous county officials also have been indicted for corruption. In the 1980s, more than 150 county commissioners in Oklahoma were convicted of defrauding taxpayers in an intricate kickback scheme. One Oklahoma county purchased enough lumber to rebuild every one of its bridges four times, yet not a single bridge was repaired.[256] New Jersey's Bergen County Utilities Authority awarded bond underwriting contracts on a no-bid basis to the investment banking firms that had made large campaign contributions to county politicians. The county ended up $600 million in debt.[257]

An FBI sting, code-named Operation Pretense, led to the convictions of a number of county supervisors in Mississippi. Those counties not only had far overpaid for heavy equipment, but, in some cases, investigators could not even find the equipment.[258] This variety of white-collar crime is virtually as old as recorded history. Officials who oversaw the building of the ancient pyramids in Egypt reportedly engaged in "creative accounting" and "cooked" the Pharaohs' ledgers regarding the costs and amounts of equipment and materials they used.[259]

Corruption at the county level can be exemplified by a pair of cases resulting in criminal convictions. The first case is that of Ronald Benoit, the Justice of the Peace in Jefferson County, Texas. One of Benoit's responsibilities was to collect fines for traffic tickets from motorists. The fact that voters kept Benoit in office for 11 years suggests that he performed this task efficiently. The problem was that he often collected the fines, dismissed the charges, then kept the money for himself. After pleading guilty to theft, he was given 2 years probation, ordered to make restitution for the thousands of dollars he stole, and required to sign an agreement never to seek elected office again.[260]

The second case is that of Andrew Hinshaw, the former tax assessor of Orange County, California. Hinshaw accepted "gifts" of expensive stereo equipment from the Tandy Corporation, parent company of the Radio Shack chain, after he had denied Tandy a favorable tax exemption. When he later changed his mind and granted the exemption, it earned him a criminal indictment. Hinshaw was convicted of bribery and sentenced to 1 to 14 years in prison.[261] A party leader demonstrated no special acumen when he assessed the damage to Hinshaw's career: "I think the conviction puts a serious crimp in his political future."[262]

Municipal Corruption.   The mindset of middle America long has harbored a "deep strain of anti-urbanism."[263] So, although graft (or, as it was once called, "boodle"[264]) can refer to bribery and payoffs at any level of government, the term usually is associated with big-city corruption. Historically—from Boss Tweed and his Tammany Hall dynasty in New York,[265] to Mayor "Big Bill" Thompson and his gangster-friendly administration in Chicago,[266] to Tom Prendergast and his ubiquitous Kansas City machine[267]—graft has always been the "common cold" of American politics.[268]

To cite just one flagrant example, a number of local officials have been accused in recent years of soliciting bribes from investment bankers in return for helping the bankers grab a piece of the lucrative ($1 billion per year) municipal bond underwriting market—a practice that has been dubbed "pay to play."[269]

Local corruption is an especially incendiary betrayal because the city represents the layer of government closest to the people.

> Local government is the testing ground for self-government. Rascals might be expected in the Sacramento capitol or in the U.S. Congress, but dishonesty in local government comes terribly close to violating the institutions that most directly concern the people.[270]

Although the urban "machine" (at least in its formerly omnipotent incarnation) may now be virtually extinct in the United States, "boodle" is definitely alive and kicking. It is estimated that, between 1970 and 1990, criminal convictions of local officials increased by 900%.[271] Graft cases have been prosecuted in most major American cities (e.g., Chicago,[272] Philadelphia,[273] Atlanta,[274] Cleveland,[275] San Diego,[276] Miami[277]), as well as a great many smaller municipalities. The mayors of Syracuse, New York,[278] and Pawtucket, Rhode Island,[279] for example, each extorted about $1 million from city contractors. In 1995, Congressman Walter Tucker, III, an ordained minister, was convicted of extorting $30,000 in bribes while he was mayor of Compton, California, earlier in the decade.[280]

But if one wishes to find truly voracious corruption in its natural habitat, little Compton is not the place to look. One must travel about 3000 miles east across the Hudson River.

New York City has a tradition of corruption that is almost mythic in magnitude. In a city as big and as rich as New York, containing such an immense municipal bureaucracy, "bribery and kickbacks have been going on since the Tweed era."[281] Tweed and his urban pirates may be long gone, but a series of sensational cases in the late 1980s illustrates the extent to which corrupt officials can still pillage a city. More than 100 individuals—including Democratic Party leaders as well as elected and appointed officials—were ensnared by state and federal investigations.[282] Graft was uncovered in at least nine city agencies, including the Housing Authority, the Taxi and Limousine Commission, and the city's Health and Hospitals Corporation.[283] The administration of Mayor Edward Koch fell into shambles.[284] Koch ceased shouting out his signature slogan: "How'm I doin'?" The answer had become painfully obvious.

The worst scandal occurred in the Parking Violations Bureau (PVB) of the New York Transportation Department.[285] In January 1986, the mayor's close friend Donald Manes, the borough president of Queens and a major force in city government, was found by police in a car near LaGuardia Airport, bleeding from both wrists. Manes claimed he had been kidnapped by two men.

Within days, Manes' protégé, Geoffrey Lindenauer, deputy director of the PVB, was arrested for extorting $5000 from a company hired to collect delinquent parking fines.[286] Lindenauer eventually would be charged with taking $410,000 in payoffs from collection agencies contracted by the PVB.[287] In the previous 2 years, the city had paid private firms $31 million to collect just $85 million in overdue parking fines,[288] so the stakes were more than ample to sustain a system of institutionalized plunder.

From his hospital bed, Manes soon admitted that his purported abduction had been a botched suicide attempt, spurred by overwhelming depression. The source of that depression became much clearer when Lindenauer entered into an agreement with prosecutors, under which most of the charges against him would be swapped for his testimony against several of his superiors, including Manes. Two days after Lindenauer's plea bargain was struck, Manes, facing certain indictment and likely imprisonment, successfully committed suicide by stabbing himself in the heart.[289]

Lindenauer's testimony was instrumental in the government's case against one of the most powerful politicians in the city, Stanley Friedman, Democratic leader of the Bronx.[290] Friedman was a part owner of a company the city was paying $22 million to supply hand-held computers to the PVB. Lindenauer had manipulated the bidding process on Friedman's behalf so that the company, Citisource, Inc., would encounter no significant competition for the lucrative contract. On top of that, Citisource had fraudulently misrepresented itself. For starters, Friedman's company claimed to have 30 employees—in reality, it had only one.

> And while the company said it had a prototype computer, it actually had nothing. Koch canceled the contract. Friedman went to City Hall and protested with amazing sangfroid. "We are virtually on target with a fine product," he explained.[291]

Friedman was convicted of federal racketeering and conspiracy charges in November 1986. The following March, he was given a 12-year prison sentence.[292] His trial painted such a vulgar picture of New York politics that when Lindenauer responded to a question during his lengthy testimony by replying, "I can't give you an honest answer on that one," the courtroom erupted in laughter.[293]

POLICE CORRUPTION

As we have seen throughout this chapter, some public officials, both elected and appointed, have bartered their influence and have used their positions to solicit or extort bribes. Police corruption shares important structural similarities with political corruption. However, there is also a fundamental difference, related to the status of the corrupters, which makes police misconduct deserving of separate consideration. Many elected officials and appointed regulators have the power to sell favors, such as lucrative government contracts, to other white-collar criminals. Law enforcers, too, have something valuable to sell—immunity from the law—but their buyers more typically are "common" (i.e., blue-collar) criminals.[294]

Like political corruption, police corruption is an illegal use of official authority for personal gain. "Personal gain" distinguishes police corruption from certain other forms of police misconduct, such as brutality or violations of constitutional rights, committed by law enforcers in pursuit of organizational goals. "Official authority" distinguishes police corruption from simple police criminality and thus excludes street crimes like rape or burglary, even though such offenses may be (and have been) committed by police officers.[295]

Periodic corruption scandals have plagued virtually every major urban police department in the United States—New York City,[296] Chicago,[297] Philadelphia,[298] Detroit,[299] Cleveland,[300] Washington, DC,[301] Dallas,[302] Miami,[303] Atlanta,[304] and New Orleans,[305] to cite just a recent sampling. A 1999 investigation of the Rampart Division of the Los Angeles Police Department uncovered a list of crimes allegedly committed by officers ranging from perjury to drug dealing to robbery to shooting unarmed suspects then framing them for assault.[306]

Moreover, police corruption exists in smaller cities and towns as well. The chief of police in Rochester, New York, for example, was convicted on drug trafficking charges in 1991.[307] The chief of the Newark, New Jersey, police department pleaded guilty in 1996 of stealing $30,000 from a police fund.[308] Four West New York, New Jersey, police officers, including the chief, pleaded guilty in 1998 to taking part in a $600,000 bribery and kickback scheme. They had coerced local merchants to install video gambling machines.[309] Fifteen officers in Inglewood, California, were sanctioned in 1994 for running a local bookmaking operation—from department telephones.[310]

The sheriff of Bristol, Virginia, a mountain town on the Tennessee border, killed himself the day after a grand jury began investigating charges against him of embezzling $377,000. The sheriff allegedly had stolen money paid to the town for housing surplus prisoners from Washington, DC, in the

Bristol jail. He had used these funds to buy a new house, several vehicles, and certificates of deposit for his children. More than $60,000 in cash was found in a desk drawer in his office.[311]

Furthermore, police corruption is not limited to municipal departments. County and state forces also have experienced their share of misappropriation. For 3 years, the chief of the Niagra County jail in upstate New York charged all his personal groceries to taxpayers through jail accounts. The former county sheriff was also sentenced for stocking his refrigerator with thousands of dollars worth of jailhouse food.[312] In 1998, the sheriff of Star County, Texas, resigned after pleading guilty to conspiracy charges. He had been referring prisoners to a local bail bondsman in exchange for kickbacks. The payments often were delivered directly to his office.[313] The biggest county law enforcement scandal involved 26 deputy sheriffs from Los Angeles County, who were convicted of skimming millions of dollars from drug money seized in their investigations.[314] Dozens of other deputies were forced to retire. In all, more than one-third of the entire elite L.A. County narcotics unit was implicated.[315]

Barker and Roebuck have devised a useful typology of police corruption.[316] They identify a number of categories, of which we will examine six:

Corruption of Authority

Corruption of authority encompasses a wide variety of unauthorized material inducements, anything from discounted underwear to free commercial sex. According to one survey, 31% of all wholesale or retail businesspersons in three major cities acknowledged that they give free or discounted merchandise, food, or services to police officers.[317] Although this practice may seem trivial compared with those uncovered in ABSCAM or Greylord, there are hidden costs. First of all, the image of law enforcement is demeaned by such behavior. As a former police officer once observed, "[T]he public generally concedes that policemen are the world's greatest moochers."[318] For a profession which depends so heavily on the respect and cooperation of the citizenry,[319] such an image cannot help. More important, acceptance of gifts or discounts—even from reputable merchants—initiates a conditioning process that can normalize other, more reprehensible, types of police corruption.[320]

Kickbacks

"In many communities, police officers receive goods, services, or money for referring business to towing companies, ambulances, garages, lawyers, doctors, [bail] bondsmen, undertakers, taxi cab drivers, service stations, [and] moving companies."[321] Some departments reputedly condone these arrangements, provided the corrupter is a legitimate businessperson,[322] whereas others consider such conduct to be a gross violation of professional ethics and apply strict sanctions.

Shakedowns

A shakedown occurs when a law enforcement officer receives a payoff in exchange for not making an arrest. Shakedowns can range in seriousness from accepting a gratuity from a "respectable" citizen trying to avoid a traffic charge to taking a bribe from an apprehended criminal bargaining for release.[323] In New York City, motorists once commonly kept $10 bills clipped to their driver's licenses. When stopped for a traffic violation, they would hand the license to the officer, who would pocket the bill and wave the driver on.[324] At the more sinister end of the continuum, New York drug pushers reportedly always carry a hefty wad of emergency cash to try to buy their way out of arrests; occasionally they succeed.[325]

The "Fix"

The most familiar violation in this category involves officers who agree to dispose of traffic tickets in exchange for a fee. A far more serious type of fix, however, entails the quashing of criminal prosecutions—in effect, a delayed shakedown. The fixer is often a detective who conducts or controls the investigation upon which the prosecution is based.

"The investigating officer usually agrees to 'sell the case,' that is, withdraw prosecution in return for some material reward; he either fails to request prosecution, tampers with the existing evidence, or gives perjured testimony."[326] According to reports, it is even possible in some police departments to fix murder cases.[327]

Opportunistic Theft

Opportunistic theft includes practices such as stealing money from arrestees or unconscious accident victims. One writer tells of a former Miami policeman who routinely stole any cash he could find from every dead body he encountered.[328] More significantly, this category also includes keeping all or part of money, property, or drugs seized as evidence in raids.[329] As the Los Angeles skimming case (mentioned earlier) illustrates, this crime potentially can involve enormous amounts of money.

Protection of Illegal Activities

Persons engaging in illegal activities and seeking to operate without police interference sometimes pay individual officers (or even entire precincts) protection money. This is especially the case with so-called victimless crimes, e.g., drugs, gambling, prostitution. Attempts to legislate morality appear to have contributed substantially to police corruption because bribes generated by victimless crimes are more easily rationalized. This enhanced capacity for neutralization was demonstrated by one officer when he discussed his attitude toward gambling payoffs: "Hell, everybody likes to place a bet once in a while. . . . Sure there are honest cops on the force . . . [b]ut most of us are re-alistic."[330] An analysis of drug payoffs describes how corrupted officers would commonly remark that "it's just drug money," implying that there is a differ-ent standard for theft of illegally generated revenues compared to theft of law-ful profits.[331]

Not all protection money, however, emanates from victimless crime, assuming there is such a thing. "Officers in some departments also receive protection payoffs from robbers, burglars, jewel thieves, confidence men, fences and forgers."[332]

How might police corruption be explained? Because complicated questions seldom inspire simple answers, numerous hypotheses have been generated. Some have rested upon structural aspects of law enforcement. Three factors in particular have been suggested most frequently: (1) structural opportunity; (2) an institutionalized code of silence; and (3) inadequate orga-nizational controls.

Structural Opportunity.   By definition, police work places officers in close proximity to a wide array of illegal activities and an abundance of illicit prof-its. Such continuous exposure inevitably yields opportunities for bribes and payoffs. "Not only can police officers offer valuable services merely by being a little less vigilant, but they also are in constant contact with people who desire those services and have no compunctions about breaking the law to purchase them."[333]

Patrol officers generally work alone or with a single partner. "Despite the quasi-military chain of command and such innovations as two-way radio, the fact is that most police supervisors most of the time cannot know what their officers are doing."[334] Law-abiding citizens are even less cognizant of po-lice activities. Crime and vice are photosensitive, so many law enforcers must work in a murky, subterranean milieu, far removed from public view. We often watch them cruise by in their patrol cars, we occasionally receive traffic citations from them, but seldom do we personally witness the police in their most serious professional role—investigating crimes and arresting criminals. Low managerial and civic visibility affords officers such wide behavioral dis-cretion that the opportunities for corruption are unavoidable.[335]

The Code of Silence.   Enhancing structural opportunity is the so-called Blue Wall of Silence[336]—a cultural norm that proscribes officers from informing on corrupt colleagues. Intense group cohesiveness greatly reduces the risk for ex-posure and thus helps attenuate the line between observer and participant. In 1997, the nation was horrified by a bestial attack on a suspect inside a New York City police station. The victim, a Hatian immigrant, was beaten, tortured, and sodomized with the wooden handle of a toilet plunger. At least 20 officers were in the vicinity when the gruesome incident transpired, "[Y]et only four officers eventually came forward and testified; no one came forward immedi-ately and none of these officers demanded immediate medical attention."[337]

The victim was left bleeding in a holding cell for 3 hours until paramedics were finally summoned. During this period, the officer who had forced the plumbing tool into the victim's anus had brandished his weapon around the station house for all to see and bragged about what he had done. He was confident that his fellow officers would cover for him.[338] A New York borough commander has compared the Blue Wall of Silence to *omerta*, the Mafia's code of secrecy.[339] "[I]t is a fact of life that telling on an officer is viewed as a betrayal worse than corruption itself."[340]

Consider the experience of New York Detective Bob Leucci. After Leucci testified against his former partners regarding skimming, shakedowns, and fixes in the Narcotics Bureau, he was transferred to internal affairs and assigned to teach routine training courses. The topic of his first lecture was surveillance techniques, but the real lesson was about the sanctity of the silence code.

> In the middle of the classroom a hand shot up.
> "What did you say your name was?"
> "Detective Leucci."
> "Are you *the* Detective Leucci?"
> "I'm Detective Leucci."
> "I don't think I have anything to learn from you," said the student. He got up and walked out of the classroom and did not come back.[341]

As Leucci discovered, violation of the perverse "loyalty over integrity" credo can carry severe group sanctions. The penalty can be a professional life sentence because the "informer" label hangs around a police officer's neck for his or her whole career.

> One rookie officer in Brooklyn saw fellow officers turn against her when she reported her partner for theft. They harassed her for years, leaving notes on her locker calling her a rat. She transferred, but abuse followed her to the next precinct.[342]

Moreover, the physical risk of accusing corrupt colleagues can be far more costly than peer ostracism. "Police officers can hold the power of life and death over one another. They have to be certain that when they radio for help, it will come."[343] A former New York City police commissioner has acknowledged that "fear of being abandoned under fire is one reason corruption persists."[344] Perhaps no single moment underscores this contention more than one which occurred in a California courtroom in 1997. A San Francisco police officer, the victim of a vicious sexual assault, was cited for contempt when she refused to testify against her alleged assailant, her ex-husband—a fellow officer. "She feared that if she spoke out against another cop, the word would be out and other officers might refuse to back her up in a dangerous situation."[345]

The Blue Wall of Silence places honest police officers, pressured to obey the code, in a Catch-22 predicament, because working alongside corrupt colleagues can sometimes be as perilous as abandonment by them. One officer has vividly described the hazardous dilemma faced by good cops who protect bad cops:

> Suppose, she said, she confronts a drug dealer on a corner who is secretly paying off her partner. She and the dealer both draw their guns. Her partner is standing behind her. Whom does he help?[346]

Organizational Controls.   Structural opportunity is further reinforced by inadequate internal controls. "Police departments simply have not provided sufficiently rigorous supervision and training on matters related to the dynamics of corruption."[347] Furthermore, many police administrators have been unwilling to confront corruption as a systemic problem, subscribing instead to the notion of a "few bad apples." The Pennsylvania Crime Commission's investigation of the Philadelphia Police Department, for example, "found that although the top administrators were not corrupt, they repeatedly ignored the pervasive nature of the problem, insisting that it existed only in isolated individual cases."[348] By reducing the level of analysis from the whole organization to the deviant member, the "bad apple" theory provides yet another layer of protection to corrupt officers. It is obviously very difficult for police leadership to fight corruption and deny its existence simultaneously.

Rather than concentrating on structural flaws, however, some explanations of corruption have stressed personality features indigenous to police officers. New recruits may bring their own constellation of traits to the job, but police work also fosters the development of certain superordinate attitudes. One survey of the research in this area concludes that there *is* a "police personality."[349] For example, "[p]olice officers tend to be somewhat more impulsive, aggressive, and willing to take risks than people in other occupational groups."[350] Each of these traits could be a desirable quality in law *enforcers*, but in the wrong mix, the same traits are also characteristic of law *breakers.*

Other studies reveal that police officers tend to feel more isolated than most people. They typically are suspicious of and defensive toward outsiders, and so choose to separate themselves from the public.[351] "Sensing the uneasiness so many of the rest of us feel in the presence of even an off-duty officer, those in police work tend to avoid social contacts with the general public and to retreat into the company of other officers."[352] Law enforcement can be a uniquely stressful and demoralizing job; the high rates of alcoholism, suicide, divorce, and domestic violence among police officers attests to this fact.[353] The hours, the uniform, the inherent danger, the acquired world-weary cynicism, along with other factors, likely encourage withdrawal from the societal mainstream. The resulting "us-versus-them" mentality could be very receptive to the transmission of a deviant tradition within a department.

Another trait that researchers have linked to the police personality is a false perception of invulnerability, stemming from the power and authority vested in the badge.[354] Many who wear the badge—even those who tarnish it—may feel safely insulated from allegations of corruption. As one officer has stated, "Who's going to take the word of a junkie over a cop?"[355] But, as the following analysis of the New York Police Department illustrates, such reckless self-assurance has created an expanding class of convicted felons consisting of "ex-cops."

The NYPD

"As long as New York City has had police, it has had police corruption."[356] In 1894, Captain Max Schmittberger, the force's preeminent bagman, made a lengthy confession before the Lexow Committee of the State Senate. According to Schmittberger, a $300 payment was required to join the force, and every subsequent promotion entailed an escalating fee demanded by the ruling Tammany Hall political machine. A lucrative precinct could cost a prospective captain $15,000, an enormous price-tag in those days. Another witness, Inspector "Clubber" Williams,[357] reluctantly acknowledged possessing a large personal fortune, a luxurious estate, and a steam-powered yacht. "Williams claimed to have accumulated his wealth through real-estate speculation in Japan—an explanation so fantastic that no one could disprove it."[358]

The Lexow Committee revealed police corruption "on a scale that remains astonishing."[359] A department-wide protection racket flourished with the full knowledge of the police chief. Yearly kickbacks from whorehouses and saloons approached $10 million[360] at a time when the average wage for skilled labor in the United States was $5.95 per week.[361]

Shortly after Theodore Roosevelt became Police Commissioner of New York City in 1895, he began firing officers who were receiving regular payoffs from the city's many brothels.[362] In 1931, Governor Franklin D. Roosevelt commissioned a special investigation, which reported widespread corruption among New York City's vice squad.[363] Both Roosevelts, products of a sheltered upper class, discovered in their adulthood what most average New Yorkers probably knew as youngsters: The NYPD has a considerable presence of corruption.

This is not to imply that most New York cops are crooked. In fact, according to former Deputy Mayor Milton Mollen, whose commission carefully studied the problem and released a detailed report in 1994, "[T]he vast majority of police officers throughout the city do not engage in corruption."[364] But even if the percentage of corrupt officers is quite small—say 3%—when a force contains 30,000 members[365] spread across 76 precincts in five boroughs, corruption that may be modest in relative terms can be considerable in absolute terms. After all, if "only" 3% of New Yorkers had the measles, it rightly would be called an epidemic.

Indeed, it must have seemed like an epidemic in 1951 when 35 New York policemen were indicted for criminal conspiracy. They were all beneficiaries of bookie Harry Gross, who reputedly spent $1 million per year on police payoffs to protect his $20-million per year gambling empire.[366]

(Continued)

In keeping with an approximate 20-year scandal cycle, the Knapp Commission of the 1970s (named for its chairman, New York attorney Whitman Knapp) revealed an entrenched system of corruption inside the NYPD. Large networks of officers collected bribes from bookies and prostitutes, often passing their payoff money up the chain of command.[367]

Undercover agents, in the employ of the commission, recorded misconduct so normalized that one almost expected Social Security taxes to be withheld from payoffs. For example, patrolman William Phillips was taped negotiating a monthly protection price with an undercover investigator he believed was an agent of an elegant New York brothel:

> "Now define the deal," says Teddy. . . . "We're going to get protection from the precinct?"
>
> "Division," reiterates Phillips. "Division, borough, and precinct. Listen, you give me the money, you're not going to have any problems, I'm telling you that right now."[368]

Confronted with such bald evidence of his guilt, Phillips (who would later go to prison for murdering a pimp) was co-opted by the Knapp Commission and became a friendly witness at its hearings. He described payoffs from every construction site in the city to ignore dust violations, from every double-parked delivery truck to look the other way, from every seedy bar to move arrests of brawlers and dope pushers out to the street so as not to jeopardize precious liquor licenses. According to Phillips, corruption had become so out of control in the NYPD, that some cops were bribing other cops.

> From rookies prying $2 a week out of impoverished Puerto Rican bodegas, to division commanders exacting $1,500 a month tithes from district gamblers, Phillips testified, hardly a cranny of the whole department is free of some kind of graft.[369]

The real money, however, was where it had always been—in vice. In the words of Officer Phillips, "I never knew a plain-clothes man yet . . . that wasn't on the 'pad.'"[370] In its final report, the Knapp Commission found that plainclothes detectives received regular payoffs, amounting to as much as $3500 per month, from each of the protected illicit operations under their jurisdiction.[371] Again, the extent to which this deviance could be normalized was striking. Newly assigned detectives had to serve a 60-day "apprenticeship" before they were entitled to a share of the bribe money. When supervisors were involved, they got a share-and-a-half. When a detective was transferred out of a precinct, he was given 2 months "severance pay" by his partners in crime.[372]

In its time, the Knapp Commission was perceived largely as a success. Courageous departmental whistleblowers like Bob Leucci, David Durk,[373] and the legendary Frank Serpico[374] became heroic figures to the public (although not, of

(Continued)

course, to their peers behind the Blue Wall). The panel's recommendation of a comprehensive shake-up within the NYPD was embraced by a new police commissioner.[375] Corruption was said to have decreased.

By the 1980s, however, rampant misconduct was back and the stakes had escalated. The bookie and the pimp, long the symbols of urban vice, were displaced in primacy by the crack cocaine dealer. "[T]he crack trade and its gusher of illicit cash [were] testing the integrity of American law enforcement as never before."[376] Police corruption, which once had consisted mainly of "grass-eaters"—as the Knapp Commission labeled officers who took graft from prostitutes and gamblers[377]—now was dominated by a new breed of "meat eaters"—cops so aggressively corrupt that they were indistinguishable from the most predatory street criminals.

A former Bronx patrolman, Bernie Cawley, explained to the Mollen Commission why he was known to his comrades as the "Mechanic":

> "Because I used to 'tune people up,'" he placidly explained. "It's a police word for beating people." Suspects? he was asked. "No, I was just beating people up in general."[378]

In 4 years on the job, Cawley claimed to have "tuned up" more than 400 persons. "Who's going to catch us?" he said, shrugging. "We're the police."[379]

For the NYPD, still recovering from its pummeling at the hands of the Knapp Commission, the worst was yet to come. The first domino tipped over in Brooklyn in 1992, when Officer Michael Dowd and five other policemen were arrested for drug-trafficking. Dowd's corruption had been the worst-kept secret in the NYPD. Over a period of 6 years, 16 complaints had been filed against him, alleging that he had been taking bribes, robbing drug dealers, and selling cocaine. Dowd came to work in a $35,000 Corvette, owned four suburban homes,[380] and was sometimes picked up by limousine at the station house for Atlantic City gambling trips—all on a salary of $400 per week.[381] Witnesses had even observed Dowd snorting cocaine off the dashboard of his patrol car.[382] "[Yet], senior officials repeatedly ignored allegations against Officer Dowd or blocked efforts to check them out."[383] When he finally was apprehended, it was by local police in Long Island, outside NYPD jurisdiction.

It was soon evident that the arrest of Dowd and his five-man "crew" was just the initial spasm of an impending avalanche. Dowd had formed a criminal organization in Brooklyn of 15 to 20 fellow officers. "Politicians and the media started asking what had happened to the system for rooting out police corruption established 21 years ago at the urging of the Knapp Commission."[384]

Dowd lived up to his billing as the most crooked cop in New York by continuing his illegal activities even after his arrest, reportedly corresponding with drug dealers from his jail cell about a planned "Butch Cassidy" escape to Central America.[385] Dowd was convicted in 1994 and received a long prison sentence. The full weight of the criminal justice system fell on him like Dorothy's house; he

(Continued)

would not even be eligible for parole for at least 11 years. He had apologized to the court for disgracing his badge and had begged for leniency, but Federal Judge Kimba Wood, who had once sent Michael Milken to prison (Chapter 6), was unimpressed with Dowd's sudden contrition. Judge Wood told Dowd that his crimes "betray an immorality so deep that it is rarely encountered."[386]

A month after Dowd's arrest, the Mollen Commission was created to assess the extent of corruption in the NYPD[387] and to determine why Dowd's superiors apparently had shut down their eyes, ears, and brains. As a result of the commission's public hearings, three more Brooklyn officers—known as the "Morgue Boys" because they divided up their loot in an abandoned coffin factory[388]—were arrested for staging a series of illegal raids on local crack houses for the purpose of stealing cash and drugs.

The corruption exposed in the Brooklyn precincts was numbing in its profligacy, but it proved to be only the warm-up act for Harlem's 30th Precinct, which the acerbic New York media soon would dub the "Dirty Thirty."[389] Persistent suspicions that the 30th Precinct was a center for rapacious brutality were confirmed in the summer of 1993, when internal affairs investigators watched through binoculars as a uniformed officer stole a kilo of cocaine from a Harlem drug dealer.

> [W]ord immediately spread on the street that the police officer, patrolman George Nova, was holding an auction. Drug runners flagged down his patrol car to put in their bids. Within hours he had three separate offers, and by early dawn he had a deal: one kilo, sold for $16,000 cash.[390]

Their surveillance of Nova had led internal affairs into a world where "police officers ran through Harlem like a gang of thugs."[391] The following March, a sting operation videotaped three of Nova's colleagues from the 30th Precinct "breaking into an apartment, beating up an occupant, searching for drugs, and stealing cash."[392] Within weeks, 11 more of the 30th's "finest" were led away in handcuffs.[393] There was nothing petty about the charges. One officer was accused of shooting a drug dealer while stealing his cocaine; another was alleged to have pocketed $100,000 while illegally searching an apartment.[394] The police commissioner walked into the 30th Precinct station house a month later and personally stripped the badges off two drug-dealing officers.[395] By the end of the year, 29 officers, one-quarter of the precinct's entire roster, had been arrested[396]—including only the second female officer ever formally charged in a major NYPD corruption case.[397]

In contrast to the mess in Brooklyn, which had been depicted as a rank-and-file crime spree, two supervisors from the "Dirty Thirty" were among those arrested.[398] One of them, Sergeant Kevin Nannery, was accused of leading a squad called "Nannery's Raiders,"[399] which would tear down apartment doors and rob drug dealers,"[400] using faked 911 calls as a pretext.[401] The supervisors' arrests highlighted the issue of accountability, which had always been so discomfiting to police administrators during corruption scandals. Deputy Inspector Thomas Sweeney, who had taken command of the 30th Precinct in April following the first wave of

(Continued)

arrests, was unusually candid in his condemnation of senior officers: "Superior officers should have known if there were violations of the law. . . . Of course they should have known."[402]

Sweeney's conclusion was shared by the Mollen Commission, when it issued its final report. That report assailed a "willful blindness" to corruption throughout the ranks of the NYPD.[403] It even suggested that perhaps as many as 40 corruption cases involving senior officers had been "buried" by the Internal Affairs Bureau.[404] According to the commission, "The principle of command accountability, which holds commanders responsible for fighting corruption, completely collapsed."[405] The report took several previous police commissioners to task, implying that they had been more interested in containing corruption scandals than containing corruption.[406]

Heightened *internal* controls was one of the two main recommendations urged by the Mollen Commission. Evidence that this advice was heeded may be inferred from the resolute response of the NYPD leadership in 1995 to another precinct out of control, this one in the Bronx. Thirteen patrol officers and three sergeants from the 48th Precinct were indicted on various counts of thievery, perjury, and brutality. One of those charged was accused of stealing $400 from a man preparing to buy a Christmas present for his mother. Another of the inductees allegedly stole a victim's dog. The police commissioner offered no cover-up; instead he quickly apologized to the people of New York. Mayor Rudolph Giuliani noted that there was no "willful blindness" on the part of the police this time; they had acted expeditiously to prevent another "Dirty Thirty" from ripening on the vine. "This is precisely what you want the Police Department to do," he said. "It is exactly what didn't happen a few years ago."[407]

The other major recommendation from the Mollen panel was a proposal to increase *external* controls,[408] through the creation of a small police commission, independent of the NYPD. That body would be empowered to perform continuous assessments of the department's systems for preventing, detecting, and investigating corruption and to conduct, whenever necessary, its own corruption investigations.[409] If the historical two-decade scandal cycle runs true to form, such a commission could be quite busy around the year 2020.

NOTES

1. Hyde's wife, Lady Cornbury, reportedly was quite a thief herself. She was notorious for going on shopping sprees—in other people's homes. If she saw something she liked, such as a piece of furniture or jewelry, she would send for it the following day, claiming it in the name of the Crown. Before long, whenever local aristocrats heard her carriage wheels turn toward their houses, they would quickly hide their valuables. (Ross, Shelley. *Fall from Grace: Sex, Scandal, and Corruption in American Politics from 1702 to the Present.* New York: Ballantine Books, 1988.)

2. One of Hyde's illegally deeded tracts was renamed Hyde Park as part of the deal. Ironically, two centuries later it would become the family home of another New York governor, Franklin Delano Roosevelt. (Ross, *op. cit.*)

3. Ross, *op cit.*

4. Rogow, Arnold and Lasswell, Harold. *Power, Corruption, and Rectitude.* Englewood Cliffs, NJ: Prentice-Hall, 1963.

5. Wilson, James Q. "Corruption: The Shame of the States." *The Public Interest* 2, 1966: 31.

6. Gillespie, Kate and Okruhlik, Gwenn. "The Political Dimensions of Corruption Cleanups: A Framework for Analysis." *Comparative Politics,* October 1991: 77–95.

7. Scott, James C. "Corruption, Machine Politics, and Political Change." *American Political Science Review* 63, 1969: 1142–1157.

8. Bunker, Stephen G. and Cohen, Lawrence E. "Collaboration and Competition in Two Colonization Projects: Toward a General Theory of Official Corruption." *Human Organization* 42, 1983: 106–114.

9. Nye, Joseph S. "Corruption and Political Development: A Cost-Benefit Analysis." *American Political Science Review* 61, 1967: 417.

10. Peters, John G. and Welch, Susan. "Political Corruption in America: A Search for Definitions and a Theory." *American Political Science Review* 72, 1978: 974–984.

11. Dean, Suzanne. "Jury Convicts Rep. Howe in Sex Solicitation Case." *Washington Post.* July 24, 1976: A1, A6.

12. Paper Says an Aide to House Unit Calls Its Head Her Lover." *New York Times.* May 23, 1976: 33.

13. Gillespie and Okruhlik, *op. cit.*, p. 79.

14. Ford, Henry J. "Municipal Corruption." *Political Science Quarterly* 19, 1904: 673–686.

15. McMullen, M. "A Theory of Corruption." *Sociological Review* 9, 1961: 82–86. See also: Werner, Simcha B. "New Directions in the Study of Administrative Corruption." *Public Administration Review.* March/April 1983: 146–154.

16. Rundquist, Barry S., Strom, Gerald S., and Peters, John G. "Corrupt Politicians and Their Electoral Support: Some Experimental Observations." *American Political Science Review* 71, 1977: 955.

17. Freund, Charles P. "What Lincoln Bedroom?" msn.com. January 24, 1997.

18. "Fund-Raising Scandal Timeline." www.reagan.com. May 13, 1998.

19. *Ibid.*

20. Drew, Elizabeth. *The Corruption of American Politics.* Seacuacus, NJ: Birch Lane Press, 1999: 61.

21. Coleman, James W. *The Criminal Elite: The Sociology of White-Collar Crime* (2nd ed). New York: St. Martin's Press, 1989.

22. *Ibid.*, p. 87.

23. Sobel, Lester A. *Corruption in Business.* New York: Facts on File, 1977.

24. Coleman, 1989, *op. cit.*, p. 90.

25. DeWaal, Caroline S. and Obester, Tricia. "Seafood Safety: Consumers and Manufacturers at Risk." *USA Today Magazine.* July 1994: 24–26.

26. "USDA Official Removed." *Houston Post.* February 9, 1995: A22.

27. Coleman, 1989, *op. cit.*, p. 90.

28. Amick, George. *The American Way of Graft.* Princeton, NJ: Center for Analysis of Public Issues, 1976.

29. Coleman, 1989, *op. cit.*

30. Amick, *op. cit.*

31. "Let's Throw the Book at Defense Bid-Riggers." *Business Week.* July 4, 1988: 128.

32. "Defense Spending: Pop Goes the Weasel." *The Economist.* June 25, 1988: 26–27.

33. Ross, Irwin. "Inside the Biggest Pentagon Scandal." *Fortune,* January 11, 1993: 88.

34. *Ibid.*

35. *Ibid.*, p. 90.

36. *Ibid.*

37. *Ibid.*

38. *Ibid.*

39. Quoted in *Ibid.*, p. 92.

40. McGrane, Reginald C. (Ed.). *The Correspondence of Nicholas Biddle Dealing with National Affairs 1807-1844.* Boston: Houghton Mifflin, 1919: 218.

41. "Rostenkowski's Downfall Ends in Prison Term." *Houston Chronicle.* April 10, 1996: 7A.

42. *Ibid.* A few months after Rostenkowski's conviction, former Congressman Joseph Kolter of Pennsylvania was sentenced to 6 months in prison for conspiring to defraud taxpayers in the House post office scandal ("Fraud Sentencing." *USA Today.* August 1, 1996: 7A). In late 2000, Rostenkowski was pardoned by President Clinton in the last days of the Clinton administration.

43. Radelat, Ana. "Congress in Crisis." *Public Citizen.* May/June, 1990: 15.

44. *Buckley v. Valeo,* 429 U.S. 1, 28 (1976).

45. Welch, William M. II. "The Federal Bribery Statute and Special Interest Campaign Contributions." *Journal of Criminal Law & Criminology* 79, 1989: 1347–1373.

46. Gillespie and Okruhlik, *op. cit.*, p. 79.

47. Weeks, Joseph R. "Bribes, Gratuities and the Congress: The Institutionalized Corruption of the Political Process, the Impotence of Criminal Law to Reach It, and a Proposal Change." *Journal of Legislation* 13, 1986: 123.

48. Barnes, Fred and Wildavsky, Rachel F. "Is Washington for Sale?" *Reader's Digest.* February 1993: 46–51.

49. Quoted in "Report Ties Cash, Politics." *Boston Globe.* January 12, 1996: 10.

50. Lawrence, Jill and Hasson, Judi. "Donations to Both Parties Skirt Limits Set by Reform." *USA Today.* October 28, 1996: 1A, 2A.

51. Miller, Alan C. and Miller, T. Christian. "Election Was Decisive in Arena of Spending: Ever Higher Sums." *Los Angeles Times.* December 8, 2000: 1A, 8A.

52. Welch, *op. cit.*, p. 1349.

53. *Ibid.*

54. Kramer, Michael. "The Best Pols Money Can Buy." *Time* 140, December 14, 1992: 49.

55. Quoted in Welch, *op. cit.*, p. 1350.

56. *Ibid.*, p. 1350.

57. Drew, Elizabeth. *Politics and Money: The New Road to Corruption.* New York: MacMillan, 1983.

58. Quoted in *Ibid.*, p. 2A.

59. Welch, *op. cit.*, pp. 1350–1351.

60. Barnes and Wildavsky, *op. cit.*, p. 45.

61. Bernstein, Alan. "DeLay Sees Limit to Lobbyists' Gifts as Attack on Free Speech." *Houston Chronicle.* April 15, 1995: 29A.

62. Ferguson, Thomas and Rogers, Joel. *Right Turn.* New York: Hill and Wang, 1986.

63. Kramer, *op. cit.*, p. 49.

64. Smith, J. Y. "Hanson Is Ordered to Prison." *Washington Post.* April 19, 1975: A7.

65. "S.E.C. Finds $4.2–Million in Gulf Bribes." *New York Times.* May 3, 1975: 15, 25.

66. Smith, Robert M. "'Illegality' Cited in Gulf Payments." *New York Times.* December 31, 1975: 1, 35.

67. Sobel, *op. cit.*

68. Quoted in Robert M. Smith, *op. cit.*, p. 1.

69. "Gulf Asks Return of Illegal Gifts." *New York Times.* March 1, 1976: 1, 46.

70. Robinson, Timothy S. "Hansen's Jail Term Revoked." *Washington Post.* April 26, 1975: A1, A4.

71. "Tonry Sentenced to Prison, Fined in Election Fraud." *Washington Post.* July 29, 1977: A8.

72. Quoted in Locy, Toni. "'Sad and Sorry Tale' of Misdeeds: 3 Years Given Ex-Lawmaker." *Houston Chronicle.* November 10, 1994: 6A.

73. *Ibid.*

74. *Houston Chronicle.* August 1, 1997: 8A.

75. Associated Press. "Republican House Seat in Jeopardy." FreeRebublic.com. April 30, 1998.

76. ABCNEWS.com. "Miller Takes Over for Kim." January 19, 1999.

77. Robinson, Thomas S. "Ex-Rep. Whalley Put on Probation." *Washington Post.* October 16, 1973: A2.

78. Robinson, Timothy S. "Ex-Congressman Faces Prison." *Washington Post.* February 1, 1977: A7.

79. Meyer, Lawrence. "Diggs Sentenced to Three Years; Could Keep Seat." *Washington Post.* November 21, 1978: A1, A10.

80. Supplementary Material. *New York Times.* September 6, 1978: 11.

81. "Ex-Rep. Clark Is Sentenced." *Washington Post.* June 13, 1979: A2.

82. Coleman, 1994, *op. cit.*

83. "Former Rep. John Dowdy Dies at 83." *Houston Post.* April 15, 1995: A23, A24.

84. Meyer, Lawrence. "Judge Fines Dowdy $25,000, Gives Him 18 Months in Prison." *Washington Post.* February 24, 1971: A5.

85. "Ex-Rep. Podell Sentenced." *Washington Post.* January 10, 1975: A10.

86. "Rep. Brasco Sentenced in Bribe Scheme." *Washington Post.* October 23, 1974: A7.

87. *Ibid.*, p. A7.

88. For a comprehensive analysis of Koreagate, see: Moore, Robin and Perdue, Lew. *The Washington Connection.* New York: Condor, 1977.

89. Halloran, Richard. "The Korea Probe Clearly Is Sinking in the West." *New York Times.* March 26, 1978: E5.

90. Halloran, Richard. "Ex-Rep. Hanna Concedes Guilt in Korea Case." *New York Times.* March 18, 1978: 1, 11.

91. Quoted in Coleman, 1994, *op. cit.*, p. 52.

92. Coleman, 1994, *op. cit.*, p. 51.

93. *Ibid.*

94. "F.B.I. Studies Flood and Passman Ties to Contracts." *New York Times.* February 23, 1978: A18.

95. Coleman, 1994, *op. cit.*

96. Lyons, Richard D. "Daniel Flood, 90, Who Quit Congress in Disgrace, Is Dead." *New York Times.* May 29, 1994: 34.

97. Quoted in *Ibid.,* p. 34.

98. *Ibid.*

99. Flood's former administrative aide was the government's key witness against him. The aide also would be instrumental in the subsequent conviction of another Pennsylvania Congressman, Joshua Eilberg, who accepted bribes from a Philadelphia hospital in exchange for helping the hospital win a $14.5 million grant from a federal antipoverty agency. (Schaffer, Jan. "Guilty Plea Ends Trial of Eilberg." *Washington Post.* February 25, 1979: A1, A11.)

100. Blumenthal, Ralph. "Clashes Said to Have Marked U.S. Discussions on Richmond." *New York Times.* August 30, 1982: A1, B4.

101. Noble, Kenneth B. "Richmond to Pay Walco $425,000 in S.E.C. Case." *New York Times.* February 10, 1982: D1, D16.

102. Carroll, Maurice. "Richmond, a Wealthy Businessman, First Entered Politics as a 'Reformer.'" *New York Times.* August 26, 1982: B2.

103. Blumenthal, Ralph. "Rep. Richmond Helped Fugitive Get Job on Payroll of House Doorkeeper." *New York Times.* February 22, 1982: B3.

104. Blumenthal, Ralph. "Lawmaker's Funds Clouded by Flaws." *New York Times.* January 18, 1982: A1, B4.

105. Blumenthal, Ralph. "Rep. Richmond Payroll Raises Ethics Questions." *New York Times.* January 19, 1982: B3.

106. Blumenthal, Ralph. "Richmond Admits Guilt in U.S. Case and Quits House." *New York Times.* August 26, 1982: A1, B2.

107. *Ibid.*

108. Fried, Joseph P. "Richmond Sentenced to a Year and a Day and Fined $20,000." *New York Times.* February 11, 1982: A1, B9.

109. Greene, Robert W. *The Sting Man: Inside ABSCAM.* New York: E. P. Dutton, 1981.

110. *Ibid.*

111. Quoted in *Ibid.,* p. 158.

112. *Ibid.,* p. 161.

113. Babcock, Charles R. "Williams Shown Boasting He Could Aid Mine Venture." *Washington Post.* April 2, 1981: A1, A11.

114. Quoted in Greene, *op. cit.* p. 184.

115. *Ibid.,* p. 187.

116. *Ibid.,* p. 194.

117. *Ibid.,* p. 194.

118. Quoted in "U.S. Says Rep. Lederer Promised 'Me' for $." *Washington Post.* January 7, 1981: p. A7.

119. Quoted in Greene, *op. cit.,* p. 207.

120. Quoted in Anderson, Jack. "Thompson and Murphy on FBI Tapes." *Washington Post.* November 10, 1980: D15.

121. Greene, *op. cit.*

122. Kiernan, Laura. "Jenrette and Stowe Guilty on 3 Counts in Abscam Trial." *Washington Post.* October 8, 1989: A1, A8.

123. Greene, *op. cit.,* p. 242.

124. *Ibid.*

125. *Ibid.*

126. Kamen, Al. "Ex-Rep. Kelly Sentenced in Abscam Case." *Washington Post.* January 13, 1984: A5.

127. Quoted in Greene, *op. cit.,* p. 244.

128. *Ibid.,* p. 249.

129. Quoted in Babcock, Charles. "Rep. Myers: Never Meant to Help 'Sheik.'" *Washington Post.* August 26, 1980: A1, A4.

130. Quoted in Babcock, Charles R. "Myers Testifies He Spent 'Sheik' Cash in 2 Weeks." *Washington Post.* August 27, 1980: A10.

131. Babcock, August 26, 1980, *op. cit,* p. A4.

132. "Lederer on Hill as Abscam Trial Jury Is Selected." *Washington Post.* January 6, 1981: A6.

133. "Rep. Lederer Resigns Seat over ABSCAM Conviction." *Washington Post.* April 30, 1981: A8.

134. Barbash, Fred. "Justices Refuse to Review 4 ABSCAM Convictions." *Washington Post.* June 1, 1983: A4.

135. "Ex-Congressman Lederer Loses Philadelphia Steamfitter Job." *Washington Post.* June 22, 1981: A26.

136. Babcock, Charles R. "Sen. Williams Dismisses His Statements on Influence as 'Just Plain Hot Air.'" *Washington Post.* April 28, 1981: A9.

137. *Ibid.*

138. Babcock, Charles R. "Senator's Claims Are Ridiculed by ABSCAM Prosecutor." *Washington Post.* April 28, 1981: A9.

139. Babcock, Charles R. "Prosecution Calls Williams 'a Corrupt Public Official.'" *Washington Post*. April 1, 1981: A9.

140. Babcock, Charles R. "Williams Convicted in ABSCAM." *Washington Post*. May 2, 1981: A1, A2.

141. Babcock, Charles R. "Williams Sentenced to 3 Years." *Washington Post*. February 17, 1982: A1, A8.

142. Peterson, Bill. "Williams, Facing Expulsion, Resigns from U.S. Senate." *Washington Post*. March 12, 1982: A1, A6.

143. Anderson, Jack. "Thompson and Murphy on FBI Tapes." *Washington Post*. November 10, 1980: D15.

144. "Thompson Given 3-year Sentence." *New York Times*. October 26, 1983: B2.

145. Anderson, Jack. "New Evidence Could Clear ABSCAM Figure." *Washington Post*. December 15, 1982: B21.

146. "Drink Flawed Jenrette's Judgment, Trial Is Told." *Washington Post*. September 25, 1980: A13.

147. Kiernan, *op. cit.*

148. Kamen, Al. "Jenrette Sentenced to 2 Years in Prison on ABSCAM Charges." *Washington Post*. December 10, 1983: A2.

149. Maxa, Rudy. "Jenrette Split: Episode II." *Washington Post*. January 13, 1981: B1, B4.

150. Babcock, Charles R. "Some Jenrette Cash Traced." *Washington Post*. January 14, 1981: A1, A5.

151. Anderson, Jack. "Kelly Spins a Spooky ABSCAM Yarn." *Washington Post*. March 31, 1980: C23.

152. Sinclair, Ward. "Kelly: Wanted to Expose 'Arabs.'" *Washington Post*. February 8, 1980: A8.

153. Greene, *op. cit.*, p. 232.

154. Anderson, Jack. "'Sting Man' May Have Kept ABSCAM Money." *Washington Post*. January 18, 1982: B23.

155. Babcock, Charles R. "Wife of Key ABSCAM Witness Is Found Hanged in Florida." *Washington Post*. January 27, 1982: A1, A12.

156. Marx, Gary T. "Who Really Gets Stung? Some Issues Raised by the New Police Undercover Work." *Crime & Delinquency* 28, 1982: 165–193.

157. Braithwaite, John, Fisse, Brent, and Geis, Gilbert. "Covert Facilitation and Crime: Restoring Balance to the Entrapment Debate." *Journal of Social Issues* 43, 1987: 5.

158. *Ibid.*

159. The entrapment debate would be reignited a few years later in the aftermath of Operation Greylord (discussed later in the chapter), another fruitful FBI sting—this one involving Chicago judges. The American Civil Liberties Union complained vigorously that Greylord's indiscriminate use of electronic surveillance techniques seriously abridged privacy rights and due process. Defenders of Greylord countered that corrupt judges, by virtue of their power and position, are so insulated against criminal liability that extraordinary measures are required in order to achieve even minimal success in policing the judiciary. (See: Shipp, E. R. "What's Proper in Policing the Judiciary?" *New York Times*. January 1, 1984: 28.)

160. Small, Joseph. "Political Ethics." *American Behavioral Scientist* 19, 1976: 543–566.

161. Rangel, Jesus. "Judge in Queens Is Found Guilty in Bribery Trial." *New York Times*. December 13, 1985: A1.

162. "Brennan Case Goes to Jurors." *New York Times*. December 12, 1985: B10.

163. Buder, Leonard. "Brennan Given a 5-year Sentence and Fined $209,000 for Bribery." *New York Times*. February 4, 1986: B3.

164. Buder, Leonard. "A Suspended Judge Pleads Guilty to Racketeering in Realty Work." *New York Times*. April 2, 1987: B3.

165. One of Smith's alleged beneficiaries was businessman John Zaccaro, husband of one-time Congresswoman and former vice-presidential candidate, Geraldine Ferraro.

166. Quoted in James, George. "Ex-Queens Judge Is Given a Year in Prison for Lying to Grand Jury." *Washington Post*. September 10, 1987: A1.

167. "4 Florida Judges Are Indicted in Federal Corruption Inquiry." *New York Times*. September 25, 1991: 16.

168. "2 Judges Guilty in Florida Corruption Inquiry." *New York Times*. April 28, 1993: A18.

169. Bentayou, Frank. "Busting Public Corruption." *American Legion Magazine* 138, April 1995: 34–35.

170. Patterson, Bill. "Operation Greylord's Scorecard Nearly Complete." *Washington Post*. August 25, 1989: A5.

171. The name Greylord was taken from a term for British judges, who wear distinctive grey wigs while presiding.

172. Kose, Kevin. "9 Are Indicted in U.S. Probe of Chicago Court Corruption." *Washington Post.* December 15, 1983: A1, A2.

173. Patterson, *op. cit.*

174. Quoted in Witt, Elder. "Is Government Full of Crooks, or Are We Just Better at Finding Them?" *Governing.* September 1989: 33.

175. Greenhouse, Linda. "Justices Consider How the Taint of a Corrupt Judge Should Be Measured and Remedied." *New York Times.* April 15, 1997: A18.

176. *Ibid.*

177. Quoted in Klose, 1985, *op. cit.*, p. A3.

178. Klose, Kevin. "Senior Judge Guilty in 'Greylord' Case." *Washington Post.* July 14, 1985: A3.

179. Lacaya, Richard. "Passing Judgment on the Judges." *Time* 127, January 20, 1986: 66.

180. "Corruption: A Club for Bribery." *Time.* June 11, 1984: 33.

181. Smith, Robert M. "Tenneco Reports 'Sensitive' Gifts in U.S. and Abroad." *New York Times.* February 15, 1976: 1, 34.

182. "Texas: Politics in Court." *The Economist.* July 25, 1987: 21–22.

183. Shannon, James. *Texaco and the $10 Billion Jury.* Englewood Cliffs, NJ: Prentice Hall, 1988.

184. Methvin, Eugene H. "Justice for Sale." *Readers Digest* 134, May 1989: 133.

185. *Ibid.*, p. 134.

186. *Ibid.*, p. 135.

187. "Bankrupt: Texaco and Texas Justice." *New York Times.* April 14, 1987. A30.

188. Quoted in Methvin, *op. cit.*, p. 134.

189. Thornton, Mary. "Senate Convicts Claiborne, Strips Him of Judgeship." *Washington Post.* October 10, 1986: A1, A18.

190. Turner, Wallace. "U.S. Judge in Nevada Convicted of Filing False Income Tax Forms." *New York Times.* October 11, 1984: 1, 13.

191. Thornton, *op. cit.*

192. McAllister, Bill. "Hastings Backers Accuse Senate of Racism in Vote." *Washington Post.* October 21, 1989: A4.

193. Marcus, Ruth. "Senate Deliberates Judge Hastings's Fate." *Washington Post.* October 20, 1989: A14.

194. Marcus, Ruth. "Senate Urged to Remove Hastings." *Washington Post.* October 19, 1989: A4.

195. Marcus, Ruth. "Senate Removes Hastings." *Washington Post.* October 21, 1989: A1, A4.

196. Seligman, Daniel. "The Case of the Crooked Bench." *Fortune* 123, March 25, 1991: 139–140.

197. Biskupic, Joan. "Familiar Words—Nixon, Impeach—But Unusual Test of Power." *Washington Post.* October 11, 1992: A3.

198. "U.S. Judge Enters Prison." *Washington Post.* March 24, 1988: A1.

199. Marcus, Frances F. "U.S. Judge is Convicted in New Orleans Bribe Case." *New York Times.* June 30, 1991: 13.

200. "U.S. Judge Is Given Prison Sentence." New York Times. September 7, 1991: 12.

201. Borkin, Joseph. *The Corrupt Judge: An Inquiry Into Bribery and Other High Crimes and Misdemeanors in the Federal Courts.* New York: Clarkson N. Potter, 1962.

202. *Ibid.*

203. Maas, Arthur. "U.S. Prosecution of State and Local Officials for Political Corruption: Is the Bureaucracy Out of Control in a High-Stakes Operation Involving the Constitutional System?" *Publius: The Journal of Federalism* 17, 1987: 199.

204. Ross, *op. cit.* As of this writing, the most recent Reagan appointee to be convicted of criminal charges was former Secretary of the Interior James Watt, who was sentenced to 5 years probation, fined $5000, and ordered to perform 500 hours of community service in 1996 for attempting to mislead a grand jury investigation of influence peddling in the Reagan administration's Department of Housing and Urban Development. Watt originally was charged with 18 felony counts but entered an agreement with the government to plead guilty to a single misdemeanor charge (Locy, Tony. "Watt Given Probation on Grand Jury Charge." *Houston Chronicle.* March 13, 1996: 8A. See also: "Washington." *USA Today.* March 13, 1996: 5A).

205. When New York Congressman Mario Biaggi was convicted in 1988 of accepting a $4-million bribe from the Wedtech Corporation in exchange for no-bid government contracts, he contended that Wedtech's true partner in corruption was

Ed Meese, who had helped the company secure a $32-million Army engine contract. After the Biaggi verdict, U.S. Attorney Rudolph Giuliani (later elected Mayor of New York City) characterized Meese as "a sleaze." (Quoted in Lardner, George Jr. and Yen, Marianne. "Twice-Convicted Biaggi Surrenders House Seat." *Washington Post*. August 6, 1988: A12.)

206. Maas, *op. cit.*, p. 199.

207. *Ibid.*

208. *Ibid.*

209. *Ibid.* For a brief description of some typical cases against legislators in four states (Arizona, South Carolina, California, and Texas), see "7 Lawmakers Charged in Bribe Sting." *Washington Post*. February 7, 1991: A7.

210. Blakey, Robert. "The RICO Civil Fraud Action in Context." *Notre Dame Law Review* 58, 1982: 237–349.

211. Kolbert, Elizabeth. "Payroll-Abuse Investigation Seen as Watershed in Albany." *New York Times*. April 6, 1987: A1, B4.

212. Maas, *op. cit.*

213. "2 Sentenced in Atlanta Airport Scheme." *New York Times*. April 16, 1994: A8.

214. Wayne, Leslie. "Investing; for Municipal Bonds, Scandals Spur Change." *New York Times*. September 18, 1993: 31.

215. "Ms. Holtzman's Duty." *New York Times*. September 11, 1993: 20.

216. Thomas, Frank and Morgan, Thomas J. "Speaker Harwood Pays $5,000 to Settle Ethics Matter, Denies He Erred." *Providence Journal-Bulletin*, September 3, 1994: A1, A5.

217. Cohen, Richard M. and Witcover, Jules. *A Heartbeat Away: The Investigation & Resignation of Vice President Spiro T. Agnew.* New York: Viking Press, 1974.

218. "Kerner arrives in Ky. to Begin 3-Year Term." *New York Times*. July 30, 1974: A11.

219. Weissman, Joel. "Kerner Gets 3-Year Jail Term." *New York Times*. April 20, 1973: A3.

220. Baker, Donald P. "Mandel Trial Judge Spurns Sentence Recommendations." *Washington Post*. October 4, 1977: C1.

221. Becker, Elizabeth and Baker, Donald. "Mandel Given Sentence of Four Years in Prison: Fine Not Imposed." *Washington Post*. October 8, 1977: A1, A8.

222. Maraniss, David A. "Mandel Given Sentence of Four Years in Prison: Has no Regrets." *Washington Post*. October 8, 1977: A1, A8.

223. Raines, Howell. "Judge Says Tennessee Governor Illegally Used His Parole Powers." *New York Times*. December 21, 1978: 21.

224. "Tennessee Governor Questioned by Grand Jury on Alleged Bribes." *New York Times*. December 23, 1978: 9.

225. "Blanton Grants Clemency to 52 Tennessee Convicts." *New York Times*. January 17, 1979: 14.

226. Raines, Howell. "Gov. Blanton of Tennessee Is Replaced 3 Days Early in Pardons Dispute." *New York Times*. January 18, 1979: 16.

227. Raines, Howell. "Even After Blanton Was Ousted, He Tried to Aid 30 More Convicts." *New York Times*. January 19, 1979: A12.

228. Maas, Peter. *Marie: A True Story.* New York: Random House, 1983: 415.

229. Shabecoff, Phillip. "Blanton Verdict in Tennessee Upset." *New York Times*. April 12, 1983: L9.

230. Reid, David. "Alabama's Baptist Governor Indicted." *Christianity Today* 37, February 8, 1993: 57.

231. "Ex-Governor of Alabama Loses Ruling." *New York Times*. April 22, 1994: A17.

232. Jefferson, James. "Tucker Gets Probation in Whitewater." *Boston Herald*, August 20, 1996: 3.

233. Hasson, Judi. "Whitewater Verdicts: Guilty." *USA Today*. May 29, 1996: 1A; Pressley, Sue Ann. "Arkansans Rally to Defense of Their Indicted Governor." *Houston Chronicle*. June 23, 1995: 6A.

234. Quoted in Page, Susan. "Arkansas Gov Will Resign, Then Appeal." *USA Today*. May 29, 1996: 3A.

235. Mathis, Nancy. "Clinton's Former Partners Convicted of Fraud." *Houston Chronicle*. May 29, 1996: 1A, 8A; Nichols, Bill. "For Clinton, Ripples of Concern." *USA Today*. May 29, 1996: 3A.

236. Quoted in Serrill, Michael. "Bad Debts, Bad Judgments." *Time*, 150. September 15, 1997: 92.

237. *Ibid*, p. 43.

238. *Ibid.*

239. *Ibid.*, p. 92.

240. *Ibid.*, p. 92.

241. "Man Was to Plead Guilty Until Pardon." *Houston Chronicle*. January 25, 2001: 10A.

242. *Ibid.*

243. "Rhode Island Ex-Governor Pleads Guilty of Bribery, Racketeering." *Houston Chronicle.* December 12, 1998: 11A.

244. Tedford, Deborah. "Edwards Guilty of Extortion." *Houston Chronicle.* May 10, 2000: 1A, 16A.

245. Zganjar, Leslie. "Casino-Licensing Graft Evidence Stacks up Against Ex-La. Governor." *Houston Chronicle.* October 1, 1998: 17A.

246. Deslatte, Melinda. "Ex-Louisiana Gove. Faces Sentencing." Yahoo!News.com. January 7, 2001.

247. Gott, Natalie. "Former La. Governor on Trial." ABCNews.com. January 10, 2000.

248. Zganjar, *op. cit.*

249. Gott, Natalie. "Trails of Money, Stacks of Cash May Cost Edwards in Latest Trial." *Houston Chronicle.* April 24, 2000: 4A.

250. Zganjar, *op. cit.*

251. Edwards' odd reference was to Monica Lewinsky's "friend" Linda Tripp, who secretly recorded phone conversations they had shared regarding Lewinsky's alleged sexual relations with President Bill Clinton.

252. Quoted in Sack, Kevin. "49ers Co-Owner Pleads Guilty to Concealing Extortion Plot." *Houston Chronicle.* October 7, 1998: 1A, 10A.

253. Quoted in Gott, *Houston Chronicle. op. cit.,* p. 4A.

254. Quoted in Gott, *Houston Chronicle. op. cit.,* p. 4A.

255. Quoted in Tedford, *op. cit.,* p. 1A.

256. Witt, Elder. "Is Government Full of Crooks, or Are We Just Better at Finding Them?" *Governing.* September 1989: 33–38.

257. *Ibid.*

258. *Ibid.*

259. Marvin, Mary Jo. "Swindles of the 1990s: Con Artists Are Thriving." *USA Today Magazine.* September 1994: 80–84.

260. "Former JP Sentenced." *Houston Chronicle.* December 6, 1995: 19A.

261. "Rep. Hinshaw Gets 1–14 Years in Jail." *Washington Post.* February 25, 1976: A12.

262. Quoted in *Ibid.,* p. A 12.

263. Callow, Alexander. *The City Boss in America.* New York: Oxford University Press, 1976.

264. "Boodle" came from *boedel,* the Dutch word for property. Some time after Nieuw Amsterdam became New York City, "boodle" was applied specifically to property misappropriated by politicians—particularly New York politicians. (Logan, Andy. "Around City Hall: Upstairs, Downstairs." *The New Yorker,* August 21, 1989: 80–86.)

265. Callow, Alexander B. *The Tweed Ring.* New York: Oxford University Press, 1966.

266. Enright, Richard T. *Capone's Chicago.* Lakeville, MN: Northstar Mascher Books, 1987.

267. Miller, Richard L. *Truman: The Rise to Power.* New York: Mcgraw-Hill, 1986.

268. Callow, 1976, *op. cit.,* p. 33.

269. Pare, Terence P. "The Big Sleaze in Muni Bonds." *Fortune* 132, August 7, 1995: 113–120.

270. *Ibid.,* p. 141.

271. Witt, Elder. "Is Government Full of Crooks, or Are We Just Better at Finding Them?" *Governing* 2, 1989: 32–38.

272. Witt, *op. cit.*

273. Groson, Lindsey. "Corruption Is Brotherly in Philadelphia." *New York Times.* November 11, 1986: E4.

274. Applebome, Peter. "Scandal Casts Shadow Over Atlanta Mayoral Race." *New York Times.* November 18, 1993: A16.

275. Hicks, Jonathan. "Subpoena Jolts Black Mayors Meeting." *New York Times.* April 27, 1991: 8.

276. "After 5 Years, Case Against Former Mayor of San Diego is Resolved." *New York Times.* January 2, 1991: A14.

277. "Miami City Official Pleads Guilty." October 10, 1996: 3A. Bacon, John. "Miami Bribe." *USA Today. USA Today.* October 30, 1996: 3A.

278. Witt, *op. cit.*

279. "Former Mayor Gets 5½ Years for Extortion." *New York Times.* February 2, 1992: B10.

280. "Congressman from California Convicted of Extortion, Resigns." *Houston Chronicle.* December 13, 1995: 14A.

281. "New York: Unhappy Days Are Here Again." *The Economist.* February 1, 1986: 21.

282. O'Connor, Colleen and McKillop, Peter. "The Big Apple Is Beset by Rotten Apples." *Newsweek* 109, March 30, 1987: 30.

283. Hornblower, Margot. "Scandals Unfold in New York." *Washington Post.* March 10, 1986: A6.

284. Newfield, Jack and Barrett, Wayne. *City for Sale: Ed Koch and the Betrayal of New York*. New York: Harper & Row, 1988.

285. Barrett, Wayne. "The Scandal that Won't Go Away." *Village Voice*. April 13, 1993: 10–12, 31–37.

286. Hornblower, Margot. "Manes Protégé Indicted in Bribery Case." *Washington Post*. February 25, 1986: A3.

287. Hornblower, March 10, 1986, *op. cit.*

288. Weiss, Phillip. "Koch and the Bosses." *The New Republic* 194, March 10, 1986: 12–15.

289. McFadden, Robert D. "Manes Is a Suicide, Stabbing Himself at Home in Queens." *New York Times*. March 14, 1986: A1, B20.

290. "Corruption Trial: A Clash of Tactics." *New York Times*. November 23, 1986: 42.

291. Weiss, *op. cit.*, p. 14.

292. Lynn, Frank. "Bronx Chief Quits and Friedman Gets 12-Year Sentence." *New York Times*. March 12, 1987: A1, B14.

293. Meislin, Richard J. "A Not Very Pretty Picture of the City." *New York Times*. November 9, 1986: E4.

294. Coleman, 1994, *op. cit.*

295. Sherman, Lawrence W. *Scandal and Reform: Controlling Police Corruption*. Berkeley: University of California Press, 1978.

296. Nelson, Jill. "Blue Plague." *New York Times*. May 20, 1994: 27.

297. "Chicago Police Officer Guilty." *New York Times*. August 11, 1994: 13A.

298. "Police Union Officials Guilty in Philadelphia." *New York Times*. February 19, 1995: 39; "Philadelphia Police Scandal Keeps Growing." *Houston Chronicle*. March 21, 1996: 12A; Smith, Jim. "Judge Sends Message: Corrupt Officers Get Long Prison Sentences." *Houston Chronicle*. April 17, 1996: 14A.

299. "A Detroit Police Corruption Probe." Vol. 114, *Newsweek*. December 18, 1989: 30. See also: "Secret Self-Service?" *The Economist*. February 16, 1991: 23.

300. Gladwell, Malcolm. "In Drug War, Crime Sometimes Wears a Badge." *Washington Post*. May 19, 1994: A1, A16.

301. Locy, Toni. "Ex-Officer Says Greed Guided Him into Net of Drug Sting." *Washington Post*. October 20, 1994: C1, C8. See also: Duggan, Paul. "D.C. Officers Plead Guilty in Drug Case." *Washington Post*. April 17, 1994: B3; Locy, Toni. "3 D.C. Officers Found Guilty in Corruption Case." *Washington Post*. November 19, 1994: B1; Harmon, John, Taylor, Troy, and Washington, Dwayne. "Stiff Sentences for Crooked Cops." *Washington Post*. May 29, 1995: A14.

302. Hollandsworth, Skip. "The Seduction of Cruiser and Bruiser." *Texas Monthly*. September 1993: 128–141.

303. Sechrest, Dale and Burns, Pamela. "Police Corruption: The Miami Case." *Criminal Justice and Behavior* 19: 294–313.

304. "First Black Woman to Run a Big City Police Force Cracks Down on Corruption." *Jet*, 88, October 2, 1995: 8–13.

305. "9 New Orleans Officers Are Indicted in U.S. Drug Case." *New York Times*. December 8, 1994: 18; Sewell, Dan. "New Orleans Police Officers Find Themselves Being Policed." *Houston Chronicle*. Houston Chronicle. April 21, 1996: 25A.

306. "Investigation to Zero In on L.A. Police." *Houston Chronicle*. September 22, 1999: 10A; Lelyveld, Nita. "Latest LAPD Scandal Taints City's Criminal-Justice System." *Houston Chronicle*. September 26, 1999: 21A. "Poor Supervision, LAPD Culture Faulted in Scandal." *USA Today*. March 2, 2000: 3A.

307. Gladwell, *op. cit.*

308. Haygood, Wil. "Billy Celester's Hard Rise, Swift, Fall." *Boston Globe*, August 11, 1996: A1, A24.

309. Johnson, Kevin. "New Breed of Bad Cop Sells Badge, Public Trust." *USA Today*. April 16, 1998: 8A.

310. Dillow, Gordon. "15 Officers Disciplined in Inglewood." *Los Angeles Times*, May 25, 1994: B1.

311. O'Harrow, Robert, Jr. "Va. Sheriff Target of Probe Commits Suicide." *Washington Post*. January 23, 1992: B1, B6.

312. Bentayou, *op. cit.*

313. Johnson, *op. cit.*

314. Reich, Kenneth. "3 More Former Deputies Guilty in Skimming." *Los Angeles Times*, August 30, 1994: B1, B4.

315. Morganthau, Tom. "Why Good Cops Go Bad." *Newsweek* 124, December 19, 1994: 30–34.

316. Barker, Thomas and Roebuck, Julian. *An Empirical Typology of Police Corruption: A Study in Organizational Deviance*. Springfield, Ill.: Charles C. Thomas, 1973.

317. Reiss, Albert J. Jr. *The Police and the Public.* New Haven: Yale University Press, 1972.

318. Quoted in Deutsch, Albert. *The Trouble with Cops.* Boston: Crown, 1955: 47–48.

319. Cooksey, Otis E. "Corruption: A Continuing Challenge for Law Enforcement." *FBI Law Enforcement Bulletin,* September 1991: 5–9.

320. Stern, Mort. "What Makes a Policeman Go Wrong?" *Journal of Criminal Law, Criminology and Police Science* 63, 1992: 98–101.

321. Roebuck, Julian and Barker, Thomas. "A Typology of Police Corruption." *Social Problems* 21, 1974: 429.

322. Barker and Roebuck, *op. cit.*

323. *Ibid.*

324. Burnham, David. "How Corruption Is Built into the System—and a Few Ideas for what to Do about It." *New York* 119, September 21, 1970: 1–18.

325. Cook, Fred J. "The Pusher Cop: The Institutionalizing of Police Corruption." *New York,* August 16, 1971: 22–30.

326. Barker and Roebuck, *op. cit.,* p. 34.

327. Roebuck and Barker, *op. cit.*

328. Messick, Hank. *Syndicate in the Sun.* New York: MacMillan, 1968.

329. Roebuck and Barker, *op. cit.*

330. Skolnick, Jerome H. *Justice Without Trial: Law Enforcement in Democratic Society.* New York: John Wiley, 1966: 208.

331. Carter, David L. "Drug-Related Corruption of Police Officers: A Contemporary Typology." *Journal of Criminal Justice* 18, 1990: 93.

332. Barker and Roebuck, *op. cit.,* p. 28.

333. Coleman, 1994, *op. cit.,* p. 45.

334. Johnston, Michael. *Political Corruption and Public Policy in America.* Monterey, Calif.: Brooks/Cole, 1982: 85.

335. *Ibid.*

336. Bragg, Rick. "Blue Wall of Silence: Graft Shielded Behind Old Code." *New York Times.* April 26, 1994: B1, B2.

337. Collins, Allyson. "Justice Won't Prevail Until Blue Wall of Police Silence Comes Down." *Houston Chronicle.* June 13, 1999: 4C.

338. *Ibid.*

339. *Ibid.*

340. *Ibid.,* p. B1.

341. Daly, Robert. *Prince of the City: The True Story of a Cop Who Knew Too Much.* Boston: Houghton Mifflin, 1978: 311.

342. Bragg, *op. cit.,* p. B2.

343. *Ibid.,* p. B2.

344. *Ibid.,* p. B2.

345. Hoover, Ken. "S.F. Cop Refuses to Testify in Sex Assault Case." *San Francisco Chronicle.* April 2, 1997: A15.

346. *Ibid.,* p. B2.

347. Carter, *op. cit.,* p. 95.

348. Coleman, 1987, 95.

349. Lefkowitz, Joel. "Psychological Attributes of Policemen: A Review of Research and Opinion." *Journal of Social Issues* 31, 1975: 7–20.

350. Johnston, *op. cit.,* p. 83.

351. Westley, William A. *Violence and the Police.* Cambridge, Mass.: M.I.T. Press, 1970.

352. Coleman, 1994, *op. cit.,* p. 45.

353. Krauss, Clifford. "Police Problems' Scale Eludes Senior Officials." *New York Times.* May 9, 1994: B3.

354. Carter, *op. cit.*

355. Quoted in Carter, *op. cit.,* p. 93.

356. Lardner, James. "The Whistle-Blower— Part I." *The New Yorker* 69, July 5, 1993: 52–56.

357. Williams' unusual nickname came from his feisty declaration that there was more law at the end of his nightstick than in all the statute books.

358. *Ibid.,* p. 58.

359. Hirschorn, Michael. "Good Cop, Bad Cop." *New York* 27, July 11, 1994: 15,

360. *Ibid.*

361. "What the Census Reveals." *New York Times.* May 2, 1894: 7.

362. Jeffers, H. Paul. *Commissioner Roosevelt: The Story of Theodore Roosevelt and the New York City Police, 1895-1897.* New York: Wiley, 1994.

363. Davis, Kenneth S. *FDR: The New York Years 1928-1933.* New York: Random House, 1985.

364. Krauss, Clifford. "Police Corruption in New York: As Expected, a Blight Returns." *New York Times.* March 21, 1994: B3.

365. The NYPD is by far the largest police department in the United States—more than $2\frac{1}{2}$ times bigger than the second largest force, Chicago's.

366. Conklin, William R. "Gross Gets 12-Year Term: Police Graft Story Bared." *New York Times.* September 28, 1951: 1, 22.

367. Krauss, March 7, 1994, *op. cit.*

368. "Cops on the Take." *Newsweek.* November 1, 1971: 43.

369. Krauss, March 7, 1994, *op. cit.*, p. B5.

370. *Newsweek,* November 1, 1971, *op. cit.,* p. 43.

371. Commission to Investigate Allegations of Police Corruption in New York City. "Police Corruption in New York: The Knapp Commission." In M. David Ermann and Richard J. Lundman (Eds.), *Corporate and Governmental Deviance: Problems of Organizational Behavior in Contemporary Society* (Second Edition). New York: Oxford University Press, 1982: 155–166.

372. *Newsweek,* November 1, 1971, *op. cit.*

373. Lardner, James. "The Whistle-Blower—Part II." *The New Yorker* 69, July 12, 1993: 39–59.

374. Maas, Peter. *Serpico: The Cop Who Defied the System.* New York: Viking Press, 1973. See also: "Serpico Testifies." *New York,* 26, April 19, 1993: 130.

375. Buckley, Tom. "Murphy Among the 'Meat Eaters'." *New York Times Magazine,* December 19, 1971: 11, 42, 44–49.

376. Morganthau, *op. cit.*, p. 30.

377. Buckley, *op. cit.*

378. Lacayo, Richard. "Cops and Robbers." *Time* 142, October 11, 1993: 43.

379. *Ibid.,* p. 43.

380. Bonfante, Jordan. "Cops and Robbers." *Time* 142, October 11, 1993: 42–43.

381. Treaster, Joseph B. "Corruption in Uniform: The Dowd Case; Officer Flaunted Corruption and His Superiors Ignored It." *New York Times.* July 7, 1994: 1.

382. Armao, Joseph and Cornfeld, Leslie U. "How to Police the Police." *Newsweek* 124, December 19, 1994: 34.

383. Treaster, *op. cit.*, p. 1.

384. Lacayo, *op. cit.*, p. 43.

385. Treaster, Joseph B. "Convicted Police Officer Receives a Sentence of at Least 11 Years." *New York Times.* July 12, 1994: 1.

386. Quoted in *Ibid.*, p. 1.

387. Wolff, Craig. "Corruption in Uniform: Chronology; Tracking Police Corruption over the Years." *New York Times.* July 7, 1994: B3.

388. "3 Officers Will Face Shakedown Charges." *New York Times.* March 8, 1994: B3.

389. "The Police: NYPD Blues." *The Economist.* April 30, 1994: 29–30.

390. Gladwell, *op. cit.*, p. A1.

391. *Ibid.,* p. A1.

392. Krauss, Clifford. "Officers Held in Police Sting after Robbery Is Videotaped." *New York Times.* March 19, 1994: 1, 27.

393. Krauss, Clifford. "11 More Officers Taken off Duties in 30th Precinct." *New York Times.* May 5, 1994: A1, B4.

394. *The Economist,* April 30, 1994, *op. cit.*

395. Pooley, Eric. "Has Bill Bratton Gone Soft?" *New York* 27, July 11, 1994: 24–26.

396. "Former 39th Precinct Officer Pleads Guilty." *New York Times.* December 20, 1994: 6.

397. Holloway, Lynette. "Equality on Police Force: Women Arrested Too." *New York Times.* October 2, 1994: 35.

398. Krauss, Clifford. "14 More Officers Arrested at a Shaken 30th Precinct." *New York Times.* September 29, 1994: A1, B3.

399. Sullivan, John. "Ex-Sergeant Is Sentenced In Police Corruption Case." *New York Times.* June 17, 1997: B3.

400. Krauss, Clifford. "At 30th Precinct, 2 Supervisors' Rise and Fall." *New York Times.* September 30, 1994: B1, B3.

401. Armao, Joseph and Cornfeld, Leslie U. "When Cops Betray Their Communities." *Newsweek* 124, December 19, 1994: 32.

402. Quoted in Krauss, Clifford. "On Their Watch: 30th Precinct Scandal Raises Issues on the Accountability of Supervisors." *New York Times.* October 3, 1994: B8.

403. Krauss, Clifford. "Corruption in Uniform: The Overview; 2-Year Corruption Inquiry Finds a 'Willful Blindness' in New York's Police Dept." *New York Times.* July 7, 1994: 1.

404. *The Economist,* April 30, 1994, *op. cit.*

405. *Ibid.,* p. 30.

406. Treaster, Joseph B. "Mollen Panel Says Buck Stops with Top Officers." *New York Times.* July 10, 1994: 21.

407. Krauss, Clifford. "16 Officers Indicted in Brutality in Bronx." *New York Times.* May 4, 1995: A4.

408. It has been argued for years that civilian review boards are one of the most effective ways to eliminate police misconduct. See, for example: Glazer, Sarah. "Police Corruption: Can Brutality and Other Misconduct Be Rooted Out?" *CQ Researcher* 5, November 24, 1995: 1041, 1043.

409. Mollen Commission. "Excerpts." *New York Times.* July 7, 1994: B2.

CHAPTER 10

Medical Crime

Doctor: You ask me if I have a God complex? Let me tell you something: I *am* God.

From *Malice* (1994). Screenplay by Aaron Sorkin and Scott Frank.

*T*here can be little doubt that the U.S. healthcare system is vulnerable to fraud, waste, and abuse. Given the wide array of private and public services, insurance plans, medical corporations, and treatment facilities, it is very difficult to pinpoint losses owing to crime in the gargantuan, trillion-dollar-per-year healthcare industry—an industry that consumes 14% of America's gross national product, making it the *largest business in the country*.[1] But even in the absence of a precise estimate, the sheer cost of medical care in America assures that even relatively small amounts of crime add up to illicit profits of sizable magnitude. Some experts estimate that up to $80 billion per year is stolen from taxpayers and insurers as a result of healthcare fraud[2] on the part of physicians and, to a lesser extent, other providers such as dentists,[3] pharmacists,[4] psychologists,[5] chiropractors,[6] and podiatrists.[7] Moreover, the dollars drained have serious physical consequences as well, especially for the most needy among us, who depend on government benefit programs such as Medicaid and Medicare.

A southern California case, one of the largest health fraud operations in history, uncovered a gang of unscrupulous doctors and medical entrepreneurs. Mobile laboratories offered "free" tests, and clinics provided misrepresented services and bogus diagnoses in a potential billion-dollar false billing scheme to defraud health insurance companies. Masterminded by Michael and David Smushkevich, two Russian immigrant brothers, the conspiracy reached its peak between 1986 and 1988, when investigators found that it encompassed 1000 separate companies and 400 bank accounts around the world.[8] The ring included a dozen people who set up hundreds of phony corporations and fake businesses to bill insurance companies and launder the money received from them.

Patients were solicited from "boiler rooms," where slick telemarketers "pitched" full physical examinations with state-of-the-art diagnostics at little or no fee. The exams were conducted in "rolling labs" at such places as health clubs, shopping malls, and retirement homes. Medical charts were falsified to make it appear that each test was essential. In one case, a 2-hour examination of an Irvine, California, woman resulted in $7500 in billings, despite the fact that she was not feeling ill and had no physical symptoms.[9] Because most insurance policies do not cover preventive procedures, patients were required to fill out medical history forms that were later "doctored" to show that the tests were medically necessary, and thus eligible for payment. Sometimes diagnostic tests were performed *before* the patient had even been examined.

About $50 million was paid by government and private insurers before the scam was detected. It unraveled, ironically, when a physician working for Pacific Mutual Insurance received a telephone solicitation from one of the boiler rooms. When he went for his "free" examination, he filled out a medical history form without being asked anything about his current health. Soon thereafter, his insurance company (and employer) received a bill for $7500, with diagnoses showing high blood pressure, diabetes, heart disease, and cancer. The doctor had none of those conditions. Authorities raided the Smushkevichs' offices and clinics 8 months later, after they received other similar complaints of fraudulent diagnoses.

One of the physicians involved in the conspiracy, Dr. William O. Kuperschmidt, was convicted on charges of mail fraud, money laundering, and racketeering, slapped with a huge $50-million fine, and ordered to forfeit two properties and all assets of a medical enterprise that included three clinics operating in southern California. Michael Smushkevich, the alleged ringleader, denied any criminal wrongdoing, arguing that the case should be handled in civil court "and focus on who determines what tests were 'medically necessary.'"[10] David Smushkevich fled to Amsterdam, while his attorney claimed that his fugitive client was "absolutely" innocent.[11] In 1993, however, both brothers were found "absolutely" guilty of multiple fraud charges.[12]

Insurers were not the only victims of the Smushkevich scam, however. There was a ripple effect that unjustly penalized innocent patients as well. One California chiropractor, who was in excellent health and an active athlete, had his application for a life insurance policy rejected months after his medical record had been smeared with unfounded diagnoses, including heart defects and obstructive pulmonary emphysema. It took him 2 years to clear his record.

Healthcare rip-offs also have substantial secondary effects on consumers and businesses in terms of higher costs for government health programs and increases in insurance premiums. The traditional medical insurance reimbursement fraud, involving a single perpetrator has changed according to authorities, and more sophisticated and costly crimes involving "cartel-type frauds" are becoming more commonplace. Criminal organizations of that type have been found all across the country.[13]

In this chapter, we will examine some of the major forms of medical crimes, relate a sample of illustrative case histories, and discuss enforcement problems as well as emerging areas for future concern.

EQUIPMENT SALES

Some of the most devious operators in the healthcare field have treated government programs such as Medicare, the government health program for the elderly, like open checkbooks. Senior citizens, the inveterate targets of so many forms of consumer fraud, are particularly susceptible to scams involving the marketing of medical products such as seat lift chairs, oxygen concentrators, home dialysis systems, and other sometimes unnecessary equipment at inflated costs. Medicare is an easy mark. It fails to account for the legitimacy of suppliers, because no documentation is required.

One case in Philadelphia, involving over 2200 fraudulent claims filed in 1988 and 1989, bilked Medicare out of millions of dollars. The companies filing the false claims, Federal Home Care and Home Health Products, were owned by Mark Mickman, the former proprietor of a television rental business. While issuing a court injunction in 1989, a federal judge labeled Mickman's operation "an out and out scam."[14] Mickman employed teenaged girls in a telemarketing scheme operated out of shopping centers in the Philadelphia area. The girls called Medicare beneficiaries who had responded to an ad offering a "free Medicare covered package." The telemarketers would then obtain Medicare numbers, and ask if they had any physical conditions or problems. If they did, Mickman's firm "could help." Although Medicare requires a 20% co-payment, they were told that Medicare would cover 100% of the cost. In a bench opinion, Judge Donald Van Artsdalen said, "Teenagers who had no medical training were making medical diagnoses upon which sophisticated, expensive equipment was being purchased for patients that neither needed nor wanted the equipment."[15]

The scam worked because doctors, whose authorization is needed for such claims, signed precompleted forms, allowing Mickman to bill Medicare successfully. Rip-off artists sometimes fake the signatures or pay off corrupt doctors to sign forms. In other instances, doctors may sign the forms mistakenly or succumb to pressure from patients to do so.

In some frauds the equipment is not only nonessential, but outrageously overpriced as well. A chunk of flimsy foam that cost a supplier about $28 was charged to Medicare as a $900 "dry floatation mattress" for bedsores. Another profit-gouging item is a transcutaneous electronic nerve stimulator (TENS), which generates electrical impulses that can control pain. The components could be bought at Radio Shack for about $50, but Medicare is sometimes billed as much as $500 per unit.[16] Prices for equipment also vary by region, allowing suppliers to set up "branch offices" that are little more than mail drops in the more profitable states.[17]

Besides the outright crooks who have intentionally conducted business in a fraudulent manner, there are firms which aggressively market their products to unsuspecting patients, while keeping barely within the technical boundaries of current law. In a variation on the classic "bait and switch" technique, medical equipment companies compile lists of beneficiaries—usually those enrolled in Medicare—by placing ads which offer free gifts or services. High-pressure salespersons call on the beneficiaries, find out their health conditions and needs, then sell them equipment and supplies. Obviously, rules which allow such deceptive practices invite fraud and abuse. As an official in the California Medical Association put it, "There's no limit to what an American entrepreneur can conjure up to sell products."[18]

HOME CARE FRAUD

Home care services constitute a relatively new area for fraud by unscrupulous providers. The trend toward outpatient treatment, shorter hospital stays, and new technologies have led to a growing home care industry. In 1997 more than 10% of Medicare beneficiaries received services from 10,000 home healthcare agencies at a taxpayer cost of $19 billion annually. "The total number of home health visits financed by Medicare doubled from 1992 to 1996, reaching 280 million."[19] Like all thieves who follow the scent of money, rip-off artists have zeroed in on this lucrative market. The home care business, as one law enforcement official in New York put it, is "attracting the sharks."[20] Medicare and Medicaid, the government insurance programs for the elderly and the poor, reportedly lose over $2 billion per year to home care fraud.[21] Private insurers undoubtedly lose many millions of dollars more.

Home care fraud is particularly difficult to investigate because it entails a plethoric menu of services provided in thousands of private residences. More than 12,500 companies provide such services, mostly to the elderly. In one case:

> [A]n individual with no experience in healthcare started a Texas home health agency in the pantry of her husband's restaurant. Inspectors found that the company had hired home health aides on the condition that they first recruit patients. The agency was suspected of providing unnecessary services and was cited for violating federal standards.[22]

One of the largest home care fraud cases was settled in New York in 1990 against Professional Care, Inc. An inside informant verified that the company had systematically overbilled the state Medicaid system. Medicaid is the federally-mandated, but state-run, program that provides medical care for the indigent. During a 4-year period, Professional Care was reimbursed for home care services performed by untrained workers, or in some instances, no workers at all. It was also found that many more hours were charged than were actually provided.[23] The firm pleaded guilty to grand larceny and falsification of business records, and its two highest officers were convicted of conspiracy. A total of $5.2 million in fines and restitution were levied.

Another major case occurred in 1995, when John Watts, Jr., owner of United Home Care Services in California, pleaded guilty of defrauding Medicare out of $1.5 million. Watts was a convicted cocaine dealer, who started United Home Care a year after his release from prison. It is indicative of the almost complete lack of regulation in the home care industry that his background was never checked when he applied for and received a California license to run a home care agency. His scam was to submit bills for services never provided to patients who were never seen. Most of his "patients," in fact, were already dead. Watts would later tell a Senate committee investigating healthcare fraud, "We didn't start out to do this. But it was just too easy."[24]

In another 1995 case, Rony Flores, owner of Casa Care Services in New York was convicted of defrauding Medicaid out of $1.25 million. Flores routinely billed Medicaid for bogus "care" provided by untrained, unqualified employees, many of whom were illegal immigrants.[25]

In 1996, Jack and Margie Mills, owners of ABC Home Health Services—one of the giants of the industry, operating in 22 states—were convicted and imprisoned for bilking Medicare out of more than $14 million. The couple had lived a lavish lifestyle, replete with private jets, luxurious mansions, magnificent jewelry, exclusive country club membership, and world travel. The problem was that all of this opulence (and more) was paid for by taxpayers. The couple were adding extravagant personal expenses to the nearly $50 million per month that ABC was billing the government. Included in the fraudulent claims was their son's BMW. Prosecutors would later say that Jack Mills had used Medicare as his own private trust fund.[26]

There is also concern over the burgeoning "home infusion services" market, in which companies provide for intravenous drugs and nutrients in the patient's residence. A 1991 New York study showed that home infusion companies sold drugs for between 157% and 1066% more than did retail pharmacies.[27] One New York company charged $9.84 for sterile water that costs $2 at a pharmacy.[28] In Washington, DC, home infusion charges double annually, owing in large part to drug markups as high as 2000%.[29] A young Massachusetts cancer patient arranged to have his final round of chemotherapy administered at home by a private provider, so he would not miss his first day of college. His family received a bill for $6450—more than 10 times what a major Boston hospital had charged for each previous infusion.[30]

AIDS treatments account for one-quarter or more of total revenues at some infusion firms.[31] The New York City Department of Consumer Affairs has charged that price gouging is particularly blatant for people with AIDS. For example, a nutritional supplement used by AIDS patients, which wholesales for about $1300 per month, was billed as high as $10,000.[32] In Seattle, one AIDS patient's bill for 45 days of in-home intravenous medication to prevent blindness and infection came to $47,000.[33]

One scam in California, perpetrated against that state's Medicaid program (Medi-Cal), bilked the government out of $9.1 million. A 3-year investigation led to charges against American Home Healthcare Products, an Oakland-based company, as a result of false claims submitted to Medi-Cal between 1987 and 1988. The company had enticed patients to swap their five monthly Medi-Cal stickers, which are used for obtaining services, in exchange for "free" incontinence supplies. The company would later overcharge Medi-Cal for supplies delivered or make up fictitious orders. The firm also double-billed nursing homes for supplies, which Medi-Cal then paid for.[34]

HOSPITAL FRAUDS

Hospital costs constitute the largest portion of the nation's healthcare expenditures. Anyone who has been hospitalized knows of the unbelievable costs of such familiar items as over-the-counter pain relievers or ordinary bandages. The usual answer given by administrators when they are questioned about what appears to be conspicuous price gouging can be summed up in one word: overhead. Indeed, when hospital accounting departments must determine the amounts charged for services and items, they take into account the costs of the building, staff, equipment, insurance, and even the unpaid bills of former patients. Thus, what seems like highway robbery to patients and their families may sometimes be defensible hospital billings.

On the other hand, things that certain hospitals do inarguably constitute mendacious, or even outright criminal, behavior. Hospitals have been known to bill patients for "ghost services"—that is, nonexistent services. And if tests are done incorrectly, the patient can end up footing the bill for the hospital's mistakes. Multiple billings may also occur, where patients are charged more than once for the same service, sometimes from different departments. Hospitals have also been known to "upcode," a practice in which facts of the actual treatment are intentionally altered so that insurance companies will pay the maximum amount for the procedure performed. Other billing tricks known as "fragmentation" or "unbundling" occur as well, whereby a number of charges can be made from what is usually a single less expensive charge for services or procedures.

"Cost shifting" is a technique which hospitals use to attract patients by offering reasonable room rates but then charging sky-high prices for ancillary items. Congressional hearings on the pricing policies of 77 Humana hospitals nationwide revealed that the chain routinely charged $9 for Tylenol tablets, $455 for nursing bras, $104 for $8-sets of crutches, $45 for saline solution (which costs the hospital 81 cents), and $1206 for esophagus tubes that wholesale for $152.[35]

As rapacious as these practices are, hospitals have also been known to engage in even more organized and avaricious schemes which add greatly to the nation's healthcare costs. For example, federal investigations have revealed that hospitals may routinely demand kickbacks from doctors, a practice under which physicians are required to make payments to the hospitals for patient referrals. Moreover, it was found that physicians who refuse to make such payments may lose the right to practice at the hospital altogether. The illegal payments are disguised in hospital records as reimbursements by the doctors for billing, marketing, or other fabricated services.[36] In one case, "radiologists had to pay half of their gross receipts to a hospital's endowment fund."[37] In another, doctors were forced to pay 25% of their profits exceeding a set amount as a condition of operating the radiology department.[38] Because such practices obviously drive up government costs, they are illegal under the regulations of Medicare and Medicaid—programs which account for almost 40% of hospital spending nationwide.[39] They are also proscribed by both civil and criminal laws. Kickbacks can increase the utilization of services, unnecessary tests and procedures, higher prices, and may lead to unethical and criminal behaviors by doctors in an effort to make back what they have lost through institutionalized extortion.

In one of the largest healthcare fraud settlements ever, National Medical Enterprises, Inc. (NME), a Santa Monica, California-based corporation which manages more than 60 substance abuse and psychiatric hospitals nationwide, paid $379 million in criminal fines, civil damages, and penalties. Previously, the company had settled numerous lawsuits, including one involving six insurers for $125 million.[40] NME had been accused of a host of illegal marketing and billing practices, including instructing hospital administrators to adopt "intake goals" designed to bring patients into the hospitals for lengthy stays and unnecessary treatments.[41] NME also settled other claims including "billing insurance programs multiple times for the same service, billing insurance programs when no service was actually provided, and billing Medicare for payments made to doctors and others that were solely intended to induce referrals of patients to the facilities."[42] According to one lawsuit, a patient entered an NME facility for a 2-week evaluation and was not allowed to leave for 11 months.[43]

A closer look at psychiatric hospital frauds will show how such scams are perpetrated.

CASE   STUDY

Psychiatric Hospitals

For many decades, American psychiatric hospitals were predominantly public institutions where mentally ill citizens were warehoused and forgotten. In the 1950s and 1960s, many patients were rendered docile through lobotomies and crude psychosurgery in which an instrument known as an "icepickalon" was inserted into the brain through an eye socket and used to dig out prefrontal tissue. "[A] good deal of the patient's personality often ended up in the operating room wastebasket."[44] Even today, some state mental hospitals are still described as "filthy, backward institutions where patients are frequently tied down, locked up, and sometimes left lying in their own excrement."[45] When inpatient insurance coverage for mental health and substance abuse problems grew in the 1970s, however, *private* for-profit psychiatric hospitals became "cash cows."

(Continued)

In the 1980s, as insurance companies were hit by exceedingly high costs in this area of coverage and began scrutinizing payments, lengths of hospital stays were shortened. Consequently, many psychiatric hospitals became increasingly desperate for patients. The need to fill beds has resulted in a veritable catalogue of fraudulent and abusive practices designed to maximize revenue: patients abducted by "bounty hunters;" patients hospitalized against their will until their insurance ran out; false diagnoses; over billing; unnecessary treatments; and kickbacks paid for the recruitment of patients.[46]

One profoundly disturbing case occurred in Texas in 1991, where 14-year-old Jeremy H. was taken from his home by two uniformed men after his younger brother lied about Jeremy's purported drug use. Jeremy was brought to Colonial Hills Hospital, a psychiatric institution in San Antonio owned by the Psychiatric Institutes of America (PIA). His family had thought the two abductors were law enforcement officers; his grandmother later told a Texas State Senate committee investigating healthcare fraud that they had acted like the "Gestapo."[47] Jeremy was detained for 6 days with no contact with his family and was released only after a state senator intervened on his behalf. It was later discovered that the "officers" who took him away were security guards employed by a private firm hired by Colonial Hills for the delivery of patients. It was also revealed that the "doctor" who had admitted Jeremy was using false credentials.

The attorney representing Jeremy's family claimed that the boy had been dragged away because he was covered for a wide range of mental health benefits under CHAMPUS (Civilian Health and Medical Program for the Uniformed Services), the federal health plan for the families of military personnel. After 6 days of "treatment," Jeremy's family received a bill for $11,000, which CHAMPUS paid. However, CHAMPUS asked the Department of Defense to investigate the case. Jeremy's abduction also spurred state legislative hearings which produced allegations of fraud and abuse at 12 other PIA facilities in Texas and a number of other national hospital chains operating in that state.[48]

Texas appears to have become a breeding ground for all sorts of shamelessly aggressive recruitment practices because of the dramatic proliferation of psychiatric hospitals there since the mid-1980s and the resulting intensity of cutthroat competition for insurance dollars. Texas may also be particularly susceptible to aggressive fraud because, according to the Texas Commission on Alcohol and Drug Abuse, about one-fifth of its adult population experiences at least one alcohol-related problem during any given year.[49] The state is saturated by formidable marketing campaigns, "with hotlines and slick billboards, television, magazine, newspaper and radio advertisements promoting the benefits of treatment for depression or alcohol and drug abuse."[50] Patient referral firms, known as "headhunters," even infiltrate local Alcoholics Anonymous groups in order to deliver prospective patients to contracted hospitals. One such firm had a quota to deliver 60 patients each month to a Fort Worth hospital.[51]

(Continued)

Houston-area school counselors have reportedly been offered reward money to refer troubled students to psychiatric treatment centers. "Public service" counselors, telephone hotlines and other "help groups" have allegedly been established by private hospitals to learn covertly about prospective patients' insurance rather than their medical needs. Those who are insured are then duped into hospital programs.[52]

Some former hospital admissions officers have contended that they were fired on the basis of their "conversion rates," the ratio of telephone inquiries converted to hospital admissions. In the words of one discharged employee, "There was tremendous pressure to get people into the hospital. I felt like a used-car salesman."[53]

Other deplorable practices include "[i]nsurance 'cash-ectomies' in which corporate psychiatric hospitals overcharge for doctor visits that last two to three minutes if they occur at all."[54] One Texas hospital reportedly charged $150 per day for the use of an ordinary television as a therapeutic device. Another scam utilizes "golden handcuff" contracts between hospitals and psychiatrists. This practice, under which psychiatrists may earn "salaries" of up to $300,000 for recruitment, has been described as the "outright buying and selling of patients."[55]

Perhaps the most despicable fraud of all involves the looting of the Texas Crime Victim's Compensation Fund, which provides for counseling and mental health treatment for crime victims and their families. According to an investigative report in the *Houston Chronicle,* hospitals may have falsified diagnoses in order to qualify for coverage under this fund. In 1991, Texas withheld payment on $3.1 million of claims to the 12 PIA (Psychiatric Institutes of America) facilities in the state. Over just a $2\frac{1}{2}$ month period, PIA had billed that amount for the questionable treatment of crime victims.[56]

Fraud charges have been brought against hospitals in many other states as well, including New Jersey, Florida, Alabama, and Louisiana. One California hospital created an employee incentive contest in which "staffers could win prizes—from a color television to a Caribbean cruise—for bringing in new patients."[57] Like Texas, California has been swamped by sleazy recruitment schemes generated by private psychiatric hospitals. A veteran administrator for one such facility has been quoted anonymously:

> I never had anybody from the corporate office ask me about the needs of a patient. All they want to know is the [hospital] census and the profits. . . . It's a whore's market.[58]

In 1992, federal investigations were launched in more than a dozen states. Not all the resulting allegations concerned illegal patient recruitment schemes. Patients who *voluntarily* sought help have claimed that they were virtually "imprisoned" in psychiatric hospitals. One such case involved a woman whose doctor referred her to a hospital in Texas after she had suffered a psychotic reaction to a pain medication. This patient thought she would be there for a day or two. Instead, her stay lasted 3 months, during which time the hospital tried to change her status from "psychiatric" to "medical," which would have increased her

(Continued)

insurance coverage from \$50,000 to \$1 million. She was also heavily sedated and kept isolated from family and visitors. Her doctor warned her that she would be kept "in a mental hospital the rest of her life"[59] if she fought for release. After her insurance was exhausted, she was finally sent home with a bill for over \$48,000.[60]

A few indignant doctors have recently come forward, relating astonishing stories of greed, ethical violations, and corruption at psychiatric hospitals. In response, hospitals have claimed that generalizing from isolated patient complaints "is extremely dangerous to people who need care."[61] Although diagnoses may change during a patient's stay, hospital officials argue that this does not mean that patients are detained for insurance purposes. But even if isolated cases may not prove that wrongdoing and fraud are the norm, they certainly offer compelling evidence that some psychiatric hospitals do take advantage of patients through predatory recruitment, kickback schemes, and false diagnoses. How many hidden cases exist remains a matter of speculation, however, because of a shrinking investigative capacity.

Insurance companies themselves have also been blamed for the skyrocketing growth of private psychiatric hospitals by offering more generous benefits for inpatient care than outpatient care.[62] A spokesperson for the American Psychological Association has described this bias toward institutionalization as "a perverse incentive where people wind up in the hospital because they can't afford outpatient care."[63]

Although the policies of some private psychiatric hospitals can be justly termed "reprehensible," it is difficult to find an adjective sufficient to describe patient abuses at certain *public* mental hospitals. For example, a federal judge has ruled that the state of Tennessee had violated the constitutional rights of developmentally disabled residents of the Arlington Developmental Center (ADC), a state-operated institution. Among other things, the judge ruled, "[P]sychiatric and psychological services were virtually nonexistent. Medical care was below any minimum standard and well below the medical malpractice standard."[64] The Justice Department estimated that at least 25 patients at ADC had died of aspiration pneumonia, an infection caused by food entering the lungs when patients are fed while lying down instead of sitting up.[65] It was further revealed that the causes of these preventable deaths had been officially recorded as heart failure or respiratory arrest. A Justice Department witness characterized this policy as a shabby subterfuge: "Everybody who dies has stopped breathing or their heart has stopped. . . . What we have here are quiet little murders."[66]

America's most malignant public repository for the developmentally disabled was Forest Haven in Washington, DC. During just a 2-year period, at least 10 Forest Haven residents died of aspiration pneumonia. The exact death toll can never be known, but the problem was believed to date back at least 20 years.[67] The total number of victims of Forest Haven's routine negligence could easily exceed 100. A former assistant attorney general for civil rights has declared that Forest Haven constituted "the deadliest known example of institutional abuse in recent American history."[68] In 1994, Forest Haven, battered by litigation, was closed forever.

SELF-REFERRALS

A major reason for the ballooning cost of medical care in the United States rests in the practice of self-referral, through which a physician sends patients for ancillary services to a company in which he or she has a financial interest. Such a custom may not be illegal, per se, but can create abundant opportunities for ethical violations in the name of extra profits. Doctors who invest in laboratories, pharmacies, surgical centers, and physical therapy facilities can earn enormous sums of money through needless referrals of patients. "As early as 1989, a government study revealed that physicians who owned diagnostic labs ordered up to 45 percent more tests than those who did not."[69] The U.S. Department of Health and Human Services estimates that one-quarter of the labs in this country are owned by doctors who refer their patients there.[70] There is also a serious matter of price-gouging. One study conducted in Florida reported that doctor-owned labs charge on the average 40% more than other labs in the state.[71]

In California, where legislation has been introduced to ban self-referrals, Congressman Pete Stark has commented:

> "Physician ownership/referral arrangements represent an exploding virus which ultimately will erode the trust patients have traditionally placed in their physicians. The sad thing is that we are quickly getting to the point where each of us is going to have to wonder if we are getting referred for a health service because we need it or because it would fatten our physician's dividend check."[72]

Self-referrals pose a transparent conflict of interest for physicians. The practice can easily open the door to fraud through the intentional provision of unnecessary but profitable services. Arnold Relman, a former editor of the distinguished *New England Journal of Medicine* has observed, "Basically, we're talking about a kickback or a bribe that has so far avoided existing regulations."[73] Relman estimates, based on a survey of doctors by the American Medical Association (AMA), that between 50,000 and 75,000 physicians have a financial interest in ancillary medical services.[74] The AMA opposes legislation to ban doctors from investing in such services, claiming (as always) that doctors know best and that self-referrals help ensure better treatment. On the other hand, it seems virtually impossible to imagine that self-referrals could be divorced entirely from the profit motive. Patients have every right to expect that their doctors will direct them to high-quality and fairly-priced services for purely medical reasons and not entrepreneurial ones.

MEDICARE FRAUD

As we have already noted, the federal Medicare program is rife with fraud and abuse. For example, Medicare spends more than $6 billion annually—roughly $30,000 per patient—on kidney dialysis treatment. This sum represents 80% of the total dialysis billing in the United States.[75] A 1995 investigative report by the *New York Times* alleges that National Medical Care, the largest chain of kidney centers in the country, cuts costs and raises profits by using obsolete and potentially dangerous dialysis machines.[76] Moreover, this callous policy is emulated by competing private kidney treatment facilities. Consequently, American dialysis patients are more than twice as likely to die in a given year as patients in Western Europe or Japan.[77]

The U.S. General Accounting Office estimates that at least 10% of total expenditures, or about $17 billion per year, is lost to fraudulent Medicare practices.[78] The list of scams that have been uncovered seems almost endless, including one in which a Beverly Hills physician had allegedly billed Medicare for over $1 million for house calls to patients who were dead.[79] In California, for example, a nursing home operator bilked Medicare out of almost $4 million and probably would have gotten away with it had he not sloppily misaddressed forged invoices from fictitious firms in "New Hamshire,"[sic] or "Lubbock, Mississippi" [Texas].[80] In Florida, senior citizens were solicited door-to-door for their Medicare numbers, supposedly to be used in a "free milk program." Instead, their ID numbers were utilized by crooks to defraud Medicare of $14 million.[81] An immigrant physician from the Dominican Republic who had ambassador status in his homeland was indicted with four other physicians for defrauding Medicare out of $25 million through false billings for nonexistent wheelchairs, hospital beds, and prescriptions over a 5-year period.[82] Dr. Rafael Gonzalez Pantaleon was convicted by a federal jury in New York on 45 counts of fraud and sentenced to more than 6 years in prison. He jumped bail and fled to his home country where he lives free while defying U.S. efforts to extradite him.[83] In an effort to drum up business at the government's expense, a home healthcare service operating in 22 states (mentioned earlier) billed Medicare for $85,000 for "gourmet popcorn," which was sent to doctors as an inducement for them to use the company's services.[84]

Medicare fraud and abuse is not limited to small or illegitimate enterprises; prominent institutions and corporations have been implicated as well. In 1995, the University of Pennsylvania agreed to pay $30 million to settle allegations that it had submitted an estimated $10 million dollars in false Medicare claims over a 6-year period. This was the largest Medicare settlement ever paid by a single healthcare provider.[85] In another major case involving two of the nation's largest clinical laboratories, the government received $39.8 million to settle fraud charges involving the submission of unnecessary laboratory tests.[86] The firms, Metwest (a subsidiary of Unilab) and Metpath (a unit of Corning, Inc.) were accused of including a cholesterol test in their basic blood analysis screening, but were billing the government separately for it without the knowledge of the physicians who ordered the test. In statements issued by the two companies, they were careful to note that the settlement "does not constitute an admission by [either company] with respect to any issue of law."[87]

The alleged violations in the Metwest/Metpath case were similar to those in a previous settlement involving National Health Laboratories, Inc., which paid the government $111.4 million—at that time the largest healthcare provider settlement in history. After a 2-year investigation initiated by a whistleblower,[88] the company pleaded guilty to two charges of submitting false claims. President and CEO Robert E. Draper forfeited $500,000 and spent 3 months in prison.[89] Investigators found that the company had charged the government $18 apiece for three tests which were supposed to be part of a single basic blood series test. Private insurers in contrast, were charged only about 65 cents for the same tests.[90]

Project Jump Start, initiated in 1993, was one of the most ambitious Medicare investigations and scrutinized 132 hospitals. The findings revealed that some of the hospitals routinely submitted phony claims to obtain Medicare payments for unapproved procedures.[91]

> [M]any of the hospitals changed billing codes for noncovered experimental devices to fool Medicare examiners into thinking they were paying for approved procedures. Atherectomies—performed to drill out plaque in clogged arteries—were commonly billed as angioplasties.[92]

A Sacramento hospital obtained Medicare reimbursement for experimental defibrillators and pacemakers by deleting the word "experimental" from forms.[93] One whistleblower has even charged that doctors actually hold seminars on how to dupe Medicare.[94]

In 2000, in the largest criminal and civil settlements ever in a Medicare fraud case, the former Columbia/HCA Healthcare Corp. agreed to pay the government $840.3 million dollars. HCA will pay $745 million to settle civil charges and an additional $95.3 million in criminal penalties. The case came to light by whistleblowers who reported that the company systematically overcharged Medicare and other government programs for years by "upcoding," where false patient diagnoses are reported in order to increase reimbursement.[95] In the criminal case, it was charged that HCA conspired to defraud the government by making false statements, paying kickbacks to doctors, and submitting false bills.[96] The Nashville-based hospital chain is the largest in the country, operating 200 facilities in 22 states. In explaining why the criminal plea bargain did not involve prison sentences for company officials, Attorney General Janet Reno stated that financial penalties were deemed to have a greater impact and were "the most effective way" to deter corporate fraud.[97] As of this writing, 50 FBI agents are continuing the investigation of HCA which may turn up additional charges and monetary penalties.[98] According to officials, the final settlement during the George W. Bush administration could be as high as $1 billion.[99]

Individual physicians can cheat the Medicare system by billing patients excessively. Three common means are overcharges, retainers, and waivers.

Overcharges

Some doctors make patients sign "contracts" for services such as surgery. These can be at rates much higher than Medicare's covered amounts, requiring patients to pay much more than required by law. In New York, for instance, a doctor can charge no more than 15% above Medicare's approved rate. Yet in one example, a 70-year-old retired truck driver illegally paid over $1100 more than required by law for hand surgery costing a total of $2601.[100] It is estimated that in 1993 alone almost 1.5 million Medicare beneficiaries were illegally over-charged, with costs totaling about $101 million.[101]

Retainers

Some doctors cheat the system by requiring new patients to pay up-front "retainers" for a package of services purportedly not covered by Medicare in order to receive comprehensive treatment. Such packages are illegal if they are knowingly sold to patients who already have such coverage in their Medicare-supplement policies.

Waivers

Doctors may ask patients to waive their right to have the physician bill Medicare directly, leaving the patient to pay for such services as telephone calls, medical conferences, and prescription refills—services which Medicare considers part of the fees it pays to doctors. Physicians can also use what is called a "global waiver," under which a number of vague services are listed that Medicare "may not" pay for. The patient is asked to pay these costs directly. The only type of waiver which is legal is one where a specific *uncovered* procedure is listed, such as cosmetic surgery.[102]

Many generic medical and health crimes can be perpetrated against Medicare, such as fraudulent equipment sales, billing for services never rendered, and providing unnecessary services. Enforcement in the Medicare program is problematic, just as it is for Medicaid and private insurers. One of the ways that fraud could be ferreted out of the system is through the vigilance of patients who report phony billings. Complaints are handled by "carriers," i.e., firms (usually insurance companies) which are paid to process Medicare claims and investigate billings that are suspicious or out of line. As budgets shrink, however, carriers are strained merely to provide the basic service of processing and paying legitimate claims, without scrutinizing potentially phony ones. Because of this, the General Accounting Office has found that even when carriers are *called by patients* with information relating to possible fraud and wrongdoing, few follow-ups will occur because there is little or no incentive for the companies to do so.[103] Examples of ignored abuses include the incredible case of an elderly man who complained that he was charged for a pregnancy test.[104]

A government investigator captured the frustration of elderly whistle-blowers when he commented, "We went looking for a paper trail and couldn't find one."[105] If carriers do not follow up on obvious and provable scams that are virtually handed to them by patients, it is difficult to believe that they can effectively police the Medicare system. This ends up costing taxpayers tens of billions of dollars per year—money that could be used to improve healthcare for the elderly or help reduce the federal deficit. FBI Director Louis J. Freeh before a Senate committee summed up the failure of government efforts to deal with fraud in public healthcare spending over the past three decades: "The problem is so big and so diverse that we are making only a small dent in addressing the fraud."[106] Given the immense costs of such crimes, Freeh's assessment underscores the importance of reform in the healthcare arena. But dismantling Medicare—a piece at a time—is not the same as reforming it. Members of Congress (who enjoy perhaps the best group health insurance plan in the world) seem to find it all too easy to cut others' healthcare benefits to save money.

As more control over government healthcare passes to the states, reflecting the renascent federalism of the 1990s, it is doubtful if fraud control will be funded in the future even at the already inadequate levels decried by Freeh. Under pressure to reduce costs, Medicare is likely to evolve into a new system of managed care, utilizing the HMO (health maintenance organization) model to regulate medical decisions.[107] HMOs, with their flat-fee structure, may very well reduce the incentive for overtreatment, but a whole new laundry list of potential offenses may fill that void, such as negligent undertreatment to reduce overhead and drive up profits.[108] Indeed, Medicare fraud has already found a home in the emerging HMO system. International Medical Centers (IMC), the largest Medicare HMO in the country at the time, declared bankruptcy in 1986 *after* receiving $360 million from the government. The company's failure was attributed to exorbitant salaries and illegal practices. After he was indicted by a federal grand jury, the founder of IMC fled the country to avoid prosecution.[109]

One investigation of Medicare practices found that 89% of the nation's hospitals regularly double-bill for services. Officials note that this does not necessarily represent criminal fraud, but rather "gaming of the system," whereby respected institutions inflate their profits at taxpayer expense. In 1997, the cost of such practices was estimated at $23 billion annually. Noted medical ethicist Arthur Caplan explains that, "Pushing the envelope to maximize reimbursement and financial gain is a much bigger problem than outright scams, hoaxes and gimmicks. . . . Medical ethics are slowly being undercut by business ethics, and in business, pushing the limit of profits is not considered a sin; it's considered a virtue."[110] The transformation that Caplan identifies suggests that without dramatic changes to the nation's healthcare system, even more government vigilance of medical providers will be necessary in the future.

MEDICAID FRAUD

As with Medicare, Medicaid violations constitute a threat to the health of Americans and to the financial resources of the nation. The program has been hammered by fraud almost since its inception. The first major scandal surfaced in 1973, when *New York Daily News* reporter William Sherman wrote a twelve-part Pulitzer Prize-winning series documenting his personal experiences posing as a patient in New York City's Medicaid clinics, known pejoratively as "Medicaid mills." A few years later, Senator Frank Moss of Utah followed suit, presenting himself as an indigent patient at several New York City clinics complaining that he had a cold. His visits led to blood and urine tests, follow-up appointments, and prescriptions to be filled at pharmacies adjacent to the clinics.[111] Moss's Congressional subcommittee concluded that Medicaid was "not only inefficient, but riddled with fraud and abuse."[112] The committee recommended that the federal government allocate funds for enforcement.

In response, Congress enacted the Medicare and Medicaid Anti-Fraud and Abuse Amendments of 1977. Among its provisions, the Amendments upgraded violations from misdemeanors to felonies and required more disclosure as to ownership of healthcare facilities.[113] Congress also passed legislation enabling states to establish Medicaid Fraud Control Units (MFCU).[114] Despite these and other attempts to crack down, however, Medicaid fraud has continued to flourish and, if anything, has grown more sophisticated. Typically, fraudulent practices involve billing for services never rendered or intentional overutilization of unnecessary services. The fee-for-service structure of Medicaid, wherein providers are paid according to the bills they submit, leaves the program open to looting. Indeed, some providers seem to treat Medicaid as a virtual license to print money. An inspector general for the Department of Health and Human Services has concluded, "A welfare queen would have to work mighty hard to steal $100,000. Somebody in the practitioner or provider community can burp and steal $100,000."[115]

It has been argued that abuses in Medicaid are even more extensive than in Medicare because of the negative feelings of some health professionals toward welfare patients, whose behavior and personal habits (and perhaps their poverty itself) are a source of contempt.[116] Indicative of this disdain is the feeble excuse offered by a dentist, whose license was suspended in 1995 because of complaints that he had physically abused patients. He was one of the largest individual Medicaid providers of any type in Texas, collecting over $600,000 from the program in 1994 alone. At his hearing before the Texas Board of Health, his defense was that he never turns away Medicaid patients, even though many of them are "dirty" and "smell bad."[117]

As a social problem, Medicaid fraud has never garnered enough official attention to be rectified. Recently, a California psychiatrist was allowed to remain in a $102,000 per year administrative position at a Los Angeles county mental health center for months after being convicted of defrauding the state Medi-Cal system of more than $150,000.[118] This figure was the product of a plea bargain; the actual amount of the fraud is believed to be $1.3 million. Typical of the many charges against the doctor was his submission of 37 claims for a patient he saw only once.[119] Official laxity was further illustrated when a New York City journalist used two "rented" Medicaid cards to obtain thousands of dollars of unnecessary medical exams, tests, and prescriptions in a short period of time. In "playing the doctors" (a term widely used by junkies and hustlers throughout the city), the reporter visited over 15 clinics and saw more than two dozen physicians, therapists, and lab technicians. While he was piling up prescriptions and bills, the reporter also observed dozens of others who were doing the same thing, most likely to resell the drugs on the black market. In New York State alone, it is estimated that "playing the doctors" costs taxpayers up to $150 million annually.[120]

Uncovered Medicaid violations merely scratch the surface of the true extent of the problem. One investigator acknowledges that the only crooks who are caught are the reckless or stupid ones, "the fish who jump into the boat."[121] Some of the blatant offenses reflect such gross arrogance that they cross the border into absurdity. Investigations have documented cases in which daily psychotherapy sessions have totaled more than 24 hours, x-rays have been taken without using film, and bills have been submitted for circumcisions done on female infants and hysterectomies performed on male patients.[122]

There is nothing farcical, however, about a truly monstrous example of Medicaid fraud, described as "shocking" by the presiding judge. This case concerned a Los Angeles ophthalmologist, Dr. Jose Manaya, who was convicted in 1984 on charges related to unnecessary eye surgeries. Unnecessary surgery, intentionally performed, is legally equivalent to assault; it can involve not only theft, but maiming and death as well.[123] Dr. Manaya had subjected poor, mostly Hispanic patients to needless cataract surgery in order to collect Medi-Cal fees of $584 per eye. Manaya went through myopic Medi-Cal patients like Sherman through Georgia; he collected about $1 million over 5 years. In one instance, a 57-year-old woman was totally blinded after he operated on her one sighted eye. Investigators discovered that when Manaya's patients had private medical insurance or were well off financially, the operations were done with skill and success. If the patients were on Medicaid, however, the surgery was performed in a quick and careless manner.[124]

Remarkably, Dr. Manaya received fervent support from many members of the medical community, who urged leniency. The response of the judge, who handed down a 4-year sentence, made his feelings clear: "It's astounding how they could write these letters. They seem to think the whole trial was a contrivance by the attorney general's office."[125] What had particularly upset him was how the letter writers, in their zeal to portray Manaya as a "victim," virtually ignored the criminally abused patients. The judge noted, "In not one of these letters has there been one word of sympathy for the true victims in this case, the uneducated, Spanish-speaking people, some of whom will never see a sunrise or a sunset again."[126]

It would be a mistake to conclude from the Manaya case that the most virulent forms of Medicaid fraud and abuse are limited to physicians only. Investigators have recently begun scrutinizing the practices of pediatric dentists who participate in Medicaid. Many of these specialists are believed to opt routinely for expensive and potentially dangerous procedures, including stainless steel crowns, hospitalization, and general anesthesia, in lieu of more conservative alternatives such as in-office fillings and local anesthesia.[127] Regulators who have sought out second opinions have found that very young patients from low-income families often require little or no work, despite the expensive treatments proposed by their Medicaid providers. One expert has concluded,

"Some of these things that are being done are just money down the drain, because these kids are going to be losing their [baby] teeth shortly."[128] As with the Manaya case, however, there is more at risk than money when greed turns reckless. The overuse of anesthesia by pediatric dentists trying to perform as much work as possible at one sitting "endangers children and could be considered child abuse."[129] In 1991, a 3-year-old Medicaid patient in Texas died of respiratory arrest "after her dentist gave her a 'cocktail' of three sedatives and injected her gums with a local anesthetic."[130] The dentist received a 30-day suspension, which is still under appeal at this writing, nearly 5 years later. In a 1994 Texas case, a *13-month-old* Medicaid patient died while under general anesthesia in a hospital where she had been put by her dentist, who planned to put crowns on four of her eight teeth.[131]

Although outrageous Medicaid violations may make headlines, a public outcry demanding a change in enforcement policies has thus far not materialized. One reason for this may be that the victims—low-income persons—do not command much respect or sympathy from an increasingly antipoor public. Another problem is that the issue of fraud is often seen as peripheral to the major tasks of containing overall costs and improving our healthcare delivery system. "In this context, overutilization of services, the core of fraud and abuse, can be seen as no more than a distraction from the major concern: The underavailability of healthcare in the United States."[132]

CASE STUDY

Medicaid Murder?

One of the nation's most bizarre Medicaid fraud cases involved Dr. Olga Romani, who arrived in the United States from Cuba in 1960. Claiming to have graduated from the University of Havana medical school (where official transcripts are unobtainable in the United States), she began practicing in Miami in 1967 while she completed her state licensing requirements. In 1974, she pleaded guilty to charges related to the unlawful practice of medicine, and received a sentence of 5 years probation.[133] The case was prosecuted after two women whom she had treated for acne complained that they were left disfigured as a result.[134] Between 1976 and 1981, Romani became the second largest Medicaid provider in Florida and operated two clinics. By 1980, she had received $184,000 in reimbursement for medical services from the state.[135] In March 1981 she was arrested on racketeering charges alleging that she had stolen more than $97,000 from Medicaid by billing for services never performed.[136] For example, Romani had billed Medicaid after purportedly treating one of her patients for diaper rash. During the trial, the patient was asked by the prosecutor whether he was in fact receiving such treatment. The jurors and spectators chuckled as Eddie James King, a 19-year-old, 220-pound Florida A&M football player, answered "No." After King had visited her twice for

(Continued)

a "cold," Romani billed Medicaid for 51 visits, claiming payments of $1885.[137] Another witness, whose Medicaid recipient number was used by the defendant to bill the state for 165 visits, testified that she had never even met Romani. After a parade of other witnesses offered similar testimony, the jury took only 1 hour to convict Romani on 24 counts of filing false claims and 24 counts of receiving payments to which she was not entitled.[138] One attorney estimated that the money stolen by Romani could have been used to treat more than 10,000 needy patients.[139] Olga Romani received a 20-year sentence in prison for Medicaid fraud, showing little emotion as the judge passed sentence.

If the Romani case had ended there, it would be a modestly interesting example of occupational crime. But there was much more to come. Soon after her sentencing, Romani became the central suspect in the murder of her partner, Dr. Gerardo DeMola, who was shot to death in his car at a hospital parking lot a few weeks before Romani's indictment on the fraud charges in 1981.[140] Romani was believed to have paid $10,000 for a contract killing because she feared that her former associate might testify against her in the fraud case.[141] Later, after she was indicted on murder charges, prosecutors produced a "hit list" which included Demola's name as well as others involved with the investigation. Romani attempted to explain away the list by claiming that it was to be delivered to a Santerian priest who had asked for the names of persons with whom she might be involved in future legal disputes.[142] Santeria, an arcane mixture Christianity and voodoo, is a Caribbean religion, which stresses the casting of spells and curses. She did not believe in Santeria, Romani contended, but wrote out the list of her "enemies" on the advice of her accountant, who said it might ease her mind.[143]

During her murder trial Romani was evasive, only marginally coherent, and did not make a credible witness. Convicted in 1983, she was sentenced to life imprisonment, with a 25-year mandatory sentence on the murder charge and received another 30 years for conspiracy.[144] The murder conviction was later overturned on procedural grounds, but Romani continues to serve time on her fraud and conspiracy convictions.

PSYCHIATRISTS—"LAST AMONG EQUALS?"

Although there are numerous examples of Medicaid fraud which have been documented in the popular media and the criminological literature,[145] psychiatrists stand out as the most frequently accused and sanctioned group among medical specialties.[146] Psychiatrists represent about 8% of all physicians but about 20% of all doctors suspended from Medicaid for fraudulent practices.[147] Some enforcement officials feel that such a finding validates their view that psychiatrists are more prone to violating the laws regulating Medicaid. This conforms to the generally low popular esteem in which psychiatrists are held relative to other medical specialists.[148]

The explanation for the overrepresentation of psychiatrists in Medicaid fraud cases, however, may be more oblique than the attribution of a greater propensity to cheat the program. Almost all doctors bill Medicaid (or any other insurance program, for that matter) for specific services rendered, such as examinations, tests, x-rays, surgeries, and the like. The issue of fraud usually centers on whether these services were actually provided to patients. The practice of psychiatry provides an exception to this pattern, which is probably responsible for their higher rate of violations found in official statistics. Psychiatrists submit bills for *time*—that is, their payments are based on the time they spend with patients (typically 50-minute "hours") and not on complex procedures or medical interventions. This distinction makes apprehension much less complicated in the case of psychiatrists, because investigators can more readily determine (sometimes using nothing but a wristwatch) if the time periods that have been billed conform to those actually spent with patients. As especially easy enforcement targets, psychiatrists as a group may thus be labeled as more "criminal" than other doctors, even though they are no more or less prone to dishonesty.

Nonetheless, documented cases of occupational crimes by psychiatrists reveal an ugly side to their specialty. Most notably, the sexual abuse of emotionally vulnerable patients by sleazy psychotherapists is a recurring infraction of both legal and professional codes. Although white-collar crime usually connotes fraud, theft, or some other form of financial misappropriation, the extortion of sexual favors in exchange for medical services clearly meets Sutherland's definitional criteria: offenses committed by relatively respectable persons within their occupational roles.[149] The number of doctors disciplined for sexual misconduct reportedly doubled between 1990 and 1994.[150] Again, psychiatrists appear to be overrepresented. In a 1986 survey, 7% of male psychiatrists and 3% of female psychiatrists reported sexual contact with a patient. In addition, about two-thirds of the respondents said they had seen at least one patient who reported having sex with another therapist, of whom only 8% had reported the incident to authorities.[151]

FERTILITY FRAUD

One of the most obnoxious types of medical malfeasance is perpetrated against women and couples who are having problems trying to conceive. Given their oftentimes heightened emotional states and willingness to try almost anything, they are particularly vulnerable to fraud and other misdeeds. "Fertility fraud" has begun to surface as a new form of crime in the medical profession, as rapid advances in knowledge and technology—sometimes outpacing ethical and legal considerations—allow for a range of offenses which simply were not possible earlier.[152] At least two chilling cases have come to light in recent years.

The first case involved a Virginia-based fertility doctor, Cecil Jacobson. Renowned as a brilliant geneticist, Jacobson, who had helped develop the amniocentesis procedure in the United States, referred to himself as "the babymaker." He told patients desperate to conceive, "God doesn't give you babies. . . . I do."[153] With patients giving him their trust—and money—Jacobson deceived them in return by telling a number of women they were pregnant when in fact they were not, and by secretly inseminating others with his own sperm.

Jacobson fathered children for numerous couples who believed they were receiving other donor sperm. Some of these mothers-to-be became suspicious, however, after receiving a tip and ordered genetic tests which showed that the doctor himself had fathered their babies. Jacobson originally denied, then later admitted, these charges. His attorney argued that "if the doctor had used his own sperm" it was done in the interest of providing the patient with a "clean and good" sample for their own protection from AIDS.[154]

Jacobson had also administered hormone treatments to some patients, which simulated the effects of early pregnancy. Women testified before the Virginia Medical Board that he had even shown them sonograms of what he said was "their fetus," including such details as heartbeats, thumb-sucking, and various movements. He even gave them snapshots of the purported fetus to keep with them. A few weeks later he would tell them that their babies had died. The U.S. attorney who prosecuted the case declared, "It's basic fraud of the cruelest sort."[155]

On March 4, 1992, Dr. Jacobson was convicted on 52 felony counts of fraud and perjury related to his impregnating patients with his own sperm and lying to others that they had become pregnant. Prosecutors produced DNA evidence showing that Jacobson had fathered at least 15 children through patients who were tested and alleged that he could have fathered up to 75 more through patients who had not come forward for testing.

Because no fraud statutes existing then covered artificial insemination, the government was forced to rely on wire and mail fraud charges; Jacobson had used the postal service and the telephone to communicate with patients for billings and appointments. On the witness stand, the doctor admitted using his own sperm to impregnate patients, but could not recall exactly how many. His lawyer argued that it did not really matter because such an act is not illegal. Jacobson stated that he had never intended to mislead patients and that he had "dedicated his life to couples who were desperate to have children."[156] Jacobson actually seemed surprised by the reaction to his behavior. Whether he truly was or not may not be that important. More telling was the insensitivity to his patients he acknowledged at his trial, "I was totally unaware of the anger, anguish and hate I have caused—until these proceedings."[157]

Jacobson received a 5-year prison sentence in 1992. At his sentencing, a former patient had this to say about the doctor's conduct: "He took away the most important thing in the world from all of us. He told us we were going to have a baby, and then it was gone."[158]

While Dr. Jacobson was deceiving patients in Virginia, the second fertility scandal was developing at the University of California, Irvine (UCI). The school's Center for Reproductive Health has become the focus of very serious allegations of widespread wrongdoing. The director of the Center, one of the foremost fertility experts in the world and creator of a revolutionary fertility technique known as "GIFT" (gamete intrafallopian transfer) has been accused, along with his two partners, of numerous violations. All three doctors are currently under investigation by local, state and federal authorities and apparently have fled the country.

The scandal was first reported by staff members in 1994 and came to public attention a year later. The university has since closed the Center and filed suit against the doctors, claiming that they have violated university policies, prescribed an unapproved fertility drug, performed research on patients without their consent, and "stole" eggs or embryos from patients in order to impregnate others.[159] One couple learned from medical records that three of their embryos had been implanted in another patient. They later discovered that they were the biological parents of twins born to that patient.[160] The victimized couple has declared, "What happened to us was nothing less than theft by doctors who acted for their own profit and prestige."[161]

After the scandal erupted, UCI began an internal investigation which suggested "irregularities" at the Center. The university, however, has been accused by some observers of dragging its feet in an attempt to control the damage to its reputation. Other critics have been even more damning, accusing the university of turning a blind eye in order to keep the prestigious—and very profitable—Center alive.[162]

There are now hundreds of fertility centers around the country, and "clinics have found that touting their success rates is their best marketing tool."[163] False promises and exaggerated claims may well have motivated the fraudulent practices at UCI. The scandal has resulted in California Senate hearings, the resignation of the UCI Medical Center's director and accusations that the university punished at least one whistleblower by demoting her.[164]

If all the imputed ethical lapses at the Center for Reproductive Health were not enough, major financial wrongdoing has also been alleged. There is a great deal of money to be made in assisted reproduction. Most procedures reportedly average about $8000.[165] An audit concluded that the three UCI doctors had failed to report nearly $1 million in income at the expense of patients, insurance companies, and the university. Auditors further charged that the doctors had kept more than $167,000 in cash disbursements and had failed to disclose more than $800,000 under a contract which required them to share some of their fees with the university.[166] During one period of time, two of the doctors reportedly were given envelopes of cash to take home with them each day. The auditors concluded that "each month the physicians split the cash amongst themselves."[167]

Efforts by the university to investigate the case were stymied by the doctors' lack of cooperation in turning over patient records. More stonewalling was revealed in 1995, when a former patient complained that the director had attempted to persuade her to sign a retroactive consent form, granting permission to donate eggs he had already removed from her 2 years earlier. When UCI officials tried to obtain these records, the director denied their requests.

After formal charges were brought against the three doctors, there were public demonstrations by patients and medical students who rallied in support of the physicians, claiming that they were dedicated and skilled practitioners. One patient who bore a healthy child through the director's GIFT technique stated in an interview, "I believe he works for God."[168]

The University of California has settled over 100 lawsuits from former patients of the fertility clinic at Irvine at a cost of over $22 million, and more cases remain to be adjudicated.[169] In 2000, the university fired both Dr. Sergio Stone,[170] who was earlier convicted of insurance fraud in connection with his activities at the fertility clinic,[171] and Dr. Ricardo Asch, who was the director of the clinic and who fled to Mexico to avoid prosecution after the scandal erupted.[172] A third physician, Dr. Jose Balmaceda was dismissed from the university earlier, and fled to Chile to avoid the same federal charges as Asch.[173] Interviewed in Mexico, where he continues making babies, Asch denied any wrongdoing, and is suing the university for back pay and for ruining his reputation.[174]

Some bioethicists argue that competition to succeed in the growing area of fertility technology could cause doctors to cut moral corners. This is all the more likely because there is little regulation in the fertility field. One expert in medical ethics at the University of Pennsylvania maintains, "There is less regulation here than there would be in the animal-breeding industry."[175]

NURSING HOME ABUSES

With people living longer and families spread farther apart, more and more Americans are forced to rely on nursing homes and other residential institutions[176] for long-term care.[177] "Nursing homes now consume eight cents of every dollar spent on healthcare."[178] In 1996, there were 1.6 million elderly Americans living in nursing homes; the figure now exceeds 2 million.[179] The industry owes its spectacular growth to the federal government, which began dispensing Medicare and Medicaid funds in the 1960s on behalf of the elderly poor.[180] Since the nursing home industry is dominated by enterprises run for profit, and its personnel are among the lowest-paid health workers, quality of care may not be an overriding consideration in many facilities. Because patients are not fully able to care for themselves, let alone confront unprincipled owners or unresponsive staff, a good deal of mistreatment has been known to occur. The attorney general of New York has reported that one of four nursing home abuse cases in his jurisdiction involve caregivers with serious criminal records. Twenty-six states, including New York, have no laws requiring criminal background checks for nursing home workers. In one case, a nursing home aide was charged with beating and groping a 92-year-old patient, before it was known that he had previously been convicted of felony assault and for killing a pet guinea pig.[181]

Elderly residents are frequently preyed upon by greedy nursing home operators and related medical and health personnel. As an Alabama county official has warned, "There are vultures out there watching for vulnerable elderly."[182] In one case reported in Houston, for example, an elderly woman was so neglected that her death was not even discovered until rigor mortis had set in. Another woman at the same facility had to be hospitalized for rat bites.[183] In 2000, state regulators in Florida banned admissions to a nursing home where an 87-year-old woman died after being bitten more than 1600 times by ants. The patient was discovered with ants swarming over her body. The staff brushed the ants off and gave her a shower. She died the next afternoon.[184]

The nursing home industry provides an environment that too often is conducive to woeful abuses against the elderly. A 1997 survey of 3000 acutely ill patients reported that given the choice between a nursing home or the grave, nearly one-third said they would rather be dead.[185] A sad history of inhumane conditions and overcharging for services—if they are provided at all—has made nursing homes the target of numerous state and federal investigations. For example, a nursing home for veterans, run by the State University of New York at Stony Brook, came under investigation by state officials less than 5 months after it opened for reportedly abusing and neglecting patients, several of whom died under questionable circumstances.[186]

Other similar scandals include the following cases:

❖ In Florida, state officials removed six elderly people from a nursing home after they found one of them suffering from deformities caused by neglect and others strapped into urine-soaked chairs or in beds covered with feces.[187] In another Florida case, an 88-year-old man, suffering from Alzheimer's disease and cancer, was restrained in bed for so many hours and subsequently developed such severe bedsores that they "ate through his skin, muscles, and bones." There is no delicate way to put it: Over a 4-month period, the patient actually rotted to death.[188]

❖ In 1990, a federal judge upheld a jury's $250,000 damage award to the family of a nursing home resident in Mississippi who was physically abused and allowed to remain in her own excrement for extended periods of time.[189]

❖ An 81-year-old man with Alzheimer's disease was reluctantly placed in an Alabama nursing home by his family. Three months later, the patient broke his hip and became permanently bedridden when he slipped on his own urine. Aides began keeping him tied up and heavily sedated. He developed bedsores and bruises, including an unexplained black eye. He had entered the home at a robust 182 pounds. When he died 2 years later—his body curled into a fetal position—he weighed 94 pounds.[190]

Some of the worst nursing home horror stories have been reported in North Carolina, where more than 50,000 patients reside in long-term care facilities. Operators of these facilities regularly contribute substantial sums of money to the campaign coffers of state and local politicians and have profited in return by slack regulation and a ineffectual sanctioning system of paltry fines.[191] Conditions are not necessarily any worse in North Carolina than in other states, but local investigative journalists there have taken an acute interest in this topic, and so there seems to be greater documentation of pervasive negligence, as the following vignettes sorrowfully recount:

❖ In 1991, an elderly nursing home resident wandered out of the building unattended, fell into a drainage ditch and drowned. The state fined the home $250.[192]

❖ In 1992, social workers found a bedsore on a nursing home patient's foot that was so infected that gangrene had developed and it had become infested with maggots. It required amputation.[193]

❖ For a period of at least 16 days, an 89-year-old nursing home patient's hands, face, and vagina swelled abnormally. The staff failed to notify a physician as her condition deteriorated. One morning, a nurse found her with "frothy mucous" around her mouth and "puffy breathing," but did not even check her vital signs or assess her condition. The patient died 25 minutes later.[194]

❖ A 65-year-old retired mill worker, crippled by arthritis and suffering from diabetes, was placed in a nursing home after he became unable to self-administer his insulin shots. For 7 days, he received the wrong dose of insulin from the staff. In addition, he was not fed until hours after his injections, which lowered his blood glucose to a dangerous level. When he eventually became unresponsive, a nurse stuck a tube down his nose and pumped orange juice into his stomach in order to raise his blood glucose level. Another nurse soon reinserted the tube for more orange juice; then the first nurse returned and pumped in still more juice. None of this had been done with a doctor's approval. Finally, paramedics were called to rush the patient to a hospital. When he coughed up orange foam in the ambulance, the paramedics found the feeding tube coiled in his mouth. It had not been taped into place, contrary to standard procedure. The liquid had emptied into his lungs instead of his stomach. Within hours, he was dead. The man had literally *drowned in orange juice.*[195]

North Carolina also contains 450 rest homes. Because this type of long-term residential facility is not legally required to provide 24-hour care, rest homes are even less regulated than nursing homes.[196] In 1991, an Alzheimer's patient disappeared from one of these places and was never found.[197] In 1992, staff members at another rest home "punished an unruly resident by slapping her, pinching her breasts, swinging her by her arms and legs, and forcing a bar of soap into her mouth."[198] The owner, the largest rest home operator in the state, was fined $500. Three weeks after checking into a rest home, another Alzheimer's patient was found hanging from her bed, "asphyxiated by a restraining device designed to keep her from getting up."[199] This time the fine was $3000—high by North Carolina standards, despite the fact that the state contributes nearly $100 million annually to its rest home industry.

According to an investigative report entitled "Is Grandma Drowsy or Is She Drugged?" many nursing homes have resorted to giving patients powerful sedatives and psychotropic drugs to keep them docile, thus increasing profits by minimizing care.[200] A major study released in 1988 by Harvard Medical School found that 58% of residents in 12 Massachusetts nursing homes were prescribed sedatives, tranquilizers, or mind-altering drugs, often in excessive doses and using more than one drug at a time.[201] Although in some cases the need for such drugs could be justified, continued understaffing and lack of mental healthcare in nursing homes was also related to their use. Staff doctors can give nurses "blank checks" for prescriptions for residents, and oftentimes families and the residents themselves are unaware of which drugs are being given.[202]

Two other studies conducted by researchers at Yale and the University of Minnesota showed that large numbers of nursing home residents "are tethered to their beds or wheelchairs or given powerful tranquilizing drugs without documentation that they are needed."[203] In 1991, an article in the *Journal of the American Medical Association* reported that the prescribing of antipsychotic drugs without an appropriate diagnosis is an established practice in nursing homes.[204]

Nursing homes are also prone to financial rip-offs, usually tied to the Medicare program. A 1995 study by the U.S. General Accounting Office uncovered widespread overcharging to Medicare for therapy services.[205] The cost of these services has increased enormously (over 100%) between 1990 ($4.8 billion) and 1993 ($10.4 billion), raising concern that some of this growth was the result of fraud and abuse. The General Accounting Office found huge markups on therapy services by rehabilitation companies, who supply therapists to the nursing homes, and by the nursing homes themselves. For example, Medicare has been charged $600 per hour or more for therapy, whereas the average salaries for occupational, physical, and speech therapists range from $12 to $25 per hour.[206]

The complaints by beneficiaries and their families, which usually relate to overcharging, have been confirmed by numerous investigations around the country. In Georgia, a Department of Justice investigation of the owner of four rehabilitation companies resulted in an indictment for submitting false claims, mail fraud, wire fraud, and money laundering. In North Carolina, rehabilitation companies have been found to bill Medicare for overpriced services as well as services never rendered at all. One extensive investigation involved abuses by one company linked to over 130 providers spread over 21 states. The company systematically charged grossly inflated amounts for services. In one instance, Medicare was billed for $8415, of which a $4580 fee was included by the billing service just for processing the claim.[207]

POLICING DOCTORS: PHYSICIAN HEAL THYSELF?

Although it should be stressed that the vast majority of physicians and other health providers are honest and dedicated to quality care, it does not take a large contingent of deviant practitioners to steal enormous sums of money or cause extensive physical harm. Control of these miscreants has been a thorny public policy issue for some time. Doctors reflexively argue that their profession is capable of policing itself. After all, who knows more about medical procedures and potential errors and mistakes than them? There is, however, at least one glaring flaw in this linear assumption. Physicians are seldom willing to report colleagues who practice medicine below generally accepted standards. Often, even in egregious cases, doctors will not come forward to identify fellow professionals who are putting patients at great risk. For example, a New York obstetrician performed a Caesarian section on a patient in 1999 and then *carved his initials in her stomach*. He later told a supervisor that he had done such a beautiful job, "he thought he should sign it."[208]

Incredibly, this weird menace continued to practice for 4 months following his custom-engraved surgery. Although he was dismissed from his staff position, neither the hospital nor any of his colleagues ever reported the bizarre incident to state authorities. His medical license was finally revoked only after he lost a $1.75-million civil judgment. Because his second initial is a Z, the media dubbed him "Dr. Zorro."[209]

Another recent case involving an 8-year-old Colorado boy, who died during minor surgery after his anesthesiologist *fell asleep* during the operation, dramatically illustrates the fatal consequences of the medical profession's traditional code of silence. This doctor had been reported to the hospital by colleagues on at least *six* prior occasions for appearing to doze during surgery. In each instance, the hospital had handled the accusations internally through its confidential peer review process.[210]

The victim's parents buried their son believing that he had died from natural causes and not at the hands of a snoozing specialist. Only after receiving an anonymous telephone call did they press for a formal investigation. The state medical board finally stripped the doctor of his license, condemning his professional conduct as "abhorrent."[211] One may well ask why it took six episodes of sleeping at the switch and the needless death of an innocent child to remove this menacing misfit.

Much like the "Blue Wall of Silence" (described in Chapter 9), which inhibits honest law enforcement officers from weeding out corrupt ones, the preceding case underscores the folly of a cultural norm that encourages the many ethical practitioners to "circle the wagons" around the few disreputable ones. Other doctors must take responsibility for dangerously deviant medical practitioners and seriously police their profession if they do not want government regulators and prosecutors to do it for them. Until physicians repudiate their self-serving "us versus them" mentality, their calls for less outside intervention seem more than a little hypocritical.

If anything, it would appear that *increased* intervention is needed. In 1994, the number of disciplinary actions taken against physicians by state medical boards reached an all-time high, topping 4000 for the first time.[212] Yet, according to a report by the Public Citizen Health Research Group, entitled *13,012 Questionable Doctors*, two-thirds of doctors disciplined in 1995 for substandard, incompetent, or negligent care were allowed to continue practicing with little or no restriction.[213] The report declares, "If airline pilots were so poorly regulated as physicians, we would have [a] plane crashing every day."[214]

Not surprisingly, among the biggest sources of disciplinary laxity are Medicare and Medicaid defrauders.[215] Reportedly, 30% of doctors barred from the Medicare program are not even penalized by state medical boards.[216]

Since the mid 1980s, as evidence of the cost and extent of medical fraud has grown, private insurance companies have also become more actively engaged in fraud detection and prevention. Yet many experts still criticize the health insurance industry for not doing enough in this area. A 1990 survey conducted by the Health Insurance Association of America found that only half of the companies questioned had formed fraud prevention units.[217] With great sums of money at risk, some skeptics believe that the industry has not moved fast enough or far enough. Part of the reason for this sluggishness is that, like with so many white-collar crimes, the costs of insurance fraud are merely passed along to consumers—in this case, in the form of higher premiums. Antifraud enforcement in government programs, where the pressure to turn a profit is absent, is even more deficient. The Health Care Financing Administration (HCFA), for example, which runs the $100-billion-plus Medicare program, has continually come under attack for being too lax and for providing loopholes for fraud to occur. The HCFA has also been criticized for taking too long to implement new laws designed to control fraud and for reducing payments to private contractors for fraud prevention.[218]

The bottom line may be, however, that there is simply too big a system to police, given the government's limited resources and half-hearted commitment. As things stand now in the world of medical crime, the "cops" are catching only a handful of the "robbers."

NOTES

1. Davis, L. J. "Medscam." *Mother Jones* 20, March 1995: 26–29.
2. Witkin, Gordon, Friedman, Doran, and Guttman, Monika. "Health Care Fraud." *U.S. News & World Report*. February 24, 1992: 34–43.
3. "Easy Prey." *Houston Chronicle*. November 20, 1995: 20A.
4. U.S. Department of Justice. "Government Fraud." 1989: 4–10.
5. Geis, Gilbert, Pontell, Henry N., Keenan, Constance, Rosoff, Stephen M., O'Brien, Mary Jane, and Jesilow, Paul. "Peculating Psychologist: Fraud and Abuse Against Medicaid." *Professional Psychology: Research and Practice* 16, 1985: 823–832.
6. Makeig, John. "Chiropractor Receives 8 Years in Fraud Case." *Houston Chronicle*. November 16, 1995: 37A.
7. Ropp, Kevin L. "Wisconsin Foot Doctor Jailed for Selling Drug Samples." *FDA Consumer* 29, 1995: 36.
8. Moffat, Susan, "Brothers Enter Guilty Pleas in Massive Insurance Fraud." *Los Angeles Times*. March 17, 1993: 12.
9. *Ibid.*
10. Witkin et al., *op. cit.*, p. 36.
11. *Ibid.*, p. 36.
12. *Ibid.*
13. Witkin et al., *op. cit.*
14. *Ibid.*
15. *Ibid.*
16. *Ibid.*
17. *Ibid.*
18. Miller, Rena. "Reimbursement Schemes Costly for Medicare." *Los Angeles Times*. June 17, 1991: A16.
19. Pear, Robert. "Audit Uncovers Medicare Fraud in Services to Homebound Elderly." *Houston Chronicle*. July 27, 1997: 12A.
20. Witkin et al., *op. cit.*, p. 38.
21. Eisler, Peter. "Home Healthcare Fraud on the Rise." *USA Today*. November 12, 1996: 1A, 2A.

22. Pear, *op. cit.*
23. *Ibid.*
24. Quoted in *Ibid.*, p. 1A.
25. *Ibid.*
26. Eisler, Peter. "Ga. Couple's Fall a Jolt to the Industry." *USA Today.* November 12, 1996: 7A.
27. *Ibid.*
28. Lord, Mary. "A High-Priced Hookup." *US News & World Report* 116, May 9, 1994: 63–69.
29. *Ibid.*
30. *Ibid.*
31. *Ibid.*
32. *Ibid.*
33. Lord, *op. cit.*
34. Fellner, Jonathan, "AG Sting Uncovers Medi-Cal Fraud," *Los Angeles Daily Journal.* November 17, 1989: 4.
35. Frantz, Douglas, "Humana Under Fire for High Markups." *Los Angeles Times.* October 18, 1991: D3.
36. Pear, Robert, "U.S. Says Hospitals Demand Physicians Pay for Referrals." *New York Times.* September 27, 1992: A1.
37. *Ibid.*, p. A1.
38. *Ibid.*
39. *Ibid.*
40. "National Medical Settlement." *New York Times.* March 9, 1994: C18.
41. Schine, Eric, and Yang, Catherine. "Migraines for National Medical." *Business Week.* September 13, 1993: 74–75.
42. "National Medical Enterprises Hit With Record Fine in Healthcare Fraud Case." *Corporate Crime Reporter.* July 4, 1994: 4.
43. Yang, Catherine and Schine, Eric. "'Put the Head in the Bed and Keep It There.'" *Business Week* (Industrial/Technology Ed.) 3341, October 18, 1993: 68–70.
44. Washington, Harriet A. "Human Guinea Pigs." *Emerge.* October 1994: 29.
45. "Mental Hospitals Blasted." *Houston Chronicle.* December 21, 1995: 23 A.
46. Witkin et al., *op. cit.*
47. *Ibid.*
48. *Ibid.*, p. 41.
49. Smith, Mark. "Law Targets Psychiatric Care System Abuses." *Houston Chronicle.* September 8, 1991: 1A, 20A.
50. Smith, Mark. "Marketing Blitz Straddles Line of Medical Ethics." *Houston Chronicle.* September 8, 1991: 20A.
51. Smith, Mark. "Profitable Addictions: Claims of 'Bounty Hunting' for Patients Probed." *Houston Chronicle.* September 8, 1991: 20A.
52. *Ibid.*
53. Smith, "Law Targets . . . ," *op. cit.*, p. 20A.
54. *Ibid.*, p. 20A.
55. *Ibid.*, p. 20A. A less formal "golden handcuff" agreement guaranteed one San Antonio psychiatrist tickets to University of Texas football games in exchange for recruitment services.
56. *Ibid.*
57. Smith, "Marketing Blitz . . . ," *op. cit.*, p. 20A.
58. Quoted in Smith, "Law Targets . . . ," p. 20A.
59. Witkin, *op. cit.*, p. 41.
60. *Ibid.*
61. *Ibid.*, p. 42.
62. Smith, "Marketing Blitz . . . ," *op. cit.*
63. Quoted in *Ibid.*, p. 20A.
64. Waas, Murray. "Bleak House." *Los Angeles Times.* April 3, 1994: 10.
65. *Ibid.*
66. Quoted in *Ibid.*, p. 10.
67. *Ibid.*
68. Quoted in *Ibid.*, p. 10.
69. Lord, *op. cit.*, p. 65.
70. Sternberg, Stephen. "Double Dipping Doctors." *Mother Jones* 18, May–June, 1993: 29.
71. *Ibid.*
72. Quoted in *Ibid.*, p. 29.
73. Quoted in Spiegel, Claire. "Doctor's Use of Own Labs: Good Ethics?" *Los Angeles Times.* February 17, 1989: 1.
74. *Ibid.*
75. Eichenwald, Kurt. "Trouble in Dialysis-Care Industry Puts Lives on the Line." *Houston Chronicle.* December 4, 1995: 3A.
76. National Medical Care is a division of W. R. Grace Corporation, one of the main defendants in the Woburn children's leukemia cluster examined in Chapter 3.
77. *Ibid.*
78. Shogren, Elizabeth. "Rampant Fraud Complicates Medicare Cures." *Los Angeles Times.* October 8, 1995: 1.
79. Bacon, John. "Fraud Claim." *USA Today.* January 14, 1998: 3A.
80. *Ibid.*
81. *Ibid.*
82. Fineman, Mark. "Fraud Case Puts New Strain on U.S. Dominican Relations." *Los Angeles Times.* February 26, 1999: A2.

83. *Ibid.*

84. Shogren, *op. cit.*

85. "Medicare Settlement Set." *Houston Chronicle.* December 13, 1995: 17A.

86. Rundle, Rhonda. "Corning Unit, Unilab Pay $39.8 million to Settle Allegations of Medicare Fraud." *Wall Street Journal.* September 14, 1993: A6.

87. *Ibid.,* p. 1.

88. Epstein, Aaron. "Blowing the Whistle." *Wichita Eagle,* March 6, 1994: 1D.

89. Sims, Calvin. "Company to Pay $111 million in Health-Claims Fraud Suit." *New York Times.* December 19, 1992: 1.

90. *Ibid.*

91. Found, Edward T. and Headden, Susan. "The Hospital Fraud Inquiry that Fizzled." *US News & World Report* 119, December 18, 1995: 42.

92. *Ibid.,* p. 42.

93. *Ibid.*

94. *Ibid.*

95. "HCA to Pay $95.3 Million Fine in Fraud Case." *Los Angeles Times.* December 14, 2000: C2.

96. Jackson, Robert L. "HCA Pleads Guilty in Medicare Fraud Case." *Los Angeles Times.* December 15, 2000: C1.

97. *Ibid.*

98. *Ibid.*

99. *Ibid.*

100. "How Medicare Patients are Bilked: Overcharges, Retainers and Waivers." *Consumer Reports.* August, 1994: 527.

101. *Ibid.*

102. *Ibid.*

103. Anderson, Jack and Van Atta, Dale. "Medicare: Whistle-Blowing in the Wind." *Washington Post.* August 21, 1991: E7.

104. *Ibid.*

105. *Ibid.,* p. E7.

106. Shogren, *op. cit.,* p. 1.

107. Gottlieb, Martin. "Medicare's Overhaul Will Place Billions into Coffers of HMOs." *Houston Chronicle.* December 10, 1995: 16A. See also: Estrich, Susan. "Politics as Usual with All the Investigations." *USA Today.* December 21, 1995: 11A.

108. Jesilow, Paul, Geis, Gilbert, and Harris, John. "Doomed to Repeat Our Errors: Fraud in Emerging Health-Care Systems." *Social Justice* 22, 1995: 125–138.

109. Abramowitz, Michael. "Collapse of a Health Plan: How Did Such a Good Idea Turn Out So Bad?" *Washington Post.* June 23, 1987: A1.

110. Zaldivar, R.A. "Who's Abusing Medicare? Not Just Crooks, Probe Finds." *Houston Chronicle.* August 26, 1997: 7A.

111. United States Senate, Subcommittee on Long-Term Care, Special Committee on Aging. *Fraud and Abuse Among Practitioners Participating in the Medicaid Program.* Washington, DC: Government Printing Office, 1976.

112. *Ibid.*

113. Hogue, Elizabeth, Teplitsky, Sanford V., and Sollins, Howard L. *Preventing Fraud and Abuse: A Guide for Medicare and Medicaid Providers.* Owings Mills, Md: National Health , 1988.

114. Jesilow et al.

115. Quoted in Witkin, *op. cit.,* p. 34.

116. Geis, Gilbert, Henry N. Pontell and Paul D. Jesilow, "Medicaid Fraud." In Scott, Joseph E. and Hirschi, Travis Hirschi (Eds.), *Controversial Issues in Crime and Justice.* Newbury Park, Calif.: Sage, 1988: 17–39.

117. Morris, Jim. "Dentist Accused of Abuse Taken off Advisory Panel." *Houston Chronicle.* December 2, 1995: 1A, 18A.

118. Meyer, Josh. "Convicted Doctor Kept on Public Payroll." *Los Angeles Times.* November 30, 1995: A3, A28.

119. *Ibid.*

120. Kennedy, Douglas. "Healthy Spoils From Very Sick System." *New York Post.* April, 18, 1995: Part III, 5.

121. *Ibid.,* p. 18.

122. Pontell, Henry N., Rosoff, Stephen M., and Goode, Erich. "White Collar Crime." In Goode, Erich (Ed.), *Deviant Behavior* (4th ed.). Englewood Cliffs, NJ: Prentice Hall, 1994: 345–371.

123. Lanza-Kaduce, Lonn, "Deviance Among Professional: The Case of Unnecessary Surgery." *Deviant Behavior* 1, 1980: 333–359. Lanza-Kaduce reports that as much as 15% of all elective surgery performed in the United States—that is, operations not involving emergencies or life-threatening circumstances—are unnecessary. For example, it is claimed that 90% of all tonsillectomies are unneeded, and 15% of all hysterectomies (surgical removal of the uterus) are said to be performed in the absence of pathology.

124. Welkos, Robert. "Doctor in Blindings Gets 4-Year Prison Term, Fine." *Los Angeles Times*. April 25, 1984: 1, 6.

125. *Ibid.*, p. 6.

126. *Ibid.*, p. 6.

127. Morris, Jim. "Cavities in the State's Dental Fraud Effort." *Houston Chronicle*. December 17, 1995: 1A, 20A.

128. *Ibid.*, p. 20A.

129. *Ibid.*, p. 20A.

130. *Ibid.*, p. 20A.

131. *Ibid.*

132. Jesilow, Paul, Henry N. Pontell, and Gilbert Geis, *Prescription for Profit: How Doctors Defraud Medicaid*. Berkeley: University of California Press, 1993: 35.

133. Eady, Brenda. "MD Claims Innocence in Medicaid Scheme." *Miami Herald*. March 29, 1981: 4B.

134. *Ibid.*

135. Messerschmidt, Al. "Witnesses Dispute Doctor's Claims." *Miami Herald*. January, 16, 1982: 2B.

136. Eady, Brenda. "Medicaid M.D. Accused of Fraud," *Miami Herald*. March 14, 1981: 1B.

137. Messerschmidt, *op. cit.*

138. Markowitz, Arnold. "Jury Takes 1 Hour to Convict Doctor of Medicaid Fraud." *Miami Herald*. January 23, 1982: 1B.

139. Personal Interview. 1990.

140. Katzenbach, John. "MD Charged in Contract Killing," *Miami Herald*. September 4, 1982: B1.

141. *Ibid.*

142. Grimm, Fred. "Alleged Hit List was for 'Voodoo Man' Doctor Says." *Miami Herald*. February 2, 1983: 1B.

143. *Ibid.*

144. Grimm, Fred. "Woman Doctor Convicted in Plot to Kill Partner, Sentenced to Life," *Miami Herald*. February 4, 1983: 1D.

145. Jesilow, Pontell, and Geis, *op. cit.*

146. Geis, Gilbert, Jesilow, Paul, Pontell, Henry, and O'Brien, Mary Jane. "Fraud and Abuse by Psychiatrists Against Government Medical Benefit Programs." *American Journal of Psychiatry* 142, 1985: 231–234.

147. *Ibid.*

148. Rosoff, Stephen M. and Leone, Matthew C. "The Public Prestige of Medical Specialties: Overviews and Undercurrents." *Social Science & Medicine* 32, 1991: 321–326.

149. Sutherland, Edwin H. *White-Collar Crime*. New York: Holt, Rinehart and Winston, 1949.

150. Hilts, Philip J. "Punished Doctors Keep on Practicing." *Houston Chronicle*. March 29, 1996: 9A.

151. Gartrell, Nanette, Herman, Judith, Olarte, Sylvia, Feldstein, Michael, and Localio, Russell. "Psychiatrist-Patient Sexual Contact: Results of a National Survey, I: Prevalence." *American Journal of Psychiatry* 143, 1986: 1126–1131.

152. In 1999, for example, a well-known Manhattan gynecologist and fertility expert was indicted on charges that he billed insurance companies for routine procedures to cover he had actually performed: fertility surgeries. It was alleged that the doctor had submitted hundreds of phony bills over a 10-year period amounting to nearly $4 million. It is believed that false billing is common among doctors who specialize in costly fertility procedures, because insurance companies often do not pay for them. The doctor strongly maintained his innocence, arguing that, "It is ridiculous that insurance companies will pay a man to have Viagra but refuse to pay for a woman to have fertility treatments." ("Case of Fraud Rivets Attention." *Houston Chronicle*. January 23, 2000: 12A.)

153. Elmer-Dewitt, Phillip. "The Cruelest Kind of Fraud." *Time*, 138, December 2, 1991: 27.

154. *Ibid.*, p. 27.

155. *Ibid.*, p. 27.

156. *Ibid.*, p. 27.

157. Quoted in Howe, Robert F. "Citing Cruel Lies by Jacobson, Judge Gives Him 5 Years, Fine." *Washington Post*. May 9, 1992: D1.

158. Quoted in "Fertility Doctor Gets Five Years." *New York Times*. May 9, 1992: 8.

159. Cowley, Geoffrey, Murr, Andrew, and Springen, Karen. "Ethics and Embryos." *Newsweek*. June 12, 1995: 66.

160. Challender, Debbie. "Fertility Fraud: Why One Mother May Never Know Her Babies." *Redbook*. December 1995: 84–87, 116–118. The UCI case is not the only recent scandal involving fertility centers. In 1995, a clinic at the University Hospital in Utrecht, the Netherlands, botched an in vitro procedure by fertilizing a woman's

eggs with sperm from both her husband *and* another man. As a result, the woman gave birth to twin boys, one white and one black.

161. *Ibid.*, p. 84.
162. Marquis, Julie. "Legislators Blast UCI's Fertility Center Role." *Los Angeles Times.* June 7, 1995: B1.
163. Challender, *op. cit.*, p. 86.
164. Kelleher, Susan and Nicolsi, Michelle. "UCI Report: Clinic Doctors Punished Whistleblower." *Orange County Register.* June 4, 1995: 1.
165. Challender, *op. cit.*
166. Wagner, Michael G. "Audit Ascribes Undue Profits to Fertility Doctors." *Los Angeles Times.* June, 5, 1995: 1.
167. *Ibid.*
168. *Ibid.*, p. 1.
169. "The Aftermath of Clinic Scandal: 106 Suits Settled, Nine More to Go." *Orange County Register.* July 4, 1999: 14.
170. Weiss, Kenneth R. "Regents Fire UCI Doctor Linked to Fertility Scandal." *Los Angeles Times.* March 16, 2000: A1.
171. Haldane, David. "Ex-UCI Fertility Doctor Sentenced in Fraud Case." *Los Angeles Times.* February 25, 1999: B6.
172. Weiss, Kenneth R. "UC Regents Fire Professor Involved in Fertility Case." *Los Angeles Times.* July 21, 2000: A5.
173. Kelleher, Susan. "Fugitive Doctor Continues Work in Mexico City." *Orange County Register.* July 4, 1999: 15.
174. *Ibid.*
175. Quoted in Weber, Tracy and Marquis, Julie. "In Quest for Miracles, Did Fertility Clinic Go Too Far?" *Los Angeles Times.* June 4, 1995: 1.
176. For example, a 2-year investigation of Pennsylvania's largest residential institution for the developmentally disabled uncovered horrifying offenses including manslaughter and sewing up patient wounds without anesthesia. It was alleged that doctors had improperly treated patients and, in one case, had ordered x-rays for a vomiting patient with a fever and whose skin had turned blue, resulting in the patient's death. "Six Doctors Charged With Abuses, Three Deaths at Home for Retarded." *Houston Chronicle.* February 27, 1999: 23A.)
177. Bates, Eric. "No Place Like Home." *Southern Exposure.* Fall 1992: 17–21.
178. *Ibid.*, p. 19.
179. Wilkes, James L. "Nursing Home Nightmares." *USA Today.* August 20, 1996: 11A.
180. *Ibid.*
181. Eisler, Peter. "Prosecutors Join Forces With Nursing Homes." *USA Today.* July 3, 1997: 3A.
182. Quoted in Calvert, Scott. "The Vulnerable Elderly." *Birmingham News.* August 15, 1993: 13A.
183. Trafford, Abigail. "The Tragedy of Care for America's Elderly." *U.S. World & News Report.* April 24, 1978: 56.
184. "Florida Penalizes Nursing Home in Ant Bite Fatality." *Houston Chronicle.* June 7, 2000: 12A.
185. Peterson, Richard. "30% Would Rather Die Than End in Nursing Home." *USA Today.* August 5, 1997: 1D.
186. McQuiston, John T. "Health Dept. Studies Reports of Abuse at Nursing Home." *New York Times.* February 29, 1992: 28.
187. "6 Found in Nursing Home Filth, Florida Says." *New York Times.* November 26, 1987: A28.
188. Wilkes, *op. cit.*, p. 11A.
189. Lewin, Tamar. "Nursing Home Damages Upheld." *New York Times.* September 5, 1990: A20.
190. Bates, *op. cit.*
191. Ready, Tinker. "Resting Uneasy." *Southern Exposure.* Fall 1992: 22–25.
192. *Ibid.*
193. *Ibid.*
194. Williams, Paige and Garloch, Karen. "Pain and Profit." *Charlotte Observer.* September 27, 1992: A1.
195. *Ibid.*
196. Ready, *op. cit.*
197. *Ibid.*
198. *Ibid.*, p. 24.
199. *Ibid.*, p. 22.
200. Findlay, Steven. "Is Grandma Drowsy, or is She Drugged?" *U.S. World & News Report.* June 12, 1989: 68.
201. *Ibid.*
202. *Ibid.*
203. Kolata, Gina. "Nursing Homes are Criticized on How They Tie and Drug Some Patients." *New York Times.* January 23, 1991: A16.
204. Jencks, Stephen F. and Clauser, Steven B. "Managing Behavior Problems in Nursing Homes." *JAMA* 265, 1991: 506–507.

205. U.S. General Accounting Office. "Medicare: Tighter Rules Needed to Curtail Overcharges for Therapy in Nursing Homes." Washington, DC: GAO/HEHS-95–23, 1995.
206. *Ibid.*
207. *Ibid.*
208. "Carving Initials into Patient Did Not End Doctor's Career." *Houston Chronicle.* January 29, 2000: 3A.
209. "Doctor Who Carved Initials Sentenced." *Houston Chronicle.* May 31, 2000: 7A.
210. Siegal, Barry. "Medicine's Fatal Code of Silence." *Los Angeles Times.* August 24, 1995: A16–A17.
211. Siegal, Barry. "A Death Cracks the Shell of Privacy." *Los Angeles Times.* August 25, 1995: A1, A22–A23. Criminal charges of reckless manslaughter have also been filed by the district attorney's office in Denver. At this writing, the case has yet to be adjudicated.
212. "Disciplining the Docs." *People's Medical Society Newsletter,* 14, 1995: 6.
213. Levy, Doug. "Many 'Bad' Doctors Evade Censure." *USA Today.* March 29, 1996: 2D.
214. Quoted in *Ibid.*, p. 2D.
215. *People's Medical Society Newsletter, op. cit.*
216. *Ibid.*
217. U.S. General Accounting Office, *op. cit.*
218. *Ibid.*

CHAPTER 11

Computer Crime

Mother: What are you doing?
Young Hacker: I'm taking over a TV network.
Mother: Finish up, honey. And get to sleep.

From *Hackers* (1995). Screenplay by Rafael Moreu.

*I*n the late nineteenth century, the French social theorist Gabriel Tarde constructed his *law of insertion,* which noted how newer criminal modes are superimposed on older ones through imitative learning and technological innovation.[1] Thus, for example, the European highwayman of the eighteenth century prepared the way for the American stagecoach bandit of the nineteenth century. Likewise, the train robber of the nineteenth century was the progenitor of the twentieth century truck hijacker. In the twenty-first century, Tarde's insight is being validated again, this time in ways Tarde himself scarcely could have imagined.

Today, the falsified ledger, long the traditional instrument of the embezzler, is being replaced by corrupted software programs. The classic weapons of the bank robber can now be drawn from a far more sophisticated arsenal containing such modern tools as automatic teller machines and electronic fund transfers. In short, white-collar crime has entered the computer age.

Computer crime has been defined broadly as "the destruction, theft, or unauthorized or illegal use, modification, or copying of information, programs, services, equipment, or communication networks."[2] Donn B. Parker, one of the country's leading computer crime researchers, offers a less formal definition of computer crime as any intentional act associated with computers where a victim suffers a loss and a perpetrator makes a gain.[3] Under these definitional guidelines, the following offenses all could be classified as computer crimes: (1) electronic embezzlement and financial theft; (2) computer hacking;

417

(3) malicious sabotage, including the creation, installation, or dissemination of computer viruses; (4) utilization of computers and computer networks for purposes of espionage; and (5) use of electronic devices and computer codes for making unauthorized long-distance telephone calls. Each of these offenses will be examined in this chapter; however, it would be instructive to consider first just how sizable this problem has become and how fast it has grown.

For obvious reasons, computer crime has a short history. Its most immediate precursor was probably the invention of the so-called blue box in the early 1960s. The blue box was an illegal electronic device capable of duplicating the multifrequency dialing system developed by AT&T. The telephone company had described its new direct-dialing technology in its technical journals, apparently confident that no one in the general public would ever read or at least understand such esoteric information. How wrong they were. "Ma Bell" became the first casualty of the first law of electronic crime: *If it can be done, someone will do it.* Motivated by a curious blend of mischievousness and greed, a cadre of young wizards tape-recorded piccolos and other high-pitched sounds, and thus created the blue box, which gave them unauthorized access to the entire Bell network. They called themselves "phone phreaks." One ingenious phreak even discovered that a giveaway whistle packaged in Cap'n Crunch cereal produced a perfect 2600-cycle tone that allowed him to place overseas telephone calls without paying charges.

Although occasional arrests were made, phone phreaking was more or less hidden from the public, both by the phreaks themselves, who feared exposure, *and* by the telephone company, which feared an epidemic. But in 1971, a popular magazine "blew the whistle" (appropriately enough!) with the publication of an explosive article entitled "Secrets of the Little Blue Box."[4]

At about this same time, the fledgling computer industry had graduated from the self-contained mainframe to interactive linkage and primitive networks. Once again, the first law of electronic crime was activated, as computer buffs now could use terminals to explore powerful mainframes that were previously off-limits. A new term entered the public lexicon: hacker. In the 1970s, the early hackers began using school computers for a variety of misdeeds, most notably the alteration of grades. However, because few schools even had computers at the time, hacking was still a relatively minor nuisance.

However, by the end of the decade, modems (devices linking computers with telephones) and computerized bulletin board services (BBSs) appeared. By the early 1980s, the home personal computer (PC) had become increasingly common. For hackers this was the missing ingredient—a high-tech skeleton key that could open a myriad of locked doors. For example, in 1985, 23 teenagers broke into a Chase Manhattan Bank computer by telephone, destroying accounting records and changing passwords. No money was stolen, but customers effectively were denied access to their own files.[5]

Predictably, the first generation of hackers, for all their mischief, were only setting the stage for far more insidious types of computer crime; what may have begun as a questionable hobby shared by a network of adolescent misfits has been co-opted by a more malevolent class of white-collar criminal.

Some individuals began employing the basic hacker methodology to break into systems, not as a vandalic prank or simply to do it, but to steal.

"Computers have created opportunities for career criminals, an increasing number of whom are becoming computer literate."[6] An early (and ongoing) example involves the planting of an unauthorized program, known as a Trojan Horse. Such a program can transfer money automatically to an illegal account whenever a legal transaction is made.[7] To many skilled thieves and embezzlers, this was akin to striking the mother lode.

How common and how costly has computer crime become? It is believed to be the fastest-growing type of crime in America.[8] A 1986 survey asked respondents if they believed that their companies were being victimized by computer crime; Only 7% said yes.[9] A 1993 survey reported that 70% of the more than 400 companies responding admitted to at least one security infringement in the previous 12 months; 24% put the financial loss per incident at more than $100,000.[10] The head of the organization which conducted the latter survey noted, "The problem is much more serious than expected."[11] Of the 150 large companies surveyed by Michigan State University in 1995, 148 said they had suffered from computer crime; 43% said they had been victimized 25 times or more.[12]

Moreover, computer crime is no longer just an American problem. It has been uncovered in both Canada[13] and Mexico[14], as well as Western European nations, such as the United Kingdom,[15] Sweden,[16] The Netherlands,[17] Germany,[18] Switzerland,[19] and Italy.[20] Viruses have been created in such distant places as Bulgaria and South Africa.[21] Hackers reportedly have proliferated in France and Israel,[22] India and Singapore,[23] and Russia (where they are called *chackers*).[24] Likewise, computer security has become a major concern in Japan,[25] Hong Kong,[26] Australia,[27] and New Zealand.[28] In one especially malignant use of computer technology, an Argentine kidnapping ring illegally accessed financial records to determine how much ransom victims could pay.[29]

Regarding cost, estimates of annual losses resulting from computer crime range from $550 million (National Center for Computer Crime Data) to $15 billion (Inter-Pact computer security organization)[30] or even higher. This remarkably wide range of estimates no doubt reflects the substantial variation which exists in defining what qualifies as computer crime. Thieves can steal anything from entire systems[31] to transportable laptop and notebook computers[32] to integrated circuits, semiconductors, or memory chips[33]—all of which can be resold for their illicit "street value." Is hardware theft computer crime? About 14 million federal tax returns are now filed electronically. In 1989, IRS agents arrested a Boston bookkeeper for electronically filing $325,000 worth of phony tax refund claims.[34] A 1993 report by the U.S. General Accounting Office warns the IRS of its potential vulnerability to a number of new electronic schemes.[35] Should this be classified as tax fraud or computer crime? The Internet offers sociopathic young malcontents an opportunity to download "The School Stopper's Textbook," which instructs students on how to blow up toilets and how to "break into your school at night and burn it down."[36] Is this criminal incitement or free speech? Dealers in child pornography utilize the

Internet and computer bulletin board services to advertise materials and exchange information.[37] Pedophiles also use the Internet to "troll" for potential victims, usually adolescent boys.[38] This is obviously felonious conduct of the most offensive sort, but can it really be considered computer crime? Computer systems have assisted the daily operations of prostitution rings.[39] Illegal gambling records are now routinely computerized.[40] Organized crime uses computers in many of its operations, from bribery to hijacking,[41] and illegal drug cartels employ computers to describe clients and distribution networks.[42] The computer has also become an indispensable tool for "laundering" drug money[43] and other organized crime revenues. Money laundering is now a $100 billion per year industry in the United States.[44] Should all those billions of dollars be considered part of the cost of computer crime?

The truth is that there is little consensus in these matters. In fact, some experts have adopted an "agnostic" position that the true cost is unknowable. To further complicate estimation, it was suggested that by the year 2000 virtually *all* business crime would conform to what now is considered computer crime.[45]

Some varieties of telemarketing fraud described in Chapter 2 have already spread to the Internet. A state securities commissioner has warned, "Don't believe that just because it's on a computer, that it's true. Computers don't lie, but the people who put messages on computers lie."[46] In 1995, for example, a 15-year-old Utah boy was charged with bilking $10,000 out of Internet users by posting phony advertisements for computer parts.[47] Penny stock swindlers post messages on "investors" bulletin boards about supposedly major developments at small companies. The object is to build interest in and increase the buying of the stock so that the price will shoot up. The people behind the fabricated messages then sell their shares at a hefty profit and leave other stockholders with near-worthless paper. This technique is known in penny stock parlance as "pump and dump." An Oklahoma con artist pumped and dumped to drive up the shares of Bagels and Buns, a publicly traded company with no assets, from 38 cents to $7.50 in just 4 months.[48]

Other crooks have masqueraded as financial advisers or licensed brokers on the Internet and solicited investments in fictitious mutual funds. One Michigan scam artist talked a New York investor into sending him $91,000 and cheated a Texas victim out of $10,000. Six months later, the Texan ruefully acknowledged his gullibility: "I was terribly embarrassed. I knew I'd been screwed."[49] Cyberspace is also stuffed with hundreds of more "exotic" investment scams—everything from wireless cable television to ostrich farming.[50]

Computers have also become the principal tool in sophisticated identity theft scams. In a recent case, for example, a suspect was charged with utilizing library computers, Web-enabled cell phones, and virtual voice mail to dupe credit bureaus into providing detailed reports on victims chosen from *Forbes'* list of the richest people in America. These data were used to gain access to credit cards and brokerage accounts. The alleged list of targets including such notable figures as Steven Spielberg, Oprah Winfrey, Martha Stewart, Ted Turner, Ross Perot, George Lucas, and Warren Buffett.[51] Police called this crime "one of the most ambitious identity-theft schemes they had ever seen."[52] A detective with the New York Police Department's computer investigation unit said of the suspect—a 32-year-old high school dropout: "He's the best I've ever found."[53]

Another gray area in estimating the losses from computer crime is software piracy. No one knows the actual cost of this offense, but a study conducted by the Software Publishers Association (SPA) claims that $7.4 billion worth of business application software was counterfeited in 1993—a figure nearly equal to the total legitimate revenues for the entire industry in that same year.[54] In addition to business applications, piracy also entails the illegal copying of software for personal use, known as "softlifting."[55] A Massachusetts BBS recently raided by the FBI had subscribers from 36 states and 11 countries, who paid $99 per year to download illegally copied personal software.[56]

Foreign piracy of American software is an extremely costly problem. Some countries provide no copyright protection at all for software, and many that do have copyright laws choose not to enforce them.[57] Computer software is predominantly an American asset (American companies control about 80% of the world market); so other nations "tend to be slow to provide protection for goods they don't produce themselves."[58] In 1993, just seven countries—South Korea, Spain, France, Germany, Taiwan, Thailand, and Poland—reportedly cost American software companies more than $2 billion. In each of these countries, pirated American software was said to account for between 75% and 90% of the total software in use.[59] The former chairman of the International Trade Subcommittee of the U.S. Senate has stated that the elimination of piracy would significantly shrink the American trade deficit.[60] An overseas dealer, for example, was selling pirated copies of the popular *Lotus 1-2-3* spreadsheet software (which usually retails for around $200) for $1.50![61] To put it in perspective, this means that for every $100 in pirated Lotus sales generated by this dealer, MicroPro, the manufacturer of Lotus, lost nearly $15,000 in legitimate sales. Similarly, in China a pirated CD-ROM containing 70 popular software programs is available for just $100. The legitimate price is $10,000 in the United States, where millions of dollars were spent to develop it.[62]

When one considers as well the vast amount of undetected software piracy certain to exist, guessing the bottom line jolts the imagination. Indeed, based on their survey of 45,000 American households, McGraw-Hill Information Systems conservatively estimates that there is one pirated copy of software for every authorized copy.[63] The SPA places the ratio at *seven to one*.[64]

A newer form of piracy involves Internet sites known as WAREZ. WAREZ sites are subterranean—although often "conspicuously subterranean"—web sites that provide copyrighted programs for downloading. With a little bit of expertise and a couple of quick clicks of a mouse, one can download thousands of dollars worth of commercial software, copyrighted computer games, even the latest movies. Most computer games are available illegally on WAREZ sites before they are even available for public release. Some recent movies, such as *Star Wars: The Phantom Menace* and *Austin Powers:*

The Spy Who Shagged Me, were available on the Internet before they were released to theaters.[65]

People who create WAREZ sites are known as "crackers" because they "crack" copy protection codes. Most of them are teenaged boys who trade WAREZ like baseball cards. They use a program called a machine code monitor, which allows them to read protected disks one byte at a time, an operation known as "boot tracing." At critical points in the sequence, they insert new instructions and "liberate" the disk. Groups such as the Inner Circle, Addiction, and the Phrozen Crew pass gigabytes of pirated software through cyberspace. WAREZ groups have even created their own brazenly illegal, "in your face" websites.[66]

As with traditional software piracy, it is difficult to put a price tag on WAREZ piracy, because no one can determine how many people are downloading illegal WAREZ and how many of them would otherwise buy legal versions. But the figure is certainly high and growing rapidly.

The ultimate cost of computer crime is further clouded because there is a huge "dark figure" of unreported cases. "Because of public humiliation, liability issues, and security inadequacies, many corporations do not report computer crime losses, especially large ones."[67] Businesses often hire so-called cyber-posses, private security firms that monitor for intrusions and identify system flaws that gave unauthorized entry, instead of reporting hacker assaults to law enforcement authorities.[68] The reason for bypassing the law is that many victims believe they stand to lose more by revealing their vulnerabilities to customers and clients than from the crimes themselves.[69] The fear of "copycat" incidents also probably discourages the reporting of security breaches.[70] Furthermore, when it is information that is stolen, rather than money, the loss may be incalculable in terms of dollars. A survey of major corporations conducted by Computer Security Institute, released in 1996, found that only 17% of those suffering electronic intrusions notified authorities.[71]

Finally, the estimation of computer crime losses perhaps is most complicated by the clandestine nature of the crimes themselves. The most proficient electronic thieves are able to cover up all traces that a crime has been committed.[72] As the president of a major computer security consulting firm has noted, "We only read about the failed computer criminals. The really successful ones are never detected in the first place."[73]

However, even if the actual computer crime loss figure can only be guessed, no one questions that the losses are enormous. A survey by ComSec, an organization of computer security professionals, reports that 36 of 300 companies responding (12%) acknowledged losses of $100,000 or more in just the first 3 months of 1993, with another 42 (14%) losing between $10,000 and $100,000. For the preceding year, 69% of respondents admitted security problems, with 53% of those problems resulting in losses of at least $10,000.[74] Once more, the findings far exceeded the predictions of the startled investigators.

But survey data and raw numbers, however robust, are an undramatic way to tell a dramatic story. To understand the dimensions and the dangers of computer crime, we must examine the crimes themselves. Let us consider in more detail the five categories of computer crime suggested earlier.

EMBEZZLEMENT AND FINANCIAL THEFT

According to recent FBI statistics, the average armed bank robbery nets $3177.[75] The Data Processing Management Association reports that the average computer crime loss may be as high as $500,000.[76] This great disparity reveals that while there are physical limitations to the potential payoff available to the blue-collar robber—large amounts of money have weight and take up space—the white-collar thief who can access the appropriate computer can steal a fortune without moving anything heavier than some decimal points. As if to demonstrate this lack of physical limitations, millions of gallons of heating oil from Exxon's Bayview refinery were misappropriated by altering computer files.[77] A gang of rogue employees in a major railroad's computerized inventory center once "stole" 200 30-ton boxcars.[78] Without a doubt, the modern thief can steal more with a computer than with a gun.[79] In addition, bank robbers must face the prospect of getting shot at; not so the computer criminal. Dillinger never had it so good.

One of the most famous bank-related computer crimes, however, did involve the physical movement of hard cash. For 3 years, beginning in 1970, the chief teller at the Park Avenue branch of New York's Union Dime Savings Bank embezzled over $1.5 million from hundreds of accounts. Despite having no formal computer training, he was able to shift nonexistent money around from account to account, falsifying quarterly interest payments and satisfying visiting auditors with remarkable ease. So slick were his manipulations that, reportedly, he had difficulty explaining the intricacies of his crime to the bank's executives after his arrest.[80] He eventually served 15 months of a 20-month sentence. At last report, he was driving a taxicab in New Jersey. None of his pilfered funds has ever been recovered.

His eventual downfall happened almost by accident, as a by-product of an entirely different case. A routine police raid on a "bookie joint" revealed that he had been betting as much as $30,000 per day on sporting events. "If his indiscreet bookmakers had not kept his name in their files, he might well have kept up his embezzlement for quite a while longer than he did."[81]

It is interesting to note that the Union Dime Savings case serves as a perfect model of criminologist Donald Cressey's earlier research on the social psychology of embezzlement. According to Cressey, embezzlers typically go through a three-stage process. In stage 1, they are faced with what they perceive to be an unshareable financial problem, that is, a need for money which they cannot share with spouses, relatives, or friends. Supporting a $30,000 per day gambling habit on an $11,000 a year salary[82] would certainly seem to qualify in this regard. In stage 2, they recognize an opportunity to solve their problem secretly. This opportunity rests in the positions of trust which they hold. A position of chief teller, of course, would provide just such an opportunity. Finally, in stage 3, they manage to avoid internalizing a criminal identity by rationalizing their acts as borrowing rather than stealing.[83] It is the curse of compulsive gamblers like the Union Dime teller to continue expecting a financial recovery, even as the debts keep mounting. As we shall see, such labored rationalization is a recurring theme among computer criminals.

Embezzlement is a traditional crime, but computers have done for it what the microwave did for popcorn. It is no coincidence that between 1983 and 1992, the pubescent years of the computer revolution—arrests for embezzlement rose 56%.[84] As one state official has observed, "All scams are old, it's merely the technology that's changing."[85] In 1991, someone, believed to be an employee, used the computer in the payroll department of a prestigious New York bank to steal $25 million without leaving a trace. As of this writing, the case remains unsolved, not because there are no suspects, but because there are too many. "[H]undreds of employees had access to the same data that appear to have made at least one of them very rich."[86] This case underscores the findings of numerous major studies which report that most computerized theft is committed by authorized users, trusted insiders, and skilled employees.[87] "The easiest way into a computer is usually the front door."[88]

Not all electronic embezzlers work for banks. An employee in the computer center of a big-city welfare department stole $2.75 million, over a 9-month period by entering fraudulent data into the computerized payroll system and thereby creating a phantom work force complete with fake social security numbers. He would intercept the weekly paychecks "earned" by the fictitious crew, endorse and cash them, and dream of early retirement. He was uncovered only when a police officer found a fistful of phony checks in his illegally parked rental car.[89]

As we have already noted, some embezzlers have employed a Trojan horse—the "bad" program concealed inside the "good" program—as a means of diverting cash into fraudulent accounts. This is the most common method used in computer fraud.[90] Dishonest programmers have also planted "trap doors" or "sleepers" into the instructions which allow them to bypass security safeguards and siphon off cash using an imposter terminal.[91] A common variation on this method involves a practice known as *"salami slicing."* This type of fraud has been around for many years and was known in the pre-byte era as "rounding down."[92] Salami techniques divert (or, in keeping with the metaphor, "slice off") very small amounts of assets from very large numbers of private accounts. The stolen assets are so small, sometimes a few cents or even just a fraction of a cent per transaction, that they do not make a noticeable dent in any single account.[93]

How many people, after all, will bother to stoop down to retrieve a dropped penny? But when multiplied over a million or so bank transactions performed at computer speed, these "dropped pennies" can turn into tens or hundreds of thousands of dollars—well worth stooping for. For example, in the 1980s an employee at an investment firm used a computer to set up false accounts and filled them by diverting three-tenths of a cent interest from actual accounts.[94] In 1992, a hacker bragged to *Forbes* magazine that he had broken into Citibank's computers and for 3 months had quietly skimmed a penny or so from each account. He boasted that when he had accumulated $200,000, he quit.

One of the more spectacular salami attacks took place in California at around the same time as the Union Dime Savings case. Over a 6-year period, the chief accountant for a large produce company siphoned more than $1.5 million from his employers. While studying computer technology, he developed a program able to add small sums to disbursement accounts in payment of phony produce orders.[95] He later claimed that his motivation was simply to receive a promised annual bonus he felt he had been cheated of.[96] He decided he was entitled to three-quarters of 1% of the company's gross, and he began looting the company at exactly that rate. "He did this by devising a special algorithm—a set of rules for making calculations—which he used as a master program to alter the company's accounting data in the computer."[97] Because this firm grossed $30 million annually, pennies became dollars, and dollars became a fortune.

When he eventually was arrested and tried, he pleaded *nolo contendere* (no contest), perhaps expecting the same sort of typically light sentence his counterpart at Union Dime Savings was to receive. Instead he was sentenced to 10 years in San Quentin and served just over 5 years. Upon release, he became—what else?—a computer consultant.

The stark difference in the punitive sanctions meted out in these two roughly equivalent embezzlement cases underscores the general public's confusion about computer crime. Depending on how a prosecutor chooses to present a case, a jury is apt to perceive a computer criminal as anything from a pathetic "nerd" gone bad to an electronic terrorist threatening the very foundation of the American way of life.

Sometimes embezzlers are not low-level or mid-level employees of a company, but those at the very top.[98] This certainly would apply to the notorious Equity Funding scandal. This case well illustrates the lack of definitional consensus regarding computer crime. Because the Equity Funding case is considered by some to primarily one of securities fraud, rather than true computer fraud, many analyses of computer crime never mention Equity Funding, although it is arguably one of the most costly white-collar crimes ever perpetrated.

In the early 1970s, the Los Angeles-based insurance firm and mutual fund company programmed its computer to issue insurance policies on people who did not exist and then sell those fake policies to other companies through a system of reinsurance customarily employed in that business to spread actuarial risk and increase cash flow.[99] This was done to inflate the price of Equity Funding stock, which had begun to fall after a spectacular run-up in the early 1960s. The scheme grew over time to epic proportions. By 1972, 65% of Equity Funding's policies were fraudulent.[100] Fictitious policyholders, or persons already dead, were carrying $3.2 billion in life insurance. Some of the conspirators were skimming from the resale proceeds, and other conspirators were skimming from the skimmers.

It has been observed that, as computer crimes go, the Equity Funding fraud was not a particularly sophisticated one and would have been uncovered sooner or later, if only because there were just too many people involved.[101] The most effective computer crimes probably are the work of a single individual or at most a small gang. Moreover, because the fraud was conducted by management itself, there was little incentive to conceal the misuse of the computer from company officials. In the final analysis, Equity Funding was simply a gigantic Ponzi scam run amok.[102]

When the computer fraud is committed by someone from outside the victimized organization, embezzlement becomes theft. Here again, banks are a frequent target. In 1980, for example, the Wells Fargo Bank of San Francisco lost $21 million, allegedly to two boxing promoters who used a computer for illegal electronic fund transfers (EFTs).[103] In 1988, seven men were convicted of stealing $70 million from the First National Bank in Chicago through fraudulent EFTs.[104] In absolute terms, this is a great deal of money, but in relative terms, it hardly makes a ripple in the more than $1 trillion that is transferred electronically by American banks each day.[105]

Probably the best-known EFT case is that of Stanley Mark Rifkin, who stole $10.2 million from California's Security National Bank in less than an hour.[106] Rifkin was a computer programmer who was creating a back-up system for Security National's wire room, the bank's communication center from where between $2 billion and $4 billion dollars are transferred every day. The purpose of the back-up system was to allow the bank to continue making EFTs even if the primary system crashed.[107] Rifkin, of course, had to learn the system intimately and, as his education continued, he began to think about robbing the bank. On October 25, 1978, he stole an employee access code from the wall of the wire room, walked to a nearly telephone booth, and transferred the $10.2 million to a New York bank and then to Switzerland. The next day, the cash was converted into diamonds.[108]

Rifkin may have been a brilliant computer programmer, but he turned out to be an inept criminal. He was arrested 10 days later after attempting to sell some diamonds in Beverly Hills. He was convicted in March, 1979 and received a sentence of 8 years in federal prison.

More recently, beginning in the mid-1980s, officials in several states began uncovering a simple but alarmingly effective form of electronic bank robbery. An individual would open an account and eventually receive computer-coded deposit slips. Near the beginning of a month, he or she would then place some of those deposit slips on the counter where blank deposit slips normally would be. When customers unknowingly used them, the money would be deposited in the criminal's account. By the time the irate customers questioned their monthly bank statements, the thieves had emptied their accounts and were nowhere to be found.[109]

Another form of electronic larceny came to light in 1987, when nine Pittsburgh teenagers were arrested for computer fraud. They had made thousands of dollars in purchases using stolen credit card numbers. They had obtained these numbers by using their PCs to break into the files of a West Coast credit card authorization services, which provided them with a lengthy list of valid credit card numbers and expiration dates.[110]

More recently, Western Union discovered that hackers had made electronic copies of the credit and debit card information from over 15,000 consumers who transferred money on the company's web site.[111] In another case, online retailer Egghead.com had to notify its 3.5 million customers (including one of the authors of this book) that their financial information had been accessed by a hacker.[112] Other recent victims include the Internet search service RealNames, whose computer containing 20,000 credit card numbers was infiltrated.[113] Hackers also put thousands of stolen credit card numbers from creditcards.com on the Internet after the company ignored a $100,000 extortion demand.[114] America Online, the world's largest Internet service provider, has fallen prey to hackers who utilized a "Trojan Horse" to gain access to member accounts.[115] Even mighty Microsoft, maybe the most alluring of all targets, was hacked in 2000. Intruders, using a program called QAZ Trojan, were able to view highly confidential source codes for future software products.[116] Microsoft CEO Bill Gates has himself been a victim. A hacker recently altered three stories on the website of the *Orange County Register* (a large southern California newspaper), making one read that Gates had been arrested for breaking into NASA computers.[117]

In 1993, one of the most brazen computer crimes in memory occurred in Connecticut. Two ex-convicts built a homemade automatic teller machine (ATM), wheeled it into a shopping mall, and planted it there for 16 days. The bogus machine even contained money for some users, thus enhancing its legitimate veneer. But despite its clever masquerade, it was just a subspecies of Trojan horse, designed to copy secret access codes from customers' ATM cards. This allowed the criminals to withdraw more than $100,000 from banks in six states.[118] They were arrested 2 months later on a variety of fraud, theft, and conspiracy charges.

HACKING

In its original sense, the word "hacker," coined at MIT in the 1960s, simply connoted a computer virtuoso. "However, beginning in the 1970s, hackers also came to describe people who hungered to know off-limits details about big computer systems—and who were willing to use devious and even illegal means to satisfy this curiosity."[119] The pioneer hackers of the 1960s and 1970s probably exemplified sociologist Edwin Lemert's classic concept of primary deviance[120]—that is, their conduct would have been described by observers as norm violating. Of course, computers were so new then, there may have been few clear norms to violate. If their intent was not to destroy private files, could they be considered vandals? If their intent was not to steal data, could they be considered thieves? Perhaps the least ambiguous way to characterize them was as trespassers.

On the other hand, there was likely little, if any, of Lemert's notion of secondary deviance[121]—that is, no deviant self-identify on the parts of the hackers themselves. Indeed, their mastery of skills that may have seemed more magic than science to the general public endowed them with a sense of intellectual elitism. "[A]mong these young computer outlaws was a sense of superiority to the bureaucrats whose systems they could so easily infiltrate."[122] As one author, commenting on the first generation of hackers, has observed, "[T]o be a computer hacker was to wear a badge of honor."[123]

Most hackers display what Jay "Buck" Bloombecker, director of the National Center for Computer Crime Data, terms a "playpen mentality."[124] They see breaking into a system as a goal, not a means to some larcenous end.

> Sipping cola and munching pizza, they work through the night, often alone, their computers linked to the outside world by modems. They share their successes with confidants whom they often know only through voice or electronic messages. Many are teenagers whose parents don't know a modem from a keyboard.[125]

At least two categories of "playpen" hackers have been identified: creative "showoffs," who break into databases for fun, rather than profit; and "cookbook hackers," the most common category, defined as computer buffs who coast along the global Internet computer network without any specific target, twisting electronic door knobs to see what systems fly open.[126] The "recipes" used by the "cookbook" hackers generally are those that have been developed by the more knowledgeable "showoffs." Many of these recipes apparently are of gourmet quality. A security analyst for AT&T has estimated that less than 5% of intrusions into computer systems by outsiders are even detected, let alone traced.[127]

Hackers might be thought of as a deviant subculture. They ascribe to a set of norms, which apparently they take very seriously, but which often conflicts with the norms of the dominant society. They have their own peculiar code of ethics, known as the "cyberpunk imperatives."[128] For instance, they believe computerized data are public property and that passwords and other security features are only hurdles to be jumped in pursuit of these communal data.[129] A famous hacker known as The Knightmare has summed up this haughty creed: "Whatever one mind can hide, another can discover."[130] There is even an ultimate proscription: "Hackers will do just about anything to break into a computer except crashing a system. That's the only taboo."[131]

Another way of looking at young hackers is from the perspective of Sykes and Matza's well-known "drift" theory of delinquency.[132] Hackers might be viewed in this manner as fundamentally conforming youths who drift into occasionally deviant behavior through the use of such "neutralizations" as the claim that they are only trying to expose lax security systems[133] or merely trying to learn more about computers.[134] These may seem like lame rationalizations, but more than one young hacker has justified his misconduct on those very grounds.

Furthermore, even the most sophomoric intentions can go terribly awry. A group of seven Milwaukee high school students, devoted electronic joy riders who called themselves the "414" gang, learned this lesson in 1983. They were from all accounts nice young men—loving sons, Eagle Scouts, exemplary students. But, in the name of "fun-and-games," they managed to break into a file at the Los Alamos, New Mexico, nuclear weapons facility and also erase a confidential file at New York's Memorial Sloan-Kettering Cancer Center.[135] When they were apprehended, they denied any criminality in their actions. Their public statements seemed to be drawn directly from Sykes and Matza's inventory of neutralization techniques: "[I]t's not our fault" [denial of responsibility]; "We didn't intend harm" [denial of injury]; "There was no security" [denial of victim].[136]

Like the fabled sorcerer's apprentice, the 414s became intoxicated with their inordinate power and failed to contemplate maturely the consequences of their actions. This sort of irresponsibility has been the hackers' bane from the very beginning. If there is such a construct as *white-collar delinquency*, then teenaged hackers are its embodiment.

Beyond the "playpen mentality," however, there is a dark side to hacking, personified by a very different species of "stunt hacker" whose motivations are undeniably malicious. One such individual revealed this dark side in an article he wrote under the ominous pen name Mr. X:

> I can turn off your electricity or phone, destroy your credit rating—even take money out of your bank account—without ever leaving the keyboard of my home computer. And you would never know I was the one ruining your life![137]

If one doubts the plausibility of Mr. X's frightening boast, consider that in 1985 seven New Jersey teenagers were arrested for stealing $30,000 worth of computer equipment, which they had billed to total strangers on hacked credit card numbers.[138] Hackers have also invaded credit files[139]—including those at TRW, the nation's largest credit information storage system.[140] In 1985, a Houston loan officer utilized the bank's credit-checking computer terminal to steal the records of a Fort Worth couple. He used that information to open 21 bogus accounts in their name and ran up bills of $50,000.[141] Anyone who has ever been victimized in this manner has experienced the living hell of the credit pariah. If one's credit rating is sabotaged, one can no longer apply for a mortgage or loans of any kind. Even renting an apartment may become impossible.[142] As one victim has lamented, "There's only one problem with having good credit. Someone may steal it."[143]

Consider as well the career of "Dr. Demonicus." A bright young man with awesome computer skills, his lack of interest in academics landed him behind the counter of a fast-food restaurant after graduating from high school. His ambition, however, soon transformed him from a classic underachiever to a wealthy alleged felon. According to the charges in a federal indictment, he would scan telephone directories for the names of presumably well-heeled doctors and lawyers, then hack the local credit bureau for their credit card numbers. He was further accused of using those numbers to buy $200,000 worth of merchandise, which he would have delivered to vacant houses held by the Department of Housing and Urban Development. Later, like a postman in reverse, he would allegedly drive his daily route and collect his packages. As of this writing, Dr. Demonicus has not yet gone to trial. If convicted, he faces up to 50 years in prison.[144]

A journalist has offered a first-person account of his own brush with identity theft, also called "true-name" computer because the criminal adopts a real identity.[145] A hacker, 1000 miles away had pulled the writer's file from a credit-reporting agency.

> In minutes . . . he had a virtual summary of my life: past addresses and employers, Social Security number, credit card numbers, mortgage information, bank accounts and all the other personal data that appear on the credit reports for me and 160 million other Americans. Armed with that information, he was able to open nearly 30 separate loan, checking and credit accounts at banks, department stores electronics retailers, appliance outlets and other merchants. And he did it as fast as kids unwrap birthday presents.[146]

Using the pilfered credit, the thief went on a $100,000 shopping spree.

Identity theft is currently exploding.[147] The Federal Trade Commission reports that it receives about 1700 calls per week to it's hotline, 1-877-ID-THEFT.[148] The entry point for identity thieves are social security numbers, the obtainment of which is like batting practice to skilled hackers. Social security numbers have become a de facto national ID card, a purpose for which they were never intended. In the 1930s, revulsion at the Nazi's "Show us your papers" mantra led Americans to insist that the new cards be clearly marked "Not for Identification."[149] But, thanks to businesses seeking quick credit checks and bureaucrats seeking blind efficiency, social security numbers today have become a kind of electronic currency. And "[with] the onset of e-commerce, pressure on people to reveal their private Social Security Numbers has increased tenfold."[150]

As more and more personal records are stored electronically, the danger mushrooms. "For a few hundred dollars anyone can buy someone's complete medical history."[151] A Maryland bank was caught using stolen records to cancel loans of customers with cancer.[152] A Federal Trade Commissioner has declared, "It is now possible to capture and use information in ways that were unimaginable a few years ago. It's an incredible risk to personal privacy."[153] Recently, for instance, a 13-year-old girl copied the names and telephone numbers of former emergency room patients from the computer at the University of Florida Medical Center. As a prank, she telephoned seven of these individuals and falsely told them that they had tested positively for the AIDS virus. One young woman thought the joke was so funny that she attempted suicide after receiving the call.[154]

Many hackers seem to be petulant egomaniacs. For example, one hacker, who calls himself Garbage Heap, has bitterly complained to *Computer-World* magazine that his talent deserves more appreciation.[155] If respect is really his goal, then Garbage Heap might want to think about picking a new pseudonym.

America's Most Wanted "Geek"

The infamous case of Kevin Mitnick is a vivid example of how a hacker can degenerate from prankster to public enemy. Like many renegade hackers, he began his deviant career in high school by breaking into the school's main computer system. Later, he managed to hack into the central computer of the entire Los Angeles Unified School District. After dropping out of school in 1981, at the age of 17, he was arrested as part of a hacker ring that had stolen key manuals from Pacific Telephone. Mitnick was prosecuted as a juvenile and placed on probation. The following year, he was in trouble again. This time he used publicly available computers at the University of Southern California to break into numerous systems, including some at the U.S. Department of Defense. His probation was revoked, and he spent 6 months in a California Youth Authority facility.[156]

Up to this point, Mitnick arguably was still more brat than criminal. He had not yet stolen money or damaged data; but a manifest pattern of escalating havoc already was emerging. Exploring private off-ramps along the information superhighway may be a challenging recreation but it does not pay the rent, and as many hackers get older they become more profit-oriented.[157] In 1988, Mitnick, now 25, was arrested for repeatedly breaking into a computer software system at the Digital Equipment Corporation in Massachusetts. He copied the software, which had cost DEC more than $1 million to develop. He further cost DEC more than $4 million in downtime. As if this were not enough, Mitnick had also broken into the computer system at Leeds University in England by telephone, using the 16 unauthorized MCI long-distance telephone account numbers in his possession.[158]

A notable aspect to this case is the way Mitnick was portrayed both by the government and the media. He became the symbol of computer crime and the future shock paranoia it generates in society. Mitnick has been labeled "the Willie Horton of computer crime,"[159] a reference to the notorious rapist who was made the symbol of violent crime during the 1988 presidential election. Even a former hacking cohort of Mitnick, known as Susie Thunder, once declared, "He's really crazy. . . . He's dangerous."[160] He was denied bail and spent $7\frac{1}{2}$ months in jail awaiting trial—a very unusual fate for a white-collar criminal. So frightened were the authorities of Mitnick's skills and potential for electronic vengeance that all his telephone calls had to be dialed by others. Finally, Mitnick entered into a plea bargain and, in 1989, received a 1-year sentence to be followed by entry into a rehabilitation program for computer addiction.

By 1993, however, Mitnick was the subject of an intense FBI manhunt.[161] He was suspected of stealing software and data from a number of leading cellular phone manufacturers. In an ironic role reversal, it is further alleged that while a fugitive, Mitnick "managed to gain control of a phone system in California that allowed him to wiretap FBI agents who were searching for him."[162] One frustrated

(Continued)

agent said of Mitnick, "He should have been locked up long ago."[163] In a 1994 telephone interview with a freelance journalist, the fugitive Mitnick discussed why he was unable to resist the temptation of technology: "People who use computers are very trusting, very easy to manipulate."[164]

On February 15, 1995, Kevin Mitnick was arrested in North Carolina and accused of violating the terms of his probation by stealing an almost inestimable number of data files and at least 20,000 credit card numbers from computers.[165] He was indicted again in 1996 on charges of stealing millions of dollars in software.[166] Eternally unrepentant, he has summed up his baleful career in four words: "I love the game."[167]

Kevin Mitnick's placement on the FBI's Ten Most Wanted list underscores how seriously hacking is now treated by the criminal justice system. Between 1986 and 1992, only 9 of 129 computer criminals convicted in California courts went to prison.[168] Today, those same courts were handing out serious time. Hacker Kevin Poulsen, for example, recently was sentenced to nearly 5 years in prison for using his computer to block all telephone calls except his own—to California radio contests. Poulsen's manipulations enabled him to win two Porsches, two Hawaiian vacations, and $22,000 dollars in cash.[169]

In 1992, a group of young hackers, ranging in age from 18 to 22 and calling themselves by such exotic names as Phiber Optik, Acid Phreak, Outlaw, and Scorpion,[170] were arrested for corrupting the databases of some of the largest corporations in America. The MOD, alternately known as the Masters of Destruction[171] or the Masters of Deception,[172] allegedly stole passwords and technical data from Pacific Bell, Nynex, and other telephone companies, Martin Marietta, ITT, and other Fortune 500 companies, several big credit agencies, two major universities, and the Educational Broadcasting Network.[173] The damage caused by these hackers was extensive. One company alone, Southwestern Bell, suffered losses of $370,000.[174]

In what resembles a high-tech parody of urban gang warfare, the MOD apparently were motivated by a fierce competition with a rival "gang," the Legion of Doom.[175] Donn B. Parker, who has interviewed Phiber Optik,[176] noted the importance of one-upmanship in the hacker subculture: "Computer hacking is a meritocracy. You rise in the culture depending on the information you can supply to other hackers."[177] Phiber Optik (John Lee) has also gleefully boasted that he could commit a crime with just five strokes on a keyboard. He claimed, for example, that he could get free limousines, airplane flights, hotel rooms, and meals "without anyone being billed." Young Mr. Optik acknowledged, however, that his time in prison had been "no fun."[178]

One of the most disturbing aspects of malicious hacking involves the area of national security. A 24-year-old hacker known as Captain Zap was arrested in 1981 for breaking into the White House's computers. In 1983, a 19-year-old UCLA student used his PC to enter the Defense Department international communications system.[179] In 1991, a gang of Dutch hackers managed to crack Pacific Fleet computers during the Persian Gulf War.[180] Two young hackers broke into computers at the Boeing Corporation—a major defense contractor[181]—and later used their home computers to examine confidential government agency files.[182] More recently, an 18-year-old Israeli hacker was accused of the most organized attack ever on the Pentagon's computer system.[183] A report from the American military's inspector-general found "serious deficiencies in the integrity and security" of a Pentagon computer used to make $67 billion per year in payments.[184]

Even more alarming is a report released by the U.S. General Accounting Office in 1996, which determined that hackers had attacked Pentagon computer systems as many as 250,000 times the previous year and had gained entry in two of every three attempts.[185] The General Accounting Office concluded, "At a minimum, these attacks are a multimillion dollar nuisance to defense. At worst, they are a serious threat to national security."[186] Members of Congress have expressed great concern over such stories, calling for tougher sanctions and the federalization of all computer crime.

In early 1998, the Pentagon's computer networks were hit by what was described as the "most organized and systematic assault"[187] ever launched against them. Although no classified documents appeared to have been tampered with, a deputy defense secretary called the matter "a very serious long-term problem."[188] A few weeks later, two California teenagers, aged 16 and 17, were arrested by the FBI and accused of the cyber-attacks. The boys, who went by the code names Makaveli and TooShort, had used "sniffer" programs to intercept Pentagon passwords. They also had placed "back-door" programs in the military computers in order to re-enter at will.[189] They had leapfrogged from their local Internet Service Provider (ISP) into the Pentagon systems, as well as systems at the University of California at Berkeley, MIT, and two sites in Mexico.[190]

Makaveli and TooShort pleaded guilty to charges of juvenile delinquency and received 3 years probation and were deprived of any unsupervised computer access. They were also ordered to perform 100 hours of community service and pay $5525 in restitution.[191] This case strongly underscores the gaping moral schism between hackers and victims. The government stressed that the boys' activities "had the potential to disrupt military communications throughout the world."[192] TooShort's lawyer argued that the hackers had no malicious intentions and were simply trying to explore advanced computer systems. He added, "I call it the Mount Everest effect. They did it to prove they could."[193]

Cyber-attacks on the government are an escalating problem. It is now believed that at least six or seven government computers are hacked successfully every day. Moreover, many government systems are invaded for months before the violation is even noticed. Recently, for example, a group called GlobalHell defaced websites operated by the White House and the Senate.[194] In 1997, a hacker interfered with the transmission of medical data from astronauts orbiting the earth.[195] In 1998, a hacker gang, called Noid, broke into military computers and were able to download software that controls the positioning of satellites.[196]

Also in 1998, the leader of still another cyber-gang, called #conflict, was arrested on charges of illegally breaking into two computers at NASA's Jet Propulsion Laboratory (JPL) in California. One of the sites was an internal e-mail server, the other involved satellite design and mission analysis of future space flights. According to federal agents, the suspect, who uses the code name Rolex, had gained access to more than 800 computers, including many at major universities, and possessed 76,000 passwords. In an act of arrogant defiance, Rolex actually used one of NASA's computers to host an Internet chat room devoted to hacking techniques.[197]

The break-ins at JPL were so serious that "one of the computers had to be taken off-line and other permanently decommissioned."[198] In addition to Rolex, #conflict's membership included Blood, Endless, Zerox, and Bomb. Among their activities was a planned attempt to rig the online voting for the annual MTV Movie Awards.

Rolex was 20 years old when he was arrested. Thus, unlike Makaveli and TooShort in the NASA break-in discussed earlier, if he is convicted it will not be for juvenile delinquency; and he will not be spanked and sent to his room without his supper, or his modem. He faces up to 16 years in prison and a fine of $375,000.[199]

Indeed, the courts appear to be increasingly inclined to treat even teenage hacking as something much more serious than puerile mischief. In 2001, a teenage hacker with the code-name Coolio, was sentenced to 9 months to 1 year in jail for breaking into a Los Angeles Police Department website. Coolio defaced the LAPD site with pro-drug slogans and images, including one depicting Donald Duck with a syringe in his arm.[200] According to the U.S. attorney prosecuting a Massachusetts teenager who had caused a system crash at a local airport and knocked out tower-to-planes communication for 6 hours, "These are not pranks. This is not like throwing spitballs at your teacher."[201]

A 16-year-old Miami hacker was recently sentenced to 6 months at a juvenile detention center for invading NASA computers as well as Pentagon computers that monitor potential for nuclear, chemical, and biological attacks.[202] The young man told the court, "Never Again. It's not worth it. Because all of it was for fun and games, and they're putting me in jail for it."[203]

C A S E   S T U D Y

The Amazing Adventures of Mafiaboy

On February 7, 2000, a coordinated cyber-attack was launched against the world's busiest e-commerce sites. The attacks began on a Monday, with a 3-hour assault on Yahoo.com, one of the world's most popular websites. They continued on Tuesday, temporarily crippling many other major sites, including Amazon.com, eBay, Buy.com,[204] ZDNet,[205] and E-trade.[206] By Tuesday night the attacks had

(Continued)

spread to a leading media site, CNN.com.[207] The magnitude of the damage was estimated to exceed $1.2 billion.[208] Security experts and the companies themselves believed that the nature of the attacks seemed too similar to be coincidental.[209] The basic mechanisms for "denial-of-service attacks" (as they are known in cybercrime parlance) are relatively simple:

> The attacker hits a site so frequently that legitimate surfers can't get in. In distributed attacks the hackers take over a large number of computers connected to the Internet and force those computers to pound the site simultaneously. The subverted computers, called 'zombies,' respond to a single command from the attacker, who conveniently hides in anonymity while the zombies do the dirty work.[210]

When the FBI launched an international manhunt for the culprit or culprits, the chief investigator joked that "computer systems were so vulnerable that any technologically savvy 15-year-old could have been behind the sabotage."[211] He was exactly right. By the following week, the FBI had zeroed in on a suspect—a 15-year-old Canadian hacker, who calls himself Mafiaboy. The ninth-grader had left a careless digital trail along with boastful dialogue in Internet chat rooms.[212] He was known to Canadian cybercrime authorities but was generally not regarded as especially sophisticated or dangerous. "Mafiaboy is known in the hacker underground as a 'script kiddie,' a beginning hacker who simply downloads attack software ("scripts") offered by Web sites, rather than creating or modifying his own software tools."[213] Scripts are available on the Internet—if one knows where to find them—and require "only that a user identify a target and decide when to commence and when to quit the attack."[214] The rest is mainly automated.

Mafiaboy, a juvenile of course under Canadian law, was arrested in June on two counts of *mischief*.[215] In a curious although unrelated sidelight to the case, Mafiaboy's father (Mafiaman?) was also arrested and charged with conspiracy to commit assault. Canadian police, who had tapped the telephones at Mafiaboy's house, heard conversations between his father and another man about plans to assault a business associate.[216]

Like so many adult criminals, Mafiaboy's downfall was largely the result of his own need to feel important. "[He] left a trail of electronic bread crumbs, using Internet chat rooms to discuss his plans for attacking Web sites and then boast about having carried out the attacks."[217] He bragged that he had hacked big computers at major American universities, including Harvard and Yale,[218] and utilized them to bombard the websites. Some of the hackers who heard Mafiaboy's loose lips (or, in this instance, "loose fingers") called the FBI.

In January 2001, nearly a year after the massive cyber-attack, the now 16-year-old Mafiaboy pleaded guilty to what had been raised to 55 counts of mischief.[219] As of this writing, the case has yet to be adjudicated, but the young Montrealer could face up to 2 years confinement in a youth center.[220]

(Continued)

Mafiaboy's "mischief" serves as an unsettling reminder of how much harm can be inflicted suddenly on the "new economy" by a reckless teenager. A former federal prosecutor, now head of an Internet security firm observed, "If a 15-year-old in Montreal can do that much damage, imagine what a concerted effort by real professionals, industrial competitors or foreign governments can do."[221]

As for Mafiaboy himself, he has been called "your smarter-than-average computer geek with one foot in the doghouse and the other foot in the computer hall of fame."[222] A 17-year-old friend marvels, "He shut down all those companies. He's got my respect."[223] A neighbor, whose daughter played in the same basketball league as Mafiaboy, articulates an ambivalent reaction, "You wouldn't want your kids to emulate him. On the other hand, he'll probably get a great job with an Internet company and make lots of money some day."[224]

VIRUSES

Another reason for so much congressional anxiety is the threat of pernicious computer viruses—once a rare phenomenon, now, some claim, approaching epidemic proportions.[225] A virus is an instructional code lodged in a computer's operating system that is designed to copy itself over and over. A virus may have four different phases: (1) *dormancy*, in which the virus does not destroy files, thus establishing a false sense of trust and complacency on the user's part; (2) *propagation*, in which the virus begins to replicate; (3) *triggering*, in which the virus is launched by some occurrence, such as a particular date; and (4) *damaging*, in which the virus carries out the actual harm intended by its author.[226] Virus writers can be motivated by any number of factors, including a desire for recognition, the furtherance of a social-political cause, or a craving for personal revenge.[227]

A computer can be infected with a virus for months or even years without the user's knowledge.[228] When an infected computer comes in contact with an uninfected piece of software, the virus is transmitted. Computerized bulletin boards are major targets for infection.[229] Viruses can also be hidden on diskettes.[230] "In today's computer culture, in which everybody from video gamesters to businessmen trades computer disks like baseball cards, the potential for widespread contagion is enormous."[231]

For example, in 1988, the previously unknown Brain virus infected over 100,000 PC disks across the United States, including about 10,000 at George Washington University alone. Embedded in the virus was the cryptic message, WELCOME TO THE DUNGEON.[232] It turned out to be the creation of two brothers operating a computer store in Pakistan. Under a bizarre retailing philosophy that might best be described as schizoid vigilantism, they were selling pirated software, then punishing their customers for buying it.[233]

Computer viruses can range from annoying to devastating. Some viruses are relatively innocuous, such as the so-called Peace virus. Designed by a 23-year-old Arizona programmer, it showed up on the screens of thousands of Macintosh computers in 1987, flashed a single peace message, then erased itself and disappeared.[234] The Peace virus, like most American computer viruses, is derived from the first-generation Stoned virus, which announces its presence by printing the message "Your PC is now stoned," followed by a demand to legalize marijuana.[235]

Like Stoned, certain viruses might be described as playful:

> A rogue program that made the rounds of Ivy League schools featured a creature inspired by *Sesame Street* called the Cookie Monster. Students trying to do useful work would be interrupted by persistent messages saying: "I want a cookie." In one variation, the message would be repeated with greater and greater frequency until users typed the letters C-O-O-K-I-E on their terminal keyboards.[236]

Far less playful, however, is the Rock Video virus that entertains unsuspecting users with an animated image of Madonna, then erases all their files and displays the ignominious taunt, YOU'RE STUPID.[237]

Sadly, most viruses wreak havoc without even offering glimpses of glamorous performers as compensation. In 1988, Robert Morris, a Cornell University graduate student, planted the infamous Internet virus which infected a vast network of 6000 computers stretching from Berkeley to Princeton to MIT and caused at least a quarter of a million dollars in damage.[238] Morris became the first person convicted under the Computer Fraud and Abuse Act of 1986.[239] He was sentenced to 3 years probation, fined $10,000, and ordered to perform 400 hours of community service.[240] This comparatively light sentence was received with hostility by some members of both the computer community and the general public.[241] Sanctioning hackers remains a controversial topic, because they are characteristically so far removed from any popular criminal stereotype. Virus authors are often adolescents, "kids who are a little bit short on social ethics."[242]

On the other hand, Morris was not a kid, and his offense was hardly trivial. It has been reported that when his virus entered the computers at the Army's Ballistic Research laboratory in Maryland, system managers feared the United States had been invaded.[243]

Some viruses appear deceptively benign. In December 1987, a seemingly harmless "Christmas Tree" virus, designed by a German student, was loosed on the world-wide IBM network. Instructions to type the word "Christmas" would flash on a terminal screen. Users who complied with this innocent-sounding request tripped a virus that ultimately infected 350,000 terminals in 130 countries. IBM had to shut down its entire e-mail system for 2 days to contain the spread.[244] According to a 1993 survey of corporations conducted by the national Computer Security Association, viruses cost American businesses $2 billion annually.[245] One-quarter of the attacks require more than 5 days to correct.[246]

Viruses are sometimes placed in so-called logic bombs. In other words, the virus program contains delayed instructions to trigger at some future date or when certain preset conditions are met, such as a specific number of program executions.[247] An early example was the Jerusalem virus, so named because it was discovered at Hebrew University. This virus, which had the potential to cause a computer to lose all its files instantly, was set to go off on the fortieth anniversary of the State of Israel. Fortunately, the virus was eradicated well before that date.[248] Additional examples are the Joshi virus, which instructed the user to type "Happy Birthday Joshi" and was set to activate on January 5, 1993, and the Casino virus, set to activate on January 15, April 15, and August 15, 1993. Casino is a particularly mischievous virus which challenges the user to a slot-machine game and damages files if the user loses.[249]

Newer "stealth" viruses are much more complex than the earlier generations just described, hiding inside the computer memory whenever an antivirus scanning program searches the hard drive.[250] One of the worst of this new breed is the Mutating Engine virus. Unleashed by a Bulgarian known as the Dark Avenger, Mutating Engine can change form every time it replicates.[251]

According to the U.S. Department of Energy, so-called macro viruses now pose a significant threat to computers. An early macro strain, Concept, became the world's number one virus in just 6 months: "Faster than any in history,"[252] according to the head of the National Computer Security Association. Concept does not destroy data—it repeatedly flashes an annoying numeral onscreen—but it is very expensive to eradicate. "Other strains overseas, notably one called Hot, are more sinister, says William Orvis of CIAC [Computer Incident Advisory Capability]. 'How much do you want to bet that they'll come here?'"[253]

Macro viruses are actually "worms." They spread so fast because they can be transmitted through e-mail and because they infect documents, rather than programs. The Melissa virus shut down thousands of e-mail servers. It was sent in the form of a Microsoft Word e-mail attachment. It copied itself, then sent out a list of Internet porn sites to the first 50 names in the victim's e-mail address book. The original virus has been traced to a posting in the Internet newsgroup alt.sex. Melissa's victims include Merrill Lynch, Paine Webber, Intel, Compaq, Lockheed Martin, Indiana University, the North Dakota state government, the U.S. Department of Energy, the daily show-business newspaper *Variety*, and even *Security* magazine.[254]

On May 4, 2000, the notorious Love Letter virus (also dubbed the "Love Bug") began attacking an estimated 45 million computers in the form of an e-mail attachment with the subject line "ILOVEYOU." Other mutations were disguised as a joke or a Mother's Day gift order. When victims open the attachment, "it begins a destructive process that overwrites system and data files and downloads a password-thieving program from the Internet."[255] While Melissa only sends itself to the first 50 names in the victim's e-mail address book, the Love Bug is far more damaging. It sends itself to all the names in all the victim's address books and it destroys files, too.[256] Estimates of the damage to e-commerce were as high as $10 billion, surpassing even the infamous worm Melissa.[257] At least four classified systems in three separate defense agencies were contaminated. One of them was the top-secret National Security Agency.[258]

Almost immediately, electronic evidence convinced U.S. investigators that the Love Bug had originated in the Philippines. They soon identified a prime suspect, code-named Spyder; he was 15 years old.[259]

Probably the best-known criminal prosecution involving a computer virus was that of Texan Donald Burleson. He worked in the computer room of a Fort Worth securities-trading firm and was responsible for assuring that the company's password system operated properly. Burleson, a man of unconventional political beliefs, was a member of a fanatical tax protest movement. He argued frequently with his employers over the issue of federal withholding tax, which he insisted not be deducted from his paycheck. In 1985, when his employers learned he was planning to sue them to force them to stop withholding his taxes, he was fired. Before turning in his keys, the enraged Burleson planted a "worm." A worm is similar to a virus, except it is not contagious and only infects its host computer.[260]

A few days later, the director of accounting discovered to his horror that "168,000 commission records no longer existed on the computer—they had been deleted from the system!"[261] This, of course, would make the month's payroll impossible to calculate. Burleson was arrested and became the first person ever tried for sabotage by virus.[262] He was convicted in 1988, fined $12,000, and placed on 7 years probation.[263]

Except for precipitating the country's first "computer virus trial,"[264] the Burleson case does not seem, upon reflection, especially remarkable. Yet it was a media sensation. This may be explained in part simply by its timing. Just a few months earlier, "the Christmas Tree virus had embarrassed IBM and introduced readers to the concept of viruses as a type of computer crime."[265] For whatever reason, computer viruses subsequently have captured the public's imagination. Perhaps the term itself, with its mad scientist imagery and plague-like connotation, has generated a strange blend of fright and titillation. In any event, the media seldom underplay a virus story. Studies reveal that the level of public interest in viruses is a direct function of increasing or decreasing media attention.[266]

Critics of the media have argued that the virus "epidemic" has been overblown, and that there are more problematic computer crime issues worthier of public concern. They cite as evidence the "media hype" over the Michelangelo virus, which was supposed to infect millions of computers worldwide on March 6, 1992 (Michelangelo's birthday) and erase everything it touched. "In the end, scattered copies of Michelangelo were found—but nowhere near the millions predicted."[267] On the other hand, futurists predict that computer extortion, using the mere threat of a "stealth" virus, will be one of the major crimes of the twenty-first century.[268]

ESPIONAGE

Although computer viruses generally receive substantial media attention, statistics reveal that the misuse of computers as tools for industrial, political, and international espionage may be a cause for greater concern. A major FBI sting operation in 1982, for instance, targeted more than 20 employees of the Hitachi and Mitsubishi corporations of Japan who were suspected of stealing data from IBM.[269] Since then, industrial espionage by means of computer has exploded, increasing by a reported 260% between 1985 and 1993.[270]

In 1992, American companies suffered losses from computer-related industrial espionage exceeding $1 billion. It is estimated that more than 85% of these crimes were committed or aided by employees. Sometimes the motive is to settle a grudge. An NBC employee embarrassed *Today* Show host Bryant Gumbel by breaking into confidential computer files and publicly releasing a nasty memo Gumbel had written about his jovial colleague, weatherman Willard Scott.[271] Sometimes the motive is simply to make some money.[272] For example, employees with access to equipment and passwords can download strategic data or client lists and sell them to unscrupulous competitors. Because of the number of company insiders with such access, as well as the number of mercenary outsiders capable of breaking through passwords and cracking data encryption, many computer networks have proved vulnerable to spying and data theft.[273]

A Canadian-based computer company filed a $5-million lawsuit in 1992 against a former employee, alleging that he copies the firm's entire customer database and used it to establish his own competing business.[274] At about that same time, computerized trade-secret data were stolen from a California technology company.[275] Six months later, the head of a rival firm and a former employee of the victimized firm were indicted on charges of conspiracy and data theft.[276] These criminal indictments were considered precedent-setting because electronic industrial espionage cases traditionally had been fought in the civil court arena.[277]

Occasionally, industrial espionage and virus infection are melded into a single computer crime. Consider the plight of the head of a British technology company whose latest product was sabotaged with a software virus by a rival exhibitor during a 1993 trade show for potential customers. In an open letter to an industry journal, this embittered executive writes in a tone more suggestive of a street crime victim:

> There is a fair chance that whoever planted the virus is reading this. . . .
> Whoever you are, I understand why your bosses told you to do it.
> Nevertheless, it was vandalism, you tried to wreck something which is very valuable to me, and I won't stand for it. I'm going to pursue this with the full weight of the law, and if I ever find out who you are, may God help you.[278]

Computers have also been used illegally to obtain confidential information "that can help or hinder political candidates at all levels of government."[279] A dramatic example of political espionage occurred in New York in 1992. The medical records of a Congressional candidate were hacked from a hospital computer by an unknown party and sent to a newspaper. Those records revealed that the candidate once had attempted suicide, and this information soon was published in a front-page story. The candidate won the election, despite the publicity regarding her medical history, but the personal aftermath of this electronic invasion of her privacy serves as a reminder of why this book is as much about victims as villains. "It caused me a lot of pain," she would later say, "Especially since my parents didn't know."[280]

Computer crime in the area of international espionage is more difficult to assess. The covert nature of spying makes it hard to determine the actual number of incidents.[281] Moreover, because by definition this brand of white-collar crime often involves material classified as secret by the government, details of certain cases probably have been concealed from public scrutiny. A few stories, however, have been reported by the media. An arrest warrant was issued in 1996 for a 22-year-old former Harvard student who allegedly used stolen university passwords to break into American military computers from his home in Argentina.[282] When a young Washington-area hacker was arrested for breaking into a Pentagon computer system, he demonstrated his proficiency to investigators by cracking an Air Force system as they looked on. It took him 15 seconds.[283]

In 1994, two hackers broke into the computers at Griffis Air Base in New York. "By the time authorities became aware of their presence five days later, the pair had penetrated seven computer systems, gained access to all information in the systems, copied files—including sensitive battlefield simulations—and installed devices to read the passwords of everyone entering the systems."[284] The two hackers were able to use the pilfered passwords to launch more than 150 intrusions through the Griffis system into other military, government, and commercial systems. In one case, they accessed a Korean computer facility. For several anxious hours, investigators did not know if the installation in question was in North or South Korea. The concern was that the North Koreans would interpret an intrusion from an American military base as act of war. To the relief of authorities, the target turned out to be the South Korean Atomic Research Institute.[285] Eventually, one of the hackers was identified as a British 16-year-old, calling himself "Datastream Cowboy." He was quickly arrested. His accomplice and mentor, still at large and known only as "Kuji," is believed to be a foreign agent.[286]

The most widely chronicled computer espionage case is that of the so-called Hanover Hackers in 1989. A group of young West German men were arrested for selling American military data to the Soviet KGB in exchange for cash and cocaine. This spy ring consisted of five members of West Germany's notorious Chaos Computer Club, which had achieved European hacking stardom in 1987 by breaking into two NASA computers.[287] The most proficient member of the Hanover group, 24-year-old Markus Hess, had illegally accessed a computer at the Lawrence Berkeley Laboratory on the University of California, Berkeley campus and had used that computer as a launch pad to access U.S. military computers at sites such as the Pentagon, the White Sands Missile Range, and the Redstone Missile Base.[288]

Of the five original Hanover Hackers, the youngest one was not charged in exchange for testifying against his friends; another was burned to death in what was either a hideous suicide or a brutal murder. The remaining three who stood trial were convicted in 1990. Germany was reuniting, the

Cold War was winding down, and no one seemed particularly anxious to lock the defendants up and throw away the keys. That they sold classified computer data to the Russians was undeniable; but just how valuable those data were was not at all clear. For one thing, the relatively small payments they received did not seem commensurate with a major espionage success. When the U.S. National Security Agency assessed the damage, one of their scientists observed in a memo, "Looks like the Russians got rooked."[289] In one of those truth-is-stranger-than-fiction twists, that scientist was Robert Morris, Sr., whose son had released the Internet virus 18 months earlier.

The sentences handed down ranged from 1 year and 8 months to 2 months. All the defendants were put on probation, because their drug problems had, in the opinion of the judges, clouded their judgment and mitigated their responsibility.[290]

International computer espionage in the United States appears to be taken more seriously than in Europe. Indeed, it has been called the single most important security issue of the 1990s.[291] This concern may have originated in the early 1980s, when the Reagan administration withdrew funding for an international research center in Vienna, because its computers were tied to other research centers in both the United States and the Soviet Union. A fear was expressed that this connection might have allowed the Russians to log in to American computers and scan for classified data.[292]

Under the Computer Fraud and Abuse Act of 1986, it is illegal to tamper with any computer system used by the federal government or by government contractors. The act empowers the FBI to investigate the damage, destruction, or alteration of any data stored in such systems.[293] A representative case occurred in 1990 when personal computers at NASA and the EPA were infected with the SCORES virus, although the FBI ultimately turned this case over to local police because of difficulty in proving the suspect's intent to contaminate government computers.[294]

The first indictment of an American hacker on espionage charges occurred in 1992. The accused spy was a computer programmer from California. He allegedly stole secret Air Force flight orders for a military exercise at Fort Bragg, North Carolina.[295] Although the value of this material to the international intelligence community is dubious, the illegal possession of classified computer data is considered espionage, "even if no attempt is made to pass it to a foreign government."[296]

As equipment becomes increasingly sophisticated, the threat of computer espionage gets more serious. Compression technology has already reached a level where an ordinary digital audio tape (which can hold text as easily as music), purchased at K-Mart for under $10, can hold about 10,000 books in digital form. With current encryption technology, the entire computerized files of the stealth bomber, for example, could be completely and imperceptibly hidden on an ordinary music cassette.[297] Science may never be able to answer the venerable conundrum about how many angels can fit on the head of a pin, but it may be on the verge of discovering just how many classified documents can fit on an 8-track cassette of Pearl Jam's greatest hits.

PHONE PHREAKING

As noted earlier in this chapter, phreaking is the oldest and most durable form of electronic crime. Among the first generation of phone phreaks, some achieved legendary status: Jerry Schneider, the shameless self-promoter who appeared on the *60 Minutes* television program in 1976 and used his telephone to raise the overdraw limit on Dan Rather's personal checking account from $500 to $10,000, as millions of viewers looked on, including a stunned Rather;[298] Joe the Whistler, blind since birth but possessing perfect musical pitch and an uncanny ability to call anywhere in the world by whistling into a receiver;[299] the six-member gang, dubbed the "Gay Phone Phreaks" by the tabloid press, who placed an untraceable $19,000, 12-hour call to Indonesia;[300] and rising above them all was the king of the phreakers: Captain Crunch.

Captain Crunch (John Draper) took his "nom-de-phreak," of course, from the breakfast cereal with the direct-dialing whistle. At the time of the famous *Esquire* article,[301] Crunch was a 28-year-old walking encyclopedia of telephony. Despite three convictions, he has never considered himself a criminal and utilizes the same neutralization techniques as his hacker brethren, claiming he performs a valuable public service by exposing weaknesses in communication systems. Captain Crunch's early ambition was to phreak legally in the employ of the phone company. Reportedly, he was quite dismayed when AT&T hired his old friend Joe the Whistler, but not him.[302]

As a devoted member of the 1960s counterculture, Captain Crunch's favorite activity was spying electronically on the government. While he was serving a 4-month prison sentence in 1977, "He tweaked the coil of an FM radio with a nail file to listen in on guards' [telephone] conversations."[303]

It is not difficult to find a perverse charm in the exploits of Captain Crunch, or those of his co-legends. Even the austere Donn Parker acknowledges personal affection for the Captain.[304] But the blend of social immaturity and grand egotism that gave the pioneer phone phreaks their "Robin Hood" images also gives them the potential to teach their extraordinary skills (intentionally or otherwise) to career criminals. Thus, Parker argues, despite their individual charms, Captain Crunch and his crew are "dangerous."[305]

Furthermore, there now exists a second generation of phone phreaks, more dangerous—and less charming—than the first. A 1993 survey by Telecommunications Advisors, Inc. (TAI) reveals that 70% of respondents report that they have been victims of telephone toll fraud.[306] TAI interprets this finding as an indication that toll fraud may be a greater risk than previously believed. As the report observes, "[I]n 1990, 70% of respondents probably did not even know what toll fraud was, but it is now a thriving underground business."[307]

A 1992 published interview with a young phone phreak reveals once more that the familiar litany of neutralization techniques continues to be recited by members of the hacker subculture. This phreak insists that fraudulent calls are of no consequence to multimillion dollar corporations[308] (denial of victim). He further asserts that his actions express his anticapitalist political beliefs. This latter claim seems to flirt with hypocrisy, because he admittedly is making a considerable profit from his crimes.

How much money can an ambitious anti-capitalist make? A 1992 Congressional committee estimated that toll fraud costs $2.3 billion annually.[309] In 1993, the International Communications Association complained to the FCC that over a 5-year period, 550 incidents of toll fraud had cost its members alone $73.5 million.[310] Long-distance carriers are reluctant to reveal how much they lose each year to computer fraud, but one expert has estimated that losses now approach $4 billion, which is of course passed on to consumers as a covert "fraud tax."[311] In 1994, an MCI employee was arrested and charged with stealing more than 100,000 calling card numbers that were used to make $50 million worth of long-distance calls. Fifty million dollars was roughly 9% of MCI's net profits for the entire year.[312]

The rapidly growing cellular telephone industry has been hit particularly hard by illegally accessed calls; losses industry wide are now at $300 million per year and climbing.[313] The drawback to cellular phones is that they can be scanned easily using an inexpensive Radio Shack scanner.[314] The numbers can then be programmed into another cellular phone, making it a "clone" of the original phone.[315] Bills in the hundreds of thousands of dollars can be run up on unsuspecting victims.[316] Cordless telephones are also considered easy prey.[317]

Here are a few examples of recent toll fraud cases:

❖ NASA (a perennial target of hackers and phreakers), reportedly lost $12 million in unauthorized calls over a 2-year period as a result of computer tampering at its Johnson Space Center in Houston.[318]

❖ The chief of police of St. Croix, U.S. Virgin Islands, was convicted in 1992 of long-distance telephone fraud. He stole and used access codes from Caribbean Automated Long-Line Services (CALLS). CALLS claimed its losses may have been as high as $185,000.[319]

❖ Also in 1992, the Christian Broadcast Network lost $40,000 to a phone phreak who had hacked into its system and regularly placed calls to Pakistan.[320]

❖ In 1995, the Pacific Mutual Insurance Company lost $250,000 to toll fraud in 4 days and Avnet, a computer service company, lost $500,000 over one long weekend.[321]

One of the most polemic aspects of toll fraud is the assessment of responsibility for illegally accessed codes. In a battle of titans worthy of Greek mythology, Japan's Mitsubishi Corporation and AT&T counter-sued in 1991 over AT&T's alleged failure to warn its customers of the potential for unauthorized use of phone systems and Mitsubishi's failure to pay a $430,000 bill accumulated by 30,000 unauthorized calls allegedly placed by phreaks who had cracked their system.[322] The two companies eventually settled out of court in 1992.

In response to the issue of liability, American insurance firms and long-distance carriers now are providing coverage against toll fraud.[323] In

1992, for example, The Travelers Corporation offered $1 million in protection for $49,000, with a $100,000 deductible. At the lowest end, a $50,000 policy was available for $2500, with a $5,000 deductible.[324] These steep premiums exemplify some of the substantial indirect costs of phone phreaking.

Another cause for concern is the movement of phone phreaks into the area of industrial espionage. The proliferation of fax machines has created one of the easiest ways to steal corporate information. Computer criminals can now break into a phone line and produce a "shadow" version of the faxes received.[325] According to security experts, most corporations currently are vulnerable to data leaks resulting from telephone espionage.[326]

Finally, a common toll fraud scheme involves sidewalk "call-sell operators," who buy stolen out-dialing access codes and use them to make or sell long-distance calls, often overseas. The charges for these calls, which can run into huge amounts of money, later show up on the victimized party's telephone bill.[327] Some of the stolen codes are purchased from "shoulder surfers," persons who hang out at airports using their eyes and ears to steal access numbers from careless business travelers making long-distance calls.[328] Most of the access codes, however, are peddled by hackers who simply program their computers to "war dial"—that is, to dial "800" numbers randomly and rapidly.[329] They are able to call tens of thousands of "800" numbers in a single night and record all those answered by the "unique carrier tone of computers."[330] "Call-sell operators" then offer customers long-distance calls via the victim's phone system. These customers are often recent immigrants, too poor to afford telephones of their own, who wish to speak to relatives and friends in their native countries. In New York City, throngs of homesick foreigners reportedly line up in front of designated phone booths where well-dressed "call-sell operators" charge them $30 to talk for 10 minutes.[331]

Antifraud systems, such as voice-recognition spectrographs, now are appearing on the market.[332] Similarly, unauthorized computer access can be obstructed through biometric technology, including retina scanners, hand print readers,[333] and DNA identification devices,[334] as well as by the development of highly sophisticated "firewall" software that shields private information from hackers and thieves.[335] But computer criminals, as Gabriel Tarde might well have predicted, respond consistently to improved security technology with improved criminal technology,[336] and they will no doubt in time find a way to keep apace. This, in turn, will encourage still more advances in security and continue a never-ending cycle of thrust and parry.

NOTES

1. Tarde, Gabriel. *The Laws of Imitation*. Gloucester, Mass.: Peter Smith, 1962. This book was originally published in 1903.
2. Perry, Robert L. *Computer Crime*. New York: Franklin Watts, 1986.
3. Parker, Donn B. *Fighting Computer Crime*. New York: Scribners, 1983.
4. Rosenbaum, Ron. "Secrets of the Little Blue Box." *Esquire* 76, October 1979: 222–226.
5. Francis, Dorothy B. *Computer Crime*. New York: Dutton, 1987.

6. Parker, Donn B. "Computer Crimes, Viruses, and Other Criminoids." *Executive Speeches* 3, 1989: 15–19.

7. Perry, *op. cit.*

8. Meyer, Michael. "Stop! Cyberthief!" *Newsweek.* February 6, 1995: 36–38.

9. McEwen, J. Thomas. "The Growing Threat of Computer Crime." *Detective.* Summer 1990: 6–11.

10. "Security Survey Reveals Huge Financial Losses," *PC User.* April 21, 1993: 20. As testimony to how fast computer crime had grown, surveys conducted just 5 years earlier had reported the cost of most computer crimes to be less than $10,000 (Gilbert, Jerome. "Computer Crime: Detection and Prevention." *Property Management* 54, March/April 1989: 64–66).

11. *Ibid.*

12. Anthes, Gary H. "Security Plans Lag Computer Crime Rate." *Computerworld* 29, November 6, 1995: 20.

13. Wood, Chris. "Crime in the Computer Age," *Maclean's* 101, January 25, 1988: 28–30.

14. Sherizen, Sanford. "The Globalization of Computer Crime and Information Security." *Computer Security Journal* 8, 1992: 13–19.

15. Sykes, John. "Computer Crime: A Spanner in the Works." *Management Accounting* 70, 1992: 55. This article notes the exploits of England's "Mad Hacker." See also: Hearnden, Keith. "Computer Crime: Multi-Million Pound Problem?" *Long Range Planning* 19, 1986: 18–26; and Evans, Paul. "Computer Fraud—The Situation, Detection and Training." *Computers & Security* 10, 1991: 325–327.

16. Saari, Juhani. "Computer Crime—Numbers Lie." *Computers & Security* 6, 1987: 111–117.

17. Norman, Adrian R. D. *Computer Insecurity.* London: Chapman and Hall, 1989.

18. Hafner, Katie and Markoff, John. *Cyberpunk.* New York: Touchstone, 1991.

19. Bird, Jane. "Hunting Down the Hackers." *Management Today.* July, 1994: 64–66.

20. Rockwell, Robin. "The Advent of Computer Related Crimes." *Secured Lender* 46, 1990: 40, 42.

21. Sherizen, *op. cit.*

22. Major, Michael J. "Taking the Byte out of Crime: Computer Crime Statistics Vary as Much as the Types of Offenses Committed." *Midrange Systems* 6, 1993: 25–28.

23. Gold, Steve. "Two Hackers Get Six Months Jail in UK." *Newsbytes.* May 24, 1993: 1–2.

24. Sherizen, *op. cit.* See also: McHugh, David. "Hackers, Pirates Thrive in Russia's Tech Underworld." *USA Today.* June 1, 2000: 17A.

25. *Ibid.*

26. McGrath, Neal. "A Cleft in the Armour." *Asian Business* 31, 1995: 26.

27. Hooper, Narelle. "Tackling the Techno-Crimes." *Rydge's.* September 1987: 112–119.

28. Ceramalus, Nobilangelo. "Software Security." *Management-Aukland* 41, 1994: 26–27.

29. Sherizen, *op. cit.*

30. Major, *op. cit.*

31. McLeod, Ken. "Combatting Computer Crime." *Information Age* 9, January 1987: 32–35.

32. Daly, James. "Out to Get You." *Computerworld* 27, March 22, 1993: 77–79.

33. Bloombecker, J. J. "Computer Ethics: An Antidote to Despair." *Mid-Atlantic Journal of Business* 27, 1991: 33–34.

34. Flanagan, William G. and McMenamin, Brigid. "The Playground Bullies Are Learning How to Type." *Forbes* 150, December 21, 1992: 184–189.

35. Quindlen, Terry H. "IRS Computer Systems Are Catching More Fishy Tax Returns: GAO Praises Agency for Reeling in Electronic Cheaters But Urges Tighter Controls." *Government Computer News* 12, 1993: 67.

36. Diamond, Edwin and Bates, Stephen. "Law and Order Comes to Cyberspace." *Technology Review* 98, October. 1995: 29.

37. Torres, Vicki. "New Puzzle: High-Tech Pedophilia." *Los Angeles Times.* March 5, 1993: B3. See also: Snider, Mike. "On-Line Users Cheer Arrests for Child Porn." *USA Today.* September 15, 1995: 1D.

38. Wickham, Shawne K. "Crimes in Cyberspace Posing New Challenges for Law Enforcement." *New Hampshire News.* March 6, 1994: 1A. See also: "Cyberspace Porn Figures in Assault Case of Two Teens." *Bay Area Advertiser* (Clear Lake, Texas). December 6, 1995: 1–2; Villafranca, Armando. "Ex-Guard Jailed in Computer Porn Case." *Houston Chronicle.*

December 6, 1995: 25A, 33A; "Disgrace Follows Child Porn Bust." *aol.com.* November 7, 1998; Rather, Dan. "Cybercrime: Oh, What a Wicked Web We Weave." *Houston Chronicle.* January 28, 2001: 6C.

39. McEwen, *op. cit.*
40. McEwen, J. Thomas. "Computer Ethics." *National Institute of Justice Reports* (U.S. Department of Justice). January/February 1991: 8–11.
41. Chester, Jeffrey A. "The Mob Breaks into the Information Age." *Infosystems* 33, March 1986: 40–44.
42. *Ibid.*
43. Moore, Richter H., Jr. "Wiseguys: Smarter Criminals and Smarter Crime in the 21st Century." *Futurist.* September/October 1994: 33–37.
44. Kerry, John. "Where Is the S&L Money?" *USA Today Magazine.* September 1991: 20–21.
45. Major, *op. cit.*
46. Flaum, *op. cit.*
47. Anthes, Gary H. "Juvenile Charged with Internet Crimes." *Computerworld* 29, May 8, 1995: 12.
48. Spears, Gregory. "Cops and Robbers on the Net." *Kiplinger's Personal Finance Magazine.* February 1995: 56–59.
49. *Ibid.*, p. 56.
50. "On-Line Investment Schemes: Fraud in Cyberspace." *Consumers' Research.* 77, August 1994: 19–22.
51. "Identity-Theft Scam Targeted Celebrities." *Houston Chronicle.* March 21, 2001: 5A.
52. *Ibid.*, p. 5A.
53. Quoted in *Ibid.*, p. 5A.
54. "Pirates' Cheat Computer Software Industry out of Billions by Illegal Copying, Study Says," *Houston Post.* July 5, 1994: C9.
55. Simpson, Penny M., Banerjee, Debasish, and Simpson, Claude L. Jr. "Softlifting: A Model of Motivating Factors." *Business Ethics* 13, 1994: 431–438.
56. Marshall, Patrick G. "Software Piracy." *CQ Researcher.* May 21, 1993: 435–448.
57. Taft, Darryl K. "Software Piracy Rates Tied to Cultural Factors." *Computer Reseller News* 585, July 4, 1994: 69, 72.
58. *Ibid.*, p. 437. Copyright protection is one of the most complicated areas of international law. Some nations take a very terri-

torial approach, usually providing protection only for works first published in that country (Forscht, Karen A. and Pierson, Joan. "New Technologies and Future Trends in Computer Security." *Industrial Management & Data Systems* 94, 1994: 30–36).

59. *Ibid.*
60. *Ibid.*
61. Elmer-DeWitt, Phillip. "Invasion of the Data Snatchers." *Time* 132, September 26, 1988: 62–67.
62. "Punishment for Pirates." *USA Today.* February 6, 1995: 10A.
63. Francis, *op. cit.*
64. Marshall, *op. cit.*
65. Rosoff, Stephen M. "Who Carez About WAREZ?: The 'Other' Software Piracy." Paper presented to the Western Society of Criminology. Hawaii, May 2000. Presumably, the cracker subculture contains moles at game producers and within the technical side of the movie industry.
66. *Ibid.*
67. *Ibid.*, p. 25.
68. Zuckerman, M. J. "Businesses Bypass Law to Fend off Hackers." *USA Today.* June 6, 1996: 3A.
69. Parker, Donn. "Computer Crime." *Financial Executive* 2, December 1986: 31–33; Fields, Gary. "Reno Seeks Increased Cybercrime Reporting." *USA Today.* June 19, 2000: 3A.
70. Didio, Laura. "Security Deteriorates as LAN Usage Grows." *LAN Times* 7, 1993: 1–2.
71. Zuckerman, *op. cit.*
72. Roufaiel, Nazik S. "White-Collar Computer Crimes: A Threat to Auditors and Organization." *Managerial Auditing* 9, 1994: 3–12.
73. Quoted in Schuyten, Peter J. "Computers and Criminals." *New York Times.* September 27, 1979: D2.
74. Didio, *op. cit.*
75. U.S. Department of Justice. "FBI Uniform Crime Reports 1991" in *Crime in the United States 1991*, 1992: 13.
76. Nawrocki, Jay. "There Are Too Many Loopholes: Current Computer Crime Laws Require Clearer Definition." *Data Management* 25, 1987: 14–15.
77. Prasad, Jyoti N., Kathawala, Yunus, Bocker, Hans J., and Sprague, David. "The Global Problem of Computer

Crimes and the Need for Security." *Industrial Management* 33, July/August 1991: 24–28.

78. Brandt, Allen. "Embezzler's Guide to the Computer." *Harvard Business Review* 53, 1975: 79–89.

79. For a detailed consideration of electronic bank robbery, see: Radigan, Joseph. "The Growing Problem of Electronic Theft." *United States Banker* 103, June 1993: 37–38; Radigan, Joseph. "Info Highway Robbers Try Cracking the Vault." *United States Banker* 105, May 1995: 66–69; Sherizen, Sanford. "Criminologist Looks into Mind of High-Tech Thief." *Bank Systems & Equipment* 25, November 1988: 80–81; Sherizen, Sanford. "Future Bank Crimes." *Bank Systems & Technology* 26, October 1989: 60, 62; Sherizen, Sanford. "Warning: Computer Crime Is Hazardous to Corporate Health." *Corporate Controller* 4, 1991: 21–24; Sobol, Michael I. "Computer Crime Trends: A Brief Guide for Banks." *Bank Administration* 63, June 1987: 52.

80. Whiteside, Thomas. *Computer Capers: Tales of Electronic Thievery, Embezzlement, and Fraud.* New York: Thomas Y. Crowell, 1978.

81. *Ibid.*

82. Conklin, John E. *"Illegal But Not Criminal": Business Crime in America.* Englewood Cliffs, NJ: Prentice-Hall, 1977.

83. Cressey, Donald R. *Other People's Money: A Study in the Social Psychology of Embezzlement.* Belmont, Calif.: Wadsworth, 1971.

84. Touby, Laurel. "In the Company of Thieves." *Journal of Business Strategy* 15, 1994: 24–35.

85. Quoted in Flaum, David. "Scams Remain the Same Except Cons Now Use Newest Toys in Thievery." *Memphis Commercial Appeal*, August 14, 1994: C3.

86. Violino, Bob. "Are Your Networks Secure?" *Information Week.* April 12, 1993: 30.

87. Alexander, Michael. "The Real Security Threat: The Enemy Within." *Datamation* 41, July 15, 1995: 30–33. See also: Alexander, Michael. "Computer Crime: Ugly Secret for Business" (Part I). *Computerworld* 24, March 12, 1990: 1, 104; Ubois, Jeff. "Risky Business." *Midrange Systems* 8, July 14, 1995: 21–22; Stuller, Jay. "Computer Cops and Robbers." *Across the Board* 26, June 1989: 13–19; Carter, Roy. "The Psychology of Computer Crime." *Accountancy* 101, April 1988: 150–151; Clemons, Keith. "Computer Security: A Growing Concern." *Computerdata* 12, January 1987: 7; Lewis, Mike. "Computer Crimes: Theft in Bits and Bytes." *Nations Business* 73, February 1985: 57–58.

88. Cheswick, William R. and Bellovin, Steven M. "Secure Your Network: Keep the Riffraff Out." *Computer Reseller News* 609, December 12, 1994: 161.

89. Brandt, *op. cit.*

90. Hancock, Wayland. "Understanding Computer Viruses (Part II)." *American Agent & Broker* 65, December 1993: 61–63.

91. Prasad et al., *op. cit.*

92. Francis, *op. cit.*

93. *Ibid.*

94. *Ibid.*

95. Whiteside, *op. cit.*

96. Disgruntled employees are believed to be responsible for as much as 25% of all computer abuse (Harper, Doug. "Computer Crime May Be Close to Home." *Industrial Distribution* 83, February 1994: 41). A potentially serious threat may have emerged as a result of the severe staff cutbacks caused by the downsizing movement in corporate America, which has produced a growing number of angry and bitter workers (Daly, *op. cit.*). See also: Crino, Michael D. and Leap, Terry L. "What HR Managers Must Know About Employee Sabotage." *Personnel* May 1989: 31–38.

97. *Ibid.*, p. 93.

98. Kabay, Mich. "Is Your Boss Tampering with Data? *Computing Canada* 18, April 27, 1992: 29.

99. Seidler, Lee. *The Equity Funding Papers: The Anatomy of a Fraud.* New York: Wiley, 1977.

100. Kabay, *op. cit.*

101. Whiteside, *op. cit.*

102. *Ibid.*

103. Thornton, Mary. "Age of Electronic Convenience Spawning Inventive Thieves." *Washington Post.* May 20, 1984: A1, A8–A9.

104. Flanagan and McMenamin, *op. cit.*

105. Adam, John A. "Data Security." *IEEE Spectrum* 229, 1992: 18–20. See also: Sherizen, Sanford. "Future Bank Crimes." *Bank Systems & Technology* 26 1992: 60, 62.

106. Schuyten, *op. cit.*

107. Bloombecker, Buck. *Spectacular Computer Crimes*. Homewood, Ill.: Dow Jones-Irwin, 1990.

108. *Ibid.*

109. Thornton, *op. cit.*

110. Roberts, Ralph and Kane, Pamela. *Computer Security*. Greensboro, NC: Compute! Books, 1989.

111. "Hackers Hit Western Union Web Site." cbs.marketwatch.com. September 10, 2000.

112. Harris, Ron. "Online Retailer Egghead.com Hacked." schwab-news.excite.com. December 22, 2000.

113. *Ibid.*

114. *Ibid.*

115. "Vandals Hack into AOL With 'Trojan Horse' Virus." *Houston Chronicle*. June 17, 2000: 1C, 3C.

116. "Hackers Pry Into Microsoft Source Code." *Houston Chronicle*. October 28, 2000: 1C, 3C.

117. "Gates a Victim of Newspaper Hacker." *Houston Chronicle*. October 12, 2000: 2A.

118. "Duo Arrested in Phony Teller Machine Scheme." *Houston Chronicle*. June 30, 1993: 6A. See also: "Automated Teller Machine Fraud Grows, and Information Is the Key." *Wilmington News Journal*. June 13, 1993: G1.

119. Roush, Wade. "Hackers Taking a Byte out of Computer Crime." *Technology Review* 98, April 1995: 34.

120. Lemert, Edwin M. *Human Deviance, Social Problems, and Social Control*. Englewood Cliffs, NJ: Prentice-Hall, 1967.

121. *Ibid.*

122. Roush, *op. cit.*, p. 34.

123. Hafner and Markoff, *op. cit.*, p. 11.

124. Quoted in Beyers, Becky. "Are You Vulnerable to Cybercrime? Hackers Tap in for Fun, Profit." *USA Today*. February 20, 1995: 3B.

125. Carr, O. Casey. "Their Call Is to Steal Over the Phone, So Beware of Hackers." *Seattle Times-Post Intelligence*. September 8, 1991: E1.

126. "'Billy the Kid' Hacker Was not a Threat to Networks." *Houston Post*. February 17, 1995: 15.

127. *Ibid.*

128. Stephens, Gene. "Crime in Cyberspace." *Futurist* 29, September 1995: 25.

129. McEwen, J. Thomas. "Computer Ethics." *National Institute of Justice Reports*. January/February 1991: 8–11.

130. Quoted in Cizmadia, Robert A. "Secrets of a Super Hacker" (Book Review). *Security Management* 38, September 1994: 197.

131. *Ibid.*, p. 9.

132. Sykes, Gresham M. and Matza, David. "Techniques of Neutralization: A Theory of Delinquency." *American Sociological Review* 22, 1957: 664–666.

133. Kabay, Mich. "Computer Hackers Are No Vigilantes." *Computing Canada* 18, 1992: 36. The claim of helping to expose lax security is not limited to juvenile hackers. Recently, a 41-year-old man, using a so-called John the Ripper Internet password-cracking tool, broke into computers at NASA's Sonny Carter Training Facility in Houston. His lawyer argued that he had performed a service for his country by calling attention to security deficiencies. The prosecutor scoffed at this claim: "Patriots don't use 'John the Ripper' to hack into government computers." (Brewer, Steve. "Man Pleads No Contest to Computer Hacking." *Houston Chronicle*. October 9, 1999: 36A.)

134. Keefe, Patricia. "Portraits of Hackers as Young Adventurers Not Convincing." *Computerworld* 26, 1992: 33.

135. O'Driscoll, Patrick. "At 17, a Pro at Testifying on Computers." *USA Today*. September 26, 1983: 2A.

136. Quoted in Francis, *op. cit.*, p. 28.

137. Quoted in Francis, *op. cit.*, p. 35.

138. *Ibid.*

139. Van Brussel, Carolyn. "Arrest of N.Y.C. Hackers Hailed as 'Breakthrough.'" *Computing Canada* 18, 1992: 1.

140. Benedetto, Richard. "Computer Crooks Spy on Our Credit." *USA Today*. July 22–24, 1984: 1A.

141. Boyd, Robert S. "In Cyberspace, Private Files Are Becoming an Open Book." *Houston Chronicle*. December 8, 1995: 3G.

142. Kirvan, Paul. "Is a Hacker Hovering in Your Horoscope?" *Communications News* 29, 1992: 48.

143. Shaw, Stephen J. "Credit Crime." *St. Petersburg Times*. August 23, 1992: 1D.

144. Meyer, *op. cit.*

145. Perry, Nancy J. "How to Protect Yourself From the Credit Fraud Epidemic." *Money* 24, August 1995: 38–42.

146. *Ibid.*, p. 1D. For a similarly harrowing first-person account, see also: Sulllivan, Stacy. "Ensnared in the Nightmare of a Missing Identity." *Houston Chronicle.* May 30, 2000: A15.

147. Henderson, Robert B. "Cyber Crimes Increase in County." *Houston Chronicle.* December 20, 2000: *This Week*, 2.

148. "Feds Cracking Down on Fake IDs." *Houston Chronicle.* January 13, 2000: A3.

149. Safire, William. "'Identity Theft' Demands Legislation." *Houston Chronicle.* May 12, 2000: A42.

150. *Ibid.*

151. Rather, Dan. "What They Know About You Certainly Can Hurt You." *Houston Chronicle.* November 21, 1999: 6C.

152. *Ibid.*

153. Quoted in Boyd, *op. cit.*, p. 3G.

154. *Ibid.*

155. Hyatt, *op. cit.*

156. Rebello, Kathy. "'Sensitive Kid' Faces Trial." *USA Today.* February 28, 1989: 1B-2B.

157. Anthes, Gary H. "Taking a Byte out of Computer Crime." *Computerworld* 29, May 22, 1995: 56.

158. *Ibid.*

159. Bloombecker, *op. cit.*, p. iv.

160. *Ibid.*, p. 142.

161. The FBI has jurisdiction to investigate computer crime cases under the federal Computer Fraud and Abuse Act of 1986 (Betts, Mitch. "Recovering from Hacker Invasion." *Computerworld* 27, January 25, 1993: 43, 45). Federal authority to prosecute computer crimes was later expanded under the Omnibus Crime Bill of 1994 (Betts, Mitch. "Statute Outlaws Viruses." *Computerworld* 28, October 10, 1994: 65).

162. Markoff, John. "Computer Pirate Still Eluding the Law." *Houston Chronicle.* July 4, 1994: 13A.

163. *Ibid.*

164. Quoted in Littman, Jonathan. "In the Mind of 'Most Wanted' Hacker, Kevin Mitnick." *Computerworld* 30, January 15, 1996: 87.

165. *Houston Post,* February 17, 1995, *op. cit.*

166. Tamaki, Julie. "Computer Hacker Faces New Federal Charges." *Los Angeles Times.* September 27, 1996: A22.

167. Quoted in Littman, *op. cit.*, p. 88.

168. Bloombecker, Jay J. "My Three Computer Criminological Sins." *Communications of the ACM* 37, November 1994: 15–16.

169. "Hacker Case." *USA Today.* April 12, 1995: 3A.

170. Brown, Bob. "Indictment Handed Down on 'Masters of Disaster.'" *Network World* 29, 1992: 34.

171. Moses, Jonathan M. "Wiretap Inquiry Spurs Computer Hacker Charges." *Wall Street Journal.* July 9, 1992: B8.

172. Thyfault, Mary E. "Feds Tap into Major Hacker Ring." *Information Week.* July 13, 1992: 15.

173. Schwartau, Winn. "Hackers Indicted for Infiltrating Corporate Networks." *Infoworld* 14, 1992: 56. See also: Daly, James. "Frustrated Hackers May Have Helped Feds in MOD Sting." *Computerworld* 26, 1992: 6.

174. Schwartau, *op. cit.* See also: Daly, James. "Wiretap Snares Alleged Hackers." *Computerworld* 26, July 13, 1992: 1, 14; "Hackers Plead Guilty." *Wall Street Journal.* March 22, 1993: B2; "Hacker is Sentenced." *Wall Street Journal.* June 7, 1993: B2.

175. Tabor, Mary B. W. "Urban Hackers Charged in High-Tech Crime." *New York Times.* July 23, 1992: A1. For a detailed account of the rivalry between the Masters of Destruction and the Legion of Doom, see: Sterling, Bruce. *The Hacker Crackdown.* New York: Bantam Books, 1992.

176. Littman, Jonathan. "Cyberpunk Meets Mr. Security." *PC-Computing* 5, 1992: 288–293.

177. Quoted in Francis, *op. cit.*, p. 25.

178. Quoted in *Ibid.*, p. 25.

179. Meddis, Sam. "Lawmakers: Pull Plug on Hackers." *USA Today.* November 4, 1983: 3A.

180. "Blabbermouth Computers." *USA Today.* July 27, 1993: 8A. During the Gulf War, hackers reportedly invaded VAX systems using computer commands to search for key phrases such as "Desert Storm" and "Patriot Missile" (Forscht and Pierson, *op. cit.*).

181. "US Charges Young Hackers." *New York Times.* November 15, 1992: 40.

182. "Feds Charge 2 in Computer Break-in." *Government Computer News.* November 23, 1992: 8.

183. "Netanyahu Lauds Teen-Age Hacker Who Broke into Pentagon Site." *Houston Chronicle.* March 20, 1998: 21A.

184. Collins, Chris. "Hackers' Paradise." *USA Today.* July 6, 1993: 5A.

185. Zuckerman, M. J. "Hackers Crack Pentagon." *USA Today.* May 23, 1996: 1A.

186. Quoted in *Ibid.*, p. 1A.

187. "Pentagon Battling 'Systematic Assault' by Hackers." *Houston Chronicle.* February 26, 1998: 15A.

188. Quoted in *Ibid.*, p. 15A.

189. "Pentagon Teen Hackers Ordered to Stay Off Line." *Houston Chronicle.* November 6, 1998: 2A.

190. *Ibid.*

191. *Ibid.*

192. Quoted in *Ibid.*, p. 2A.

193. Quoted in *Ibid.*, p. 2A.

194. Goldman, John. J. and McFarlane, Usha L. "Man Accused of Hacking into NASA Computers." *Los Angeles Times.* July 14, 2000: A15.

195. *Ibid.*

196. *Ibid.*

197. *Ibid.*

198. *Ibid.*

199. *Ibid.*

200. Frothingham, Stephen. "Teen Hacker 'Coolio' Pleads Guilty." schwab-news. excite.com. January 2, 2001.

201. Quoted in: "Hacker Case." *USA Today.* March 19, 1998: 3A.

202. "Teenage NASA Hacker Facing Jail, Says It Wasn't Worth It." *USA Today.* September 25, 2000: 3A.

203. Quoted in *Ibid.*, p. 3A.

204. Richtel, Matt and Robinson, Sara. "Hacking Wave Hits High-Profile Sites on Internet." February 9, 2000: 1C, 12C.

205. Leonhard, Woody. "The New Internet Security Threat." *Smart Business.* July 2000: 102–118.

206. Iwata, Ed. "Digital Trail, Chat Room Boasts Led to Teen Hacker." *USA Today.* February 16, 2000: 3B.

207. Richtel and Robinson, *op. cit.*

208. Leonhard, *op. cit.*

209. Richtel and Robinson, *op. cit.*

210. Leonhard, *op. cit.*, p. 105.

211. Johnson, Kevin, Zuckerman, M. J., and Solomon, Deborah. "Online Boasting Leaves Trail." *usatoday.com.* June 7, 2000.

212. Iwata, *op. cit.*

213. *Ibid.*, p. 3B.

214. Anwar, Yasmin. "Hacker Known as Mischievous Kid." usatoday.com. June 7, 2000.

215. Johnson, Kevin and Zuckerman, M.J. "Teen Arrested in E-Commerce Hacks." usatoday.com. June 7, 2000.

216. "Hacker's Father Nabbed for Assault Plans." usatoday.com. June 7, 2000.

217. Johnson et al.

218. "Hacker 'Mafiaboy' Pleads Guilty." usatoday.com. January 18, 2001.

219. *Ibid.*

220. Johnson, Kevin. "'Mafiaboy' Trying to Stare Down Prosecutors." usatoday.com. December 5, 2000.

221. Quoted in Johnson et al.

222. Anwar, *op. cit.*

223. Quoted in *Ibid.*

224. Quoted in *Ibid.*

225. Powell, Douglas. "Mopping Up After Michelangelo." *Toronto Globe and Mail.* March 7, 1992: D8.

226. Greenberg, Ross M. "Know Thy Viral Enemy." *Byte.* June 1989: 175–180.

227. "Hot on the Trail of Virus Writers." *USA Today.* May 7, 2001: 3D.

228. Hancock, *op. cit.*

229. "Operations: A Viral Epidemic." *Credit Union Management.* 12, May 1989: 28.

230. Hancock, Wayland. "Computer Viruses (Part 2)." American *Agent & Broker* 60, September 1988: 14–18.

231. Elmer-DeWitt, Phillip. "Invasion of the Data Snatchers." *Time* 132, September 26, 1988: 63.

232. *Ibid.*, p. 62–67.

233. *Ibid.*

234. *Ibid.*

235. Powell, *op. cit.*

236. *Ibid.*, p. 66.

237. *Ibid.*

238. Bloombecker, *op. cit.*

239. Alexander, Michael. "Supreme Court Refuses Morris Appeal." *Computerworld* 25, October 14, 1991: 14.

240. Hafner and Markoff, *op. cit.*

241. Daly, James. "Virus Vagaries Foil Feds." *Computerworld* 27, July 12, 1993: 1. 15.

242. Powell, *op. cit.*, p. D8

243. *Ibid.*

244. Bloombecker, *op. cit.*

245. Daly, July 12, 1993, *op. cit.*

246. *Ibid.*

247. Adams, Tony. "Of Viruses and Logic Bombs (Part I)." *Australian Accountant* 58, May 1988: 83–85.

248. Elmer-DeWitt, *op. cit.*

249. Daly, James. "Viruses Ringing in the New Year." *Computerworld* 27, 1992: 79.

250. Hyatt, Josh. "Computer Killers." *Boston Globe*. March 3, 1992: 35.

251. Powell, *op. cit.*

252. Kim, James. "Virus Strain New 'Hazard' to Computers." *USA Today*. March 1–3, 1996: 1A.

253. Quoted in *Ibid.*, p. 1A.

254. Kornblum, Janet. "Widespread Melissa Virus Snarls E-Mail Servers." *USA Today*. March 30, 1999: 1B.

255. Silverman, Dwight. "PC Users Left Lovestruck by Vicious Virus." *Houston Chronicle*. May 5, 2000: 1A, 18A.

256. *Ibid.*

257. *Ibid.*

258. "FBI Says It Has ID'd Virus Suspect." www.msnbc.com. May 5, 2000.

259. *Ibid.*

260. Garfinkel, Simson L. "Lax Security Lets Hackers Attack." *Christian Science Monitor*. October 13, 1989: 12–13.

261. Bloombecker, *op. cit.*

262. Lewyn, Mark. "First 'Computer Virus' Trial Starts Today." *USA Today*. September 6, 1988: 3B.

263. Lewyn, Mark. "Computer Verdict Sets 'Precedent.'" *USA Today*. September 27, 1988: 1A.

264. Joyce, Edward J. "Time Bomb: Inside the Texas Virus Trial." *Computer Decisions* 20, December 1988: 38–43.

265. Bloombecker, *op. cit.*, p. 104.

266. Zalud, Bill. "Doing the Virus Hustle." *Security* 27, 1990: 42–44.

267. Burgess, John. "Viruses: An Overblown Epidemic?" *Washington Post*, December 30, 1992: F1, F3.

268. Moore, *op. cit.*

269. Parker, 1983, *op. cit.*

270. Lee, Moon. "The Rise of the Company Spy." *Christian Science Monitor*. January 12, 1993: 7.

271. Lopez, Ed. "Can Your Computer Keep Secrets?" *Miami Herald*. March 13, 1989: Business Section, p. 1.

272. Rothfeder, Jeffrey. "Holes in the Net." *Corporate Computing* 2, 1993: 114–118.

273. Violino, *op. cit.*

274. Buchok, James. "$5M Suit Filed Over Database Copying Claim." *Computing Canada* 18, 1992: 1–2.

275. O'Connor, Rory J. "High-Tech Cops Wade Through Digital Dump of Information." *San Jose Mercury News*, October 24, 1992: 10D-11D.

276. Groves, Martha. "2 Indicted on Trade-Secret Theft Charges." *Los Angeles Times*. March 5, 1993: D1.

277. Ratcliffe, Mitch. "Symantec Execs Face Felony Rap in Borland Case." *MacWEEK* 7, 1993: 1–2.

278. "Jules." "On the Use of Weapons." *EXE* 10, 1993: 52–53.

279. Forcht and Pierson, *op. cit.*, p. 32.

280. Hasson, Judi. "Access to Medical Files Reform Issue." *USA Today*. July 27, 1993: 1A–2A. In 1995, legislation was introduced in the U.S. Senate aimed at protecting the privacy of patients' health records. The senator who sponsored the bill argued, "Doctors and nurses and pharmacists may know things about us we don't even tell our spouses or friends." (Quoted in Boyd, *op. cit.*, p. 3G).

281. Lee, *op. cit.*

282. Rosenberg, Carol. "Argentine Unmasked as Computer Hacker." *Houston Chronicle*. March 30, 1996: 8A.

283. Roush, *op. cit.*

284. Zuckerman, M. J. "Hacker Pair Illustrate Pentagon's Vulnerability." *USA Today*. May 23, 1996: 3A.

285. *Ibid.*

286. *Ibid.*

287. Hafner and Markoff, *op. cit.*

288. Stoll, Clifford. *The Cuckoo's Egg*. New York: Doubleday, 1989.

289. Hafner and Markoff, *op. cit.*

290. Stoll, *op. cit.*

291. *Ibid.*

292. Hafner and Markoff, *op. cit.*

293. Belts, Mitch. "Recovering From Hacker Invasion." *Computerworld* 27, 1993: 45.

294. "Dallas Police Investigate Suspect in Spreading of Computer Virus." *Houston Post*. December 29, 1990: 19.

295. Markoff, John. "Hacker Indicted on Spy Charges." *New York Times*. December 8, 1992: 13.

296. *Ibid.*, p. 13.

297. Kelly, Kevin. "Cyberpunks, E-Money, and the Technologies of Disconnection." *Whole Earth Review*. Summer 1993: 40–59.

298. Bloombecker, *op. cit.*

299. Parker, 1983, *op. cit.*

300. *Ibid.*

301. Rosenbaum, *op. cit.*

302. Parker, 1983, *op. cit.*

303. *Ibid.*

304. *Ibid.*

305. *Ibid.*, p. 180.

306. Daly, James. "Toll Fraud Growing." *Computerworld* 27, 1993: 47–48.

307. *Ibid.*, p. 47.

308. Herman, Barbara. "Yacking with a Hack: Phone Phreaking for Fun, Profit, & Politics." *Teleconnect* 10, 1992: 60–62.

309. Quinn, Brian. "$2.3 Billion: That's About How Much Toll Fraud is Costing Us a Year (Maybe More)." *Teleconnect* 10, 1992: 47–49. See also: Taff, Anita. "Users Call for Toll Fraud Laws to Distribute Losses." *Network World* 9, 1992: 27–28.

310. Dodd, Annabel. "When Going the Extra Mile Is Not Enough." *Network World* 10, 1993: 49–50.

311. Titch, Steven. "Get Real About Fraud." *Telephony* 227, October 17, 1994: 5.

312. *Ibid.*

313. McMenamin, Brigid. "Why Cybercrooks Love Cellular." *Forbes* 150, 1993: 189.

314. Panettieri, Joseph C. "Weak Links: For Corporate Spies, Low-Tech Communications Are Easy Marks." *Information Week.* August 10, 1992: 26–29.

315. Flaum, *op. cit.*

316. Kapor, Mitchell. "A Little Perspective, Please." *Forbes* 15, June 21, 1993: 106,

317. *Ibid.*

318. Rill, Derick. "Hackers Reach Out and Touch NASA." *Houston Post.* December 6, 1990: A22.

319. Luxner, Larry. "V.I. Official Convicted in Fraud Case." *Telephony* 222, 1992: 20–22.

320. Lewyn, Mark. "Phone Sleuths Are Cutting Off the Hackers: Corporations and Phone Companies Join to End Long-Distance Fraud." *Business Week.* July 13, 1992: 134.

321. Falconer, Tim. "Cyber Crooks." *CA Magazine* 128, December 1995: 12–17.

322. "AT&T, Mitsubishi Settle Phone Suit." *Washington Post.* October 13, 1992: C3.

323. Daly, James. "Get Thee Some Security." *Computerworld* 27, 1993: 31–32. See also: Daly, James. "Out to Get You." *Computerworld* 27, 1993: 77–79.

324. Brown, Bob. "Insurer Adds Phone Fraud Protection." *Network World* 9, 1992: 1–2.

325. Panettieri, *op. cit.*

326. *Ibid.*

327. Urbois, Jeff. "Saving Your Company From Telephone Fraud." *MacWEEK* 6, 1992: 22.

328. Marvin, Mary Jo. "Swindles in the 1990s: Con Artists Are Thriving." *USA Today Magazine.* September 1994: 80–84.

329. Colby, Richard. "Anatomy of a Toll Fraud." *Portland Oregonian.* July 5, 1992: 1.

330. Jahnke, Art. "The Cops Come to Cyberspace." *Boston Magazine.* November 1990: 90.

331. *Ibid.*

332. Quinn, *op. cit.*

333. Falconer, *op. cit.*

334. Stephens, *op. cit.*

335. Cheswick, William R. and Bellovin, Steven M. *Firewalls and Internet Security: Repelling the Wily Hacker.* Reading, Mass.: Addison-Wesley, 1994.

336. For example, criminologist Gene Stephens has warned that the development of virtual-reality technology portends fantastic new varieties of computer fraud: "In the future, a virtual-reality expert could create a hologram in the form of a respected stockbroker or real estate broker, then advise clients in cyberspace to buy certain stocks, bonds, or real estate. Unsuspecting victims acting on the advice might later find that they had enlarged the coffers of the virtual-reality expert, while buying worthless or nonexistent properties" (Stephens, *op. cit.*, p. 27).

Conclusions

Larry the Liquidator: We have a responsibility. A responsibility to our employees, to our community. What will happen to them? I got two words for that: Who cares?

From *Other People's Money* (1991). Screenplay by Alvin Sargent.

C rime committed within a privileged class was a favorite dramatic theme of Shakespeare. Yet even the sapient Bard seemed at times perplexed by the enigma of elite corruption:

O, that deceit should dwell
In such a gorgeous palace!

Romeo and Juliet. Act III, Scene 2[1]

In the preceding chapters, we have explored many corrupt "palaces"—from the lavish offices of predaceous swindlers, to the ornate cathedrals of religious hucksters, to the stately chambers of porcine legislators. By now it may seem that the authors have endeavored to document a simple fact: People are basically greedy and dishonest and, given half a chance, will steal anything they can. Such an interpretation, however, would be far from accurate. Most people, most of the time, do *not* engage in fraud, embezzlement, bribery, and cover-ups. Rather, these acts involve persons occupying certain societal roles and transpire only under certain conditions. In this final chapter, we will consider some of the factors that give rise to white-collar criminality, along with some changes that need to be made in order to control it.

We will also re-examine both official and public responses to white-collar crime. Many commentators have suggested that white-collar crime flourishes because of a generally tepid reaction by law enforcement and other government agencies. Why does it seem that so many upperworld criminals are never brought to justice? Why do those few who are sanctioned seem to receive punishments so remarkably lenient? Moreover, why do convicted white-collar offenders suffer so little of the stigma and opprobrium that the citizenry attaches to "common" criminals? These are important questions that need to be addressed.

We will investigate, too, the consequences of white-collar crime. We briefly noted some of the injuries inflicted by these offenses. Here we expand that discussion, focusing on the human and environmental destruction, the economic costs, and the social damage wrought.

CAUSES OF WHITE-COLLAR CRIME

Today, just as Sutherland observed more than a half-century ago, scholarly theories of crime still overwhelmingly emphasize street crimes and the characteristics of those who commit them. Much effort has gone into searching for the peculiar physiological or psychological traits that differentiate the criminal from the noncriminal—from Lombroso's early notion of the "born" criminal,[2] to Freud's concept of the underdeveloped conscience,[3] to more recent attempts to locate violent lawbreakers at the low end of the IQ distribution curve.[4] A review of such literature reveals that white-collar offenders generally are left out of the theoretical picture.

Moreover, conventional theories of crime often have a tautological quality in that they define criminality in terms of the same factors they posit as causes. If crime is defined as acts committed by young, low-income males who score low in IQ tests, then explaining those acts through theories that stress age, poverty, and cognitive capacity is not very illuminating. Furthermore, the fact that upperworld criminals are typically older, more affluent, and superior in measured intelligence raises questions that cannot be answered by such circular reasoning. The elucidation of elite criminality requires a revised definition of crime and a higher level of analysis.[5]

Such an approach is not concerned with explanations that focus on "types" of people. It is assumed, in other words, that white-collar criminals are not significantly different, in terms of their personality or psychological make-up, than other people. Therefore, one need not attempt to create a profile of the "typical" white-collar criminal. Indeed, one of the striking things about white-collar offenders is how similar they are to "respectable" members of society.

As we have seen, the epidemic of financial scandals that scarred the 1980s spread its infection across Washington, Wall Street, and even the once-staid S & L industry. Was this, as Chapter 6 suggests in its examination of insider trading, the inevitable outgrowth of a "greed culture" that dominated American society during that decade? Culture, from the sociological viewpoint, is certainly important; however, but many sociologists are uncomfortable with purely cultural explanations of behavior, preferring instead to look for underlying social structural causes. They study the structural relationships that exist among individuals within the context of societies, institutions, and organizations.

Thus, in attempting to identify the causes of white-collar crime, we will focus on three basic levels of sociological analysis. We will see how *societies, institutions,* and *organizations* generate the opportunity, motives, and means for white-collar criminality.

Societal Causes

This is the level of analysis in which cultural explanations of white-collar crime are rooted. Of course, all criminal acts are committed by individuals. But as sociologists emphasize, individual decisions are always made in larger societal contexts that present and provide support for particular options, making behavior that might otherwise seem unethical or unlawful appear as reasonable and legitimate. Ironically, when individuals engage in white-collar crime, although they are breaking the law, they are often *conforming* to cultural values, such as the accumulation of wealth.

In 1938, the noted American sociologist, Robert Merton, published an article that was to become famous, entitled "Social Structure and Anomie," in which he wrote: "[C]ontemporary American culture continues to be characterized by a heavy emphasis on wealth as a basic symbol of success, without a corresponding emphasis on the legitimate avenues on which to mark towards this goal."[6] At the same time, in Merton's view, American culture places negative sanctions on those who fail to achieve material success, attributing their failure to personal deficiencies and character flaws such as laziness. Merton observed that one response to this pressure is for certain individuals to turn to more "innovative" means to succeed, including, in some cases, criminal activities.[7] It is very significant that, in Merton's formulation, the standard of material success is not objective, but exists on a sliding scale, so that even the relatively well-off may feel their aspirations are blocked and may thus resort to crime to achieve culturally-defined goals.

In a similar vein, criminologist James W. Coleman has written more recently that the ultimate sources of white-collar criminality lie in the "culture of competition" that pervades American society. Coleman describes our industrial economy as one that includes a market structure which not only produces profits and losses, but winners and losers.[8] The result is a "win at any cost" morality that encourages even the scrupulous entrepreneur or executive to bend the rules—or to engage in outright fraud and deception—in order to stay ahead of the competition. And while these pressures may be found in any society that produces "surplus wealth,"—that is, wealth beyond what is required for subsistence—they are felt most acutely in advanced capitalist societies like ours, where upward mobility is regarded as a right.

These cultural views on the virtue of materialism also find support in economic theories, most notably in the writings of the eighteenth century philosopher Adam Smith. In his classic *The Wealth of Nations* (1776), Smith wrote:

> It is not from the benevolence of the butcher, the brewer, or the baker, that we expect our dinner, but from their regard to their own interest. We address ourselves, not to their humanity but to their self-love, and never talk to them of our own necessities but of their advantages.[9]

To Smith, it was this natural pursuit of self-interest that created, in his famous phrase, "the invisible hand of the marketplace" and ensured social order and prosperity. More than 200 years later, Ivan Boesky, whose criminal exploits are chronicled in Chapter 6, echoed the same sentiments in his commencement speech to the graduating class of the University of California business school: "You can be greedy and still feel good about yourself."[10]

Adam Smith's extolment of the individual accumulation of wealth has been refined further in contemporary economics, most prominently by Milton Friedman. From the perspective of Friedman and his apostles, people are "utility maximizers" guided by the rational pursuit of self-interest in free markets. In Friedman's opinion, concepts like "the social responsibility of business" are oxymorons, because corporations should have but one goal: to make a profit.[11]

Far from being an esoteric abstraction, known only to a select group of academics, this acquisitive creed is transmitted to the real world of commerce through business schools, where future executives are indoctrinated with its self-justifying precepts. Studies of MBA students have found that they often internalize the values implicit in Friedman's economic vision. One survey of graduate business students reported that "many students were willing to do whatever was necessary to further their own interests, with little or no regard for fundamental moral principles."[12]

Neoclassical economics provides individuals with ready-made rationalizations for their behavior. This is what sociologist C. Wright Mills referred to as "vocabularies of motives," the verbal means by which people can justify and account for their behavior.[13] These accounts can be used to explain away criminal acts of all sorts. White-collar offenders frequently employ what theorists Gresham Sykes and David Matza call "techniques of neutralization,"[14] mechanisms that allow them to annul any potential guilt or internal conflict stemming from conduct on their part that breaks laws to which they claim ostensible allegiance. A 1987 marketing study concluded that neutralization plays a major role in unethical business practices.[15]

The five commonly recognized neutralization techniques are:[16]

1. *Denial of Responsibility.* Offenders argue that they are not personally accountable for their actions because of overriding factors beyond their control. For example, ghetto price-gougers typically justify usurious interest rates on the grounds that low-income consumers are "deadbeats."
2. *Denial of Injury.* Offenders contend that their misconduct causes no direct suffering. For example, producers of the rigged television quiz shows insisted

that they merely had enhanced the dramatic appeal of innocuous programs designed only to entertain.

3. *Denial of Victim.* Offenders claim that violated parties deserved whatever happened. For example, many computer hackers maintain that anyone leaving confidential data files unprotected is really at fault for any subsequent break-ins.

4. *Appeal to Higher Loyalties.* Offenders depict their conduct as the by-product of an attempt to actualize a higher value. For example, Richard Nixon and Oliver North portrayed their respective crimes as acts of patriotism.

5. *Condemning the Condemners.* Offenders seek to turn the tables on their accusers by claiming to be the true victims. For example, S & L crook Charles Keating repeatedly blamed regulators, prosecutors, politicians, journalists, and just about everyone else—everyone, that is, except himself.

In their avowals of innocence, corporate criminals also draw on what has been termed the "folklore of capitalism"[17] to recast themselves as misunderstood visionaries or persecuted dissidents. At the zenith of his career when he was moving billions of dollars through the economy, junk bond impresario Michael Milken was fond of portraying himself as an agent of social change, a "social engineer" whose activities were restructuring society.[18]

In a similar manner, some white-collar criminals try to evoke images of the frontier. They liken themselves to pathfinders, blazing new trails through unchartered business terrain. This theme was sounded by a pair of notorious environmental criminals in an interview they gave from federal prison. Prior to their incarceration, the Colbert brothers ran a successful company which purchased toxic chemical wastes from American manufacturers and then illegally dumped them in underdeveloped countries. In their interview, the Colberts steadfastly denied any guilt:

> "We were, in a sense, innovators ahead of the times. . . . We're basically pioneers in the surplus chemical business, which is something that's a necessary business for society."[19]

Institutional Causes

Although culture may provide the rationalizations for white-collar crime, specific institutions provide the means and opportunities. Not all industries are contaminated by fraud. For instance, higher education, an institution with which the authors are intimately familiar, experiences very little fraud (with the exception of rare cases of plagiarism and falsified research) simply because there is very little to be gained through deception. On the other hand, industries like the popular music business (Chapter 5), where sales for a single album may reach many millions of dollars, afford considerable incentive for bribery and corruption. At the same time, the unregulated character of the record industry and the individualistic basis of decision making by music broadcasters also provide ample opportunity for illegal conduct. Thus, certain industries are structured in such a way as to provide both the incentives and the opportunities for white-collar crime and, therefore, one must examine that structure to discover root causes.

The concept of "criminogenic industries" is used to describe the factors that facilitate fraud in industries like the music business. Needleman and Needleman state that the defining feature of criminogenic industries is that "their internal structures—economic, legal, organizational and normative—play a role in generating criminal activity within the system, independent at least to some degree from the criminal's personal motives."[20] The automobile industry, for example, has been described as "criminogenic" because it has a market structure characterized by a high concentration of manufacturers who exert control over the distribution process[21] and because excessive pressures from manufacturers on dealers to increase sales[22] create the conditions that give rise to extensive fraud and abuse at the retail level. Likewise, the largely unregulated and decentralized nature of automotive repair makes it another prime area for deceptive practices. As we saw in Chapter 2, numerous investigations have found that overcharging, billing for unnecessary work, and the sale of phantom parts are common practices at auto repair shops around the country—findings that may come as no surprise to any car owner who has ever left a mechanic's shop feeling pummeled by the bill.

One of the clearest illustrations of institutional criminogenesis was the debasement of Wall Street in the 1980s. The "merger mania" of the era was orchestrated by investment banks and law firms whose members were privy to valuable information about impending deals. The restricted nature of that information and the tremendous profits it could yield created both the opportunity and the incentive for insider trading.

Organizational Causes

In many white-collar crimes, the motivation is straightforward—individual material gain. This would be the case, for example, when a Sheraton Corporation food buyer recently was sentenced to 15 months in prison for taking "hundreds of thousands of dollars" in kickbacks from produce wholesalers.[23] It would also certainly be the case with many of the notorious criminals portrayed in these pages, such as Charles Ponzi, Ivan Boesky, or Jim Bakker.

However, in many of the other cases discussed in this book, individuals carried out the criminal schemes, but the ultimate benefit went to a larger organization, typically a corporation. A basic distinction in the analysis of white-collar crime is between what is known as "occupational crime" and what is labeled "corporate crime."

Clinard and Quinney[24] defined occupational crime as "offenses committed by individuals in the course of their occupations and the offenses of employees against their employers" and corporate crime as "offenses committed by corporate officials for their corporation and the offenses of the corporation itself." Occupational crime would include bank employees who embezzle, physicians who defraud health benefit programs, mechanics who overcharge or bill for needless services, and politicians who accept bribes and kickbacks.

Corporate crimes, on the other hand, usually are more complex and involve individuals who violate the law to advance the interests of the organization. Corporate crime already has been designated the "crime of choice" for the twenty-first century.[25]

In preceding chapters, we have examined numerous instances of corporate crime. The illegal dumping of hazardous waste by companies that were well-aware of the serious consequences, the knowing exposure of workers to unsafe conditions, and the deliberate sale of dangerous products are all examples of corporate crime, where the offenses frequently were carried out by supervisors and managers who claimed to be "just following orders."

More recently, the idea of corporate crime has been extended into more traditional categories of criminal law, such as homicide. In Chapter 3, we considered the infamous Pinto case, in which the Ford Motor Company was charged with "reckless homicide" after three teenagers died when their Pinto burst into flames after being rear-ended by another vehicle. Although Ford eventually was acquitted—largely because of a procedural technicality—a significant legal precedent was set in the area of corporate criminal liability.

Some criminologists have sought to extend the concept of corporate liability to encompass organizations of all types, including government agencies and even nonprofit organizations. Schrager and Short[26] distinguished "organizational crime" from individual offenses by defining it as illegal acts committed by "an individual or a group of individuals in a legitimate formal organization in accordance with the operative goals of the organization." Other theorists have used similar terms, such as "organizational deviance"[27] and "elite deviance."[28]

Whatever the terminology, organizational crime also includes acts of governmental deviance described in Chapter 8, such as the FBI's unlawful surveillance and persecution of American citizens, the burglaries, dirty tricks, and cover-ups overseen by the White House in the Watergate scandal, and the abuses of power precipitated by the Iran-Contra affair. To this list one could add the well-documented involvement of the CIA in drug trafficking around the world, particularly in Southeast Asia and Latin America.[29] These were all illegal activities undertaken by individuals on behalf of the covert agenda (but not the mandated goals) of official agencies and political administrations.

Why do some organizations promote "deviance" while others do not? Sometimes it is simply a matter of the greed of the individuals leading the organization. For example, Mickey Monus, co-founder and president of the 300-unit Phar-Mor drugstore chain, was convicted in 1995 of a mammoth fraud and embezzlement scheme that drove his own company into bankruptcy.[30]

C A S E   S T U D Y

The Mickey Monus Club

The flamboyant Mickey Monus was well-known for his extravagant lifestyle. His palatial home even featured a full-sized indoor basketball court.[31] In fact, Monus was such a rabid basketball fan that he launched his own professional league, the World Basketball League (WBL) in 1987.[32] The WBL was a financial fiasco from the start and folded in 1992. The only reason it lasted that long was that Monus siphoned off $10 million from Phar-Mor to keep the league afloat.[33]

But embezzling $10 million to save a minor-league sports operation was only a moderately interesting sidebar to the real story; because Monus was a major-league crook. By keeping two sets of books—one actual, one "doctored"—Monus, assisted by several other Phar-Mor insiders, was able to misstate the company's sales and earnings and thus defraud investors and creditors out of more than $1 billion.[34] *Newsweek* called it "the biggest corporate fraud this century."[35]

Monus was convicted in federal court on 48 separate counts and handed a whopping 20-year prison sentence. He would have to wait at least 17 years for parole.[36] In a statement to the presiding judge, Monus declaimed his farewell address to the troops:

> The important thing is not the numbers to me . . . but the employees—all those dedicated, loyal and highly motivated people. I want them to know the sorrow and regret that I have. The sorrow and regret will live with me for the rest of my life.[37]

Those 20,000 "dedicated, loyal" employees—many now out of work—doubtless shared Monus's "sorrow and regret" when Phar-Mor fell under bankruptcy protection and began closing stores.

In a sordid postscript, Monus was indicted for jury tampering in 1997, while he was serving his prison sentence and living with his sorrow and regret. Monus allegedly had bribed a juror during his first trial in 1994, which had deadlocked on all charges.[38]

Not all organizational deviance conforms to the "greedy leader" model, however. In many cases, it has more to do with the environment in which the organization operates. Some sociologists have carried Merton's notion of blocked aspirations to a higher level of analysis, suggesting that a particularly significant aspect of a criminogenic corporate environment is the "strain" placed on organizations. A case study of organizational misconduct by another drug store chain concluded that organizations, like individuals, may seek illegal means to achieve economic success when legitimate avenues are blocked and when opportunities are available to attain material goals unlawfully.

Executives of the chain reportedly ordered employees to falsify Medicaid claims after state officials had rejected earlier claims for administrative reasons. Those executives believed that reimbursement for the false claims was "owed" to the company.[39] A survey of retired middle managers from Fortune 500 companies reported that the most important cause of unlawful or unethical practices in their corporations, according to respondents, was the pressures applied by top management to show profits and reduce costs.[40]

C A S E   S T U D Y

Olde Whine in New Bottles

A prime example of a deviant corporate culture was revealed at the Olde Discount Corp., a leading discount brokerage chain. The company and three of its senior officials, including its founder and chairman, were fined more than $5 million by the SEC for fraudulent sales practices. The Commission found that Olde "willfully violated the antifraud provisions of the federal securities laws."[41] The SEC determined that "Olde's compensation, production, hiring, and training policies *created an environment* that enabled the firm's brokers to engage in abusive sales practices, such as churning, unauthorized and unsuitable trading, and lying to customers" [emphasis added].[42] The SEC further ruled that Olde's compensation and production policies "created an environment where the pressure to sell overshadowed customer suitability determinations."[43]

Under its compensation policies, Olde gave substantially higher payouts to its brokers for selling special venture stocks—that is, stocks recommended by Olde—than for other stocks. "Olde's compensation system induced its brokers to sell those stocks in which they had the greatest financial interest without considering the suitability of such stocks for their customers."[44]

Olde's production policies created overt pressure to sell. In order to maintain their commission privileges, Olde brokers were required to sell an average of two new special venture stock positions—worth at least $20,000—every day.[45] By requiring brokers to push special venture stocks or run the risk of termination or lower commissions, Olde ensured that its brokers would aggressively sell special venture stocks. In addition, Olde brokers needed to convince each of their customers to buy at least one Olde recommended stock every 6 months. Customers not meeting this criterion would be reassigned.[46]

Olde's hiring and training practices encouraged its brokers to use high-pressure sales techniques. Brokers were taught to "cross-sell"—that is, "to convince customers who wanted to buy non-Olde recommended stocks, on which brokers received little compensation, to buy special venture stocks instead."[47]

Brokers were told, "Why let someone buy a stock you're not going to get paid on?" Brokers were taught to create "a sense of urgency" and to tell customers

(Continued)

that if they did not buy immediately, they would not be able to get the stock tomorrow. Brokers were to continue to "pitch" a stock to their customers until they agreed to buy. Brokers were also taught to use sales scripts that contained false statements, such as "the price of the stock is going up" and that the broker had been "watching the stock for two years." In addition, brokers were told to make misleading statements to customers concerning the financial interest of Olde.[48]

Working in such a criminogenic environment, it is easy to see why Olde brokers at various branch offices throughout the country engaged in what the vhairman of the SEC termed "egregious" abuses and practices that "put the firm and its brokers in conflict with the interests of its clients."[49]

Organizations like Olde Discount not only provide the context for white-collar crimes but often the means to commit them. In practice, then, it may be very difficult to distinguish between acts that promote the goals of an organization from those that primarily benefit individuals, since, in many cases, "individuals and their organizations often reap mutual advantage from criminal conduct."[50] In fact, organizations can be used by members as "weapons" in the commission of crimes. As researchers in one study observed, "[O]ccupation and organization are to the world of white-collar crime what the knife and the gun are to street crimes."[51] Thus, elements like size, ownership form, and administrative structure can be used by organizational members to commit and later hide their crimes. This notion was applied to a study of fraud among insolvent S & L's which found that "those institutions that were stock-owned . . . were the sites and vehicles for the most frequent, the most costly and the most complex (as measured by the number of individuals involved) amounts of white collar crime."[52]

RESPONSES TO WHITE-COLLAR CRIME

Given the abundant opportunities that many persons have to engage in white-collar crime, it is interesting that more people do not. The most obvious reason for this is the fear of punishment. Despite the fact that relatively few individuals who cheat on their taxes are ever actually prosecuted, the knowledge that some have been (including the treasurer of the United States, as described in Chapter 1) is enough to keep most of us reasonably honest when we submit out tax forms in April. In other words, many citizens do not cheat on their taxes simply because of strong moral compunctions but because the law *deters* them. Classical criminological notions of deterrence rest on the fundamental utilitarian premise that people will seek pleasure and avoid pain. Thus, when the potential risks associated with a behavior, such as a crime, outweigh the potential gains, an individual will decide rationally against the behavior. Much of our criminal law is based on this assumption about human nature.

A central concern about white-collar crime is that the risk-reward ratio is out of balance—that is, the potential rewards greatly outweigh the risks. Given the low probability of apprehension and the likelihood of light punishment, white-collar crime appears to be a "rational" course of action in many cases.

The sometimes indifferent response to white-collar criminals stands in sharp contrast to the harsh punitive treatment customarily accorded to street criminals, a contrast summed up in Jeffrey Reiman's pithy observation that "the rich get richer and the poor get prison."[53] The comparative leniency shown white-collar offenders has been attributed to several factors related to their status and resources, as well as to the peculiar characteristics of their offenses. First, the relatively high educational level and occupational prestige of many white-collar offenders is seen as creating a "status shield" that protects them from the harsh penalties applied with greater frequency to "common" criminals. Many judges identify with defendants whose background and standing in the community are similar to their own. When three former executives of C. R. Bard Corporation, one of the world's largest medical equipment manufacturers, were convicted in 1996 of conspiring to test unapproved heart surgery catheters in human patients, the sympathetic judge reluctantly sentenced them to 18 months in federal prison. He almost seemed to be scolding the jury when he said, "I don't regard the defendants as being evil people or typical criminal types."[54] The U.S. attorney who prosecuted the case could not have disagreed more. He characterized the callous executives as "evil people doing evil things . . . for money."[55]

A second leniency factor punctuates one of the world's worst-kept secrets—that life is seldom fair. White-collar defendants' higher incomes enable them to secure expensive legal counsel, whose level of skill and access to defensive resources is generally unavailable to lower-income defendants.

Finally, white-collar crimes frequently involve complicated financial transactions in which the victims are either aggregated classes of unrelated persons, such as stockholders, or large government agencies, such as the IRS, neither of which engender the kind of commiseration that individual victims of street crimes can elicit from judges and juries.

Anecdotal evidence from a number of recent cases seems to support the proposition that white-collar criminals receive lighter sanctions. Michael Milken's initially tough 10-year sentence was later cut to 3 years, and he was released after serving only 24 months in a minimum security facility. Likewise, two of the most notorious S & L crooks in Texas, Don Dixon and "Fast Eddie" McBirney, whose corrupt savings and loans eventually cost the taxpayers $3 billion, had their original sentences substantially reduced.[56]

Evidence of a more empirical nature also supports the leniency hypothesis. A study of persons suspected by federal regulators in Texas and California to be involved in serious S & L crimes revealed that only 14% to 25% were ever indicted. The study also examined the sentences imposed in S & L cases involving mean losses of a half-million dollars and found that the average sentence was 3 years—significantly less than the average prison terms handed to convicted burglars and first-time drug offenders in federal court.[57] It would appear that burglars and first-time drug offenders are considered by the courts to be more serious threats to public security than are thrift looters who can destabilize the entire economy.

A study of California Medicaid providers convicted of defrauding that state's healthcare system produced similar findings (Chapter 10). It reported that, compared with a control group of "blue-collar" offenders charged with grand theft (the same charge leveled at the Medicaid fraud offenders), the Medicaid fraud defendants—many of whom were physicians—were less than half as likely to be incarcerated. This disparity is made even more conspicuous by the fact that the median financial losses from the Medicaid offenses were more than 10 times the median losses from the control group's crimes.[58]

On the other hand, it should be noted that although the findings from these kinds of focused studies may seem clear, the results yielded by broader analyses of class-based sentencing differentials are less consistent. Although many studies have supported the leniency hypothesis,[59] others have reported no evidence that higher-status defendants are punished any less severely than lower-status ones.[60] Some have even produced the contrary finding that higher-status defendants receive longer, not shorter, sentences.[61] Thus, the issue of social status and punitive leniency remains unresolved.[62]

Furthermore, can we say that the preferential treatment of high-status defendants—even if it exists—is necessarily a bad thing? The presumption that differential sentencing has a deleterious effect on our system of justice and on society in general has been challenged by certain economists. In a provocative article entitled, "Do We Punish High Income Criminals Too Heavily?", John Lott answers his own question with an emphatic "Yes." Lott argues that, because wealthy defendants experience a proportionately greater decline in income following a criminal conviction than do poorer defendants, their punishment will be unduly harsh if they receive the same sentences as their low-income counterparts who are convicted of the same crimes.[63] The solution he recommends is to allow upperworld criminals to "buy justice"—that is, to use their lighter sentences to offset the more serious extra-legal sanctions they face.[64] For example, suppose that a bank president and a bank teller are each convicted of embezzlement and sentenced to 2 years in prison. Suppose further that, upon release, the bank president's annual income declines 90%, from $1 million to $100,000 and the teller's annual income declines "only" 50%, from $20,000 to $10,000. According to Lott's extraordinarily curious notion of justice, the bank president should have been "compensated" for his or her greater loss of income by a shorter sentence.

Critics of Lott's "wealth maximization" approach contend that using money as his unit of measure "violates the principle of the equality of individuals before the law."[65] Furthermore, "wealth maximization arguments seem to assume that wealthy offenders suffer from "collateral penalties"—that is, society punishes white-collar criminals in ways that go far beyond the courtroom, such as a dramatic alteration of their standing in the community and their ability to earn a living. One of the flaws in such reasoning is that its underlying premise may be false, at least in many cases. After interviewing several dozen convicted white-collar criminals who had completed their sentences about their post-release lifestyle, *Forbes* magazine concluded that, "U.S. society is forgiving and often forgetting about white-collar convictions."[66] One of those interviewed was David Begelman, who was convicted of embezzlement in 1978 when he ran Columbia Pictures.[67] Within months of his conviction, he was back in the movie business, running MGM Studios and he later went on to become a successful independent film producer.[68]

Further evidence of the forgiving attitude of business toward professionals who cheat and defraud clients is found in an SEC study of "rogue brokers," persons who had been the subject of official investigations for violating securities laws. The SEC found that many of the brokers had little difficulty securing jobs after their brushes with the law; in fact, two-thirds were still employed in the securities industry.[69] Likewise, the Medicaid fraud study cited earlier reported that only 12% of the convicted doctors had their licenses to practice medicine revoked.[70]

Moreover, in some states the laws actually protect the wealth of convicted white-collar criminals. Just before Martin Siegel was indicted in New York for insider trading (Chapter 4), he moved his family to Florida, where he purchased a $3.25-million beachfront home. Perhaps Siegel just preferred mild Florida winters to those in New York, but it seems more likely that he was trying to safeguard his assets from the onslaught of impending litigation by taking advantage of a Florida law that prohibits the seizure of a person's legal residence. This archaic statute, originally enacted as a populist measure to prevent banks from displacing homesteaders, has resulted in Florida becoming a haven for white-collar criminals seeking to shelter their loot from the government by "investing" in expensive mansions.[71]

EFFECTS OF WHITE-COLLAR CRIME

Chapter 1 noted that people often fail to express the kind of outrage over corporate crime that they do over street crimes because it is usually more difficult to visualize the damage wrought by white-collar offenses. In addition, television often ignores or downplays corporate crime because those crimes lack the dramatic elements that fit the needs of the electronic media: clearly defined victims and villains; illegal actions that are easily understood and can be described in quick sound bytes; motivations like jealousy and rage that can be vividly portrayed; and heroes in the form of police or prosecutors, who apprehend and then punish those responsible. In contrast, white-collar crimes are frequently confusing; the perpetrators, because of their social status, are not easy to cast as lawbreakers; the injury caused by these crimes (as in the case of toxic dumping, for example) may take years to develop; and the resolution of the cases often occurs outside of criminal courts and away from television cameras in private negotiations between offenders and anonymous government officials. For these reasons, television often shows little interest in cases of corporate criminality, while at the same time deluging us with sensational stories of murder, mayhem, and madness.

Nonetheless, as this book has stressed repeatedly, the effects of white-collar crimes are in many ways more serious than those of "common" crime.

These harmful consequences fall into three categories: environmental and human costs; economic costs; and social costs. Let us consider each of these effects in more detail.

Environmental and Human Costs

The kinds of dire prophecies of environmental destruction issued by ecologists are usually shrugged off by most Americans as alarmist hyperbole—until disasters like the Exxon Valdez or Love Canal occur. Only then does the public recognize the terrible threat posed by industrial irresponsibility. Corporate apologists often depict these events as tragic but unpredictable "accidents" that no amount of legislation could prevent. After the 1984 Union Carbide catastrophe at Bhopal, India (Chapter 3), when a storage tank containing deadly gas burst and killed at least 2500 people, some American magazines actually portrayed Union Carbide as the "victim," expressing concern over the impact of the disaster on the company's reputation and future profitability. In contrast, Indian publications all focused on the true victims and consistently referred to the event as a "crime."[72]

The American media's unwillingness to see such disasters as manifestations of corporate crime was also evident in their response to the tragic 1991 fire at the Imperial chicken processing plant in North Carolina (Chapter 4) that killed 26 workers, who were trapped inside because management had chained the emergency exits shut to prevent employee pilferage. Despite the eventual manslaughter conviction of the plant's owner, the media tended not to focus on criminal culpability but on an alleged breakdown in government safety regulations, particularly the failure of OSHA to inspect the plant adequately.[73]

Economic Costs

One of the more immediate effects of corporate criminality is the drag it places on the economy. Chapter 1 pointed out that the annual costs to Americans from all white-collar crimes runs into hundreds of billions of dollars; the total from personal fraud alone is more than $40 billion. In certain industries, the costs are especially high. For instance, the General Accounting Office has estimated that at least $100 billion (10% of the nearly $1 trillion spent by Americans on healthcare every year) is lost to fraud and abuse.[74]

Who pays these costs? Are they equally shared by all members of society? Should some groups, particularly those who may have profited from the crimes, absorb a larger share of the cost? The evidence indicates that the burden is *not* shared equally across society but is shifted to the middle- and lower-income segments of the population. Because these costs are typically passed on to taxpayers, they represent a "regressive tax" imposed on those individuals least able to pay. At the same time, companies victimized by white-collar crime or slapped with punitive fines for their own offenses pass the costs on to consumers.

Chapter 7 noted that the multibillion cost of bailing out failed S & L was paid for mainly through the issuance of government bonds, which eventually must be redeemed by taxpayers. In theory, the progressive nature of the American tax structure means that wealthy citizens would pay a higher proportion of their incomes to cover the bill. In reality, however, the loopholes and tax shelters enjoyed by high-income individuals means that the bulk of the burden will fall on the middle class.

The S & L bailout also forced reductions of government spending in other areas, notably the social services frequently needed by low-income persons, none of whom had benefited from the extraordinarily high interest rates that corrupt thrifts paid to depositors during the I-got-mine years of the "greed decade." In contrast, the government chose to cover all lost deposits of the bankrupt S & Ls (not just those under $100,000, as the law required). This meant, for example, that many wealthy depositors were able to reap the benefits of the high interest rates offered S & Ls without assuming any of the risks when they failed.[75] The economic elite, who never miss an opportunity to rail contemptuously against welfare payments to the poor, thus became the shameless beneficiaries of the biggest "entitlement" program ever implemented by the U.S. government.

An illustration of how the economic costs of white-collar crime can generate a "ripple effect" is provided by the bankruptcy of Orange County, California. Because of fraud and gross mismanagement in one self-indulgent venue, every city, town, and school district in the United States will have to pay more to borrow money from now on.[76]

C A S E   S T U D Y

The Orange County Bankruptcy

On December 6, 1994, officials of Orange County, California, one of the most affluent areas in the country, made an announcement that shocked the nation. The arch-conservative Board of Supervisors had declared the county bankrupt, with financial losses amounting to between $1.5 billion and $2 billion. It was the largest municipal failure in history. Known for its upscale lifestyle, Mediterranean climate, and attractive beaches, Orange County also has a less savory reputation. On frequent occasions, federal authorities have referred to it as the "fraud capital of the United States." As a hotbed of investor frauds (Chapter 2), S & L failures (Chapter 7), and other assorted economic crimes, the bankruptcy merely underscored what many people already knew about Orange County. Simply put, white-collar crime is a way of life there.

The county's collapse, dramatic enough because of its sheer size, was that much more injurious because of the numerous municipalities, school districts, public agencies, and private citizens who had invested in the once fabled County Investment Pool. The pool had produced spectacular returns for years before taking a nosedive in value. Run by former county treasurer, Robert Citron, the pool had

(Continued)

outperformed all other government investments in the state and the nation by such a large margin that Citron became known as a "financial guru." Citron, a college dropout and the lone Democrat in a staunchly Republican administration, played the role of master money manager in a government simultaneously hungry for revenues yet fiercely antitaxation. As former county supervisor Thomas Riley put it, "This is a person who has gotten us millions of dollars. I don't know how the hell he does it, but it makes us all look good."[77] Little did Riley know that these words, spoken only months before the county declared bankruptcy, would soon ring hollow to investors in the failed fund.

Despite numerous warnings from public and private sources, Riley and his colleagues on the board of supervisors refused to acknowledge what should have been obvious to even those untrained in high finance: The way Citron performed his "magic" was by taking enormous risks with public funds. Instead, local politicians ignored recommendations for increased oversight of the treasurer's office. As long as Citron "did whatever he did," elected officials could rest comfortably knowing that they would not have to ask constituents to cough up additional taxes to pay for public services. In a place where tax hikes occur about as often as Viva Castro rallies, politicians had plenty of incentive to shut their eyes.

Admittedly, this head-in-the-sand strategy worked very well for a while. Citron's portfolio generated about $500 million above what would have been earned using the state's more conservative investment approach.[78]

Citron's purported financial acumen, however, was later exposed as an unquestioning dependence on the advice of investment brokers, most notably, the giant firm of Merrill Lynch. In testimony before a state senate committee investigating the bankruptcy, Citron said he was there "simply to tell the truth."[79] He expressed apologies to the people of Orange County for following the wrong course and for his over-reliance on the advice of others. The "financial guru" now claimed that he was a vestal investor debauched by the wolves of Wall Street:

> I had never, nor have I ever, owned a share of stock. My primary training was on-the-job. Due to my inexperience, I placed a great deal of reliance on the advice of market professionals. This reliance increased as the number and types of investments permitted by the Government Code were liberalized, and as financial instruments became more complex. . . . [I]n retrospect, I wish I had more education and training in complex government securities.[80]

In a further twist that could only be considered weird, it was later learned that among those "others" consulted by Citron were a 900-number psychic and a mail-order astrologer, who gave him interest-rate predictions.[81]

Betting that interest rates would remain low, Citron invested heavily through the use of derivatives, which would pay high returns as long as interest rates remained depressed. Derivatives are complex financial instruments whose value is tied to something extrinsic, such as interest rates or stock indices. The chairman of the American stock exchange has called derivatives "the 11-letter

(Continued)

four-letter word."[82] According to *Fortune* magazine, "[T]he nightmare of Orange County . . . brought to life the dread of many Wall Streeters, a major loss of public money linked to derivatives. Many of these derivatives bear the fingerprints of Merrill Lynch."[83]

Merrill Lynch officials, however, noted that they had warned Citron about his portfolio on numerous occasions and were not willing to shoulder the blame for the pool's collapse. Nevertheless, Merrill Lynch profited mightily by selling derivatives and other securities to the county and underwriting bond transactions. On two different occasions the investment house sold the county an additional $277 million[84] and $855 million[85] of the very derivatives that they later claimed they had warned him about.

Orange County acted like a compulsive gambler, while Merrill Lynch and other brokerage houses behaved like croupiers offering an acquisitive community new chances to spin the wheel.[86] Once the county was "hooked" on its source of revenue, brokers could divert blame from themselves by providing written documentation that they had warned of the risks involved and thus were in compliance with vague securities laws. When asked why they continued to sell these shaky investments to Citron after their own analysis showed potential danger, a Merrill Lynch spokesman would only say, "Well, that's a legitimate question."[87] Unfortunately, the legitimate answer has yet to be ascertained, and huge lawsuits have been filed against the firm.

To compound the disaster, the county leveraged (i.e., "borrowed") $12 billion in public money in order to maximize the profits on its investments. After all, "the more you invest, the more you can earn"[88]—or lose.

> And what was the public purpose of those borrowings? It was to give county agencies, cities and school and water districts a little extra in their budgets. That way, government officials and county residents could get around the realities of life in a time of stern voter resistance to taxes and vocal protests about the size of government.[89]

By pleading guilty to six counts, including misappropriation of public funds and making false material statements in connection with the sale of securities, Citron reluctantly accepted some responsibility for the debacle. He did not, however, cause the debacle by himself, nor was he the only person involved who broke the law. Other individuals have been indicted,[90] and current and former supervisors have been charged by the SEC with "official wrongdoing," the highest civil sanction short of being indicted. Numerous officials have resigned, and more still more criminal indictments and administrative charges are inevitable. At this writing, the SEC and FBI are still investigating the case, and Citron has yet to be sentenced, pending his cooperation with prosecutors. It is becoming clearer, however, that Citron was merely the hapless technician in a triangle of power that linked Wall Street with Orange County's visible and invisible governments.[91]

(Continued)

The incredible lack of oversight and the bungling greed that was exposed in the bankruptcy provide important lessons for municipal finance. Remarkably, many economists, just as in the case of the S & L scandal, prefer not to label such activities as "real" crimes. For example, in characterizing the bankruptcy, the dean of the business school at a local university described the county as "a living laboratory of financial mismanagement and government ineptitude—if not outright irresponsibility."[92] This is certainly not a flattering depiction, but mismanagement, ineptitude, and irresponsibility are not crimes. Fraud, however, is a crime, and fraud is what Robert Citron pleaded guilty to.

Similarly, as if to completely deny the role of white-collar crime in the worst government bankruptcy ever, the first academic book on the collapse, which focuses on Citron and his ill-fated derivatives, *does not even mention the terms "crime" or "fraud"* nor acknowledge their significance in the bankruptcy.[93] Such lenient analysis tends to characterize financial wrongdoings as a consequence of the "risky business" present in everyday financial transactions. Given the strong evidence to the contrary, that point of view is at best incomplete and potentially misleading; at worst it can form the basis of misguided and highly destructive public policy.

One does not need Citron's psychic reader to recognize that a criminogenic environment conducive to fraud existed in Orange County, which allowed for the ensuing financial disaster. To ignore the role of white-collar crime in the bankruptcy and instead assign the explanation to "risky business," is to disregard the existence of the *real* political, economic, and social contexts within which such events take place. Presciently capturing the "real" Orange County, a fitting epitaph was coined years ago by a wise comic-strip possum named Pogo: "We have met the enemy, and he is us."

Other municipalities, most of them far less prosperous and guilty of no wrongdoing, have to share the bill for the Orange County debacle because municipal investors must now consider bankruptcy and default a feasible alternative to debt. In other words, Orange County has raised the level of risk for lenders, who will accordingly demand higher interest from *all* municipal bond issuers. This may be an affront to distributive justice, but it is no surprise. The diffusion of accountability is a common by-product of fiscal recklessness. Consider, for example, all the commercial banks that failed in the 1980s owing to fraud and abuse. Federal regulators were able to cover the costs of those failures, while avoiding a direct S & L-type bailout, by raising the premiums paid to federal deposit insurance funds by member institutions. The increased expenditure was then passed on by banks to customers in the form of higher interest rates on credit card balances, without any corresponding increase in the interest paid to depositors on their savings accounts. In effect, this transfer of debt represented a silent bailout of the banking industry funded by consumers.[94]

The same sort of buck-passing is also seen in a wide variety of other businesses, where the costs of white-collar crime are absorbed by consumers in the form of higher prices for goods and services. Malfeasant corporations always try to portray themselves somehow as "victims"—of unfair regulations, political persecution, or whatever—but it is ultimately ordinary citizens who pay the tab. In this way, white-collar crime contributes to the widening economic gap between the "haves" and the "have nots" in American society.

Social Costs

In addition to the environmental damage, the human destruction, and the economic losses, there are other less tangible but very serious social consequences of white-collar crime. The impact of upperworld criminality tends to radiate, influencing people's attitudes toward society and each other. Chapter 1 observed how persistent, unpunished corporate and governmental corruption can produce feelings of cynicism among the public, remove an essential element of trust from everyday social interaction, delegitimate political institutions, and weaken respect for the law. One could identify many specific effects—as previous chapters have done—but a negative consequence still remaining for consideration is the relationship between white-collar offenses and other forms of crime. There is a connection, both direct and indirect, between "crime in the suites" and "crime in the streets."

White-collar criminality surely encourages and facilitates other types of crime. Indirectly, the existence of elite lawbreaking promotes disrespect for the law among ordinary citizens and provides ready rationalizations for potential street criminals seeking to justify their misconduct. Underclass youths who see or hear about local politicians taking bribes, police officers stealing drugs, or merchants cheating customers are able to minimize the harms caused by their own crimes by arguing that "everybody's doing it," or "we're no worse than anybody else," or "that's the way the system works." For many poor, young urbanites, crime among the rich and powerful affirms the futility of legitimate work and demonstrates the monetary and status rewards that accompany illegal activities. This cynical world-view was vividly articulated by a member of a Puerto Rican street gang in Chicago:

> We grew up at a time when people were making money and making it quick. You know, we saw on television people getting rich overnight. Then we saw, you know, you had the white-collar criminals—you know the guys who are just like us but never get caught, except that everybody knows that they are crooks. You had all these guys becoming filthy rich. And what do you think that's going to tell us? Shit, it didn't tell me to go and get a job at McDonalds and save my nickels and dimes.[95]

For such young offenders from the underclass, it seems, a life of hustling on the streets represents a "rational" alternative to the limited opportunities offered to them by legitimate society, just as Merton had proposed seven decades ago.

White-collar criminality also promotes other forms of crime in more direct ways. One of the allegations from the Iran-Contra hearings (Chapter 8), for example, was that a number of small banks with ties to organized crime were used by American officials to channel funds illegally to the Nicaraguan Contras.[96]

Organized crime, in fact, has long depended on corruption for its existence. In 1895, the Lexow Commission, investigating the New York Police Department, reported that "money and promise of service to be rendered are paid to public officials by the keepers or proprietors of gaming houses, disorderly houses or liquor saloons . . . in exchange for promises of immunity from punishment or police interference."[97] Nearly 75 years later, the President's Commission on Law Enforcement and Administration of Justice reached the same conclusion: "All available data indicate that organized crime flourishes only where it has corrupted local officials."[98] From organized crime's point of view, this relationship is functional—bribery of cops and politicians enables it to conduct its illicit business free of official interference.[99] From the perspective of society and the victims of organized crime, however, this depraved symbiosis is wholly dysfunctional.

White-collar criminal activities support the illegal drug industry as well. Corrupt banks are central to the operations of the international cartels that import billions of dollars in cocaine and other drugs into the United States each year. Given the cash-heavy nature of drug sales, distributors and retailers are faced with the inevitable problem of converting huge amounts of cash into forms that can be more easily invested or transported overseas. Federal law requires that financial institutions must report all transactions of $10,000 or more. This creates a dilemma for drug dealers who may accumulate millions of dollars in cash. But for a price, unscrupulous bankers can "launder" that money, converting it into more legitimate forms without reporting it to the authorities. At a time when banks are coming under increased scrutiny, drug dealers are turning to other financial institutions, like insurance companies, to launder their cash.[100] Money laundering, of course, is not limited to drug dealers but can be found anywhere that a group that has a need to disguise its sources of income—most notably with the operators of gambling casinos in the United States, who launder cash skimmed from profits in order to evade taxes.[101]

CONTROLLING WHITE-COLLAR CRIME

When the new Republican majority won control of Congress in 1994, it quite naturally sought to impose its self-reliant philosophy—enunciated in its "Contract With America"—on the public. Many citizens, unhappy with the status quo, embraced this pact; but others managed to control their enthusiasm. Critics contend that, beneath the Contract's seductive rhetoric, one finds the same vision espoused by Adam Smith and his disciples: a society dominated by the marketplace; a society in which the government has limited power to protect consumers; a society in which citizens have few legal recourses to challenge the ascendancy of corporations; and a society in which the people essentially must place their trust in the "good will" of bankers, manufacturers, brokers, and the other conductors of the free market.

The Contract was a blueprint for a laissez-faire economy. One of its clauses proposed a moratorium on new governmental regulations and would subject all existing regulations—including such areas as environmental pollution, employee safety, and consumer protection—to a cost-benefit analysis to determine if they impede commerce in any way. Those rules determined to be too "costly" would be eradicated.[102]

Securities regulation was a major target of the Contract. Legislation has already been proposed (unsuccessfully) to downgrade the SEC's original watchdog function. Such an action would effectively have enfeebled much of the investor protection law that has underpinned U.S. capital markets for decades.[103] Another clause, approved by Congress in 1995 under the guise of "tort reform," made the recovery of money lost to securities fraud extremely difficult in federal court. The bill included a much higher burden of proof of intent and penalties for persons who sue and do not win.[104]

The Contract also called for the capping of product liability awards by juries. Vocal critics of America's tort system, such as former Vice-President Dan Quayle, contend that the willingness of juries to make excessive multi-million dollar awards to plaintiffs strangles the economy by discouraging companies from introducing new products. A common example used to support this argument is that of Monsanto, which has developed a patented phosphate-fiber substitute for asbestos but has kept if off the market because it fears potential lawsuits. In fact, the EPA believes this asbestos substitute to be as carcinogenic as asbestos, so Monsanto's decision not to sell it may be based on sound corporate policy, not intimidation.[105] Nevertheless, Quayle and his cohorts seem intent on bestowing blanket immunity on manufacturers by exploiting the universal unpopularity of ambulance-chasing lawyers.

There is another notable aspect to the Contract With America. It called for the implementation of much harsher punishment for "street" criminals but said virtually nothing about the punishment of white-collar offenders.

Deregulation represents a movement in exactly the wrong direction in the fight against white-collar crime. When the corporate establishment—through its congressional surrogates—tells the American people, "We want to get government off *your* backs," they almost always mean, "We want to get government off *our* backs"—a very different proposition. It is impossible to imagine how the absence of an SEC could have prevented the insider trading epidemic, or how the elimination of banking restrictions would thwart another S & L crisis, or how doing away with the EPA would render future Love Canals less likely. Advocates of laissez-faire solutions do point out, with some justification, that government regulations have already failed to prevent the afore-mentioned calamities. Yet, calling for their abolishment because they have been less than entirely successful seems dangerous and absurd. If budget slashing forces regulatory agencies to cut back on enforcement, prosecutors "may well find that the cuffs are on them."[106]

But if deregulation moves us in the wrong direction, then what might the right direction be? A number of suggestions to curb white-collar criminality can be offered, requiring changes of three types: legal, institutional, and social.

Legal Changes

It has been proposed that new laws that impose tougher penalties on white-collar criminals might well deter some potential offenders. More punitive federal sentencing guidelines have resulted in more white-collar crime convictions—8050 in 1994, up 6% in 24 months.[107] But whether this new toughness serves as a general deterrent is not at all clear. Current laws likely fail to deter because white-collar offenders are aware of the frequent lack of vigorous enforcement and the relatively low probability that their crimes will be detected or punished severely. A federal prosecutor has declared, "You deal with white-collar crime the same way as street crime. You try to raise the likelihood they will be caught and punished."[108] Stricter application of existing guidelines would also serve to redress the sentencing imbalance between white-collar and traditional "common" criminals.[109]

The system of regulatory codes and administrative agencies that monitor corporate conduct and respond to criminal violations is another important part of the legal apparatus is. Some scholars believe that we do not need more regulation; rather, we need "smarter" regulation. Simply applying harsher laws to corporations and individuals, they argue, will only produce a subculture of resistance within the corporate community "wherein methods of legal resistance and counterattack are incorporated into industry socialization."[110] Regulation works best when it is a "benign big gun"—that is, when regulators can speak softly but carry big sticks in the form of substantial legal penalties.[111]

A hierarchical structure of sanctions also has been proposed, in which the first response to misconduct consists of advice, warnings, and persuasion; then escalates to harsher responses culminating at the top of the pyramid, in what is termed "corporate capital punishment" or the dissolution of the offending company.[112] The goal of this model is compliance: "Compliance is thus understood within a dynamic enforcement game where enforcers try to get commitment from corporations to comply with the law and can back up their negotiations with credible threats about the dangers faced by defendants if they choose to go down the path of non-compliance."[113] The strength of such a system is that it works at multiple levels and holds all the actors involved—"executive directors, accountants, brokers, legal advisers, and sloppy regulators"[114]—accountable for criminal misconduct.

Institutional Changes

Preceding chapters have highlighted numerous examples of "criminogenic industries"—industries whose structure and traditional practices seem to encourage, or even embrace, criminal behavior. Any successful preventive strategy must therefore seek to "deinstitutionalize" white-collar crime, that is, to remove its institutional sources. This is by no means an easy task. About 20% of the 1000 largest American corporations already have "ethics officers" who help formulate codes of proper conduct.[115] A *Wall Street Journal* reporter, however, has written that these codes "are little more than high-sounding words on paper."[116]

Sociologist Amitai Etzioni has suggested that a better way to encourage ethical business conduct is to "foster associations and enforce moral codes somewhat like those of lawyers and physicians" in the business community.[117] Such associations would lack legal authority, but they could discipline violators through public censure and other informal control mechanisms.

Another way to change the environment in which corporate organizations do business is to create internationally agreed upon standards of conduct. This would be particularly important in the case of American companies that operate in—and often export white-collar crimes to—foreign countries. The most significant step in this direction has been the United Nation's attempt to draw up a Code of Conduct for multinational corporations. That document sets standards of acceptable behavior for global firms. Among other things, the Code calls upon these corporations to abstain from corrupt practices, such as political bribery, and to carry out their operations in an environmentally sound manner.[118] With these same goals in mind, the Clinton administration has proposed a code of ethics for American firms operating overseas. Known as the Model Business Principles, this code encourages companies to adopt more scrupulous behavior abroad by "providing a safe and healthy workplace . . . pursuing safe environmental practices . . . and complying with U.S. laws prohibiting bribery."[119]

Neither of these proposed codes establishes any authority to sanction violators; they are merely guidelines. Enforcement is left up to individual nations. This could be a significant weakness. As we have seen, some underdeveloped countries have shown a willingness to tolerate egregious abuses by American corporations, either because of official corruption or out of desperation for economic growth. Nevertheless, these efforts represent a first step toward battling white-collar crime in a global economy.

Social Changes

Earlier in this chapter, it was suggested that Americans tend to have very strong feelings about crime and criminals but are often ambivalent in their responses to those convicted of white-collar offenses. As noted, many corporate lawbreakers have received the support of their colleagues and other prominent members of their community. Even after their convictions, they were quickly accepted back into legitimate society, suffering few of the stigmas and resentments that other types of convicted felons routinely experience. Indeed, it almost seems that we extend a begrudging respect to those who are clever and bold enough to fleece us out of millions. But if we are ever to gain control over white-collar crime, these attitudes must change.

Criminologist John Braithwaite argues that the broader corporate milieu need to be transformed. Braithwaite calls for the creation of a "communitarian corporate culture" in which organizations draw "everyone's attention to the failings of those who fall short of corporate social responsibility standards [shaming], while continuing to offer them advice and encouragement to improve [reintegration]."[120] A simple, yet very effective, form of "shaming" that can be employed when corporations violate the law is adverse publicity—spreading information about misconduct to consumers, who could then express their disapproval by refusing to patronize the offending company.[121] Braithwaite's ideal corporation, "well integrated into the community and therefore amenable to the pressures of social control,"[122] stands in dramatic contrast to Friedman's model of an amoral corporation, divorced from obligations to the community and inevitably producing a criminogenic environment.

Many of the old assumptions about the utility of business ethics are now being challenged. "Most people act unethically for two reasons: to make more money and to beat the competition."[123] But according to a number of more recent studies, an ethical culture can actually make a business *more* successful. Walker Research, which tests employees perceptions about their employers, reports "an attitudinal link between perceptions of ethics and a company's ability to hold on to employees."[124] According to a 1999 Walker report:

> [C]ompanies viewed as highly ethical by their employees were six times more likely to keep their staff members. On the other hand, 79 percent of employees who questioned their bosses' integrity said they felt trapped at work or uncommitted, or were likely to leave their jobs soon—sobering news in an economy where holding on to every good employee counts.[125]

Moreover, another study found that businesses with a "strong culture of shared values"[126] tend to be more profitable than other companies. "Companies with a strong sense of values see revenue grow four times faster, jobs get created seven times faster, and stock prices increase 12 times faster."[127]

Another way to change the culture of tolerance for white-collar crime is to alter the socialization of future captains of industry. One logical place to look is to the elite MBA programs where many American business leaders are trained. A few years ago, a class at the Columbia Business School was divided into groups for a simulated negotiation game. Each team was given time to plan its bargaining strategy in private. One group actually planted a "bug" in the room where another group was holding its strategy meeting.[128] A survey of students at the University of Virginia's Darden Graduate School of Business Administration reported that "71 percent believed that being ethical can be personally damaging."[129] In 1990, an annual show at Michael Milken's alma mater, the University of Pennsylvania's prestigious Wharton School, featured a student playing the role of class valedictorian. At her mock "graduation" ceremony, she stepped away from the podium, grabbed a microphone and explained musically how she had made it to the top of her class, to the tune of Michael Jackson's hit song "Beat It."

I cheated, cheated
Cheated, cheated,
And Maybe I sound conceited,
You're probably angry,
I'm overjoyed,
I work on Wall Street,
You're unemployed.[130]

A number of reformers have called for the integration of rigorous ethical analyses into the curricula of business schools.[131] The sad reality, however, is that by that point it may already be too late. Some MBA programs have begun to offer business ethics courses, either as electives or in some cases as requirements[132]; but whether such reform will have any measurable future impact on corporate morality seems a long shot at best. At one leading business school, an elective called "Managing in the Socially Responsible Corporation" is reportedly ridiculed by students as a useless "touchy-feely" course.[133] A former chairman of IBM has declared, "If an MBA candidate doesn't know the difference between honesty and crime, between lying and telling the truth, then business school, in all probability, will not produce a convert."[134]

Accordingly, pedagogic indoctrination needs to be expanded beyond MBA programs. Critical analyses of commercial and governmental practices should be incorporated into classrooms at all levels of the educational system.[135] As teachers, the attitude that the authors find most common among our students is one of apathy and cynicism, captured in statements like, "What's the difference? The system's rigged anyway," or "What can you do? All politicians are corrupt." This kind of resignation is self-fulfilling and ultimately self-defeating; it allows upperworld criminality to continue without resistance and with the tacit acceptance of its victims. Students and the public at large have to understand that, although business and political corruption are pervasive, they are not unstoppable. Ordinary citizens do possess the means to counter these practices, even if it is only through collective acts like voting against crooked politicians or shunning products from manufacturers that poison the environment.

Recently, pension funds representing the interests of thousands of employees have begun to flex their muscles as large stockholders. When Salomon Brothers was uncovered rigging the treasury bond market in 1991 (Chapter 1), the California Public Employees Retirement System suspended its investment activities with that firm.[136] Similarly, in 1992, the New York City Employees Retirement System used its influence as a major shareholder in the Reebok Corporation to force a reduction of the extravagant $33 million salary paid to the company's chairman.[137] Both these illustrations suggest the substantial power that citizens can wield over corporations when they pool their economic clout.

Like death, taxes, and *I Love Lucy,* white-collar crime may always be with us. Measures such as those just outlined will not entirely extirpate the problem, but they can help to make it less commonplace and to minimize its fallout. If nothing else, raising the public's consciousness of the depth, dynamics, and disaster of white-collar crime—as this book has tried to do—can hopefully reshape people's view of events like the insider trading scandal and S & L crisis, the tragedy of carcinogenic pollution, and other licensed assaults on the quality of life in the United States.

Larry the Liquidator, in the fictional dialogue quoted at the opening of this chapter, asks: "Who cares?" Larry and the real-life villains he symbolizes deserve an answer. Every law-abiding citizen, every innocent victim, every one of us who has looked on while neo-Vandals in custom-tailored suits have sacked America need to join voices in million-part harmony and assert that *we* care.

NOTES

1. Shakespeare, William. *Romeo and Juliet.* New York: Bantam Books, 1980: 69.

2. Lombroso, Cesare. *Crime, Its Causes and Remedies.* Henry P. Horton (Trans.) Boston: Little, Brown, 1911.

3. Freud, Sigmund. *A General Introduction to Psycho-Analysis.* Joan Riviere (Trans.) New York: Liveright, 1935.

4. Herrnstein, Richard and Murray, Charles. *The Bell Curve: Intelligence, and Class Structure in America.* New York: Free Press, 1994.

5. In sharp contrast to this contention, two well-known criminologists, Michael Gottfredson and Travis Hirschi, have argued provocatively, albeit unpersuasively, that white-collar crime is no different in its essential nature than street crime and that a distinct theory is therefore unnecessary. *All* crime, they maintain, is essentially the result of individual traits, most notably low self-control. (Gottfredson, Michael and Hirschi, Travis. *A General Theory of Crime.* Stanford, Calif.: Stanford University Press, 1990.)

6. Merton, Robert K. "Social Structure and Anomie." In Robert Merton, *Social Theory and Social Structure.* Glencoe, Ill.: The Free Press, 1957: 131–160.

7. *Ibid.*

8. Coleman, James W. *The Criminal Elite* (3rd Ed.). New York: St. Martin's, 1994.

9. Smith, Adam. *The Wealth of Nations,* Vol. 1. New York: P.F. Collier, 1902: 56–57.

10. Barol, Bill. "The Eighties Are Over." *Newsweek* 110, January 4, 1988: 40–48.

11. Friedman, Milton. "The Social Responsibility of Business Is to Increase Its Profit." *New York Times Magazine.* September 13, 1990: 32.

12. Wood, John, Lonenecker, Joseph M., and Moore, Carlos. "Ethical Attitudes of Students and Business Professionals: A Study of Moral Reasoning." *Journal of Business Ethics* 7, 1988: 249–257. See also: Walker, Janet. "'Greed Is Good' . . . or Is It? Economic Ideology and Moral Tension in a Graduate School of Business." *Journal of Business Ethics* 11, 1992: 273–283.

13. Mills, C. Wright. "Situated Actions and Vocabularies of Motive." *American Sociological Review* 33, 1968: 46–62.

14. Sykes, Gresham and Matza, David. "Techniques of Neutralization." *American Sociological Review* 22, 1957: 664–670. For empirical applications of this concept to white-collar crime, see: Rothman, Mitchell and Gandossy, Robert. "Sad Tales: The Accounts of White-Collar Defendants and the Decision to Sanction." *Pacific Sociological Review* 25, 1982: 449–473; Benson, Michael. "Denying the Guilty Mind: Accounting for Involvement in White Collar Crime." *Criminology* 27, 1989: 769–794.

15. Vitell, Scott J. and Grove, Stephen J. "Marketing Ethics and the Techniques of Neutralization." *Journal of Business Ethics* 6, 1987: 433–438.

16. From Sykes and Matza, *op. cit.*

17. Thurmon, Arnold. *The Folklore of Capitalism.* New Haven, Conn.: Yale University Press, 1937.

18. Bailey, Fenton. *The Junk Bond Revolution.* London: Fourth Estate, 1991.

19. Center for Investigative Reporting. *Global Dumping Ground*. Washington, DC: Seven Locks Press, 1990: 37.

20. Needleman, Martin and Needleman, Carolyn. "Organizational Crime: Two Models of Criminogenesis." *Sociological Quarterly* 20, 1979: 517.

21. Leonard, William and Weber, Marvin. "Automakers and Dealers: A Study of Criminogenic Market Forces." *Law and Society Review* 4, 1970: 407–424.

22. Farberman, Harvey. "A Criminogenic Market Structure: The Automobile Industry." *Sociological Quarterly* 16, 1975: 438–457.

23. Foderaro, Lisa W. "Former Sheraton Food Buyer Is Sentenced for Kickbacks." *New York Times*. July 12, 1997: B25.

24. Clinard, Marshall and Quinney, Richard. *Criminal Behavior Systems* (2nd Ed.). Cincinnati, Ohio: Anderson, 1986: 189.

25. Johnston, Jeffrey L. "Following the Trail of Financial Statement Fraud." *Business Credit* 97, October 1995: 48.

26. Schrager, Laura and Short, James F., Jr. "Toward a Sociology of Organizational Crime." *Social Problems* 25, 1978: 411–412.

27. Ermann, David and Lundman, Richard. "Deviant Acts by Complex Organizations: Deviance and Social Control at the Organizational Level of Analysis." *Sociological Quarterly* 19, 1978: 55–67.

28. Simon, David and Eitzen, Stanley. *Elite Deviance*. Boston: Allyn and Bacon, 1982.

29. McCoy, Alfred. *The Politics of Heroin: CIA Complicity in the Global Drug Trade*. Brooklyn, NY: Lawrence Hill Books, 1991.

30. Collins, Glenn. "Ousted Phar-Mor President Found Guilty in $1 Billion Fraud." *New York Times*. May 26, 1995: D3.

31. Schroeder, Michael and Schiller, Zachary. "A Scandal Waiting to Happen." *Business Week* 3280, June 24, 1992: 32–36.

32. Monus was also one of the original owners of the Colorado Rockies Major League Baseball team. He was forced to sell his stake in the franchise when the Phar-Mor scandal erupted.

33. Brookman, Faye. "Deep Discounter Phar-Mor Declares Bankruptcy." *Drug Topics* 136, September 7, 1992: 84–85; Star, Marlene G. "Phar-More Ills Hurt Strategy." *Pension & Investments* 20, August 17, 1992: 3, 31.

34. Fallon, Geoffrey D. "Yes, Virginia, Some Companies Do Commit Fraud." *Across the Board* 32, 1994: 33; Vachon, Michael. "Phar-Mor Disaster Shakes Private Market Investors." *Investment Dealers Digest* 58, August 10, 1992: 15–16; Freudenheim, Milt. "Phar-Mor Says Profit Was Faked." *New York Times*. August 5, 1992: D1.

35. Solomon, Jolie. "Mickey's Secret Life." *Newsweek* 120, August 31, 1992: 70–72.

36. "Monus, Co-Founder of Phar-Mor, Gets a 20–Year Sentence." *Wall Street Journal*. December 4, 1995: B5.

37. Quoted in *Ibid.*, p. B5.

38. "Founder of Phar-Mor, in Prison, Is Indicted." *New York Times*. June 26, 1997: D2.

39. Vaughan, Dianne. *Controlling Unlawful Organizational Behavior*. Chicago: University of Chicago Press, 1983.

40. Clinard, Marshall. *Corporate Ethics and Crime*. Beverly Hills, Calif.: Sage, 1983.

41. "Olde Discount Settle Sales Practice Abuses Suit." www.sec.gov. September 10, 1998.

42. *Ibid.*

43. *Ibid.*

44. *Ibid.*

45. *Ibid.*

46. *Ibid.*

47. *Ibid.*

48. *Ibid.*

49. Quoted in *Ibid.*

50. Wheeler, Stanton and Rothman, Mitchell. "The Organization as Weapon in White-Collar Crime." *Michigan Law Review* 80, 1982: 1405.

51. *Ibid.*, p. 1426.

52. Tillman, Robert and Pontell, Henry. "Organizations and Fraud in the Savings and Loan Industry." *Social Forces* 4, 1995: 1458.

53. Reiman, Jeffrey. *The Rich Get Richer and the Poor Get Prison: Ideology, Crime and Criminal Justice* (4th Ed.). Boston: Allyn and Bacon, 1995.

54. Quoted in Ranalli, Ralph. "Execs Get 18 Months in Med-Testing Flap." *Boston Herald*. August 9, 1996: 20.

55. Quoted in *Ibid.*, p. 20. Moreover, Barry Goetz has addressed the important issue of class bias in the enforcement of laws concerning white-collar crime. He argues that the phenomenon of "arson-for-profit" has been relegated to a "nonissue" status by law enforcement which

reflects not only selectivity by the state, but also has important implications for understanding both equity issues and class bias in enforcement and state processes. (Goetz, Barry. "Organization as Class Bias in Local Law Enforcement: Arson-for-Profit as a "Nonissue." *Law and Society Review* 31:3, 1997: 557–587).

56. Hightower, Susan. "S & L Swindlers Get Early Withdrawal from Prison." *San Diego Union-Tribune.* July 31, 1994: I1.

57. Pontell, Calavita, and Tillman, *op. cit.*

58. Tillman, Robert and Pontell, Henry. "Is Justice 'Collar-Blind'? Punishing Medicaid Provider Fraud." *Criminology* 53, 1988: 294–302.

59. For example: Hagan, John and Nagel, Ilene. "White-Collar Crime, White-Collar Time." *American Criminal Law Review* 20, 1982: 259–289; and Hagan, John, Nagel, Ilene, and Albonetti, Celesta. "Differential Sentencing of White-Collar Offenders." *American Sociological Review* 45, 1980: 802–820.

60. Benson, Michael and Walker, Esteban. "Sentencing the White-Collar Offender." *American Sociological Review* 53, 1988: 294–302.

61. For example: Wheeler, Stanton, Weisburd, David, and Bode, Nancy. "Sentencing the White-Collar Offender: Rhetoric and Reality." *American Sociological Review* 50, 1982: 641–659; and Weisburd, David, Waring, Elin, and Wheeler, Stanton. "Class, Status, and the Punishment of White-Collar Criminals." *Law and Social Inquiry* 15, 1990: 222–243.

62. Using criminal defendants who are physicians as a model, Rosoff has argued that the customary "status shield" can be transformed into a target, under certain circumstances, particularly when the offense is a "common" crime rather than a white-collar crime.

63. Lott, John. "Do We Punish High Income Criminals Too Heavily?" *Economic Inquiry* 30, 1992: 583–608. See also: Baum, Sandy and Kamas, Linda. "Time, Money, and Optimal Criminal Penalties." *Contemporary Economic Policy* 13, October 1995: 72–79.

64. Lott, John. "Should the Wealthy Be Able to 'Buy Justice'?" *Journal of Political Economy* 95, 1987: 1307–1316.

65. Baum, Sandy and Kamas, Linda. "Time, Money, and Optimal Criminal Penalties." *Contemporary Economic Policy* 13, October 1995: 74.

66. Machan, Dyan and Button, Graham. "Beyond the Slammer." *Forbes,* November 26, 1990: 284–288.

67. McClintick, David. *Indecent Exposure: A True Story of Hollywood and Wall Street.* New York: Morrow, 1982.

68. *Ibid.*

69. U.S. Securities and Exchange Commission, Division of Market Regulation. "The Large Firm Project." 1995.

70. Tillman and Pontell, *op. cit.*

71. "Rich Debtors Finding Shelter Under a Populist Florida Law." *New York Times.* July 25, 1993: A1.

72. Lynch, Michael, Nalla, Makesh, and Miller, Keith. "Cross-Cultural Perceptions of Deviance: The Case of Bhopal." *Journal of Research in Crime and Delinquency* 26, 1989: 7–35.

73. Wright, John, Cullen, Francis, and Blankenship, Michael. "The Social Construction of Corporate Violence: Media Coverage of the Imperial Food Products Fire." *Crime & Delinquency* 41, 1995: 20–36.

74. Witkin, Gordon, Friedman, Doran, and Guttman, Monika. "Health Care Fraud." *U.S. News & World Report,* February 24, 1992: 34–43.

75. "Who Should Pay for the S & L Bailout?" *New York Times.* September 21, 1990: A31.

76. Petruno, Tom and Flanigan, James. "Orange County in Bankruptcy." *Los Angeles Times.* December 7, 1994: D1.

77. Jorion, Philippe. *Big Bets Gone Bad: Derivatives and Bankruptcy in Orange County.* San Diego: Academic Press, 1995: 7.

78. Brazil, Jeff, Wilogren, Jodi, and Lait, Matt. "O.C. Bankruptcy: Study Casts Doubt on Citron's Financial Record," *Los Angeles Times.* January 8, 1995: A1.

79. Quoted in *Los Angeles Times.* "Orange County Bankruptcy: Key Excerpts From Testimony by Citron, Stamenson." January 16, 1995: A2.

80. *Ibid.*, p. 22

81. Nyhan, David. "'95 Offers Many Lessons for What *Not* to Do in '96." *Boston Globe.* December 31, 1995: 82.

82. Quoted in Loomis, Carol J. "Untangling the Derivatives Mess." *Fortune* 131, May 20, 1995: 50. Another example of the peril of

derivatives occurred in 1994–1995, when the financial press began excoriating Bankers Trust New York for allegedly deceiving corporate derivatives clients about the extent of their losses. Three companies, Procter & Gamble, Gibson Greetings, and Mead, Corp., reportedly suffered combined losses of $172 million ("The Tangled Tale of the Tape." *Institutional Investor.* 29, April 1995: 42–43; Baldo, Anthony. "Sweeping the Street." *Financial World* [Special Issue]. August 16, 1994: 61–63).

83. *Ibid.*, p. 51.

84. Brazil, Jeff. "Merrill's Responsibilities Key to Orange County Suit; Crisis." *Los Angeles Times.* January 15, 1995: A1.

85. Henderson, Nell and Fromson, Brett D. "Merrill Lynch: The Broker Behind Orange County." *Washington Post.* December 10, 1994: F1.

86. In an unrelated 1996 case, investment banker Mark Ferber was convicted of 58 charges relating to illegal kickbacks he had received from Merrill Lynch. A federal jury in Boston ruled that Ferber, who had made millions advising public agencies on municipal finance, had misrepresented himself to clients as unbiased at the same time he was selling his influence to Merrill Lynch for hundreds of thousands of dollars (Nealon, Patricia. "Ferber Is Guilty of Selling Influence." *Boston Globe.* August 10, 1996: A1, A6).

87. Brazil, *op. cit.*

88. Petruno and Flanigan, *op. cit.*, p. D1.

89. *Ibid.*, p. D1.

90. "3rd Orange County Official Charged." *USA Today.* December 14, 1995: 3A.

91. Davis, Mike. "Bankruptcy on the Backs of the Poor: Rotten Orange County," *Nation* 260(4) January 30, 1995: 121.

92. Aigner, Dennis. *UCI Journal* 4, 1995: 2.

93. Jorion, *op. cit.*

94. U.S. Congress, House Committee on Banking, Finance, and Urban Affairs, Subcommittee on Consumer Affairs and Coinage. "H.R. 2440, Credit and Charge Card Disclosure Amendments of 1991." 102nd Congress, Second Session, October 9, 1991.

95. Quoted in Padilla, Felix. *The Gang as an American Enterprise.* New Brunswick, NJ: Rutgers University Press, 1992: 103.

96. Brewton, Pete. *The Mafia, CIA & George Bush.* New York: Time Books, 1994.

97. New York Senate. *Report and Proceedings of the Senate Committee Appointed to Investigate the Police Department of the City of New York.* Albany, NY: 1895: 6.

98. U.A. President's Commission on Law Enforcement and Administration of Justice. *Task Force Report: Organized Crime.* Washington, DC: U.S. Government Printing Office, 1967: 6.

99. Merton, Robert K. *Social Theory and Social Structure.* Glencoe, Ill.: Free Press, 1957.

100. U.S. Congress, House Committee on Banking, Finance, and Urban Affairs. "Federal Government's Response to Money Laundering." May 25, 1993.

101. Block, Alan and Scarpitti, Frank. "Casinos and Banking: Organized Crime in the Bahamas." *Deviant Behavior* 7, 1986: 301–312.

102. Gillespie, Ed and Schellhas, Bob (Eds.). *Contract With America.* New York: Time Books, 1994.

103. Cooke, Stephanie. "SEC Under Attack." *Euromoney* 317, September 1995: 84–88.

104. Stein, Ben. "Insecurities Trading." *Los Angeles Magazine* 41, January, 1996: 31–33.

105. "Business: Not Guilty." *Economist.* 326, February 13, 1996: 63–64.

106. Lee, Charles S. "Bit Crime, Big Time." *Newsweek* 126, December 11, 1995: 59.

107. *Ibid.*

108. Quoted in Langberg, Mike. "White Collar Crime Erodes Faith in Business." *San Jose Mercury News.* February 12, 1989: 1E.

109. *United States Code Congressional and Administrative News.* 98th Congress, Second Session, 1984, Vol. 4. St. Paul, MN: West.

110. Ayres, Ian and Braithwaite, John. *Responsive Regulation.* Oxford: Oxford University Press, 1992: 20.

111. *Ibid.*

112. Fisse, Brent and Braithwaite, John. *Corporations, Crime and Accountability.* Cambridge: Cambridge University Press, 1993.

113. *Ibid.*, p. 143.

114. *Ibid.*, p. 230.

115. Yenkin, Jonathan. "Ethics Officers Manage Companies' Morals." *Orange County Register,* August 29, 1993: Business Section, p. 1.

116. Rakstis, Ted J. "The Business Challenge: Confronting the Ethics Issue." *Kiwanis Magazine,* September 1990: 30.

117. Etzioni, Amitai. *Public Policy in a New Key.* New Brunswick, NJ: Transaction, 1993: 103.

118. U.S. Congress, Senate Committee on Foreign Relations, Subcommittee on International Economic Policy, Trade, Oceans and Environment. "U.N. Code of Conduct on Transnational Corporations." 101st Congress, Second Session, October 11, 1990.

119. "White House Unveils Its Overseas Code of Corporate Conduct." *Los Angeles Times.* March 28, 1995: D1.

120. Braithwaite, John. *Crime, Shame and Reintegration.* New York: Cambridge University Press, 1989.

121. Coffee, John. "No Sound to Damn, No Body to Kick: An Unscandalized Inquiry into the Problem of Corporate Punishment." *Michigan Law Review* 79, 1981: 424–429.

122. Braithwaite, 1989, *op. cit.,* p. 144

123. Galvin, *op. cit.,* p. 99.

124. *Ibid.,* p. 99.

125. *Ibid.,* p. 99.

126. *Ibid.,* p. 99.

127. Quoted in *Ibid.,* p. 99.

128. Marks, Peter. "Ethics and the Bottom Line." *Chicago Tribune Magazine.* May 6, 1990: 26.

129. Rakstis, *op. cit.,* p. 30.

130. Marks, *op. cit.,* p. 26.

131. See, for example: Etzioni, *op. cit.*

132. Fraedrich, John P. "Do the Right Thing: Ethics and Marketing in a World Gone Wrong." *Journal of Marketing* 60, January 1996: 122–123.

133. Marks, *op. cit.*

134. Quoted in Mulligan, Hugh A. "Ethics in America." *Richmond Times-Dispatch.* April 6, 1989: F1

135. For example, Denise A. Monroe has designed a creative social science lesson for elementary school teachers, from which young students can learn about defective consumer products and false advertising (Monroe, Denise A. "Let the Manufacturer Beware." *Journal of School Health* 64, February 1994: 83–84).

136. "California Resumes Business Activities with Salomon Unit." *Wall Street Journal.* November 11, 1992: B5.

137. "Reebok Vote on Pay Issue." *New York Times.* May 6, 1992: 2.

Index

Goldman, William, 292
Goldman Sachs, 227
Goldwater, Barry, 311
Gonzalez, Henry, 278, 282
Gore, Albert, 134
government
    cyber-attacks on, 433–434
    religion and, 207
    See also political corruption
graft, 361
Graham, Billy, 206, 209
Gray, Ed, 281, 282
Gray, L. Patrick, III, 324
Great American Life Insurance Company of
        Cincinnati, 263
Great Electrical Conspiracy, 72–74
Great Salad Oil Swindle, 8–9
Greenspan, Alan, 281
Griffen, Merv, 237
Grigson, James, 109–110
Gross, Harry, 369
Grumman Corporation, 218, 238–239
Guarasci, Richard, 161
Guevara, Jose Luis, 352
Gulf Oil Corporation, 343
Gulliver's Travels (Swift), 44
Gumbel, Bryant, 440
Guthrie, Woody, 8

H

H. J. Heinz Company, 103–104
Haberman, Steve, 132
hacker, meaning of term, 418
hacking, 427–436
Hadacol, 122
Hahn, Jessica, 203
Hakim, Albert, 308, 312, 313
Halcion, 107–111
Haldeman, H. R., 323, 325, 327, 328
Hall, Eustace, 38
Hall, Fawn, 311, 312
Hamilton, Joseph, 303
Hanna, Richard, 345
Hanover Hackers, 441–442
Hansen, "Erv," 277
Hansen, George, 343–344
Harper, Robert N., 117–118
Harris, Billy Bob, 218–219
Hastings, Alcee, 354
Hastings, James, 344
Hays, Wayne, 338
hazardous waste, export of, 147–148
Healthcare Financing Adminis-
        tration, 411

healthcare industry
    equipment sales fraud, 386–387
    fertility fraud, 403–406
    fraud in, 384–386
    home care fraud, 387–389
    hospital fraud, 389–393
    nursing home abuses, 406–409
    overview of, 384
    psychiatrists, 402–403
    self-referrals, 394
    self-regulation of, 409–411
Helms, Richard, 325
Hemlock, Michigan, 142–143
Henkel, Lee, 280
Henvick, Don, 199, 200
Hess, Markus, 441
Hinshaw, Andrew, 361
Hoffenberg, Steven, 5
Hoffman-LaRoche, 65
hoisting equipment, 166–167
Holland, Deborah J., 38
Holtzman, Elizabeth, 356
home care fraud, 387–389
home equity loan scams, 55
Home Health Products, 386
Home Shopping Network, 58
homicide
    corporate crime as, 460
    criteria for, 176, 178
Honduras, 309
Hooker Chemical Corporation, 133, 134
Hoover, J. Edgar, 316–321
Hopewell, Virginia, 156
Hormel, 102
hospital fraud, 389–393
Howe, Allan, 338
Hubbard, Carroll, Jr., 344
Humbard, Rex, 198
Humphrey, Hubert, 325
Humphreys, Roger, 357
Hunt, E. Howard, 324, 325
Hunt, Guy, 357
Hurwitz, Hal, 260
Hyde, Edward, 337
Hyde Park, New York, 134

I

IBM, 72
identity theft, 420–421, 430
Illinois v. O'Neill (1985), 174–176, 177, 178
Imperial Food Products, 174
incarceration
    for environmental crime, 154–155
    for workplace conditions, 173
indirect cost of white-collar crime, 472